Political Power and the Urban Crisis

2nd edition

ALAN SHANK
State University of New York at Geneseo

Holbrook Press, Inc.   Boston

Books by Alan Shank

NEW JERSEY REAPPORTIONMENT POLITICS: STRATEGIES
AND TACTICS IN THE LEGISLATIVE PROCESS

POLITICAL POWER AND THE URBAN CRISIS, FIRST EDITION

EDUCATIONAL INVESTMENT IN AN URBAN SOCIETY
(*with Melvin R. Levin*)

Library of Congress Catalog Card Number: **72-87406**

Dedicated to my wife, Bernice,
and my children,
Steven and Naomi

Contributors

ADVISORY COMMISSION ON INTERGOVERNMENTAL RELATIONS (Article 25) is a 26-member committee of officials representing federal, state, and local governments, and private citizens, created by a 1959 Act of Congress to discuss emerging public problems that are likely to require intergovernmental cooperation.

RUSSELL BAKER (Article 20), was a journalist with the Washington Bureau of *The New York Times* from 1954 to 1962. He is presently the very witty and urbane columnist of "Observer," which has appeared on the *Times* editorial page since 1962.

EDWARD C. BANFIELD (Article 1) is William R. Kenan, Jr., Professor at the University of Pennsylvania. Formerly, he was Henry Lee Shattuck Professor of Urban Government at Harvard University, where he wrote extensively on city politics in such books as *Urban Government* (1961, 1969), *Political Influence* (1961), and *City Politics* (1963). His most recent book is *The Unheavenly City* (1970).

DAVID L. BIRCH (Article 5) is Assistant Professor of Business Administration at the Harvard Business School.

RICHARD P. BURTON (Article 24) is an economist-planner on the senior research staff of the Urban Institute in Washington, D.C.

JAMES P. CAMPBELL (Article 10) served as co-director of the Task Force on Law and Law Enforcement of the National Commission on the Causes and Prevention of Violence, which issued its report on *Law and Order Reconsidered* in 1969.

DEMETRIOS CARALEY (Article 40) is Professor of Political Science at Barnard College and the graduate Faculties of Columbia University.

JAMES S. COLEMAN (Article 31) is professor of social relations at The Johns Hopkins University.

RALPH W. CONANT (Article 27) is director of the Institute of Urban Studies at the University of Houston, president of the Southwest Center for Urban Research in Houston, and was formerly associate director of the Lemberg Center for the Study of Violence at Brandeis University.

LINDA AND PAUL DAVIDOFF (Article 38) are urban planners with the Suburban Action Institute in White Plains, New York.

ANTHONY DOWNS (Article 4) is senior vice-president and a member of the board of directors of the Real Estate Research Corporation and a consultant to the RAND Corporation, the Urban Institute, the Brookings Institution, the Ford Foundation, and a number of Federal agencies. He also served as a consultant to the National Advisory Commission on Civil Disorders. He is the author of several books, including *An Economic Theory of Democracy* (1957) and *Urban Problems and Prospects* (1970).

MAX FRANKEL (Article 26), a *New York Times* reporter since 1952, has been chief Washington correspondent since 1968 with major emphasis on American foreign policy.

ROBERT M. FRENCH (Article 22) is Associate Professor of Sociology at Florida State University.

HERBERT J. GANS (Article 12) is Professor of Sociology at Columbia University. He formerly taught at the Massachusetts Institute of Technology and was a Faculty Associate at the Harvard-MIT Joint Center for Urban Studies. Professor Gans has written on urban problems in such books as *The Urban Villagers* and *The Levittowners* (1967).

NEIL N. GOLD (Article 38) is an urban planner with the Suburban Action Institute in White Plains, New York.

FRED I. GREENSTEIN (Article 13) is Professor of Political Science at Wesleyan University, where he has written widely on party politics and political socialization in such books as *The American Party System and The American People* (1970), *Children and Politics* (1969), and *Personality and Politics* (1969).

EDWARD GREER (Article 19) is Director of the Urban Affairs Program at Wheaton College, where he has edited *Black Liberation Politics* (1971). Mr. Greer also served as Director of Program Coordination under Mayor Richard Hatcher in Gary, Indiana.

FERNE K. KOLODNER (Article 29) is a member of the Community Planning Staff in the Office of the Commissioner, Social Security Administration, Department of Health, Education, and Welfare. She has had extensive experience in community organization and in planning local and neighborhood community action programs.

MILTON KOTLER (Article 11) is a Resident Fellow at the Institute for Policy Studies in Washington, D.C. He is the author of *Neighborhood Government* (1969).

SANFORD KRAVITZ (Article 29) is Dean of the School of Social Welfare at the State University of New York at Stony Brook. Previously, he was Associate Professor of Social Planning at Brandeis University and Associate Director of the Community Action Program, Office of Economic Opportunity.

HARVEY LIEBER (Article 34) is an Assistant Professor and an academic director of the Washington Semester Program, School of Government and Public Administration, The American University, Washington, D.C. He was an American Society for Public Administration Fellow with the Federal Water Pollution Control Administration during 1968–1969.

JOHN V. LINDSAY (Article 23) has been Mayor of New York City since 1965. In 1969, Mayor Lindsay wrote about the political and public policy issues of the nation's largest city in *The City*.

THEODORE J. LOWI (Article 14) is University Professor and John L. Senior Professor, Joint Appointments, in the Department of Government and History, Cornell University. Formerly, he was Professor of Political Science at the University of Chicago. His books include *At the Pleasure of the Mayor* (1964) and *The End of Liberalism* (1969).

RICHARD L. MAULLIN (Article 17) is a member of the social science department of the RAND Corporation in Santa Monica, California where his research focuses principally on Latin American politics. He also works as a volunteer in managing election campaigns.

DANIEL P. MOYNIHAN (Article 35) recently appointed United States Ambassador to India, is Professor of Education and Urban Politics at Harvard University, where he has written extensively on urban problems in such books as *Beyond the Melting Pot* (1963), and *Maximum Feasible Misunderstanding* (1969). From 1969–1971, Professor Moynihan served as President Nixon's Chairman of the Urban Affairs Council and later as Presidential Counselor.

NATIONAL COMMISSION ON URBAN PROBLEMS (Article 2) was appointed by President Lyndon B. Johnson on January 12, 1967, to review and recommend solutions regarding zoning, housing, building codes, taxation, and development standards with special emphasis on low-income housing.

NEWSWEEK (Article 9) periodically publishes special reports on the moods and attitudes of different segments of the nation's people.

RICHARD M. NIXON (Articles 36 and 39) is the 37th President of the United States.

MICHAEL NOVAK (Article 8) teaches "social ethics" at the State University of New York at Old Westbury.

MICHAEL PARENTI (Articles 7 and 15) is Associate Professor of Political Science at the University of Vermont in Burlington.

JACK ROSENTHAL (Article 3) is a national urban correspondent for *The New York Times*.

LEE SLOAN (Article 22) is Associate Professor of Sociology at Brooklyn College of the City College of New York.

ELMER B. STAATS (Article 30) is Comptroller General of the United States and chief of the U.S. Government Accounting Office.

DAVID P. STANG (Article 28) served as co-director of the Task Force on Law and Law Enforcement of the National Commission on the Causes and Prevention of Violence, which issued its report on *Law and Order Reconsidered* in 1969.

GEORGE STERNLIEB (Article 33) is director of the Center for Urban Policy Research, Rutgers University, New Brunswick, New Jersey. He has done considerable analysis of slum housing and written several books, including *The Tenement Landlord* (1966).

GEORGE A. WILEY (Article 37) is Executive Director of the National Welfare Rights Organization.

JAMES Q. WILSON (Article 18) is Professor of Government at Harvard University. From 1963–1966, he was Director of the Harvard-MIT Joint Center for Urban Studies. His extensive writings on urban politics include *Negro Politics* (1960), *The Amateur Democrat* (1962), *City Politics* (1963), and *Varieties of Police Behavior* (1968).

JOSEPH F. ZIMMERMAN (Article 21) is Professor of Political Science at the Graduate School of Public Affairs, State University of New York at Albany. One of his most recent books is *Subnational Politics, second edition* (1970).

Contents

Preface to the Second Edition   **xiii**

Preface to the First Edition   xvi

part I

Emergence of an Urban Nation

1. URBAN AMERICA   How Is the Metropolis Developing?

   Introduction   3

   Questions for Discussion and Debate   9

   1. The Logic of Metropolitan Growth
      Edward C. Banfield   11

   2. The Urban Setting: Population, Poverty, and Race
      National Commission on Urban Problems   34

   3. The Outer City: U.S. in Suburban Turmoil
      Jack Rosenthal   70

   4. The Future of American Ghettos
      Anthony Downs   77

   5. The Changing Economic Function
      David L. Birch   91

   6. Property Taxes and the Public Schools: *Serrano v. Priest*
      California State Supreme Court   102

   Suggestions for Further Reading   121

2. PEOPLE AND CITIES: Polarization or Consensus?

    Introduction   125

    Questions for Discussion and Debate   129

    7. Ethnic Politics and the Persistence of Ethnic Identification
        Michael Parenti   131

    8. White Ethnic
        Michael Novak   148

    9. Report from Black America
        Editors of Newsweek   159

   10. Radical Black Militancy
        James S. Campbell   172

   11. Neighborhood Self-Government
        Milton Kotler   180

   12. We Won't End the Urban Crisis Until We End 'Majority Rule'
        Herbert J. Gans   186

    Suggestions for Further Reading   200

part II

Political Power in Metropolitian Areas

3. CITY GOVERNMENT AND POLITICS: What Is the Nature of Political Participation, Leadership, and Conflict?

    Introduction   205

    Questions for Discussion and Debate   211

   13. The Changing Pattern of Urban Party Politics
        Fred I. Greenstein   212

   14. Machine Politics—Old and New
        Theodore J. Lowi   230

15. Power and Pluralism: A View from the Bottom
    Michael Parenti   241

16. Mayoral Leadership by a Modern Boss-Politician
    Alan Shank   269

17. Los Angeles Liberalism
    Richard L. Maullin   276

18. The Mayors vs. the Cities
    James Q. Wilson   300

19. The "Liberation" of Gary, Indiana
    Edward Greer   315

20. If Nixon Were Mayor
    Russell Baker   336

Suggestions for Further Reading   339

4. METROPOLITICS: Is Intergovernmental Cooperation Possible?

Introduction   348

Questions for Discussion and Debate   353

21. Metropolitan Reform in the U.S.: An Overview
    Joseph F. Zimmerman   355

22. Black Rule in the Urban South?
    Lee Sloan and Robert M. French   378

23. For New National Cities
    John V. Lindsay   392

24. The Metropolitan State
    Richard P. Burton   396

25. Revenue Sharing: An Idea Whose Time Has Come
    *Advisory Commission on Intergovernmental
    Relations*   407

26. Revenue Sharing Is a Counterrevolution
    Max Frankel   419

Suggestions for Further Reading   431

part III

The Urban Crisis

5. URBAN PROBLEMS AND POLICIES OF THE 1960's: Riots, Police, Poverty, Employment, Education, Housing, and Environment

Introduction   437

Questions for Discussion and Debate   443

27. Patterns of Civil Protest: Ghetto Riots
     Ralph W. Conant   445

28. The Police and Their Problems
     David P. Stang   460

29. Community Action: Where Has It Been? Where Will It Go?
     Sanford Kravitz and Ferne K. Kolodner   486

30. The Closing of Job Corps Centers
     Elmer B. Staats   501

31. Equality of Educational Opportunity
     James S. Coleman   518

32. School Busing: Swann v. Board of Education
     United States Supreme Court   531

33. Housing Abandonment: What Is to Be Done?
     George Sternlieb   540

34. Public Administration and Environmental Quality
     Harvey Lieber   557

6. THE CITIES AND THE FEDERAL SYSTEM: Public Policies for the 1970's

Introduction   575

Questions for Discussion and Debate   578

35. Toward a National Urban Policy
     Daniel P. Moynihan   579

36. Presidential Message on Welfare Reform
     Richard M. Nixon   599

37. NWRO Proposals for a Guaranteed Adequate Income
     George A. Wiley   609

38. The Suburbs Have to Open Their Gates
     *Linda and Paul Davidoff and
     Neil N. Gold*   621

39. Federal Policies and Equal Housing Opportunity
     Richard M. Nixon   637

40. Is the Large City Becoming Ungovernable?
     Demetrios Caraley   656

Suggestions for Further Reading   674

INDEX   687

Preface to the Second Edition

Four years have passed since the first edition of *Political Power and the Urban Crisis* was published. I remain convinced that the solution of our critical urban problems should be the nation's top priority. Nearly every argument advanced in the preface to the first edition continues to occupy the center stage of our public debates. In fact, not only has the urban crisis not been effectively tackled, but also even more issues and actors have appeared on the scene since 1969. The environmentalists and the consumer advocates, such as Ralph Nader, have brought attention to the incredible fouling of the country's air and water, the shoddy practices of many big corporations in producing poor quality products, and the misleading claims of commercial advertising on television. In addition to the nation's large black minority, other disadvantaged groups, including Mexican-Americans and American Indians, have become quite vocal in dramatizing the discrimination against them and their lack of opportunities to participate fully in our society. While large-scale ghetto riots have receded since the tremendously destructive city conflagrations of 1967, the crime rate has soared nearly out of sight, effective gun control legislation remains a hope rather than a fact, and all of us have been made painfully aware of the eroding and self-destructive dangers of the drug culture.

The second edition of *Political Power and the Urban Crisis* continues the call for action set forth in the first edition by offering its readers relevant, topical articles which demonstrate that the crisis of the cities is in no small way related to the nature of urban political power. To emphasize the goals of poignancy, timeliness, and controversy, as well as to keep apace with the most recent urban developments, the second edition contains, with two exceptions, an entirely new selection of articles. Chapter 2 now analyzes the questions of ethnicity, polarization and consensus among diverse groups, and possible strategies for political coalitions. The six chapter introductions and the listings in "Suggestions for Further Reading" have been substantially revised. Finally, three new features are added: First, following each chapter introduction is a series of "Questions for Discussion and Debate." Second, an index and, third, a list of contributors appear for the first time.

The nationwide response to *Political Power and the Urban Crisis* by a long list of colleges, universities, and faculty has been truly gratifying. In my own courses, particularly in the Boston University Overseas Graduate Programs in Brussels, Belgium, and Heidelberg, Germany (1969–1970), the student reactions to the controversies and public policy issues of the first edition not only stimulated lively class discussions but also resulted in some very worthwhile, informative, and provocative research papers.

As with my acknowledgments in the first edition, I wish again to express my deep appreciation to the many contributors who have made this second edition possible. The staff at Holbrook Press, especially Paul Conway and John DeRemigis, have facilitated my efforts with their encouragement, promptness, editorial assistance, and first-rate professional advice. Barry Fetterolf, a former Holbrook Press editor, remains my chief mentor, whose confidence in me originally spurred the development of this book. I owe a special note of thanks to my academic critics and reviewers, particularly to Robert Lineberry of the University of Texas at Austin for his most helpful suggestions to include several outstanding articles and to Donald Zauderer of American University for recommending the conceptual framework for many of the chapter introductions. On the home front, William F. Wacenske, a Geneseo student, provided me with many hours of good clerical assistance in compiling materials for the second edition.

Finally, I wish to thank the many students whom I have taught and directed for the past three years at Boston University, the Boston University Overseas Graduate Program, and the State University College of New York at Geneseo for their warm and frequently enthusiastic responses. In particular, I express gratitude to A. Edward Elmendorf (now with the World Bank), Larry Daugherty (a management consultant in Brussels), and David Kerwin (a Canadian school teacher) for their intelligent and critical suggestions which have affected my own thinking on the nature of urban problems. After all, to achieve many of the solutions and new courses of action proposed in this book, it will take the efforts of bright, capable, and committed young people who move from the classroom to direct involvement with the problems of the nation.

Alan Shank

Geneseo, N. Y.

August 1972

Preface to the First Edition

THE URBAN CRISIS is the greatest domestic problem facing America today. Race is the key to understanding the magnitude of our urban problems. Cities have become, at an ever-increasing pace, the location of the poor, lower class, underprivileged, unskilled, and in recent times, growing numbers of angry and militant Negroes. On the other hand, our suburbs contain millions of white Americans who enjoy unmatched affluence: rising family incomes, high levels of educational achievement, good jobs, and single-family homes. Barring any dramatic reversals of current trends, the future of our metropolitan areas will be characterized by this central city-suburban cleavage, which is rooted in both racial and class differences.

Can anything be done to make America an indivisible nation with "liberty and justice for all"? This book of selected essays provides an opportunity to examine various responses to the urban crisis by government and private enterprise. The essays were chosen, for the most part, to explore in depth the human side of urban problems. The urban crisis is defined in terms of the massive concentration of impoverished Negroes living in deteriorating and decaying central city ghettos. Neither can the Negro poor be blamed for their conditions, nor must the response to their demands for change be simply one of "law and order." Persistent and massive Negro impoverishment in the cities is a disease that reflects either a failure of our social and governmental institutions or a profound weakness in our economic system. It is time to deal with critical urban problems in a comprehensive and successful way.

A major assumption throughout this book is that government and private enterprise *can* solve urban problems connected with education, employment, and housing. The essential ingredients for a massive, concerted, and energetic effort are creative leadership and a sense of urgency in reordering our national priorities. It was clear in the spring of 1969 that the Vietnam War and the difficulties of reordering national priorities by the Nixon Administration were the major obstacles of federal government initiative toward urban problems. There was simply not enough money available to spend on domestic needs while the War and heavy defense spending continued. Whether the cessation of hostilities in Vietnam would permit a full-scale attack on urban problems remained an open question. In any case, the lack of comprehensive and well-financed short-term and long-term programs appeared to increase the possibility of tensions in our cities before any notable improvements were likely. Americans seemed to accept the inevitability of riots in Negro ghettos.

The challenge of urban America lies in reconciling the demands for "law and order" with the malaise of impoverished Negroes. Racial harmony, equal opportunity, and the good life are all possible if men of good will get together and act in an effective and responsible manner. It *is* possible to mobilize the resources now available in the public and private sectors of the economy to meet our urban problems. But do we still have time to give the Negro his chance to become a part of the mainstream of American society? When will government and private enterprise fulfill their responsibilities to alleviate the urban crisis? And, if we already have many solutions to our urban problems, do we also have the will and the courage to carry them out?

The experts who explore and analyze urban problems in this book represent a wide variety of outlooks. They are drawn from the fields of government, social science, and journalism. Their essays have been selected for poignancy, timeliness, and controversy. Urban problems are complex, and the experts are often in sharp disagreement. Neither their analyses of problems nor their suggested solutions should be accepted at face value. Much can be gained by debating the merits of various plans and programs. Those who use this book are encouraged to enter into the debate in order to evaluate the strengths and weaknesses of alternative ideas and approaches to urban problems.

The book is divided into three major parts with a total of six chapters. Part I, "Emergence Of An Urban Nation," contains selections on metropolitan area developments and discussion of population trends, with special emphasis on the problems of Negro city residents. Part II, "Political Power In Metropolitan Areas," deals with the government and politics of cities and suburbs, together with responses to urban problems by the federal and state governments. Part III, "The Urban Crisis," analyzes the key problems of education, employment, and housing and indicates the kinds of solutions that are necessary.

Short introductory essays precede each of the six chapters. The editor's comments are brief, since the essays are largely self-explanatory. Finally, there are a series of annotated suggested readings offered for further analysis of urban problems.

The editor wishes to express deep appreciation to the contributors of this volume for their cooperation and assistance. The staff at Holbrook Press, and particularly Barry Fetterolf and Beverly Malatesta, provided me with constant encouragement to complete the book in record time.

It is hoped that the essays concerning the nature, problems, programs, and prospects of our urban centers will lead to a better understanding and appreciation for those who critically investigate, examine, and analyze the urban crisis while using this book.

Alan Shank
Boston, Mass.
April 1969

PART 1

Emergence of an Urban Nation

Chapter 1

Urban America

How Is The Metropolis Developing?

The United States has indisputably become an urban nation. Our economic strength and productive capacity are concentrated in metropolitan areas where more than two-thirds of our population now lives. The private sector of the economy has contributed to the considerable affluence of most white, middle-class Americans. However, all levels of government—federal, state, and local—encounter complex problems of public policy involving highly controversial issues, such as the seemingly irreconcilable cleavages between blacks and whites, between central cities and suburbs, and between the forces of change and the forces of reaction.

The five articles in this chapter introduce the major urban challenges of the 1970's. Over time, the metropolis has been shaped by various factors that have resulted in determining where people decide to live. Public policy may be viewed as the response of government to these metropolitan growth patterns: What are the major transformations that have influenced the metropolis? What are the basic causes for these metropolitan changes? What are the possible consequences of governmental response to public demands?

In the first selection, Edward C. Banfield contends that the metropolis is a product of demographic, technological, and economic imperatives which can be traced to the nineteenth century industrial revolution. Metropolitan growth is thus the result of predetermined pressures created by our marketplace economy. First, the expansion of cities outward from core areas because of increases in population causes intense competition for housing and industrial location. Second, the development of transportation technology enables the upwardly mobile middle class to separate place of work from residence by traveling long distances over superhighway complexes. Third, the unequal distributions of wealth and income among different urban classes permit the more affluent groups to move outside the central cities and live in single-family suburban homes, while the less affluent groups remain in older central city housing which has been vacated by the white middle class.

Arguing the "logic" of these metropolitan growth forces, Professor Banfield believes that the range of governmental alternatives for policy makers is severely restricted. Local decision makers cannot do very much about influencing individual choices in the metropolis. Government is restrained by the collective decisions of individuals who move more or less freely throughout metropolitan areas.

The statistical surveys offered by the National Commission on Urban Problems (Article 2) appear to confirm Professor Banfield's views on metropolitan population expansion. The commission estimates that by 1985 the national population will have increased by 40 to 50 million, 81 per cent of which will occur in metropolitan areas. However, these demographic imperatives reveal serious imbalances in our society. Within central cities there are continuing increases in nonwhite population, much of which is disadvantaged, dependent, and poverty stricken. Poverty areas within the cities appear to be stagnating: Higher concentrations of the poor, less employment and housing, and fewer educational opportunities than in the past are growing phenomena in these areas. By becoming concentrations of the disadvantaged, many ghettos are no longer the way stations for upward mobility that they were for previous urban ethnic and religious groups.

The central cities might seek assistance from the more prosperous suburbs, but this help does not seem likely to be forthcoming. For more than twenty years, the white middle class has been abandoning the cities and moving to the suburbs. Both the National Commission on Urban Problems (Article 2) and Jack Rosenthal (Article 3) indicate that the suburbs now have an overall population advantage over the older central cities in most metropolitan areas. However, suburbanites and suburban government generally refuse to share responsibility for solving central city problems. Why? Historically, an anti-urban bias has pervaded American political thought and public attitudes. Cities were thought to be evil and wicked, while the virtues of the farm and the countryside were praised. When anti-urbanism is coupled with racial prejudice, we can begin to understand the plight of the inner cities. Most suburbanites view the central city as a collection of run-down and deteriorating neighborhoods inhabited by threatening groups who cause breakdowns in community order. While many suburban dwellers formerly lived in the cities, they no longer wish to associate with nonwhite lower-class and "alien" elements. Instead, suburban attitudes result in closing a ring around the inner cities, creating a serious "apartheid" problem in the metropolitan housing market. Suburbia becomes separated from the cities, even though the two are economically interdependent. Cities may continue to be a source of suburban commuter employment, but living outside of the central cities becomes the realization of the true American dream: more open space, a single-family home, and good schools for children.

Can fleeing to the suburbs relieve the middle class from responsibility for the plight of the urban poor? Tom Wicker, a *New York Times* columnist, suggests that attempts to escape from America's social problems may be a self-delusion:

> The real point is that there is, in fact, no place to hide from the kind of society we have created, or allowed to develop. The blacks and the poor didn't make their society; it put them in their present places. The city doesn't make modern life unpleasant; modern life is rendering the city intolerable. The suburbs, the weekend house, the island in the sea or the woods can't be walled off against change and turmoil growing out of the kind of people we are and the kind of lives we lead; they can only delude the hopeful.*

What are the prospects for alleviating racially segregated living conditions in metropolitan areas? Anthony Downs (Article 4) argues that *status quo* policies of the past and ghetto improvement strategies have neither reduced the concentrations of slum dwellers nor provided sufficient opportunities for disadvantaged groups to enter the mainstream of American society. By maintaining the present levels of social welfare programs, government cannot do very much about

---

* *The New York Times* (November 28, 1971), Section 4, p. 11, col. 6. Copyright © 1971 by The New York Times Company. Reprinted by permission.

eliminating the adverse underlying conditions of racial segregation, alienation, or violence. Ghetto improvement might be compatible with demands for black political power, but at the same time various housing, employment, education, and social service programs must be significantly expanded. There must be greater incentives for increased private capital investment. Also, programs to upgrade ghettos might lead to an intensified level of conflict between program administraters and black militants who demand community control.

Downs suggests that a ghetto dispersal policy might be the most feasible long-range alternative for ending urban poverty and racial discrimination. If nonwhites were encouraged to leave the slums and to relocate in the suburbs, there would be greater opportunities for them to find new jobs, send their children to better schools, and experience the advantages of living in an integrated society. Ghetto dispersal should be accompanied with positive incentives for minority groups, including rent supplements, home ownership supplements, or other forms of direct cash subsidies. Also, suburban communities would have to be assured that the influx of low-income groups would not disturb the prevailing socioeconomic environment. Dispersal would seek to promote the advantages of living in better neighborhoods without changing community character or creating new ghettos.

While Downs provides considerable food for thought with his ghetto-dispersal proposal, several critical problems remain to be solved before the policy can be implemented. Downs' basic premise is that racial isolation is the key obstacle preventing nonwhites from enjoying the benefits of American affluence. However, there is a substantial difference between achieving racial integration by law or court decisions and attaining racial integration that is genuinely supported by local customs and community attitudes. Black power advocates might resist ghetto-dispersal programs designed by whites. They might consider dispersal a way of undercutting minority efforts to gain community control of local institutions. Second, ghetto leaders could argue that population dispersal does not eliminate the root causes of institutional racism in America. Third, civil rights leaders, white liberals, government officials, blacks, and other minorities might be divided over the use of the racial or ethnic quotas that seem implicit in such a policy. Who would decide the quotas? Are quotas only another form of discrimination? Fourth, will suburbs accept even a small increase of inner-city ghetto residents? Before blacks,

Puerto Ricans, Chicanos, and other entrapped minorities believe that suburbs will actually welcome them, they will have to be convinced that dispersal is more than a set of promises. This factor means that suburbs will have to modify restrictive land use, zoning, planning, and other real estate practices that make it difficult for moderate and low-income families to purchase or rent housing outside of the central cities.

Even with the numerous political and sociological reservations associated with ghetto dispersal, there are strong *economic* reasons to develop public policies that encourage more heterogeneous population mixes in the metropolis. In Article 5, David L. Birch shows that central cities no longer function as all-purpose economic systems. In the economic life cycle of cities, population density and land costs increase while new job opportunities develop in the suburbs. Why? New economic growth is more feasible outside the central cities, particularly as more land is available at less cost and superhighway intersections provide easy access to and from suburban centers. Thus, manufacturing, wholesaling, and retailing activities will abandon the cities and move to the suburbs. We can thus expect that the cities will become elite and specialized service centers for white-collar workers. Disadvantaged minorities cannot improve their economic status unless they gain access to the real sources of available jobs. These new jobs will be in the suburbs, not in the central cities.

The outward movement of jobs, commerce, and industry in metropolitan areas has not been accompanied by changes in local government tax structures. Instead, cities and suburbs continue to rely heavily on property taxes to raise more than 85 per cent of local government revenues. The metropolis is characterized by diverse tax bases, tax rates, and expenditure needs. The proliferation and fragmentation of local taxing authorities results in significantly different levels of public services from one jurisdiction to the next. Faced with the prospects of nonwhite majorities, central cities are forced to find new sources of revenue to support costly social welfare programs. Poverty-stricken groups are the most dependent on municipal government for public assistance, but they are the least able to pay for such needs. At the same time, the middle-class exodus to the suburbs has not only undercut the central city's tax base but also required suburbia to construct expensive public facilities which require high taxes from homeowners.

Urban economist Dick Netzer indicates several critical defects of local property taxes.[1] First, when compared with sales taxes, property taxes represent a very high percentage of annual housing costs, with rates exceeding 25 per cent or more. Second, property taxes are regressive, since they are levied on the value of property rather than on the owner's ability to pay. Thus moderate and low-income home-owners are forced to assume a greater tax burden in relation to their income than are more affluent families. Third, local reliance on property taxes produces "fiscal zoning" practices. Communities attempt to exclude moderate and low-income renters, for example, by establishing such restrictive regulations as large lots for new hous-ing or by limiting apartment buildings to one- and two-bedroom units. The goal is to discourage families with numerous school-age children who might not pay their proportionate share of local public school taxes. Finally, various suburbs often seek to provide location incentives for new commerce and industry by offering lower tax rates. The result may be that such communities are discouraged from rais-ing taxes to finance improved local public services.

The California Supreme Court's important ruling on property tax inequities relating to public schools may provide a dramatic turn-about in future state and local tax policies. On August 30, 1971, the court declared in *Serrano v. Priest* (Article 6) that California's pub-lic school financing system violates the Fourteenth Amendment of the United States Constitution because it denies equal protection of the law to school-age children. In his opinion Justice Sullivan con-cludes that wealth may no longer be used to determine the quality of public education. Traditionally, differences in tax bases among vari-ous school districts result in significantly different levels of revenue to support education. Such a situation is inherently discriminatory because "affluent districts can have their cake and eat it too: They can provide a high quality education for their children while pay-ing lower taxes. Poor districts, by contrast, have no cake at all."

Since the California Supreme Court offered no remedies in its decision, it remains to be seen how the state legislature will respond in changing the tax structure for local schools. Without abolishing local property taxes, the legislature could require minimum and maximum levels of tax effort and spending to be the same for all districts. Thus all districts would tax and spend at the same rates. If a district exceeded the maximum expenditure per school-age child, the excess could be distributed to poorer districts. If a district could not produce the minimum revenues required for good quality education, the state could make up the difference with additional financial assistance. A second possible reform might be for the state to assume all responsibility for financing public schools. By so doing, the state would relieve localities of setting their own tax rates and provide for a more equitable distribution of tax revenues to all school districts.

Management of conflict, adequate provision of public services, and viability of local governments in metropolitan areas are continuing and important public policy issues. However, more public concern and increased citizen participation alone will not cure the urban malaise without a corresponding effort to reallocate public resources. When cities, suburbs, and metropolitan areas overcome their financial and taxation difficulties, it may be possible to bring about reconciliation between various ethnic, racial, and religious groups. Until then, all that our public decision makers can do is to try to keep the lid on the seriously divisive political and sociological issues that threaten to tear apart the fabric of our society. Metropolitan politics today focuses upon managing conflict while local governments are challenged by the demands of various discontented groups. The American metropolis may no longer have time to experiment with new approaches to solving problems: The tensions mount, and the resources for solutions remain absent. And no one seems completely satisfied with the public authority and leadership now in power in our metropolitan areas.

NOTES

1. *Economics and Urban Problems* (New York: Basic Books, Inc., 1970), pp. 191–196.

QUESTIONS FOR DISCUSSION AND DEBATE

1. Professor Banfield argues that there are predictable metropolitan growth imperatives which are largely the result of certain economic forces and private, individual choices. What role, if any, can public officials have in managing future urban development patterns? Is there any demographic, sociological, or political evidence that past and current metropolitan growth trends are in fact destroying American cities?

2. In the past, the nation's central cities provided many opportunities for disadvantaged ethnic and religious minorities to enter the mainstream of American society. Is the present condition of most urban nonwhites comparable to similar situations in the past? If not, what special circumstances limit the opportunities of today's disadvantaged groups living in the central cities?

3. What are the comparative advantages and disadvantages of maintaining the present levels of governmental programs for the inner-city poor?

4. If anti-urbanism is a persistent theme in American political thought, are there any apparent conflicts between the American preferences for large-scale corporate concentrations in the private sector and for small-scale or decentralized suburban living?

5. State as many pro and con arguments as you can in response to the following proposition: Ghetto dispersal may be opposed for political and social reasons, but there are strong economic advantages to such a policy.

6. In the economic life cycle of cities, there are several important trends that affect the metropolis. What are the implications of these trends for the future economy of the nation?

7. If the property tax is reformed, will local communities lose control over their own affairs, such as providing public services at specific levels? Should most public services be controlled locally, or are there others that might be better provided on an area-wide metropolitan basis?

8. What are the moral, political, and legal bases for concluding that differences in tax revenues among various school districts result in unconstitutional discrimination against school-age children?

ARTICLE 1

The Logic of Metropolitan Growth

Edward C. Banfield

Much of what has happened—as well as of what is happening—in the typical city or metropolitan area can be understood in terms of three imperatives. The first is demographic: if the population of a city increases, the city must expand in one direction or another—up, down, or from the center outward. The second is technological: if it is feasible to transport large numbers of people outward (by train, bus, and automobile) but not upward or downward (by elevator), the city must expand outward. The third is economic: if the distribution of wealth and income is such that some can afford new housing and the time and money to commute considerable distances to work while others cannot, the expanding periphery of the city must be occupied by the first group (the "well-off") while the older, inner parts of the city, where most of the jobs are, must be occupied by the second group (the "not well-off").

The word "imperatives" is used to emphasize the inexorable, constraining character of the three factors that together comprise the logic of metropolitan growth. Indeed, the principal purpose of this chapter is to show that, given a rate of population growth, a transportation technology, and a distribution of income, certain consequences must inevitably follow; that the city and its hinterland must develop according to a predictable pattern and that even an all-wise and all-powerful government could not change this pattern except by first changing the logic that gives rise to it. The argument is not that nothing can be done to improve matters. Rather, it is that only those things can be done which lie within the boundaries— rather narrow ones, to be sure—fixed by the logic of the growth process. Nor is it argued that the only factors influencing metropolitan development are those that relate to population, technology, and income. Countless others also influence it. Two of these other factors are of key importance, even though they are not part of the logic of the process. They will be discussed in the following two chapers (on class culture and race).

This chapter, highly schematic, describes in a generalized way how most American cities, small as weil as large, have developed and are still developing, but it does not describe completely (or perhaps even accurately) how any *particular* city has developed. The city under discussion here is a highly simplified model. Its residents have no class, ethnic, or racial attributes (they will acquire them in the next two chapters). They are neither rich nor poor; instead, they are "well-off" or "not well-off," depending upon whether or not they can afford to buy new homes and to commute a considerable distance— requiring, say, half an hour or more—to work. . . .

The logic of metropolitan growth began unfolding the moment the cities were founded and it has not changed since. More than a century ago, in 1857, a select committee of the state legislature described the forces that were shaping New York. These were, as the committee made clear, the same forces that had always been shaping it. And they were the same ones that are shaping it and other cities still:

> As our wharves became crowded with warehouses, and encompassed with bustle and noise, the wealthier citizens, who peopled old "Knickerbocker" mansions, near the bay, transferred their residence to streets beyond the din; compensating for remoteness from their counting houses, by the advantages of increased quiet and luxury. Their habitations then passed into the hands, on the one side, of boarding house keepers, on the other, of real estate agents; and here, in its beginning, the tenant house became a real blessing to that class of industrious poor whose small earnings limited their expenses and whose employment in workshops, stores, and about the wharves and thoroughfares, rendered a near residence of much importance. At this period, rents were moderate, and a mechanic with family could hire two or more comfortable and even commodious apartments, in a house once occupied by wealthy people, for less than half what he is now obliged to pay for narrow and unhealthy quarters. This state of tenantry comfort did not, however, continue long; for the rapid march of improvement speedily enhanced the value of property in the lower wards of the city, and as this took place, rents rose, and

accommodations decreased in the same proportion. At first the better class of tenants submitted to retain their single floors, or two and three rooms, at the onerous rates, but this rendered them poorer, and those who were able to do so, followed the example of former proprietors, and emigrated to the upper wards. The spacious dwelling houses then fell before improvements, or languished for a season, as tenant houses of the type which is now the prevailing evil of our city; that is to say, their large rooms were partitioned into several smaller ones (without regard to proper light or ventilation), the rates of rent being lower in proportion to space or height from the street; and they soon became filled, from cellar to garret, with a class of tenantry living from hand to mouth, loose in morals, improvident in habits, degraded or squalid as beggary itself.[1]

What was happening in New York (and elsewhere as well) was the expansion of the city outward under the pressure of growth at its center. Typically, land closest to the point of original settlement (always the point most accessible to waterborne transportation) became the site of the central business district. Great accessibility to wharves, markets, shops, and offices, and later to railheads, meant that commercial and industrial activities had to be located there; the closer a site was to the most accessible center, the more it tended to be worth. Accordingly, most people lived on the outskirts of the central business district, where land prices were not prohibitively high. Only the very rich, to whom the price of land did not matter, and the very poor, who occupied undesirable sites near factories and wharves and endured great overcrowding, lived in the very center of the city.

As the central business district grew, it absorbed the residential neighborhoods adjacent to it. The people who lived in them were pushed outward into unsettled or sparsely settled districts where land prices were still low. To say that they were "pushed" makes it sound as if they went against their wills. Probably most were glad to go. Those who owned their homes profited from the rise in prices; they could sell an old house close to the business district for enough with which to build a new and bigger one at the periphery of the city.

Much of the housing taken over in this way was torn down to make room for factories, stores, and offices. Some, however, was converted to more intensive residential use. When the only transportation was by horse, almost everyone lived within walking distance of his job in the central business district. Even afterward, when one could take a trolley to work, factory workers and office and store clerks generally preferred to pay relatively high rents for crowded quarters from which they could walk to work rather than spend the time and money to commute from neighborhoods where rents were lower. The central business district was therefore ringed with rooming houses and tenements. These establishments could afford the expensive land because they used it intensively. At the end of the last century, for example, some lodging houses in Chicago accommodated (if that is the word) as many as a thousand lodgers a night.

As the populations and income of the city grew, so did the number and proportion of those (the "well-off") who could afford new homes. In the nature of the case, most new homes had to be built at the periphery of the expanding city, where there was vacant land. Until the end of the Civil War, transportation in all large cities was by horsecar;[2] therefore, new housing had to be fairly close in and consisted largely of "three-deckers" (upper-story porches decking the front and rear of four-story tenements). Soon, however, it became feasible to build farther out. The first elevated steam railroads were built in New York in the 1870's, and twenty years later every sizable city had an electric trolley system.[3] Railroads and trolleys enabled more people to commute and to commute larger distances; the farther out they went, the cheaper the land was and the larger the lot sizes they could afford. One- and two-family houses became common.

Wherever this outward movement of the well-off passed beyond the legal boundaries of the city, it created special problems. As early as 1823, Cincinnati officials complained that people living on the edge of the town did not contribute their fair share of taxes, and a few years later the council of St. Louis, which had the same problem, petitioned the state legislature to enlarge the city to include the settlers just beyond its borders who had "all the benefits [sic] of a City residence without any of its burdens."[4] Many cities were enlarged, thus postponing—in some instances almost to the present—the emergence of an acute problem of city-suburb relations. The motives that impelled people to move outward were essentially the same, however, whether the boundaries of the city were near in or far out, and the strength of the outward movement seems to have been roughly the same in every era and in every place. The "flight to the suburbs" is certainly nothing new.[5]

The movement of the well-off out of the inner city was always regarded (as it had been by the select committee in New York) as both portent and cause of the city's decline. The well-off were sure that without their steadying and elevating influence the city would drift from bad to worse and become "the prey of professional thieves, ruffians, and political jugglers."[6] As a committee of leading Bostonians explained in the 1840's:

An individual's influence is exerted chiefly in the place where he resides. Take away from the city a hundred moral and religious families, and there will be taken away a hundred centers of moral and religious influence, though the constituted heads of those families spend the greatest part of their time in the city, and hold in the metropolis the greatest proportion of their property. Those who remove their residence from the city, remove also their places of attendance on public worship, and the children of those families are removed from our primary and higher schools, public and private.... They are not here to visit the poor and degraded, and by their example and conduct to assist in resisting the tide of iniquity that is rolling in on us.[7]

People said that they moved because the city was no longer habitable: they could not stand its dirt, noise, and disorder, not to mention the presence near them of "undesirable" people. (When they moved beyond the borders of the city, they added political corruption and high taxes to this list.) Actually, they would have moved anyway, although not in all cases quite so soon, even if the inner city had been as clean and fresh as a field of daisies. They would have moved sooner or later because, as the city grew, the land they occupied would have to be used more intensively. Or, to put it another way, they would have moved because only the very rich could afford to forego the advantage of much cheaper land on the outskirts.

As the well-off moved outward, the "not well-off" (meaning here those who could not afford new houses or the time and money to travel half an hour to work) moved into the relatively old and high-density housing left behind. Indeed, it was in part the pressure of their demand for this housing that caused the well-off to move as soon as they did. The result in many places was to thin out the most overcrowded districts ("rabbit-warrens," the reformers of the 1880's called them) adjacent to warehouses, factories, stores, and offices.

Had the supply of the not well-off not been continually replenished by migration from abroad and from the small towns and farms of this country, the high-density tenement districts would have emptied rapidly at the end of the last century as incomes rose and more people moved outward. As it happened, however, immigration continually brought new workers who, for at least a few years—until they, too, could move on—were glad to take refuge in the housing that the others had left behind.

Heavy as it was, migration to the city seldom fully offset the decentralizing effect of the commuter railroad and the trolley and of the expansion of commercial and industrial land uses near the city's center. In many cities the densest slums were either displaced by stores, offices, and factories or drained to reasonable densities by improvement of transportation, or both. The Basin tenement area of Cincinnati, for example, lost one-fourth of its population between 1910 and 1930, a period of rapid growth for the rest of the city. In Chicago, New York, and Philadelphia much the same thing happened.[8]

In the first half of the twentieth century the process of growth was accelerated by changes of technology, although its character was not changed in any essential way. Invention of the mechanical refrigerator, along with a vast increase in the variety of inexpensive canned foods, reduced the number of boardinghouses and restaurants. Dispersal of factories was brought about by the use of heavy-duty power transmission cables and, even more, of the assembly line (horizontal processes required more land). Probably of equal importance was the introduction of cheap and rapid highway transportation.[9] By 1915 nearly 2.5 million automobiles were in use; five years later there were 1.1 million trucks. The automobiles facilitated the creation of residential neighborhoods still farther out from the central business district, and the trucks cut factories loose from railheads (and thus from the center of the city also). Stupendous sums were spent for automobiles and for highways, in effect subsidizing the development of the hinterland.

The federal government gave outward expansion a further push when during the Depression it created the Federal Housing Administration. As was noted in the previous chapter, FHA's assistance (and later the Veterans Administration's as well) went mostly to those who bought new homes. For the most part these were in outlying neighborhoods of the central city or in the suburban ring, the only places where vacant land was plentiful. Had it been disposed to do so, FHA might have stimulated the renovation of existing housing and thus the refurbishing of the central cities. If it had done this, it would have assisted many of the not well-off, a category that included most Negroes as well as other minority group members. In fact, it did the opposite: it subsidized the well-off who wanted to leave the central city, while (by setting neighborhood and property standards that they could not meet) refusing to help the not well-off to renovate their central-city houses.[10]

The Depression slowed down but—thanks to the FHA—did not stop the outward movement of the well-off. It did, however, interrupt and even reverse the flow into the city of the not well-off. In the 1920's more than four million immigrants had come from abroad, the great majority of them settling in the larger cities. There also had been a considerable movement of Negroes from the rural South to the large cities of the North, especially New York. (The Negro population of New York more than doubled in this decade, rising from 152,467 to 327,706, and Harlem, which had only recently been occupied by outward-bound, second-generation Jews and Italians, was suddenly transformed.[11]) When the Depression struck, people not only stopped coming to the city but left it in large numbers to go "back to the land" and back to the old country. Now, partially drained and no longer being replenished, the inner city began to stagnate. Neighborhoods that had been packed a few years before were more or less depopulated; people who lived in them no longer expected to follow the "tenement trail" out of the city. They seemed to have been left permanently behind and it appeared to some people that a new and serious problem had arisen. As Edith Elmer Wood explained in a bulletin written for the Public Works Administration in 1935:

> The blighting effect of slums on human lives and human character was less acute during the period of immigration and rapid population growth than it is now. Newcomers sought the cheapest and therefore the worst housing, literally pushing out, and necessarily into something better, the last previous immigrant wave. They were able to afford the move because rapidly expanding population meant rapidly expanding jobs. . . . Living in the slums was a temporary discomfort, cheerfully endured, because of an animating faith that prosperity and comfort were just ahead. . . .
>
> Since immigration stopped, all that has changed. The situation has become static. A superior family climbs out here and there, but it is the exception, not the rule, and for every one that goes up, another must come down. Discouragement or bitterness has taken the

place of hope. It is only recently that we have seen a generation reach manhood and womanhood which was born and bred in our city slums, which has known no home but a dingy tenement, no playground but the city streets. And worst of all, it has little hope of attaining anything better except by the short-cuts of crime.[12]

The "defense boom" and then World War II quickly filled the inner city to overflowing once again. Now the well-off could not move away because of controls on residential construction; at the same time, large numbers of workers, most of them unskilled, came from small towns and farms until all the inner city housing that could possibly be used was occupied. A huge amount of new factory capacity was built in two or three years, most of it at the periphery of the city but within its borders. Had this expansion taken place under normal circumstances, most of the new factories would have been located in the suburban ring, beyond the borders of the city. The effect of the war, therefore, was to slow down somewhat the decentralization of the city.

As soon as wartime controls were lifted, the logic of growth reasserted itself. A huge pent-up demand on the part of the well-off, whose numbers had been swelled by formation of new families, wartime prosperity, and the home-loan provisions of the "G.I. Bill of Rights," burst forth in a mass exodus from the city to the suburbs: between 1940 and 1950 some 2.3 million persons moved out of the twelve largest central cities. Not all of these people went to the suburbs, of course, and 2.3 million was only 12 percent of the total population of these cities; nevertheless, the sudden outward surge was unprecedented in scale. As had happened before, when the well-off left, the not well-off moved into the housing left behind. The most nearly well-off of them took the best of it and left the housing that they vacated for others below them on the income ladder, who in turn passed their housing down to still others. Many of those in this housing queue—practically all those at the "far" end of it—were Negroes (in New York, Puerto Ricans also; in Los Angeles, Oakland, and some other cities, Mexicans also).

The heavy, rapid Negro migration to the city in the war and postwar years changed the situation markedly. In 1940 nearly three-quarters (72 percent) of the nation's Negroes lived in the South; twenty years later a little more than half (54 percent) lived there. The Negro had always been rural, but by 1960 he was urban: one-half of all Negroes lived in central cities; in the 1950 to 1960 decade in every one of the fifty largest central cities, the percentage of Negroes in the population rose.[13]

Massive as it was, this new migration into the large cities did not quite offset the movement of the well-off out of them. Consequently, by 1960 there was ample housing of a sort for most of those seeking it. Much of it was of a very good sort, built only thirty or forty years before and still structurally sound. All that was wrong with much of it was that it was out-of-date, aesthetically and otherwise, by the standards of the well-off—standards that had risen rapidly during the war and postwar prosperity. The not well-off very quickly occupied the better housing that came on the market. In the past, the least well-off had lived in compact, high-density districts. Now they spread out in all directions, leapfrogging neighborhoods here and there, covering miles and miles.[14]

By no means all of the well-off left the city. Some who could afford any rent lived in luxury apartments, a gold coast along the central business district. The number of such people was bound to grow, but not enough to change the inner city fundamentally. In the outlying neighborhoods, heads of families often remained even when they could afford to move; people getting along in years saw no point in moving from neighborhoods in which they had lived so long and to which they had become attached. It was their children and their boarders who moved away to the suburbs. On the lower East Side of New York in the early 1960's there were still some neighborhoods occupied mainly by remnants of the Jewish immigration of the early 1900's and the Puerto Rican immigration of the 1920's,[15] but the population of such neighborhoods was thinning out. The later migrants, mostly Negroes (and in New York, Puerto Ricans), had in most cases come to the city as young adults or children and were a remarkably fast-growing and fast-spreading population.

Looking at the neighborhoods they had left a decade or two before, suburbanites were often dismayed at what they saw—lawns and shrubbery trampled out, houses unpainted, porches sagging, vacant lots filled with broken bottles and junk. To them—and, of course, even more to the scattering of "old residents" who for one reason or another remained—these things constituted "blight" and "decay." To the people who were moving into these neighborhoods from old tenements and shanties, however, the situation appeared in a very different light. Many of them cared little or nothing for lawns and had no objections to broken bottles; they knew, too, that the more "fixed up" things were, the higher rents would be. What mattered most to them was having four or five rooms instead of one or two, plumbing that worked, an inside bathroom that did not have to be shared with strangers down the hall, and central heating. To the least well-off, "blight" was a blessing. They were able, for the first time in their lives, to occupy housing that was comfortable.

Although the appearance of neighborhoods declined as they were occupied by lower-income groups, the quality of housing in the central city as a whole improved dramatically. Housing was repaired and improved on a wholesale scale during the postwar years, some of it by government programs but more of it through the normal processes of consumer spending. Although differences in Census definition make precise comparisons impossible, more than half the housing in metropolitan areas that was substandard in 1949 was put in sound condition during the next ten years through structural repairs or by plumbing additions. At the end of the decade, some families still lived in housing that was appallingly bad, but their number was now small and getting smaller every year.[16]

The improvement resulting from the repair of substandard housing and the handing down of good housing by the well-off was widespread. This fact can be seen from the gains made by Negroes, the worst-housed group in the population, as shown in the table.

Percentage of Negro Families Occupying Substandard Housing[17]

Metropolitan Area	1950	1960
New York	33.8	23.0
Chicago	59.3	25.4
Philadelphia	42.8	13.8
Los Angeles	19.0	6.2
Detroit	29.3	10.3
St. Louis	75.0	39.4
Washington, D.C.	33.9	13.6
San Francisco-Oakland	25.6	14.9

By discarding housing that was still usable, the well-off conferred a great benefit upon the not well-off. Like many benefits, however, this one had hidden costs: in order to use the discarded housing, one had to live where it was; all too often this meant living where there were not enough jobs.

The central business district—and with it the central city as a whole—had long been losing its monopoly of accessibility. As the population at the periphery of the city grew, there was increasing support for large stores and other facilities that could compete with those of the central business district. People no longer had to go downtown for almost everything. At the same time, improvements in transportation, especially the building of expressways and of major airports that were some distance from the city, made it easier than before to get from one part of the metropolitan area to another without going downtown. Also, manufacturing always tended to move outward to cheaper land; beginning in the early 1930's, increases in plant size and improvements in materials-handling techniques hastened this movement. More and more manufacturers wanted single-story plants with horizontal material flows and aisles wide enough to permit mechanical handling of materials. This usually compelled them to move their operations to a less congested area close to a center of long-distance truck hauling.[18] After the Second World War, much manufacturing, and much retailing and wholesaling as well, moved out of the city.

The central business district retained its advantage of accessibility with respect to activities involving frequent face-to-face communication. Top executives had to be near to each other and to the bankers, lawyers, advertising men, government officials, and others with whom they dealt frequently; consequently, they kept their headquarters downtown. The rest of their operations—factories as well as record-keeping—they sent to the suburbs, where land was cheaper and clerical help easier to find, or to other areas altogether.

By far the biggest concentration of jobs for the unskilled was still in or near the central city. Service workers (for example, watchmen and elevator operators) were concentrated downtown, and "laborers" worked in the nearby industrial suburbs. There were not enough such jobs to go around, however, now that so high a proportion of the city's population consisted of the unskilled. Most of the *new* jobs for the unskilled, moreover, were in the suburban ring; that was where almost all the growth was taking place. Unskilled workers, most of whom lived near the downtown part of the central city, would have been happier had the jobs not moved outward. The outward movement of jobs did not leave them stranded, however;

except in three or four of the largest metropolitan areas, a worker could travel from his inner city dwelling to a job anywhere on the outer perimeter of the metropolitan area in no more than half an hour. The radial pattern of highway and rail transportation, although not planned for the purpose, was ideal from the standpoint of workers who were characteristically needed for a few days first in one suburb and then in another, the second being perhaps on the opposite rim of the metropolitan area from the first. "Reverse commuting"—that is, traveling from an inner city residence to a suburban job—became common among the unskilled workers of the central city. The advantage of living near the center of a radial transportation system may have been a major cause—conceivably as great a one as racial discrimination—of the failure of many workers to move to the suburbs.[19]

At some future time—a very distant one perhaps—the logic of metropolitan growth will have to change. Conceivably, the urban population may stop growing, or technology may change so as to make it cheaper to build upward than outward, or government may redistribute income to such an extent that everyone can afford to buy a new house and to commute a considerable distance to work. If none of these changes occurs, the supply of vacant land into which the metropolis can expand will run out. None of these changes seems likely to occur in the foreseeable future, however. Essentially the same logic that shaped the growth of the city in the past may therefore be expected to shape that of the metropolitan area in the future. It is, in fact, already clear that the urban population will grow: the children of the postwar baby boom are already reaching adulthood, and a new, "second-generation" baby boom may be about to begin. Migration to the cities from the rural South will not be as great as it was during and after the war, but it will be substantial. In 1960 there were slightly less than half as many Negroes on farms and in rural areas as there had been in 1950, and a relatively high proportion of these people were too old to migrate or had long since decided not to. The birthrate in the rural South, however, was high —high enough to keep a large stream of migrants moving to the cities.[20]

Immigration from abroad will also contribute to the cities' growth. In 1968 it accounted for more than one-fifth (22.1 percent) of the total

United States population increase; about half the immigrants were un-skilled or semiskilled workers and their families.

If present trends continue, there will not only be more people in the cities in the next two or three decades, but a higher proportion of them will be well-off. By the year 2000, according to the Council of Economic Advisers, the average American family will have an annual income of about $18,000 (in 1965 prices).[21] In this very affluent society, housing will probably be discarded at an even faster rate than now, and the demand for living space will probably be greater. In the future, then, the process of turnover is likely to give more and better housing bargains to the not well-off, encouraging them to move ever farther out-ward and thus eventually emptying the central city and bringing "blight" to suburbs that were new a decade or two ago. To the "pull-ing" effect of these bargains will be added two "pushing" ones: the physical deterioration of housing in the central city (which, being the oldest, has been in use the longest) and the clearance activities of urban renewal and public works programs, which are expected to displace between half a million and two million families between 1965 and 1975. Among those moving outward from the central city will be large numbers of Negroes. Efforts to keep them in the central city where their voting strength can be exploited are bound to fail, as are efforts to distribute them throughout white nieghborhoods. In their quest for liv-ing space and jobs, well-off Negroes, like the well-off in other groups, will move into the suburban ring, in some places leapfrogging white suburbs to create their own and in others occupying suburbs vacated by better-off Negroes or whites. As better-off suburbanites make ready to move farther out into the suburban ring in search of larger lots, they will relax zoning and other restrictions that have excluded the less well-off from suburban communities; as the need to find customers for their "downgraded" properties grows, less and less exhortation will be needed to convince them of the soundness of the principle of open occupancy. Despite these movements, however, large numbers of Negroes will continue to live in the central city for at least several decades.

If there is any check on outward expansion, it is probably the limited supply of vacant land. This supply will be used up faster than ever, not only because more people will be able to afford land, but also because they will be able to afford larger lots. (In the New York metropolitan region, for example, the next six million people to move to new homes in the outlying suburbs are expected to take as much land as the previous sixteen million took. Two-thirds of the land in these suburbs is now zoned for single-family houses on lots of a half acre or more.[22]) It will be many years before the frontier of vacant land is reached, however. (Even in the New York region, where the demand is greatest, the supply is expected to last for at least another generation.[23]) And when it is at last reached, the outward movement will not stop abruptly; instead, two- and three-acre lots will probably be subdivided into half-acre ones, permitting movement from the older, higher-density rings of settlement to continue for some time. As the supply of vacant land diminishes, however, the price of it will rise, and this will dampen the desire to use it lavishly. That the outlying suburbs of New York and other cities are zoned for large lots therefore indicates little about the density at which they will actually be built; the zoners there may not have anticipated how costly land would become and how sobering an effect this would have upon prospective buyers. In fact, the dampening effect of higher land prices in the suburbs has been operating for some time. Of the new dwelling units started in 1966, 32.8 percent were in apartment houses for three or more families; ten years before, the comparable figure was only 8.7 percent.

As the price of vacant land in the suburbs goes up, that of land and buildings in the central city will go down. As was pointed out earlier, the central business district—and with it the central city as a whole—has been losing the monopoly of accessibility that made its land so valuable. As the exodus of commerce, industry, and population continues, the value of real estate in the central city will decline. Urban renewal will tend to slow this down: so long as it appears likely that the government will buy deteriorating property at its present market value, that value is not likely to fall. In a few favored parts of a city, renewal may hold values steady. But it probably cannot hold them steady throughout the whole of a large city—and it certainly cannot steady them in *all* large cities. The amount of subsidy that this enterprise would require is far beyond what anyone would consider tolerable.

If the populations of the inner cities are not again replenished by low-income immigrants—an uncertain condition, since, as the example of Cuba shows, a Latin American dictator may at any time send hundreds of thousands fleeing north—the time will come when cleared land in the depopulated central city will be worth less than vacant land in the heavily populated suburbs. When this time comes, the direction of metropolitan growth will reverse itself: the well-off will move from the suburbs to the cities, probably causing editorial writers to deplore the "flight to the central city" and politicians to call for government programs to check it by redeveloping the suburbs.

Recently, some tendencies toward recentralization have appeared.[24] First, advances in electronic data processing are making some offices into "paper-processing factories"; these employ unskilled workers at the bottom of the white-collar occupational ladder in jobs such as key punch operator. Second, "the computer and the recent technological advances in teleprocessing and time-sharing have also strongly reinforced the ability of a business enterprise to retain its head office and management in a centralized location in the face of ever wider decentralization of operations."[25] Third, huge expenditures are being made on scientific research and development. Much of this work does not require great land space, is independent of manufacturing and materials locations, and is best done in close proximity to universities.

The central city is not at all likely to regain its old monopoly on accessibility, however. At most, it will be one of several nuclei in a metropolitan area over which business activity and residential occupance are, as compared to the "old-fashioned" city, rather evenly and thinly spread.

Despite recentralizing tendencies, it is idle to talk of bringing large numbers of the well-off back into the central city. For the city to compete as a residential area with the suburbs, large districts of it would have to be completely rebuilt at very low densities. This is out of the question so long as people are living in these districts. To be sure, the government might build new housing somewhere else (where?) for the residents of the old neighborhoods and move them to it, forcibly if necessary. It might then tear down the existing structures and put up new ones, creating neighborhoods that would attract the well-off back from the suburbs. This plan would be fantastically expensive, of course, since it would mean destroying a great deal of useful housing, as well as stores, factories, churches, schools, and other facilities. Doing this would be insane if the purpose were nothing more than "civic patriotism" or the wish to confer benefits on the well-off.

A case might perhaps be made for a wholesale exchange of population between the central city and the suburbs on the ground that the preservation of democratic institutions requires it. But if such were the purpose, the redeveloped central city could not be occupied solely or even mainly by the well-off—rich and poor, black and white, would have to be settled in proximity to one another, sharing schools and other facilities, the object being to improve the quality of the community by their association. An undertaking of this sort would have the justification of aiming at an important public good. Whether it would, within reasonable probability, secure that good is doubtful, however. For one thing, it would be hard to give the well-off the space necessary to bring them back from the suburbs and still have room for the large number of the not well-off who would have to be accommodated. If, as is all too likely, one of the requirements of the well-off was that they be insulated from "undesirables," then obviously the reoccupation of the city by them could not be brought about on terms that would serve any public purpose. Even on the most favorable view of the possibilities—that is, assuming that stable, integrated neighborhoods could be created—the wisdom of, in effect, throwing a large part of the city's physical plant on the scrap heap might well be questioned.

To build "new towns" (actually small cities) when doing so involves abandoning or underutilizing existing facilities would be an even more costly venture since not only housing, schools, churches, and stores, but everything else as well—factories, streets, water and sewer lines—would have to be built new from the ground up. Here again, one may say that if the object is to create an integrated community, and if that object can be attained in this way and in no other that entails smaller costs (so that abandoning existing streets, sewer lines, and the like is unavoidable), the money is well spent. That the undertaking would be immensely expensive is beyond question, however.[26]

The impracticability of attracting large numbers of the well-off back into the central city before land prices there have become competitive with those in the suburbs (and without the use of large subsidies) can be seen from New York City's experience with a "demonstration" project. This project involved two blocks on West Ninety-fourth and Ninety-fifth streets near Central Park. The owners of the brownstone buildings in these blocks were given the choice of either bringing their buildings up to a high standard or selling them to someone—either a private purchaser or the City—who would. In May 1960, the letters to the owners went out. Nearly ten years later (September 1969) the City had bought eighteen of the buildings. Four of them were offered for sale to qualified bidders at auction in 1963, but only one was bid upon and that by only one bidder. In 1965 the City announced that it had arranged negotiated sales to eighteen "sponsors" who would rehabilitate the buildings and create a racially integrated neighborhood. The sponsors would pay from $21,000 to $34,000 for the buildings, which was about 10 percent less than their estimated market value. Since they were in very poor condition ("nothing but four walls," said Mrs. Kenneth B. Clark, who with her husband was one of the sponsors), rehabilitation costs would be high—about $15,000 per floor, making the total cost of a building (all were either four or five floors) at least $80,000.[27] By the end of 1967, only four buildings had actually passed out of the City's hands, and all but one of the original sponsors had withdrawn; for some of the buildings as many as three sponsors had come and gone. By the summer of 1969, the City still had possession of seven buildings. The cost of rehabilitation had by now risen to about $20,000 per floor, and the City was hoping to sell the remaining buildings at about 50 percent of their current market value. Of course, even if the buildings had all been bought up immediately at market prices, nothing much would have been "demonstrated," for the City's real problem was not to induce a few very prosperous families to live near the center of Manhattan but to bring tens of thousands of moderately well-off families back to such unglamorous places as Brooklyn and the Bronx.

The three imperatives listed at the beginning of this chapter—namely, rate of population growth, technology of transportation, and distribution of income—place stringent limits on policy. Except as it may relax one or more of them and so change the logic of metropolitan growth, government—even the wisest and most powerful government—must work within the limits set by these imperatives. It may hasten or delay the unfolding of the logic of growth and it may make such adaptations—very important ones sometimes—as are possible within it. But given the premises, it cannot prevent the conclusions from following.

Consider the case of New York City. The state legislative committee of 1857, whose report was quoted earlier, confidently asserted that "wise and simple laws," if only they had been adopted in time, would have checked or prevented the evils it deplored. With such laws, it said, "the city of New York would now exhibit more gratifying bills of health, more general social comfort and prosperity and less, far less expenditure for the support of pauperism and the punishment of crime." It blamed the authorities of an earlier time for not having passed the necessary laws; those authorities, it said, "were unmindful of the future public good, precisely as we, in our day and generation, are pertinaciously regardless of our posterity's welfare."[28]

Perhaps the authorities were unmindful of the future public good. Whether they were or were not does not matter much; they could not, in any case, have changed the imperatives of population growth, transportation technology, and income level, and it is these factors that account not only for their failure to change the pattern of growth but also for the failure of authorities in later times as well, including, of course, the committee of 1857 itself.

What, one wonders, are the wise and simple laws that would have saved the situation if only they had been made soon enough? The idea of controlling land use by a zoning ordinance is a recent one, but suppose that when Manhattan was first settled an ordinance had limited the spread of warehouses, factories, and other objectionable land uses. If such an ordinance had been made and enforced, the old Knickerbocker mansions would still be standing—but there would be no city. Nor, if *all* towns had made and enforced such ordinances, would there be cities anywhere. If towns are to grow into cities and cities into metropolises, old residential districts necessarily must decline and disappear.

Suppose, again, that in the city's earliest days the authorities had enacted a housing code requiring the demolition of all substandard dwellings. (The committee of 1857 did, in fact, propose a regulation against the renting of cellars.[29]) Such a code, if enforced, would have prevented the city from growing fast and from ever becoming a metropolis.[30] In order to grow fast, the city had to become a center of warehouses, shops, and factories, which meant that it had to have a plentiful supply of cheap labor, which meant that it had to have a plentiful supply of housing that such labor could afford. If all the housing had been decent by the standards of the time, some of the labor required for the city's growth could not have afforded to live in the city at all.[31]

It may be argued that if the city had insisted, adequate housing would have been provided and the extra cost in effect added to the wage bill and so passed on to the consumer. But no city could have added very much to its wage bill without worsening its competitive position vis-à-vis other areas. Had all places provided adequate housing, the city would have been under a cost handicap, and its development would have been impeded accordingly. The fundamental fact was that it would have cost more to provide adequate housing in the city than elsewhere. (To be sure, had the extra costs been imposed upon the affluent *regardless of where they lived,* the city would not have been handicapped, but because of political boundaries and other institutional arrangements this was not a real possibility.)

If society had been willing to accept a curtailment of the rate of economic growth for the sake of preventing overcrowding and bad housing in the city, it could have prevented people who could not support themselves properly from coming to the city at all. By restricting the supply of labor in the city, the authorities could have forced the price of it up. Keeping the farm boys on the farms and stopping immigration of all but skilled workers from abroad could have checked or prevented the evils that the committee deplored. But, of course, the growth of New York would also have been checked or prevented. The old Knickerbocker mansions might still be there, but the Statue of Liberty would not be.

It was impossible both to allow unrestricted immigration and to eliminate substandard housing. If free to do so, people would come to the cities from the rural backwaters of this country, and from abroad, and they would keep on coming until the opportunities in the city as they perceived them were no better than those in the places where they were. Since opportunities in much of the world were extremely poor, the movement into the city was bound to be massive and to continue almost indefinitely if allowed. Improving conditions in the city while allowing migration to continue freely could have no effect but to establish the final equilibrium at a different point—i.e., one at which *more* of the poor would have come to the city. As Jacob A. Riis wrote in *The Poor in Great Cities* (1895), if it were possible for New York to "shut her door against the immigration of the world and still maintain the conditions of today, I should confidently predict a steady progress that would leave little of the problem for the next generation to wrestle with. But that is only another way of saying, 'if New York were not New York.' "[32]

If the authorities had been able to find a miraculously cheap and fast means of transporting large numbers of people from the factory district to the outskirts of the city, the evils that the select committee deplored would easily have been ended. For a time, in fact, reformers in New York thought the subway might accomplish wonders. ("If the happy day ever comes when a poor man can be carried to the green fields of Long Island, New Jersey, or Westchester County for five cents, then a wonderful change will take place," one of them wrote.[33]) The subway and the trolley did put an end to "rabbit warrens," but in the large cities it was still necessary, despite the new transportation technology, for many people to be crowded together close to the factories, stores, and offices. In 1893 a member of the American Economic Association declared that the confident belief of a few years before that rapid transit would solve New York's housing problems was now seen to be a vain hope.[34]

So long as large numbers of workers had to live near their jobs, it was impossible to avoid high rents and overcrowding in the large cities, a conclusion that the reformers of every generation fought manfully against but finally had to accept. It was impossible, a city commission concluded in 1900, to design a tenement house that was both adequate and commercially feasible; moreover, legislation to require the conversion of existing tenements to other uses was not practicable.[35] And in 1955 a mayor's committee estimated that about a million persons (268,000 families) would be displaced if the multiple-dwelling code was strictly enforced.[36]

Redistributing income was another possibility, and it, too, was tried. Subway and highway construction was subsidized, as was the purchase of new homes. Insofar as these and other measures put people in the class of the well-off who would otherwise not have gotten there so soon, they hastened the decongestion of the city. But since they had to be paid for by taxes—taxes that were not imposed only on the super-well-off—these measures must have had some contrary and offsetting effect as well. In any event, migration into the city always replenished at least partially the "class of tenantry living from hand to mouth, loose in morals, improvident in habits, degraded and squalid as beggary itself." Redistribution of income could not eliminate poverty in the city so long as opportunities in any part of the world were conspicuously worse off than in the city, and so long as people were free to move to it.

NOTES

1. "Report of the Select Committee Appointed to Examine into the Condition of Tenant Houses in New York and Brooklyn," transmitted to the Legislature March 9, 1857 (Albany, N.Y.), pp. 11–12. Excerpts of this report appear in Glaab, *The American City.*

2. In the Boston area, however, more than 20,000 passengers a day were being carried in and out of the city, by ferry and otherwise, as early as 1847. Oscar Handlin, *Boston's Immigrants,* rev. ed. (Cambridge, Mass.: Harvard University Press, 1959), p. 18.

3. Blake McKelvey, *The Urbanization of America* (New Brunswick, N.J.: Rutgers University Press, 1963), pp. 78–79. See also Glaab, *The American City,* p. 178; and Sam B. Warner, Jr., *Streetcar Suburbs* (Cambridge, Mass.: Harvard University Press and M.I.T. Press, 1962).

4. Richard C. Wade, *The Urban Frontier* (Chicago: University of Chicago Press, Phoenix Books, 1964), p. 307.

5. In Philadelphia the outward movement was proportionately greater between 1860 and 1910 than between 1900 and 1950 (Hans Blumenfeld, "The Modern Metropolis," *Scientific American* 213 [September 1965]: 67). For an account of Philadelphia's early pattern of growth, which was not that of the ideal type described in the text, see Sam B. Warner, Jr., *The Private City* (Philadelphia: University of Pennsylvania Press, 1968), ch. 3.

6. Edward Crapsey, *The Nether Side Of New York* (New York: Sheldon and Company, 1872), p. 9.

7. Quoted in J. Leslie Dunstan, *A Light to the City* (Boston: Beacon Press, 1966), p. 91.

8. Mabel L Walker, *Urban Blight and Slums* (Cambridge, Mass.: Harvard University Press, 1938), pp. 132–133.

9. Constance McLaughlin Green, *The Rise of Urban America* (New York: Harper & Row, 1965), pp. 132–133.

10. Davis McEntire, *Residence and Race* (Berkeley: University of California Press, 1960), pp. 300–301. FHA discriminated against Negroes until well into the Truman administration. Afterward it discriminated again them in *effect* by insisting on very low-risk loans.

11. Gilbert Osofsky, *Harlem: The Making of a Ghetto* (New York: Harper & Row, 1963), p. 128.

12. Edith Elmer Wood, *Slums and Blighted Areas in the U.S.,* Administration of Public Works, Housing Division Bulletin Number 1 (Washington, D.C.: U.S. Government Printing Office, 1935), p. 19.

13. Leo F. Schnore, *The Urban Scene* (New York: The Free Press, 1965), pp. 256–257.

14. McEntire, *Residence and Race,* ch. 3

15. Raymond Vernon, *Metropolis 1985* (Cambridge, Mass.: Harvard University Press, 1960), p. 141.

16. On the comparability of 1950 and 1960 Census data, see Bernard J. Frieden, "Housing and National Urban Goals: Old Policies and New Realities," in James Q. Wilson, ed., *The Metropolitan Enigma* (Cambridge, Mass.: Harvard University Press, 1968), pp. 166–168.

Substandard housing is "dilapidated" or lacks one or more plumbing facilities. *Dilapidated* housing does not provide safe and adequate shelter and endangers the health, safety, and well-being of the occupants because it has one or more "critical defects," on a combination of lesser ones, or is of inadequate original construction. *Critical defects* are those that indicate continued neglect and serious damage to the structure (p. 163).

Frieden (p. 173) divides the Census income categories into groups representing roughly the bottom third ($0–1,999 in 1950, $0–2,999 in 1960), middle third ($2,000–3,999 in 1950, $3,000–5,999 in 1960), and upper third ($4,000 and above in 1950, $6,000 and above in 1960). The percentage of families in each third living in substandard housing was as follows:

	1950 (percent)	1960 (percent)
Upper third	12	4
Middle third	30	14
Lower third	53	36

17. The table is adapted from data presented by Bernard J. Frieden in *The Future of Old Neighborhoods* (Cambridge, Mass.: M.I.T. Press, 1964), p. 24.

18. See the chapter on technological change by Boris Yavitz in Eli Ginsburg et al., *Manpower Strategy for the Metropolis* (New York: Columbia University Press, 1968), especially pp. 49–55.

19. It will be understood that the account that has been given of metropolitan development refers to an ideal type. Concretely, the older (Eastern and Midwestern) cities conform to the type much better than do the newer (Western and Southwestern) ones. Los Angeles, which had practically no history prior to the automobile and truck, conforms hardly at all. Chicago is fairly representative of most large metropolitan areas.

20. Between 1960 and 1968 the number of Negroes living in central cities increased from 9.7 million to 11.9 million, while the number of whites dropped by almost 2 million. Between 1960 and 1966 whites had been leaving central cities at a rate of about 150,000 per year, but the rate rose to almost 500,000 per year between 1966 and 1968. Negroes had been moving into central cities at a rate of about 400,000 per year between 1960 and 1966; this rate declined to about 100,000 per year in the 1966–1968 period. In this latter period, the Negro metropolitan population *outside* central cities increased by about one million persons—an increase of 35 percent over the number of Negroes living in those areas in 1960. As of 1968, 54 percent of the total Negro population of the United States lived in central cities and about 15 percent in suburbs. U.S. Bureau of the Census, *Current Population Reports,* Population Characteristics, Series P-20, No. 181, "Population of the United States by Metropolitan-Nonmetropolitan Residence: 1968 and 1960" (Washington, D.C.: U.S. Government Printing Office, 1969), pp. 1–3, tables A, B, and D.

21. *Economic Report of the President,* transmitted to the Congress, January 1965 (Washington, D.C.: U.S. Government Printing Office, 1965), p. 169.

22. Robert Weaver in New York City Planning Commission, "The Future by Design," (multilithed transcript of symposium, October 1964), p. 169.

23. Raymond Vernon, *The Myth and Reality of Our Urban Problems* (Cambridge, Mass.: Harvard University Press, 1962), p. 33.

24. See Yavitz, in Ginsburg et al., *Manpower Strategy,* pp. 58–61.

25. Ibid., p. 59.

26. The financial troubles of Reston, Va., are described by Monroe W. Karmin in *The Wall Street Journal*, October 13, 1967, p. 1.

27. The *New York Times* of October 18, 1966, gives an account of a couple who purchased a brownstone at 155 West Ninety-first street, paying $30,000 for the house and investing another $55,000 in reconstruction and improvements. Presumably, this building, which had been a rooming house, was purchased from a private party.

28. Glaab, *The American City*, p. 11.

29. Ibid. Other measures proposed by the Committee were regulations to insure easy egress from tenements in case of fire, prevention of prostitution and incest by requiring a sufficient number of rooms per family and by prohibiting subletting, and prevention of drunkenness "by providing for every man a clean and comfortable home" (p. 3).

30. Code enforcement and rent control, along with apprehension about civil disorder, are held responsible for decreases in land values in Harlem in the last ten years. Because of vigorous enforcement of the building code, many buildings are vacant and have been vandalized. (*New York Times*, April 28, 1968).

31. Before the arrival of the Irish, Handlin remarks with reference to Boston, "the rigid labor supply had made industrialization impossible." (By "rigid" he presumably means one that demanded and got relatively high wages.) And the Irish, he adds, could not have been housed without cellar holes. *Boston's Immigrants*, pp. 82, 110).

32. Jacob A. Riis, in Robert A. Woods et al., *The Poor in Great Cities* (New York: Scribner's, 1895), p. 88.

33. William T. Elsing, "Life in New York Tenement Houses as Seen by a City Missionary," in *The Poor in Great Cities*, p. 76.

34. Marcus T. Reynolds, *The Housing of the Poor in American Cities* (New York: American Economic Association, March and May 1893), p. 109.

35. *Reports of the Industrial Commission, Immigration*, Vol. XV (Washington, D.C.: U.S. Government Printing Office, 1901), p. 491.

36. Morris Eagle, "The Puerto Ricans in New York City," in Nathan Glazer and Davis McEntire, eds., *Studies in Housing and Minority Groups* (Berkeley: University of California Press, 1960), p. 176.

The Urban Setting: Population, Poverty, and Race

National Commission on Urban Problems

The urban problems this Commission has studied are directly related to the size and nature of the American population, its distribution and mobility, and the social and economic handicaps faced by certain of its segments. Shortages of housing, difficulties of urban financing, jurisdictional gaps and conflicts among local governments, harmful zoning and land-use policies—all these arise directly or indirectly from the increasing number of people, their residential locations and their ability to move to other locations.

The findings and recommendations which constitute this report of the Commission are based in part on the analyses and projections regarding population, poverty, and race which are summarized below.

THE CHANGES IN OUR POPULATION

The Population Explosion

The first national census, in 1790, counted 4 million persons in the new Nation. Now, at the end of 1968, the population exceeds 200 million, and it may reach 300 million by the end of the century—only 30 years away.

As Chart I demonstrates, the steady growth in U.S. population has slowed markedly only once—during the great depression. The annual growth rate dropped to a low of 0.7 percent in 1936, rose to a high of 1.83 percent in 1947, rose again to 1.81 in 1956, and has

Reprinted from *Building The American City*, pp. 40–53. Report of the National Commission on Urban Problems to the Congress and to the President of the United States, 91st Congress, 1st Session, House Document No. 91–34, December 12, 1968. Washington: U.S. Government Printing Office.

declined steadily since. The 1967 rate was 1.07 percent. (See table 29.)

The population study[1] upon which our discussion is based relies on the next-to-lowest census projection of the birth rate.[2] Even on this conservative basis, the study projects a 41 percent increase in population from 1960 to 1985.

The nonwhite population has a higher birth rate than the white population and will, if present trends continue, increase more rapidly in all regions; by 1985, it will form almost 14 percent of the population. The rate of increase in the South will be masked by the rate of departure; because of its already high nonwhite population, however, the South will (according to recent trends) have the largest absolute increase in nonwhite population—39 percent of the entire nonwhite increase in the United States. (The nonwhite population is 92 percent Negro, but also includes Orientals, American Indians, Polynesians,

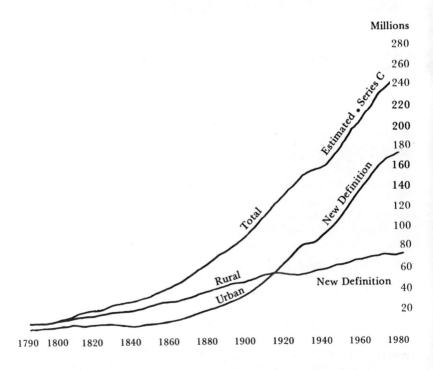

CHART 1. Total U.S. population, urban and rural, 1790–1960 and estimated 1985.

TABLE 1. U.S. Population by Region and Color; 1960 and Projected 1985
[Population in thousands]

Region and color	Population 1960	Population 1985	Percent increase	Percent distribution, by color, 1985
United States	179,323	252,185	40.6	100.0
White	158,832	217,714	37.1	86.3
Nonwhite	20,491	34,471	68.2	13.7
Northeast	44,678	58,517	31.0	100.0
White	41,522	52,269	25.9	89.3
Nonwhite	3,155	6,248	98.0	10.7
North central	51,619	65,723	27.3	100.0
White	48,003	59,228	23.4	90.1
Nonwhite	3,617	6,495	79.6	9.9
South	54,973	78,910	43.5	100.0
White	43,477	62,016	42.6	78.6
Nonwhite	11,496	16,894	47.0	21.4
West	28,053	49,035	74.8	100.0
White	25,830	44,201	71.1	90.1
Nonwhite	2,223	4,834	117.5	9.9

Source: Patricia L. Hodge and Philip M. Hauser, "The Challenge of America's Metropolitan Population Outlook, 1960 to 1985," Research Rept. No. 3, National Commission on Urban Problems, Washington, D.C., 1968, p. 19.

Eskimos, and other races. Puerto Ricans and Mexican-Americans are classified as white in census data.)

Recently released census figures, based on a population sampling in March 1968, reveal a tendency toward a more even distribution of the Nation's nonwhite population over the period 1940 to 1968.

The Population Implosion

The change from a predominantly rural to a predominantly urban nation occurred about five decades ago. (See table 30.) At the time of the first census in 1790, 95 percent of the people lived on farms, or in places of less than 2,500 inhabitants. Only 5 percent lived in urban places of 2,500 or more. The 1920 census showed that America had become an urban nation: a majority lived in urban areas. The concentration of people on relatively small portions of land—even the sprawling suburbs are dense compared to rural areas—has been described as an implosion.

By 1960, 70 percent of the population lived in urban places, and 63 percent lived in metropolitan areas. The metropolis, or the SMSA,[3] has come to characterize the pattern of American settlement. Roughly defined, it encompasses a city of more than 50,000 and the counties which contain it and maintain a certain economic and social dependence on it. The suburban counties, may, and often do, contain rural "pockets," but the preponderance of metropolitan population lives in settlements with an urban character. (The term "central city" refers to a municipality of 50,000 or more at the center of the metropolis; it is a political jurisdiction, and should not be confused with "downtown," "core," or "slum area.")

It is estimated that 71 percent of the total U.S. population will live in metropolitan areas by 1985. Most of the projected population growth—65.2 million, or 80.6 percent of it—will occur inside all metropolitan areas as defined in 1967.

Table 3, based on recent trends, shows that in the next 16 years the South—the only section of the country which is now about evenly split between urban and rural population—will probably make the greatest leap toward urbanization. The West is expected to join the already highly urban Northeast as a region which is four-fifths metropolitan.

TABLE 2.   Percent Distribution of the Negro[1] Population by Region 1940, 1950, 1960, 1966, and 1968

	1940[2]	1950[2]	1960	1966	1968
United States	100	100	100	100	100
Northeast	11	13	16	17	18
North central	11	15	18	20	22
South	77	68	60	55	53
West	1	4	6	8	8

[1] Includes only the 92 percent of nonwhite population which is Negro.

[2] Data exclude Alaska and Hawaii.

Note: Percentages may not add to 100 percent because of rounding.

Source: "Recent Trends in Social and Economic Conditions of Negroes in the United States," U.S. Department of Commerce, Bureau of the Census, series P–23, No. 26, BLS Rept. No. 347, July 1968.

TABLE 3.   Percent of Population in Metropolitan Areas by Region; 1960 and Projected 1985

Region and metropolitan status	1960	1985	Change
United States:			
Metropolitan	63.0	70.6	+ 7.6
Nonmetropolitan	37.0	29.4	− 7.6
Northeast:			
Metropolitan	79.1	80.9	+ 1.8
Nonmetropolitan	20.9	19.1	− 1.8
North Central:			
Metropolitan	60.0	67.9	+ 7.9
Nonmetropolitan	40.0	32.1	− 7.9
South:			
Metropolitan	48.1	58.5	+10.4
Nonmetropolitan	51.9	41.5	−10.4
West:			
Metropolitan	71.8	81.6	+ 9.8
Nonmetropolitan	28.2	18.4	− 9.8

Source: Hodge-Hauser, op. cit., p. 9.

Loss of Population Dominance by the Central City

Geographically the city, in the old sense of a concentrated urban settlement, is eating up more and more of the countryside. In fact, large metropolitan areas have begun to meet at their fringes, and the term *megalopolis* has been invented to describe clusters of metropolitan areas. The traditional image of the large central city surrounded by peripheral territory and scattered small towns is, in most instances, no longer valid. The jurisdictions outside the central city are growing rapidly, while growth of the central city has slowed sharply. If present trends are projected, central cities will grow in population by only about 13 percent by 1985, but the suburban rings will grow by 106 percent. Put another way, 89 percent of all metropolitan growth will be in the suburbs.

Table 4 shows how the balance of population growth has gradually shifted since the 1900's from the city to the suburb. This parallels the population trend from predominantly rural to predominantly

TABLE 4.   Percent of Growth Within Metropolitan Areas, 1900–1960

	Metropolitan total	Central city [a]	Suburban ring
1900–1910	32.0	37.1	23.6
1910–20	25.0	27.7	20.0
1920–30	27.1	24.3	32.3
1930–40	8.8	5.6	14.6
1940–50	22.6	14.7	35.9
1950–60	26.3	10.7	48.5

[a] The projections for central cities are within fixed geographic boundaries of 1960, making no allowance for annexations or city-county consolidations between 1960–1985. See Hodge-Hauser, op. cit., Methodology, p. 85.

Source: U.S. Census of Population, 1960: Standard Metropolitan Statistical Areas, PC(3)–1D, table 1.

urban, and both trends have been associated with the advent of the automotive age.

Presumably by the late 1960's, these trends already tipped the balance of metropolitan population in favor of the suburbs. In 1950, 41 percent of the people, in metropolitan areas lived in suburbs; by 1960 that share was up to 49 percent, and the figure projected for 1985 is 63 percent.

TABLE 5.   Percent of Metropolitan Area Population in the Suburban Ring, by Region, 1950, 1960, and Projected 1985

	1950 [1]	1960 (A)[1]	1960 (B)[2]	Projected 1985 [3]
United States	41	53	49	63
Northeast	43	51	51	61
North central	37	50	47	63
South	40	53	43	60
West	49	61	55	69

[1] In terms of 1950 boundaries of central cities, within SMSA's as defined in 1960.

[2] In terms of 1960 boundaries of central cities, within SMSA's as defined in 1960.

[3] In terms of 1960 boundaries of central cities, within SMSA's as defined in 1967.

Note: To the extent of central city annexations between 1960 and 1985, the projected proportions would be reduced.

Source: Hodge-Hauser, op. cit., p. 31.

No Longer a Melting Pot

The dominant central city of earlier decades contained within it a broadly diverse ethnic, racial, and economic mix. The recent trend, however, has been for these various groups to settle out into separate political jurisdictions. Within the metropolis, the central city retains most of the nonwhites and the majority (63 percent) of the metropolitan poor. Among the separate suburban jurisdictions, social and economic differences are often accentuated by the development of such homogeneous units as the low-income suburb, the industrial enclave, and the affluent commuter community.

Separation of color. The central cities, which already contain half of the Nation's nonwhite population, will contain an even greater share of the nonwhite residents in the future if the trends of the last few decades are maintained. Projections of these trends indicate, however, that while the percentage of nonwhites would almost double between 1960 and 1985 in the central cities, it would rise only slightly in the

TABLE 6.   Percent of U.S. Population That Is Nonwhite, in Central City and Suburban Ring, by Region, 1960 and Projected 1985

Region and residence	Percent non-white, 1960	Percent non-white, 1985
United States:		
Central city	17.8	30.7
Ring	5.2	6.1
Northeast:		
Central city	13.8	26.4
Ring	3.1	3.7
North central:		
Central city	17.1	32.0
Ring	2.8	2.2
South:		
Central city	26.0	38.8
Ring	11.7	13.2
West:		
Central city	13.0	23.3
Ring	4.9	5.3

Source: Hodge-Hauser, op. cit., p. 31.

TABLE 7.   Concentration of U.S. Nonwhite Population by Region, 1960 and Projected 1985

Region	In metropolitan areas [1]		In central cities of metropolitan areas	
	1960	1985	1960	1985
United States	64.4	78.3	50.5	58.4
Northeast	93.9	94.5	76.0	77.4
North central	89.7	91.5	78.8	81.9
South	45.7	63.9	34.1	42.2
West	77.9	89.6	53.5	59.1

[1] 1960 boundaries of SMSA's used for 1960; 1967 boundaries used for 1985.
Source: Hodge-Hauser, op. cit., p. 28.

suburbs. The South would remain the region of highest nonwhite central city concentration, but other regions would not be far behind by 1985.

If past trends persist, by 1985 more than three-fourths of the Nation's Negroes will live in metropolitan areas, and 58 percent of them will live in the central cities. The average will be far higher outside the still largely rural South.

In 1960, 78.5 percent of the nonwhites in metropolitan areas lived in central cities. Thus, more than 1 out of 5 nonwhites lived in the suburbs, but formed only 5 percent of the suburban population.[4]

There is limited recent evidence of some shift in the long-term trends upon which the foregoing projections are based. The Census Bureau's sample survey during the first quarter of 1968 reports a leveling off in the increase of Negro population in metropolitan central cities between 1966 and 1968, changing the ratio of Negroes to whites in central city and suburbs. But this apparent shift in trend would have to deepen and grow to change the prospects sharply.

Separation by income level.   Suburbs tend to have a larger proportion of middle- and upper-income residents than do their central cities, and a smaller percentage of families below the poverty level. The pattern is not a simple one and varies with the size of the metropolitan area. In the five largest SMSA's (population 3 million or more) —New York, Los Angeles-Long Beach, Chicago, Philadelphia,

TABLE 8.   Percent of Families Within Central Cities and Suburbs with Incomes under $3,000 or over $10,000 in Metropolitan Areas in 1959

Families by Income	Central city	Suburban ring
Less than $3,000 income	17.6	12.5
More than $10,000 income	16.5	21.2

Source: U.S. Bureau of the Census, U.S. Census of Population, 1960: Selected Area Reports, Standard Metropolitan Statistical Areas, Final Report PC(3)–1D, quoted in "Fiscal Balance in the American Federal System," Advisory Commission on Intergovernmental Relations, Washington, D.C. 1968.

and Detroit—the separation by income level is much sharper than the nationwide average.

THE IMPACT OF POPULATION CHANGES

Black Majorities

The study made for the Commission indicates the prospect of a further net drop in the white population of metropolitan central cities and a further rise in the nonwhite population.

Continuation of recent trends would produce Negro majorities by 1985 in New Orleans, Richmond, Chicago, Philadelphia, St. Louis, Detroit, Cleveland, Baltimore, and Oakland. Already, Newark, Gary, and Washington, D.C., are more than half Negro.[5]

In the absence of conscious, emphatic public policy, there appears to be little likelihood of a major shift in nonwhite population from central city to suburb. Recent Census Bureau figures show the nonwhite proportion in the suburbs holding steady at about 5 percent, and the Commission study projects a rise to only 6.1 percent by 1985. Moreover, even the slight movement of Negroes to the suburbs is likely to involve those who already are at a relative economic and social advantage, thereby reinforcing the trend toward concentration of the poor and socially handicapped in the central cities.

Suburban Population Dominance

According to the latest Census Bureau figures, the central city has gone in 8 years from a nationwide numerical advantage over the suburbs to a distinct disadvantage—from 105 percent of the suburb's population to only 84 percent.[6] If the trends of recent years persist, it will decline to about 58 percent by 1985. (A relative disadvantage will hold true in every region, ranging from 44 percent to 66 percent.) [7]

The political effects are difficult to predict with certainty, because there are two opposing trends:

On the face of it, in terms of numbers of voters, the balance of political power has shifted to the suburbs, and where their interests are as one, they may be expected to make their weight felt at the statehouse, in Congress, and in national elections.

On the other hand, the suburban ring is fragmented into many separate political jurisdictions, often with sharply different social and economic characteristics, as noted before. In the decades to come, it is likely that many large suburban cities will find more in common with the central city than with other, smaller suburbs. The giant metropolitan complexes of the future will include large outlying municipalities, "suburbs" in name only, some of which will be more populous than many present-day central cities (there were 83 suburban municipalities with a population of over 50,000 in 1960).[8] Even now many such suburban cities are suffering almost the full range of urban problems.

Changes in the Age Structure

Not only the size of population, but the size of various age groups will affect every facet of American life. Even with a declining birth rate, the United States will have an increase in the total population by 1985, and an increase in each age group, although the increases will be most notable for the 15–44 and over-65 age groups.

Almost all of the persons in these two age categories had already been born in 1968. There will be a sizable increase by 1985 in the number of young people, especially nonwhite young people, at the

TABLE 9. Percent Increases in Total and in Nonwhite Population by Age Group, in United States and in Metropolitan Areas, 1960–85

	Total	Under 15	15–44	45–64	65 and over
United States	40.6	30.5	57.2	19.0	50.8
Nonwhites	68.2	59.5	91.8	33.5	63.4
Total SMSA	57.8	49.1	74.0	31.3	75.5
Nonwhites	104.5	100.7	123.9	60.4	118.8
Total central city	12.7	13.9	24.9	−11.5	13.3
Nonwhites	94.5	91.8	112.4	52.5	108.7
Total suburban ring	105.9	81.1	125.2	84.7	164.5
Nonwhites	140.7	131.4	167.0	91.3	154.6

Source: Hodge-Hauser, op. cit., pp. 36 and 42.

most vigorous age. Taken with the projected continued concentration of the poor and the nonwhites in the central cities, this is one of the most potentially important domestic trends of the next several decades.

THE POOR IN AMERICA

The number of Americans living in poverty[9] is declining while the total population continues to grow. About 13 million fewer persons were poor in 1967 than in 1959, and the percentage of the poor in the total population dropped from 22.1 percent to 13.3 percent during the same period. This is a remarkable but little-noted achievement—a 33-percent reduction in the number of the poor in less than a decade, and an even greater proportional decrease when the rise in the population is taken into account.

Despite this notable rate of progress, almost 26 million persons remain in poverty, and many of them are the "hard-core poor" whose circumstances are not readily improved by traditional antipoverty measures. However, the same assumption might have been made for the 39 million poor in 1959; more progress may be possible than has previously been thought.

TABLE 10.   Incidence of Poverty, Selected Years, 1959–67

	Number of individuals below poverty level	Percent below poverty level
1959	38,940,000	22.1
1963	35,290,000	18.9
1966	29,657,000	15.3
1966 [1]	28,781,000	14.9
1967 [1]	25,929,000	13.3

[1] Using a revised definition which reflects improvements in statistical procedures used in processing the income data.
Source: U.S. Department of Commerce, Bureau of the Census, "Family Income Advances, poverty Reduced in 1967," Series P–60, No. 55, Aug. 5, 1968, table 2, p. 4.

Who Are the Poor?

Certain groups are readily identifiable as major components of the poverty population—nonwhites, the aged, members of female-headed families, members of large families, and members of families whose heads are unemployed or underemployed.

The white and nonwhite poor. There are twice as many whites as nonwhites[10] in the Nation's total poverty population, but the incidence of poverty is much higher among nonwhites than among whites. In 1967, 41 percent of the nonwhite population was poor, compared with 12 percent of the white population. Nonwhites thus constitute a far larger share of the poverty population (31 percent) than of the American population as a whole (12 percent). Moreover, the nonwhite proportion of the poverty population has been increasing, slowly but steadily, since the first racial count was made in 1959; it was 28 percent then, and 32 percent by 1967.[11]

Both nonwhite and white poor are declining, however, both in numbers and in percentages of total population.

The aged. Persons aged 65 years or over made up 18 percent of the 29.7 million poor in 1966, although this age group formed only 7 percent of the total population.

TABLE 11.   Persons Below the Poverty Level, 1959–1967

	Number (in millions)		Percent of respective population	
	Nonwhite	White	Nonwhite	White
Year:				
1959	10.7	28.2	55	18
1960	11.4	28.7	55	18
1961	11.6	26.5	55	17
1962	11.6	25.4	54	16
1963	11.2	24.1	51	15
1964	10.9	23.4	49	14
1965	10.5	21.4	46	13
1966	9.6	20.1	41	12
Based on revised methodology:				
1966	9.3	19.5	40	12
1967	8.3	17.6	35	10

Source: U.S. Department of Commerce, Bureau of the Census, and U.S. Department of Health, Education, and Welfare, Social Security Administration.

The aged bear a disproportionate share of the poverty burden. One obvious reason is that fewer of them are in the labor force. Another is that women are likely to be poorer than men at all ages, and women form a greater proportion of those 65 and older than they do of any other age group. Almost two-thirds of the aged poor are women.

Persons living alone also are more likely to be poor than those who live in or with a family, and a majority of the elderly poor live alone or with just one other person. The number is increasing: between 1959 and 1966, the number of elderly men and women living alone or with nonrelatives rose by one-third. Paradoxically, this is probably partly a reflection of rising income (from social security benefits and related programs) so that "more of them had enough to try going it alone, choosing privacy, albeit the privacy of poverty, rather than being an 'other relative' in the home of their children."[12]

The large poor family. In 1966 a child in a large family (five or more children) was $3\frac{1}{2}$ times as likely to be poor as the child in a one- or two-child family. Almost half of the poor children were in families with five or more children.[13] The number of large poor families has

TABLE 12. Living Arrangements of Aged Noninstitutional Population in March, 1967, by Sex and Poverty Status in 1966

	Incidence of poverty (percent)	Total	In poor house- holds
		(in millions)	
All aged 65 or over	29.9	17,937	5,372
Living alone	55.3	4,878	2,697
In family units	20.5	13,059	2,675
Men	24.9	7,784	1,934
Living alone	44.0	1,285	565
In family units	21.1	6,499	1,369
Women	33.9	10,152	3,437
Living alone	59.3	3,593	2,132
In family units	19.9	6,559	1,305

Source: "Counting the Poor: Before and After Federal Income-Support Programs," by Mollie Orshansky, 1966, as reprinted from Joint Economic Committee Print, "Old-Age Income Assurance, pt. 11: The Aged Populations and Retirement Income Programs," December 1967, table 13, p. 109.

diminished slightly since 1959, when there were 1.1 million such families. In 1966 there were 0.9 million, and indications in the March 1968 sample survey of the census are that the number had decreased to 0.8 million in 1967.[14]

A growing proportion of the children in these families, however, suffered the added disadvantage of lacking a father—18 percent in 1959, 29 percent in 1966, and 34 percent in 1967.[15] Moreover, in 1967, the sample showed that 48 percent of the large poor families were nonwhite (although nonwhite form only 12 percent of the total population). The majority (65 percent) of these nonwhite families were headed by women.[16]

Households headed by a woman. Households, even small ones, headed by women seem particularly prone to poverty. Between 1959 (the first year for which poverty family statistics are available) until 1966, the incidence of poverty for female-headed households dropped slightly, but improvement has not been nearly as great as that for households headed by men. And the proportion of poor households headed by a female seems to be growing. In 1959, of all poor house-

TABLE 13. Composition of All Families, Selected Years, 1950 to 1968

(Percent)

Year	Husband-wife		Other male head		Female head [1]	
	Non-white	White	Non-white	White	Non-white	White
1950	77.7	88.0	4.7	3.5	17.6	8.5
1955	75.3	87.9	4.0	3.0	20.7	9.0
1960	73.6	88.7	4.0	2.6	22.4	8.7
1966	72.7	88.8	3.7	2.3	23.7	8.9
1967	72.6	88.7	3.9	2.1	23.6	9.1
1968	69.1	88.9	4.5	2.2	26.4	8.9

[1] Female heads of families include widowed and single women, women whose husbands are in the armed services or otherwise away from home voluntarily, as well as those separated from their husbands through divorce or marital discord. In 1968, divorce and separation accounted for 47 percent of the nonwhite female family heads and 34 percent of the white.

Source: U.S. Department of Commerce, Bureau of the Census.

holds, 5.4 million were headed by women and 8 million by men. By 1966 the number of poor households headed by men had dropped by 2.4 million but the number headed by women stayed about the same, so that women-headed households accounted for almost half of all poor families.[17]

In 1966, of the total number of female-headed families in the country, 35.0 percent were poor, while 9.8 percent of male-headed families lived in poverty.[18] A breakdown of figures by race reveals the far worse plight of the nonwhite family headed by a woman. In 1966, in the Nation as a whole, 60.2 percent of all nonwhite female-headed families lived in poverty as compared with 27.7 percent of white female-headed families. And the percentage of nonwhite families headed by a female appears to be growing.

The unemployed and the underemployed. Poverty measured by income obviously has a close relationship to employment. And, as one might expect, a profile of the unemployed is similar to that of the poor population itself.

a. *Race*. The higher incidence of poverty among nonwhites is accompanied by an unemployment rate that has been at least twice that of whites since 1954.

The special disadvantage of the Negro in regard to employment appears to have accompanied his move to urban areas. In 1940 (when 41 percent of Negro males were employed in agriculture, where unemployment rates were low) the nonwhite unemployment rate was slightly less than the white rate. It should be noted, however, that while unemployment rates in agriculture were low, so were wages, so that employment did not necessarily spell economic well-being. Furthermore, in agriculture, underemployment is almost as serious a problem as unemployment. Negroes were leaving the farms, however. Since 1930 the proportion of Negroes living in cities has nearly doubled. So by 1960 only 9.1 percent of the experienced nonwhite labor force remained in agriculture.[19]

The lowest point of Negro unemployment reached in the years since World War II was 4.5 percent in 1953, but with the end of the Korean war the rate doubled and then remained high throughout the 1950's and early 1960's. In 1958 and 1961, both recession years, nonwhite unemployment rose above 12 percent. Since 1954 the 2 to 1 unemployment ratio has become a stubborn economic fact of life. (See table 14.)

b. *Youth*. An important development is the very high rate of teenage unemployment—especially high for nonwhite teenagers. This could prove to be an increasingly explosive problem if the population projections cited earlier in this chapter are borne out.

In 1948 the Negro teenage unemployment rate was 7.6 percent, compared to a white teenage rate of 8.3 percent. The white rate has since increased somewhat, but the rate for nonwhite teenagers has more than tripled.

c. *Women versus men*. Among the poor, women outnumbered men by 8 to 5 in 1966—a ratio that reached 2 to 1 for those above age 65. Women at the head of families were three and a half times as likely to be poor as male family heads, and they were even more disadvantaged if they had children under 6 to look after.[20] The unemployment rate for women was much higher than that for men in 1966.

49

TABLE 14.   Unemployment Rates,[1] 1948–67, and 1968 (First 6 Months)

	Nonwhite	White	Ratio: Nonwhite to white
1948	5.2	3.2	1.6
1949	8.9	5.6	1.6
1950	9.0	4.9	1.8
1951	5.3	3.1	1.7
1952	5.4	2.8	1.9
1953	4.5	2.7	1.7
1954	9.9	5.0	2.0
1955	8.7	3.9	2.2
1956	8.3	3.6	2.3
1957	7.9	3.8	2.1
1958	12.6	6.1	2.1
1959	10.7	4.8	2.2
1960	10.2	4.9	2.1
1961	12.4	6.0	2.1
1962	10.9	4.9	2.2
1963	10.8	5.0	2.2
1964	9.6	4.6	2.1
1965	8.1	4.1	2.0
1966	7.3	3.3	2.2
1967	7.4	3.4	2.2
1968 (First 6 months seasonally adjusted)	6.8	3.2	2.1

[1] The unemployment rate is the percent unemployed in the civilian labor force.
Source: U.S. Department of Labor, Bureau of Labor Statistics, as published in "Recent Trends in Social and Economic Conditions of Negroes in the United States, July 1968.

d. *Central city versus suburban residents.* A study by the Bureau of Labor Statistics using census data collected in 1967 in the 20 largest metropolitan areas in the United States reveals a much higher unemployment rate in central cities than in suburban areas. This might be expected, in view of the high concentration of nonwhites (with a 2 to 1 national unemployment ratio) in central cities. Although nonwhites formed about 25 percent of the potential labor force, they accounted for 40 percent of the unemployed in central cities.[21] More than half (54 percent) of the labor force of the 20 largest SMSA's work in suburban areas, and 95 percent of this suburban labor force is white[22]—even though the suburban rings of these metropolitan

TABLE 15. Unemployment Rates and Total Figures for Teenagers (Aged 16–19), by Color, 1959–67

	White		Nonwhite	
	Rate (percent)	Total	Rate (percent)	Total
1957	10.6	401,000	19.1	96,000
1958 [1]	14.4	541,000	27.4	138,000
1962	13.3	580,000	25.3	142,000
1963	15.5	708,000	30.0	170,000
1964	14.8	708,000	27.3	165,000
1965	13.4	705,000	26.5	171,000
1966	11.2	651,000	25.4	186,000
1967	11.0	633,000	26.3	202,000

[1] 1958 marked the beginning of a new era of higher unemployment; the 1958–62 period displayed a relatively constant rate.

Source: Compilation of Census Bureau data as published in "Employment and Earnings," and Monthly Report of the Labor Force, Bureau of Labor Statistics, Department of Labor.

areas contain relatively large cities and many towns that are not bedroom suburbs.[23]

There was a considerable difference in the white unemployment rate between the city and the suburb, but for nonwhites the difference was relatively insignificant.[24] It was difficult for nonwhites to obtain a job in either area.

e. *Central city commuters.* One of the reasons for the concentration of Negroes in the central city was the availability of jobs. Now, however, increasing numbers of jobs are being located in the suburbs, where they are less accessible to central city residents. A 1967 report issued by the Department of Labor shows that between 1954 and 1965 more than half of all new industrial and mercantile buildings constructed in metropolitan areas in the United States were being built outside central cities—and this movement appeared to be accelerating. The study showed that from 1960 to 1965 at least 62 percent (by value) of the permits for new industrial buildings were issued for construction in the suburbs; the figure was 52 percent for mercantile buildings.[25]

Census data for five large metropolitan areas show that central

TABLE 16.   Employment of Heads of Families, 1966, by Sex and Poverty Status of Head

[In percent]

	All male heads of families	All female heads of families	Female heads of poor families	Male heads of poor families
Worked all year	74	35	19.0	38.0
Worked part year	15	23	29.0	27.0
Unemployed			54.8	23.1

Source: "Counting the Poor: Before and After Federal Income-Support Programs," (1966); Joint Economic Committee print, "Old-Age Income Assurance, pt. II: The Aged Population and Retirement Income Programs," December 1967, P. 211; pp. 192–193.

cities either lost jobs or gained them in very small proportion to the gains made by suburbs.

Who is filling the new jobs in the suburbs? Journey-to-work data collected on five major metropolitan areas by the Census Bureau suggest that it is not the central city Negroes.

Commuting from the central cities of these five metropolitan areas to suburban jobs is both time consuming and costly. A study on commuting in these five metropolitan areas reveals that a central city ghetto dweller in Philadelphia would have to spend $6.60 a week for commuter tickets and change buses three times, at the least, in order to get to a job in neighboring Montgomery County. If he lived near the railroad station and if his job were close to the station in Montgomery County he could cut the cost to $4.80 a week.

In Baltimore, the cost for traveling by public transportation

TABLE 17.   Unemployment, by Color, in 20 Largest SMSA's, 1967

	National percentage	Central city percentage	Suburban percentage
Total	3.8	4.7	3.3
White	3.4	3.7	3.1
Nonwhite	7.4	7.6	7.0

Source: Paul O. Flaim, "Jobless Trends in 20 Largest Metropolitan Areas," Monthly Labor Review, May 1968, vol. 91, No. 5, table 2, p. 18, and table 3, p. 21.

TABLE 18.   Employment Pattern (1951–65)

Number of new jobs

	City	Suburbs	Metropolitan area
Baltimore	1,450	86,086	87,536
New York	127,753	387,873	515,626
Philadelphia	−49,461	215,296	165,835
St. Louis	−61,800	141,911	80,111
San Francisco	9,346	185,742	195,089

Source: "County . Business Patterns," U.S. Census Bureau, as quoted in "The Impact of Housing Patterns on Job Opportunities," National Committee Against Discrimination in Housing, New York, 1968.

from the central city to a suburban job ranges from approximately $4 a week for a 40-minute ride (each way) to $15 a week and an hour's ride each way to Annapolis.

In St. Louis, it would take from 3 to 4 hours per day, at a cost of about $6.50 a week, for a worker to get from the ghetto area to the McDonnell Aircraft Corp. and back. To many of the St. Louis suburban job centers there is no public transportation at all.

TABLE 19.   Nonwhite Commuting from Central City to Suburban Jobs (1960)

Percent of work force

	Nonwhite male commuters	Central city nonwhite males	Total suburban employ-ment, 1959	Total suburban employ-ment,[1] 1959
Baltimore	9,546	16.0	6.9	138,069
New York	7,007	3.1	1.3	524,799
Philadelphia	8,570	8.6	1.8	480,821
St. Louis	3,156	9.0	1.4	233,505
San Francisco	7,272	15.3	2.0	370,790

[1] Employment data by county not available for 1960.

Source: U.S. Census of Population, 1960, "Journey to Work: County Business Patterns," 1959, as quoted in "The Impact of Housing Patterns on Job Opportunities," National Committee Against Discrimination in Housing, New York: 1968.

In New York, it costs $30 a month to commute on the Long Island Railroad.

Commuting between Hunter's Point in San Francisco and a Contra Costa County job in the East Bay area would require three to four transfers, 4 to 5 hours of traveling time per day, and some $15 a week. To commute from Alameda or West Oakland to the Contra Costa County jobs would take at least 4 hours a day and cost about $11.50 a week.[26]

The McCone report on the Watts riots cited inadequate and costly public transportation as a major influence in creating a sense of isolation and frustration in the south central Los Angeles area.

Existing in-and-out commuter public transit systems are generally not suited to "reverse commuting." Central city residents, white or Negro (except domestics), can seldom use the "empty backhaul" of a commuter bus or train to get to a suburban job. Private automobiles are the most common means used to get to work in this county, but many employable central city dwellers cannot afford cars or even car pools to take them to suburban jobs.

The high unemployment rate of central-city nonwhites is, however, not wholly attributable to central-city-to-suburb commuting problems. White-collar jobs, which are generally increasing at a faster rate than blue-collar jobs, are in the main locating in central cities.[27] But it is this source of employment—which would not involve the commuting difficulties just described—that the nonwhite finds largely inaccessible to him because of a lack of skills or outright discrimination.

If these obstacles were overcome, white-collar employment could form a major source of employment for central city Negroes. Hearings held in January 1968 by the Equal Employment Opportunity Commission in New York City indicate, however, that white-collar employment discrimination is a serious problem for central city Negroes.

f. *Residents of poverty areas.* At the Commission hearings in Los Angeles, author and social scientist Nathan Glazer said:

> . . . our slum problems are not primarily physical problems; they are complex social problems related to the fact that the slumdwelling population in our cities is increasingly Negro. Thus, when foreign visitors see our slums, they are reacting only partly to their physical conditions—they are reacting to the sight of men lounging about

without employment, children playing without supervision, youth without any apparent useful employment. They are reacting to a social as well as a physical scene.[28]

In 1967 the unemployment rate in poverty areas was 9.4 percent for nonwhites and 6 percent for whites.[29] National rates were 7.3 percent for nonwhites and 3.4 percent for whites. A wide disparity can be seen between unemployment rates in ghetto areas and in the total metropolitan areas in which they are located.

g. *The Underemployed.* The unemployment rate takes into account only those who are not working but who are actively seeking employment. It does not count the poor who have other job-related problems, nor those who are not participants in the labor force. And these underemployed form a substantial part of the poverty population.

TABLE 20.   Unemployment Rates, Ghetto Areas and Surrounding Metropolitan Areas, 1966

		Unemployment rate (percent)	
SMSA	Ghetto area	Ghetto [1]	SMSA [2]
Boston	Roxbury	6.9	3.7
Cleveland	Hough and surrounding neighborhood	15.6	3.5
Detroit	Central Woodward	10.1	4.3
Los Angeles	South Los Angeles	12.0	6.0
New York	Harlem	8.1	4.6
	East Harlem	9.0	
	Bedford-Stuyvesant	6.2	
Philadelphia	North Philadelphia	11.0	4.3
Phoenix	Salt River Bed	13.2	
St. Louis	North Side	12.9	4.5
San Antonio	East and West Sides	8.1	
San Francisco-Oakland	Mission-Fillmore	11.1	5.2
	Bayside	13.0	

[1] As of November 1966.

[2] Average for year ending August 1966.

Source: 1967 Manpower Report of the President, p. 75; metropolitan area data based on special tabulation of data from the Current Population Survey, published in "The Impact of Housing Patterns on Job Opportunities," National Committee Against Discrimination in Housing, New York 1968.

(i) The working poor: Work may be the key to economic well-being, but it does not guarantee it. For many of the poor, what is needed is not so much *more* jobs but *better* ones—with higher pay, more secure tenure, and more opportunity for advancement.

In 1966, one out of every four poor families was headed by a man who had worked throughout the entire year. Of the 3 million men under 65 who headed poor families, half were "fully employed" in terms of time on the job. Their low-paying jobs resulted in poverty-level living for the 8 million members of their families—one-third of all the poor who were not living alone.

Since the poverty measuring rod takes family size into account, one might assume that numerous children rather than low income was the main cause of the poverty status of these "fully employed" men. But in 1965, three-fifths of such poor but fully employed men had no more than three children to support.[30]

Incidence of poverty is closely related to type of job held. High poverty rates are associated with farming and unskilled labor for men and domestic service for women.

(ii) Subemployment: A special survey undertaken by the Labor Department in 14 of the worst ghetto areas of the country in November 1966, revealed that while unemployment rates were very high, this standard measure of joblessness did not take into account other very severe problems related to being out of work. As a result, a new method of measuring joblessness was developed: the subemployment index.[31] Table 21 shows the inordinately high subemployment rates for 11 ghetto areas, and compares them with the standard unemployment rates. The average subemployment rate for all the cities was 34.6 percent, which would mean that 1 in every 3 residents of these ghetto areas in the labor force was unemployed, employed part time, or employed at poverty-level wages.[32]

Unemployment is a major cause of poverty, but subemployment may be a greater one. In 1966, in metropolitan areas alone, there were 2.393 million adults and 2.384 million children under 18 living in poor households headed by *employed* males aged 18 to 65. They constituted almost one-third of all poor persons in metropolitan areas, while only 1 out of every 7 poor persons in metropolitan areas lived in households having a male head under age 65 who was unemployed. Low wages, then, rather than joblessness was the cause of the greater amount of poverty in metropolitan areas.

TABLE 21.   Subemployment Rate and Unemployment Rate in 11 Ghetto Areas, 1966

[In percent]

	Unemployment	Subemployment
Boston	6.9	24
Cleveland	15.6	49
New Orleans	10.0	45
New York:		
Harlem	8.1	29
East Harlem	9.0	33
Bedford-Stuyvesant	6.2	28
Philadelphia	11.0	34
Phoenix	13.2	42
St. Louis	12.9	39
San Antonio	8.1	47
San Francisco	11.1	25

Source: U.S. Department of Labor, as published in "The Impact of Housing Patterns on Job Opportunities," National Committee Against Discrimination in Housing, New York, 1968, p. 18.

Where Are the Poor?

Trends in the distribution of the Nation's poverty population—in terms of regions, urban and rural concentrations, and metropolitan area locations—are an important aspect of the urban problems encompassed by the Commission's work.

Regional Distribution

About half of the Nation's poor lived in the South in 1966. The South, still the least urban region of the United States, was also the location of two-thirds of the nonwhite poor and two-fifths of the white poor.

Similar statistics collected 2 years earlier indicated that the nonwhite poor were concentrated even more heavily in the South than they were in 1966, but are now beginning to spread out through the country.[33] The short-term trend, however, would indicate that the

TABLE 22.   The Distribution of Poor U.S. Families, by Region and
Color, 1966

[In percent]

Region	All families	White families	Nonwhite families
Northeast	17.0	19.0	12.0
North Central	20.7	23.0	14.7
South	48.5	42.1	64.7
West	13.8	15.9	8.5
Total	100.0	100.0	100.0

Note: Not all percentages will total 100 percent because of rounding.

Source: "The Shape of Poverty, 1966," by Mollie Orshansky, reprinted from the Social Security Bulletin, March 1968, table 6.

proportion of those in poverty, white and nonwhite, was lessening everywhere except in the Northeast, where the percentage of nonwhite poor was apparently increasing.[34]

The Countryside and the Metropolis

The part of the United States that is not metropolitan includes farm, nonfarm, and even some urban plans not included in the 1967 count of 228 U.S. SMSA's. Since 1920 this vast area has held less than half of the U.S. population, and it now holds only about a third. But it contains about half of the poor—although comparison with the 1964 figures would indicate that this proportion is decreasing.[35]

TABLE 23.   Percent of the Regional Population in Poverty, by Color, 1966

Region	All families	White families	Nonwhite families
Northeast	8.6	7.4	24.9
North Central	9.2	8.0	24.5
South	19.7	14.6	46.9
West	10.1	9.1	21.1

Source: "The Shape of Poverty in 1966," op. cit.

Metropolitan areas as a whole have 65 percent of the population but only 51 percent of the poor; in nonmetropolitan areas the figures are 35 percent of the population and 49 percent of the poor.

The City and the Suburb

Within metropolitan areas the poor tend to concentrate in the central cities. The high percentage of metropolitan poor in central cities is due to the fact that the great majority of nonwhite poor live in these central cities. Almost half of the white poor live in the suburbs.

The suburbs do not carry their share of the total poor. With 35 percent of the U.S. population, they have only 20 percent of the poor. The number of poor in the central city is roughly in proportion to its share of the total population; the small towns and rural places, as mentioned above, carry a disproportionate burden that makes up for the light load of the suburbs.

The incidence of poverty in the suburbs is about half that in the central city. Even a nonwhite, living in the suburbs, is a little less likely to be poor than a nonwhite in the central city. However, he is still almost four times more likely to be poor than is a suburban white.

Poverty Pockets in and around Cities

A special survey was made in the spring of 1966 of households (families plus individuals living alone) within "poverty areas" des-

TABLE 24.   Location of the Metropolitan Poor by Color, 1966

[Numbers in millions]

	Total		White poor		Nonwhite poor	
	Number	Percent	Number	Percent	Number	Percent
Central city	9.5	63	5.3	53	4.2	82
Suburban ring	5.7	37	4.8	47	.9	18
Total	15.2	100	10.1	100	5.1	100

Source: Orshansky, Counting the Poor.

TABLE 25.   Distribution of Total Population, Contrasted with Distribution of Total Poor, Population, by Type of Place, 1966

	All persons		White persons		Nonwhite persons	
	Percent of total U.S. population	Percent of U.S. poor	Percent of total U.S. population	Percent of U.S. poor	Percent of total U.S. population	Percent of U.S. poor
Metropolitan	64.7	51.0	64.3	50.0	67.9	53.2
Central city	30.2	31.5	27.0	26.5	53.4	43.6
Ring	34.6	19.5	37.3	23.5	14.5	9.6
Nonmetropolitan	35.3	49.0	35.7	50.0	32.1	46.8
	100.0	100.0	100.0	100.0	100.0	100.0

Source: "Counting the Poor: Before and After Federal Income-Support Programs," (Population estimates derived from special tabulation made by the Bureau of the Census from the Current Population Survey for March, 1967).

ignated according to the 1960 census data, in both the central cities and the suburbs of the 101 largest metropolitan areas.[36] It is apparent that nonwhite families are concentrated in poverty areas much more than are white families, whatever the income level. Only 11 percent of white families (data do not include individuals living alone) lived in these poverty areas in 1965; by contrast 58 percent of all nonwhite SMSA families lived there.

TABLE 26.   Percentage of Population That Is Poor by Type of Place, 1966

	All poor	White poor	Nonwhite poor
Metropolitan	12.1	9.3	32.0
Central city	16.2	11.7	33.0
Ring	8.6	7.6	28.2
Nonmetropolitan	21.4	16.8	59.3

Source: "Counting the Poor: Before and After Federal Income-Support Programs," op. cit.

Moreover, the concentration of nonwhite families in poverty areas is increasing. (These data include the suburban poverty pockets, with their low proportion of nonwhite residents. The concentration of nonwhites of all incomes in central city poverty areas is always substantially greater than the average of the two areas indicates.)

In 1960, 37 percent of the families in poverty areas were black; 5 years later the proportion had risen to 41 percent.[37] A corollary of the concentration of nonwhites in poverty areas is that nonwhite families of all economic levels are thrown together in the poverty areas. Such areas thus begin to assume the character of the classic ghetto. Historically, a ghetto was the section of a city within which a particular ethnic group was confined, and outside which its members were not permitted to live, regardless of income or social status. Using the term "ghetto" to mean a poverty area is inaccurate. The concentration of Negroes, of course, is not as absolute a confinement as it was in the ghetto of the Middle Ages. Many Negroes of high income and cultural levels, however, have found it difficult to follow the American pattern of gradual integration into the larger community. Fifty-two percent of nonpoor nonwhite families lived in poverty areas in 1965, contrasted with only 10 percent of the nonpoor whites.[38]

As one would expect, the percentage of households (families and individuals living alone) below the poverty line is much greater within these poverty areas than it is outside, although poor families are still a minority even within poverty areas. Nearly one-fifth of the households in central cities are poor, but nearly one-third of those in central city poverty areas are below the poverty line. Even in the suburbs, almost a quarter of the households in poverty pockets are poor, compared to only about an eighth of the residents of suburbia as a while.

The incidence of poverty among individuals living alone in cities, and especially in poverty areas is greater than that among families, ranging from one-third to nearly half everywhere. The pattern is repeated (except for single nonwhites) in the suburban ring. Very probably, this is the statistical reflection of the plight of elderly individuals, white and nonwhite, described earlier.

Other population subgroups overrepresented in these poverty areas in 1965 were: families headed by women, families with a head 14 to 24 years old, large families (seven or more), families dependent

TABLE 27. Proportion of Families and Individuals in 100 Largest SMSA's and Their Poverty Areas Who Were Poor in 1965

[In percent]

	Central cities		Outside central cities	
	Total	Poverty areas	Total	Poverty areas
Total households	19.7	33.4	11.7	23.1
Families	13.4	27.2	7.5	18.0
White	9.4	18.6	6.7	15.1
Nonwhite	28.9	35.8	24.8	29.5
Individuals alone	36.0	44.9	34.3	46.8
White	34.5	43.5	33.3	43.5
Nonwhite	42.0	47.1	46.3	(1)

1 Base less than 65,000 people.

Source: "Incidence of Poverty in 1965 Among Families and Unrelated Individuals by Color, for the United States, by Detailed Residence Categories," Survey of Economic Opportunity, Bureau of the Census.

on income other than earnings (presumably on social security or public assistance), and families whose head was unemployed, semiskilled or unskilled.

The character of poverty areas changed in the 5-year period 1960–65 in ways that somewhat parallel developments in the central city as a whole. Considerable numbers of white families left. Among the nonwhite residents, the total number of families increased

TABLE 28. Population Subgroups as Part of Total and as Part of Poverty Areas of 100 Largest SMSA's, 1965

	Percent of total	Percent of poverty areas
Female-headed families	11.4	20.4
Families with head aged 14–24	6.0	8.1
Large families	6.5	9.9
Families with source of income not earnings	8.3	13.4
Head unemployed, semiskilled, or unskilled	43.9	67.6

Source: "Characteristics of Families Residing in Poverty Areas Within Large Metropolitan Areas," table 1.

slightly, but the total number of those families who were poor dropped by about the same percentage. The situation in 1965, therefore, reflected an area of more concentrated black residence that included more of the Negro middle class.[39]

CONCLUSIONS

Most Americans are economically better off today than they were 10 or even 5 years ago. An era of unprecedented national prosperity has been shared in by most segments of the population. Fewer Americans—white, black, Indian, Puerto Rican, Mexican-American, oriental—are poor, according to much statistical evidence. This evidence has led some to conclude that the urgent urban problems which fall within the scope of this Commission's assignment are on the way to resolving themselves. A closer examination reveals, however, that certain of these problems persist and, indeed, are becoming more acute in the absence of concerted remedial action.

More people. The sheer concentration of population in city and suburb is, in itself, an urban problem, for more people—regardless of their social or economic condition—means a demand for more schools, more water and sewers, more transportation, more police protection, more of all the services that are part of urban living. Municipal administrations are finding it difficult to run fast enough to stand still; but the next 15 years will add another 40 to 50 million persons to the population, and 81 percent of this growth is expected to occur within metropolitan areas.

The suburban advantage. The suburban ring has a majority of the residents of the metropolitan area. It also has less than its proportionate share of the poor, and only 5 percent of American nonwhites. Part of the reason that this considerable section manages to retain its present character is that little low-cost housing is being built there; indeed, little low-cost housing is built anywhere, but the central city, so far, has the only substantial stock of housing depreciated far enough to provide a supply of housing, however unsatisfactory, for low-income whites and nonwhites. The suburbs, however, contain nearly half the *white* metropolitan poor—a figure which suggests that the suburbs discriminate more on the basis of race than on the basis of economic status.

Increased nonwhite population in central city. The central city has 32 percent of the Nation's poor, and more than half of the Nation's nonwhites. Figures on the change in location of the poor are too recent to be reliable, but it seems clear that the concentration of nonwhites of all income levels is increasing in the central city. The prospect is that the political base of many of our larger cities, in the South, Northeast, and West, will be that of a black majority by 1985. Since the incidence of poverty is much higher among nonwhites than whites, the fiscal implication for the central city is not hopeful.

Poverty area stagnation. The urban slum has, in American experience, been a way station to a better life for its inhabitants. Now, however, instead of sending forth the residents that characterize it today—the urban nonwhites—the city poverty area appears to be concentrating them still further. The nonwhite component of central city poverty areas has increased decidedly; their high proportion of poor households appears to be nearly stationary. Apparently there is a hard core of nonwhite families whose situation improves slowly, if at all. According to an expert witness before the hearings of this Commission, the problem in urban slums is less a matter of housing than the entire social and economic history of American nonwhites:

> Whatever may have been the case in other countries and in other times, our slum problem is not primarily a problem of specific facilities: it is a problem related to the existence in this Nation, and increasingly in our cities, of a large, depressed population, which has suffered from discrimination, segregation, poor education.
>
> Our slums have always varied, depending on who lived in them. We have lived with German slums, Irish slums, Jewish slums, Italian slums. We are now living in an age of Negro slums. Each group has been a participant in creating an environment which to some extent reflected its experience. Now we have a group that has suffered from the worst experience, with the worst effects—and the environment it has helped to create reflects that experience.[40]

The problems of particular groups. Certain groups in our society have special difficulties—the elderly, women who head families, children in large families, and, of course, the unemployed and underemployed. Although the white poor outnumber the nonwhite poor two to one, the nonwhite poor form a larger than proportionate share of these hard-core categories. Seen in this light, the age group projections made in the Commission's population study[41] are rather ominous:

The dependent age groups—those under 15, and those over age 65—will increase rapidly if present trends continue, especially among the nonwhites. There will be one and a half times the present number of elderly, white and nonwhite, in the suburbs by 1985, and the nonwhite elderly in the central cities will double in number. This age group formed nearly one out of five of the poor in 1966. The group that will grow least will be that aged 45 to 64.

The group that will grow most rapidly—fortunately perhaps, since they must shoulder most of the burden of support for the dependent groups—will be the relatively young working force, aged 15 to 44. The very growth of this age group, however, engenders potential problems. These are the childbearing years, the most vigorous years, and the years in which jobs must be found and held. The increase in this group will be greatest in the suburbs, *but may be felt*

TABLE 29.   Net Population Growth Rates, 1935 to 1967

1935 [1]	.80	1952	1.69
1936 [1]	.71	1953	1.70
1937 [1]	.79	1954	1.78
1938 [1]	.91	1955	1.76
1939 [1]	.89	1956	1.81
1940	.92	1957	1.72
1941	1.03	1958	1.67
1942	1.27	1959	1.65
1943	1.31	1960	1.63
1944	1.15	1961	1.64
1945	1.04	1962	1.51
1946	1.53	1963	1.43
1947	1.83	1964	1.36
1948	1.72	1965	1.22
1949	1.71	1966	1.14
1950	1.63	1967	1.07
1951	1.74		

---

[1] For the 48 States excluding armed forces overseas.

Source: Current Population Reports—Population Estimates, Estimates of the population of the United States and components of change: 1940 to 1968. Series p. 25, No. 398, July 31, 1968, U.S. Bureau of the Census.

TABLE 30. Growth in Total U.S. Population, in Urban and Rural Population, 1790-1960

Year:	Total (in thousands)	Decade rate	Urban (in thousands)	Rate	Rural (in thousands)	Rate
1790	3,929	—	202	—	3,728	—
1800	5,308	35.1	322	59.4	4,986	31.0
1810	7,240	36.4	525	94.0	6,714	34.6
1820	9,638	33.1	693	32.0	8,945	33.2
1830	12,866	33.5	1,127	62.6	11,739	31.2
1840	17,069	32.7	1,845	63.7	15,224	29.6
1850	23,192	35.9	3,544	92.1	19,648	29.0
1860	31,443	35.6	6,217	75.3	25,227	28.3
1870	39,818	26.6	9,902	59.2	28,656	13.5
1880	50,156	26.0	14,130	42.6	36,026	25.7
1890	62,948	25.5	22,106	56.4	40,841	10.5
1900	75,995	20.7	30,160	36.4	45,835	12.2
1910	91,972	21.0	41,999	39.2	49,973	9.0
1920	105,711	14.9	54,158	28.9	51,553	3.1
1930	122,775	16.1	68,955	27.3	53,820	4.3
1940	131,669	7.2	74,424	7.9	57,246	6.3
1950 [1]	150,698	14.5	96,468	29.6	54,230	−5.2
1960 [1]	179,323	18.5	125,269	22.9	54,054	−.3

[1] New definition including unincorporated parts of urban areas.

Source: Statistical Abstract of the United States, 1968, Table 1; Historical Statistics of the United States, Colonial Times to 1957, U.S. Bureau of the Census, Series A-195209; Statistical Abstract of the U.S., 1968, Table 14 (for 1960 figures).

most severely in cities. Nonwhites in this age group will more than double, and yet this group suffers more from unemployment, cannot move to the suburbs, and finds even commuting to suburban jobs difficult.

Americans are better off today than a decade ago. The general prosperity has reduced unemployment; most importantly, however, the American public has taken great collective steps in the last 10 years, through governmental and private action, to improve the lot of the poor in jobs, health, education, and housing. These actions have had a marked effect. But there are still almost 26 million Americans in poverty. We cannot be content to ignore their distress in the midst of the well-being of the rest of America.

The changing character of the central city relates to more people and growth of particular categories of its residents. The more rapid growth of the suburban areas underlines the likelihood that the problems faced by the central city today will be shared by suburbia tomorrow. They are, indeed, problems that confront every American.

NOTES

1. Patricia L. Hodge and Philip M. Hauser, "The Challenge of America's Metropolitan Population—1960 to 1985." Research Report No. 3, National Commission on Urban Problems, U.S. Government Printing Office, Washington, D.C., 1968.

2. The Bureau of the Census has presented four series of population projections, the "A" series assuming the highest birth rate, the "D" series the lowest. This report utilizes the "C" series. The authors of the Commission's study felt that the "best" of the four 1985 Census projections was the one employing the next to lowest birth rate. They preferred this to the lowest on the ground that the large numbers of children born during the post-war baby boom are just now approaching marriage, and it is not yet possible to predict with any certainty that the total number of children they will bear will be fewer than those born by the "wave" preceding them.

3. A *Standard Metropolitan Statistical Area (SMSA)* is "a county or group of contiguous counties (except in New England, towns and cities rather than counties are used in defining habitants or more or twin cities with a combined population of at least 50,000. In addition, other contiguous counties are included in an SMSA if, according to certain criteria, they are essentially metropolitan in character and are socially and economically integrated with the central city. In New England, towns and cities rather than counties are used in defining SMSA's." U.S Bureau of the Census, *Statistical Abstract of the United States: 1967*, (88th edition) Washington, D.C., 1967.

4. Hodge-Hauser, *op. cit.*, p. 26.

5. *Report of the National Advisory Commission on Civil Disorders*, U.S. Government Printing Office, Washington, D.C., March 1, 1968, p. 216.

6. "Recent Trends in Social and Economic Conditions of Negroes in the United States," U.S. Department of Commerce, Bureau of the Census, Series P–23, No. 26, July, 1968, p. 4.

7. Hodge-Hauser, *op. cit.*, pp. 14 and 16.

8. 1960 Hodge-Hauser, op. cit., pp. 36 and 42.

9. The definition of poverty used in this chapter is that developed by the Social Security Administration. It is an income measurement taking into account family size, number of children, and farm-non-farm residence. The basis of the poverty income determination is the nutritionally sound "economy" food plan designed by the Department of Agriculture for "emergency or temporary use when funds are low." The income measurement is based on the assumption that a family should spend no more than a third of its income on food. The poverty thresholds are adjusted annually to reflect changes in price levels.

For 1966 a nonfarm family of four would be classified as poor if its income was $3,335 or below.

10. Statistics for the nonwhite" population include more than Negroes but can be taken as a general measurement of the Negro population since Negroes form about 92 percent of the nonwhite population. Statistics for areas with high concentrations of Japanese and Chinese as well as Negroes can, however, be misleading, for Chinese and Japanese are at the opposite end of the spectrum from Negroes for almost all economic and social data. As Daniel Moynihan points out in "Employment, Income, and the Ordeal of the Negro Family," (Daedalus, Fall 1965, p. 769), "Japanese and Chinese have twice as large a proportion of their populations going to college as do whites; Negroes have a little less than half. Negroes have twice as high a rate of unemployment as do whites; Chinese and Japanese have half. In 1960, 21 percent of Negro women who had ever married were separated, divorced, or had their husbands absent for other reasons, as against 6 percent of Chinese. A consequence of these figures is that statistics for nonwhites generally understate the degree of unemployment among Negroes as well as the extent of family disorganization, and the gap that separates them from the white world."

On the other hand, the "white" category includes Puerto Ricans and Mexican-Americans, who are socio-economically similar to Negroes in many respects. The latter distortion is not as statistically significant, however, because the number of white so far exceeds the number of nonwhites.

11. "Family Income Advances, Poverty Reduced in 1967," U.S. Department of Commerce, Bureau of the Census, Series P-60, No. 55, August 5, 1968, p. 4, table 2.

12. Mollie Orshansky, "The Shape of Poverty, 1966," reprinted from the Social Security Bulletin, U.S. Department of Health, Education and Welfare, U.S. Government Printing Office, Washington, D.C., March 1968, p. 8.

13. *Ibid.*, p. 9.

14. "Family Income Advances, Poverty Reduced in 1967," *op. cit.*, p. 7, table 7.

15. According to a preliminary Census Survey.

16. "Family Income Advances. Poverty Reduced in 1967."

17. "The Shape of Poverty, 1966," p. 5, table 2.

18. *Ibid.*, p. 11, table 6.

19. Daniel P. Moynihan, "Employment, Income, and the Ordeal of the Negro Family," *Daedalus*, Journal of the American Academy of the Arts and Sciences, Fall 1965, p. 751.

20. Mollie Orshansky, "Counting the Poor: Before and After Federal Income-Support Programs," reprinted from Joint Economic Committee Print. *Old Age Income Assurance*, Part II, December 1967, U.S. Congress, p. 206.

21. Paul O. Flaim, "Jobless Trends in Twenty Largest Metropolitan Areas," *Monthly Labor Review*, U.S. Department of Labor, Bureau of Labor Statistics, May 1968, Vol. 91, No. 5, p. 27.

22. *Ibid.*, pp. 19–20.

23. For example, Yonkers (191,000 population in 1960) in the New York ring, and Camden, New Jersey (1960 population, 117,000) in the Philadelphia ring. (See Paul. O. Flaim, op. cit., p. 20).

24. The standard error for the suburban nonwhite unemployment rate is relatively large. The range for this rate (5.9–8.1) and the range for the nonwhite central city rate (7.1–8.1 percent) overlap considerably. It is therefore possible

that there is no difference at all between the two rates. See Paul O. Flaim, *op. cit.*).

25. Dorothy K. Newman, "The Decentralization of Jobs," *Monthly Labor Review*, May 1967.

26. Commuting time and cost data obtained from, The Impact of Housing Patterns on Job Opportunities, National Committee Against Discrimination in Housing, New York, 1968, pp. 27–29.

27. In 1950, the total number of blue-collar workers in the United States exceeded the number of white-collar workers by about one million. By 1966, white-collar workers exceeded blue-collar workers by more than 5.5 million. By 1975, there will be almost 12 million more white-collar jobs than there were in 1964. The increase in blue-collar jobs will be only 4.4 million. Bureau of Labor Statistics, America's Industrial and Occupational Manpower Requirements, 1964–75, prepared for the National Commission on Technology, Automation and Economic Progress.

    Between 1954 and 1965 the increase in white-collar jobs took place largely within central cities.

28. Nathan Glazer, *Hearings Before the National Commission on Urban Problems*, Vol. 2, p. 240.

29. *The Impact of Housing Patterns on Job Opportunities, op. cit.*, p. 15.

30. "The Shape of Poverty, 1966," op. cit., p. 15.

31. The subemployment index covers an entire employment hardship area and takes into account not only the traditionally "unemployed" (those actively seeking work but unable to find it) and the working poor (heads of households earning less than $60 a week and individuals over 65 earning less than $56 a week); but also those working part time but seeking full-time jobs; half the number of nonparticipants in the male age group 20–64 who are not in the labor force, and a "conservative and carefully considered estimate of the male 'undercount' group."

    A special survey taken in 1966, described in footnote 36 below, revealed that a very large number of ghetto residents of working age were not counted in the labor force of the metropolitan areas surveyed.

32. *The Impact of Housing Patterns on Job Opportunities, op. cit.*, pp. 18–20.

33. Mollie Orshansky, "More About the Poor in 1964," reprinted from the *Social Security Bulletin*, U.S. Department of Health, Education and Welfare, Social Security Administration, May 1966, table 22.

34. *Ibid.*

35. Mollie Orshansky, "The Poor in City and Suburb, 1964," reprinted from the *Social Security Bulletin*, U.S. Department of Health, Education and Welfare, Social Security Administration, December 1966, p. 5, table 4.

36. A special study of the 1960 Census data was made by the Census Bureau for the Office of Economic Opportunity on family and per capita income rankings. In addition, another special study began in 1965 of "poverty areas" in the 101 SMSA's with a 1960 population of 250,000 or more using census tracts, the smallest area for which the necessary socio-economic information was available (many of the smaller SMSA's were either partially tracted or not tracted at all). One of these large SMSA's, Davenport-Rock Island-Moline, Iowa, Ill., was found to have no poverty areas at all.

    All census tracts were ranked according to five equally-weighted poverty-linked characteristics: (1) Percent of families with income under $3,000 in

1959; (2) Percent of children under age 18 not living with both parents; (3) Percent of persons age 25 or older with less than 8 years of education; (4) Percent of unskilled males employed; and (5) Percent of housing units dilapidated or lacking some or all plumbing. Those in the lowest quartile were designated "poor" tracts and "poverty areas" depended on the number and duration of existence of contiguous poverty tracts. There were 193 poverty areas designated in 100 SMSA's.

Next, a national sample survey was made in the Spring of 1966 by the Census Bureau for OEO, covering about 80,000 households. The study included the annual March Current Population Survey, the Monthly Labor Survey, and a special sample run specifically for this study. All 80,000 households families and unrelated individuals) were classified as being in or out of a Poverty Area.

37. Supplementary Reports, PC(81)–54, U.S. Department of Commerce, Bureau of the Census, November 13, 1967; Table A; and Arno I. Winard, "Characteristics of Families Residing in Poverty Areas Within Large Metropolitan Areas," Bureau of the Census, June 15, 1967, Table 1.

38. *Ibid.*

39. *Ibid.*

40. Nathan Glazer, *op. cit.*, p. 240.

41. Hodge-Hauser, *op. cit.*

ARTICLE 3

The Outer City: U.S. in Suburban Turmoil

Jack Rosenthal

Rapidly, relentlessly, almost unconsciously, America has created a new form of urban settlement. It is higher, bolder and richer than anything man has yet called city.

Tranfixed by the image of bedroom towns in the orbit of true cities, most Americans still speak of suburbs. But a city's suburbs are no longer just bedrooms. They are no longer mere orbital satellites. They are no longer sub.

Reprinted from *The New York Times* (May 30, 1971), p. 1, col. 2–3, and p. 28, col. 3–8. © 1971 by The New York Times Company. Reprinted by permission.

They are broad, ballooning bands, interlinked as cities in their own right. In population, jobs, investment, construction, stores, political power—all the measurements that add up to "urban"—the old inner city is now rivaled, often surpassed, by the new.

This is the Outer City.

VAST CHANGES NOTED

And from its massive, centerless development, repeated again and again across the country, spring the most serious implications for the quality of urban life.

In 1940, suburbs contained 27 million people; 2 of every 10 Americans; 19 million fewer than the cities. Now they contain 76 million; almost 4 of every 10; 12 million more than the cities that spawned them.

Once-rustic fringe villages now have their own zip codes, area codes, big league stadiums. They are the sites of luxury hotels and industrial plants, fine stores and corporate offices.

In New York, the population remains about equally divided between urban and suburban. But elsewhere the suburbs are already two, three, four times more populous than the inner cities they surround.

Commonly, 40, 50 and even 60 percent of those who live in a city's suburbs also work in them. Half, or more, of every retail dollar is spent in the suburbs. More than 8 of every 12 dollars spent on housing construction is spent in the suburbs. About two-thirds of all industrial construction is in the suburbs, in the outer cities of the nation.

Visits and interviews in five geographically representative areas —Baltimore, Cleveland, Los Angeles, Houston and Atlanta—showed that the suburbs are individual, diverse communities with a diversity of problems. In the distant exurban greenery, planners worry about how to channel new growth. In closer suburbs officials struggle to show that age need not bring decay. In the closest, decay has already begun.

But taken together, the suburbs have, like New York's, become informally federated in many areas. Their residents use the suburbs collectively: as a city, a centerless city.

Mrs. Ada Mae Hardeman is a Californian who says she doesn't really know where she is from:

"I live in Garden Grove, work in Irvine, shop in Santa Ana, go to the dentist in Anaheim, my husband works in Long Beach, and I used to be president of the League of Women Voters in Fullerton."

She doesn't much mind. "I don't miss central city pleasures out here in spread city. Honestly, I have to say I love it."

NOW THE BELTWAYS

Now such independence of the city is being massively fortified with concrete. Broad beltways already encircle 10 large cities and will soon rim 70 more—the accidental new main streets of the outer cities.

And the residents of the outer cities have become so independent of the inner cities that it is common to hear people brag that they haven't been downtown in months, even years.

Still, like many inner-city residents who think that the urban world revolves around downtown, they do not concede that the suburban rings constitute an alternate city.

They prize the array of urban facilities of their outer city. But many, as in parts of New York's Westchester County and Northern New Jersey, still identify with the image of the pastoral town.

They are alarmed by the consequences of their own growth, like increasing density and pollution. But they still cling to the governmental forms of isolated villages.

FEDERAL ACTION ENDORSED

They are increasingly willing—even, surprisingly, in the most conservative communities—to endorse *Federal* action to assuage the poverty and blight left behind in the inner cities. But, otherwise, they shrink from these problems often with indifference, sometimes with anger.

Tormented city officials, like Larry Reich, the Baltimore city planner, may denounce what they regard as unfairness:

"The city of Baltimore makes the suburbs possible because we carry the burdens of the old, poor, black and deviants. Why should we keep carrying the burden?"

But in the suburbs, many people quote with unabashed candor the old troopship cry: "Pull up the ladder, Jack, I'm on board."

SEE HOW THEY GROW

And the new outer cities continue—rapidly, centerlessly—to grow:

For all the vitality of downtown Houston, the fashion center is not downtown. Tiffany's in Houston now is a block from the Loop beltway, one small segment of a $300-million retail, commercial and hotel development called City Post Oak. Even in the twilight, the rows of plaza light globes, like luminous pearls, only soften the staggered concrete shapes behind them which stretch outward for eight blocks and upward for 22 stories.

It was once second-rate farmland out amid the slash pine and red clay 15 miles from Atlanta's old warehouse district. Now H. C. Patillo, who calls himself merely a medium-size local builder, has developed an industrial park, serving local and national concerns alike. It contains long, low, attractive plants, 103 of them, on a 2,000-acre tract.

Roosevelt Field, the lonely little Long Island airport from which Charles Lindbergh took off for Paris in 1927, is now the Roosevelt Shopping Center, one of the East's largest. In place of the tiny crowd that watched the Spirit of St. Louis disappear into the morning fog are the crowds of housewives shuttling from Macy's to Gimbel's.

In Orange County, Calif., once a sprawling bedroom for Los Angeles, Newport Center, a vast alabaster oasis, gleams against the tan foothills near the Pacific. The floor space in the fashion stores and 18-story office towers already nearly equals that of Manhattan's Pan Am Building, and they are 49 miles from downtown Los Angeles.

"Everybody thinks a city needs to have a center," says Richard Baisden, a political scientist at the new University of California at Irvine. "Well, why does it? Downtown has ceased to have any real relevance. Its functions have dissipated and decentralized out to where the people are."

This decentralization, it is evident from the visits to five metropolitan areas, is nearly complete.

The barges, boxcars and industries that once gave the inner city its pre-eminence, and jobs, have not disappeared. But now they are rivaled by tractor-trailer rigs, beltways and fork-lift trucks that make desirable such low-rent industrial plants as the Pattillo development in Atlanta.

A HOME AT LAST

The central cities, their variety of apartments, flats and homes growing old, are no longer the sole, or even the most desirable, location of housing. For millions, the automobile and Federal insurance for new housing in outlying areas have crystallized the American dream.

"The suburban house," says Edgardo Contini, a noted Los Angeles urbanist, "is the idealization of every immigrant's dream—the vassal's dream of his own castle.

"Europeans who come here are delighted by our suburbs, even by the worst sprawl. Not to live in an apartment! It is a universal aspiration to own your own home."

'RIBBON OF GOLD'

The movement of people, in turn, has sped the outward spiral of shopping, a movement so rapid that in some cities, total suburban retail sales now far exceed those in the inner city.

And now have come the circumferential highways, what Baltimore calls the Beltway, Houston the Loop, Atlanta the Perimeter— and what one developer calls "the ribbon of gold."

Pasadena, Tex., near the Houston Loop beltway, expects to double and redouble its population. This growth will come, says Mayor Clyde Doyal, despite the fact that "we have no bus station, no railroad, no airport; what we've got is a freeway."

In Atlanta, people call the Perimeter the lifeline to development of the outer city. "People are learning to use it, learning to drive faster by driving farther," says Harold Brockey, president of Rich's. "No one says it took me 10 miles to get here; they say it took me 15 minutes."

The beltways are generating yet another level of growth. Suburban development once meant tract homes, schools and flat shopping centers. Now it is typified by monumental complexes like Mario Doccolo's $22 million Hampton Plaza in suburban Towson, Md.

Why did he build this gleaming, round, 29-story tower of tan stone—with offices, fine shops and condominium apartments—in the suburbs?

Because, Mr. Doccolo says, *"This* is the city. They're getting out of Baltimore. People go there to do what they have to do and then— zoom!—back out to the suburbs.

"I could see Mohammed wasn't going to the mountain anymore, so I said, 'Let's build the mountain out here.' That's what I bet on."

Thus the outer city: people, houses, plants, jobs, stores, space, greenery, independence.

NOT COMPLETE YET

But it is not, at least not yet, the complete city.

Some functions are still left to the inner city. Rapid high-rise office development in many cities testifies to one. White collar professionals—lawyers, brokers, bankers, government workers—still require frequent face-to-face contact, a central verbal marketplace.

Inner cities also remain culture centers. But many suburban residents are willing to do without downtown museums, theaters and symphonies, satisfying their cultural needs at outlying universities or amateur performances.

Most notably, the inner cities, despite the erosion of their economic strength, are still called on to perform a major social function: caring for the needy and societizing the poor.

The inner city remains the haven where the rural migrant, the poor black, the struggling widow can find cheap housing, health care, welfare and orientation to the complexities of urban life.

The burden of this function, clear from the straining budgets of every major city, prompts officials everywhere to talk of the swelling new outer cities as parasites.

ABANDONMENT CHARGED

"The middle class has entirely abandoned the city," says Norman Krumholtz, Cleveland's lean, intense planning director. "Twenty years down the road, it's perfectly conceivable that the city will be just one great big poorhouse."

Where, asks Baltimore's Larry Reich, are the blacks in the suburbs? It is a rhetorical question. He knows the suburbs are less than 7 percent black, compared with the city's 47 percent.

Where, he asks, do hippies, many of them children of the suburbs, congregate? Where is the suburban skidrow? Where is the fairness?

In Orange County, Calif., the black population is less than 1 percent. Yet nearly 7,000 of the county's 10,000 blacks are concentrated in beleagured Santa Ana.

In Cleveland, a suburban-dominated regional council, overriding city protests, voted a new freeway that would chew up more of the city's eroding tax base.

The speaker is a suburban city manager in California, but his words convey the sentiments of outer-city residents across the country:

"Social problems in the city? People here would say, 'Sympathy, yes. But willingness to help? That's their tough luck. That's their problem.' "

ARTICLE 4

The Future of American Ghettos

Anthony Downs

In the past few years, responsible authorities at many levels of government in the United States have increasingly focussed their attention upon the widening gap between conditions of life enjoyed by most Americans and those prevalent in the ghetto areas of our central cities. Earlier hearings conducted by this Subcommittee have dramatically described the complicated tangle of problems and undersirable conditions which dominate life in these ghettos. The apparent failure of existing federal, state, and municipal programs to stem certain adverse trends in ghettos has led some observers to conclude that the present individual-program approach is qualitatively wrong. That is, the past federal policy of developing a specific program carried out by a particular agency in response to some identifiable need—such as the need for vocational education or for public housing —has not succeeded in stemming the disadvantageous trends in any large city. Therefore, it is suggested, some alternative, entirely new approach should be developed in the future.

In my opinion, this conclusion does not necessarily follow from the failure of existing programs to stem the tide of deterioration, blight, cultural malaise, and violence in ghetto areas. It is at least equally conceivable that such failure results from the puny scale of past and present programs in relation to the magnitude of the adverse forces involved. Thus, it may not be the type of approach used by the federal government which has been wrong, but rather the unwillingness of the federal government and local governments to develop the full potentialities of those programs which are part of

Reprinted from Statement of Anthony Downs, "The Future of American Ghettos," in *Federal Role in Urban Affairs*, Part 17, pp. 3483–3490. Hearings before the Subcommittee on Executive Reorganization of the Committee on Government Operations. U.S. Senate, 90th Congress, 1st Session, April 20–21, 1967. Washington: U.S. Government Printing Office.

that approach, by operating them at much larger scale. Or perhaps both these factors are involved in the evident failure of our efforts to "turn the tide."

This conclusion that *scale* is just as important as *quality of program* is supported by an examination of the role of slums and ghettos in human history. No society in history which contained large urban settlements has been without miserable slums in which conditions were far worse than those in U.S. central cities today. Moreover, no society has ever even attempted to eliminate both poverty and all social discrimination against particular ethnic and nationality minorities. Ideological statements asserting that elimination of poverty and discrimination is official policy have been made in many societies, including our own and the Soviet Union. But merely stating a desired outcome is certainly not the same as pursuing an effective program to achieve it.

It is certainly true that the U.S. has reduced the incidence of poverty to lower levels than in any previous society. Nevertheless, for the United States government to adopt an official objective of *eliminating* slums and ghettos in our cities is an extraordinarily serious step. Pursuing such a policy effectively would involve changes in our economy and social structure of a profound nature. These changes would not only require major reallocations of money and manpower, but also alterations in the value structures of both the poor and racial minority groups on the one hand, and the middle- and upper-income and racial majority groups on the other. Furthermore, since no society has ever seriously attempted to attain such a goal before, there are really no precedents to follow. Personally, I am very much in favor of our adopting such a goal. But I believe we should do so with full recognition of the depth of change which a commitment to this objective actually involves.

Today there is a great deal of talk about a "crisis" in our cities. It is difficult to measure the quality of life in cities at any time; so it is doubly difficult to determine whether conditions are any worse today than they have been in the past. As far as I know, most conditions of life in cities have been steadily improving if looked at over any relatively long perspective, such as 50 to 100 years. The two glaring exceptions to this generalization are the levels of mass violence and air pollution, which have certainly grown worse in the past few years. However, with these exceptions, I believe it is misleading to speak of a "crisis" in our cities as though most trends are at some point of discontinuity which poses a grave and immediate threat to society. On the contrary, in terms of absolute standards of living, the vast majority of persons living in both cities and suburbs have in the past decade experienced rapidly improving conditions in almost every respect.

However, it is true that the aspirations of some groups—particularly those who have been at the bottom of the economic heap for so long—have risen even faster than their actual living standards. In the past, most revolutionary violence has occurred only after actual standards of living have begun to improve for even the poorest persons—but their expectations rose even faster. So if there is a crisis in our cities, it should be viewed as resulting from a disparity between aspirations and performance, rather than a complete failure of performance. In fact, I do not believe our response to the ghetto problem should be based upon conceiving of it as a crisis which momentarily threatens us. Rather, I believe we should take a much longer-run view. We should treat our response as requiring a major alteration in the very structure of our society designed to eliminate or at least substantially improve a fundamental but undesirable condition which has existed in all urban societies since history began.

KEY BACKGROUND FACTS

Before discussing possible strategies for reacting to ghetto conditions, I would like to set forth certain fundamental facts which any strategy must take into account. These can be briefly summarized as follows:

Ambiguity of the Term "Ghetto"

The word "ghetto" has two very different connotations which are easily confused. Historically, it meant an area in which certain ethnic groups were compelled to live. This meaning today carries over into the concept of a ghetto as an area to which members of an ethnic minority, particularly Negroes, are residentially restricted by social, economic, and physical pressures exerted by the rest of society. In this meaning, a ghetto can contain wealthy and middle-income residents as well as poor ones. However, the word "ghetto" has also recently come to mean an area in which urban poor people live, regardless of race or color. Since most urban poor people are white, this meaning has very different connotations from the first meaning. Thus, in 1960 there were 10.3 million nonwhites living in central cities. Since they were highly segregated residentially, this number serves as a good estimate of the 1960 ghetto population derived from the first or racial meaning of this word. This means that about half of all U.S. nonwhites lived in central-city ghettos in 1960. On the other hand, if we take the poverty definition, the total number of poor persons in 1960 (those with 1959 incomes under $3,000) who lived in central cities was 8.2 million. Moreover, approximately 66 percent of these persons were white and 34 percent were nonwhite.

Nonwhites as a group have a much higher incidence of poverty than whites and a much higher fraction of nonwhites live in central cities. Hence there is clearly an important relationship between these two definitions of "ghetto." Nevertheless, they are not the same, and considerable confusion arises from failure to distinguish clearly between them. In the remainder of my own analysis, I will use the word in its racial sense unless otherwise noted.

Racial Ghettos Are Now Rapidly Expanding

Any policies designed to cope with the ghetto must recognize the fact that concentrations of nonwhite population—particularly Negroes—in our central cities are not only failing to shrink, but are growing rapidly. In 1950, there were 6.3 million nonwhites living in central cities. In 1960, there were 10.3 million. This represents an increase of 63.5 percent, or an average of 400,000 persons per year. In the same decade, the white population of central cities went from 42.0 million to 47.6 million, an increase of 5.6 million, or 13.3 percent. However, in the largest central cities, the white population actually declined while the nonwhite population rose sharply.

Since 1960, Negro populations of central cities have continued to grow rapidly, and Negroes have continued to reside almost entirely in segregated neighborhoods. Our field surveys in Chicago show that 1,080 blocks were more than 25 percent Negro in 1950. From 1954 to 1960, 1,344 more blocks shifted from less than 25 percent Negro to more than 25 percent Negro, or 2.6 blocks per week. From 1960 through 1966, 1,101 additional blocks so shifted, or 3.5 blocks per week. There has been no significant drop in the number of dwelling units per block involved, so Negro expansion has apparently not slowed down at all.

Some recent tentative estimates we have made indicate that the central city nonwhite population for the whole U.S. will be about 14.3 million in 1968, and could rise to as high as 20.4 million by 1978. These estimates assume continued nonwhite immigration to central cities at about the same rate as occurred from 1950 to 1960. But even if we cut our estimate of net inmigration in half, the 1978 nonwhite central city population would still be about 19.2 million.

Such growth has critical implications for a great many policy objectives connected with ghettos. For example, it has been suggested that school district boundaries should be manipulated so as to counteract de facto segregation by creating districts in which many Negroes and many whites will jointly reside. This solution is practical over the long run only when there is reasonable stability in the total size of these two groups. But when one group is rapidly expanding in a city where there is no vacant land to build additional housing, then the other group must contract, unless there are sharp rises in density, which are not occurring. Therefore, as the nonwhite population expands in cities where vacant land no longer exists, the white population inevitably falls. So possibilities for ending de facto segregation in this manner inexorably shrink as time passes. For this and other reasons, no policy towards ghettos can afford to ignore this rapid expansion of the nonwhite population.

The Total Size of Ghettos in Relation to the Nation

Although a great deal of attention has been focussed upon ghettos in the last few years, they are still a relatively small fraction of the total population in the U.S. Taking the racial definition of ghettos as central-city nonwhite population, there were about 10.3 million persons in ghettos in 1960, or only about 5.7 percent of the total U.S. population. Furthermore, the number of persons now in ghettos, and the likely increase in that number in the future, are very small compared to the number of persons who will be added to the second focal point of urban problems—the suburban growth area—in any given future period. The Census Bureau Series D population estimate indicates that the total U.S. population in 1980 will be 226 million, as compared to 180.6 million in 1960. If we assume that about 90 percent of this increase will occur in the suburban portions of our metropolitan areas, that indicates a growth of approximately 40.9 million persons in those 20 years. In contrast, the ghetto (i.e., nonwhites in central cities, can be expected to increase by about 11.2 million from 1960 to 1980 (under a high immigration assumption) to a total level of about 21.5 million. Thus, the growth of the ghetto will be only one-quarter as large as the growth of suburban population. In fact, the *growth* in suburban population from 1960 to 1980 will be *twice as large* as the *total* ghetto population by 1980.

These facts are significant for two reasons. First, it may be difficult to create widespread political support for ghetto-improvement programs which have a very high per capita cost but are aimed at well under 10 percent of the total population. Second, it would be a mistake to focus all of our leadership talents, financial resources, and policy energies devoted to urban problems on ghettos alone when peripheral expansion of metropolitan areas will involve vastly more people. However, it is certainly true that the people who will be involved in the growth of suburbs have tremendously greater capacity to look out for their own interests than those who reside in ghettos.

The Complexity of Ghetto Problems

No single category of programs can possibly be adequate to cope with the tangled problems that exist in ghettos. In my opinion, any ghetto-improvement strategy must concern itself with at least the following kinds of issues: jobs and employment, education, housing, health, personal safety and crime prevention, and income maintenance for dependent persons. A number of other programs could be added, but I believe these are the most critical.

The Location of New Jobs

Most new employment opportunities are being created in suburban portions of our metropolitan areas, not anywhere near central city ghettos. Furthermore, this is a trend likely to continue indefinitely into the future. It is true that downtown office-space concentrations in a few large cities have created additional jobs near ghettos. But the outflow of manufacturing jobs has normally offset this addition significantly—and in some cases has caused a net loss of jobs in central cities. If we are going to provide jobs for the rapidly expanding ghetto population, particularly jobs which do not call for high levels of skills, we must somehow bring these potential workers closer to the locations of new employment opportunities. This can be done in three ways: by moving job locations so new jobs are created in the ghetto, by moving ghetto residents so they live nearer to the new jobs, or by creating better transportation between the ghetto and the locations of new jobs. The first alternative—creating new jobs in the ghetto—will not occur in the future under normal free-market conditions, in my opinion. However, any ghetto-improvement strategy must face the problem of linking up persons who need employment with those firms which can provide it.

BASIC ANTI-GHETTO STRATEGIES

There are three basic strategies which the United States may adopt towards ghettos. Before describing them, I want to point out that these strategies apply to individual metropolitan areas. Therefore, it is at least theoretically possible to adopt different strategies toward the ghetto in different metropolitan areas. In fact, I believe that there are some strong reasons why this would be an excellent idea. Moreover, since these strategies are not mutually exclusive, they can be adopted in various mixtures. This further strengthens the case for using a variety of approaches across the country. However, for purposes of analysis, it is fruitful to examine each of these strategies as though it were to be the sole instrument for coping with ghetto problems in all cities.

The Status Quo Strategy

The first strategy is to do nothing more than we are doing. I certainly do not wish to imply that present federal and local efforts in the anti-poverty program, the public housing program, the urban renewal program, health programs, educational aid programs, and many others are not of significant benefit to residents of ghettos. Nevertheless, as earlier testimony before this Subcommittee has pointed out, these programs have not succeeded in stemming the various adverse trends operating in ghetto areas. Therefore, the strategy of continuing our present policies and our present level of effort is essentially not going to alter current conditions in ghettos. This may make it seem silly for me to label a continuation of present policies as a specific anti-ghetto strategy. Yet I wish to emphasize the fact that failure to adopt effective policies is still a strategy. It is certainly not a successful one, but nevertheless it is an expression of our commitment and attitude towards the ghetto. If we maintain our current programs, segregated areas of residence in our central cities will continue to expand rapidly, to spawn violence, and to suffer from all of the difficult problems that have been described in previous hearings. The dedicated efforts now being made by thousands of federal, state, municipal, and private workers will indeed ameliorate conditions of life for many individuals residing in ghettos. But in my opinion, they will not "turn the tide" so as to cause any basic changes in the situation.

The Ghetto-Improvement Strategy

The second fundamental anti-ghetto strategy I call the ghetto-improvement strategy. This approach is aimed at dramatically improving the quality of life within the confines of present ghetto areas. I presume that any such policy would apply to the poverty meaning of ghetto more than the racial meaning. That is, any ghetto-improvement strategy would aim at upgrading the lowest-income and most disadvantaged citizens of our central cities, regardless of race. Nevertheless, nearly half of such persons are nonwhites. So the ghetto-improvement strategy would still concentrate heavily upon the same areas as if it were to follow a racial policy.

It is important to realize that the ghetto-improvement strategy would not end racial segregation. It would help many Negroes attain middle class status, and thus make it easier for them to leave the ghetto if they wanted to. Undoubtedly many would. But, by making life in central city ghettos more attractive without creating any strong pressures for dispersal of the nonwhite population, such a policy would increase the inmigration of nonwhites into central cities. This would speed up the expansion of racially segregated areas in central cities.

The basic idea underlying this strategy is to develop federally-financed programs that would greatly improve the education, housing, incomes, employment and job training, and social services received by ghetto residents. This would involve (a) vastly expanding the scale of present programs, (b) changing the nature of many of them because they are now ineffective or would be if operated at a much larger scale, and (c) creating incentives for a much greater participation of private capital in ghetto activities. Such incentives could include tax credits for investments made in designated ghetto areas, wage subsidies connected with on-the-job training but lasting longer than such training so as to induce employers to hire unskilled ghetto residents, rent or ownership supplements for poor families enabling them to rent or buy housing created by private capital, and others.

The ghetto-improvement strategy is consistent with a current ideology that has come to be called "black power" viewpoint. This viewpoint has been criticized by many, and some of its defendants have misused it to incite violence. Yet it is certainly an intellectually respectable and defensible position. This argument states that the American Negro population needs to overcome its feelings of powerlessness and lack of self-respect. It can do so by gaining control of the political machinery which has jurisdiction over the areas where Negroes live. Such assumption of local power would be fully consistent with the behavior of previous nationality groups, such as the Irish in New York and Boston. They, too, came up from the bottom of the social and economic ladder, where they had been insulted and discriminated against, by gaining political and economic control over the areas in which they lived. According to this view, a fully integrated society is not really possible until the Negro minority has developed its own internal strength. Therefore, the ideal society in which race itself is not an important factor would come much later. It could exist only after Negroes had gained power and self-respect by remaining in concentrated areas over which they could assume control and direction. This view contends that a future in which central cities were primarily Negro and suburbs almost entirely white would be an advantage rather than a disadvantage.

Although the ghetto-improvement strategy and the "black power" viewpoint are consistent, they are not identical. The "black power" viewpoint does not inherently require the kind of environment-enriching policies which are the heart of the ghetto-improvement strategy. In fact, present trends are already operating to make the conditions sought by "black power" advocates come true. Thus the proponents of "black power" do not need to do anything but wait for ghetto growth to allow their ideology to come into dominance in many of our large central cities, or at least in portions of them. On the other hand, the ghetto-improvement strategy would not deliberately discourage middle-class Negroes from leaving the ghetto, as would advocates of "black power."

The Dispersal Strategy

The third basic anti-ghetto strategy is what I call the dispersal strategy. Its key assumption is that the problems of the ghetto cannot be cured as long as millions of nonwhites, particularly those with low incomes and other significant disadvantages, are required or persuaded to live together in segregated ghetto areas. The dispersal strategy contends that large numbers of nonwhites should be given strong incentives to move from central cities into suburban areas, including those in which no nonwhites presently reside. To illustrate what I mean by "large numbers," let me postulate one version of the dispersal strategy, which I call the "constant-size ghetto strategy." This strictly hypothetical strategy aims at stopping the growth of existing ghettoes by dispersing enough nonwhites from central cities to suburbs (or peripheral central city areas) to offset potential future increases in that growth. Taking the period from 1968 through 1973, our estimates show that the nonwhite population of all U.S. central cities would, in the absence of any dispersal strategy, expand from 14.3 million to somewhere from 16.7 to 17.1 million, depending upon rates of immigration. Thus, if dispersal of nonwhites were to take place at a large enough scale to keep central city ghettos at their 1968 level during the five subsequent years, there would have to be a movement of between 2.4 and 2.8 million nonwhites into the suburbs. This amounts to between 480,000 and 560,000 per year. The suburban nonwhite population in all 212 metropolitan areas grew a total of only 74,000 per year during the decade from 1950 to 1960. In that decade, the white population of suburban portions of our metropolitan areas (the so-called urban fringe) increased by about 1,626,000 persons per year. Certainly some of this population increase was caused by an exodus of whites from central cities in response to the growth of nonwhite population therein. If future nonwhite population growth in central cities were stopped by a large-scale dispersion policy, then white population growth of the suburbs would be definitely smaller than it was from 1950 to 1960. Thus, a policy of dispersion of this magnitude would mean that future suburban population growth would be somewhere between 25 and 33 percent nonwhite, as compared with less than 5 percent nonwhite in the decade from 1950 to 1960.

Clearly, such dispersal would represent a radical change in existing trends. Not only would it stop the expansion of nonwhite ghettos in central cities, but also it would inject a significant nonwhite population into many presently all-white suburban areas. It is certainly true that policies of dispersal would not necessarily have to be at this large a scale. Dispersal aimed not at stopping ghetto growth, but merely at slowing it down somewhat, could be carried out at a much lower scale. Yet even such policies would represent a marked departure from past U.S. practices.

Such a departure would be necessary for any significant dispersal of nonwhites. Merely providing the *opportunity* for nonwhites to move out of ghettos would not result in many moving, at least not in the short run. Even adoption of a vigorously-enforced nationwide open-occupancy law applying to all residences would not greatly speed up the present snail's-pace rate of dispersion. Experience in those states which have open occupancy ordinances decisively proves this conclusion. Hence positive incentives for dispersion would have to be created in order to speed up the rate at which nonwhites move from central cities and settle in suburban areas. Such incentives could include rent supplements, ownership supplements, and other devices which essentially attach a subsidy to a person. Then, when the person moves, he and the community into which he goes get the benefit of that subsidy. This creates incentives both for him to move, and for the community to accept him.

Why should we even consider this radical strategy as one of the alternatives to which we should give serious attention? I believe there are four reasons. First, future job-creation is going to be primarily in suburban areas, but the unskilled population is going to be more and more concentrated in central city ghettos unless we effect some dispersion. Such an increasing divergence between where the workers are and where the jobs are will make it ever more difficult to create anything like full employment for ghetto residents. In contrast, if those residents were to move into suburban areas where they would be exposed to more knowledge of job opportunities and would have to make much shorter trips to reach them, they would have a far better chance of getting employment.

Second, the recent Coleman Report on equality of achievement in education reaches a *tentative* conclusion that it is necessary to end the clustering of lower-income Negro students together in segregated schools in order to improve their education significantly. As I understand the report, it implies that the most significant factor in the quality of education of any student is the atmosphere provided by his home and by his fellow students both in and out of the classroom. When this atmosphere is dominated by members of deprived families, the quality of education is ineradicably reduced—at least within the range of class size that has ever been tried on a large scale. Therefore, if we are to provide effective educational opportunities for the most deprived groups in our society to improve themselves significantly, we must somehow expose them to members of other social classes in their educational experience. Since there are not enough members of the Negro middle class "to go around," so to speak, this means some intermingling of children from the deprived groups with those from not-so-deprived white groups, at least in schools. Because of the transportation difficulties of bussing the large number of students in the hearts of central cities to suburban areas, it makes sense to accomplish this objective through some residential dispersion.

Third, continued concentration of large numbers of nonwhites under relatively impoverished conditions in ghettos may lead to unacceptably high levels of crime and violence in central cities. The outbreak of riots mostly in nonwhite areas in our central cities in the past few years is unprecedented in American history. No one is sure about what really causes these explosive events. Yet it is hard to avoid the conclusion that continuing to concentrate masses of nonwhite population in ghettos dominated by poverty and permeated with an atmosphere of deprivation and hopelessness will certainly not remove those causes, whatever they are.

Fourth, a continuation of ghetto growth will, over the next three or four decades, produce a society more racially segregated than any in our history. We will have older, blighted central cities occupied by millions of nonwhites, and newer, more modern suburban areas occupied almost solely by whites. Prospects for moving from that situation to a truly integrated society in which race is not a factor in key human decisions are not very encouraging. In fact, by that time we will be faced with a fantastically more massive dispersal problem than we are at present if we really want to achieve a society integrated in more than just words.

In my opinion, the four reasons stated above are sufficiently compelling so that we should seriously consider the merits—and costs—of a dispersal strategy.

I am fully aware that such a strategy may now seem fantastically impractical to responsible politicans like yourselves. I realize that the dispersal of nonwhites from ghettos to the suburbs through a deliberate federal policy presupposes radical changes in existing attitudes among both suburban whites and central city nonwhites. The history of the last fifty years clearly shows that, in spite of our social mobility, we Americans are extremely sensitive to class differentiations. We deliberately develop class-stratified suburban areas, using zoning, tax rates, lot-size requirements, and other devices to exclude persons considered farther down the ladder of social and economic prominence. As each group and each family moves upward in our mobile society, it becomes very concerned about creating social distance between itself and those now below it—including those who were once equal to it.

I am not deploring these historic traditions of self-improvement and protection of amenities and privileges which have been won through hard work and perseverance. Nevertheless, it is at least possible that the social objective of upgrading the lowest and most deprived groups in our society cannot be accomplished if we simultaneously insist upon maintaining rigid class distinctions by geographic area. The best dispersal policy would be one which did not change the dominant socio-economic character of the receiving suburban areas, but which allowed new groups of inmigrants to benefit from that character. This implies that newcomers would comprise a minority in each area into which they went. This would be the most desirable form of dispersion, because it would enable the group that was already there to maintain nearly intact their conception of the proper standards for that community, while sharing the benefits of those standards with others. Even this change in attitude, however, presupposes a shift in values of profound magnitude among white middle-class Americans. Furthermore, I doubt that most nonwhites today want to live in white communities in which they would be relatively isolated from other nonwhites. There is no very good empirical evidence one way or the other, but it is my opinion that most Negroes prefer to live with other Negroes, just as the evidence clearly suggests that most Jews want to live with other Jews. How would a dispersal strategy cope with this preference?

I do not pretend to have any pat answer to that question, or to many of the other disturbing questions raised by the concept of a dispersal strategy. Yet the alternatives to such a strategy—alternatives we are now pursuing—could conceivably lead us to equally grave changes in values. For example, if there is an extremely significant increase in violence in nonwhite ghettos which spills over into all-white areas, it is at least conceivable that the white population will react with harshly repressive measures which would significantly restrict individual freedoms. This, too, would call for a basic shift in our values, but one which I regard with much more alarm than the one required by a dispersal strategy. Yet it is not an improbable consequence of our continuing our present strategy. In fact, in this age of rapid technological change, it is naive to suppose that there will not in the future be very significant alterations in attitudes which we presently take for granted.

The Changing Economic Function

David L. Birch

As Raymond Vernon pointed out ten years ago,[1] on the surface there is little or no reason why economic activity should be located in the central city. Vernon found that, with a few exceptions, wage rates are practically indistinguishable between central city and suburb. He also found few, if any, advantages for businesses in the city in terms of space costs, transportation costs, and taxes. Manufacturing floor space in the central city is slightly more expensive in small quantities and a great deal more expensive in large quantities. Even taking into account the extra conveniences that must be built into new suburban locations, such as parking, shopping facilities, and cafeterias, space costs are more or less equal between city and suburb.

With rising congestion in the cities, rapid construction of circumferential highways, and the granting of advantageous city rates to suburban shippers, the cost advantage to a manufacturer or wholesaler of a central-city distribution point may no longer be substantial. For a retailer, the bulk of whose customers will not drive more than twenty minutes to get to his store, a central-city location can be a distinct disadvantage. Taxes in the central city are somewhat higher, and the differential can be expected to continue as the cities' needs continue to outstrip their resources.

With all these disadvantages in space costs, transportation costs, and taxes, how do we explain the tremendous concentrations of economic activity found in today's central cities?

The first, and most obvious, explanation is that the central cities are where it all started. In the days when transportation was difficult and slow and the advantages of a harbor or a railroad intersection

Reprinted from David L. Birch, *The Economic Future of City and Suburb*, pp. 3–15. CED Supplementary Paper Number 30. Copyright © 1970 by the Committee for Economic Development. Reprinted by permission of the Committee for Economic Development.

were great, the geographically concentrated city was the best solution for men of affairs and their families. *The* place to close a financial deal was the Cosmopolitan Club or Frank's Delicatessen. Out-of-town guests expected to be entertained at the 21 Club. Investments depreciate slowly and customs change slowly. If the central cities claimed no measurable economic advantages today, we would still not expect the concentrations that developed during the late nineteenth and early twentieth centuries to disperse rapidly.

But we must look beyond historical geography if we are to explain why so many central cities are still growing at a rapid pace. The search for a positive explanation led Vernon to identify three factors: (1) the communication factor, (2) the costs of uncertainty, and (3) the external economies of scale.

As Vernon saw it, face-to-face communication is very important to the small manufacturer who is dealing in a nonstandard product on a tight schedule. The producer of legal briefs or women's clothes or the seller of fresh produce must engage in all the subtleties of showing his product to the customer, reaching an agreement on the spot, and delivering the product—all in a very short period of time. The head-quarters of business firms need to be in close personal contact with the bankers, the underwriters, and the stock brokers who provide them with funds, with the lawyers who protect and advise them, with the officers of other firms with whom they do business, and with a host of specialized suppliers. Taken together, the people in these firms constitute a number of closely knit communities that depend upon day-to-day personal communication to get things done. An entire community can be moved physically, as was the produce market in Paris and the garment industry in Amsterdam, but it must remain as a community in order to sustain the human relationships on which it depends.

Minimizing the costs of uncertainty by locating in a congested urban complex is once again primarily the concern of the small producer of nonstandard products. The small machine shop owner or the producer of advertising brochures is constantly seeking new business that may require the use of new materials and processing techniques. The risk of investing in equipment to produce his own materials for any particular order is very great as compared with the short-term savings he might obtain. He would much prefer to be in a position to call on a diversity of competing suppliers, despite the extra cost. Likewise, the man who runs a specialized lathe or printing process needs a great diversity of customers to assure him of steady production. He cannot afford to be dependent upon one or two customers whose individual needs for his special product might vary a great deal. This interacting group of suppliers and producers forms a community in which one relies on the other to minimize risk.

External economies of scale have long been put forth as a rationale for concentration. The city can provide for the smaller firm what the larger, suburban company might have to provide for itself, or do without. The smaller firm contracts, either directly or through taxation, for the partial use of a subway or an airport, a freight distribution service or a sewage disposal plant. Collectively, these smaller firms bargain together for lower shipping rates. They hire a part-time electrician by purchasing his services by the hour. Because the central cities are able to offer this opportunity to share large fixed costs, they serve as breeding grounds for small firms. Vernon was not surprised to find that 69 percent of small plants were located in central cities, whereas only 45 per cent of their larger, more self-sufficient counterparts were situated in such centers. It is no accident that new firms spring up and die in the central cities at about twice the rate that they do in the suburbs. The ease of getting started is much greater when the burdens of getting started can be shared.

The advantages of close personal communication, lower costs of uncertainty, and external economies of scale are obviously greater for some firms than for others. Wholesalers and service firms, which tend to deal in specialized, nonstandard products, cannot completely ignore the advantages of a central location and thus tend to be more content in the central city. However, retailers, taking advantage of a short shopping radius, and manufacturers, attracted by the efficiencies of single-story plants, have increasingly located in the suburbs.

THE CITY'S INCREASING SPECIALIZATION

Attempts to document these observed trends have been frustrated for years because of the inadequate level of detail contained in census and other data. Detailed employment data for most central cities and suburban areas are available only for retail trade, wholesale trade, manufacturing, and selected services, which, in combination, account for only 55 per cent of total metropolitan employment and 58 per cent of central-city employment.

Accepting for the moment these shortcomings, an analysis of the four employment categories for which data are available supports our Darwinian assumption that some forms of activity survive better than others in a central-city environment, and that services survive the best. Looking at Figure 1, we note that, for a sample of seventy-three Standard Metropolitan Statistical Areas (SMSA's), representing 75 per cent of the total metropolitan population,[2] there have been recent absolute declines in retail trade, relatively slow growth in wholesaling and manufacturing, and rather greater growth in service jobs.

As a further check on this pattern, we must look to "other services," a category which includes most nonbusiness organizations, such as hospitals, law offices, schools, and nonprofit membership organizations (ranging from the Knights of Columbus to the Elks to CORE). We must also examine jobs in such fields as finance, insurance, real estate, and government. Together, these additional sectors account for

---

FIGURE 1.   Growth of Central City Employment by Major Industry Groups: 1948–1963

Distribution and Mean Annual Percentage Change for Seventy-Three SMSA's

Employment Category	Per Cent of Total Central City Employment in 1963	Mean Annual Percentage		Change 1958–63
		1948–54	1954–58	
Retail trade	20.0	0.8	1.8	−0.9
Wholesale trade	5.7	1.6	2.3	1.4
Manufacturing	27.5	3.6[a]	1.1	1.6
Selected services	5.0	2.3	4.7	2.4

[a] Data pertain to 1947–1954.

Sources: National Planning Association, *Economic and Demographic Projections for Two Hundred and Twenty-Four Metropolitan Areas,* Regional Economic Projections Series, Report No. 67–R–1, Vol. I, II, and III; U.S. Department of Commerce, Bureau of the Census, *County Business Patterns,* 1948, 1956, and 1958; and U.S. Department of Commerce, Bureau of the Census, *Census of Manufactures and Census of Business,* selected reports for various years, 1954–1963. See Appendix II, p. 41.

FIGURE 2.   Change in Central City Employment by Selected Categories: 1948–1967

Distribution and Mean Annual Percentage Change for Eight Central Cities[a]

Employment Category	Per Cent of Total Central-City Employment in 1963	Mean Annual Percentage 1948–56	Change 1956–67
Finance	3.1	4.0	4.1
Insurance and real estate	3.9	1.8	−0.2
Government[b]	11.4	n.a.	2.0
Other services[c]	13.4	4.0	15.7

[a] Baltimore, Denver, New Orleans, New York, Philadelphia, St. Louis, San Francisco, and Washington, D.C.

[b] Data pertain to 1957–1962.

[c] Includes medical, legal, educational, and miscellaneous business services, as well as nonprofit membership organizations.

Sources: See Figure 1.

approximately 32 per cent of central-city employment, raising our over-all coverage to about 90 per cent.

Unfortunately, the data for these additional sectors are quite sketchy. There are only eight SMSA's for which central-city statistics are available, and then only because county and city boundaries happen to coincide in these eight instances, thus opening up the detailed data ordinarily available for counties. The figures for the eight cities reveal some support for the concept of growing central-city specialization in service-type jobs. In Figure 2, we note that hospitals, schools, and law offices are growing much more rapidly as a group than is any sector yet examined. The financial sector is also expanding quite rapidly. Government employment is growing more slowly, and there appears to be a trend for insurance and real estate organizations to abandon the city for greener pastures.

If these differential growth rates are as persistent over the next fifteen to twenty years as they have been since 1948—and in the absence of dramatic changes in transportation or communication, we have every reason to believe that they will be—then it is reasonable to expect that the central cities will continue to become economic specialists. They will increasingly serve as the home for the hospital, the corporate headquarters, and the state office building.

The degree to which these trends persist will depend, of course, to a certain extent upon the relative growth of the sectors within the economy as a whole. If our greatest expansion as a nation over the next twenty to thirty years were to be in manufacturing or retail trade, rather than services, then the prospects for continued central-city growth would be diminished. However, one comprehensive projection, made by the National Planning Association, suggests otherwise. The NPA estimates summarized in Figure 3 indicate that it is the services (aggregated in this case), the financial community, and the government that can expect the greatest growth through at least 1975.

FIGURE 3.   Growth of U.S. Employment by Major Categories Since 1950, Projected to 1975

Average Annual Rate of Change

Employment Category	Actual 1950–57	Actual 1957–62	Projected 1962–75
Retail trade	0.3%	0.8%	1.9%
Wholesale trade	0.9	0.6	1.9
Manufacturing	1.6	−0.3	1.2
Services	2.7	3.5	2.9
Finance insurance and real estate	3.6	2.7	3.2
Federal government	2.2	1.9	0.1
State and local government	3.4	4.5	4.2

Sources: See Figure 1.

Thus, it can be assumed from the available evidence that, in aggregate, central cities will experience substantial growth in the white-collar, service-type job categories. As manufacturers, wholesalers, and retailers settle elsewhere, the effect of the growth in services will be to alter the mix of activities going on in central cities, which, in turn, will quite probably have an influence on the kinds of people living there.

THE SUBURB VERSUS THE CITY

Before we examine the residential function of cities, there remain two important economic questions. First, how are cities faring relative to suburbs in terms of economic growth rates? A basic consideration here is whether cities are capturing the bulk of the region's service jobs, and hence becoming service centers, or whether their specialization merely reflects an internal shift. Second, are all cities—large and small, young and old, north, south, and west—behaving in roughly the same fashion, or can we expect differences?

It is clear that the suburbs are growing much faster than the cities, despite the absolute gains of the central cities. As can be seen by a comparison of Figure 4 with Figure 2, suburban growth rates are much higher (sometimes by a factor of ten or more) than those of the central city.

FIGURE 4.   Growth of Suburban Employment by Major Industry Groups: 1948–1963

Mean Annual Percentage Change for Seventy-Three SMSA's

Employment Category	1948–1954	1954–1958	1958–1963
Retail trade	1.8%	15.5%	11.3%
Wholesale trade	4.5	17.6	9.4
Manufacturing	10.5[a]	6.3	9.9
Selected services	8.9	18.1	13.8

[a] Data pertain to 1947.

Sources: See Figure 1.

This rapid suburban expansion has had a predictable effect on the central-city share of total metropolitan employment: without exception, the central-city percentage is declining. (See Figure 5.) The difference in the central-city share as between one type of employment and another is less predictable, and perhaps more informative. In particular, the central city's relatively high share of service and financial jobs suggests that the city, by specializing in service work, has been able to attract and hold a great percentage of all high-

FIGURE 5. **The Central City's Changing Share of Urban Employment: 1948–1967**

Percentage

Employment Category	1948	1954	1956	1958	1963	1967
Sample of Seventy-three SMSA's[a]						
Retail trade	78.9%	77.6%		72.4%	64.0%	
Wholesale trade	87.3	86.4		82.4	78.5	
Manufacturing[b]	65.9	64.4		60.8	57.6	
Selected services	88.6	83.1		79.5	75.0	
Sample of Eight SMSA's[c]						
Other services	81.4		83.6%			72.1%
Finance	90.4		86.8			82.9
Insurance and real estate	92.7		89.2			80.2
Government	n.a.		66.0			59.7

[a] Statistics for sample of seventy-three SMSA's described in Appendix I.
[b] Data pertain to 1947.
[c] Statistics for sample of eight SMSA's described in Figure 2.
Sources: See Figure 1.

priced service jobs in the region. It thus appears to be functioning as an elite service center.

THE LIFE CYCLE OF THE CITY

It must be emphasized, however, that not all central cities are undergoing the same kind of transformation at the same rate. If we compare large smsa's (over 500,000 people) with smaller ones (less than 500,000 people), it is clear that cities in smaller smsa's are growing much more rapidly than cities in larger smsa's for each employment category. (See Figure 6.) In particular, manufacturers still appear to find the central cities of smaller metropolitan areas attractive, which would suggest that the problems of locating suitable building sites for efficient, one-story plants are not so acute.

Size, of course, is only one basis for comparing cities, and it is not a particularly useful one for prediction purposes. Intuitively, we would expect Phoenix and Albany, which are almost identical in

FIGURE 6.   Growth of Central City Employment by Size and Age of SMSA: 1948–1963[a]

Percentage Change for Seventy-Three SMSA's by Major Industry Groups

	Old SMSA's	Middle-Aged SMSA's	Young SMSA's	Average
Retail Trade				
Large SMSA's	−11.1%	19.8%	73.5%	4.2%
Smaller SMSA's	−13.0	11.7	26.5	18.6
Average	−11.2	15.7	37.7	9.5
Wholesale Trade				
Large SMSA's	4.1	43.9	111.6	23.6
Smaller SMSA's	17.0	26.5	54.2	42.2
Average	4.9	35.2	67.9	30.5
Manufacturing				
Large SMSA's	− 0.8	59.6	284.1	42.0
Smaller SMSA's	−10.9	52.6	89.8	69.9
Average	− 1.4	56.1	136.0	52.3
Selected Services				
Large SMSA's	31.5	56.6	162.1	50.6
Smaller SMSA's	21.2	37.8	67.8	54.3
Average	30.9	47.2	90.2	52.0

[a] "Old" SMSA's qualified as SMSA's before 1900; "middle-aged," between 1900 and 1930; and "young," after 1930. "Smaller" SMSA's have a population of less than 500,000; "large" SMSA's contain over 500,000 people.

Sources: See Figure 1.

size, to have quite different futures. Likewise, we might well anticipate different patterns for such matched pairs as Buffalo and Houston, or San Diego and Cincinnati. For one thing, we would expect the younger city in each case to have lower densities and more room for expansion. In point of fact, the densities of these cities are roughly one-half the densities of the older cities. Furthermore, we would expect the younger cities to be built around road networks, rather than around the railroads and harbors of the earlier cities. The combination of open room for new housing and new plants and the greater efficiency of moving from the one to the other should give these younger cities a distinct advantage in attracting jobs and the people to fill them.

There is nothing to suggest, however, that young cities can avoid the life cycle that older cities have experienced. As today's young cities "fill up," new technology will favor the still newer SMSA's, which will be able to incorporate recent advances from the start. The young cities of 1970 will become the older cities of 2050 and, in the process, more than likely will pass through the typical phases of growth, saturation, and eventually stabilization and decline.

To test this conjecture, SMSA's were further grouped according to the year in which each qualified as an SMSA. The resulting categories were: old (before 1900), middle-aged (1900–1930), and young (after 1930). The results strongly support the life-cycle notion. As can be seen in Figure 6, invariably the older the SMSA, the less rapidly it is growing in economic terms. Of particular interest is the absolute decline of retail trade and manufacturing in the older cities. In sharp contrast is the rapid growth of central-city manufacturing in the younger cities regardless of size. If anything, these young cities are captializing on their roads and open spaces to become manufacturing rather than service specialists. And, as might be predicted from a life cycle model, the older a city gets, the less its tendency to rely on manufacturing for growth.

This suggests a sequence whereby younger cities chew up low-density land at a good clip with manufacturing floor space, parking lots, and road networks. The other economic functions develop more slowly. As the city ages and becomes more densely populated, central-city land becomes more expensive, and manufacturing declines in significance, as does retail and wholesale trade. Services, in contrast, appear to thrive on concentration, for all the reasons indicated earlier, and, through a process of self-selection and survival, emerge as the dominant economic force in the older, larger cities. The tendency of central cities to become elite service centers appears, like rheumatism and decaying teeth, to be a strong function of age.

One effect of this life cycle phenomenon will be to redistribute the location of economic activity over time. Most of the younger, growing metropolitan areas are found in the South and the West. Whereas at present these younger areas account for only about 25 per cent of total employment, over time their much greater growth rates will give them an increasing share of the nation's gross national product. Conversely the significance of the large northern metropolitan centers, which served as the nuclei of urban growth during the first half of this century, will decline in a relative sense. Companies will not automatically locate their headquarters in New York or Philadelphia or Chicago. A young man will no longer have to "make it" in *the* big city. There will be a larger number of significant and growing economic concentrations to choose from.

Summarizing, we can envision a future that is quite different from the past. The central city is no longer able to function as a general-purpose economic system. Specialization is taking place within the city and within the SMSA, particularly in the older areas. Those organizations which can thrive on the advantages that concentration and a large city government can offer are thriving. Others are leaving or, more importantly, not locating there in the first place.

The extent to which specialization takes place appears closely related to the age of the area in which the city is located. While central cities in older areas are declining absolutely in most non-service jobs, cities in younger areas are growing quite rapidly across the board. Since the younger areas are located primarily in the South and the West, one result of this life-cycle effect will be to alter substantially the location of economic growth during the next fifty years. The pillars of American urban society during the first half of the century will have to accept a relatively lesser role in the future.

NOTES

1. Raymond Vernon, *The Changing Economic Function of the Central City* (New York: Committee for Economic Development, 1959).

ARTICLE 6

Property Taxes and the Public Schools: Serrano v. Priest

California State Supreme Court

We are called upon to determine whether the California public school financing system, with its substantial dependence on local property taxes and resultant wide disparities in school revenue, violates the equal protection clause of the Fourteenth Amendment. We have determined that this funding scheme invidiously discriminates against the poor because it makes the quality of a child's education a function of the wealth of his parents and neighbors. Recognizing as we must that the right to an education in our public schools is a fundamental interest which cannot be conditioned on wealth, we can discern no compelling state purpose necessitating the present method of financing. We have concluded, therefore, that such a system cannot withstand constitutional challenge and must fall before the equal protection clause.

Plaintiffs, who are Los Angeles County public school children and their parents, brought this class action for declaratory and injunctive relief against certain state and country officials charged with administering the financing of the California public school system. Plaintiff children claim to represent a class consisting of all public school pupils in California, "except children in that school district, the identity of which is presently unknown, which school district affords the greatest educational opportunity of all school districts within California." Plaintiff parents purport to represent a class of all parents who have children in the school system and who pay real property taxes in the county of their residence.

Defendants are the Treasurer, the Superintendent of Public Instruction, and the Controller of the State of California, as well as

Reprinted from *Congressional Record,* 92d Congress, 1st Session, Vol. 117, No. 139 (September 23, 1971), pp. E9965–E9970. Washington: U.S. Government Printing Office. Footnotes and other citations are omitted from text.

the Tax Collector and Treasurer, and the Superintendent of Schools of the County of Los Angeles. The county officials are sued both in their local capacities and as representatives of a class composed of the school superintendent, attending public schools in many other districts of the State . . ." The financing scheme thus fails to meet the requirements of the equal protection clause of the Fourteenth Amendment of the United States Constitution and the California Constitution in several specified respects.

In the second cause of action, plaintiff parents, after incorporating by reference all the allegations of the first cause, allege that as a direct result of the financing scheme they are required to pay a higher tax rate than taxpayers in many other school districts in order to obtain for their children the same or lesser educational opportunities afforded children in those other districts.

In the third cause of action, after incorporating by reference all the allegations of the first two causes, all plaintiffs allege that an actual controversy has arisen and now exists between the parties as to the validity and constitutionality of the financing scheme under the Fourteenth Amendment of the United States Constitution and under the California Constitution.

Plaintiffs pray for: (1) a declaration that the present financing system is unconstitutional; (2) an order to remedy this invalidity; and (3) an adjudication that the trial court retain jurisdiction of the action so that it may restructure the system if defendants and the state Legislature fail to act within a reasonable time. . . .

I

We begin our task by examining the California public school financing system which is the focal point of the complaint's allegations. At the threshold we find a fundamenal statistic—over 90 percent of our public school funds derive from two basic sources: (a) local district taxes on real property and (b) aid from the State School Fund.

By far the major source of school revenue is the local real property tax. Pursuant to article IX, section 6 of the California Constitution, the Legislature has authorized the governing body of each county, and city and county, to levy taxes on the real property within a school district at a rate necessary to meet the district's annual education budget. The amount of revenue which a district can raise in this manner thus depends largely on its tax base—i.e., the assessed valuation of real property within its borders. Tax bases vary widely throughout the state; in 1969–1970, for example, the assessed valuation per unit of average daily attendance of elementary school children ranged from a low of $103 to a peak of $952,156—a ratio of nearly 1 to 10,000.

The other factor determining local school revenue is the rate of taxation within the district. Although the Legislature has placed ceilings on permissible district tax rates, these statutory maxima may be surpassed in a "tax override" election if a majority of the district's voters approve a higher rate. Nearly all districts have voted to override the statutory limits. Thus the locally raised funds which constitute the largest portion of school revenue are primarily a function of the value of the realty within a particular school district, coupled with the willingness of the district's residents to tax themselves for education.

Most of the remaining school revenue comes from the State School Fund pursuant to the "foundation program," through which the state undertakes to supplement local taxes in order to provide a "minimum amount of guaranteed support to all districts. . . ." With certain minor exceptions, the foundation program ensures that each school district will receive annually from state or local funds, $355 for each elementary school pupil and $488 for each high school student.

The state contribution is supplied in two principal forms. "Basic state aid" consists of a flat grant to each district of $125 per pupil per year, regardless of the relative wealth of the district. "Equalization aid" is distributed in inverse proportion to the wealth of the district.

To compute the amount of equalization aid to which a district is entitled, the State Superintendent of Public Instruction first determines how much local property tax revenue would be generated if the district were to levy a hypothetical tax at a rate of $1 on each $100 of assessed valuation in elementary school districts and $.80 per $100 in high school districts. To that figure, he adds the $125 per pupil basic aid grant. If the sum of those two amounts is less than the foundation program minimum for that district, the state contributes the difference. Thus, equalization funds guarantee to the poorer districts a basic minimum revenue, while wealthier districts are ineligible for such assistance.

An additional state program of "supplemental aid" is available to subsidize particulary poor school districts which are willing to make an extra local tax effort. An elementary district with an assessed valuation of $12,500 or less per pupil may obtain up to $125 more for each child if it sets its local tax rate above a certain statutory level. A high school district whose assessed valuation does not exceed $24,500 per pupil is eligible for a supplement of up to $72 per child if its local tax is sufficiently high.

Although equalization aid and supplemental aid temper the disparities which result from the vast variations in real property assessed valuation, wide differentials remain in the revenue available to individual districts and, consequently, in the level of educational expenditures. For example, in Los Angeles County, where plaintiff children attend school, the Baldwin Park Unified School District expended only $577.49 to educate each of its pupils in 1968–1969; during the same year the Pasadena Unified School District spent $840.19 on every student; and the Beverly Hills Unified School District paid out $1,231.72 per child. The source of these disparities is unmistakable; in Baldwin Park the assessed valuation per child totaled only $3,706; in Pasadena, assessed valuation was $13,706; while in Beverly Hills, the corresponding figure was $50,885—a ratio of 1 to 4 to 13. Thus, the state grants are inadequate to offset the inequalities inherent in a financing system based on widely varying local tax bases.

Furthermore, basic aid, which constitutes about half of the state educational funds, actually widens the gap between rich and poor districts. Such aid is distributed on a uniform per pupil basis to all districts, irrespective of a district's wealth. Beverly Hills, as well as Baldwin Park, receives $125 from the state for each of its students.

For Baldwin Park the basic grant is essentially meaningless. Under the foundation program the state must make up the difference between $355 per elementary child and $47.91, the amount of revenue per child which Baldwin Park could raise by levying a tax of $1 per $100 of assessed valuation. Although under present law, that difference is composed partly of basic aid and partly of equalization aid, if the basic aid grant did not exist, the district would still receive the same amount of state aid—all in equalizing funds.

For Beverly Hills, however, the $125 flat grant has real financial significance. Since a tax rate of $1 per $100 there would produce $870 per elementary student, Beverly Hills is far too rich to qualify for equalizing aid. Nevertheless, it still receives $125 per child from the state, thus enlarging the economic chasm between it and Baldwin Park.

II

Having outlined the basic framework of California school financing, we take up plaintiffs' legal claims. Preliminarily, we reject their contention that the school financing system violates article IX, section 5 of the California Constitution, which states, in pertinent part: "The Legislature shall provide for a *system of common schools* by which a free school shall be kept up and supported in each district at least six months in every year. . . ." Plaintiffs' argument is that the present financing method produces separate and distinct systems, each offering an educational program which varies with the relative wealth of the district's residents.

We have held that the word "system," as used in article IX, Section 5, implies a "unity of purpose as well as an entirety of operation, and the direction to the legislature to provide 'a' system of common schools means *one* system which shall be applicable to all the common schools within the state." However, we have never interpreted the constitutional provision to require equal school spending; we have ruled only that the educational system must be uniform in terms of the prescribed course of study and educational progression from grade to grade.

We think it would be erroneous to hold otherwise. While article IX, section 5 makes no reference to school financing, section 6 of that same article specifically authorizes the very element of the fiscal system of which plaintiffs complain. Section 6 states, in part: "The Legislature shall provide for the levying annually by the governing board of each county, and city and county, of such school district taxes, at rates . . . as will produce in each fiscal year such revenue for each school district as the governing board thereof shall determine is required . . ."

Elementary principles of construction dictate that where constitutional provisions can reasonably be construed to avoid a conflict, such an interpretation should be adopted. This maxim suggests that section 5 should not be construed to apply to school financing; otherwise it would clash with section 6. If the two provisions were found irreconcilable, section 6 would prevail because it is more specific and was adopted more recently. Consequently, we must reject plaintiff's argument that the provision in section 5 for a "system of common schools" requires uniform educational expenditures.

III

Having disposed of these preliminary matters, we take up the chief contention underlying plaintiffs' complaint, namely that the California public school financing scheme violates the equal protection clause of the Fourteenth Amendment to the United States Constitution.

As recent decisions of this court have pointed out, the United States Supreme Court has employed a two-level test for measuring legislative classifications against the equal protection clause. "In the area of economic regulation, the high court has exercised restraint, investing legislation with a presumption of constitutionality and requiring merely that distinctions drawn by a challenged statute bear some rational relationship to a conceivable legitimate state purpose.

"On the other hand, in cases involving 'suspect classifications' or touching on 'fundamental interests,' the court has adopted an attitude of active and critical analysis, subjecting the classification to strict scrutiny. Under the strict standard applied in such cases, the state bears the burden of establishing not only that it has a *compelling* interest which justifies the law but that the distinctions drawn by the law are *necessary* to further its purpose."

A. Wealth as a Suspect Classification

In recent years, the United States Supreme Court has demonstrated a marked antipathy toward legislative classifications which discriminate on the basis of certain "suspect" personal characteristics. One factor which has repeatedly come under the close scrutiny of the high court is wealth. "Lines drawn on the basis of wealth or property, like those of race, are traditionally disfavored." Harper v. Virginia Bd. of Elections (1966). Invalidating the Virginia poll tax in *Harper,* the court stated: "To introduce wealth or payment of a fee as a measure of a voter's qualifications is to introduce a capricious or irrelevant factor." "[A] careful examination on our part is especially warranted where lines are drawn on the basis of wealth . . . [a] factor which would independently render a classification highly suspect and thereby demand a more exacting judicial scrutiny."

Plaintiffs contend that the school financing system classifies on the basis of wealth. We find this proposition irrefutable. As we have already discussed, over half of all educational revenue is raised locally by levying taxes on real property in the individual school districts. Above the foundation program minimum ($355 per elementary student and $488 per high school student), the wealth of a school district, as measured by its assessed valuation, is the major determinant of educational expenditures.

Although the amount of money raised locally is also a function of the rate at which the residents of a district are willing to tax themselves, as a practical matter districts with small tax bases simply cannot levy taxes at a rate sufficient to produce the revenue that more affluent districts reap with minimal tax efforts. For example, Baldwin Park citizens, who paid a school tax of $5.48 per $100 of assessed valuation in 1968–1969, were able to spend less than half as much on education as Beverly Hills residents, who were taxed only $2.38 per $100.

Defendants vigorously dispute the proposition that the financing scheme discriminates on the basis of wealth. Their first argument is essentially this: through *basic* aid, the state distributes school funds equally to all pupils; through *equalization* aid, it distributes funds in a manner beneficial to the poor districts. However, state funds constitute only one part of the entire school fiscal system. The foundation program partially alleviates the great disparities in local sources of revenue, but the system as a whole generates school revenue in proportion to the wealth of the individual district.

Defendants also argue that neither assessed valuation per pupil nor expenditure per pupil is a reliable index of the wealth of a district or of its residents. The former figure is untrustworthy, they assert, because a district with a low total assessed valuation but a miniscule number of students will have a high per pupil tax base and thus appear "wealthy." Defendants imply that the proper index of a district's wealth is the total assessed valuation of its property. We think defendants' contention misses the point. The only meaningful measure of a district's wealth in the present context is not the absolute value of its property, but the ratio of its resources to pupils, because it is the latter figure which determines how much the district can devote to educating each of its students.

But, say defendants, the expenditure per child does not accurately reflect a district's wealth because that expenditure is partly determined by the district's tax rate. Thus, a district with a high total assessed valuation might levy a low school tax, and end up spending the same amount per pupil as a poorer district whose residents opt to pay higher taxes. This argument is also meritless. Obviously, the richer district is favored when it can provide the same educational quality for its children with less tax effort. Furthermore, as a statistical matter, the poorer districts are financially unable to raise their taxes high enough to match the educational offerings of wealthier districts. Thus, affluent districts can have their cake and eat it too: they can provide a high quality education for their children while paying lower taxes. Poor districts, by contrast, have no cake at all.

Finally, defendants suggest that the wealth of a school district does not necessarily reflect the wealth of the families who live there. The simple answer to this argument is that plaintiffs have alleged that there is a correlation between a district's per pupil assessed valuation and the wealth of its residents and we treat these material facts as admitted by the demurrers.

More basically, however, we reject defendants' underlying thesis that classification by wealth is constitutional so long as the wealth is that of the district, not the individual. We think that discrimination on the basis of district wealth is equally invalid. The commercial and industrial property which augments a district's tax base is distributed unevenly throughout the state. To allot more educational dollars to the children of one district than to those of another merely because of the fortuitous presence of such property is to make the quality of a child's education dependent upon the location of private commercial and industrial establishments. Surely, this is to rely on the most irrelevant of factors as the basis for educational financing.

Defendants, assuming for the sake of argument that the financing system does classify by wealth, nevertheless claim that no constitutional infirmity is involved because the complaint contains no allegation of purposeful or intentional discrimination. Thus, defendants contend, any unequal treatment is only de facto, not de jure. Since the United States Supreme Court has not held de facto school segregation on the basis of race to be unconstitutional, so the argument goes, de facto classifications on the basis of wealth are presumptively valid.

We think that the whole structure of this argument must fall for want of a solid foundation in law and logic. First, none of the wealth classifications previously invalidated by the United States Supreme Court or this court has been the product of purposeful discrimination. Instead, these prior decisions have involved "unintentional" classifications whose impact simply fell more heavily on the poor.

For example, several cases have held that where important rights are at stake, the state has an affirmative obligation to relieve an indigent of the burden of his own poverty by supplying without charge certain goods or services for which others must pay. In Griffin v. Illinois the high court ruled that Illinois was required to provide a poor defendant with a free transcript on appeal. Douglas v. California held that an indigent person has a right to court-appointed counsel on appeal.

Other cases dealing with the factor of wealth have held that a state may not impose on an indigent certain payments which, although neutral on their face, may have a discriminatory *effect*. In Harper v. Virginia Bd. of Elections the high court struck down a $1.50 poll tax, not because its *purpose* was to deter indigents from voting, but because its *results* might be such. We held in In re Antazo that a poor defendant was denied equal protection of the laws if he was imprisoned simply because he could not afford to pay a fine. In summary, prior decisions have invalidated classifications based on wealth even in the absence of a discriminatory motivation.

We turn now to defendants' related contention that the instant case involves at most de facto discrimination. We disagree. Indeed, we find the case unusual in the extent to which governmental action *is* the cause of the wealth classifications. The school funding scheme is mandated in every detail by the California Constitution and statutes. Although private residential and commercial patterns may be partly responsible for the distribution of assessed valuation throughout the state, such patterns are shaped and hardened by zoning ordinances and other governmental and-use controls which promote economic exclusivity. Governmental action drew the school district boundary lines, thus determining how much local wealth each district would contain. Compared with *Griffin* and *Douglas*, for example, official activity has played a significant role in establishing the economic classifications challenged in this action.

Finally, even assuming arguendo that defendants are correct in their contention that the instant discrimination based on wealth is merely de facto, and not de jure, such discrimination cannot be justified by analogy to de facto racial segregation. Although the United States Supreme Court has not yet ruled on the constitutionality of de facto racial segregation, this court eight years ago held such segregation invalid, and declared that school boards should take affirmative steps to alleviate racial imbalance, however created. Consequently, any discrimination based on wealth can hardly be vindicated by reference to de facto racial segregation, which we have already condemned. In sum, we are of the view that the school financing system discriminates on the basis of the wealth of a district and its residents.

B. Education as a Fundamental Interest

But plaintiffs' equal protection attack on the fiscal system has an additional dimension. They assert that the system not only draws lines on the basis of wealth but that it "touches upon," indeed has a direct and significant impact upon, a "fundamental interest," namely education. It is urged that these two grounds, particularly in combination, establish a demonstrable denial of equal protection of the laws. To this phrase of the argument we now turn our attention.

Until the present time wealth classifications have been invalidated only in conjunction with a limited number of fundamental interests—rights of defendants in criminal cases and voting rights. Plaintiff's contention—that education is a fundamental interest which may not be conditioned on wealth—is not supported by any direct authority.

We, therefore, begin by examining the indispensable role which education plays in the modern industrial state. This role, we believe, has two significant aspects: first, education is a major determinant of an individual's chances for economic and social success in our competitive society; second, education is a unique influence on a child's development as a citizen and his participation in political and community life. "[T]he pivotal position of education to success in American society and its essential role in opening up to the individual the central experiences of our culture lend it an importance that is undeniable." Thus, education is the lifeline of both the individual and society.

The fundamental importance of education has been recognized in other contexts by the United States Supreme Court and by this court. These decisions—while not *legally* controlling on the exact issue before us—are persuasive in their accurate factual description of the significance of learning.

The classic expression of this position came in Brown v. Board of Education (1954), which invalidated de jure segregation by race in public schools. The high court declared: "Today, education is perhaps the most important function of state and local governments. Compulsory school attendance laws and the great expenditures for education both demonstrate our recognition of the importance of education to our democratic society. It is required in the performance of our most basic public responsibilities, even service in the armed forces. It is the very foundation of good citizenship. Today it is a principal instrument in awakening the child to cultural values, in preparing him for later professional training, and in helping him to adjust normally to his environment. In these days, it is doubtful that any child may reasonably be expected to succeed in life if he is denied the opportunity of an education. Such an opportunity, where the state has undertaken to provide it, is a right which must be made available to all on equal terms."

The twin themes of the importance of education to the individual and to society have recurred in numerous decisions of this court. Most recently in San Francisco Unified School Dist. v. Johnson, where we considered the validity of an anti-busing statute, we observed, "Unequal education, then, leads to unequal job opportunities, disparate income, and handicapped ability to participate in the social, cultural, and political activity of our society." Similarly, in Jackson v. Pasadena City School Dist., which raised a claim that school districts had been gerrymandered to avoid integration, this court said: "In view of the importance of education to society and to the individual child, the opportunity to receive the schooling furnished by the state must be made available to all on an equal basis."

When children living in remote areas brought an action to compel local school authorities to furnish them bus transportation to class, we stated: "We indulge in no hyperbole to assert that society has a compelling interest in affording children an opportunity to attend school. This was evidenced more than three centuries ago, when Massachusetts provided the first public school system in 1647. And today an education has become the *sine qua non* of useful existence. . . . In light of the public interest in conserving the resource of young minds, we must unsympathetically examine any action of a public body which has the effect of depriving children of the opportunity to obtain an education."

And long before these last mentioned cases, in Piper v. Big Pine

School Dist., where an Indian girl sought to attend state public schools, we declared: "[T]he common schools are doorways opening into chambers of science, art, and the learned professions, as well as into fields of industrial and commercial activities. Opportunities for securing employment are often more or less dependent upon the rating which a youth, as a pupil of our public institutions, has received in his school work. These are rights and privileges that cannot be denied." Although *Manjares* and *Piper* involved actual exclusion from the public schools, surely the right to an education today means more than access to a classroom.

It is illuminating to compare in importance the right to an education with the rights of defendants in criminal cases and the right to vote—two "fundamental interests" which the Supreme Court has already protected against discrimination based on wealth. Although an individual's interest in his freedom is unique, we think that from a larger perspective, education may have far greater social significance than a free transcript or a court-appointed lawyer. "[E]ducation not only affects directly a vastly greater number of persons than the criminal law, but it affects them in ways which—to the state—have an enormous and much more varied significance. Aside from reducing the crime rate (the inverse relation is strong), education also supports each and every other value of a democratic society—participation, communication, and social mobility, to name but a few."

The analogy between education and voting is much more direct: both are crucial to participation in, and the functioning of, a democracy. Voting has been regarded as a fundamental right because it is "preservative of other basic civil and political rights. . . ." The drafters of the California Constitution used this same rationale—indeed, almost identical language—in expressing the importance of education. Article IX, section 1 provides: "A general diffusion of knowledge and intelligence being essential to the preservation of the rights and liberties of the people, the Legislature shall encourage by all suitable means the promotion of intellectual, scientific, moral, and agricultural improvement." At a minimum, education makes more meaningful the casting of a ballot. More significantly, it is likely to provide the understanding of, and the interest in, public issues which are the spur to involvement in other civic and political activities.

The need for an educated populace assumes greater importance as the problems of our diverse society become increasingly complex. The United States Supreme Court has repeatedly recognized the role of public education as a unifying social force and the basic tool for shaping democratic values. The public school has been termed "the most powerful agency for promoting cohesion among a heterogenous democratic people . . . at once the symbol of our democracy and the most persuasive means for promoting our common destiny." In Abington School Dist. v. Schempp (1963), it was said that "Americans regard the public schools as a most vital civic institution for the preservation of a democratic system of government."

We are convinced that the distinctive and priceless function of education in our society warrants, indeed compels, our treating it as a "fundamental interest."

First, education is essential in maintaining what several commentators have termed "free enterprise democracy"—that is, preserving an individual's opportunity to compete successfully in the economic marketplace, despite a disadvantaged background. Accordingly, the public schools of this state are the bright hope for entry of the poor and oppressed into the mainstream of American society.

Second, education is universally relevant. "Not every person finds it necessary to call upon the fire department or even the police in an entire lifetime. Relatively few are on welfare. Every person, however, benefits from education . . ."

Third, public education continues over a lengthy period of life —between 10 and 13 years. Few other government services have such sustained, intensive contact with the recipient.

Fourth, education is unmatched in the extent to which it molds the personality of the youth of society. While police and fire protection, garbage collection and street lights are essentially neutral in their effect on the individual psyche, public education actively attempts to shape a child's personal development in a manner chosen not by the child or his parents but by the state. "[T]he influence of the school is not confined to how well it can teach the disadvantaged child; it also has a significant role to play in shaping the student's emotional and psychological makeup."

Finally, education is so important that the state has made it compulsory—not only in the requirement of attendance but also by assignment to a particular district and school. Although a child of wealthy parents has the opportunity to attend a private school, this freedom is seldom available to the indigent. In this context, it has been suggested that "a child of the poor assigned willy-nilly to an inferior state school takes on the complexion of a prisoner, complete with a minimum sentence of 12 years."

C. The Financing System Is Not Necessary to Accomplish a Compelling State Interest

We now reach the final step in the application of the "strict scrutiny" equal protection standard—the determination of whether the California school financing system, as presently structured, is necessary to achieve a compelling state interest.

The state interest which defendants advance in support of the current fiscal scheme is California's policy "to strengthen and encourage local responsibility for control of public education." We treat separately the two possible aspects of this goal: first, the granting to local districts of effective decision-making power over the administration of their schools; and second, the promotion of local fiscal control over the amount of money to be spent on education.

The individual district may well be in the best position to decide whom to hire, how to schedule its educational offerings, and a host of other matters which are either of significant local impact or of such a detailed nature as to require decentralized determination. But even assuming arguendo that local administrative control may be a compelling state interest, the present financial system cannot be considered necessary to further this interest. No matter how the state decides to finance its system of public education, it can still leave this decision-making power in the hands of local districts.

The other asserted policy interest is that of allowing a local district to choose how much it wishes to spend on the education of its children. Defendants argue: "[I]f one district raises a lesser amount per pupil than another district, this is a matter of choice and preference of the individual district, and reflects the individual desire for lower taxes rather than an expanded educational program, or may reflect a greater interest within that district in such other services that are supported by local property taxes as, for example, police and fire protection or hospital services."

We need not decide whether such decentralized financial decision-making is a compelling state interest, since under the present financing system, such fiscal free will is a cruel illusion for the poor school districts. We cannot agree that Baldwin Park residents care less about education than those in Beverly Hills solely because Baldwin Park spends less than $600 per child while Beverly Hills spends over $1,200. As defendants themselves recognize, perhaps the most accurate reflection of a community's commitment to education is the rate at which its citizens are willing to tax themselves to support their schools. Yet by that standard, Baldwin Park should be deemed far more devoted to learning than Beverly Hills, for Baldwin Park citizens levied a school tax of well over $5 per $100 of assessed valuation, while residents of Beverly Hills paid only slightly more than $2.

In summary, so long as the assessed valuation within a district's boundaries is a major determinant of how much it can spend for its schools, only a district with a large tax base will be truly able to decide how much it really cares about education. The poor district cannot freely choose to tax itself into an excellence which its tax rolls cannot provide. Far from being necessary to promote local fiscal choice, the present financing system actually deprives the less wealthy districts of that option.

It is convenient at this point to dispose of two final arguments advanced by defendants. They assert, first, that territorial uniformity in respect to the present financing system is not constitutionally required; and secondly, that if under an equal protection mandate relative wealth may not determine the quality of public education, the same rule must be applied to all tax-supported public services.

In support of their first argument, defendants cite Salsburg v. Maryland (1954) and Board of Education v. Watson. We do not find these decisions apposite in the present context, for neither of them involved the basic constitutional interests here at issue. We think that two lines of recent decisions have indicated that where fundamental rights or suspect classifications are at stake, a state's general freedom to discriminate on a geographical basis will be significantly curtailed by the equal protection clause.

The first group of precedents consists of the school closing cases, in which the Supreme Court has invalidated efforts to shut schools in one part of a state while schools in other areas continued to operate. In Griffin v. School Board (1964) the court stated: "A state, of course, has a wide discretion in deciding whether laws shall operate statewide or shall operate only in certain counties, the legislature 'having in mind the needs and desires of each.' . . . But the record in the present case could not be clearer that Prince Edward's public schools were closed . . . for one reason, and one reason only: to ensure . . . that white and colored children in Prince Edward County would not, under any circumstances, go to the same school. Whatever nonracial grounds might support a State's allowing a county to abandon public schools, the object must be a constitutional one. . . ."

Similarly, Hall v. St. Helena Parish School Board held that a statute permitting a local district faced with integration to close its schools was constitutionally defective, not merely because of its racial consequences: "More generally, the Act is assailable because its application in one parish, while the state provides public schools elsewhere, would unfairly discriminate against the residents of that parish, irrespective of race. . . . [A]bsent a reasonable basis for so classifying, a state cannot close the public schools in one area while, at the same time, it maintains schools elsewhere with public funds."

The *Hall* court specifically distinguished *Salsburg* stating: "The holding of Salsburg v. State of Maryland permitting the state to treat differently, for different localities, the rule against admissibility of illegally obtained evidence no longer obtained in view of Mapp. v. Ohio, . . . Accordingly, reliance on that decision for the proposition that there is no constitutional inhibition to geographic discrimination in the area of civil rights is misplaced. . . . [T]he Court [in *Salsburg*] emphasized that the matter was purely 'procedural' and 'local.' Here, the substitutive classification is discriminatory. . . ."

In the second group of cases, dealing with apportionment, the high court has held that accidents of geography and arbitrary boundary lines of local government can afford no ground for discrimination among a state's citizens. Specifically rejecting attempts to justify unequal districting on the basis of various geographic factors, the court declared: "Diluting the weight of votes because of place of residence impairs basic constitutional rights under the Fourteenth Amendment just as much as invidious discriminations based upon factors such as race or economic status, Griffin v. Illinois, Douglas v. California. . . . The fact that an individual lives here or there is not a legitimate reason for overweighting or diluting the efficacy of his vote." (Reynolds v. Sims) If a voter's address may not determine the weight to which his ballot is entitled, surely it should not determine the quality of his child's education.

Defendants' second argument bolls down to this: if the equal protection clause commands that the relative wealth of school districts may not determine the quality of public education, it must be deemed to direct the same command to all governmental entities in respect to all tax-supported public services; and such a principle would spell the destruction of local government. We unhesitatingly reject this argument. We cannot share defendants' unreasoned apprehensions of such dire consequences from our holding today. Although we intimate no views on other governmental services, we are satisfied that, as we have explained, its uniqueness among public activities clearly demonstrates that *education* must respond to the command of the equal protection clause.

We, therefore, arrive at these conclusions. The California public school financing system, as presented to us by plaintiff's complaint supplemented by matters judicially noticed, since it deals intimately with education, obviously touches upon a fundamental interest. For the reasons we have explained in detail, this system conditions the full entitlement to such interest on wealth, classifies its recipients on the basis of their collective affluence and makes the quality of a child's education depend upon the resources of his school district and ultimately upon the pocketbook of his parents. We find that such financing system as presently constituted is not necessary to the attainment of any compelling state interest. Since it does not withstand the requisite "strict scrutiny," it denies to the plaintiffs and others similarly situated the equal protection of the laws. If the allegations of the complaint are sustained, the financial system must fall and the statutes comprising it must be found unconstitutional.

V

Defendants' final contention is that the applicability of the equal protection clause to school financing has already been resolved adversely to plaintiffs' claims by the Supreme Court's summary affirmance in McInnis v. Shapiro and Burruss v. Wilkerson. The trial court in the instant action cited *McInnis* in sustaining defendants' demurrers.

The plaintiffs in *McInnis* challenged the Illinois school financing system, which is similar to California's, as a violation of the equal protection and due process clauses of the Fourteenth Amendment because of the wide variations among districts in school expenditures per pupil. They contended that *"only* a financing system which apportions public funds according to the educational needs of the students satisfies the Fourteenth Amendment."

A three-judge federal district court concluded that the complaint stated no cause of action "for two principal reasons: (1) the Fourteenth Amendment does not require that public school expenditures be made only on the basis of pupils' *educational needs,* and (2) the lack of judicially manageable standards makes this controversy non-justiciable." The court additionally rejected the applicability of the strict scrutiny equal protection standard and ruled that the Illinois financing scheme was rational because it was "designed to allow individual localities to determine their own tax burden according to the importance which they place upon public schools." The United States Supreme Court affirmed per curiam with the following order: "The motion to affirm is granted and the judgment is affirmed." No cases were cited in the high court's order; there was no oral argument.

Defendants argue that the high court's summary affirmance forecloses our independent examination of the issues involved. We disagree.

Since *McInnis* reached the Supreme Court by way of appeal from a three-judge federal court, the high court's jurisdiction was not discretionary. In these circumstances, defendants are correct in stating that a summary affirmance is formally a decision on the merits. However, the significance of such summary dispositions is often unclear, especially where, as in *McInnis*, the court cites no cases as authortiy and guidance. One commentator has stated, "It has often been observed that the dismissal of an appeal, technically an adjudication on the merits, is in practice often the substantial equivalent of a denial of certiorari." Frankfurter and Landis had suggested earlier that the pressure of the court's docket and differences of opinion among the judges operate "to subject the obligatory jurisdiction of the court to discretionary considerations not unlike those governing *certiorari*." Between 60 and 84 percent of appeals in recent years have been summarily handled by the Supreme Court without opinion.

At any rate, the contentions of the plaintiffs here are significantly different from those in *McInnis*. The instant complaint employs a familiar standard which has guided decisions of both the United States and California Supreme Courts: discrimination on the basis of wealth is an inherently suspect classification which may be justified only on the basis of a compelling state interest. By contrast, the *McInnis* plaintiffs repeatedly emphasized "educational needs" as the proper standard for measuring school financing against the equal protection clause. The district court found this a "nebulous concept"—so nebulous as to render the issue nonjusticiable for lack of " 'discoverable and manageable standards.' " In fact, the nonjusticiability of the "educational needs" standard was the basis for the *McInnis* holding; the district court's additional treatment of the substantive issues was purely dictum. In this context, a Supreme Court affirmance can hardly be considered dispositive of the significant and complex constitutional questions presented here.

Assuming, as we must in light of the demurrers, the truth of the material allegations of the first stated cause of action, and considering in conjunction therewith the various matters which we have judicially noticed, we are satisfied that plaintiff children have alleged facts showing that the public school financing system denies them equal protection of the laws because it produces substantial disparities among school districts in the amount of revenue available for education.

The second stated cause of action by plaintiff parents by incorporating the first cause has, of course, sufficiently set forth the constitutionally defective financing scheme. Additionally, the parents allege that they are citizens and residents of Los Angeles County; that they are owners of real property assessed by the county; that some of defendants are county officials; and that as a direct result of the financing system they are required to pay taxes at a higher rate than taxpayers in many other districts in order to secure for their children the same or lesser educational opportunities. Plaintiff parents join with plaintiff children in the prayer of the complaint that the system be declared unconstitutional and that defendants be required to restructure the present financial system so as to eliminate its unconstitutional aspects. Such prayer for relief is strictly injunctive and seeks to prevent public officers of a county from acting under an allegedly void law. Plaintiff parents then clearly have stated a cause of action since "[i]f the . . . law is unconstitutional, then county officials may be enjoined from spending their time carrying out its provisions. . . ."

Because the third cause of action incorporates by reference the allegations of the first and second causes and simply seeks declaratory relief, it obviously sets forth facts sufficient to constitute a cause of action.

By our holding today we further the cherished idea of American education that in a democratic society free public schools shall make available to all children equally the abundant gifts of learning. This was the credo of Horace Mann, which has been the heritage and the inspiration of this country. "I believe," he wrote, "in the existence of natural law, or natural ethics—a principle antecedent to all human institutions, and incapable of being abrogated by any ordinance of man . . . which proves the *absolute right* to an education of every human being that comes into the world, and which, of course, proves the correlative duty of every government to see that the means of that education are provided for all. . . ."

The judgment is reversed and the cause remanded to the trial court with directions to overrule the demurrers and to allow defendants a reasonable time within which to answer.

SULLIVAN, J.

We concur: Wright C. J.; Peters, J.; Tobriner, J.; Mosk, J.; Burke, J.

DISSENTING OPINION BY McCOMB, J.

I dissent. I would affirm the judgment for the reasons expressed by Mr. Justice Dunn in the opinion prepared by him for the Court of Appeal in *Serrano* v. *Priest.*

McCOMB, J.

SUGGESTIONS FOR FURTHER READING

I. General Introduction

Adrian, Charles R., and Charles Press. *Governing Urban America.* 3d ed. Chapters 1 and 3. New York: McGraw-Hill Book Company, 1968. (Urban developments and local government ideology.)

Banfield, Edward C., and James Q. Wilson. *City Politics,* Part I. New York: Random House, Inc., Vintage Books, 1963. (Background to the study of city politics.)

Blumenfeld, Hans. "The Modern Metropolis." In *Cities, A Scientific American Book.* Pp. 40–57. New York: Alfred A. Knopf, Inc., 1967. (Urbanization in America and Europe from a regional planning perspective.)

Bollens, John C., and Henry J. Schmandt. *The Metropolis.* 2d ed. Chapters 1 and 2. New York: Harper & Row, Publishers, Inc., 1970. (Urban developments in a metropolitan context.)

Dahl, Robert A. "The City in the Future of Democracy." *American Political Science Review* 61 (1967):953–970. (An argument that the Greek city-state provides a model for enhanced civic participation in modern cities.)

Ginger, Ray, ed. *Modern American Cities.* A New York Times Book. Chicago: Quadrangle Books, Inc., 1969. (A collection of essays on urban developments in America.)

Greer, Scott. *Governing the Metropolis.* Chapters 1 and 3. New York: John Wiley and Sons, Inc., 1962. (Urban developments and proliferation of governments in metropolitan areas.)

Herson, Lawrence J. R. "The Lost World of Municipal Government." In *Urban Government: A Reader in Administration and Politics,* edited by Edward C. Banfield. Pp. 3–18. New York: The Free Press, 1961. (A critical evaluation of municipal government literature and its public administration biases.)

Mumford, Lewis. "In Defense of the City." In *Metropolitan Politics,* edited by Michael N. Danielson. Pp. 20–27. Boston: Little, Brown and Co., 1966. (A pessimistic outlook on the results of metropolitan sprawl together with arguments for reconsidering the classic values of urban life.)

Reich, Charles A. *The Greening of America.* New York: Random House, Inc., 1970. (A radical attack on the corporate state's neglect of human values together with a defense of the youth-hippie culture.)

Starr, Roger. *The Urban Choices: The City and Its Critics.* Baltimore: Penguin Books, Inc., 1967. (A strong, but sometimes questionable, attack on contemporary city critics and suggested solutions to city problems with major emphasis on New York City.)

U.S., Congress, House of Representatives, *Metropolitan America: Challenge to Federalism,* 89th Congress, 2d Session, October, 1966, pp. 1–11. (An analysis of the conflicts among metropolitan governmental units relative to public service demands and local government taxing capabilities as stated by the Advisory Commission on Intergovernmental Relations.)

"What Kind of City Do We Want?" *Nation's Cities* 5 (1967):17–23, 45–47. (The debate of thirty-three urban experts that central cities must not be permitted to deteriorate any further.)

II. Historical Development of Cities

Branyan, Robert L., and Lawrence H. Larsen, eds. *Urban Crisis in Modern America.* Problems in American Civilization. Lexington, Mass.: D. C. Heath and Co., 1971. (A collection of essays on urban problems.)

Dorsett, Lyle W., ed. *The Challenge of the City, 1860–1910.* Problems in American Civilization. Lexington, Mass.: D. C. Heath and Co., 1968. (A collection of essays on the Progressive era in urban development.)

Green, Constance McLaughlin. *American Cities in the Growth of the Nation.* New York: Harper & Row, Publishers, Inc., Colophon Books, 1965. (Essays on American city development with emphasis on the movement of population westward from colonial times to the present.)

Mumford, Lewis. *The City in History.* Pp. 446–481. New York: Harcourt, Brace and World, Inc., 1961. (An encyclopedic history of cities with the selected reading providing insight on city developments during the Industrial Revolution.)

Tager, Jack, and Park D. Goist. *The Urban Vision.* Homewood, Ill.: The Dorsey Press, 1970. (Selected essays on American urban developments from 1860 to 1965.)

Wade, Richard C. "The City in History—Some American Perspectives." In *Urban Life and Form,* edited by Werner Z. Hirsch. Pp. 59–79. New York: Holt, Rinehart and Winston, Inc., 1963. (A brief summary of American urban developments from colonial times to the present.)

III. The Grass Roots Philosophy in American Local Government

Elazar, Daniel J. "Are We a Nation of Cities?" *The Public Interest* 4 (1966): 42–58. (An argument that America is a nation of small towns because of the continuing attachment to Jeffersonian ideals.)

———. *Cities of the Prairie: The Metropolitan Frontier and American Politics.* New York: Basic Books, Inc., 1970. (A historical analysis of ten mid-western metropolitan "civil" communities with emphasis on cultural, political, and suburban developments.)

Goodnow, Frank. "The Historical Development of the City's Position." In *Urban Government,* edited by Edward C. Banfield. Pp. 42–56. New York: The Free Press, 1961. (A history of the reasons for city dependence on state legislatures.)

Lyford, Joseph P. *The Talk in Vandalia.* New York: Harper & Row, Publishers, Inc., Colophon Books, 1965. (A discussion by residents of a small farming town in Illinois about the problems of rural living in the mid-twentieth century.)

Martin, Roscoe C. *Grass Roots.* New York: Harper & Row, Publishers, Inc., Colophon Books, 1962. (An examination of the defense of small town government which concludes that many weaknesses exist, according to various tests of efficiency and economy.)

Rourke, Francis E. "Urbanism and American Democracy." *Ethics* 74 (1964): 255–268. (The continuing effects of Jeffersonian attitudes on American city development.)

Syed, Anwar. *The Political Theory of American Local Government.* Chapters 2, 3, and 4. New York: Random House, Inc., 1966. (A comparison of local self-government ideals with the dependency of cities on state legislatures by examining Dillon's rule in depth.)

Vidich, Arthur J., and Joseph Bensman. *Small Town in Mass Society.* Garden City, N. Y.: Doubleday and Co., Inc., Anchor Books, 1960. (An important sociological study of "Springdale," indicating that decision-making processes by small town governments may conflict with classical notions of democratic theory.)

White, Morton and Lucia. *The Intellectual versus the City.* New York: The New American Library, Inc., Mentor Books, 1964. (A history of the anti-urban bias in American thought.)

IV. Local Property Taxes and the Public Schools

Advisory Commission on Intergovernmental Relations. *Who Should Pay for Public Schools? Washington,* D.C.: U.S. Government Printing Office, October, 1971. (The results of ACIR Conference concerning how much to spend on schools, how to raise revenues, and how to spend money where the needs are greatest and in a way that will get the most results.)

Coons, John E. "Equal Dollars for School Districts." *The New York Times* (November 1, 1971):41, cols. 3–6. (An analysis of *Serrano v. Priest* with the suggestion that the California legislature might establish minimum and maximum tax and expenditure efforts for public schools.)

Howe, Harold. "Anatomy of a Revolution." *Saturday Review* (November 20, 1971):84–88, 95. (A discussion of the California Supreme Court ruling within the framework of public education problems and prospects.)

Netzer, Dick. *Economics and Urban Problems.* Pp. 191–196. New York: Basic Books, Inc., 1970. (A critique of local property taxes and their effects on local services.)

Wise, Arthur E. "The California Doctrine." *Saturday Review* (November 20, 1971):78–83. (A legal and constitutional analysis of *Serrano v. Priest.*)

Chapter 2

People and Cities
Polarization or Consensus?

With more than two hundred million inhabitants, urban America is such a vast, diverse, and expansive nation that it is not surprising to find so many different attitudes, beliefs, and opinions on public issues. In the past, elected leaders skillfully built effective political alliances by appealing to the basic democratic principles underlying our society. But the decade of the 1960's saw growing frustration and alienation among the American electorate. Not only were three important and inspiring leaders assassinated—John F. Kennedy, Robert F. Kennedy, and Martin Luther King—but we also discovered that America was a country torn by dissension, the Vietnam War, ghetto riots, black power separatists, youthful rebels, and a growing malaise among the white majority all proved to be polarizing factors.

The first three selections of this chapter discuss the contemporary causes of political polarization as they affect the urban milieu. The underlying theme is the attitudes and perceptions of diverse segments of our population in regard to their welfare and the factors that contribute to it. What are the problems which different ethnic and racial groups face as members of American society? What are the sources of these problems? In terms of perceptions, what are the areas of similarity and dissimilarity between individuals of diverse racial, class, and ethnic groups?

If an attempt is to be made to deal directly with the underlying causes of urban problems, it seems clear that a consensus among diverse groups in the society is necessary for political action. Michael Parenti (Article 7) analyzes the continuing ethnic group basis of American politics. While many middle-class Americans are undifferentiated in their life styles, they continue to have an attachment to their national origins and religious ties. Parenti draws an important distinction between the outward appearances of Americanization (which he calls acculturation) and the persistence of ethnic identification. White America may not be as assimilated as is commonly believed. The melting pot theory is largely a myth, since there are still a large variety of ethnic variations and attitudes, a considerable parallel system of ethnic social institutions, and strong psychological feelings of minority group identity. Even when different groups move from the cities to the suburbs, they retain friendships and associations with people of similar backgrounds. For these reasons, it is not surprising that political candidates often stress ethnic ties in electoral campaigns.

In a personalized view of America's white ethnics, Michael Novak (Article 8) examines the basic causes of political, social, and intellectual alienation among these urbanized groups. He describes the Eastern and Southern European Poles, Italians, Greeks, and Slavs as unassimilated and distrustful of those who control the mainstream of American power and prestige. They believe that the major financial and governmental decisions are made by an "Ivy League" power elite, while the press, mass media, and literary world largely reflect the ideas of Jewish intellectuals.

The white ethnics have worked hard to achieve their present situation. When they first arrived in America at the turn of the twentieth century, the Irish, Italians, East Europeans, and Jews all faced severe hardships. They were fiercely resisted by older city residents. These newcomers had to make substantial personal and group efforts to gain an economic niche in American cities.

Novak stresses the essential differences between the city ethnics and native white Americans. The ethnics are predominantly Catholic, while the nativists are Protestant. Additionally, each group is suspicious of the other because of their different cultural heritages and fears. At the same time, the ethnics and the nativists are conservative, patriotic, and distrustful of intellectuals who, in Novak's view, have sought to homogenize them, destroy their cultural roots, and accuse them of racist attitudes towards blacks and other minorities. Novak ends his article with a plea for preserving ethnic diversity so that liberal democracy can evolve without submerging different ideas, cultures, and attitudes in an undifferentiated and powerless mass.

Perhaps one of the greatest sources of discontent and hostility among the blue-collar working class is the black minority. Their loudest complaint is that the pace of black economic, social, and political progress has been increased by white liberals who do not ever consider the urban and economic status of white ethnics. The white worker feels victimized and neglected by the innovative, black-oriented social reforms of the 1960's. He seems ready to turn to "law and order" advocates who promise to pay more attention to his plight.

In contrast, the black minority, as shown in the 1969 *Newsweek* survey (Article 9), considers the pace of social and economic improvement to be much too slow. The vast majority of American blacks still aspire to a place in the open society, but they view America's international, military, and defense commitments as serious detractions from governmental attention to pressing domestic problems. Black hopes and aspirations are still part of a revolution of rising expectations, but there is also a new culture, a sense of togetherness, and "soul." Most of all, many blacks are becoming convinced that their goals are best realized by effective political action and participation. They believe that the ballot box, not racial violence, will open doors into American society.

Having identified the needs and goals of different groups in the urban milieu, we turn next to alternative strategies for political, social, and economic change. What is the range of political strategies? Should individuals work within or outside traditional channels? Is it possible to strengthen minority group identity by militant activism, while at the same time seeking to develop workable political alliances with other groups? Which holds the greatest prospect for black development and progress—black separatism or a coalition among different segments of the population bridging racial and ethnic considerations? Is it possible to build a new, progressive majority for social, economic, and political change? Can city government be made more responsive by encouraging community control and neighborhood self-rule? Can the system of majority rule respond to the demands of disenchanted and alienated minorities?

One alternative strategy is black militancy, a continuing theme in city politics, which emphasizes the crucial importance of self-determination and the acceptance of blacks on their own terms in city political life. In fact, efforts to achieve political recognition through a new style of leadership has now extended beyond the black community to other minorities, including Puerto Ricans, Chicanos, American Indians, and white ethnics. In Article 10, James S. Campbell identifies the basic goals and tactics of radical black militancy, which include cultural autonomy, political autonomy, and self-defense. Ironically, the thrust for black cultural independence appears remarkably similar to the position of the white ethnics described by Michael Novak in Article 8. Urban blacks are reacting against "neocolonial" domination by American middle-class values which they think destroy the Afro-American cultural heritage. Second, political autonomy is an effort to build a political base of strength in the black community that will enable black leaders to exercise power effectively on behalf of their constituents. In this regard, black political militancy is a drive for separatism, a tactic by which the minority community will close ranks behind its leaders before entering into political coalitions with whites. Self-defense is the most controversial and potentially the most dangerous of militant tactics. The argument is that the neocolonial white army, the police, must not be permitted to brutalize, harass, or stifle minority group efforts for self-determination. While there is much to be said for police intimidation of black activists, the inevitable result of self-defense tactics has been violent confrontation between ghetto revolutionaries and the police. Rather than achieving their goals, such militants invariably have been killed, imprisoned, or exiled. For example, consider the large numbers of Black Panther leaders who have been captured by the police.

A variation of the political autonomy strategy is community control or neighborhood self-government. In his testimony before the Senate Subcommittee on Executive Reorganization (Article 11), Milton Kotler argues that slum conditions cannot be attacked separately, since poor housing, schools, and employment conditions constitute a unified political order of repression which residents cannot change in any legal way. Kotler calls the neighborhood self-governing decision a new approach to organize impoverished minorities. In his view, people must have the authority to decide their own political future. In effect, he emphasizes the importance of town meeting government in city neighborhoods. This process, he feels, will incorporate principles of political freedom for ghetto residents in the decision-making process. Kotler's proposal has several basic assumptions, which may or may not apply to all slum neighborhoods. These include (1) the similar characteristics of neighborhood residents and their consequent attachment to neighborhood boundaries; (2) the motivation and mobilization of residents to participate in the decision-making process; and (3) the availability of sufficient financial and technological resources to bring about changes in the slums. Additionally, Kotler's proposals for neighborhood self-rule are close to the ghetto improvement strategy criticized by Anthony Downs in Article 4 (Chapter 1). In their implementation they might also face some of the considerably difficult problems encountered by the Community Action Programs of the War on Poverty, which will be discussed in Chapter 5.

If Kotler's strategy for neighborhood self-rule is a microscopic view of urban problems, Herbert Gans (Article 12) is more concerned with the nationwide implications of the urban crisis. Gans argues that our major urban dilemmas—poverty, segregation, and urban decay—are national crises that transcend local governmental control. Furthermore, they involve fundamental problems of institutional resistance to change in a democratic society. While it might be possible to organize slum communities for self-determination, what would be their relationship with the corporate centralization and complex bureaucratic decisional mechanisms of the larger society? Although citizens have long been urged to be active in their communities and neighborhoods, they often find that their actual participation is limited to activity in organized groups or lobbies that do not always represent their best interests. Such a system creates outvoted minorities who may turn to disruptive tactics to dramatize their plight. To overcome this tyranny of the majority, Gans recommends a reconsideration of majority rule. He contends that minority groups should be represented fairly on all governmental levels and consulted directly in decisions that directly affect their lives. Gans would not do away with majority rule, but he would require a new system of proposing and executing decisions that would both recognize and protect the needs of disaffected minority groups.

QUESTIONS FOR DISCUSSION AND DEBATE

1. Michael Parenti's distinction between the concepts of acculturation and social assimilation raises a number of interesting chal-

lenges to the traditional melting pot theory. After identifying as many racial, ethnic, and religious city immigrants as you can, make a case for their acculturation or assimilation. Is the Parenti distinction applicable to all of these groups? If not, why not?

2. Social and economic mobility in American cities is often attributed to personal self-improvement or the "bootstraps" theory. Are there any dependent urban groups who can no longer rely on their "bootstraps" for upward mobility? Why is this the case?

3. Michael Novak describes the white ethnics as basically conservative and Democratic in their political preferences. Does this mean that there is almost no way that white ethnics and blacks can form a political alliance?

4. Black power and black militancy are controversial terms in American political rhetoric. Assume the roles of a white ethnic, a white liberal, and a black ghetto resident, and define black power and black militancy.

5. What are the differences, if any, between Kotler's arguments for neighborhood self-government and those for grass-roots democracy in the suburbs. Is the basic problem in America today one of government that is too large in scale or one of too many fragmented local governments?

6. In proposing modifications of majority rule, would you favor a system of proportional representation? Weighted voting? Concurrent majorities? In a democratic society, what are the alternatives for balancing a possibly tyrannical majority wth a possibly tyrannical minority? If minorities are often prevented from influencing decisions, what happens when majority decisions are ignored?

Ethnic Politics and the Persistence of Ethnic Identification

Michael Parenti

A question that has puzzled students of ethnic politics can be stated as follows: in the face of increasing assimilation why do ethnics continue to vote as ethnics with about the same frequency as in earlier decades? On the basis of his New Haven study, Robert Dahl observes that ". . . in spite of growing assimilation, ethnic factors continued to make themselves felt with astonishing tenacity."[1] Nevertheless, he asserts, "the strength of ethnic ties as a factor in local politics surely must recede."[2] Dahl sets up a "three-stage" model to describe how political assimilation will follow a more general social assimilation. However, one of his co-researchers, Raymond Wolfinger, demonstrates in a recent article in this REVIEW[3] that ethnic voting patterns persist into the second and third generations, and that "at least in New Haven, all the social changes of the 1940's and 1950's do not seem to have reduced the political importance of national origins."[4] The same observation can be made of religious-ethnic identities, for as Wolfinger notes, citing data from the Elmira study, social mobility in no way diminishes the religious factor as a determinant of voting behavior; in fact, in the case of upper and middle class Catholics and Protestants, religion seems to assume a heightened importance as a voting determinant.[5] Wolfinger marshals evidence to support the arresting proposition that, melting pot or not, ethnic voting may be with us for a long time to come, a finding which craves explanation.

Part of the reason for the persistence of ethnic voting may rest in the political system itself. Rather than being a purely dependent vari-

Reprinted from Michael Parenti, "Ethnic Politics and the Persistence of Ethnic Identification," *American Political Science Review*, Vol. 61, No. 3 (September 1967), pp. 717–726. Reprinted by permission of the American Political Science Association and Michael Parenti.

able, the political system, i.e., party, precinct workers, candidates, elections, patronage, etc., continues to rely upon ethnic strategies such as those extended to accommodate the claims of newly-arrived ethnic middle-class leadership; as a mediator and mobilizer of minority symbols and interests, the political system must be taken into account.[6]

Wolfinger suggests several further explanations, which may be briefly summarized as follows: (a) "Family-political identification." Voting studies show that as many as four-fifths of all voters maintain the same party identification as did their parents, a continuity which is not merely a reflection of similar life conditions but is in part ascribable to the independent influence of primary group relations.[7] (b) "Critical elections theory." The emergence of highly salient ethnic candidates and issues may cause a dramatic realignment so that a particular party becomes the repository of ethnic loyalty even after the ethnically salient candidate and issues have passed.[8] (c) "Historical after-effects." Partisan affiliations, as Key and Munger have demonstrated for Indiana, persist generations after the reasons for their emergence have ceased to be politically relevant. Thus "even when ethnic salience has faded, . . . its political effects will remain."[9] (d) "Militant core-city residue." The ethnic community may retain a group awareness despite a growing class heterogeneity because the assimilationist-minded will advance to the suburbs while those among the upwardly mobile who choose to stay in the ethnic city settlements are more likely to be the most strongly in-group oriented.[10]

Several comments are in order before we proceed further: of the above explanations, there seems to be some question as to whether (a), (b) and (c) are concerned with independent variables. It does seem that the Key-Munger historical after-effect idea in (c) is an extension of the "fixation" of the "crucial elections" notion in (b) and that both must rest in large part on the strong inheritance and continuity of family partisan identifications in (a). Explanation (d), while suggestive, is wanting in substantiating data. What evidence we have does not necessarily support the "militant core-city residue" idea, and certainly does not lend substance to the image of a homogenized, assimilated suburbia, as we shall see below. Nevertheless, the above hypotheses submitted by Wolfinger may serve as useful explanations for the political continuity of all social groups, ethnics included.[11]

Yet, after all is said and done, I cannot free myself from the suspicion that perhaps a false problem has been created which can best be resolved by applying certain analytic and theoretical distinctions, supported by data that extend beyond the usual voting studies. If, in fact, it can be demonstrated that assimilation is not taking place, then the assimilation theory as propounded by Dahl, along with Wolfinger's alternate explanations are somewhat beside the point. And the question, why do ethnics continue to vote as ethnics despite increasing assimilation, becomes the wrong one to ask—because the answer may simply be that minorities are not assimilating. At first glance, such an assertion seems to violate the evidence of our senses. Have not old-world immigrant cultures all but disappeared? Are not the ethnics scattering into homogeneously Americanized suburbs? Is not the educational level of the national minorities continually increasing? Are not ethnic occupational distributions changing? etc.

The confusion rests, I submit, in the failure—common to many of us political scientists, and even to some sociologists and anthropologists—to make a conceptual distinction between "acculturation" and "assimilation." The distinction is crucial in reading correct meaning into our data and in guiding us to fruitful theoretical conclusions. For while it is established that ethnics have accommodated themselves to American styles and customs (acculturation) by the second generation, and while perhaps they may enjoy increased occupational and geographic mobility, it is not at all clear that they are incorporating themselves into the structural-identificational-group relations of the dominant society (assimilation). On close examination we find that the term "assimilation," as commonly used, refers to a multiplicity of cultural, social and identificational processes which need closer scrutiny.[12]

I. ACCULTURATION AND ASSIMILATION

At the outset, it is necessary, as Talcott Parsons and others have urged, to distinguish between *cultural* and *social* systems: the cultural is the system of beliefs, values, norms, practices, symbols and ideas (science, art, artifacts, language, law and learning included); the social is the system of interrelations and associations among individuals and groups. Thus a church, family, club, informal friendship group, or formal organization, etc., composed of individuals interracting in some kind of context involving roles and statuses are part of the *social* system, or one might say, represent particular sub-societal systems within the society; while the beliefs, symbols, and practices mediated and adhered to by members of the church, family, club, etc., are part of the *cultural* system or sub-cultural systems within the total culture. By abstracting two analytically distinct sets of components from the same concrete phenomena we are able to observe that, although there may often be an important interraction, the order of relationships and the actions and conditions within one are independent of those in the other. Attention to this independence increases analytical precision.[13]

What was considered as one general process becomes a multi-faceted configuration of processes. And if it can be said that there is no inevitable one-to-one relationship between the various processes, and that imperatives operative in one system are not wholly dependent upon the other, then ethnic political behavior becomes something less of a mystery. *For ethnic social sub-systems may persist or evolve new structures independent of the host society and despite dramatic cultural transitions in the direction of the mainstream culture.*

Since early colonial times, nearly every group arriving in America has attempted to reconstruct communities that were replications of the old world societies from which they had emerged. With the exception of a few isolated sectarian enclaves such as the Hutterites, the Amish and the Hasidic, they failed to do so. If culture is to be represented as the accumulated beliefs, styles, solutions and practices which represent a society's total and continuing adjustment to its environment, then it would seem to follow that no specific cultural system can be transplanted from one environment to another without some measure of change. Unable to draw upon a complete cultural base of their own in the new world, and with no larger constellation of societal and institutional forces beyond the ghetto boundaries to back them, the immigrants eventually lost the battle to maintain their indigenous ways. By the second generation, attention was directed almost exclusively toward American events and standards, American language, dress, recreation, work, and mass media, while interest in old world culture became minimal or, more usually, non-existent. To one extent or another, all major historical and sociological studies of immigration and ethnicity document this cultural transition of the American-born generation.

However, such acculturation was most often *not* followed by social assimilation; the group became "Americanized" in much of its *cultural* practices, but this says little about its *social* relations with the host society. In the face of widespread acculturation, the minority still maintained a social sub-structure encompassing primary and secondary group relations composed essentially of fellow ethnics. A study of a Polish-American industrial town illustrates this cultural-social distinction. The Polish children treat their immigrant parents with either patronization or contempt, speak American slang, are addicted to American popular music, and popular culture, accept fully the American way of piling up money and material goods when possible. Yet they keep almost all their social contacts within the confines of the Polish-American community and have no direct exposure to, and little interest in, middle-class American society.[15] Similar findings were made by Whyte and Gans in their respective studies—done twenty years apart—of Italian-American communities in Boston. American styles, language, sports and consumption patterns predominated, but interpersonal relations and social group structures were almost exclusively Italian-American in both the North End of the 1940's and the West End of the 1960's.[16]

From birth in the sectarian hospital to childhood play-groups to cliques and fraternities in high school and college to the selection of a spouse, a church affiliation, social and service clubs, a vacation resort, and, as life nears completion, an old-age home and sectarian cemetary—the ethnic, if he so desires, may live within the confines of his sub-societal matrix—and many do.[17] Even if he should find himself in the oppressively integrated confines of prison, the ethnic discovers that Italian, Irish, Jewish, Negro and Puerto Rican inmates coalesce into distinct groups in "a complex web of prejudices and hostilities, friendships and alliances."[18]

Hollingshead, in a study of New Haven, discerned vertical social divisions based on race, religion and national origin along with the expected horizontal cleavages due to income and residence. Cutting across the class strata were the parallel dissections of the black and white worlds, with the latter further fissured into Catholic, Jewish and Protestant components which, in turn, sub-divided into Irish, Italian, Polish, etc. Within this highly compartmentalized world were to be found the ethnic associational patterns.[19]

II. HETEROGENEITY WITHIN THE HOMOGENEOUS SOCIETY

Could not such unassimilated sub-structures be more representative of a time when urban areas were segmented into ghettos untouched by post-war affluence, upward occupational mobility and treks to the suburbs? This is the question which seems to anticipate both Dahl and Wolfinger. In actuality, while individual ethnics have entered professional and occupational roles previously beyond their reach, minority group mobility has not been as dramatic as it often supposed. A comparison of first and second generation occupational statuses as reported in the 1950 national census shows no evidence of any substantial convergence of intergroup status levels. The occupational differences among ethnic groups, with the Irish as a possible exception, remain virtually the same for both generations, leading C. B. Nam to observe that even with the absence of large-scale immigration, "the importance of nationality distinctions for the American stratification system will remain for some time to come."[20] If today's ethnics enjoy a better living standard than did their parents, it is because there has been an across-the-board rise throughout America. Fewer pick-and-shovel jobs and more white collar positions for minority members are less the result of ethnic mobility than of an overall structural transition in our national economy and the composition of our labor force.[21]

Furthermore, despite the popular literature on the hopeless homogeneity of suburbia,[22] suburbs are not great *social* melting pots. Scott Greer, after noting the breakup of some of the central city ethnic communities, cautions: "The staying force of the ethnic community (in suburbia) must not be underestimated." The good Catholic, for instance, "can live most of his life, aside from work, within a Catholic environment,"[23] in a sub-societal network of schools, religious endogamy, family, church, social, athletic and youth organizations, and Catholic residential areas. Similarly, Robert Wood observes that suburbs tend toward ethnic clusters. In the more "mixed areas," ethnic political blocs are not unknown. As in the city, the tension between the older resident and the newcomer sometimes reinforces ethnic political alignments and ethnic social identifications.[24] Minority concentrations are less visible in suburban than in urban areas because less immigrant and second-generation persons reside there. Lieberson's study of ten major metropolitan areas shows that the groups most highly segregated from native whites in the central city are also most residentially concentrated in the suburbs, so that suburban patterns bear a strong similarity to those found in the city.[25]

Finally, residential segregation is not a necessary prerequisite for the maintenance of an ethnic sub-societal structure; *a group can maintain ethnic social cohesion and identity, while lacking an ecological basis.*[26] The Jews of Park Forest live scattered over a wide area and "participate with other Park Foresters in American middle-class culture," that is, they clearly are acculturated. Yet in one year a Jewish sub-community consisting of informal friendship groups, a women's club, a B'nai B'rith lodge and a Sunday School had emerged. Similarly distinct Lutheran and Catholic social groupings also had developed in which national origin played a large part. (Religion, according to Herbert Gans, was not the exclusive concern of any of the three groups.)[27]

The neighborhood stores, bars, coffee-shops, barber shops, and fraternal clubrooms which serve as social nerve centers in the ecologically contiguous first-settlement urban areas are difficult to reconstruct in the new topography of shopping centers and one-family homes, but they are frequently replaced by suburban-styled church, charity and social organizations, informal evening home-centered gatherings and extended family ties kept intact over a wide area with the technical assistance of the omnipresent automobile. The move to second and third settlement areas and the emergence of American-born generations, rather than presaging an inevitable process of disintegration has led to new adjustments in minority organization and communication. *Even when most of the life-styles assume an American middle-class stamp, these in-group social patterns reinforce ethnic identifications and seem to give them an enduring nature.* Today identifiable groups remain not as survivals from the age of immigration but with new attributes many of which were unknown to the immigrants.[28] In short, changes are taking place in ethnic social patterns, but the direction does not seem to be toward greater assimilation into the dominant Anglo-American social structure.

In addition to the movement of ethnics from first settlement areas to the surrounding suburbs there is a smaller "secondary migration" to the Far West. What little evidence we have of this phenomenon suggests that highly visible acculturation styles do not lead to the loss of ethnic consciousness. The numerous Italian, Armenian, Greek, Finnish and Jewish sub-societal organizations, to cite the West Coast groups that have come to my attention, suggest that structural assimilation into the Anglo-Protestant mainstream is far from inevitable in the "newer America." Friedman, observing how the Jews in Alberquerque are so well integrated as to be "almost indistinguishable from the community at large," then goes on to describe a Jewish network of social organizations such as Hadassah, B'nai B'rith, Shul, Temple, etc.[29] The strenuous efforts made by West Coast Greek-Americans on behalf of Mayor Christopher of San Francisco, including appeals that reached segments of the Greek community in New York, indicate that old-style political ethnic appeals are not unknown in California. The recent gubernatorial contest in Nevada, with its appeals to Mormons, Catholics and Italians, moved one observer to comment that "the Nevada campaign made it clear once again that American elections more often than not are heavily dependent on a maze of ethnic, religious and minority group voting factors that few candidates discuss in public."[30] At the same time, the emerging political articulation of Mexican-Americans throughout the Far West should remind us that growing acculturation often leads to *more* rather than less ethnic political awareness.[31]

In general terms, the new "affluence," often cited as a conductor of greater assimilation, may actually provide minorities with the financial and psychological wherewithal for building even more elaborate parallel sub-societal structures, including those needed for political action. In prosperous suburban locales, while the oldest and most exclusive country clubs belong to old-stock Protestant families, the newer clubs are of Jewish or varying Catholic-ethnic antecedents. Among Chicago's debutantes, established "society," primarily Anglo-Protestant, holds a coming-out at the Passavant hospital ball. Debutantes of other origins make do with a Presentation Ball (Jewish), a Links Ball (Negro) and the White and Red Ball (Polish). Similar developments can be observed in numerous other urban and suburban regions.[32] Rather than the expected structural assimilation, parallel social structures flourish among the more affluent ethnics. Increasing prosperity among Catholics has been accompanied by an increase in Catholic institutional and social organizations including a vast parochial education system,[33] and the proliferation in sectarian higher education often means a heightened ethnic consciousness. Thus Lenski finds, after controlling for income and party affiliation, that parochially educated Catholics tend to be more doctrinally orthodox and politically conservative than [publicly] educated Catholics.[34]

If ethnic social relations show this notable viability, it might also be remembered that ethnic sub-cultures have not been totally absorbed into mainstream America. Numerous writers have observed the influence of ethnic cultural valuations of political life, causing one to conclude that not only is there slim evidence to show that assimilation is taking place, but there is even some question as to whether acculturation is anywhere complete.[35] Acculturation itself is a multi-faceted process, and even as American styles, practices, language, and values are adopted, certain ethnic values and attitudes may persist as a vital influence; for instance, the attitude that fellow-ethnics are preferable companions in primary group relations.

That ethnic sub-cultures may still operate as independent variables in political life can be seen in the recent Wilson and Banfield study. In twenty referenda elections held in seven major cities between 1956 and 1963 for expenditures to pay for public services such as hospitals, schools and parks, it was found that the groups which, because of their income level, would pay little or nothing while benefitting most, were least likely to support such services namely Poles, Czechs, Italian, Irish and other ethnics.[36] Conversely, upper-income White Protestants and Jews, the very groups that would be paying the costs while benefitting least, were the strongest supporters of these proposed expenditures. The correlations are too compelling for one to assume that the voters of all groups were acting out of ignorance of their actual material interests. More likely, the authors conclude, there is something in the White Protestant and Jewish subcultural belief systems which tends "to be more public-regarding and less private—(self or family) regarding" than in the other ethnic sub-cultures.[37] In sum, *cultural belief systems or residual components of such systems may persist as cultural and political forces independently of objective and material factors.*[38]

III. IDENTIFICATIONAL DURABILITY

From the time he is born, the individual responds to cultural cues mediated by representatives that help shape his personal character structure. As Parsons suggests, beside the distinction made between the cultural and social systems, one must take into account the personality system.[39] Insofar as the individual internalizes experiences from earlier social positions and sub-cultural matrices, his personality may act as a determinant—or character interpreter—of his present socio-cultural world. To apply that model to our present analysis: ethnic identifications are no matter of indifference even for the person who is both culturally and socially assimilated to the extent that his professional, recreational, and neighborhood relations and perhaps also his wife are of the wider White Protestant world. A holiday dinner at his parents' home may be his only active ethnic link, or it may be— as Stanley Edgar Hyman said when asked what being Jewish meant to him—nothing more than "a midnight longing for a hot pastrami sandwich"; yet it is a rare person who reaches adulthood without some internalized feeling about his ethnic identification. Just as social assimilation moves along a different and slower path than that of acculturation, so does identity assimilation, or rather non-assimilation enjoy a pertinacity not wholly responsive to the other two processes.

There are several explanations for the persistence of individual ethnic identity in such cases. First, even if the available range of social exposure brings a man into more frequent contact with out-group members, early in-group experiences, family name and filial attachments may implant in him a natural awareness of, and perhaps a pride in, his ethnic origins. An individual who speaks and behaves like something close to the Anglo-American prototype may still prefer to identify with those of his own racial, religious or national background because it helps tell him who he is. For fear of "losing my identity" some individuals have no desire to pass completely into a "nondescript" "non-ethnic" American status. In an age of "mass society" when the "search for identity" concerns many, an identification which is larger than the self yet smaller than the nation is not without its compensations.[40]

Furthermore, the acculturated ethnic may be no more acceptable to the nativist than the unacculturated. Since the beginning of our nation, the native population has wanted minority groups to acculturate or "Americanize," a process entailing the destruction of alien customs and appearances offensive to American sensibilities. But this was not to be taken as an invitation into Anglo-American primary group relations. (It seems that nativists well understood the distinction between acculturation and assimilation.) To be sure, there is little to suggest that the host society has been a gracious host.[41] Even if full social acceptance is won without serious encounters with bigotry, it is unlikely that from childhood to adulthood one will have escaped a realization that some kind of stigma is attached to one's minority identity, that one is in some way "marginal."[42] Ethnic identifications are, after all, rarely neutral. Few things so effectively assure the persistence of in-group awareness as out-group rejection, and much of the ethnic cradle-to-grave social structure, often considered "clannish," is really defensive.[43] The greater the animosity, exclusion and disadvantage, generally the more will ethnic self-awareness permeate the individual's feelings and evaluations. For groups enjoying some measure of acceptance ethnicity plays an intermittent rather than constant role in self-identity, whereas for those groups which have experienced maximum hostility and oppression—for instance, the Negro American —the question of ethnic identification takes on a ubiquitous quality, there being few instances when, for real or imagined reasons, race does not define, shape or intrude upon both the ordinary business of living and the extraordinary business of politics.[44]

As long as distinctions obtain in the dominant society, and the foreseeable future seems to promise no revolutionary flowering of brotherly love, and as long as the family and early group attachments hold some carry-over meaning for the individual, ethnic identifications and ethnic-oriented responses will still be found even among those who have made a "secure" professional and social position for themselves in the dominant Anglo-Protestant world.

IV. CONCLUSION

By way of concluding I may summarize my major propositions and discuss their broader political and theorectical applications.

1. If the wrong question is asked, then the answers are irrelevant. If our conceptual and analytic tools are insufficient, then we fail to do justice to our data. The question of why ethnics continue to vote as ethnics despite increasing assimilation focuses on a false problem because minority groups are not assimilating. Using an admittedly simplified application of Parson's model, we arrive at the hypothesis that the cultural, social and personality systems may operate with complex independent imperatives to maintain ethnic consciousness. *Assimilation involves much more than occupational, educational and geographic mobility.* From the evidence and analysis proffered in the foregoing pages, there is reason to believe that despite a wide degree of second and third generation acculturation: (1) residual ethnic cultural valuations and attitudes persist; acculturation is far from complete; (2) the vast pluralistic parallel systems of ethnic social and institutional life show impressive viability; structural assimilation seems neither inevitable nor imminent; (3) psychological feelings of

minority group identity, both of the positive-enjoyment and negative-defensive varieties, are still deeply internalized. In sum, ethnic distinctiveness, can still be treated as a factor in social and political pluralism.

Dahl's assertion that the Germans, Irish, Jews and Italians of New Haven are entering into the "third stage of assimilation" in which middle-class jobs, neighborhoods, ideas, associates and styles of life make ethnicity a negligible factor, and Wolfinger's assertions that "ethnic consciousness is fading; it is already faint in some parts of the country and for some ethnic groups," and that "continuing increases in education, geographic dispersion, intermarriage and inter-group contacts are all likely to reduce ethnic consciousness,"[45] should be scruntinized carefully. We can see that (a) increases in education have not necessarily led to a diminished ethnic consciousness; indeed, the increase in sectarian education often brings a heightened ethnic consciousness.[46] (b) Increases in income and adaptation to middle-class styles have not noticeably diminished the viability and frequency of ethnic formal and informal structural associations. Such stylistic changes as have occurred may just as easily evolve *within* the confines of the ethnically stratified social systems, thereby leading to a proliferation of parallel structures rather than absorption into Anglo-Protestant social systems. (c) Geographical dispersion, like occupational and class mobility has been greatly overestimated. Movement from the first settlement area actually may represent a transplanting of the ethnic community to suburbia. Furthermore, as we have seen, even without the usual *geographic* contiguity, *socially* and *psychologically* contiguous ethnic communities persist. (d) Inter-group contacts, such as may occur, do not necessarily lead to a lessened ethnic awareness; they may serve to activate a new and positive appreciation of personal ethnic identity. Or intergroup contacts may often be abrasive and therefore conducive to ethnic defensiveness and compensatory in-group militancy. Perhaps intermarriage, as a genetic integration (for the offspring) will hasten assimilation; where hate has failed, love may succeed in obliterating the ethnic. But intermarriage remains the exception to the rule, and in the foreseeable future does not promise a large-scale structural group assimilation. Furthermore, in the absence of pertinent data, we need not assume that the offspring of mixed marriages are devoid of ethnic identifications of one kind or another.

2. While not denying what was granted earlier, namely that the political system itself may be an instigator and fabricator of ethnic

appeals, we would do well to avoid common overstatements along these lines. It is quite true that politicians are capable of amazing alertness to ethnic sensibilities even in instances where such sensibilities fail to materialize.[47] Yet in the light of the above discussion it would be unduly hasty to conclude that politicians betray a "cultural lag" or perceptual laziness by their continued attention to ethnic groups. The political organization attempting to mobilize support faces the problem of having to construct definitions of its constituency which will reduce the undifferentiated whole into more accessible, manageable, and hopefully more responsive components. The politician, then, is not completely unlike the scientific investigator—if we may allow ourselves an extended analogy—who in dealing with a mass of data must find some means of ordering it into meaningful and more manipulatable categories. More specifically, he must find means of making his constituency accessible to him in the most economical way. Given the limited availability of campaign resources and the potentially limitless demands for expenditure, the candidate is in need of a ready-made formal and informal network of relational sub-structures within his constituency. He discovers that "reaching the people" is often a matter of reaching particular people who themselves can reach, or help him reach, still other people.

A growing acculturation may have diminished the salience of the more blatant ethnic appeals, and the candidate knows that a nostalgic reference to the old country no longer strikes the resonant note it did thirty years ago; indeed, it may elicit a self-consciously negative response from the American-born generations. But he also should know that social assimilation (whether he calls it that or not) is far from an accomplished reality, as he finds himself confronted with leaders and members from a wide melange of ethnic associations, be they professional, business, labor, veteran, neighborhood, educational, church, charitable, recreational or fraternal. Unhampered by any premature anticipations of assimilation, the politician can work with what is at hand. Even if "ethnic issues," as such, do not emerge in a campaign, ethnic social life provides him with ready-made avenues to constituent audiences, audiences which—no matter how well acculturated—are not noted for their indifference to being courted by public figures.

That many urban and suburban politicians persist in giving attentive consideration to minority social groupings in American-born constituencies, then, may be due less to their inveterate stupidity than to the fact that ethnic sub-structures and identifications are still extant, highly visible and, if handled carefully, highly accessible and responsive. The political practitioner who chooses to ignore the web of formal and informal ethnic sub-structures on the presumption that such groupings are a thing of the past does so at his own risk.

3. Historically, the theoretical choice posed for the ethnic has been either isolated existence in autonomous cultural enclaves or total identificational immersion into the American society. We have seen that neither of these "either-or" conditions have evolved. In 1915, Woodrow Wilson observed: "America does not consist of groups. A man who thinks of himself as belonging to a particular national group in America has not yet become an American."[48] As was so often the case when he addressed himself to the problem of national minorities, Wilson took the simple view. His was the commonly accepted assumption that a person's identity or position in the social system were indivisible qualities; therefore, identity choices were mutually exclusive. But in reality a person experiences cumulative and usually complementary identifications, and his life experiences may expose him to some of the social relations and cultural cues of the dominant society while yet placing him predominantly within the confines of a particular minority sub-structure. For the ethnic, a minority group identity is no more incompatible with life in America and with loyalty to the nation than is any regional, class, or other particular group attachment. A pluralistic society, after all, could not really exist without pluralistic sub-structures and identities. Ethnics can thus sometimes behave politically as ethnics while remaining firmly American. It may be said that minorities have injected a new meaning into a national motto originally addressed to the fusion of thirteen separate states: *e pluribus unum,* a supreme allegiance to, and political participation in, the commonality of the Union, with the reserved right to remain distinct unassimilated entities in certain limited cultural, social and identificational respects.

The disappearance of ethnicity as a factor in political behavior waits in large part upon total ethnic structural-identificational assimilation into the host society. Perhaps even in that far-off future "when national origins are forgotten, the political allegiances formed in the old days of ethnic salience will be reflected in the partisan choices of totally assimilated descendants of the old immigrants."[49] If so, then the forces of political continuity will once more have proven themselves, and ethnicity will join long-past regional ties, wars, depressions, defunct political machines, deceased charismatic leaders and a host of other half-forgotten forces whose effects are transmitted down through the generations to shape the political continuities and allegiances of all social groups. But before relegating them to the history of tomorrow, the unassimilated ethnics should be seen as very much alive and with us today.

NOTES

1. Robert Dahl, *Who Governs?* (New Haven: Yale University Press, 1961), p. 59.
2. *Ibid.*, p. 62. See also pp. 32–62 inclusive.
3. Raymond E. Wolfinger, "The Development and Persistence of Ethnic Voting," this REVIEW 59 (December, 1965) , 896–908.
4. *Ibid.*, p. 907.
5. *Ibid.*, see also Bernard R. Berelson *et al.*, *Voting* (Chicago: University of Chicago Press, 1954) , p. 65.
6. Besides the studies cited in Wolfinger, *op. cit.*, and his own data on New Haven, almost all the literature on the relationship between the political machine and the ethnic lends support to this proposition.
7. Cf. Wolfinger *op. cit.*, p. 907 and the studies cited therein. Also Herbert Hyman, *Political Socialization* (New York: The Free Press of Glencoe, 1959), and much of the work done by Fred I. Greenstein.
8. Here Wolfinger is applying Key's hypothesis. See V. O. Key, Jr. "A Theory of Critical Elections," *Journal of Politics*, 17 (February, 1955), 3–18.
9. The quotation is from Wolfinger, *op. cit.*, p. 908. See also V. O. Key and Frank Munger, "Social Determinism and Electoral Decision: the Case of Indiana," in Eugene Burdick and Arthur J. Brodbeck (eds.), *American Voting Behavior* (Glencoe, Ill.: The Free Press, 1959), pp. 281–299.
10. Wolfinger, *loc. cit.*
11. For a more extended and systematic treatment of the question of political continuities and discontinuities see Seymour M. Lipset *et al.*, "The Psychology of Voting: An Analysis of Political Behavior," in Gardner Lindzey (ed.), *Handbook of Social Psychology*, Vol. II (Cambridge, Mass.: Addison-Wesley, 1954), pp. 1124–1170.
12. For instance, Wolfinger uses the term "assimilation" synonymously with "general acculturation and occupational differentiation," in the same body of propositions, *op. cit.*, p. 906.
13. A. L. Kroeber and Talcott Parsons, "The Concepts of Culture and of Social System," *American Sociological Review*, 23 (October, 1958), 582–583; also Talcott Parsons, *The Social System* (Glencoe, Ill.: The Free Press, 1951).
14. See for instance: Oscar Handlin, *Boston's Immigrants, A Study in Acculturation* (Cambridge: Harvard University Press, rev. ed. 1959); Oscar Handlin, *The Uprooted* (New York: Grosset and Dunlap, 1951) ; R. E. Park and H. A. Miller, *Old World Traits Transplanted* (New York: Harper, 1921) ; W. I. Thomas and F. Znaniecki, *The Polish Peasant in Europe and America*, 5 vols. (Boston: Badger, 1918–20); E. V. Stonequist, *The Marginal Man, A Study in Personality and Culture Conflict* (New York: Scribner, 1937); W. L. Warner and Leo Srole, *The Social Systems of American Ethnic Groups* (New Haven:

Yale Univ. Press, 1945); William Foote Whyte, *Street Corner Society* (Chicago: University of Chicago Press, 1943); Herbert J. Gans, *The Urban Villagers* (New York: Free Press of Glencoe), 1962.

15. Arnold W. Green, "A Re-examination of the Marginal Man Concept," *Social Forces*, 26 (1947), 167–171.

16. Whyte, *op. cit.*, and Gans, *op. cit.*, A socially unassimilated pluralism is readily visible in many areas of American life. Thus, in a single weekend in New York separate dances for persons of Hungarian, Irish, Italian, German, Greek and Polish extractions are advertised in neighborhood newspapers and the foreign language press.

17. See Milton M. Gordon, *Assimilation in American Life* (New York: Oxford University Press, 1964), p. 34; also Erich Rosenthal, "Acculturation without Assimilation?" *American Journal of Sociology* 66 (November, 1960), 275–288; Amitai Etzioni, "The Ghetto—a Re-evaluation," *Social Forces* (March, 1959), 255–262; J. Milton Yinger, "Social Forces Involved in Group Identification or Withdrawal," *Daedalus*, 90 (Spring, 1961), 247–262; Y. J. Chyz and R. Lewis, "Agencies Organized by Nationality Groups in the United States," *The Annals of the American Academy of Political and Social Science*, 262 (1949).

18. M. Arc, "The Prison 'Culture' From the Inside," *New York Times Magazine*, February 28, 1965, p. 63.

19. August B. Hollingshead, "Trends in Social Stratification: A Case Study," *American Sociological Review*, 17 (1952), 685 f; see also Gans, *op. cit.*; Warner and Srole, *op. cit.*, for further evidence of ethnic sub-societal systems.

20. C. B. Nam, "Nationality Groups and Social Stratification in America," *Social Forces*, 37 (1959), p. 333. The assumption that Negroes have been enjoying a slow but steady economic advance is laid to rest by Dale Hiestand, *Economic Growth and Employment Opportunities for Minorities* (New York: Columbia University Press, 1964).

21. See Lewis Corey, "Problems of the Peace: IV. The Middle Class," *Antioch Review*, 5, 68–87.

22. For instance William H. Whyte, *The Organization Man* (Garden City: Doubleday, 1957); A. C. Spectorsky, *The Ex-Urbanites* (New York: J. B. Lippincott, 1955).

23. Scott Greer, "Catholic Voters and the Democratic Party," *Public Opinion Quarterly*, 25 (1961), p. 624.

24. Robert C. Wood, *Suburbia, It's People and Their Politics* (Boston: Houghton Mifflin Co., 1958), p. 178. As impressive as is the trek to the suburbs, more recent developments should not go unrecorded. Of great significance, and hitherto unobserved because it is of such recent occurrence is the effect of the revised and liberalized national origins quota system of our immigration laws. Direct observation of immigration into several of the Italian and Greek communities in New York during 1965–66 leaves me with the conviction that the ethnic core-city community is far from declining. In certain urban centers, such as the Brownsville section of New York, the gradual depletion of old ethnic neighborhoods is being amply and visibly counterbalanced by new injections of Polish refugees, along with Italian, Greek and Latin American immigrants who not only reinforce the core-city neighborhoods but frequently lend them certain first-generation touches reminiscent of an earlier day.

25. Stanley Lieberson, "Suburbs and Ethnic Residential Patterns," *American Journal of Sociology*, 67 (1962), 673–681.

26. See Etzioni, *op. cit.*, for a discussion of this point.

27. Herbert J. Gans, "Park Forest: Birth of a Jewish Community," *Commentary*, 7 (1951), 330–339.

28. Cf. Etzioni, *op. cit.*, p. 258; also Nathan Glazer and Daniel P. Moynihan, *Beyond the Melting Pot* (Cambridge: M.I.T. and Harvard University Press, 1963), pp. 13–16.

29. Morris Friedman, "The Jews of Albuquerque," *Commentary*, 28 (1959), 55–62.

30. Tom Wicker, "Hidden Issues in Nevada," *The New York Times*, July 23, 1966.

31. See Joan W. Moore and Ralph Guzman, "The Mexican-Americans: New Wind from the Southwest," *The Nation*, May 30, 1966, pp. 645–648.

32. *Cf.*, E. Digby Baltzell, *The Protestant Establishment, Aristocracy and Caste in America* (New York: Random House, 1964), p. 357; and "Life and Leisure," *Newsweek*, December 21, 1964.

33. John Tracy Ellis, *American Catholicism* (Chicago: University of Chicago Press, 1956), *passim*; also James P. Shannon, "The Irish Catholic Immigration," in Thomas T. McAvoy (ed.), *Roman Catholicism and The American Way of Life* (Notre Dame: University of Notre Dame Press, 1960), pp. 204–210.

34. Gerhard Lenski, *The Religious Factor* (Garden City, N.Y.: Doubleday, 1963, rev. ed.), pp. 268–270.

35. Cf. Wesley and Beverly Allinsmith, "Religious Affiliation and Politico-Economic Attitude," *Public Opinion Quarterly*, 12 (1948), 377–389; Lawrence Fuchs, *The Political Behavior of the American Jews*, (Glencoe, Ill.: The Free Press, 1956).

36. James Q. Wilson and Edward C. Banfield, "Public Regardingness As a Value Premise in Voting Behavior," this REVIEW, 58 (December 1964), 876–887.

37. *Ibid.*, pp. 882–885. Wilson and Banfield offer no delineation of these sub-cultural ingredients. For an attempted analysis of the components of religious belief systems which are politically salient see Michael Parenti, "Political Values and Religious Culture: Jews, Catholics and Protestants," *The Journal for the Scientific Study of Religion*, (forthcoming).

38. For the classic statement of this proposition see Max Weber, *The Protestant Ethic and the Spirit of Capitalism* (New York: Scribner's Sons, 1958). For application of this proposition to the American scene see Seymour Martin Lipset, *The First New Nation* (New York: Basic Books, 1963), pp. 110–129.

39. Parsons actually constructs a four-systems model which includes the social, cultural, personality and physiological systems; the fourth system is not immediately pertinent to our discussion. See Talcott Parsons, "Malinowski and the Theory of the Social System" in R. Firth (ed.), *Man and Culture* (London: Routledge and Kegan Paul, 1960).

40. See Gordon, *op. cit.*; also Gans, "Park Forest," *op. cit.*

41. See Baltzell, *op. cit.*, for a study of White Protestant exclusiveness; also Gordon, *op. cit.*, pp. 111–12.

42. For supporting data see Michael Parenti, *Ethnic and Political Attitudes: Three Generations of Italian Americans*, unpublished Ph.D. dissertation, Yale University, 1962) ; also Gordon W. Allport, *The Nature of Prejudice* (Garden City, N.Y.: Doubleday, 1958).

43. Hansen observes: "When the natives combined to crush what they considered the undue influence of alien groups they committed a tactical error, for the newcomers, far from being crushed were prompted to consolidate their hitherto scattered forces": Marcus Lee Hansen, *The Immigrant in American History* (New York: Harper and Row, 1960 ed.), p. 136.

44. Race consciousness is, James Q. Wilson notes, "an ever-present factor in the thought and action of Negroes of all strata of society," and is "the single most consistent theme in Negro discussion of civic issues." *Negro Politics: The Search for Leadership* (Glencoe: Free Free Press), p. 170. It is true, however, that members of any one group, because of individual experiences and per-

sonalities, may vary as to the amount of emphasis they place upon their ethnic status: see Aaron Antonovsky, "Toward a Refinement of the 'Marginal Man' Concept," *Social Forces*, 35 (1956), 57–62, for a study of in-group attitudes among Jewish males; also Irwin Child, *Italian or American? The Second Generation in Conflict* (New Haven: Yale University Press, 1943). To my knowledge there exists no quantifiable cross-group comparative study of in-group awareness. The impression one draws from non-comparative studies as implied above is that the groups most disliked by the wider society harbor the greatest number of individuals of militant ethnic self-awareness.

45. Dahl, *op. cit.*, pp. 35–6; *Wolfinger op. cit.*, p. 908.
46. Lenski, *loc. cit.* Lenski's entire study points to the persistence of sub-cultural religio-ethnic variables in political and economic life. The transition away from the Democratic Party by Catholics is not, as Wolfinger seems to suggest, a symptom of assimilation; in fact, by Lenski's data, it is a manifestation of a growing commitment to religious conservatism.
47. See, for instance, the study of balanced ticket calculations in a New York statewide campaign in the concluding chapter of Glazer and Moynihan, *op. cit.*
48. Quoted in Oscar Handlin, *The American People in the Twentieth Century* (Boston: Beacon Press, 1963, rev. ed.), p. 121.
49. Wolfinger, *loc. cit.*

ARTICLE 8

White Ethnic

Michael Novak

Growing up in America has been an assault upon my sense of worthiness. It has also been a kind of liberation and delight.

There must be countless women in America who have known for years that something is peculiarly unfair, yet who have found it only recently possible, because of Women's Liberation, to give tongue to their pain. In recent months, I have experienced a similar inner thaw, a gradual relaxation, a willingness to think about feelings heretofore shepherded out of sight.

I am born of PIGS—those Poles, Italians, Greeks, and Slavs, non-English-speaking immigrants, numbered so heavily among the workingmen of this nation. Not particularly liberal, nor radical, born into a history not white Anglo-Saxon and not Jewish—born outside what in America is considered the intellectual mainstream. And thus privy to neither power nor status nor intellectual voice.

Those Poles of Buffalo and Milwaukee—so notoriously taciturn, sullen, nearly speechless. Who has ever understood them? It is not that Poles do not feel emotion: what is their history if not dark passion, romanticism, betrayal, courage, blood? But where in America is there anywhere a language for voicing what a Christian Pole in this nation feels? He has no Polish culture left him, no Polish tongue. Yet Polish feelings do not go easily into the idiom of happy America, the America of the Anglo-Saxons and, yes, in the arts, the Jews. (The Jews have long been a culture of the word, accustomed to exile, skilled in scholarship and in reflection. The Christian Poles are largely of peasant origin, free men for hardly more than a hundred years.) Of what shall the man of Buffalo think, on his way to work in the mills, departing from his relatively dreary home and street? What roots does he have? What language of the heart is available to him?

The PIGS are not silent willingly. The silence burns like hidden coals in the chest.

All four of my grandparents, unknown to one another, arrived in America from the same county in Slovakia. My grandfather had a small farm in Pennsylvania; his wife died in a wagon accident. Meanwhile, a girl of fifteen arrived on Ellis Island, dizzy, a little ill from witnessing births and deaths and illnesses aboard the crowded ship, with a sign around her neck lettered "PASSAIC." There an aunt told her of the man who had lost his wife in Pennsylvania. She went. They were married. Inheriting his three children, each year for five years she had one of her own; she was among the lucky, only one died. When she was twenty-two, mother of seven, her husband died. And she resumed the work she had begun in Slovakia at the town home of a man known to us now only as "the Professor": she house-cleaned and she laundered.

I heard this story only weeks ago. Strange that I had not asked insistently before. Odd that I should have such shallow knowledge of my roots. Amazing to me that I do not know what my family suffered, endured, learned, hoped these past six or seven generations. It is as if there were no project on which we all have been involved. As if history, in some way, began with my father and with me.

Let me hasten to add that the estrangement I have come to feel derives not only from a lack of family history. All my life, I have been made to feel a slight uneasiness when I must say my name. Under challenge in grammar school concerning my nationality, I had been instructed by my father to announce proudly: "American." When my family moved from the Slovak ghetto of Johnstown to the WASP suburb on the hill, my mother impressed upon us how well we must be dressed, and show good manners, and behave—people think of us as "different" and we mustn't give them any cause. "Whatever you do, marry a Slovak girl," was other advice to a similar end: "They cook. They clean. They take good care of you. For your own good."

When it was revealed to me that most movie stars and many other professionals had abandoned European names in order to feed American fantasies, I felt only a little sadness. One of my uncles, for business reasons and rather late in life, changed his name too, to a simple German variant. Not long, either, after World War II.

Nowhere in my schooling do I recall an attempt to put me in touch with my own history. The strategy was clearly to make an American of me. English literature, American literature; and even the history books, as I recall them, were peopled mainly by Anglo-Saxons from Boston (where most historians seemed to live). Not even my native Pennsylvania, let alone my Slovak forebears, counted for very many paragraphs. I don't remember feeling envy or regret: a feeling, perhaps, of unimportance, of remoteness, of not having heft enough to count.

The fact that I was born a Catholic also complicated life. What is a Catholic but what everybody else is in reaction against? Protestants reformed "the Whore of Babylon," others were "enlightened" from it, and Jews had reason to help Catholicism and the social structures it was rooted in to fall apart. My history books and the whole of education hummed in upon that point (during crucial years I attended a public, not a parochial, school): to be modern is decidedly not to be medieval; to be reasonable is not to be dogmatic; to be free is clearly not to live under ecclesiastical authority; to be scientific is not to attend ancient rituals, cherish irrational symbols, indulge in mythic practices. It is hard to grow up Catholic in America without becoming defensive, perhaps a little paranoid, feeling forced to divide the world between "us" and "them."

We had a special language all our own, our own pronunciation for words we shared in common with others (Augustine, contemplative), sights and sounds and smells in which few others participated (incense at Benediction of the Most Blessed Sacrament, Forty Hours, wakes, and altar bells at the silent consecration of the Host); and we had our own politics and slant on world affairs. Since earliest childhood, I have known about a "power elite" that runs America: the boys from the Ivy League in the State Department, as opposed to the Catholic boys from Hoover's FBI who, as Daniel Moynihan once put it, keep watch on them. And on a whole host of issues, my people have been, though largely Democratic, conservative: on censorship, on Communisism, on abortion, on religious schools . . . Harvard and Yale long meant "them" to us.

The language of Spiro Agnew, the language of George Wallace, excepting its idiom, awakens childhood memories in me of men arguing in the barbershop, of my uncle drinking so much beer he threatened to lay his dick upon the porch rail and wash the whole damn street with steaming piss—while cursing the niggers in the mill, below, and the Yankees in the mill, above: millstones he felt pressing him. Other relatives were duly shocked, but everybody loved Uncle George: he said what he thought.

We did not feel this country belonged to us. We felt fierce pride in it, more loyalty than anyone could know. But we felt blocked at every turn. There were not many intellectuals among us, not even very many professional men. Laborers mostly. Small businessmen, agents for corporations perhaps. Content with a little, yes, modest in expectation. But somehow feeling cheated. For a thousand years the Slovaks survived Hungarian hegemony, and our strategy here remained the same: endurance and steady work. Slowly, one day, we would overcome.

A special word is required about a complicated symbol: sex. To this day my mother finds it hard to spell the word intact, preferring to write "s--." Not that much was made of sex in our environment. And that's the point: silence. Demonstrative affection, emotive dances, exuberance Anglo-Saxons seldom seem to share; but on the realities of sex, discretion. Reverence, perhaps; seriousness, surely. On intimacies, it is as though our tongues had been stolen. As though in peasant life for a thousand years the context had been otherwise. Passion, yes; romance, yes; family and children, certainly; but sex, rather a minor part of life.

Imagine, then, the conflict in the generation of my brothers, sister, and myself. (The book critic for the *New York Times* reviews on the same day two new novels of fantasy: one a pornographic fantasy to end all such fantasies [he writes], the other about a mad family representing in some comic way the redemption wrought by Jesus Christ. In language and verve, the books are rated even. In theme, the reviewer notes his embarrassment in reporting a religious fantasy, but no embarrassment at all about the preposterous pornography.) Suddenly, what for a thousand years was minor becomes an all-absorbing investigation. It is, perhaps, one drama when the ruling classes (I mean subscribers to *The New Yorker,* I suppose) move progressively, generation by generation since Sigmund Freud, toward consciousness-raising sessions in Clit. Lib., but wholly another when we stumble suddenly upon mores staggering any expectation our grandparents ever cherished.

Yet more significant in the ethnic experience in America is the intellectual world one meets: the definition of values, ideas, and purposes emanating from universities, books, magazines, radio, and television. One hears one's own voice echoed back neither by spokesmen of "Middle America" (so complacent, smug, nativist, and Protestant), nor by "the intellectuals." Almost unavoidably, perhaps, education in America leads the student who entrusts his soul to it in a direction that, lacking a better word, we might call liberal: respect for individual conscience, a sense of social responsibility, trust in the free exchange of ideas and procedures of dissent, a certain confidence in the ability of men to "reason together" and to adjudicate their differences, a frank recognition of the vitality of the unconscious, a willingness to protect workers and the poor against the vast economic power of industrial corporations, and the like.

On the other hand, the liberal imagination has appeared to be astonishingly universalist, and relentlessly missionary. Perhaps the metaphor "enlightenment" offers a key. One is initiated into light. Liberal education tends to separate children from their parents, from their roots, from their history, in the cause of a universal and superior religion. One is taught, regarding the unenlightened (even if they be one's Uncles George and Peter, one's parents, one's brothers perhaps), what can only be called a modern equivalent of *odium theologicum.* Richard Hofstadter described anti-intellectualism in America, more accurately in nativist America than in ethnic America, but I have yet to encounter a comparable treatment of anti-unenlightenment among our educated classes.

In particular, I have regretted and keenly felt the absence of that sympathy for PIGS that simple human feeling might have prodded intelligence to muster: that same sympathy that the educated find so easy to conjure up for black culture, Chicano culture, Indian culture, and other cultures of the poor. In such cases, one finds, the universalist pretensions of liberal culture are suspended: some groups, at least, are entitled to be both different and respected. Why do the educated classes find it so difficult to want to understand the man who drives a beer truck, or the fellow with a helmet working on a site across the street with plumbers and electricians, while their sensitivities race easily to Mississippi or even Bedford-Stuyvesant?

There are deep secrets here, no doubt, unvoiced fantasies and scarcely admitted historical resentments. Few persons, in describing "Middle Americans," "the Silent Majority," or Scammon and Wattenberg's "typical American voter," distinguish clearly enough between the nativist American and the ethnic American. The first is likely to be Protestant, the second Catholic. Both may be, in various ways, conservative, loyalist, and unenlightened. Each has his own agonies, fears, betrayed expectations. Neither is ready, quite, to become an ally of the other. Neither has the same history behind him here. Neither has the same hopes. Neither is living out the same psychic voyage. Neither shares the same symbols or has the same sense of reality. The rhetoric and metaphors differ.

There is overlap, of course. But country music is not a polka; a successful politician in a Chicago ward needs a very different "common touch" from the one used by the county clerk in Normal; the urban experience of immigration lacks that mellifluous, optimistic, biblical vision of the good America that springs naturally to the lips of politicians from the Bible Belt. The nativist tends to believe with Richard Nixon that he "knows America and the American heart is good." The ethnic tends to believe that every American who preceded him has an angle, and that he, by God, will one day find one too. (Often, ethnics complain that by working hard, obeying the law, trusting their political leaders, and relying upon the American Dream they now have only their own naïveté to blame for rising no higher than they have.)

It goes without saying that the intellectuals do not love Middle America, and that for all the good warm discovery of America that preoccupied them during the 1950s, no strong tide of respect accumulated in their hearts for the Yahoos, Babbitts, Agnews, and Nixons of the land. Willie Morris, in *North Toward Home*, writes poignantly of the chill, parochial outreach of the liberal sensibility, its failure to engage the humanity of the modest, ordinary little man west of the Hudson. The intellectual's map of the United States is succinct: "Two coasts connected by United Airlines."

Unfortunately, it seems, the ethnics erred in attempting to Americanize themselves, before clearing the project with the educated classes. They learned to wave the flag and to send their sons to war. (The Poles in World War I were 4 per cent of the population but took 12 per cent of the casualties.) They learned to support their President—an easy task, after all, for those accustomed abroad to obeying authority. And where would they have been if Franklin Roosevelt had not sided with them against established interests? They knew a little about Communism, the radicals among them in one way, and by far the larger number of conservatives in another. Not a few exchange letters to this day with cousins and uncles who did not leave for America when they might have, whose lot is demonstrably harder and less than free.

Finally, the ethnics do not like, or trust, or even understand the intellectuals. It is not easy to feel uncomplicated affection for those who call you "pig," "fascist," "racist." One had not yet grown accustomed not to hearing "Hunkie," "Polack," "Spic," "Mick," "Dago," and the rest. At no little sacrifice, one had apologized for foods that smelled too strong for Anglo-Saxon noses, moderated the wide swings of Slavic and Italian emotion, learned decorum, given oneself to education American style, tried to learn tolerance and assimilation. Each generation criticized the earlier for its authoritarian and European and old-fashioned ways. "Up-to-date" was a moral lever. And now when the process nears completion, when a generation appears that speaks without accent and goes to college, still you are considered pigs, fascists, and racists.

Racists? Our ancestors owned no slaves. Most of us ceased being serfs only in the last 200 years—the Russians in 1861. What have we got against blacks or blacks against us? Competition, yes, for jobs and homes and communities; competition, even, for political power. Italians, Lithuanians, Slovaks, Poles are not, in principle, against "community control," or even against ghettos of our own. Whereas the Anglo-Saxon model appears to be a system of atomic individuals and high mobility, our model has tended to stress communities of our own, attachment to family and relatives, stability, and roots. We tend to have a fierce sense of attachment to our homes, having been homeowners less than three generations: a home is almost fulfillment enough for one man's life. We have most ambivalent feelings about suburban assimilation and mobility. The melting pot is a kind of homogenized soup, and its mores only partly appeal to us: to some, yes, and to others, no.

It must be said that we think we are better people than the blacks. Smarter, tougher, harder working, stronger in our families. But maybe many of us are not so sure. Maybe we are uneasy. Emotions here are delicate. One can understand the immensely more difficult circumstances under which the blacks have suffered, and one is not unaware of peculiar forms of fear, envy, and suspicion across color lines. How much of all this we learned in America, by being made conscious of our olive skin, brawny backs, accents, names, and cultural quirks, is not plain to us. Racism is not our invention; we did not bring it with us; we found it here. And should we pay the price for America's guilt? Must all the gains of the blacks, long overdue, be chiefly at our expense? Have we, once again, no defenders but ourselves?

Television announcers and college professors seem so often to us to be speaking in a code. When they say "white racism," it does not seem to be their own traditions they are impugning. Perhaps it is paranoia, but it seems that the affect accompanying such words is directed at steelworkers, auto workers, truck drivers, and police—at us. When they say "humanism" or "progress," it seems to us like moral pressure to abandon our own traditions, our faith, our associations, in order to reap higher rewards in the culture of the national corporations —that culture of quantity, homogeneity, replaceability, and mobility. They want to grind off all the angles, hold us to the lathes, shape us to be objective, meritocratic, orderly, and fully American.

In recent years, of course, a new cleavage has sprung open among the intellectuals. Some seem to speak for technocracy—for that alliance of science, industry, and humanism whose heaven is "progress." Others seem to be taking the view once ascribed to ecclesiastical conservatives and traditionalists: that commitment to enlightenment is narrow, ideological, and hostile to the best interests of mankind. In the past, the great alliance for progress sprang from the conviction that "knowledge is power." Both humanists and scientists could agree on that, and labored in their separate ways to make the institutions of knowledge dominant in society: break the shackles of the Church, extend suffrage to the middle classes and finally to all, win untrammeled liberty for the marketplace of ideas. Today it is no longer plain that the power brought by knowledge is humanistic. Thus the parting of the ways.

Science has ever carried with it the stores and symbols of a major religion. It is ruthlessly universalist. If its participants are not "saved," they are nonetheless "enlightened," which isn't bad. And every single action of the practicing scientist, no matter how humble, could once be understood as a contribution to the welfare of the human race; each smallest gesture was invested with meaning, given a place in a scheme, and weighted with redemptive power. Moreover, the scientist was in possession of "the truth," indeed of the very meaning of and validating procedures for the word. His role was therefore sacred.

Imagine, then, a young strapping Slovak entering an introductory course in the Sociology of Religion at the nearby state university or community college. Is he sent back to his Slovak roots, led to recover paths of experience latent in all his instincts and reflexes, given an image of the life of his grandfather that suddenly, in recognition, brings tears to his eyes? Is he brought to a deeper appreciation of his Lutheran or Catholic heritage and its resonances with other bodies of religious expeience? On the contrary, he is secretly taught disdain for what his grandfather *thought* he was doing when he acted or felt or imagined through religious forms. In the boy's psyche, a new religion is implanted: power over others, enlightenment, an atomic (rather than a communitarian) sensibility, a contempt for mystery, ritual, transcendence, soul, absurdity, and tragedy; and deep confidence in the possibilities of building a better world through scientific understanding. He is led to feel ashamed for the statistical portrait of Slovak immigrants which shows them to be conservative, authoritarian, not given to dissent, etc. His teachers instruct him with the purest of intentions, in a way that is value free.

To be sure, certain radical writers in America have begun to bewail "the laying on of culture" and to unmask the cultural religion implicit in the American way of science. Yet radicals, one learns, often have an agenda of their own. What fascinates *them* among working-class ethnics are the traces, now almost lost, of *radical* activities among the working class two or three generations ago. Scratch the resentful boredom of a classroom of working-class youths, we are told, and you will find hidden in their past some formerly imprisoned organizer for the CIO, some Sacco/Vanzetti, some bold pamphleteer for the IWW. All this is true. But supposing that a study of the ethnic past reveals that most ethnics have been, are, and wish to remain, culturally conservative? Suppose, for example, they wish to deepen their religious roots and defend their ethnic enclaves? Must a radical culture be "laid on" them?

America has never confronted squarely the problem of preserving diversity. I can remember hearing in my youth bitter arguments that parochial schools were "divisive." Now the public schools are attacked for their commitment to homogenization. Well, how *does* a nation of no one culture, no one language, no one race, no one history, no one ethnic stock continue to exist as one, while encouraging diversity? How can the rights of all, and particularly of the weak, be defended if power is decentralized and left to local interests? The weak have ever found strength in this country through local chapters of national organizations. But what happens when the national organizations themselves—the schools, the unions, the federal government—become vehicles of a new, universalistic, thoroughly rationalized, technological culture?

Still, it is not that larger question that concerns me here. I am content today to voice the difficulties in the way of saying what I wish to say, when I wish to say it. The tradition of liberalism is a tradition I had to acquire, despite an innate skepticism about many of its structural metaphors (free marketplace, individual autonomy, reason naked and undisguised, enlightenment). Radicalism, with its bold and simple optimism about human potential and its anarchic tendencies, has been, despite its appeal to me as a vehicle for criticizing liberalism, freighted with emotions, sentiments, and convictions about men that I cannot bring myself to share.

In my guts, I do not feel that institutions are "repressive" in any meaning of the word that leaves it meaningful; the "state of nature" seems to me, emotionally, far less liberating, far more undifferentiated and confining. I have not dwelt for so long in the profession of the intellectual life that I find it easy to be critical and harsh. In almost everything I see or hear or read, I am struck first, rather undiscriminatingly, by all the things I like in it. Only with second effort can I bring myself to discern the flaws. My emotions and values seem to run in affirmative patterns.

My interest is not, in fact, in defining myself over against the American people and the American way of life. I do not expect as much of it as all that. What I should like to do is come to a better and more profound knowledge of who I am, whence my community came, and whither my son and daughter, and their children's children, might wish to head in the future: I want to have a history.

More and more, I think in family terms, less ambitiously, on a less than national scale. The differences implicit in being Slovak, and Catholic, and lower-middle class seem more and more important to me. Perhaps it is too much to try to speak to all peoples in this very various nation of ours. Yet it does not seem evident that by becoming more concrete, accepting one's finite and limited identity, one necessarily becomes parochial. Quite the opposite. It seems more likely that by each of us becoming more profoundly what we are, we shall find greater unity, in those depths in which unity irradiates diversity, than by attempting through the artifices of the American "melting pot" and the cultural religion of science to become what we are not.

There is, I take it, a form of liberalism not wedded to universal Reason, whose ambition is not to homogenize all peoples on this planet, and whose base lies rather in the imagination and in the diversity of human stories: a liberalism I should be happy to have others help me to find.

Report from Black America

Editors of Newsweek

Over the last decade, the Negro revolution has been the single most
dynamic force in American society—a movement so volatile that it
could in a few short years thrust up leaders as disparate as the Rev.
Dr. Martin Luther King and Malcolm X, slogans as contradictory as
"We Shall Overcome" and "Burn, Baby, Burn." Today, black Americans are torn between the hard-won assumptions of the past and what
may be the harsh realities of the future. "It is a beautiful and an ugly
thing through which we are going," says Negro intellectual Bayard
Rustin. And neither Rustin nor any other American—black or white
—can say with assurance where the Negro revolution may be heading.

How wide does the current black ferment run—and how has it
changed Negro dreams and aspirations? Has the traditional goal of
integration lost its grip on the rank and file? Who are the influential
new voices? Do they speak for the silent? Behind the fashionably
aggressive rhetoric of separatism and reparations is there realistic hope
for racial reconciliation in America? And on what terms?

On the answers to such questions rests the future direction of
the Negro movement—and perhaps the fate of the nation itself. To
try to find those answers, *Newsweek* undertook a full-scale survey of
Negro attitudes, using both public-opinion sampling and in-depth
journalistic probing. The resulting "Report from Black America" represents the first such definitive reading of the Negro mood since 1966
and the third in a *Newsweek* series begun in 1963.

The years since the last *Newsweek* survey have been among the
most tumultuous in modern American history—a time of warfare at
home and abroad, of political assassination and social upheaval. For

American Negroes, the impact of events has been intense and potentially traumatic. In three short years, a whole constellation of black leaders (including King and Stokely Carmichael) has passed from the scene, the war on poverty has all but succumbed to the war in Vietnam, a black cultural renaissance has flowered in dimensions unprecedented since the 1920s, black power has made itself felt at the polls (by Carl Stokes in Cleveland, Richard Hatcher in Gary, and Charles Evers in Fayette, Miss.) along with the white backlash (in Minneapolis, Los Angeles, and, to a certain extent, in New York City last week).

Yet the fundamental goals and the enduring optimism of the black rank and file remain basically stable. The *Newsweek* Poll found that the vast majority of American Negroes still aspires to a place in an open society—one in which integration is a free option rather than a faint hope. There is a prevalent feeling of progress—especially on economic issues—coupled with the conviction that progress has been too slow. Violence is still rejected as a tactic by most blacks, but a significant number thinks that rioting has been justified, and a majority believes the disorders have advanced black aspirations.

Although his nonviolent philosophy has lost ground since his murder, Martin Luther King is even more highly regarded in death than in life. At the same time, blacks seem to be shedding their illusions about what white America will do for them. Increasingly, Negroes feel that whites will make concessions only under pressure— and a remarkable 21 per cent so despair of significant gains that they are favorably disposed to the fantasy of a separate black nation within the boundaries of the U.S. The cutting edge of disaffection is keenest among the under-30 black population of the North.

Indeed, although they may be several strides ahead of the rank and file, the new generation of younger black leaders plainly echoes the concerns and the attitudes of those coming of age in the Northern slums. They know who they are ("Identity is not a problem anymore," says California Assemblywoman Yvonne Brathwaite), and they know what they want to accomplish. Most count it a healthy sign that Negro leadership today is much more a mosaic than a monolith. "The Movement is surely fragmented," says Atlanta's Julian Bond, at 29 perhaps the most promising of all the new voices, "but in many ways it's a beneficial fragmentation. It means that if you're an integrationist and you have a program then you feel free to work on it, a separatist has his program to work on—and so on. All these things complement each other—and on very crucial and key issues there's a great deal of unanimity."

There is a good deal of unanimity among the younger leaders— if not precisely to the ecumenical degree Bond suggests. In truth, integrationists get scant encouragement from black sophisticates these days, partly out of ideological conviction and partly out of the belief that integration is a practical impossibility right now. "You white folks wouldn't let it happen," says welfare organizer George Wiley.

Instead, the thrust now is toward a self-reliant brand of separatism coupled with a concerted drive to capture political and economic control of the ghetto and its institutions. "The neighborhoods are there to be taken," says a budding Philadelphia pol, gazing at a precinct map of the slums. And in Los Angeles, a black self-help activist adds: "Community control is where it's at." Gary's Mayor Richard Hatcher neatly unifies the twin themes. "What black people are saying is that if you call control of your own neighborhood separatism, then we have separatism all over this country," he says. "What's so unusual about people saying, 'We're going to control our own turf'? That's not separatism—that's good old Americanism."

Beyond the Hatchers, of course, there are far more incendiary voices, prone to far more destructive tactics. Still, the cry of "Burn, baby, burn," has all but disappeared from the militant vocabulary. "Black people have wised up," says Watts community worker Ferman Moore. "We're not going to give anyone a chance to slaughter our kids."

And so, as the nation slid into yet another summer last week, the apprehensions bred by Watts and Detroit and Newark were somewhat muted. Across the country, officials agreed that the hot weather was certain to bring some sort of trouble to the cities—perhaps a spate of guerrilla forays or police ambushes. But the larger question transcended the potential for violence. It was—as it has been since the birth of the Republic—whether the Negro's enduring dream of an open society would finally be redeemed by white America.

ANGRY—BUT THEY STILL HAVE A DREAM

Fifteen years after the Surpreme Court decision against segregation in the schools, six years after the flood tide of nonviolent protest in

Birmingham, five years after the first of the ghetto riots in Harlem, barely a year after the death of Martin Luther King, in the midst of a welling white backlash, the extraordinary revolution of the Negro American goes on. Its guiding impulse is not, as the most impassioned blacks and the most inflamed whites imagine, to burn down the U.S. or to secede from it—though a desperate minority professes itself willing to do either, or both. All the cheated hopes and false starts and bad advice have left black Americans a trace sadder, a bit wiser, several shades blacker—and more impatient now than they have ever been. Yet the most striking fact of all about their struggle today is how tenaciously they have kept the faith in nonviolent action as the means and an open America as the end—and how widely they believe, on the most mixed evidence, that they are in fact winning.

By 63 per cent to 21 per cent, blacks feel they can win equality without violence, and they favor integration—in housing, for example, by 74 per cent to 16 per cent. And their abiding sense of optimism is reflected in the large majority (70 per cent) who say that blacks have made progress in the last five years, and the almost equal number who believe that they will be still better off five years from now.

It is, of course, as dangerous to speak of The Negro as it would be to generalize about The White—and more dangerous still for white Americans to take undue comfort in the enduring moderation of the majority. The third *Newsweek* Poll of black America—conducted by The Gallup Organization among a cross section of 977 blacks from Harlem to Lisbon, La., to Tacoma, Wash.—may indeed be most meaningful for the differences it reveals. It shows, for example, that Southerners tend to be more hopeful than Northerners, Northerners more militant than Southerners—and Northern young people by far the angriest blacks of all. It reveals that far from being a proletariat up in arms, the poorest blacks are by and large the most conservative and that both a sense of grievance and a taste for action actually rise with income and education—a certain confirmation that the Negro's struggle remains a revolution of rising expectations.

Perhaps as significant as any of its findings, the *Newsweek* Poll discloses small but real increases in nearly every index of bitterness and alienation and despair. One black in five wishes for a separate Negro nation within the U.S.; one in seven doesn't consider America worth fighting for in a world war; and one in four thinks Negroes should arm themselves. Social change, even in a democratic society, is less often initiated by majority vote than by minority action; activist minorities brought the school-desegregation case, marched against the dogs and hoses in Birmingham, lit the fires that set Harlem and Watts and Detroit ablaze. Minorities can create a crisis, alter the vocabulary with which crises are discussed—and often the activist fraction can write the terms on which crises can be settled.

Yet it is equally true that Negro Americans believe they are on the move now as never before—more so even than at the height of the great hallelujah days of 1963. The top-priority problems, as blacks see them, are jobs (cited by 51 per cent), education (39 per cent) and housing (36 per cent). But three out of five feel they have made progress in the past five years on the job and in getting their children better educated, and half say their housing is improved. The sense of progress is predictably higher in the South, where blacks have won tangible victories over Jim Crow, but it is nevertheless high in the gateless Northern ghettos as well. And it is matched across the nation by the Negro's expectations of things to come: no fewer than two-thirds expect their lot to be better still in five years.

But black America's optimism stops far short of euphoria: 59 per cent—up 16 points in three years—think the pace of progress too slow, and only 22 per cent count themselves satisfied. The black man's sense that he is discriminated against—that he pays higher prices and more rent than whites, that he is paid lower wages for equal work, that he has less chance at college and the really good jobs—is if anything keener than it was in the 1966 *Newsweek* survey. And the new poll is filled with pained personal testimony. Employment? "On my job," says a 40-year-old Atlanta factory worker, "they hire whites off the street and give them a better job than Negroes who have been there five or ten years." Schools? "When most of our children finish high school, they don't go no further," says a Lisbon, La., housewife of 35. "The high school don't teach no trade, so they can't get a job because they don't know how to do nothing." Crime in the streets? "The crime rate among our people—it's awful," sighs an elderly Atlanta housewife. The implacability of white America? "The Man," says the 55-year-old lady manager of a Houston hamburger shop, "doesn't want the Negroes to be freed. He has a knife in our back and he won't let us be."

Negroes, moreover, have come to regard Vietnam as their own particular incubus—a war that depletes their young manhood and saps the resources available to healing their ills at home. The black

HOW ATTITUDES HAVE CHANGED		
	1966	1969
Local police are harmful to Negro rights	33%	46%
Negroes should oppose the war in Vietnam because they have less freedom to fight for	35%	56%
The Federal government is helpful to Negro rights	74% (LBJ)	25% (Nixon)
Draft laws are unfair to Negroes	25%	47%

backlash against the war is one of the most striking turnabouts since the 1966 poll: the notion that blacks ought to oppose the war because they have less freedom in the U.S.—a 35 per cent minority slogan then—has become a 56–31 majority sentiment today.

The reasons for the switch are plain. Negroes are persuaded 2 to 1 that their young are fighting a disproportionate share of the war—and by 7 to 1 that Vietnam is directly pinching the home-front war on poverty. There are tugs in the other direction; a solid and rising majority in this age of unabashed black pride, for example, sees the war as evidence that Negroes make better combat soldiers than whites. But the anti-war tide is nonetheless powerful. It has helped, in the space of three years, to reverse the old Negro majority view that the military gives black youth a better break than they can get in civilian life. And it has infected the black's already jaundiced view of Richard Nixon's Administration. "He said he would end the war, and then he goes to Florida to rest all the time," says a 21-year-old shipping clerk in Thomasville, N.C. "And I got a draft notice yesterday . . ."

A further hazard of being black is to have whites incessantly ask what the Negroes want *now*. The answer, though it is sometimes blurred by the turned-off rhetoric of separation, is changeless and utterly unremarkable: an equal—and integrated—place in the life of mainstream America. The separatist streak in black America today is stronger than in the two previous *Newsweek* Polls—and quite possibly stronger than at any time since the pioneer nationalist Marcus Garvey's gaudy back-to-Africa crusades of the 1920s. A solid 69 per cent reject the idea of a separate Negro nation. "Separation," says a 24-year-old Kansas City woman credit clerk, "is segregation." But 21 per cent embrace the idea of partition and 12 per cent quite seriously expect it—a psychic dropout rate that almost certainly would surprise even the most ardent of the ghetto's proliferating street-corner black nationalists.

THE GOAL: AN OPEN SOCIETY

Would rather send children to an integrated school	**YES 78%**	NO 9%
Would rather live in an integrated neighborhood	**YES 74%**	NO 16%
Negroes should have a separate nation in the U.S.	YES 21%	**NO 69%**
Negroes will make more progress by running their own schools, businesses and living in their own neighborhoods rather than by integrating	YES 13%	**NO 78%**

Undecided omitted

Yet the vision of escape to some black Zion co-exists with the aspiration of the overwhelming majority to the last measures of full citizenship. Today's proud Negroes, by an overwhelming 84–10 per cent, reject the idea of preferential treatment in hiring or college admissions in reparation for past injustices. And what they want as much if not more than ever is integration—by 82–11 at work, by 78–9 in the schools, by nearly as heavy a majority in housing. Not all Negroes are keen on having whites live next door. Some take comfort in the community of blackness thrust upon them by segregation ("We understand each other," says a 20-year-old Pittsburgh telephone-equipment worker) and others candidly acknowledge that Negroes can be prejudiced, too ("I don't have anything against whites," says a 26-year-old Baltimorean dryly, "but I think they should stay to themselves"). But the majority will not be satisfied until that last barrier comes down. "I love everybody," says a 36-year-old Oakland utility repairman, casting his vote for integrated neighborhoods—and the widely held view among Negroes is that the feeling would fast become mutual if only so many whites were not so afraid of letting them live too close.

For his own part, the Negro's affection for himself has probably never been higher. If they have failed to make a case for separation, the generation of militant leaders fathered by Malcolm X and brought to flower by Stokely Carmichael have turned Negroes on to blackness with electrifying impact. What do members of the race prefer to be called? "Black" is still not the first choice—Negro remains the most popular—but it has had a great vogue among the Northern city-dwellers, the young and the relatively affluent. The current standings in the game of the names:

	Like most	Like least
Negro	38%	11%
Colored people	20	31
Blacks	19	25
Afro-American	10	11
Don't care	6	6
Not sure	7	16

Also in vogue: natural hair styles (though the sample is split pro and con) and, to a lesser extent, Afro clothes such as Dashikis (which switch on the young but turn off most elders). And, however it is packaged, Negroes are overwhelmingly convinced that they have that unique something called "soul"—an *élan vital* they define as anything from natural rhythm to a stoicism bred of their long and tragic passage in white America. The phrase "black is beautiful"—Martin Luther King's catch-up contribution to the explosion of race consciousness signaled by Carmichael—strikes three out of four as a simple statement of fact. Carmichael's "black power" remains as fuzzy and as various in definition as ever. "It means we shall overcome—right now," says a Philadelphia truck driver of 42. "It means I am somebody," says a 47-year-old mover in Burton, S.C. "It means money, baby, and success," says a Denver real-estate man, also 47. But whatever it means, Negroes like the way it sounds. They recoiled from the slogan (37 to 25) three years ago, when it was mint-fresh from the Meredith march in Mississippi and still a bit scary, but they favor it, 42–31, today.

Whether as a cause or as a consequence of their celebration of blackness, Negroes are a bit less trusting in the good faith and goodwill of whites. The black man retains his benign view of those white groups and institutions that have seemed to him to care; the antipoverty program and the U.S. Supreme Court rank particularly high, and the liberal tradition of the Jews has prevailed thus far over the anti-Semitic demagogy of some ghetto militants. (Jews are rated favorably by 2 to 1 and actually fare rather better than whites generally.) But a bit of a chill shows through in the black man's diminished good feelings about Congress, trade unions, college students, state governments, the mass media. In the urban North, his regard for the police—never affectionate—has soured so badly that 56 per cent suspect them of brutality. For the first time since the Eisenhower years, Negroes feel orphaned by Washington. "Nixon don't really care for Negroes," says a young Pittsburgh shoe salesman. And if the charge is unjust, the President has yet to live it down: blacks assign him a 51–23 negative rating, and one of the more charitable among them—a 42-year-old Dorchester, Mass., housewife—offers gingerly, "He just got in office. He's done no harm yet."

And yet an infectious optimism pervades even the Negro's cooled-off view of his white brethren. He is deeply suspicious of The Man: 69 per cent are convinced that whites are either hostile or indifferent—up 15 points in three years—and only 20 per cent believe they really mean him well. Nor do a majority of Negroes believe that Northern whites are any more kindly disposed toward blacks than Southerners are. Yet in spite of it all, a solid 54 per cent are persuaded that whites have gotten better in the past five years—and a fatter 61 per cent expect them to improve even more in the next five. There are, in this sanguine view, touches of innocence ("White people," says a Philadelphia schoolteacher hopefully, "are beginning to dig us") and experience ("I've seen the times we couldn't do anything right," says a Lisbon, La., factory worker, "but now they think we can"). And there is as well the conviction, particularly among the activist young, that whites will improve as much as blacks force them to. "The black man now is determined to get equal rights by whatever means necessary," says a 28-year-old secretary in Oakland. "The white man *must* change—or face the violence."

Negroes would still rather proceed by persuasion, but the majority who think they can prevail by reason alone has shrunk from 51–24 to 46–34 in three years. And they are by no means certain how to proceed. They are convinced that they owe what they have won so far not to white charity but to black action: 68 per cent believe that marching, picketing and demonstrating have helped, and roughly two Negroes in five remain ready to march, picket or demonstrate again. Blacks are by no means ready to drop their white allies and band together strictly on color lines, as many black-power leaders have urged. "They ain't enough of us," says a 66-year-old Harlem pensioner, and a Pittsburgh housewife wondered: "How we gonna get something when we ain't got nothing? Colored folks won't help you—they can't. When you ain't got nothing and the white folks got it all, you got to work with them to get what they got."

But how? Negroes may have begun to sense that the old protest styles are obsolescent; the pool of potential volunteers, in any event, has shrunk since 1966. Conventional politics offers one alternative métier—a doubly attractive one with the advent of the Carl Stokeses and the Richard Hatchers in the cities—and blacks overwhelmingly agree that their best bet is to work within the regular parties, not as a separate black caucus. Yet a very nearly schizoid streak has crept into their view of party politics. A robust 76 per cent consider themselves Democrats—higher even than in the Kennedy-Johnson years—but only 62 per cent think the Democrats will do the most for Negroes. The spill-off goes not to the Republicans (only 7 per cent of the blacks in the Nixon era identify with the party of Abraham Lincoln) but to the cynics—the 24 per cent who doubt it really makes much difference who wins.

A measure of black America's quandary is the fact that King, in death, remains by far the most revered Negro leader—and that no one alive is even close. King's standing today has passed from hero-worship to beatification: he is rated favorably by 95 per cent of the sample, excellent by 83 per cent. The martial young loved King as much as the walk-soft old, the North as well as the South. King was too important to Negroes for them to credit the official theory that his assassination was the work of a single man. Fully 82 per cent insist that a conspiracy was involved—and 67 per cent do not believe that white America has yet put the case to full and honest investigation.

The question now is who will move into the vacuum left by King's death—and the answers, fourteen months later, remain very much open. The new-breed radicals—the advocates of separation and the apostles of armed revolution—have reached perhaps a militant tenth or so of black America but not the masses. Malcolm X and Stokely Carmichael have important personal followings among the restive young, and so do the Black Panthers. ("Black people are sick of the racist pigs in this country," says a Pittsburgh college student. ". . . If we can't win our freedom and equality any other way, there's always the gun.") But Malcolm is dead, Stokely dabbling with exile in Africa, the Panther Party decimated by run-ins with the law—and all of them rank far down on a list gauging the leaders' popularity.

Yet, far from filling the breach, the insiders—the old-style race diplomats who remain persuaded that the walls of Jericho can best be toppled from within—have slipped in the past three years. The NAACP still stands second only to King, but its excellent rating has tumbled 21 points, and the Urban League's stock is off 10. King's nominal inheritor, Ralph David Abernathy, gets A grades from 26 per cent of the blacks and B or better from 64 per cent—enough to establish him, principally by virtue of succession, as probably the most popular living activist but not as heir to King's enormous national following. The exemplars of the new black politics—notably Cleveland's Mayor Stokes and Georgia state legislator Julian Bond, the onetime SNCC activist who wowed the 1968 Democratic National Convention—have captured the imaginations of many Negroes. But, on the other hand, they cannot yet seriously be rated leaders of America's Negro masses.

King's death thus may have ended the era of the "Negro spokesman"—that time when, at least in the imagining of many whites, one man could be said to speak with authority for black people generally. And many Negroes envision a far gloomier consequence—the possibility that King's nonviolent ideals may have died with him. "What did nonviolence do for *him*?" an 18-year-old Andrews, Texas, girl asks bitterly. King, of course, would have argued that that was not the question; he always understood that he might die for his faith. But Negroes now generally agree (by 52–30) that his nonviolent strategy is in fact losing whatever tenuous hold it has left.

They would far prefer that this were not so—but five violent summers have left both those who favor rioting and those who do not full of fatalistic doubts that the fire in the streets can soon be quenched. And black America, in sharp contrast to whites, views the riots to date with the most ambivalent moral and pragmatic feelings. Those who say they would actually join a riot have dwindled from 15 per cent in 1966 to 10 per cent today—an indication perhaps that a taste for the chaos of street war diminishes with experience. Yet Negroes will not wholly disown either the riots or the rioters. Nearly half of black America doubts that the riots have been justified, but roughly a third thinks they were—a substantial constituency for the view that rioting is a legitimate extension of the rights struggle. ("There is," says a 42-year-old Philadelphia machinist, "a time for everything. Sometimes a brick must be thrown.") Neither do blacks share the widely held white view that the riots are principally the work of hoodlum elements; two-thirds agree that at least some and perhaps most of the rioters have been good citizens. And, good guys or bad, justified or not, Negroes believe (by 40–29) that the

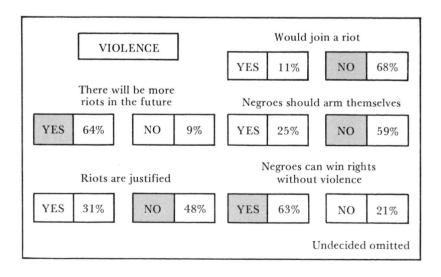

VIOLENCE		Would join a riot	
		YES 11%	NO 68%
There will be more riots in the future		Negroes should arm themselves	
YES 64%	NO 9%	YES 25%	NO 59%
Riots are justified		Negroes can win rights without violence	
YES 31%	NO 48%	YES 63%	NO 21%
			Undecided omitted

riots have helped more than they have hurt—that, much as it saddens the majority to say so, rioting works.

And yet the Negro American clings to his extraordinary faith that his cause can somehow be made to prevail without violence. He feels helpless to keep riots from happening (blacks agree, 64–9, that there will be more in the months ahead), and some bleakly predict violence in chilling new forms: sabotage, perhaps, or terrorism, or open racial war. Violence, moreover, is by no means without its proponents. "We got to get to *all* white people," says a 43-year-old Pittsburgh housewife, "and some of them, honey, only listen to violence."

The will of the majority is otherwise: the black man believes, 3 to 1, that he can win short of war. The conviction is part realism ("We have nothing to fight with," says a Denver government printer) and part romance ("We *are* winning without violence," says a young Kansas City steelworker). And it is most of all predicated on the belief that white America will respond to peaceful petitioning by the black ninth of the nation. Fifteen years after the school desegregation decision, six years after the battle of Birmingham, five years after that first explosion in Harlem, barely a year after the death of Martin Luther King, in the midst of a welling white backlash, a black waitress in Kansas City muses, "I used to feel that nonviolence was the way. But now I'm changing, and I don't know why. I guess I'm beginning to think violence is the only thing white people understand." A volatile minority of black America has long since come round to her point of view—and the single most important message of the majority is that it remains up to white America to prove that she is wrong.

Radical Black Militancy

James S. Campbell

In the effort to achieve freedom, equality and dignity, Negroes in America have repeatedly engaged in militant action and have continuously experimented with a wide variety of tactics, ideologies, and goals: insurrection and riot, passive resistance and non-violence, legal action and political organization, separatism and integration—all these and many others have been tried by black people in every period of our history. Black protest in America today is a similarly complex phenomenon. Many black leaders are working quietly but effectively "within the system" toward the same basic goals—black wellbeing and dignity—as those who have adopted more militant tactics. Even that part of the larger black protest movement which is now called "black militancy" is a complex, many-dimensioned phenomenon, and violence is only one part of it.

Three major themes stand out in contemporary black militancy:

1. Cultural autonomy and the rejection of white cultural values;
2. Political autonomy and community control; and
3. "Self-defense" and the rejection of non-violence.

Each of these three themes is a cluster of ideas, values and activities which are shared in widely varying degrees and combinations by different groups and individuals. Those who we call "radical black militants," and who are the main focus of this chapter, are Negroes who embrace notions of "self-defense" which include illegal retaliatory violence and guerrilla warfare tactics.

Reprinted from "American Society and the Radical Black Militant," in *Law and Order Reconsidered*, pp. 81–85, 108–111, co-directors James S. Campbell, Joseph R. Sahid, and David P. Stang. Vol. 10, National Commission on the Causes and Prevention of Violence Staff Study Series. Washington, D. C.: U.S. Government Printing Office, 1969.

1. *Cultural autonomy.* The movement toward black cultural autonomy and rejection of white cultural values mixes both indigenous and international influences. Looking backward at the long history of white domination in this country, and outward at what is seen as contemporary American "neocolonialism," black militants increasingly question the traditional values of American culture. From the Negro perspective, the performance of this country under the dominance of Western cultural values must seem far less impressive than it looks in white perspective, and militant blacks are now looking to their own cultural heritage as a source of affirmation of a different set of values.

Supported by the revival of awareness of African history and culture, militant blacks have grown more and more impatient with what is seen as the attempt of American institutions such as the universities, the schools and the mass media to impose white cultural standards which ignore or deprecate the independent cultural heritage of Afro-Americans. A SNCC position paper proclaims:

> The systematic destruction of our links to Africa, the cultural cut-off of blacks in this country from blacks in Africa are not situations that conscious black people in this country are willing to accept. Nor are conscious black people in this country willing to accept an educational system that teaches all aspects of Western Civilization and dismisses our Afro-American contribution . . . and deals with Africa not at all. Black people are not willing to align themselves with a Western culture that daily emasculates our beauty, our pride and our manhood.

2. *Political autonomy.* Contemporary black militancy is oriented strongly to the idea of black community control and the development of independent black political bases. The effort of the militants to overcome black powerlessness, while at the same time largely rejecting participation in traditional political avenues and party organizations, is a result of several influences.

Perhaps most important has been the failure of traditional politics to afford an effective means by which black leaders can exercise power on behalf of their constituencies. A recent study of Chicago politics, for example, showed that of a total of 1,088 policy-making positions in federal, state and local government in Cook County, only 58, or 5 percent, were held by Negroes in 1965, although blacks comprised at least 20 percent of the county's population. Nationwide, the

number of black elected officials is estimated at less than 0.02 percent
of the total of 520,000 elected officials—despite the fact that blacks are
just under 12 percent of the population. ("Traditional politics" may
yet prove responsive to black leadership aspirations, however: in
1965 when the Voting Rights Act went into effect there were but 72
black elected officials in the 11 Southern states; after the 1968 elections that number had increased more than fivefold to 388.)

Another major factor influencing the militants' thrust for black
political autonomy is the fact that residential segregation has created
the conditions for effective black political organization. Residential
segregation has meant that, in the black belt of the South as well as
in the urban North and West, blacks occupy whole districts *en bloc*.
With the growing concentration of blacks in the central cities and of
whites in the suburbs, more and more cities are developing black
majorities: in the next 15 years the number of major cities with Negro majorities will rise from 3 to 13.

A third factor in the drive toward black community control is
the sharpened political perception that control over the centers of
decision-making means control over the things about which decisions
are made, such as housing, employment, and education, as well as
other focal points of black protest like the police and the welfare
apparatus. Black power theorists like Stokely Carmichael and Charles
Hamilton believe that such control can be achieved only through
independent black political organizations:

> Before a group can enter the open society, it must first close ranks.
> By this we mean that group solidarity is necessary before a group
> can operate effectively from a bargaining position of strength in a
> pluralistic society. Traditionally, each new ethnic group in this society
> has found the route to social and political viability through the orga-
> nization of its own institutions with which to represent its needs
> within the larger society.

3. *"Self-defense."* The civil rights movement of the 1950's and
early 1960's stressed non-violence and what some called "passive
resistance." But civil rights workers in the South sometimes found
that they could not depend upon local or even federal officials for
protection against violent attacks by the Ku Klux Klan and other
white terrorist groups. Local police and sheriffs were often only half-
heartedly concerned with the welfare of rights workers, and in a few
instances at least were even active participants in terrorist groups. As

a result, in the mid-1960's a number of civil rights activists and their local allies began to arm themselves, and local defense groups sprang up in several black communities in the South.

At this time the focus of black protest began to shift to the ghettoes of the North, and expanded notions of self-defense soon arose. After the Watts riot of 1965, local Negroes formed a Community Action Patrol to monitor police conduct during arrests. (A UCLA survey showed that three fourths of the Negro males in the Watts area believed that the police used unnecessary force in making arrests.) In 1966, a small group of Oakland blacks carried the process a step further by instituting armed patrols. From a small group organized on an ad hoc basis and oriented to the single issue of police control, the Black Panther Party for Self-Defense has since grown into a national organization with a ten-point program for achieving political, social and economic goals—and with an evident willingness to resort to violence when it appears that only force and coercion will be successful in attaining the Party's goals.

The confrontation between radical black militants and some elements of the police has escalated far beyond self-defense and has in some cases become a bloody feud verging on open warfare. Aggressive attacks by black radicals on the police obviously far exceed any lawful right of self-defense (just as some of the instances of police aggression against black radicals are clearly unlawful), but the radicals nonetheless believe their attacks to be legitimate and to fall within "self-defense" when that concept is properly understood. As a militant leader argues, "We have been assaulted by our environment." This "assault" is considered to neutralize moral restraints against the use of counter-violence, which is thus seen by the radicals not as aggression but still as "defensive" retaliation.

How easily violence against police and other symbols of authority can be perceived as legitimate by radical black militants was demonstrated in the thoughts expressed before the Violence Commission by a moderate Negro leader:

> For you see, Mr. Chairman, what most people refer to as violence in the ghetto, I refer to as self defense against the violence perpetrated on the ghetto. Dr. King's widow has put it well: "In this society," she said on Solidarity Day, "violence against poor people and minority groups is routine."
>
> I must remind you that starving a child is violence. Suppressing a culture is violence. Neglecting school children is violence. Punish-

ing a mother and her child is violence. Discriminating against a working man is violence. Contempt for poverty is violence. Even the lack of will power to help humanity is a sick and sinister form of violence.

The people of the ghetto, Mr. Chairman, react to this violence in self defense. Their self defense is becoming more violent because the aggressor is becoming more violent. . . .

RESPONSES TO RADICAL BLACK MILITANCY

What are the principles which should guide the nation in dealing with the problem of radical black militancy? What are the policy implications of our analysis of the nature and causes of this phenomenon?

First: because radical black militancy is a highly complex phenomenon, with many different causes, no unbalanced, one-dimensional solution is possible—whether it be a program of intensified law enforcement or a program of expanded social reform.

Our analysis of radical black militancy has been an effort both to see this phenomenon in the perspective of the larger militant movement and to uncover the different kinds of factors which have operated to produce a commitment to illegal violence on the part of a small but significant element in the black community. We have seen that the radicals' destructive notions of "self-defense" or guerrilla warfare are often interwoven with constructive ideas in the areas of politics and culture. We have seen that in the rise of radical black militancy there has been a strong political factor—the new black radical leaders who have emerged following the failure of the society to respond adequately to the civil rights movement in the mid-1960's; there has been an ideological factor—the spread of revolutionary "anti-colonial" propaganda; there has been an economic factor—the frustration bred by living conditions in the racial ghettoes; there has been a psychological factor—the violent emotions unleashed as blacks break out of their dependent position. Moreover, underlying all these elements has been the historic institutional legacy of white supremacy and black subordination which has decisively shaped the Negro experience in America, including the recent emergence of a virulent radical black militancy.

In the face of complexities of this magnitude, it is impossible to believe that any one-dimensional package of solutions can effectively meet the problem of radical black violence. Improved law enforcement can undoubtedly deter and apprehend some radicals who engage in illegal violence—but the policeman and the judge have little power to check the spread of an ideology, to improve economic conditions or to alleviate psychological pressures. Vigorous efforts to secure the political rights of Negroes and accelerated social reforms in employment, education and housing can undoubtedly open the doors of opportunity and constructive citizenship for increasing numbers of blacks who might otherwise be tempted to violence—but in the short run incendiary leaders, violent ideologies and black rage can prove dismayingly unresponsive to well-meaning programs of social and political reform. Radical black militancy is not a one-sided problem—and it does not admit of one-sided solutions.

> *Second: because radical black militancy is, like urban rioting, a phenomenon deeply rooted in the enduring legacy of white supremacy and Negro subordination, we must continue and intensify our national commitment to secure the full and equal inclusion of black citizens into all aspects of American life.*

In order for there to be a remission in the cancerous growth of black violence, we must have unprecedented national action in support of the goal of black dignity and equality. Today's violent racial outbursts and race hatred are the outgrowth of fundamental attitudes, customs and institutions—both white and black—that have worked their way into our society for centuries. Today we reap what we have sown. We need action—in the words of the Kerner Commission, "compassionate, massive and sustained, backed by the will and resources of the most powerful and richest nation on this earth"—to create quickly, as a nation, what we as a nation have destroyed through centuries of slavery and segregation: the necessary preconditions for equal black participation in American life.

The movement to secure the inclusion of black citizens in all aspects of American life must be continued and intensified. In particular, obstacles must be removed which block the opportunities for duly elected—rather than self-appointed—black leaders to enter into the political process and to seek to advance the interests of their constituencies. The demand of local black communities for greater control over decisions that affect them and for "self-determination" is not inconsistent with the fundamental goal of inclusion. Rather, this demand is consistent with the historic commitment of the United States to democratic, local decision-making, as well as with the realities of the process by which other minority groups have made their way into the mainstream of American life. Unless the political rights of the "inner city" are respected and new local government structures are found under which these rights can be exercised, then radical black militancy will continue to attract more and more Negroes at the expense of the goal of peaceful inclusion of black and white in a single society functioning according to universally accepted political processes.

> *Third: because radical black militancy is a powerful ideological force among Negroes in the lower socio-economic brackets, the efforts which must be made to control the violence of black radicals must also involve attention to the effect of such efforts on the legitimacy of the existing social order.*

The radical black militant who attacks a policeman or bombs a college building is not simply a common criminal. He is indeed a criminal, but he is different from the burglar, the robber or the rapist. He is acting out of a profound alienation from society. He believes that the existing social and political order in America is not legitimate and that black people in America are being held in "colonial bondage" by "an organized imperialist force." Thus he is able to interpret his act of violence not as a crime but as a revolutionary (or "pre-revolutionary") act. As an isolated occurrence, this distorted interpretation would not be significant—but the interpretation is sustained by an articulated ideology that is today competing with traditional American values for the minds and hearts of the rising generation of black ghetto residents.

Whenever the police illegally harass a radical black militant leader, whenever the courts fail to accord such a person equal justice under law, whenever political leaders advocate indiscriminate suppression of all expressions of discontent, then the anti-colonial ideology gains new adherents: new proof appears to have been given that the social order in the United States is inherently and unalterably oppressive of the black race. On the other hand, when leaders of undoubted goodwill and decency vacillate in the condemnation and control of unlawful black violence because of the grievances underlying it, or when responsible authorities minimize or conceal the seriousness of the violent crime problem among ghetto Negroes so as not to be "racists," then such leaders seem to admit that the social order is so burdened with an ineradicable "guilt" as to be almost unworthy of preservation: this too feeds revolutionary violence. To deal effectively with the developing ideology of radical black militancy, we shall have to have able and effective leaders, skilled in the practice of statecraft, who will energetically strengthen, and not impair, the legitimacy of the institutions for whose preservation and improvement they are responsible.

Fourth: because radical black militancy is but one highly visible aspect of our total racial problem, uncommon courage and compassion will be required of the American people if the necessary steps toward solution are to be taken.

America's racial problem, of which radical black militancy is but one highly visible aspect, is grave and deep. It may be, however, that today we as a nation understand for the first time the full, terrible dimensions of this problem and what it has done to our people, both black and white. Perhaps we realize that its solution will require far more of us than merely to recover old values or to improve on old techniques. Perhaps we now see that racial peace and justice will require us, white and black alike, in fact to transcend our whole history—to create, often painfully, new institutions, new customs, new attitudes, in which the old self-validating judgment of white supremacy and black inferiority will be finally superseded.

Uncommon courage and compassion will be required from all our people if this challenge is to be met. We must all do what is right because it is right—not in the vain hope that it will quickly put an end to violence. A nation does not easily find its way out of a problem of this magnitude: we shall have to have the courage and the compassion to try and fail and try again, to see it through, to hold together, until we finally become, for the first time, one society, black and white, together and equal.

Neighborhood Self-Government

Milton Kotler

Mr. Chairman, members of the committee, I wish to thank you for inviting me to comment on the urban crisis and recommend an approach, born of years of thought and the past several years of hard practice, in the ECCO project in Columbus, Ohio, which could be of substantial value in rebuilding our slums and of achieving a better city for all.

The facts of urban poverty and despair in our slums and ghettoes are in: housing is rotten, unemployment is great, education is poor, health is bad, and so on. These factors compose a menacing condition. Yet, there is some encouragement in this committee's systematic deliberation on this question of rebuilding the slums, as well as recent legislative development representing a commitment of our government to apply some of the wealth and know-how of this nation to attack this urban crisis.

Between existing despair and new hope, the question is: How is this task to be done? What is the proper method of action to rebuild our slums? What is the proper role of different agents of change, public and private, federal, state, and local, to best assist this method? The crucial issue is our ability to understand the urban crisis and conceive a method of change. All too often we are strong in wealth and short in concept. Our real test is to find the proper concept of change and efficiently apply our resources to that method.

Out of my thought and experience in the actions of different communities to correct poverty and slum conditions, the proper concept of change is *neighborhood self-governing decision*. The neighbor-

Reprinted from Statement of Milton Kotler in *Federal Role in Urban Affairs*, Part 9, pp. 2054–2057. Hearings before the Subcommittee on Executive Reorganization of the Committee on Government Operations. U.S. Senate, 89th Congress, 2d Session, December 6, 1966. Washington: U.S. Government Printing Office.

hood, constituted as a non-profit tax-exempt, democratically-structured, corporation with its own assembly, officials, and revenues is the principal agent of change to rebuild our slums into a legal community of culture, freedom, and prosperity. The neighborhood must become a legal community of self-help and self-governing decisions with the sufficient capacity to relate to other organizations, public and private, for the resources and technical assistance, required to build a better city.

In current comment on this question of urban crisis and in testimony by others before you, the word *neighborhood* and its role has constantly sprung up. Notwithstanding the skepticism of academicians and experts about the existence of neighborhoods and their viability in a technological age, the neighborhood today is a living concept and image of the actual practice of ordinary people's lives. Granted it is often weak, but it is still the last remaining principle of public confidence in people's lives, particularly poor people. The neighborhood must be strengthened by organization and legal incorporation. It must be legitimized by democratic structure and public authority over resources to decide and act on specific local matters of the neighborhood, be it of 7,000 or 100,000. The neighborhood, as a legal community, must become the principal agent of rebuilding its locality and governing the public matters, principally social service, which touch the lives of that locality. Further, neighborhood corporations responsible to its residents through democratic structure, as well as responsible to outside authorities through its legal agency, may start a motion toward neighborhood government so strongly needed in today's mass urban society.

Our cities today are often larger than our states were in an earlier day. New York City, itself, is larger than the nation in population at its inception. To paraphrase Jefferson, for a concept of future direction—divide the cities into neighborhood governments. The neighborhood government, legally instituted, and democratically-constituted, will some day decide those matters of essential local concern and coordinate their activities at a city level on larger questions requiring city-wide uniformity. That future direction of neighborhood government is a subject of new federalism which we should begin thinking about. For the moment, however, let us practically build its precurser, the neighborhood corporation, as the new democracies of our cities, and as legal agents of self-governing decision and action in rebuilding our slums. It is in behalf of this new structure of community action that I wish to address my remarks and recommend some ways in which the federal government can assist this new growth.

While the facts are out on the despairing condition of our slums, it remains for us to understand what the constellation of poor housing, education, employment, health, means to its people. These are not simply bad conditions which are each open to separate improvement. Rather, these impoverished, material conditions impose a unified style of public life and civil disorder in the slum. These conditions constitute in our slums a political order of oppression which the residents of the slums are powerless to change in any legal way. Despair then, is their principle of public order. All hope is forced underground. The people cannot decide their own public life. Their public life is administered from outside. No expert approach from the outside, with technologically improved talent and resources, administered more systematically or efficiently, will change this basic condition of oppression and despair. The only thing that will change the slum is the people's own decision through the legal structure of their neighborhood corporation about those matters that intimately touch their lives. Technology has never been a substitute for political freedom and liberty.

There is new thought today and new efforts to tackle each of the different impoverished conditions of slum life. New approaches to education, new approaches to housing, new approaches to job training, etc.—new approaches to all these problems have been devised from without and are now proposed for administration from without, directly upon the slum community. These approaches may change things, but I doubt if they will improve things. At best, their inspiration is technological, and their shortcoming is political oversight. Americans will always insist on the right to decide the public matters of their community.

We grant material conditions are poor, but they cannot be improved in behalf of social peace and order simply by new technological design and administration. Neighborhood decision is essential. With such self-governing decision, the people will get behind the program, because it is their own plan of improvement. Their own commitment.

There is another way to state the simple truth: to change life which is poor toward greater dignity, prosperity and hope. We must work not with people's despair but with their hope. This is the human approach to urban change in a free society. An effective program of change in the slums must work with and build upon what no slum can kill—namely, people's humanity and freedom. And, today, the field of humanity and popular hope in the slums is the territory of their neighborhood community. The expression of hope is through neighborhood decision. Structure that hope into the neighborhood corporation, and let that hope exercise itself legally and practically upon the material conditions of poverty. If the impoverished conditions of slum life are indeed political, the method of change is simply political freedom which incorporates for decision and uses the resources of technology and the wealth of a nation to do the task.

1. The neighborhood area must be organized as a tax-exempt corporation based on one man–one vote membership of residents.
2. It must be territorially bound and can be based on resident populations of 7,000–25,000. In our largest cities, density can even support self-governing corporations of 100,000. But, always its membership must be based on the citizenship principle of residence.
3. It must be democratically structured on the basis of assembly, officials, and funding.
4. It must be formed to govern some real public matter and program.

The neighborhood corporations must have authority to govern certain matters of social service or economic development that intimately affect their local life. The neighborhood corporation must relate in its practice of decision and of management of services to all appropriate public and private agencies and organizations. It must be a part of the way of performing public services in the city.

This argument is practical as it reflects two years of experience and hard practice in the development of the ECCO project in Columbus, Ohio. I would like to briefly describe the major lines of that development as it suggests a model program for poor communities of other cities, and the role in which different agencies, public and private, can assist this development.

ECCO, the East Central Citizens Organization, is today a tax-exempt neighborhood corporation of 7,000 residents in a poor area of Columbus. Its territory is one square mile. Its population is 70% Negro and 30% white. Unemployment is high. The median income is $3,000. Housing is largely substandard and in many other respects, its community corresponds with poverty areas elsewhere. Today, however, ECCO is no longer a desperate slum, because of its corporation, and the action and decision of its citizens in assembly, council, and administration in deciding the affairs of that community. ECCO is a poor community building its prosperity through dignity and independence. For the first time in the lives of its residents, that neighborhood community is an integral part of the life of its city.

How was it formed; how does it govern; and what does it do?

How Was It Formed?

A church in that area transferred its settlement agency to neighborhood control. The neighborhood incorporated on a one man–one vote membership of residents, 16 years of age and above, to receive that settlement, gain funding for it and govern its activities. Today, that center is no longer a settlement in the typical traditional sense. It is the seat of ECCO's self-governing corporate development currently engaged in wide-ranging social services. It is the seat of the neighborhood polity, in assembly, council, and administration for community decision, development and new social undertakings in housing, health, manpower training, economic development, legal service, etc.

How Does It Govern?

The programs and activities of ECCO's democratically structured corporation is today funded at $350,000, with the early expectation of an additional $130,000 grant. The ultimate authority of that corporation is its assembly of membership which elects a council, authorizes and terminates programs, and has powers of investigation and law-making through frequent meetings. Its elected council is its executive arm and appoints an administration with assembly power of removal. That, in broad outline, is its constitution.

What Has It Done?

Programmatically, ECCO is running a wide range of services and is awaiting funding now for further service components, as well as negotiating on new programs in health and housing.

As important as its self-developed programs are, ECCO is also the place of a vibrant political life. ECCO, in assembly, council, committees, and neighborhood block groups meets nearly every night to deliberate and decide the life of its community. Through its staff, ECCO works every day and night in community development always building the momentum of its public decision on the basis of the real needs and real communication of its people. ECCO is a *vita-activa*—a total, active life of public concern and engagement.

Of still equal importance to program development and the political life of its new independence born of governing public matters, ECCO is also engaged in the everyday task of building the relationship of its neighborhood to the agencies and organizations, public and private, of its City of Columbus. It is on the board of the local Community Action Organization; it is represented on the Mayor's Advisory Committee; it is on the Police Advisory Committee, its relationship to the city is complex and endless.

ECCO is *town meeting government,* and the federal government funded it. Last year, an anti-poverty demonstration grant, under Section 207, funded the governing structure of the ECCO neighborhood corporation. This included stipends to the elected council and the general cost of corporate administration. That grant did not include the cost of service program operation. The test under that grant was whether supporting a governing structure could enable the ECCO corporation to gain funding from other agencies and sources. ECCO has done this. The Youth Committee of ECCO developed a self-governing youth program which gained funding from the Office of Juvenile Delinquency. That program is currently operating with wide involvement of the youth and is now currently developing a large manpower training program for unemployed youth in the neighborhood. The ECCO program committee developed a center proposal covering a range of service program components in education, daycare, welfare, etc. That program was approved by the Columbus Community Action Organization and now awaits funding from the regional office under the new appropriations. ECCO's program development will continue to grow and test out the question of what essential program authority is within the capacity of the neighborhood corporation to effectively govern and operate.

ECCO has the support of its people and the city.
There are no riots in ECCO because ECCO has the authority to decide and govern affairs.

Politicians do speak to ECCO in assembly and council. There is communication between the people of ECCO and city and state leadership because ECCO, too, is a corporate government doing public things.

ECCO is self-help through legal community, self-governing authority, and public and private funding. It has the resources and disposition to hire the best administrative skill and professional help where needed because the people have the authority to decide.

The success of ECCO over the past two years, in program, political life, and relationship to the city suggests the model value of the neighborhood corporation in other cities as a principal agent of rebuilding our slums from an oppressed community into independent corporate communities of decision and viable economy.

The experience of ECCO suggests a general method by which the federal government can enable the formation and development of neighborhood corporations in other cities, and promote new healthy relationships between the neighborhoods and their city.

The real object of our concern is how the poor community, through neighborhood corporations, can become principal agents of urban change in rebuilding the slums; and thereby become integral parts of their city engaged in the common task of general freedom and prosperity.

ARTICLE 12

We Won't End the Urban Crisis Until We End 'Majority Rule'

Herbert J. Gans

In 1962, a group of us, planners and social scientists, assembled a book of essays about the city, and we called it "The Urban Condi-

Reprinted from *The New York Times Magazine* (August 3, 1969), pp. 12–14, 20, 24–28. © 1969 by The New York Times Company. Reprinted by permission.

tion." Had the book been published only a couple of years later, it would probably have been entitled "The Urban Problem," and today it would surely come out as "The Urban Crisis." But these catch phrases are misleading, for they divert attention from the real issues. Although American cities are in deep trouble, the real crisis is not urban but national, and stems in large part from shortcomings in American democracy, particularly the dependence on majority rule.

The troubles of the city have been catalogued in long and by now familiar lists, but I would argue that, in reality, they boil down to three, *poverty and segregation*, with all their consequences for both their victims and other urban residents; and *municipal decay*, the low quality of public services and the declining tax revenues which are rapidly leading to municipal bankruptcy. Moreover, the first two problems are actually the major cause of the third, for the inability of the poor to pay their share of keeping up the city, as well as the crime and other pathology stimulated by poverty and segregation have brought about much of the municipal decay. In addition, the fear of the ghetto poor has recently accelerated the middle-class exodus, thus depriving cities of an important source of taxes at the very moment their expenditures have been increased by the needs of the poor. Consequently, the elimination of urban poverty and segregation would go far toward relieving the other problems of the city.

Neither poverty and segregation nor municipal decay are unique to the city, however; indeed, they are often more prevalent in rural areas. More important, all three problems are caused by nationwide conditions. Poverty is to a considerable extent a by-product of the American economy, which is today growing only in the industries and services that employ the skilled, semi-professional and professional worker, and, in fact, many of the unskilled now living in urban slums were driven out of rural areas where the demand for their labor had dried up even earlier than in the cities. Municipal decay is similarly national in cause, for small communities can also no longer collect enough in taxes to provide the needed public services, and their populations, too, are becoming increasingly poor and black as the nationwide suburbanization of the middle class proceeds.

In short, the so-called urban crisis is actually an American crisis, brought on largely by our failure to deal with the twin evils of poverty and segregation. This failure has often been ascribed to a lack of national will, as if the country were an individual who could pull himself together if he only wanted to, but even the miraculous emergence of a national consensus would not be sufficient, for the sources of our failure are built into our most important economic and political institutions.

One major source of failure is the corporate economy, which has not realized, or been made to realize, that the rural and urban unskilled workers it has cast aside are part of the same economic process which has created affluence or near-affluence for most Americans. As a result, private enterprise has been able to improve productivity and profit without having to charge against its profit the third of the population which must live in poverty or near-poverty. Instead, government has been left the responsibility for this by-product of the economic process, just as it has often been given the task of removing the waste materials that are a by-product of the production process.

But government has not been able or willing to require private enterprise—and its own public agencies—to incorporate the employable poor into the economy. Not only is there as yet little recognition among the general public or most of our leaders of the extent to which urban and rural poverty result from the structure of the economy, but private enterprise is powerful enough to persuade most people that government should take care of the poor or subsidize industry to create jobs for them.

However, government—whether Federal, state or local—has not been able or willing to absorb responsibility for the poor either, and for several important political reasons.

First, most voters—and the politicians that represent them—are not inclined to give the cities the funds and powers to deal with poverty, or segregation. This disinclination is by no means as arbitrary as it may seem, for the plight of the urban poor, the anger of the rebellious, and the bankruptcy of the municipal treasury have not yet hurt or even seriously inconvenienced the vast majority of Americans.

Rural and small-town America make little use of the city anyway, except for occasional tourist forays, and the city financial institutions which play an influential part in their economies are not impaired in their functioning by the urban condition. Suburbanites may complain about the dirt, crime and traffic congestion when they commute to city jobs, but they can still get downtown without difficulty, and, besides, many of their employers are also moving out to the suburbs.

But even the city-dwellers who are neither poor nor black can pursue their daily routines unchanged, for most of them never need to enter the slum areas and ghettos. Only the urbanites who work in these areas or live near them are directly touched by the urban condition—and they are a small minority of America's voters.

Second, many Americans, regardless of where they live, are opposed to significant governmental activity on behalf of the poor and black—or, for that matter, to further governmental participation in the economy. Not only do they consider taxes an imposition on their ability to spend their earnings, but they view governmental expenditure as economic waste, whereas private enterprise expenditures are proudly counted in the Gross National Product. The average American taxpayer is generous in paying for the defense of the country and for projects that increase American power and prestige in the world, be it a war in Vietnam or a moon shot, but he is often opposed to governmental activities that help anyone other than himself. The very corporations and workers whose incomes depend on government contracts often fight against Federal support of other activities and groups—and without ever becoming aware of the contradiction.

Consequently, many taxpayers and voters refuse to see the extent to which governmental activities create jobs and provide incomes, and how much government subsidizes some sectors of American life but not others. By and large, these subsidies go to people who need them less: there are tax exemptions for home-owners, Federal highway programs and mortgage insurance for suburbanites; direct subsidies to airlines, merchant shipping, large farms, colleges and college students; and of course, the depletion allowance for oil producers. Grants to the poor are fewer and smaller; the most significant one is public welfare, and it is called a handout, not a subsidy.

Subsidies are generally provided not on the basis of merit but power, and this is a *third* reason for the lack of action in the cities. Even though many Americans live in the city, urban areas and their political representatives have relatively little power, and the poor, of course, yet less. The poor are powerless because they are a minority of the population, are often difficult to organize, and are not even a homogeneous group with similar interests that could be organized into an effective pressure group.

The cities are relatively powerless because of the long-time gerrymandering of American state and Federal governments in favor of rural and small-town areas. As a result, rural-dominated state legislatures can use the tax receipts of the cities to subsidize their own areas, and Congressmen from these areas have been able to outvote the representatives of urban constituencies. The Supreme Court's requirement of one man–one vote is now bringing about reapportionment, but it may be too late for the cities. As more and more Americans leave for the suburbs, it appears that the cities will not be able to increase their power, for voters and politicians from rural and suburban areas who share a common interest in not helping the cities can unite against them.

In effect, then, the cities and the poor and the black are politically outnumbered. This state of affairs suggests the *fourth* and perhaps most important reason for the national failure to act: the structure of American democracy and majority rule.

America, more so than other democratic nations in the world, runs its political structure on the basis of majority rule. A majority vote in our various political institutions determines who will be nominated and elected to office, what legislation will be passed and funded, and who will be appointed to run the administering and administrative agencies. Of course, the candidates, laws and budgets which are subject to the vote of the majority are almost always determined by minorities; the only men who can run for office these days are either affluent or financed by the affluent groups who donate the campaign funds, and the legislation these men vote on is often suggested or even drafted by campaign-fund donors or other small groups with specific interests in government action. Properly speaking then, American democracy allows affluent minorities to propose, and the majority to dispose.

There is nothing intrinsically conspiratorial about this phenomenon, for it follows from the nature of American political participation. Although every citizen is urged to be active in the affairs of his community and nation, in actual practice participation is almost entirely limited to organized interest groups or lobbies who want something from government.

As a result, legislation tends to favor the interests of the organized: of businessmen, not consumers, even though the latter are a vast majority; of landlords, not tenants; doctors, not patients. Unorganized citizens may gripe about the lack of consumer legislation or even the defense budget, but only when their interests are similar and immediately threatened so that they can organize or be organized are they able to affect governmental affairs.

This is not to say that governmental decisions often violate the wishes of a majority of Americans, for, by and large, that majority is usually happy—or at least not too unhappy—with the decisions of its governments. The almost $100-billion spent annually for defense and space exploration are appropriated because, until recently, the majority of the voters wanted a victory in Vietnam and a man on the moon before the Russians. There is no Federal mass-transit program because the majority of Americans, even in the cities, prefer to use their cars; and Congress can pay more attention to a small number of tobacco farmers and producers than to the danger of cigarette smoking because the majority is not sufficiently concerned about this danger, and, as a recent study showed, many heavy smokers do not even believe that smoking leads to cancer or heart disease.

But while the American political structure often satisfies the majority, it also creates outvoted minorities who can be tyrannized and repressed by majority rule, such as the poor and the black, students, migrant workers and many others. In the past, such minorities have had to rely on the goodwill of the majority, hoping that it would act morally, but it generally offered them only charity, if that much. For example, the majority has granted the poor miserly welfare payments, and then added dehumanizing regulations for obtaining and spending the funds.

Today, many outvoted minorities have tired of waiting for an upturn in public altruism and are exerting political pressure on the majority. Thus, the poor and the black have been organizing their own pressure groups, forming coalitions with more powerful minorities (like the progressive wing of the labor movement) and getting support from liberals, other advocates of social justice and guilty whites. Indeed, such methods enabled the poor and the black to achieve the civil rights and antipoverty programs of the nineteen-sixties.

Even so, these gains, however much of an improvement they represent over the past, remain fairly small, and have not significantly improved the living conditions of large numbers in the slums and ghettos. Moreover, the activities of ghetto demonstrators and rioters have cooled some of the ardor of white liberals and trade unionists, and it is questionable whether many other groups would derive much benefit from coalition with poor or black organizations. Like all outvoted minorities, they can offer little to a coalition except the moral urgency of their cause.

Consequently, the poor and the black are caught in an almost hopeless political bind, for any programs that would produce significant gains, such as a massive antipoverty effort, an effective assault on segregation or even a workable community control scheme, are likely to be voted down by the majority, or the coalitions of minorities that make up majorities in American political life. *Moreover, since the poor and the black will probably always be outvoted by the majority, they are thus doomed to be permanently outvoted minorities.*

But if I am correct in arguing that the urban condition cannot be improved until poverty and segregation are eliminated or sharply reduced, it is likely that *under the present structure of American government there cannot be and will not be a real solution to the problem of the cities.*

The only other source of power left to outvoted minorities is *disruption,* upsetting the orderly processes of government and of daily life so as to inconvenience or threaten more powerful groups. This explains why the ghettos have rebelled, why young people sometimes resort to what adults consider to be meaningless delinquency, or students to occupations of school buildings, or working-class people to occasionally violent forms of white backlash.

Although disruption is bitterly attacked as antisocial by defenders of the existing social order, strikes were also once considered antisocial, but are now so legitimate that they are no longer even thought of as a form of disruption. The disrupters of today do not strike, but their methods have not been so unproductive as their opponents would have us believe. The ghetto rebellions have been responsible for stimulating private enterprise to find jobs for the so-called hard-core unemployed; the sit-ins—as well as the organizational activity—of the Welfare Rights movement have won higher grants for welfare recipients in some cities and have helped to arouse the interest of the Nixon Administration in re-examining the Federal welfare program; and the uprisings by college and high school students have been effective in winning them a voice in their schools.

Needless to say, disruption also has disadvantages: the possibility that it will be accompanied by violence and that it will be followed by counter-disruption—for example, police or vigilante violence—and by political efforts of more powerful groups to wipe out the gains achieved through disruption. Thus, the backlash generated by the ghetto rebellions has been partly responsible for the cutback in anti-poverty and civil-rights efforts, and the disruptions by welfare recipients and college students are now producing repressive legislation against both groups. But disruption also creates serious costs for the rest of society, particularly in terms of the polarization of opposing groups, the hardening of attitudes among other citizens, and the hysterical atmosphere which then results in more repressive legislation. Clearly, disruption is not the ideal way for outvoted minorities to achieve their demands.

Nevertheless, disruption has become an accepted political technique, and may be used more widely in the nineteen-seventies, as other groups who feel they are being shortchanged by American democracy begin to voice their demands. Consequently, perhaps the most important domestic issue before the country today is whether outvoted minorities—in the cities and elsewhere—must resort to further disruption, or whether more peaceful and productive ways of meeting their needs can be found.

If the outvoted minorities are to be properly represented in the political structure, two kinds of changes are necessary. First, they must be counted fairly, so that they are actually consulted in the decision-making process, and are not overpowered by other minorities who would be outvoted were they not affluent enough to shape the political agenda. But since even a fairer counting of the voters would still leave the outvoted minorities with little influence, ways of restricting majority rule must be found when that rule is always deaf to their demands.

Majority rule is, of course, one of the unquestioned traditions of American political life, for the first axiom of democracy has always been that the majority should decide. But democracy is not inviolably equivalent to majority rule, for government of the people, by the people and for the people need not mean that a majority is "the people." Indeed, despite its traditional usage in democracies, majority rule is little more than an easily applied quantitative formula for solving the knotty problems of how the wishes of the people are to be determined. Moreover, traditions deserve to be re-examined from time to time, particularly if society has changed since they came into being.

And American society has changed since its government was

created. What might be called *majoritarian democracy* was adopted when America was a small and primarily agrarian nation, with a great degree of economic and cultural homogeneity, few conflicting interest groups, and a since-rejected tradition that the propertyless should have fewer rights than the propertied. As a result, there were few serious disputes between majorities and minorities, at least until the Civil War, and majoritarian democracy could be said to have worked. Today, however, America is a highly heterogeneous and pluralistic nation, a society of minority groups, so to speak, and every important political decision requires an intense amount of negotiation and compromise so that enough minorities can be found to create a majority coalition. And even then, America is so pluralistic that not all minorities can be accommodated and must suffer all the consequences of being outvoted.

America has been a pluralistic society for almost a century, but the shortcomings of majority rule have not become a public issue before, mainly because previous generations of outvoted groups had other forms of redress. The outvoted of the past were concentrated among poor ethnic and racial minorities, as they are today, but in earlier years the economy needed their unskilled labor, so that they had less incentive to confront the majority, except to fight for the establishment of labor unions. Moreover, they had little reason even to think about majority rule, for government played a smaller role in the economy and in their lives.

Now all this has changed. When governmental policies and appropriations very nearly decide the fate of the poor, the black, draft-age college students, disadvantaged high school students, and not so affluent blue-collar workers, such groups must deal with government; and more often than not, their demands are frustrated by the workings of majority rule.

Thus, it becomes quite pertinent to ask whether majoritarian democracy is still viable, and whether the tradition of majority rule should not be re-examined. If three-fourths of the voters or of a legislative body are agreed on a course of action, it is perhaps hard to argue against majority rule, but what if that rule seriously deprives the other fourth and drives it to disruption? And what if the majority is no more than 55 per cent, and consists only of an uneasy and temporary coalition of minorities? Or if the remaining 45 per cent are unable to obtain compromises from the slender majority?

I believe that the time has come to modernize American democracy and adapt it to the needs of a pluralistic society; in short, to create a *pluralistic democracy*. A pluralistic form of democracy would not do away with majority rule, but would require systems of proposing and disposing which take the needs of minorities into consideration, so that when majority rule has serious negative consequences, outvoted minorities would be able to achieve their most important demands, and not be forced to accept tokenism, or resort to despair or disruption.

Pluralistic democracy would allow the innumerable minorities of which America is made up to live together and share the country's resources more equitably, with full recognition of their various diversities. Legislation and appropriations would be based on the principle of "live and let live," with different programs of action for different groups whenever consensus is impossible. Groups of minorities could still coalesce into a majority, but other minorities would be able to choose their own ways of using public power and funds without being punished for it by a majority.

It would take a book to describe how the American political system might be restructured to create a pluralistic democracy, but I can suggest some specific proposals toward this goal. They fall into two categories: those that incorporate outvoted minorities into the political structure by increasing the responsiveness of governments to the diversity of citizen interests—and to all citizens; and those which restrict majority rule so as to prevent the tyrannization of minorities. Many of my proposals have drawbacks, and some are outright utopian, but I suggest them more to illustrate what has to be done than to provide immediate feasible solutions.

The responsiveness of governments can be increased in several ways.

First, the one man-one vote principle must be extended to all levels of government and the political parties. County and municipal bodies need to be reapportioned to eliminate gerrymandering of the poor and the black; party leaders, high and low, should be elected by party members, and party candidates should be nominated by primaries, rather than by conventions or closed meetings of party leaders.

Second, the seniority system must be abolished in all legislatures, so that politicians can no longer obtain undue power simply because their own districts re-elect them time after time. The power of committee chairmen who may represent only a small number of voters to block legislation wanted by a larger number must also be eliminated.

Third, the administrative agencies and their bureaucracies must become more accountable, perhaps by replacing appointive officers with elective ones, or by requiring such bodies to be run by elected boards of directors.

Fourth, all election campaigns should be funded by government to discourage the near-monopoly that wealthy individuals now have in becoming candidates, and to prevent affluent interest groups from making demands on candidates as a price for financing their campaigns. If equal amounts—and plenty of free television time—were given to all candidates, even from third, fourth and fifth parties, the diversity of the population would be better represented in the electoral process. This might lead to election by plurality rather than majority, although in a highly diverse community or state such an outcome might not be undesirable, and runoffs can always be required to produce a final majority vote.

Fifth, methods by which the citizenry communicates with its elected representatives ought to be improved. Today, legislators tend to hear only from lobbyists, people in their own social circles, and the writers of letters and newspaper editorialists—a highly biased sample of their constituencies. Indeed, the only way an ordinary citizen can communicate is by organizing or writing letters. Of course, such methods make sure that a legislator hears only from deeply interested citizens, protecting him from being overwhelmed by too much feedback, but they also discriminate against equally interested people who cannot organize or write.

One possible solution is for governments to make postage-free forms available for people who want to write letters to their representatives, to be picked up in banks, post offices, stores and taverns. Another solution is for governments to finance the establishment of regular but independently run public-opinion polls on every major issue, so that government officials can obtain adequate feedback from a random sample of their constituents, and not only on the few issues a handful of private pollsters today decide are worth polling about.

Yet another solution is for governments to encourage people to organize politically, by allowing them to claim as tax deductions the dues and contributions to lobbying organizations (other than political parties). Limits on the size of such deductions would have to be set to prevent affluent minorities from using their funds to gain extra power; and organizations of the poor, whose members cannot afford to pay dues and do not benefit from tax deductions, could be given government grants if they could prove that two-thirds of their members were poor.

Feasible methods for increasing the power of minorities at the expense of majority rule are more difficult to formulate. One approach is to enhance the power of existing institutions that represent minority interests—for example, the courts and Cabinet departments. If constitutional amendments to establish an economic and racial bill of rights could be passed, for instance, a provision giving every American citizen the right to a job or an income above the poverty-line, the power of the poor would be increased somewhat.

Cabinet departments also represent minority interests, particularly at the Federal and state levels, although more often than not they speak for affluent minorities. Nevertheless, if the Office of Economic Opportunity were raised to full Cabinet status and a Department of Minorities established in Washington, at least some new legislation and higher appropriations for the poor and the black would result. In other Cabinet departments, new bureaus should be set up to represent the interests of outvoted minorities; in Housing and Urban Development (now dominated by builders and mayors), to look after the needs of slum dwellers; in Health, Education and Welfare, to deal with the concerns of patients, students and welfare recipients, respectively. Moreover, the policy-making boards that I suggested earlier to oversee Cabinet departments and other administrative agencies should include their clients. Thus, all school boards should include some students; welfare departments, some welfare recipients; and housing agencies, some residents of public housing and F.H.A.-supported projects.

The financial power of poor minorities could be increased by extending the principles of the progressive income tax and of school-equalization payments to all governmental expenditures. Funding of government programs could be based in part on the incomes of eventual recipients, so that the lower their income, the higher the government grant. Poorer communities would thus obtain more Federal money per capita for all public services, and subsidies for mass transit programs would automatically be higher than for expressways to suburbia.

In addition, changes in the electoral system would be needed. One solution would be election by proportional representation. P.R. has not been popular in America, partly because it wreaks havoc with the two-party system, but it is not at all clear whether a pluralistic society is best served by a two-party system to begin with. Proportional representation by race or income would go against the American grain, but as long as racial and economic integration seems to be unachievable in the near future, this solution might be more desirable than forcing the poor or the black to resort to disruption.

Actually, proportional representation is already practiced informally in many places; in New York City, election slates have always been "balanced" to include candidates from the major ethnic and religious groups. Perhaps we should even think about proportional representation by occupational groups, for job concerns are often uppermost in the voters' choices. After all, many pro-Wallace factory workers voted for Humphrey at the last minute, realizing that their job interests were more important than their fear of black militancy.

Another approach would restrict majority rule directly, by making all elections and voting procedures in legislative branches of government go through a two-step process, with majority rule applying only to the final step. This system, somewhat like the runoff used in some state and municipal elections, would require that if any legislative proposal or appropriation obtains at least 25 per cent of the total vote, it must be revised and voted on again until it is either approved by a majority or rejected by 76 per cent of the voting body. In the meantime, compromises would have to be made, either watering down the initial proposal so that a majority could accept it, or satisfying other demands of the minority through the time-honored practice of log-rolling so that they would allow 76 per cent of the voting body to reject the original proposal.

For example, if at least a quarter of a Congressional committee supported a strong negative income tax, it is likely that the second vote would produce at least a weaker version of the tax that the majority could live with. Of course, such a system would work only if outvoted minority groups were able to elect representatives in the first place. (Also, it is always possible that legislators who favored a highly regressive income tax or segregationist policies would be able to obtain legislation for *their* minorities, but if an economic and racial bill of rights were added to the Constitution, such legislation would be thrown out by the courts.)

Outvoted minorities can also achieve greater political power by the alteration of existing political boundaries and powers so that they could even become majorities in their own bailiwicks. Current proposals for decentralization and community control are boundary-altering schemes with just this political consequence, and some of the disadvantages of these schemes today could be alleviated by my previous proposal for progressive methods of government funding to provide more money to poorer communities.

But the concept of redrawing boundaries ought to be applied more broadly, for many existing political subdivisions are anachronistic. For example, it is difficult to justify the existence of many of the states as political units today, and it might be useful to think about creating smaller and more homogeneous units in highly urbanized parts of the country, perhaps of county size, particularly in order to reduce the number of outvoted minorities. (Norman Mailer has suggested just that in proposing statehood for New York City.)

Along the same line, the old idea of replacing geographical political units by groupings along economic and other interests deserves re-examination. For instance, the welfare recipient's lot would probably be improved if he or she became part of a regional governmental body of welfare recipients which could determine how the welfare system ought to be run.

Sometimes, outvoted minorities are tyrannized because their demands are diametrically opposed to the majority's. When this happens within a school or other institution, the minority should have the right to secede, establishing its own institution without being financially punished by the majority. If some parents want a Summerhill education for their children, they should be given tax money to start their own school, just as determined black nationalists should be free to build their own community if and when public aid for new towns becomes available. In a pluralistic nation, all impulses for diversity that do not clearly harm the rest of society should be encouraged.

Finally, changes in the rules of the political system must be supplemented by changes in the economic system, for ultimately it is the major obstacle to improving the lot of many outvoted minorities—and even of the unorganized majority. Some of my earlier proposals are equally applicable here.

The one-man, one-vote principle might be extended to stockholders who elect corporate boards of directors; a Cabinet department to represent consumers and other corporate customers should be set up; feedback from stockholders and customers to the corporate "legislature" should be improved, and they, as well as workers, should sit on corporate boards. In an era when many firms are subsidized by government contracts and tax credits, it is certainly possible to argue that at least such firms should become more democratic.

Most of the proposals for a pluralistic democracy are purposely intended to enhance the power of poor and black minorities; for, as I noted earlier, this seems to me the only way of solving the problems of the cities. But such a democracy is needed by all minorities who stand in danger of being outvoted by a majority, whatever their income or color. As the current demands of more people for greater equality and more control over their lives accelerate, and the role of government in society continues to mount at the same time, the need for more political pluralism will become increasingly urgent. What we so inaccurately describe as the urban crisis is in reality the beginning of a national political crisis. But it is also an opportunity for Americans to develop new ways of living together.

SUGGESTIONS FOR FURTHER READING

I. Ethnic and Social Aspects of Urban Politics

Bailey, Harry A., Jr., and Ellis Katz, eds. *Ethnic Group Politics*. Columbus, Ohio: Charles E. Merrill Publishing Co., 1969. (Collection of articles concerning ethnicity and city politics.)

Bollens, John C., and Henry J. Schmandt. *The Metropolis*. 2d ed. Chapter 3. New York: Harper & Row, Publishers, Inc., 1970. (Social anatomy of metropolitan residents.)

Fuchs, Lawrence H., ed. *American Ethnic Politics*. New York: Harper & Row, Publishers, Inc., Harper Torchbooks, 1968. (Thirteen articles and essays on ethnicity, immigration, and political implications.)

Gans, Herbert J. *The Urban Villagers*. New York: The Free Press, 1962. (Analysis of second generation Italians in West End section of Boston faced by massive urban renewal project.)

Glazer, Nathan, and Daniel P. Moynihan. *Beyond the Melting Pot: The Negroes, Puerto Ricans, Jews, Italians and Irish of New York City.* Cambridge, Mass.: The M.I.T. Press, 1963. (Problems and prospects of major ethnic, racial, and religious groups of New York City.)

Glazer, Nathan. "The Peoples of America." *The Nation* 201 (1965):137–141. (The replacement of the traditional melting pot thesis in the cities by white backlash against blacks and the flight of the white middle class to the suburbs.)

Greer, Scott. *Governing The Metropolis.* Chapter 3. New York: John Wiley and Sons, Inc., 1962. (Comparisons and contrasts of city immigrants in 1900 and today.)

Litt, Edgar. *Ethnic Politics in America.* American Government Series. Glenview, Ill.: Scott, Foresman and Company, 1970. (Reinterpretation of American ethnic politics in the light of today's ethnic and social conflicts.)

Wolfinger, Raymond E. "The Development and Persistence of Ethnic Voting." *American Political Science Review* 59 (1965):896:908. (Support for the claim that urban ethnic bloc voting continues when middle-class status is attained by attractive ethnic candidates.)

II. Race and Migration in Metropolitan Areas

Autobiography of Malcolm X. New York: Grove Press, Inc., 1966. (First nine chapters: Malcolm drifting through various cities. Last ten chapters: his role as the protest leader of the Black Muslims.)

Beardwood, Roger. "The Southern Roots of Urban Crisis." *Fortune* 78 (1968):80–87, 151–152, 155–156. (Description of how blacks are forced off farms as government policies do not assist them.)

Brown, Claude. *Manchild in the Promised Land.* New York: The New American Library, Inc., Signet Books, 1965. (Autobiographical account of Claude's life and escape from Harlem by his own efforts.)

Cleaver, Eldridge. *Soul on Ice.* New York: Dell Publishing Co., Inc., Delta Books, 1968. (Powerfully written essays by the refugee of the Black Panther Party.)

Grodzins, Morton. *The Metropolitan Area as a Racial Problem.* Pittsburgh: University of Pittsburgh Press, 1958. (An exposition of how black-white polarization in cities and suburbs results in segregated housing patterns that will continue unabated without government programs.)

Handlin, Oscar. *The Newcomers: Negroes and Puerto Ricans in a Changing Metropolis.* Garden City, N. Y.: Doubleday and Co., Inc., Anchor Books, 1962. (An examination of the difficulties of new city immigrants because of inadequate education and ineffective community organization.)

Tilly, Charles. "Race and Migration to the American City." In *The Metropolitan Enigma,* edited by James Q. Wilson. Pp. 124–146. Washington, D. C.: U.S. Chamber of Commerce, 1967. (An exposition of the fact that black city immigrants do not cause problems until they have lived in cities for a while.)

III. Special Problems of Black City Immigrants

Clark, Kenneth B. *Dark Ghetto: Dilemmas of Social Power*. New York: Harper & Row, Publishers, Inc., Harper Torchbooks, 1967. (Highly recommended and important analysis of social and psychological aspects of black slum life.)

Hunter, David R. *The Slums: Challenge and Response*. New York: The Free Press, 1968. (A comprehensive examination of slums and government programs to combat urban poverty.)

Kristol, Irving. "The Negro Today Is like the Immigrant Yesterday." *The New York Times Magazine*, September 11, 1966, pp. 50–51, 124–142. (An argument that black city residents are more comparable to impoverished urban ethnic groups of the past than to present-day white middle-class suburbanites.)

Rainwater, Lee, and William L. Yancey. *The Moynihan Report and the Politics of Controversy*. Cambridge, Mass.: The M.I.T. Press, 1967. (An anthology of the controversial U.S. government report about the pathology of disorganized black family life together with a wide range of responses by social scientists, the press, government, and civil rights leaders.)

Silberman, Charles E. *Crisis In Black and White*. New York: Random House, Inc., Vintage Books, 1964. (Highly recommended study of underlying causes of black-white problems. One of the most concise and readable books on black developments in America.)

PART 2

Political Power in
Metropolitan Areas

Chapter 3

City Government and Politics

*What Is the Nature of Political
Participation, Leadership,
and Conflict?*

Central cities of metropolitan areas are facing unparalleled problems today. Municipal governments and urban political parties must respond to competing demands and pressures exerted by a changing electorate and social structure. We are presently witnessing dramatic confrontations in urban political life. Older city residents cling to a style of politics that seeks to preserve neighborhood stability. These people fiercely resist change that threatens community values. "White backlash" is evident, especially in transitional city neighborhoods where the character of residential patterns and the composition of the public school population is rapidly changing. At the same time, many blacks living in decaying slums are rallying around the battle cry of "Black power," which in a very important sense refers to community control of local social, economic, and political institutions.

A central purpose of municipal government should be to enhance the general welfare by providing maximum opportunity for all while preserving individual liberty. As conflicting demands are placed on city governments, it becomes increasingly difficult to strike a proper balance between the goals of opportunity and liberty. It should be made clear, however, that our cities have faced political cross-pressures for a long time. Black demands for political power are only the most recent example of group cohesion in the urban arena. A persistent feature of urban politics (at least since 1850) has been the requirement for accommodation between established city dwellers and various groups of newcomers.

One of the earliest attacks on central city government and politics was directed at the corruption and evil of the boss and the political machine. Following the great waves of European immigration to American cities after 1850, city politicians found it increasingly difficult to adapt chaotic, uncoordinated, and decentralized municipal institutions to the demands of a rapidly expanding urban population.

Fred I. Greenstein (Article 13) examines the pros and cons of the boss phenomenon. Bosses established informal governments to operate alongside the unresponsive formal institutions. The older literature of city government tended to be harshly critical of the scandal, corruption, bribery, and payoffs associated with the boss. While this was certainly not "good government" in a reformist sense, the old-style political machine assisted newcomers in the process of becoming assimilated and "Americanized."

Reform movements, which began around the turn of the twentieth century, directed efforts at eradicating the worst abuses of boss rule and machine politics. The reformers placed major emphasis on institutional changes. It was thought that good government could be achieved by altering the structure of city government rather than by reforming city political parties. Such an attitude was only natural, since "politics" was considered to be an unnecessary evil. But it was ironic that the drive for "efficiency and economy" in city government resulted in divorcing popular control from the administration of public policies.

Greenstein indicates that municipal reform is the product of the Progressives, who were highly influential in changing the institutional structure of city government from 1890 to the 1920's. Additionally, the New Deal programs of the Roosevelt Administration during the 1930's changed the character of local politics. Poverty-stricken groups began to turn their attention to social welfare agencies for assistance rather than to seek help from machine politicians. As the power and influence of the old-style city machines waned, the social welfare agencies became dominant in the provision of city services. Theodore J. Lowi (Article 14) characterizes the shift of power from the party machines to the social welfare agencies in terms of an emerging "bureaucratic city-state." City bureaucracies have replaced party machines and, in doing so, have become new-style machine organizations in their own right. These new-style machines are "islands of functional power," organized around specific social welfare services and clientele.

The administrative machines are not centralized to the same extent as the older political machines were. Rather, each large agency provides specific services. Formal legal authority and bureaucratic management characterize the operation of these power centers rather than voter mobilization and a material reward exchange system. Such bureaucratic mechanisms may be relatively slow in responding to the demands of different groups in the cities. In fact, protest actions against faceless and depersonalized social welfare agencies may prove more frustrating to dissatisfied citizens than direct participation in the electoral arena.

In addition to party machines, municipal reform, and bureaucratic power, "community power structure" can be used as the framework within which to examine the pattern of urban politics. Who controls American cities? Who really runs things? Is it a monolithic power structure which acts in its own self-interest? Is the leadership group more concerned with business and financial issues than it is with political and social welfare matters? Or, is the leadership broadly representative of the masses? Are politicians and mayors the "real" community leaders? How can local leaders best be identified? How are decisions made? Who participates in the decision-making process?

The academic debate between *elitists* and *pluralists* has dominated the literature of community power. Led by Floyd Hunter's study of Atlanta, the elitists contend that power and influence are tightly controlled by a covert structure of economic interests (businessmen, bankers, financiers, etc.). In contrast, in a study of New Haven, Connecticut, the pluralist school of Robert A. Dahl concluded that power is dispersed among multiple centers of influence seeking different objectives. In particular, Mayor Richard Lee formed an executive-centered coalition which effectively balanced the political, social, and economic interests of New Haven while it promoted concrete results that apparently could not have been achieved otherwise.

Michael Parenti (Article 15) is especially concerned with the pluralist assertions that the city political arena is relatively open to all groups who wish to participate. In his review of the literature and penetrating case studies of activist efforts among Newark's black community, Parenti concludes that it is nearly impossible for impoverished minorities to have any meaningful influence over the crucial decisions that directly affect them. In fact, he discovers that lower-income groups exercise no influence over elites, that they can never prevail in a power struggle, and that most critical issues are never openly debated. He observes that the key issues concerning the black community are in fact "non-issues." In other words, the agenda for political discussion is controlled by elites who do not wish to come to grips with the pressing problems of the poor. Therefore, it is not very surprising that inner-city blacks are skeptical about the alleged advantages of participating in a system where they can never have effective input in the decision-making process. In addition to providing important insights into the alienated attitude of the poor toward government, such a conclusion raises serious questions about the validity of placing trust and confidence in the ability of elected leaders to respond to their constituencies.

In response to Professor Parenti's challenging observations, what are big-city mayors capable of accomplishing in today's urban arena? What are the major issues of recent city elections? Are the inner-city minorities quiescent or have they begun to mobilize behind new-style leaders and candidates? What are the critical obstacles to effective mayoral leadership?

In contrast to the party reformers, Mayor Richard J. Daley of Chicago (Article 16) is the single best example of a modern boss-politician leader. He is also perhaps the most powerful Democratic party mayor in the United States. In 1971 Daley was re-elected to his fifth four-year term with 70 per cent of the popular vote. Daley's party leadership comes from his unchallenged supremacy as chairman of the Cook County Democratic Party Committee. From this position he imposes extensive centralization on an extremely decentralized and fragmented local governmental system. His leadership style in city hall has encompassed both administrative reforms and considerable downtown construction. Chicago's mayor is part of a local ruling coalition which includes the business and commercial elite and labor union leaders. But to maintain a good business climate, Mayor Daley has recently found it increasingly necessary to take a hard line on "law and order" in the black ghettoes. Militant leaders in the black community, along with liberals and party dissidents, have been challenging Daley's entrenched leadership.

The Los Angeles mayoral election of 1969 (Article 17) focused directly on the "law and order" issue and racial polarization among city voters. Mayor Samuel W. Yorty, an unabashed maverick Democrat, was seeking re-election to a third term. His leading opponent was Thomas Bradley, a former Los Angeles policeman and a black city councilman. Bradley was a soft-spoken moderate who campaigned against corruption in city government while arguing for new social welfare programs to benefit the blacks and the Mexican-Americans. After Bradley had won a surprising 42 per cent of the vote against Yorty's 26 per cent in the first nonpartisan contest, Yorty unleashed an unrestrained racist and reactionary attack against him. Yorty's anti-black campaign rhetoric typified the "devil theory" in California politics: An allegedly victimized public official blames his powerlessness on certain dangerously "anti-American" forces that are undermining society. By convincing Los Angeles voters that Bradley was linked with the Black Panthers, the Students for a Democratic Society, and the Communist party, Yorty was able to polarize the electorate and win 53 per cent of the vote in the runoff election. Bradley did not effectively answer Yorty's charges until after the final results were tallied.

Unlike both Daley and Yorty, several big-city mayors have tried to cope directly with the racial crisis and the urban malaise by developing innovative social welfare programs and encouraging meaningful community participation in local decision making. However, as James Q. Wilson indicates in Article 18, such mayors may find that support for their programs comes primarily from an "audience" that is significantly different from the local voting constituency. The mayor's audience consists of federal agencies and large foundations which provide grants to the cities, the mass media, and socially-minded suburban residents, none of whom can vote for the mayor. This audience provides the mayor with resources and support, while the voters remain severely polarized, divided, and discontented.

Mayors John V. Lindsay and Richard Hatcher both face considerable leadership dilemmas as a result of the audience-constituency dichotomy. During his two terms as chief executive of the nation's largest city, Mayor Lindsay has become a symbol of the progressive, concerned urban leader. But Lindsay may have a split political image: On the one hand, he is extolled as the foremost national spokesman for the cities and the poor. On the other hand, Lindsay may not be very effective in managing New York City's day-to-day problems, such as inadequate finances, crime, corruption, poverty, and urban decay. In fact, New York City may be ungovernable, and Lindsay can only hope to perform a holding action until he gets more help from both the federal and New York State governments.

When Richard Hatcher was elected mayor of Gary, Indiana, in 1967, he became (along with Carl Stokes of Cleveland) one of the first new black chief executives of a northern, industrial city. Hatcher's election came with the price tag of a bitter, divisive battle with the Lake County Democratic machine. While he successfully united the black community politically, Hatcher found the first year of his administration troubled with severe internal bureaucratic problems requiring not only local expertise but also considerable program assistance from the federal government. Edward Greer (Article 19) questions whether Hatcher can remain a "soul" mayor while he concentrates on reorganizing the city administration to make it more responsive to public needs. Hatcher's overwhelming re-election to a second term in 1971 appears to confirm that he kept community support. Unlike Mayor Lindsay, Hatcher is able to bridge the gap between the conflicting goals of his constituency and his audience.

What would happen if a big-city mayor traded places with the president? Which is the more difficult job: chief executive of a large central city or the United States government? Russell Baker's humorous account of Richard M. Nixon's ordeals as New York City mayor (Article 20) shows us that even the best of intentions by a leader who disavows the existence of urban problems cannot make the urban crisis go away. There is also an element of truth in Baker's satire, since one's perspective of urban problems changes considerably the closer one gets to the heart of the crisis.

The future of city government and politics will depend on the extent to which the concerns of dissafected minorities are accommodated with the will of the majority. Whether the city's white population and governmental leaders will work for a new approach to the issues of race and poverty remains an open question. In any case, the lack of agreement between majority rule and minority demands can only serve to aggravate an already deteriorating urban political crisis.

QUESTIONS FOR DISCUSSION AND DEBATE

1. Even though municipal reformers may have correctly criticized the worst abuses of old-style political machines, did the party bosses provide any positive benefits for the European immigrants in terms of social welfare?

2. Considering the many efforts that have been made to achieve political, electoral, institutional, and administrative reform in American cities, which do you consider to have been the most effective and which the least effective in terms of balancing city-wide and neighborhood needs?

3. In considering contemporary varieties of urban political power, identify several of the critical problems that arise from the clash between black power and the bureaucratic city-state.

4. Community power analyses make several basic assumptions regarding elitist or pluralist decision-making structures in American cities. According to Parenti, the lower classes are largely excluded from both influence structures. Do you agree? If so, what can be done to change this situation?

5. For many years, Mayor Daley has been very successful in resisting the efforts of reformers and blacks to change the Chicago Democratic party. Why?

6. Sam Yorty defeated Thomas Bradley in the 1969 Los Angeles mayoral contest. What were the major political factors that accounted for Bradley's defeat?

7. When mayoral candidates decide to run independent political campaigns, what strategies and tactics will be most likely to achieve success? What problems will these candidates have after being elected?

8. According to Wilson, several contemporary mayors are faced by audience-constituency conflicts. Compare and contrast the relative successes and problems of Mayors Lindsay and Hatcher in resolving these conflicts.

9. Why do you think that more attention has been paid to presidential leadership roles and styles than to mayoral leadership roles and styles? Can the study of mayoral leadership provide useful insights into contemporary urban problems?

The Changing Pattern of Urban Party Politics

Fred I. Greenstein

Highly organized urban political parties are generally conceded to be one of America's distinctive contributions to mankind's repertory of political forms. Just as the two major national parties in the United States are almost universally described in terms of their *dis*organization—their lack of an authoritative command structure—the municipal parties have, until recently, been characterized by most observers in terms of their hierarchical strength. E. E. Schattschneider once summarized this state of affairs in the memorable image of a truncated pyramid: a party system which is weak and ghostlike at the top and solid at the bottom.[1]

This essay deals with the disciplined, largely autonomous local political parties which sprang up in many American cities in the nineteenth century. Much of the literature on these political configurations is heavily pejorative, concerned more with excoriation than explanation. Even the basic nomenclature, "boss" and "machine," is laden with negative connotations, although recently there has been a turn toward nostalgic romanticization of the "vanishing breed" of city bosses.[2]

Here, for reasons which I shall indicate, the attempt shall be to delineate rather than to pass moral judgment: What was the nature of old-style urban party organization? Why did this political pattern develop and how did it operate? What contributed to its short-run persistence in the face of reform campaigns? Under what circumstances have such organizations disappeared and under what circumstances have they continued into the present day—or even undergone

Reprinted from Fred I. Greenstein, "The Changing Pattern of Urban Party Politics," *The Annals*, Vol. 353 (May, 1964), pp. 2–13. Copyright © 1964 by The American Academy of Political and Social Science. Reprinted by permission of the publisher and Fred I. Greenstein.

renaissances? What are the present-day descendants of old-style urban party organizations?

Analytic delineation invariably involves oversimplification. This is doubly necessary in the present case, because our knowledge of the distribution of types of local party organization is scant. We have no census of local political parties, either for today or for the putative heyday of bosses and machines. And there is reason to believe that observers have exaggerated the ubiquity of tightly organized urban political parties in past generations, as well as underestimated somewhat their contemporary prevalence.

OLD-STYLE PARTY ORGANIZATION: DEFINITIONAL CHARACTERISTICS

Ramney and Kendall have persuasively argued that the imprecision and negative connotations of terms like "boss" destroy their usefulness. What, beyond semantic confusion, they ask, can come from classifying politicians into "bosses" versus "leaders"? Such a distinction leads to fruitless preoccupation with the purity of politicians' motives rather than the actuality of their behavior; it overestimates the degree to which figures of the past such as Richard Croker, William Tweed, and Frank Hague were free of public constraints; and it obscures the fact that *all* effective political leaders, whether or not they are popularly labeled as bosses, use quite similar techniques and resources.[3]

Granting these points, it still seems that a recognizable and noteworthy historical phenomenon is hinted at by the venerable terms "boss" and "machine." If the overtones of these terms make us reluctant to use them, we might simply speak of an "old style" of party organization with the following characteristics:

1. There is a disciplined party hierarchy led by a single executive or a unified board of directors.
2. The party exercises effective control over nomination to public office, and, through this, it controls the public officials of the municipality.
3. The party leadership—which quite often is of lower-class social origins—usually does not hold public office and sometimes does not even hold formal party office. At any rate, official position is not the primary source of the leadership's strength.

4. Rather, a cadre of loyal party officials and workers, as well as a core of voters, is maintained by a mixture of material rewards and *nonideological* psychic rewards—such as personal and ethnic recognition, camaraderie, and the like.[4]

THE RISE OF OLD-STYLE PARTY ORGANIZATION

This pattern of politics, Schattschneider comments, "is as American as the jazz band . . . China, Mexico, South America, and southern Italy at various times have produced figures who played roles remotely like that of the American boss, but England, France, Germany, and the lesser democracies of Europe have exhibited no tendency to develop this form of political organization in modern times."[5] What then accounted for the development of old-style party organization in the United States?

The Crokers, Tweeds, and Hagues and their organizations probably could not have arisen if certain broad preconditions had not existed in American society and culture. These include the tradition of freewheeling individualism and pragmatic opportunism, which developed in a prosperous, sprawling new society unrestrained by feudalism, aristocracy, monarchy, an established church, and other traditional authorities. This is the state of affairs which has been commented on by countless observers, even before de Tocqueville, and which has been used to explain such disparate phenomena as the failure of socialism to take hold in the United States, the recurrence of popularly based assaults on civil liberties, and even the peculiarly corrosive form which was taken by American slavery.[6]

It also is possible to identify five more direct determinants of the form that urban party organization took in the nineteenth century, three of them consequences of the Industrial Revolution and two of them results of political institutions and traditions which preceded industrialization.

Massive Urban Expansion

Over a relatively brief span of years, beginning in the mid-nineteenth century, industrial and commercial growth led to a spectacular rise in the number and proportion of Americans concentrated in cities. A thumbnail sketch of urban expansion may be had by simply noting the population of urban and rural areas for each of the twenty-year periods from 1840 to 1920:

	Urban Population	Rural Population
	(in millions)	
1840	1.8	15.2
1860	6.2	25.2
1880	14.1	36.0
1900	30.1	45.8
1920	54.2	51.6

These statistics follow the old Census Bureau classification of areas exceeding 2,500 in population as urban. Growth of larger metropolitan units was even more striking. In 1840 slightly over 300,000 Americans lived in cities—or, rather, a single city, New York—with more than a quarter of a million residents; by 1920 there were twenty-four cities of this size, containing approximately 21 million Americans.

The sheer mechanics of supporting urban populations of this magnitude are, of course, radically different from the requirements of rural life. There must be extensive transportation arrangements; urban dwellers are as dependent upon a constant inflow of food and other commodities as an infant is on the ministrations of adults. A host of new administrative functions must be performed as the population becomes urbanized: street construction and maintenance, bridges, lighting, interurban transportation, sanitary arrangements, fire-fighting, police protection, and so forth. Overwhelming demands suddenly are placed on governments which, hitherto, were able to operate with a minimum of effort and activity.

Disorganized Forms of Urban Government

The forms of government which had evolved in nineteenth-century America were scarcely suitable for meeting the demands of mushrooming cities. Governmental structures reflected a mixture of Jacksonian direct democracy and Madisonian checks and balances. Cities had a multitude of elected officials (sometimes they were elected annually), weak executives, large and unwieldy councils and boards. The formal organization of the cities placed officials in a position permitting and, in fact, encouraging them to checkmate each other's efforts to make and execute policies. Since each official was elected by appealing to his own peculiar constituency and had little incentive to co-operate with his associates, the difficulties caused by the formal limitations of government were exacerbated. In a period when the requirements for governmental action were increasing geometrically, this was a prescription for chaos.

Needs of Businessmen

A third aspect of mid-nineteenth-century American society which contributed to the formation of old-style party organizations was the needs of businessmen. There was an increasing number of merchants, industrialists, and other businessmen, licit and illicit, who needed— and were willing to pay for—the appropriate responses from city governments. Some businessmen wanted to operate unrestrained by municipal authority. Others desired street-railway franchises, paving contracts, construction work, and other transactions connected with the very growth of the cities themselves.

Needs of Dependent Populations

The needs of the bulk of the nineteenth-century urban population were not for profits but for the simple wherewithal to survive and maintain a modicum of dignity. It is difficult in the relatively affluent society of our day to appreciate the vicissitudes of urban life several generations ago: the low wages, long hours, tedious and hazardous working conditions, and lack of security which were the lot of most citizens. Even for native-born Americans, life often was nasty and brutish. But many urbanites were first- and second-generation immigrants who, in addition to their other difficulties, had to face an alien culture and language. Between the Civil War and the First World War, the United States managed somehow to absorb 25 million foreigners.

Unrestricted Suffrage

Urban dwellers were not totally without resources for their own advancement. The American tradition of unrestricted male franchise was, in the long run, to work to their advantage. Although it doubtless is true that few city dwellers of the day were aware of the importance of their right to vote, politicians *were* aware of this. Because even the lowliest of citizens was, or could become, a voter, a class of politicians developed building upon the four conditions referred to above: the requirements of organizing urban life, the inability of existing governments to meet these requirements, the presence of businessmen willing to pay for governmental services, and of dependent voting populations in need of security from the uncertainties of their existence.

The old-style urban party leader was as much a product of his time and social setting as was the rising capitalist of the Gilded Age. Building on the conditions and needs of the day, the politician had mainly to supply his own ingenuity and co-ordinating ability in order to tie together the machinery of urban government. If a cohesive party organization could control nominations and elect its own agents to office, the formal fragmentation of government no longer would stand in the way of municipal activity. The votes of large blocs of dependent citizens were sufficient to control nominations and win elections. And the financial support of those who sought to transact business with the city, as well as the revenues and resources of the city government, made it possible to win votes. The enterprising politician who could succeed in governing a city on this basis was a broker *par excellence;* generous brokers' commissions were the rule of the day.

The importance of out-and-out vote-buying on election day as a source of voter support can easily be overestimated. Party organizations curried the favor of voters on a year-long basis. In a day when "better" citizens espoused philosophical variants of Social Darwinism, urban politicians thought in terms of an old-fashioned conception of the welfare state. In the familiar words of Tammany sachem George Washington Plunkitt:

> What holds your grip on your district is to go right down among the poor families and help them in the different ways they need help. I've got a regular system for this. If there's a fire in Ninth, Tenth or Eleventh Avenue, for example, any hour of the day or night, I'm

usually there with some of my election district captains as soon as the fire engines. If a family is burned out I don't ask whether they are Republicans or Democrats, and I don't refer them to the Charity Organization Society, which would investigate their case in a month or two and decide they were worthy of help about the time they are dead from starvation. I just get quarters for them, buy clothes for them if their clothes were burned up, and fix them up 'til they get things runnin' again. It's philanthropy, but it's politics, too—mighty good politics. Who can tell how many votes one of these fires bring me? The poor are the most grateful people in the world, and, let me tell you, they have more friends in their neighborhoods than the rich have in theirs.[7]

With numerous patronage appointees (holders not only of city jobs but also of jobs with concerns doing business with the city), party organizations could readily administer this sort of an informal relief program. And, unlike many latter-day charitable and governmental relief programs, the party's activities did not stop with the provision of mere physical assistance.

I know every man, woman and child in the Fifteenth District, except them that's been born this summer—and I know some of them, too. I know what they like and what they don't like, what they are strong at and what they are weak in, and I reach them by approachin' at the right side.

For instance, here's how I gather in the young men. I hear of a young feller that's proud of his voice, thinks that he can sing fine. I ask him to come around to Washington Hall and join our Glee Club. He comes and sings, and he's a follower of Plunkitt for life. Another young feller gains a reputation as a baseball player in a vacant lot. I bring him into our baseball club. That fixes him. You'll find him workin' for my ticket at the polls next election day. Then there's the feller that likes rowin' on the river, the young feller that makes a name as a waltzer on his block, the young feller that's handy with his dukes—I rope them all in by givin' them opportunities to show themselves off. I don't trouble them with political arguments. I just study human nature and act accordin'.[8]

This passage reflects some of the ways in which party activities might be geared to the *individual* interests of voters. *Group* interests were at least as important. As each new nationality arrived in the city, politicians rather rapidly accommodated to it and brought it into the mainstream of political participation. Parties were concerned with the votes of immigrants virtually from the time of their arrival. Dockside naturalization and voter enrollment was not unknown.

But if the purpose of the politicians was to use the immigrants, it soon became clear that the tables could be turned. In Providence, Rhode Island, for example, a careful study of the assimilation of immigrant groups into local politics shows that, within thirty years after the arrival of the first representative of a group in the city, it began to be represented in the councils of one or both parties. Eventually, both of the local parties came to be dominated by representatives of the newer stocks. Thus, in 1864 no Irish names appear on the lists of Democratic committeemen in Providence; by 1876 about a third of the names were Irish; by the turn of the century, three-quarters were Irish. In time, the Republican party became the domain of politicians of Italian ancestry.[9] Perhaps the most dramatic example to date of urban party politics as an avenue of upward social mobility was in the antecedents of President Kennedy, whose great-grandfather was an impoverished refugee of the Irish potato famine, his grandfather a saloon keeper and a classical old-time urban political leader, his father a multimillionnaire businessman, presidential advisor, and ambassador to the Court of St. James's.

When the range of consequences of old-time party organizations is seen, it becomes apparent why moral judgments of "the boss and the machine" are likely to be inadequate. These organizations often were responsible for incredible corruption, but they also—sometimes through the very same activities—helped incorporate new groups into American society and aided them up the social ladder. The parties frequently mismanaged urban growth on a grand scale, but they *did* manage urban growth at a time when other instrumentalities for governing the cities were inadequate. They plied voters, who might otherwise have organized more aggressively to advance their interests, with Thanksgiving Day turkeys and buckets of coal. But, by siphoning off discontent and softening the law, they probably contributed to the generally pacific tenor of American politics. It seems fruitless to attempt to capture this complexity in a single moral judgment. One can scarcely weigh the incorporation of immigrant groups against the proliferation of corruption and strike an over-all balance.

WHY REFORMERS WERE "MORNIN' GLORIES"

Stimulated by high taxes and reports of corruption and mismanagement on a grand scale, antiboss reform movements, led by the more prosperous elements of the cities, became increasingly common late in the nineteenth century. Compared with the regular party politicians of their day, reformers were mere fly-by-night dilettantes— "mornin' glories."[10] They lacked the discipline and the staying power to mount a year-long program of activities. Perhaps more important, the values of the reformers were remote from—in fact, inconsistent with—the values of the citizens whose support would be needed to keep reform administrations in office. Reformers ordinarily saw low taxes and business-like management of the cities as the exclusive aim of government. To the sweatshop workers, grinding out a marginal existence, these aims were at best meaningless, at worst direct attacks on the one agency of society which seemed to have his interests at heart.

THE DECLINE OF OLD-STYLE PARTY ORGANIZATION

Although in the short run old-style party organizations were marvelously immune to the attacks of reformers, in recent decades the demise of this political form has been widely acclaimed. Because of the absence of reliable trend data, we cannot document "the decline of the machine" with precision. The decline does seem to have taken place, although only partly as a direct consequence of attempts to reform urban politics. Events have conspired to sap the traditional resources used to build voter support and to make voters less interested in those resources which the parties still command.

Decline in the Resources of Old-Style Urban Politicians

Most obviously, job patronage is no longer availabe in as great a quantity as it once was. At the federal level and in a good many of the states (as well as numerous cities), the bulk of jobs are filled by civil service procedures. Under these circumstances, the most a party politician may be able to do is seek some minor form of preferment for an otherwise qualified job applicant. Furthermore, the technical requirements of many appointive positions are sufficiently complex to make it inexpedient to fill them with unqualified personnel.[11] And private concerns doing business with the cities are not as likely to be sources of patronage in a day when the franchises have been given out and the concessions granted.

Beyond this, many modern governmental techniques—accounting and auditing requirements, procedures for letting bids, purchasing procedures, even the existence of a federal income tax—restrict the opportunities for dishonest and "honest" graft. Some of these procedures were not instituted with the explicit purpose of hampering the parties. Legislation designed deliberately to weaken parties *has*, however, been enacted—for example, nomination by direct primary and nonpartisan local elections, in which party labels are not indicated on the ballot. Where other conditions are consistent with tight party organization, techniques of this sort seem not to have been especially effective; old-style parties are perfectly capable of controlling nominations in primaries, or of persisting in formally nonpartisan jurisdictions. But, together with the other party weakening factors, explicit antiparty legislation seems to have taken its toll.

Decline of Voter Interest in Rewards Available to the Parties

Even today it is estimated that the mayor of Chicago has at his disposal 6,000 to 10,000 city patronage jobs. And there are many ways of circumventing good government, antiparty legislation. An additional element in the decline of old-style organization is the increasing disinterest of many citizens in the rewards at the disposal of party politicians. Once upon a time, for example, the decennial federal census was a boon to those local politicians whose party happened to be in control of the White House at census time. The temporary job of door-to-door federal census enumerator was quite a satisfactory reward for the party faithful. In 1960 in many localities, party politicians found census patronage more bother than boon; the wages for this task compared poorly with private wages, and few voters were willing to put in the time and leg work. Other traditional patronage jobs—

custodial work in city buildings, employment with departments of sanitation, street repair jobs—were becoming equally undesirable, due to rising levels of income, education, and job security.

An important watershed seems to have been the New Deal, which provided the impetus, at state and local levels as well as the federal level, for increased governmental preoccupation with citizen welfare. The welfare programs of party organizations were undercut by direct and indirect effects of social security, minimum wage legislation, relief programs, and collective bargaining. And, as often has been noted, the parties themselves, by contributing to the social rise of underprivileged groups, helped to develop the values and aspirations which were to make these citizens skeptical of the more blatant manifestations of machine politics.

VARIETIES OF CONTEMPORARY URBAN POLITICS

Nationally in 1956, the Survey Research Center found that only 10 per cent of a cross section of citizens reported being contacted personally by political party workers during the year's presidential campaign. Even if we consider only nonsouthern cities of over 100,000 population, the percentage is still a good bit less than 20.[12] This is a far cry from the situation which would obtain if party organizations were well developed and assiduous. But national statistics conceal a good bit of local variation. A survey of Detroit voters found that only 6 per cent of the public remembered having been approached by political party workers; in fact, less than a fifth of those interviewed even knew that there *were* party precinct officials in their district.[13] Reports from a number of other cities—for example, Seattle and Minneapolis—show a similar vacuum in party activity.[14]

In New Haven, Connecticut, in contrast, 60 per cent of the voters interviewed in a 1959 survey reported having been contacted by party workers.[15] The continuing importance of parties in the politics of this municipality has been documented at length by Robert A. Dahl and his associates.[16] New Haven's Mayor Richard C. Lee was able to obtain support for a massive urban redevelopment program, in spite of the many obstacles in the way of favorable action on such programs elsewhere, in large part because of the capacity of an old-style party organization to weld together the government of a city with an extremely "weak" formal charter. Lee commanded a substantial majority on the board of aldermen and, during the crucial period for ratification of the program, was as confident of the votes of Democratic aldermen as a British Prime Minister is of his parliamentary majority. Lee was far from being a mere creative creature of the party organization which was so helpful to him, but he also was effectively vetoed by the party when he attempted to bring about governmental reforms which would have made the mayor less dependent upon the organization to obtain positive action.[17]

Further evidence of the persistence of old-style party activities came from a number of other studies conducted in the late 1950's. For example, in 1957 party leaders from eight New Jersey counties reported performing a wide range of traditional party services, in response to an ingeniously worded questionnaire administered by Professor Richard T. Frost.[18]

Services Performed by New Jersey Politicians

The Service	Percentage Performing It "Often"
Helping deserving people get public jobs	72
Showing people how to get their social security benefits, welfare, unemployment compensation, etc.	54
Helping citizens who are in difficulty with the law. Do you help get them straightened out?	62

There was even some evidence in the 1950's of a rebirth of old-style urban party activities—for example, in the once Republican-dominated city of Philadelphia, where an effective Democratic old-style organization was put together. Often old-style organizations seem to exist in portions of contemporary cities, especially the low-income sections. These, like the reform groups to be described below, serve as factions in city-wide politics.[19]

Why old-style politics persists in some settings but not others is not fully clear. An impressionistic survey of the scattered evidence suggests, as might be expected, that the older pattern continues in those localities which most resemble the situations which originally spawned strong local parties in the nineteenth century. Eastern industrial cities, such as New Haven, Philadelphia, and many of the New Jersey cities, have sizable low-income groups in need of traditional party services. In many of these areas, the legal impediments to party activity also are minimal: Connecticut, for example, was the last state in the union to adopt direct primary legislation, and nonpartisan local election systems are, in general, less common in industrial cities than in cities without much manufacturing activity.[20] Cities in which weak, disorganized parties are reported—like Seattle, Minneapolis, and even Detroit (which, of course, *is* a manufacturing center of some importance)—are quite often cities in which nonpartisan institutions have been adopted.

SOME NEW-STYLE URBAN POLITICAL PATTERNS

In conclusion, we may note two of the styles of politics which have been reported in contemporary localities where old-style organizations have become weak or nonexistent: the politics of nonpartisanship and the new "reform" factions within some urban Democratic parties. Both patterns are of considerable intrinsic interest to students of local government. And, as contrasting political forms, they provide us with further perspective on the strengths and weaknesses of old-style urban politics.

The Politics of Nonpartisanship

The nonpartisan ballot now is in force in 66 per cent of American cities over 25,000 in population. Numerous styles of politics seem to take place beneath the façade of nonpartisanship. In some communities, when party labels are eliminated from the ballot, the old parties continue to operate much as they have in the past; in other communities, new local parties spring up to contest the nonpartisan elections. Finally, nonpartisanship often takes the form intended by its founders: no organized groups contest elections; voters choose from a more or less self-selected array of candidates.

In the last of these cases, although nonpartisanship has its intended effect, it also seems to have had—a recent body of literature suggests[21]—a number of unintended side effects. One of these is voter confusion. Without the familiar device of party labels to aid in selecting candidates, voters may find it difficult to select from among the sometimes substantial list of names on the ballot. Under these circumstances, a bonus in votes often goes to candidates with a familiar sounding name—incumbents are likely to be re-elected, for example—or even candidates with a favorable position on the ballot. In addition, campaigning and other personal contacts with voters become less common, because candidates no longer have the financial resources and personnel of a party organization at their disposal and therefore are dependent upon personal financing or backing from interest groups in the community.

Nonpartisan electoral practices, where effective, also seem to increase the influence of the mass media on voters; in the absence of campaigning, party canvassing, and party labels, voters become highly dependent for information as well as advice on the press, radio, and television. Normally, mass communications have rather limited effects on people's behavior compared with face-to-face communication such as canvassing by party workers.[22] Under nonpartisan circumstances, however, he who controls the press is likely to have much more direct and substantial effect on the public.

Ironically, the "theory" of nonpartisanship argues that by eliminating parties a barrier between citizens and their officials will be removed. In fact, nonpartisanship often attenuates the citizen's connections with the political system.

The Reform Democrats

The doctrine of nonpartisanship is mostly a product of the Progressive era. While nonpartisan local political systems continue to be adopted and, in fact, have become more common in recent decades, most of the impetus for this development results from the desire of communities to adopt city-manager systems. Nonpartisanship simply is part of the package which normally goes along with the popular city-manager system.

A newer phenomenon on the urban political scene is the development, especially since the 1932 presidential campaign, of ideologically motivated grass-roots party organizations within the Democratic party.[23] The ideology in question is liberalism: most of the reform organizations are led and staffed by college-educated intellectuals, many of whom were activated politically by the candidacy of Adlai Stevenson. In a few localities, there also have been grass-roots Republican organizations motivated by ideological considerations: in the Republican case, Goldwater conservatism.

New-style reformers differ in two major ways from old-style reformers: their ideological concerns extend beyond a preoccupation with governmental efficiency alone (they favor racial integration and improved housing and sometimes devote much of their energy to advocating "liberal" causes at the national level); secondly, their strategy is to work within and take control of the parties, rather than to reject the legitimacy of parties. They do resemble old-style reformers in their preoccupation with the evils of "bossism" and machine politics.

There also is an important resemblance between the new reform politican and the old-style organization man the reformer seeks to replace. In both cases, very much unlike the situation which seems to be stimulated by nonpartisanship, the politician emphasizes extensive face-to-face contact with voters. Where reformers have been successful, it often has been by beating the boss at his own game of canvassing the election district, registering and keeping track of voters, and getting them to the polls.[24]

But much of the day-to-day style of the traditional urban politician is clearly distasteful to the new reformers: they have generally eschewed the use of patronage and, with the exceptions of campaigns for housing code enforcement, they have avoided the extensive service operations to voters and interest groups which were central to old-style party organizations. For example, when election district captains and other officials of the Greenwich Village Independent Democrats, the reform group which deposed New York Democrat County Leader Carmine DeSapio in his own election district, were asked the

Services Performed by New York Reform Democrats[25]

The Service	Percentage Performing It "Often"
Helping deserving people get public jobs	0
Showing people how to get their social security benefits, welfare, unemployment compensation, etc.	5
Helping citizens who are in difficulty with the law. Do you help get them straightened out?	6

same set of questions about their activities used in the New Jersey study, strikingly different responses were made.

The successes of this class of new-style urban party politician have vindicated a portion of the classical strategy of urban party politics, the extensive reliance upon canvassing and other personal relations, and also have shown that under some circumstances it is possible to organize such activities with virtually no reliance on patronage and other material rewards. The reformers have tapped a pool of political activists used by parties elsewhere in the world—for example, in Great Britain—but not a normal part of the American scene. One might say that the reformers have "discovered" the British Labor constituency parties.

It is where material resources available to the parties are limited, for example, California, and where voter interest in these resources is low, that the new reformers are successful. In practice, however, the latter condition has confined the effectiveness of the reform Democrats largely to the more prosperous sections of cities; neither their style nor their programs seem to be successful in lower-class districts.[26] The areas of reform Democratic strength are generally *not* the areas which contribute greatly to Democratic pluralities in the cities. And, in many cities, the reformers' clientele is progressively diminishing as higher-income citizens move outward to the suburbs. Therefore, though fascinating and illuminating, the new reform movement must at least for the moment be considered as little more than a single manifestation in a panorama of urban political practices.[27]

CONCLUSION

The degree to which *old-style* urban party organizations will continue to be a part of this panorama is uncertain. Changes in the social composition of the cities promise to be a major factor in the future of urban politics. If, as seems possible, many cities become lower-class, nonwhite enclaves, we can be confident that there will be a continuing market for the services of the service-oriented old-style politician. Whether or not this is the case, many lessons can be culled from the history of party politics during the years of growth of the American cities—lessons which are relevant, for example, to studying the politics of urbanization elsewhere in the world.[28] In the nineteenth century, after all, the United States was an "emerging," "modernizing" nation, facing the problems of stability and democracy which are now being faced by countless newer nations.

NOTES

1. E. E. Schattschneider, *Party Government* (New York, 1942), pp. 162–169.

2. Among the better known accounts are Frank R. Kent, *The Great Game of Politics* (Garden City, N. Y., 1923, rev. ed., 1930); Sonya Forthall, *Cogwheels of Democracy* (New York, 1946); Harold F. Gosnell, *Machine Politics* (Chicago, 1937); and the many case studies of individual bosses. For a recent romanticization, see Edwin O'Connor's novel, *The Last Hurrah* (Boston, 1956).

3. Austin Ranney and Willmoore Kendall, *Democracy and the American Party System* (New York, 1956), pp. 249–252.

4. This last definitional criterion explicitly departs from the characterization of a "machine" in James Q. Wilson's interesting discussion of "The Economy of Patronage," *The Journal of Political Economy*, Vol. 59 (August, 1961), p. 370n., "as that kind of political party which sustains its members through the distribution of material incentives (patronage) rather than nonmaterial incentives (appeals to principle, the fun of the game, sociability, etc.)." There is ample evidence that for many old-style party workers incentives such as "the fun of the game," "sociability," and even "service" are of central importance. See, for example, Edward J. Flynn, *You're the Boss* (New York, 1947), p. 22; James A. Farley, *Behind the Ballots* (New York, 1938), p. 237; and the passage cited in note 8 below. The distinction between "material" and "nonmaterial" incentives would probably have to be discarded in a more refined discussion of the motivations underlying political participation. So-called material rewards, at base, are nonmaterial in the sense that they are valued for the status they confer and for other culturally defined reasons.

5. *Op. cit.*, p. 106.

6. See, for example, Edward A. Shils, *The Torment of Secrecy* (Glencoe, Ill., 1956) and Stanley M. Elkins, *Slavery* (Chicago, 1959, reprinted with an introduction by Nathan Glazer, New York, 1963).

7. William L. Riordon, *Plunkitt of Tammany Hall* (originally published in 1905: republished New York, 1948 and New York, 1963; quotations are from the 1963 edition), pp. 27–28.

8. *Ibid.*, pp. 25–26.

9. Elmer E. Cornwell, Jr., "Party Absorption of Ethnic Groups: The Case of Providence, Rhode Island," *Social Forces*, Vol. 38 (March, 1960), pp. 205–210.

10. Riordon, *op. cit.*, pp. 17–20.

11. Frank J. Sorauf, "State Patronage in a Rural County," *American Political Science Review*, Vol. 50 (December, 1956), pp. 1046–1056.

12. Angus Campbell, Philip E. Converse, Warren E. Miller, and Donald E. Stokes, *The American Voter* (New York, 1960), pp. 426–427. The statistic for non-southern cities was supplied to me by the authors.

13. Daniel Katz and Samuel J. Eldersveld, "The Impact of Local Party Activity on the Electorate," *Public Opinion Quarterly*, Vol. 25 (Spring, 1961), pp. 16–17.

14. Hugh A. Bone, *Grass Roots Party Leadership* (Seattle, 1952); Robert L. Morlan, "City Politics: Free Style," *National Municipal Review*, Vol. 38 (November, 1949), pp. 485–491.

15. Robert A. Dahl, *Who Governs?* (New Haven, 1961), p. 278.

16. *Ibid.*; Nelson W. Polsby, *Community Power and Political Theory* (New Haven, 1963); Raymond E. Wolfinger, *The Politics of Progress* (forthcoming).

17. Raymond E. Wolfinger, "The Influence of Precinct Work on Voting Behavior," *Public Opinion Quarterly*, Vol. 27 (Fall, 1963), pp. 387–398.

18. Frost deliberately worded his questionnaire descriptions of these services favorably in order to avoid implying that respondents were to be censured for indulging in "machine tactics." Richard T. Frost, "Stability and Change in Local Politics," *Public Opinion Quarterly*, Vol. 25 (Summer, 1961), pp. 231–232.

19. James Q. Wilson, "Politics and Reform in American Cities," *American Government Annual, 1962–63* (New York, 1962), pp. 37–52.

20. Phillips Cutright, "Nonpartisan Electoral Systems in American Cities," *Comparative Studies in Society and History*, Vol. 5 (January, 1963), pp. 219–221.

21. For a brief review of the relevant literature, see Fred I. Greenstein, *The American Party System and the American People* (Englewood Cliffs, N. J., 1963), pp. 57–60.

22. Joseph T. Klapper, *The Effects of Mass Communication* (New York, 1960).

23. James Q. Wilson, *The Amateur Democrat* (Chicago, 1962).

24. There is another interesting point of resemblance between old- and new-style urban party politics. In both, an important aspect of the motivation for participation seems to be the rewards of sociability. Tammany picnics and New York Committee for Democratic Voters (CDV) coffee hours probably differ more in decor than in the functions they serve. An amusing indication of this is provided by the committee structure of the Greenwich Village club of the CDV; in addition to the committees dealing with the club newsletter, with housing, and with community action, there is a social committee and a Flight Committee, the latter being concerned with arranging charter flights to Europe for club members. See Vernon M. Goetcheus, *The Village Independent Democrats: A Study in the Politics of the New Reformers* (unpublished senior distinction thesis, Honors College, Wesleyan University, 1963), pp. 65–66. On similar activities by the California Democratic Clubs, see Robert E. Lane, James D. Barber, and Fred I. Greenstein, *Introduction to Political Analysis* (Englewood Cliffs, N. J., 1962); pp. 55–57.

25. Goetcheus, *op. cit.*, p. 138.

26. DeSapio, for example, was generally able to hold on to his lower-class Italian voting support in Greenwich Village; his opponents succeeded largely by activating the many middle- and upper-class voters who had moved into new high-rent housing in the district.

27. Probably because of their emphasis on ideology, the new reform groups also seem to be quite prone to internal conflicts which impede their effectiveness. One is reminded of Robert Michels' remarks about the intransigence of intellectuals in European socialist parties. *Political Parties* (New York, 1962, originally published in 1915), Part 4, Chap. 6.

28. **On the significance** of the American experience with old-style urban politics for the emerging nations, see Wallace S. Sayre and Nelson W. Polsby, "American Political Science and the Study of Urbanization," Committee on Urbanization, Social Science Research Council, mimeo, 1963, pp. 45–48.

ARTICLE 14

Machine Politics—Old and New

Theodore J. Lowi

The political machine is an institution peculiar to American cities. Like the militant party elsewhere, the American machine as a classic type is centralized, integrated, and relatively ruthless. But there the similarity ends.

Machines have been integrated from within, as fraternities; they do not arise out of opposition to the state or to a hostile class. The power of the machine rested upon being integrated in a dispersed, permissive, and unmobilized society. Integrated, however, in a special American way.

The most militant parties of Europe have depended upon homogeneity—enforced if necessary. Machines have developed ingenious techniques for capitalizing upon ethnic and racial heterogeneity. Militant parties have typically been based on common ends at the center, holding the periphery together by fear. The machines were based upon a congeries of people with uncommon ends, held together at the center by logrolling and at the periphery by *fraternité, egalité,* and ignorance.

As to the significance of the machine for the development of the American city, the returns are still not in. Typically, it was the European observers who were the first to appreciate this unusual, Amer-

Reprinted by permission of the author and the publisher from Theodore Lowi, "Machine Politics—Old and New," in Harold F. Gosnell, *Machine Politics: Chicago Model* (Second Edition, 1968), © 1937, 1968, by the University of Chicago Press. This article is a 10-page version of Professor Lowi's *foreword,* which appeared in *The Public Interest,* No. 9 (Fall 1967), pp. 83–92.

ican phenomenon. Ostrogorski, Bryce, Weber, Michels, Schumpeter, and Duverger each in his own way made an outstanding effort to appreciate the peculiarities of urban democracy in America. Harold F. Gosnell, in *Machine Politics: Chicago Model* (1937), was one of the very first Americans to join that distinguished company with any- thing approaching a systematic treatment of the subject. (By this standard, the muckrakers do not count.)

However, Gosnell was limited by the fact that there was in his time, insufficient experience with alternative forms of big city politics. Too few big cities in the United States had been "reformed" in suf- ficient degree to provide any basis for comparison.

In the 1960's, sufficient time has passed. The machine is nearly dead, and we have experienced lengthy periods of Reform govern- ment. We can now see the machine in perspective.

How does it shape up?

CHICAGO AND NEW YORK

We can begin to introduce perspective by immediately setting aside Gosnell's claim that the Chicago experience on which his book was based is representative. It is the very uniqueness of Chicago's ex- perience with the machine that gives his study such value. It is New York that is the representative big city, not Chicago. Its representa- tiveness derives from the fact that it has experienced Reform in a way that Chicago has not. In 1967, political power in Chicago still has an extremely strong machine base; political power in New York has an entirely new and different base. As New York was being revolution- ized by the New Deal and its successors, the structure of Chicago politics was being reaffirmed. When New York was losing its last machine and entering into a new era of permanent Reform, Chicago's political machine was just beginning to consolidate. New York be- came a loose, multi-party system with wide-open processes of nomina- tion, election, and participation; Chicago became a tight, one-party system. New York sought to strengthen a weak mayor who already operated under a strong-mayor government; Chicago has had the opposite problem of an already strong mayor in a weak-mayor gov- ernment.

To evaluate the machine we must ask whether, by surviving, machine politics in Chicago in any way distorted that city's growth and development. How much change would there have been in Chicago's history if the nationalization of politics had made possible in Chicago, as it did in virtually every other big American city, ways of "licking the ward boss" and altering precinct organization, means of loosening the hold of the county organization on city hall, power for liberating the personnel and policies of the professional agencies of government? We cannot answer these questions for Chicago because the basis of machine strength still exists there, and the conditions for its continuity might well continue through the remainder of the century. However, we may be able to answer them, at least better than before, by looking at Chicago from the vantage point of New York's experience.

Populism and Efficiency

New York city government, like government in almost all large American cities except Chicago, is a product of Reform. It is difficult to understand these cities without understanding the two strains of ideology that guided local Reform movements throughout the past three-quarters of a century. *Populism* and *efficiency,* once the foundation of most local insurgency, are now almost universally triumphant. These two tenets are now the orthodoxy in local practice.

Populism was originally a statement of the evils of every form of bigness in the city, including big business, big churches, big labor, as well as big political organizations. Decentralization was an ultimate goal. In modern form, it has tended to come down to the aim of eliminating political parties, partisanship, and if possible "politics" itself.

Efficiency provided the positive program to replace that which is excised by populist surgery. The doctrine calls essentially for the centralization and rationalization of government activities and services to accompany the decentralization of power. Some Reformers assumed that services do not constitute power. Others assumed the problem away altogether by positing a neutral civil servant who would not abuse centralized government but who could use it professionally to reap the economies effected by rationalization and by specialization. That was the secret of the business system; and, after all, the city is rather like a business. ("There is no Republican or Democratic way to clean a street.")

While there are many inconsistent assumptions and goals between the doctrines of populism and efficiency, they lived well together. Their coexistence was supported by the fact that different wings of the large, progressive movement they generated were responsible for each. Populism was largely the province of the working class, "progressive" wing. Doctrines of efficiency were very much the responsibility of the upper class wing. Populism resided with the politician-activists. Efficiency was developed by the intellectuals, including several distinguished university presidents, such as Seth Low, Andrew Dickson White, Harold Dodd, and pre-eminently, Woodrow Wilson, who, while still a professor of political science, wrote a classic essay proclaiming the virtues of applying Prussian principles of administration in the United States.

These two great ideas were, by a strange and wonderful chemistry, combined into a movement whose influence forms a major chapter of American history. Charters and laws have been enacted that consistently insulate city government from politics, meaning party politics. It has become increasingly necessary, with each passing decade, to grant each bureaucratic agency autonomy to do the job as each commissioner saw fit, as increasingly appointments were made of professionals in each agency's fields.

On into the 1960's, the merit system extends itself "upward, outward, and downward," to use the Reformers' own rhetoric. Recruitment to the top posts is more and more frequent from the ranks of those who have made careers in their agencies, party backgrounds increasingly being a mark of automatic disqualification. Reform has succeeded in raising public demand for political morality and in making "politics" a dirty word. A "good press" for mayors results from their determination to avoid intervening in the affairs of one department after another. The typical modern mayor is all the more eager to co-operate because this provides an opportunity to delegate responsibility. Absolution-before-the-fact for government agencies has become part of the mayoral swearing-in ceremony.

Reform has triumphed and the cities are better run than ever before. But that is, unfortunately, not the end of the story, nor would it have been the end of the story even had there been no Negro revolution. The triumph of Reform really ends in paradox: *Cities like New York became well-run but ungoverned.*

The New Machines

Politics under Reform are not abolished. Only their form is altered. *The legacy of Reform is the bureaucratic city-state.* Destruction of the party foundation of the mayoralty cleaned up many cities but also destroyed the basis for sustained, central, popularly-based action. This capacity, with all its faults, was replaced by the power of professionalized agencies. But this has meant creation of new bases of power. Bureaucractic agencies are not neutral; they are only independent.

Modernization and Reform in New York and other cities has meant replacement of Old Machines with New Machines. The bureaucracies—that is, the professionally organized, autonomous career agencies—are the New Machines.

Sociologically, the Old Machine was a combination of rational goals and fraternal loyalty. The cement of the organization was trust and discipline created out of long years of service, probation, and testing, slow promotion through the ranks, and centralized control over the means of reward. Its power in the community was based upon services rendered to the community.

Sociologically, the New Machine is almost exactly the same sort of an organization. But there are also significant differences. The New Machines are more numerous, in any given city. They are functional rather than geographic in their scope. They rely on formal authority rather than upon majority acquiescence. And they probably work with a minimum of graft and corruption. But these differences do not alter their definition; they only help to explain why the New Machine is such a successful form of organization.

The New Machines are machines because they are relatively irresponsible structures of power. That is, each agency shapes important public policies, yet the leadership of each is relatively self-perpetuating and not readily subject to the controls of any higher authority.

The New Machines are machines in that the power of each, while resting ultimately upon services rendered to the community, depends upon its cohesiveness as a small minority in the midst of the vast dispersion of the multitude.

The modern city has become well-run but ungoverned because it has, according to Wallace Sayre and Herbert Kaufman, become comprised of "islands of functional power" before which the modern mayor stands denuded of authority. No mayor of a modern city has predictable means of determining whether the bosses of the New Machines—the bureau chiefs and the career commissioners—will be loyal to anything but their agency, its work, and related professional norms. Our modern mayor has been turned into the likes of a French Fourth Republic Premier facing an array of intransigent parties in the National Assembly. These modern machines, more monolithic by far than their ancient brethren, are entrenched by law, and are supported by tradition, the slavish loyalty of the newspapers, the educated masses, the dedicated civic groups, and, most of all, by the organized clientele groups enjoying access under existing arrangements.

Organized Decentralization

The Reform response to the possibility of an inconsistency between running a city and governing it has been to assume the existence of the Neutral Specialist, the bureaucratic equivalent to law's Rational Man. The assumption is that, if men know their own specialties well enough, they are capable of reasoning out solutions to problems they share with men of equal but different technical competencies. That is a very shaky assumption indeed. Charles Frankel's analysis of such an assumption in Europe provides an appropriate setting for a closer look at it in modern New York; ". . . different [technical] elites disagree with each other; the questions with which specialists deal spill over into areas where they are *not* specialists, and they must either hazard amateur opinions or ignore such larger issues, which is no better . . ."

During the 1950's, government experts began to recognize that, despite vast increases in efficiency flowing from the defeat of the Old Machine, New York city government was somehow lacking. These concerns culminated in the 1961 Charter, in which the Office of Mayor was strengthened in many impressive ways. But it was quickly discovered that no amount of formal centralization could definitively overcome the real decentralization around the Mayor. It was an organized disorganization, which made a mockery of the new Charter. The following examples, although drawn from New York, are of virtually universal application:

1. Welfare problems always involve several of any city's largest agencies, including Health, Welfare, Hospitals, etc. Yet during more

than 40 years, successive mayors of New York failed to reorient the Department of Health away from a "regulative" toward a "service" concept of organization. And many new aspects of welfare must be set up in new agencies if they are to be set up at all. The new poverty programs were set up very slowly in all the big cities—except Chicago.

2. Water pollution control has been "shared" by such city agencies as the Departments of Health, Parks, Public Works, Sanitation, Water Supply, and so on. No large city, least of all New York, has an effective program to combat even the local contributions to pollution. The same is true of air pollution control, although for some years New York has had a separate Department for this purpose.

3. Land-use patterns are influenced one way or another by a large variety of highly professional agencies. It has proven virtually impossible in any city for one of these agencies to impose its criteria on the others. In New York, the opening of Staten Island by the Narrows Bridge, in what may be the last large urban frontier, found the city with no plan for the revolution that is taking place in property values and land uses in that borough.

4. Transportation is also the province of agencies too numerous to list. Strong mayors throughout the country have been unable to prevent each from going its separate way. To take just one example: New York pursued a vast off-street parking program, at a cost of nearly $4,000 per parking space, at the very moment when local rail lines were going bankrupt.

5. Enforcement of civil rights is imposed upon almost all city agencies by virtue of Federal, state, and local legislation. But efforts to set up public, then City Council, review of police processes in New York have been successfully opposed by professional police officials. Efforts to try pairing and busing on a very marginal, experimental basis have failed. The police commissioner resigned at the very suggestion that values other than professional police values be imposed upon the Department, even when the imposition came via the respected tradition of "legislative oversight." The Superintendent of Education, an "outsider," was forced out; he was replaced by a career administrator. One education journalist at that time said: "Often . . . a policy proclaimed by the Board [of Education], without the advice and consent of the professionals, is quickly turned into mere paper policy. . . . The veto power through passive resistance by professional administrators is virtually unbeatable. . . ."

The decentralization of city government toward its career bureaucracies has resulted in great efficiency for the activities around which each bureaucracy was organized. The city is indeed well-run. But what of those activities around which bureaucracies are not organized, or those which fall between or among agencies' jurisdictions? For these, as suggested by the cases above, the cities are suffering either stalemate or elephantiasis—an affliction whereby a particular activity, say, urban renewal or parkways, gets pushed to its ultimate "success" totally without regard to its importance compared to the missions of other agencies. In these as well as in other senses, the cities are ungoverned.

The 1961 Election

Mayors have tried a variety of strategies to cope with these situations. But the 1961 mayoralty election in New York was the ultimate dramatization of the mayor's plight. This election was a confirmation of the New York system, and will some day be seen as one of the most significant in American urban history. For New York, it was the culmination of many long-run developments. For the country, it may be the first of many to usher in the bureaucratic state.

The primary significance of the election can be found in the spectacle of a mayor attempting to establish a base of power for himself in the bureaucracies. The Mayor's running mate for President of the City Council had been Commissioner of Sanitation, a position which culminated virtually a lifetime career of the holder in the Department of Sanitation. He had an impressive following among the sanitation men—who, it should be added, are organized along precinct lines. The Mayor's running mate for Comptroller had been for many years the city Budget Director. As Budget Director, he had survived several Administrations and two vicious primaries that pitted factions of the Democratic Party against one another. Before becoming Director he had served for a number of years as a professional employee in the Bureau. The leaders of the campaign organization included a former, very popular Fire Commissioner who retired from his commissionership to accept campaign leadership and later to serve as Deputy Mayor, and a former Police Commissioner who had enjoyed a strong following among professional cops as well as in the local Reform movement. Added to this was a new and vigorous party, the

Brotherhood Party, which was composed in large part of unions with broad bases of membership among city employees. Before the end of the election, most of the larger city bureaucracies had political representation in the inner core of the new Administration.

For the 1961 election, Mayor Wagner had put his ticket and his organization together just as the bosses of old had done. In the old days, the problem was to mobilize all the clubhouses, districts, and counties in the city by putting together a balanced ticket about which all adherents could be enthusiastic. The same seems true for 1961, except that by then the clubhouses and districts had been replaced almost altogether by new types of units.

The main point is that destruction of the machine did not, in New York or elsewhere, eliminate the need for political power. It simply altered what one had to do to get it. In the aftermath of twenty or more years of "modern" government, it is beginning to appear that the lack of power can corrupt city hall almost as much as the possession of power. Bureaucracy is, in the United States, a relatively new basis for collective action. As yet, none of us knows quite how to cope with it.

What If . . . .?

These observations and cases are not brought forward to indict Reform cities and acquit Chicago. They are intended only to put Chicago in a proper light and to provide some means of assessing the functions of the machine form of collective action.

Review of Reform government shows simply and unfortunately that the problems of cities, and the irrational and ineffectual ways city fathers go about their business, seem to obtain universally, without regard to form of government or type of power base. All cities have traffic congestion, crime, juvenile delinquency, galloping pollution, ghettos, ugliness, deterioration, and degeneracy. All cities seem to be suffering about equally from the quite recent problem of the weakening legitimacy of public institutions, resulting in collective violence and pressures for direct solution to problems. All cities seem equally hemmed in by their suburbs and equally prevented from getting at the roots of many of their most fundamental problems. Nonpartisan approaches, even the approaches of New York's Republican mayor to Republican suburbs and a Republican governor, have failed to prevent rail bankruptcy in the vast Eastern megalopolis, to abate air or water pollution, to reduce automobile pressure, or to ease the pain of the middle-class Negro in search of escape from his ghetto.

The problems of the city seem to go beyond any of the known arrangements for self-government. However, low public morality and lack of what Banfield and Wilson call "public-regardingness" may be a function simply of poor education and ethnic maladjustment. The Old Machine and its abuses may just have been another reflection of the same phenomena. If that is so, then passage of more time, and the mounting of one socio-cultural improvement after another, might have reformed the machines into public-regarding organs, if they had been permitted to survive.

Are there any strong reasons to believe that real reform could have come without paying the price of eliminating the popular base of political action? Intimations can be found in the last of the machine-recruited leaders of Tammany, Carmine DeSapio and Edward Costikyan. Each was progressively more public-regarding than any of his predecessors. Indeed, Costikyan was a model of political responsibility for whom the new New York had no particular use. However, for this question the best answers may lie in looking afresh at Gosnell's Chicago. With a scientific rigor superior to most political analysis of the 1960's, his book goes further than any other single work to capture what political behavior was like under Old Machine conditions. The sum total of his findings, despite Gosnell's own sentiments, does not constitute a very damning indictment of the Chicago machine—if contemporary experience is kept clearly in mind.

CHICAGO IN PERSPECTIVE

Even amidst the most urgent of depression conditions, the machine in Chicago does not seem to have interfered with the modest degree of rationality distributed throughout the United States. Take for instance the case of voting behavior on referendum proposals, the most issue-laden situation an electorate ever faces. Gosnell criticized the referendum as generally subject to fraud and other types of abuse, and most particularly so in Chicago during the 1920's and '30's. But even so, his figures show that the electorate, despite the machine, did not behave indiscriminately. The theory that universal suffrage provides no check against the irresponsible acceptance of financing schemes which pass the real burden on to future generations is simply not borne out in Chicago. Conservative appeals by the propertied were effective. Over a twelve-year period, including six fat years and six lean years, 66 local bond issues were approved and 48 were rejected. Those rejected included some major bond issues offered for agencies whose leaders had become discredited. Other types of issues show responsiveness to appeals other than local precinct or county organizations. As the antiprohibition campaign began to grow, so did the vote on the prohibition repealer. Clear irrationalities tended to be associated primarily with highly technical proposals involving judicial procedure or taxation, but this is true everywhere, and to much the same degree.

In a bold stroke, Gosnell also tried to assess the influence of the newspapers, the best source for rational—at least nonmachine—voting decisions. For this particular purpose Gosnell's data were weak, but fortunately he was not deterred from asking important questions merely for lack of specially designed data. Factor analysis helped Gosnell tease out of census tract data and newspaper subscription patterns a fairly realistic and balanced sense of the role of the local newspapers. Gosnell was led to conclude that the influence of news media is limited, but that this was a limitation imposed far less by the machine than by the extent to which newspapers were regularly read. Newspaper influence on issues was measurably apparent wherever daily readership was widely established—the machine notwithstanding. Here again is suggested the possibility that real machine domination rested upon a level of education and civic training that was, at the very time of Gosnell's research, undergoing a great deal of change.

Taking all the various findings together, and even allowing for abuses that were always more frequent in cities than towns, and probably more frequent in Gosnell's Chicago than other cities, we can come away from Gosnell's analysis with a picture not at all at odds with V. O. Key's notion of the "responsible electorate."

Gosnell felt his book to be an indictment of machine politics. But today, looking at the Chicago experience from the vantage point of New York's, one feels less able to be so sure.

Power and Pluralism:
A View from the Bottom

Michael Parenti

It is said we live in a pluralistic society, and indeed a glance at the social map of America reveals a vast agglomeration of regional, class, occupational, and ethnic associations all busily making claims upon state, local, and national governing agencies. If by pluralism we mean this multiplicity of public and private interests and identities, then America—like any modern society of size and complexity—is pluralistic. Used in this broad sense, the term is not particularly arresting for those political scientists interested in determining the extent to which power is democratically operative in America. However, if by "pluralism" we mean that the opportunities and resources necessary for the exercise of power are *inclusively* rather than exclusively distributed and that neither the enjoyment of dominance nor the suffering of deprivation is the constant condition of any one group, then the question of whether ours is a pluralistic society is not so easily resolved.

The protracted debate between "pluralists" and "anti-pluralists" is testimony to the difficulties we confront. After investigating "concrete decisions" at the community and national levels, the pluralists conclude that participation in decision making is enjoyed by a variety of competing groups operating in specific issue-areas often in response to the initiatives of democratically elected officials. No evidence is found to support the claim that a corporate "power elite" rules over an inarticulate mass. If there are elites in our society, they are numerous and specialized, and they are checked in their demands by the institutionalized rules of the political culture and by the compet-

Reprinted from *The Journal of Politics*, Vol. 32, No. 3 (August 1970), pp. 501–530, by permission of the publisher and author.

ing demands of other elites, all of whom represent varying, if sometimes overlapping, constituencies.[1] Conflict is multilateral and ever-
changing, and the "bulk of the population consists not of the mass but
of integrated groups and publics, stratified with varying degrees of
power,"[2] and endowed with "a multitude of techniques for exercising
influence on decisions salient to them."[3]

Not long after this theory became the accepted view in American political science, anti-pluralist critics began voicing certain
reservations. The anti-pluralists remain unconvinced that influence
and benefits are widely distributed, and that political and administrative officers operate as guardians of the unorganized majorities and
as the controllers, rather than the servants, of important interests
groups.[4] While not defending the idea of a monolithic power elite,
they question whether elites are mutually restrained by competitive
interaction, observing that many of the stronger elites tend to predominate in their particular spheres of activity more or less unmo-
lested by other elites.[5] Not only are elites often unchecked by public
authority on the most important issues affecting them, but in many
instances *public* decision-making authority has been parcelled out to
private interests on a highly inegalitarian basis.[6] The anti-pluralists
further criticize the pluralists for failing to take notice of the "powers
of pre-emption"; is it not true, for instance, that corporate leaders
often have no need to involve themselves in decision-making efforts
because sufficient anticipatory consideration is given to their interests
by office-holders?[7] Attention, therefore, should be directed to the
"nondecision," "non-issue" powers such as the power to predetermine
the agenda and limit the scope of issue conflict, and the power to
define and propagate "the dominant values . . . myths, rituals and
institutions which tend to favor the vested interests of one or more
groups relative to others."[8]

The pluralists respond to these last few criticisms by noting that
theories about unuttered anticipatory reactions, invisible participants,
and hidden values cannot be scientifically entertained. We may conjure an "infinite regress" of imaginary powers operating behind the
observable decision makers, the pluralists say, but we can study
empirically only what is visible, and only those who can be observed
making decisions or engaging in activity bearing directly upon decision making can be said to share power.

Now I, for one, have no quarrel with the dictum that we observe
only the observable, but it may be suggested that what the pluralists

have defined as "observable" is not all that meets the eyes of other researchers. Particularly troublesome to me is the relative absence of lower-strata groups from most community-power studies and the ease with which their absence is either ignored or explained away.

Let me begin with a fundamental pluralist proposition, viz., only those who participate in the decision process share in the exercise of power. If true, then it would follow that those who do *not* participate in decision making do *not* share power. This latter proposition, however, is treated rather equivocally by most pluralists. If the non-participants are of the upper classes, it is concluded that they are non-influential. But if the non-participants are from the lower income groups, it is usually maintained that they exercise "indirect" influence.

The New Haven investigation conducted by Robert Dahl and his former student, Nelson Polsby, represents one of the most important of the pluralists' community studies and, for the moment, I shall concentrate on what is revealed in that work. Dahl and Polsby discover that New Haven's active decision makers consist primarily of civic and political leaders centering around the mayor; only a few of these participants are members of the "economic elite." For one to argue that municipal authorities are under the power of the economic elite one must demonstrate, according to Polsby, that upper-class members "customarily give orders to political and civic leaders" which are obeyed, or that they regularly and successfully block policies, or that they place "their own people in positions of leadership." Finding to his own satisfaction that none of these conditions obtain in New Haven, Polsby concludes that the upper class is not preponderantly influential.[9] The only way to determine whether actors are powerful, he says, is to observe a sequence of events demonstrating their power: "If these events take place, then the power of the actor is not 'potential' but actual. If these events do not occur, then what grounds have we to suppose that the actor is powerful? There appear to be no scientific grounds for such an assumption." Those who assign "a high power potential to economic dominants" are therefore "indulging in empirically unjustified speculation."[10]

What, then, of the lower-strata groups that do not participate in decision making? The New Haven study shows that only a miniscule fraction of the citizenry engage in any activity bearing directly upon community decisions and that none of the decision makers are drawn from lower-income groups, white or black.[11] The non-participant, however, exercises "a moderate degree of indirect influence" through his power to elect officials or—if he does not vote—through his "influential contact" with those who do vote, presumably relatives and friends.[12] The vote is an effective popular control because "elected leaders keep the real or imagined preferences of constituents *constantly in mind* in deciding what policies to adopt or reject."[13] Most people, Dahl observes, "use their political resources scarcely at all," some not even bothering to vote; hence they never fully convert their "potential influence" into "actual influence."[14] They do not exert themselves because they feel no compelling need to participate. To assume that citizens, especially of the lower class, should be politically active is, Polsby says, to make "the inappropriate and arbitrary assignment of upper and middle-class values to all actors in the community."[15] There are "personally functional" and habitual reasons for lower-class withdrawal having nothing to do with political life. Polsby further assures us that "most of the American communities studied in any detail seem to be relatively healthy political organisms which means that there are bound to be considerable conservatism and self-preservation rather than innovation and demand for change within the system."[16]

Here it seems we are confronted with a double standard for the measurement of power. (1) Despite the fact that large corporation leaders and other economic notables control vast resources of wealth and property that affect the livelihoods, living standards, and welfare of the community, it cannot be presumed that they exercise indirect or potential influence over political leaders. Furthermore, it is unscientific to speak of political leaders as having anticipatory reactions to the interests of these economic elites. There must be discernible evidence of upper-class participation and victory in specific policy conflicts. But (2) it may be presumed that the unorganized, less-educated, lower-income voters exercise an indirect influence over decisions to which they have no easy access and about which they often have no direct knowledge. They accomplish this by evoking in the minds of political leaders a set of "constant" but unspecified anticipatory reactions to the voters' policy preferences, preferences that are themselves frequently unspecified and unarticulated.

If it may be postulated, without the benefit of empirical research that ordinary voters exercise indirect controls over decisions, then we can conclude that any community in America that holds elections is, by virtue of that fact, pluralistic. We have thereby presumed to know precisely the things that need to be empirically determined: to whose needs and imperatives do elected officials respond, as measured by which actual decisions and outcomes?

If, however, lower-class groups do not participate in decision-making activities, how can we determine the extent of their influence, if any, over actual decisions? And what meaning can we ascribe to their non-participation? I would suggest that instead of declaring them to be an unknown but contented entity, we should directly investigate the less privileged elements of a community to determine why they are not active, and what occurs when they attempt to become active. Studies of policy struggles involving lower-strata groups are a rarity in the literature of American political science partly because the poor seldom embark upon such ventures[17] but also because our modes of analysis have defined the scope of our research so as to exclude the less visible activities of the underprivileged. "The case study approach to power location should not be discredited," Todd Gitlin reminds us, "but why are only certain cases studied?"[18]

What I shall attempt to do in the following case studies of three "issue-areas" is to observe power "from the bottom up." I shall not attempt any detailed analysis of the maneuvers and interactions within official circles normally considered a central part of the "decision-making process"; rather the focus will be on actors who try to influence decisions from afar, the active non-elites who attempt to overcome the social distance that separates the subject of politics from the object by trying to participate both in the creation of an issue-agenda and in issue-decisions. Any assessment of non-elite influence should take into account actual outcomes: that is to say, to determine whether the protest group does or does not prevail we need to look at the effects of the contested decision. A view from the bottom requires a shift in emphasis away from studying process as an end in itself divorced from substantive effects (who governs?) and toward some empirical consideration of substantive effects (who gets what?). The presumptions are that substantive effects are, after all, what make the decision process a meaningful and important topic of study, and that they are certainly an essential variable for political actors whose efforts otherwise cannot be properly understood.

Many questions of broad theoretical import might be entertained when investigating the limits and realities of lower-class power and participation. Attention in the present study will be directed primarily to the following theoretical considerations: Is the present political system, as pluralists contend, responsive to the interests of all groups that seek to exercise influence through legitimate channels? And do the protest groups that represent the more acutely deprived strata suffer liabilities within the political system of a kind not usually accounted for in the pluralist theory?

II

Early in the summer of 1964, at the invitation of a private welfare group, 13 members of the Students for a Democratic Society went into the lower Clinton Hill neighborhood in Newark's South Ward and in cooperation with local residents formed the Newark Community Union Project (NCUP), an organization intended to assist ghetto people in the building of a social-protest movement.

The lower Clinton Hill area was turning into an all-black area whose outward appearance of greenery and trees did not quite hide the underlying conditions of overcrowding, poverty, underemployment, and insufficient public services.[19] The already strained housing conditions were further aggravated by the influx of displaced persons whose previous neighborhoods were being obliterated by urban-renewal projects. Nevertheless, as is the case with many large ghettos, the population was somewhat heterogeneous, including in addition to the very poor some relatively comfortable wage-earners, semi-professional and even professional people who remained in the South Ward because of racial discrimination or personal preference.

The NCUP organizers began making contacts with the poorer residents, hoping to find specific issues that would bring people together and involve them in community action.[20] The people who came to NCUP meetings, numbering from 25 to 80 on different occasions, and others interviewed in their homes or on street corners almost invariably expressed anger and distress about such problems as job discrimination, job shortages, poor wages, garbage- and snow-removal services, inadequate schools, rent gouging, police brutality, merchant overpricing, etc. "I am mad," said one, "I am angry when I see my people living the way they do." Coupled with these feelings was the widespread conviction that protest efforts would meet with frustration, and that the voices of the poor would not be heard, and if heard, not heeded. "What's the use?" "Nothing can ever get changed." "Why get your hopes up?" were some of the more common remarks. Nevertheless, some 15 residents and seven white students were resolute enough to give almost full-time efforts, staying with NCUP for the duration of its existence, ("This time the poor man's going to do something for himself," said one resident). Another 25 blacks were intensely active for periods extending from several months to half a year, and still scores of others involved themselves intermittently. It may be roughly estimated that as many as 150 residents participated in some major or minor way over a two-and-a-half year period in public demonstrations, rent strikes, meetings, and other organizational activities.[21]

The problems to which organizers could address themselves were varied and enormous. Several considerations determined priorities: first, what did the people themselves feel most strongly about; second, were there visible targets and goals; third, was there some chance of success? During a period extending from 1964 to 1966 efforts focused primarily on the following issues.

Issue #1 Housing

The poor in the South Ward area paid monthly rents ranging from $115 to $135 for the privilege of living without benefit of proper heating and water facilities in small sub-divided apartments in deteriorated, ill-lit, unpainted, rat-infested buildings. Groups of tenants organized by NCUP made several trips to municipal housing authorities to complain of conditions, winning nothing more than promises to "look into things." Subsequent visits to the Human Rights Commission induced that agency to send inspectors to the buildings in question. The inspectors found evidence of widespread building-code violations (as many as 125 in one apartment house), filed reports and sent copies to the landlords in question. Lacking enforcement powers of its own, the Commission took no further actions. After two months had passed without any response from the building owners, NCUP began organizing rent strikes in some of the worst buildings in an eight-block area. This action led several of the landlords, including South Ward City Councilman, Lee Bernstein, to make minor repairs in a few buildings. But most owners did not respond during the first month of the strike and none attempted any major improvements.[22] A visit by protestors to the mayor's office in turn produced a visit by Mayor Addonizio to one of the apartment houses; the rent-strike issue had by now won some passing attention in the local press. After taking due note of conditions, the mayor and his team of observers returned to city hall where, in the words of one tenant, "They made us a lot of promises but they didn't carry any out." NCUP protestors, joining forces with a local anti-poverty group, resorted to picketing the suburban home of one of the worst slumlords, an action taken over the protests of Councilman Bernstein who described the peaceful picketing as "disgraceful behavior."

After two months, the landlords whose buildings were affected by the rent strike began issuing eviction notices. One tenant, Mrs. Ida Brown, a mother of five children, was forcibly barred from her apartment by her landlord and two city detectives. When Mrs. Brown protested and attempted to enter her apartment, she was arrested and charged with assault and battery.[23] Her arrest was sufficient to persuade a number of other tenants that they had better withdraw from participation in the rent strike. Still other tenants, with the threat of eviction hanging over them, eventually moved out—their places quickly taken by other poor families—or complied with the law and resumed rent payments. Fear of arrest, forceful eviction, and legal prosecution, combined with a growing realization that nothing was being won except promises from public officials and threats from landlords, eventually proved effective in breaking the momentum of the rent-strike campaign. "There is," a resident accurately concluded, "no way us tenants, no legal way we can fight a landlord."[24] The ghetto residents learned what many always had suspected: some laws, such as those dealing with the collection of rents, the eviction of tenants, and the protection of property, were swiftly enforceable, while other laws, such as those dealing with flagrant violations of building and safety codes and the protection of people, were unaccountably unenforceable.

The rent strikes ebbed in Newark as in other cities without winning improvements in living conditions, without creating a permanent tenant's movement, and without getting the city and the courts to change their methods of dealing with slumlords. With nothing to show for their months of strenuous organizing, NCUP volunteers turned to a smaller and ostensibly more manageable issue.

Issue #2 A Traffic Light

Given the ghetto's immense needs, the desire for a traffic light on Avon Avenue might have seemed almost frivolous, but neighborhood feelings were surprisingly strong on this issue: too many children had been maimed and killed by speeding vehicles, and people found it hazardous to cross the avenue. For most residents the traffic light was literally a matter of life and death. In a few weeks NCUP collected 350 signatures on a petition, held a block rally, and waged call-in and letter-writing campaigns directed at the mayor and the City Council. Such efforts eventually earned the residents an audience with Mayor Addonizio who, confronted with a strong and well-organized community demand, agreed that a traffic light would be installed forthwith, contigent only upon City Council approval. The residents departed from the meeting in a hopeful spirit. But after another month of inaction NCUP sent another delegation to city hall this time to be told that a traffic light would cost $24,000 and was therefore too expensive, an argument that even the municipal authorities soon discarded as untenable. The protestors took to blocking traffic and picketing at the Avon Avenue intersection. On several occasions police dispersed the demonstrators with little difficulty, because most participants were hesitant to force a confrontation and expose themselves to arrest. A few "Stop" signs were installed on the side streets leading into Avon Avenue, a gesture that did nothing to slow down the main artery traffic, although it served to forestall further demonstrations as people awaited the impending light. Municipal officials gave repeated assurances that a traffic light would soon be placed, as one said, "If only you'll just be a little patient." After several more months of inaction and several more visits to city hall, it was revealed that the mayor had no authority to install a traffic light; the matter fell under state jurisdiction and had been referred to Trenton.

The protestors took to the streets again; this time attempts to block traffic led to the arrest of a few demonstrators. Municipal traffic officials continued to send assurances that the permit was "going through." But it remained for the State Bureau of Motor Vehicles to demonstrate how best to thwart the petitioners. State authorities informed NCUP organizers that they could not install a light until they had undertaken an extensive study of traffic conditions at the intersection. Data would be needed to demonstrate that a certain number of accidents—only of a kind that a light could prevent—occurred on Avon Avenue over a given period. Since no one in the community, including police and medical authorities, had kept complete records of vehicle and pedestrian mishaps, there was no proof that a light was needed; only an independent study of forthcoming fatalities and injuries could decide the matter. Despite this professed commitment to empirical research, state traffic authorities seemed unable to indicate when they might initiate the requisite survey. (Soon after this position was enunciated, white residents in a nearby middle-class neighborhood were able to get a traffic light installed 28 days after submitting a petition of approximately fifty signatures.)

Three years later, at the time of this writing, there is still no light, children are still hit by speeding vehicles at the intersection, and state officials have yet to begin their exhaustive study. More than ten months of intensive protest by lower Clinton Hill residents had produced another defeat.

Issue #3 Electoral Contest

"Why didn't you go to the local politicians for help on the rent strike and the traffic light?," I asked a number of the neighborhood organizers. "Are you kidding! They hate us! They call us trouble-makers," exclaimed one, "They are whites, Toms, and heavies. They want to run us out of town," said another. "What could they have done?," a white student conjectured in retrospect, "They knew coop-tation in the Democratic Party wouldn't silence us. We couldn't be bought off. So they were out to defeat us—even on a little thing like a traffic light." The Democratic party regulars were viewed as either indifferent or unsympathetic to ghetto needs. On the few occasions when they showed themselves responsive to the poor, it was in the performance of petty favors. They might "look into" a complaint by a mother that her welfare checks were not arriving, but they would not challenge some of the more demeaning and punitive features of the welfare system nor the conditions that fostered it. They might find a municipal job for a faithful precinct worker, but they would not advance proposals leading to a fundamental attack on ghetto unemployment. They might procure an apartment for a family but they would not ask the landlord, who himself was often a party con-tributor, to making housing improvements, nor would they think of challenging his right to charge exorbitant rents. The party regulars, whether white or Negro, seemed prepared to "look into" everything except certain of the more harrowing realities of slum life.

An opportunity to challenge them seemed to present itself in the autumn of 1965 when the United Freedom Ticket (UFT), a coalition of dissident blacks, Puerto Ricans, and "civil-rights oriented whites," asked NCUP to support the insurgency candidacy of George Richardson, a black man and a former Democratic assemblyman who had broken with the party because of its unwillingness to confront the problems of slum housing and police brutality. Richardson was "sort of a politician" to some NCUP people, and "no great prize in his political views," but he compared most favorably to his Democratic opponent whom one UFT supporter described as "the ultimate Uncle Tom." After some debate, NCUP decided to support the United Freedom Ticket which, in addition to Richardson, was running two other black candidates for State Assembly offices. After the failure of the rent-strike and traffic-light campaigns, a frontal assault at the polls seemed the only recourse: "We are tired of protesting and losing, so we're going right into politics," explained one organizer who hoped that NCUP's coalition with the UFT would increase the efficacy of both groups. Even if the Democratic incumbents were not defeated, a serious electoral challenge might make them somewhat more responsive to reformist pressure.

It was anticipated by some of the NCUP people that the campaign would provide an opportunity for creating a community-wide dialogue on fundamental issues. "Organizing the people" was, first of all, a matter of devising means of reaching and talking to persons who had never been reached before; the campaign seemed to offer just such an occasion. But faced with the necessity of swiftly reaching large numbers of people, and equipped with only limited resources, the challengers soon found themselves resorting to the traditional techniques of sound truck, leaflets, and slogans. Even so, not more than one-third of the contested area was covered and less than one-third of the voters were actually approached by UFT volunteers.

"We've got that one thing that can take it away from [the bosses]" Candidate Richardson said, "the vote." Not many residents believed him. Campaigning for "decent housing," "more and better jobs," and "freedom," the UFT found itself burdened by the very sins it was trying to fight: too many years of unfulfilled pledges by too many candidates had left people immune to political promises. Some residents felt threatened by appeals for direct involvement: "I don't know anything about politics. I don't want to have anything to do with it," was a typical response. Many had never heard of the UFT and were hesitant about an unknown ingredient. Still others indicated their sympathy for the third party's goals but were quick to voice their skepticism: "We've had our people in there before and they couldn't do nothing." The many expressions of cynicism and distrust reported by UFT canvassers might be summarized as follows: (1) Reformers were politicians, and therefore were as deceptive and insincere as other politicians. (2) Even if sincere, reformers were eventually "bought off" by those in control. (3) Even if not "bought off," reformers remained helpless against the entrenched powers: what could the UFT do even if it won all three contested seats? The conviction that "politics" could not deliver anything significant left many of the poor unresponsive, even if not unsympathetic, toward those who promised meaningful changes through the ballot box.

Of the blacks who voted, the greater number were the "better-to-do" elements—ministers, funeral directors, small businessmen, postal and clerical workers, and some skilled workers. A sizable number were beholden to, or related to those beholden to, the Democratic organization for jobs or for positions within the party that brought a modicum of social prestige. Often both resented and respected by poorer residents, the local ward politicians cultivated a wide range of acquaintances and traded on "friends and neighbors" appeals. They repeatedly stressed that a vote for the UFT might bring a Republican victory, and while many voters entertained no great expectations about the Democrats, they did fear that the Republicans might in some nameless way create still greater difficulties for blacks.[25] For some middle- and lower-middle-class blacks the act of voting was valued as a manifestation of civic virtue comparable to saluting the flag or singing the national anthem, a mark of good citizenship status reflecting well upon those Negroes who achieved it.[26]

Both the Democratic and Republican organizations provided substantial funds for neighborhood workers who saturated the black and white precincts with posters, party literature, and door-to-door canvassing, and who manned the fleet of cars to transport voters to and from the polls on election day. Even with these efforts, less than half of the registered blacks bothered to vote (as against almost two-thirds of the whites in the contested areas). The UFT ticket was thoroughly defeated, running well behind both major parties and polling less than five percent of the vote.

This description of events in Newark cannot be concluded without some mention of the role played by community officials. In statements to the press and sometimes to the protestors themselves, municipal officials voiced a dedication to the best interests of the people. It would have been remarkable had they professed anything else, but their behavior sometimes did betray their words. The methods they utilized to defeat NCUP on the rent-strike and traffic-light issues were familiar ones—the insistence that the problem in question needed elaborate investigation, the claim that the issue was not within a given authority's jurisdiction, the posing of rigorous and time-consuming legalistic procedures, the ritualistic appearance of a public official to investigate the question—followed by disingenuous promises that a solution was at hand, and the constant admonition that the protestors should exercise restraint and patience. "They just moved to go through the motions, to make us think they were moving," said one black man. "The city," concluded a white youth, "did a masterful job of destroying us. After a while we didn't know who was the target . . . we were always promised something to take the steam out [of us]. . . . They just wore us down with a run-around."[27]

The protestors also were subjected to a series of unsavory harassments. A replica of the *NCUP Newsletter,* printed by unknown individuals and containing what purported to be admissions of perverted sexual practices and communist affiliations falsely attributed to NCUP volunteers, was mailed to some 500 *NCUP Newsletter* subscribers. NCUP was infiltrated by at least one undercover agent who was ejected from the organization after admitting to being in the pay of an unnamed municipal personage. It was apparently through his efforts that the newsletter subscription list was obtained. A black detective, who quit the police force out of disgust for the racism he had encountered, confirmed the strong suspicions of NCUP workers that their telephone was being tapped by the police. On one occasion three NCUP girls were evicted from their three-bedroom apartment on charges of maintaining an unsanitary premise, sleeping on the floors, and conducting sex orgies. The landlord's letter containing these accusations was reprinted by a City Councilman and circulated among members of the Council and other municipal authorities. NCUP itself was evicted from its original storefront office, without being given a reason for the action. On another occasion threatening calls on the telephone by unidentified voices were followed by the breaking of NCUP office windows. Police repeatedly entered the office and arrested NCUP workers on disorderly conduct or loitering charges. A municipal judge once instructed one organizer brought before him to "go back to Russia." Other workers were arrested without cause while lawfully picketing a local food store accused of overpricing. Within a period of a few days, six black teenagers who assisted in routine NCUP tasks and who were planning a youth organization were arrested coming to and from the NCUP office. When Jesse Allen, a mild-mannered black leader of NCUP, went to the fifth precinct station to inquire on their behalf, he, too, was placed under arrest. Two of the youths who were arrested were convicted of breaking probation, and each was made to serve two years in prison.

The only conceivably friendly gesture directed toward NCUP in the several years of its existence came in the late spring of 1967 when Mayor Addonizio and Police Chief Spina sent letters asking the organizers to help "keep a cool summer" in the ghetto. The ensuing summer riots sent a number of NCUP people into hiding because, as two of them testify, a highly placed state official gave warning that police would be "out to get the radicals." These precautions did not prevent several NCUP workers from being arrested soon after the disorders and charged with conspiracy to riot and arson, charges that were subsequently dropped for lack of evidence.

By the end of 1967 NCUP ceased functioning. Several of the whites moved on to SDS organizing or to community action programs in other cities; others got jobs in Newark. Some of the activist blacks became involved in running a community center set up by the Union Community Corporation, an anti-poverty group under OEO sponsorship. They now found their energies absorbed in minor administrative tasks and were no longer involved in protest action. NCUP dissolved without ever coming close to achieving its central objective: the building of a viable local social movement that could exercise influence and win changes in community conditions and in the system that fostered those conditions.

In his study of young radicals, Kenneth Keniston made an observation that might serve as a summary description of the white and black activists in Newark: "What is most impressive is not their secret motivation to have the System fail, but their naive hope that it would succeed, and the extent of their depression and disillusion when their early reformist hopes were frustrated."[28] Some of the people who were engaged in NCUP have long since discarded their earlier hopes about the viability of the system, thereby recalling to mind an observation made by Christian Bay in 1965: "If budding western-democracy-type pluralist institutions turn out to benefit only the middle and upper classes—as in many Latin American countries—then we should not be surprised if idealistic students and others with a passion for social justice . . . become disposed to reject the forms of pluralist democracy altogether."[29]

III

The events in Newark provide us with a view of community power that qualifies the pluralist picture in several important respects. The following discussion attempts to summarize the findings and analyze some of the wider implications of this study.

1. For the urban blacks of Newark who had the temerity to fight city hall there exists the world of the rulers and the world of the ruled, and whether or not the first world is composed of a monolithic elite or of intramurally competing groups does not alter the fact that the blacks find themselves inhabiting the second. What impresses them and what might impress us is that the visible agents of the ruling world, a "plurality of actors and interests"—as represented by the municipal and state housing officials, motor vehicle and transit authorities, the landlords and reality investors, the mayor, the City Council, the political machines, the courts, and the police—displayed a remarkable capacity to move in the same direction against some rather modest lower-class claims.

It is one thing to conclude that power is not the monopoly of any one cohesive power elite and another to contend that it is broadly distributed among countervailing and democratically responsive groups. The belief that lower-strata groups exercise a constant, albeit indirect, power remains an article of faith rather than a demonstrated proposition at least with regard to the issues investigated in this study. Banfield's assertion that community decision makers operate "on the principle that everyone should get something and no one should be hurt very much," and Dahl's view that "all active and legitimate groups in the population can make themselves heard at some crucial stage in the process of decision," do not seem to be borne out.[30] Nor were we able to detect the "multitude of techniques for exercising influence on decisions" that Polsby believes are readily available to any group willing to engage in political competition.[31]

It may be that decision makers are responsive to lower-class pressures that are less visible than those observed in this study, but, as the pluralists would warn us, we should not embark upon an infinite regress of conjectures about covert influences. If Newark's officials were favorably influenced by the ghetto poor it must have been in ways so subtle as to have escaped the attention of both the researcher and the poor themselves. Since the data indicate that a lower-class group exercises no successful influence when *active*, I find no compelling reason to entertain the conclusion that the group wields power through unspecified means when *inactive*.

The data on Newark are consistent with the suggestion, offered by Edelman and Lipsky, that students of power and protest make a distinction between symbolic reassurances and substantive goods; the former are almost always more readily allocated to protesters and are usually designed for the purpose of deflecting the protest.[32] The few "positive" responses made by Newark's officials cost little in time, energy, and support; they were the appropriate "reciprocal noises," to use Dahl's term, intended primarily as substitutes for more tangible allocations. The familiar delaying tactics used by public officials are, Lipsky observes, "particularly effective in dealing with protest groups because of [the group's] inherent instability."[33] And the group's instability is, he adds, due to its dependence on the political resources of "third parties." This study of Newark shows, however, that even when a group demonstrates unusual durability—the NCUP persisted for three years—it still may be unable to outlast the decision makers. The latter can, so to speak, wait forever, and on many issues they would prefer to do so, while the protest group, *no matter how organizationally stable,* must start producing results if it is ever to attract a stronger following.

The idea that nothing succeeds like success is well understood by the challenged authorities. Often their unwillingness to make tangible allocations is due less to any consideration of immediate political expenditure than to their concern that present protests are but a prelude to more challenging and more costly demands. The traffic light (unlike the housing issue) hardly represented an appropriation that would have strained municipal resources or threatened the interests of more powerful groups, but a victory for the protestors might have strengthened precisely the kind of oppositional activity that Newark's officials wanted to discourage.

2. One of the most important aspects of power is the ability not only to prevail in a struggle but to predetermine the agenda of struggle, that is, to determine whether certain questions ever reach the competition stage. Assertions about the impossibility of empirically

studying these "nondecisions" need to be reexamined. Many "non-decisions" are really decisions of a sort, specifically to avoid or prevent the emergence of a particular course of action.[34] Much of the be-havior of Newark's officials can be seen as a kind of "politics of pre-vention," to use Harold Lasswell's term, a series of decisions designed to limit the area of issue conflict. More extensive study of the atti-tudes, actions, and inactions of municipal authorities toward lower-strata claims might reveal a startling number of instances in which office-holders avoid politically difficult responses to lower-class pres-sures. "The problem of politics," according to Lasswell, "is less to solve conflicts than to prevent them." Too much inclusiveness of "all the interests concerned arouses a psychology of conflict which produces obstructive, fictitious and irrelevant values," a situation best avoided when social administrators and political leaders learn to dampen by skillful tactics those issues that they judge to be detrimental to the public interest.[35] Newark offers an example of how "the politics of prevention" is practiced in the less than antiseptic world of a munici-pality.

Direct observation of lower-class groups may bring to light other instances of "nondecisions" and "non-issues," specifically those result-ing from the actual and anticipated discouragements suffered by peo-ple at the lower level of the social structure. In classic democratic theory and in much of the pluralist literature attention has been focused primarily on the presumed capacity of political leaders to anticipate the interests of various constituencies, but perhaps a more significant determinant of the conflict agenda can be found in the anticipatory reactions of lower-strata groups toward those who govern. In Newark, for instance, no attempt was made to organize protest around a number of real grievances. "If we couldn't even get a lousy traffic light with half the neighborhood out there screaming for it," explained one NCUP worker, "how could we hope to fight the corporations and the unions . . . or even the school system?" Protest groups remain inactive in certain areas because, given the enormity of the conditions needing change and the strength of the interests oppos-ing change, they see no opportunity for effective protest.[36] For them the agenda is predetermined by preferences and powers other than their own.

The same might be said of isolated individuals. Only a small percentage of the lower Clinton Hill residents were active in the various NCUP projects. According to one view, most sternly enun-

ciated by Polsby, there is no reason to assume that politically quiescent people suffer deprivations unless they express actual grievances.
But this ostensibly empirically-minded position harbors an a priori
assumption, for, in fact, individuals may remain politically quiescent
(1) because they feel no deprivation or (2) because they feel real
and urgent deprivations but are convinced that protest is futile and,
hence, give no political expression to their grievances. One can decide
which is the case only by empirical investigation of the social group
in question.[37] Any widely felt deprivation discovered by the investigator that fails to become an issue because the deprived don't have
the ability to force a confrontation may be considered a "non-issue";
these "non-issues" (or anticipatory reactions) are *empirically visible*
even if, by their nature, they tend to be *politically invisible*.

The unwillingness of so many people in Newark to make any
kind of political commitment can be partly attributed to the limitations on the time and energy of the poor.[38] Working long hours for
low pay, deprived of a host of services that middle-class whites take
for granted, many residents have neither the physical nor psychic
energy to engage in the demanding tasks of community organizing.
Many do not feel personally capable and confident enough to ask
their neighbors or themselves to participate actively. In a way that
most white people cannot appreciate, fear is a palpable ingredient in
the lives of the black poor; many are deterred by fear of eviction,
legal harassment, prosecution, police assault, and by a more diffuse
and ubiquitous fear of the powers that be.

If I were to offer any one explanation for non-participation it
would be the profound and widespread belief of so many ghetto
residents that there exists no means of taking effective action against
long-standing grievances, and that investments of scarce time, energy,
money, and, perhaps most of all, hope serve for nought except to
aggravate one's sense of affliction and impotence. In this case, non-
participation is an expression of what Kenneth Clark describes as
"the psychology of the ghetto with its pervasive and total sense of
helplessness,"[39] a pattern of anticipatory reactions that attempt to
avoid direct exposure to, and competition against, unresponsive and
unsympathetic authorities.

The contention that the poor are not really discontent else they
would register a protest vote at election time presupposes among other
things that the poor share or should share the middle-class belief that
the ballot is an effective and meaningful means of changing the

condition of their lives and their community. But, recalling Polsby's warning, we must guard against "the inappropriate and arbitrary assignment of upper and middle-class values to all actors in the community." We might also avoid treating lower-class non-participation as a self-generated entity, a manifestation of some innate subcultural habit or lack of civic virtue, and allow ourselves the notion that attitudes of defeatism and withdrawal are fostered by conditions within the socio-economic system and to that extent are accurate representations of the systemic realities and everyday-life conditions faced by the black poor.[40]

With that in mind, we might question the consistency and ease with which public-opinion surveys report that lower-strata individuals are more apathetic and less informed than citizens from better educated upper-income groups. If by "apathy" we mean the absence of affect and awareness, then many ghetto blacks, while non-participants in the usual political activities, can hardly be described as "apathetic." Apathy should not be confused with antipathy and alienation.[41] As to the finding that lower-class people are "less informed," what impressed me most about the poor, often semi-literate, blacks I talked to (residents of Newark and also of New York and more recently New Haven) was the extent to which they had a rather precise notion of what afflicted them and certainly a better sense of the difficulties and deprivations that beset the black community than the whites have in the same cities, many of whom refused to accept the legitimacy of black complaints.[42]

Whether a group appears apathetic and ill-informed depends on the kinds of questions it is being asked. Perhaps survey research, not unlike I.Q. testing, inadvertently reflects the cultural and class biases of the dominant society by focusing on those questions that are defined by the white middle-class world as "public issues." Something of the same criticism can be made of community power research of the last 15 years. That researchers have been able to study so many American cities and find so few deep-seated grievances tells us more about their research models than about urban reality. By confining themselves to issues pursued by politically visible interests they have rarely reached the muted lower strata.[43] "Rigid adherence to a conceptual schema," Charles McCoy notes in his critical appraisal of pluralism, "restricts the range of the political scientist's observable data so that he may fail to see what is taking place outside his frame of reference."[44]

3. If "inequalities in political resources remain, they tend to be *noncumulative*," some pluralists believe, since no one group either monopolizes or is totally deprived of the attributes of power.[45] Even if lacking in money and leadership, the lower strata still have the power of numbers. Thus it may be argued that the failure of NCUP and the UFT to mobilize sufficient numbers of poor people tells us only that they were unable to tap the ghetto's power resources and not that such resources are non-existent.

The contention that the slum constituency is ineffective because it fails to mobilize its numerical strength is something of a tautology. It is to say that the poor will have power if and when they act in such a way as to have power—presumably in sufficient numbers with sufficient energy. But the only way we can determine "sufficiency" is by noting that the poor prevail on a given issue. By that approach, they can never be judged powerless. If they win on any issue, then they have power; if they lose, they still have power but sufficient numbers have not made sufficient use of it. One cannot imagine a situation in which sufficient numbers have acted and lost; the proposition is established by definition rather than by observation and is non-falsifiable.

Moreover, to contend that the lower strata have a potential power that would prevail should they *choose* to use it presumes that their non-participation is purely a matter of volition. The volition argument is given its more familiar and vulgar expression by those who dismiss the inequalities of opportunity in economic life: "Anyone can make his fortune if he puts his mind and effort to it." The antecedent conditions that are crucial determinants of performance merely become a matter of self-willed doggedness.[46] The argument overlooks the fact that the ability to take effective advantage of an opportunity, the ability to convert potentiality into actuality, is itself a crucial power. The actualization of any potential power requires the use of antecedent resources, and just as one needs capital to make capital, so one needs power to use power. This is especially true of the power of numbers insofar as the opportunity to achieve political effectiveness by activating large numbers of people, especially lower-class citizens, within the normal channels of group politics, necessitates a substantial command of time, manpower, publicity, organization, legitimacy, knowledgeableness, and—the ingredient that often can determine the availability of these resources—money. Aside from its more circumspect influences, money is needed for the acquisition of elected office. "Probably the most important direct contribution" to political leaders, according to Dahl himself, "is money." The "most important indirect contribution is votes . . ."[47] The power of numbers, then, is an influence that is highly qualified by material and class considerations.

For the poor of Newark, the situation closely approximates one of "cumulative inequalities," to use Dahl's term. If the poor possessed the material resources needed to mobilize themselves, they would not be poor and would have less need to organize their numbers in a struggle to win services that the economic and political systems readily grant to more favored groups. Can the dispossessed who desire inclusion in the decision process gain access to political office without the capital needed to mobilize and activate their numbers? There seems no easy answer to this question. The problem of "political capital accumulation" is compounded by the fact that, unlike the indigent in many other countries, the poor in America are a minority and therefore even when mobilized for electoral participation may have only a limited impact. The power of numbers can be employed with countervailing efficacy by the majority that identifies itself with the "haves" and against the "have nots."

Furthermore, in places like Newark, the one institution theoretically designed to mobilize and respond to the demands of the unorganized lower strata—the local political party—fails to do so. One of the hallowed teachings of American political science is that the political party is the citizens' means of exercising collective power; the stronger the party system, the more ably will it affect the polyarchic will. But the party organization in Newark is less a vehicle for democratic dialogue and polyarchic power than a pressure group with a rather narrowly defined interest in the pursuit of office, favor, and patronage. Moved to collective activity only at election time, local politicians seem most possessed with the overriding task of securing and advancing their own positions and maintaining the ongoing equilibrium.

Party politicians are inclined to respond positively not to group *needs* but to group *demands*, and in political life as in economic life, *needs* do not become *marketable demands* until they are backed by "buying power" or "exchange power" for only then is it in the "producer's" interest to respond. The problem with most lower-strata groups is that they have few political resources of their own to exchange.[48] NCUP's protest action failed to create the kinds of inducements that would have made it in the political leaders' interest to take positive measures. The withholding of rent payments, the street-corner demonstrations, the momentary disruptions of traffic and the feeble electoral challenge were treated by the politicians of Newark not as bargaining resources but as minor nuisances that were not to be allowed to develop into major threats. Concessions to the troublemakers might have led to demands for even greater reallocations and eventually would have challenged the interests of groups endowed with far more political "buying power."

4. Not only do party regulars have little inclination to entertain the kinds of issues that might incur the wrath of higher political leaders or powerful economic interests, but they also try to discredit and defeat those reformers who seek confrontations on such issues.[49] Questions about poverty, urban squalor, unemployment, the tax structure, and the ownership, control, and uses of private and public wealth do not win the attention of most urban political organizations. But the sins of the politician are more than personal ones, for the forces that limit him also circumscribe most of political life. The very agenda of legitimate conflict is shaped by widely accepted and unquestioned belief systems and power distributions that predispose the decision maker to view the claims of certain groups as "reasonable" or "essential" and the claims of other groups as "questionable" or "outrageous." The systemic norms and rules governing political procedures operate with something less than egalitarian effects. To say that the political system is governed by "the rules of the game" is to apply an unfortunate metaphor. In most games the rules apply equally to all competitors, but in political life the symbolic norms, standards, and practices that govern traditional forms of political competition are themselves part of the object of competition. Rules that regulate procedures and priorities in any social system cannot be extricated from the substantive values and interests that led to their construction. Rather than being neutral judgments, they are the embodiment of past political victories and, as such, favor those who have "written" them. Many of the past struggles of dispossessed groups have involved actions that, until legalized as part of the rules, were treated as crimes against property and against the Constitution; these actions have included collective bargaining, boycotts, strikes, sit-downs, and the demand to legislate standards for wages, hours, and other working conditions. Many of the earlier efforts in the labor movement were directed toward legalizing certain methods of protest and competition, thereby changing the rules so as to allow for more effective participation in

future competitions.[51] Those who contend that a commitment to the rules is a precondition for democratic politics[52] overlook the fact that for some groups such a commitment is tantamount to accepting a condition of permanent defeat since certain of the rules as presently constituted (e.g., the rent laws) are, in fact, the weapons of a dominant interest.

We can conclude that the existence of protest activity should not be treated as a sure manifestation of a pluralistic influence system. Even if the thought is incongruent with the pluralist model, it should come as no surprise to political scientists that the practices of the political system do not guarantee that all groups will have accessibility to the loci of decision making, and that the ability to be heard in a debate, even when achieved, is not tantamount to the sharing of power. If American communities are governed democratically, then let it be said that democracy, like any other form of government, is a power system that allocates its values and priorities most favorably to those who have the most power, to those who have the wherewithal to take best advantage of systemic arrangements. The political order that emerges may prove to be "functional" and "workable" without contributing to the well-being of large segments of the population. Those who are most needful of substantive reallocations are, by that very fact, usually farthest removed from the resources necessary to command such reallocations and least able to make effective use of whatever limited resources they possess.

NOTES

1. Robert Dahl's *Who Governs?* (New Haven: Yale University Press, 1961) remains the most intelligent and important pluralist statement, one that can still be read with profit even by those who disagree with it. Other pluralist views may be found in Arnold Rose, *The Power Structure* (New York: Oxford University Press, 1967); Edward Banfield, *Political Influence* (New York: The Free Press, 1961); David Riesman *et al.*, *The Lonely Crowd* (Garden City, N. Y.: Doubleday Co., 1955); Nelson Polsby, *Community Power and Political Theory* (New Haven: Yale University Press, 1963); David Truman, *The Governmental Process* (New York: Alfred A. Knopf, 1953).

2. Rose, *Power Structure*, 6.

3. Polsby, *Community Power*, 118.

4. For data and critical analysis supporting the anti-pluralist position see Grant McConnell, *Private Power and American Democracy* (New York: Alfred A. Knopf, 1966) and the many studies cited therein; see also, Paul Baran and

Paul Sweezy, *Monopoly Capital: An Essay on the American Economic and Social Order* (New York: Monthly Review Press, 1966); Ralph Miliband, *The State in Capitalist Society* (New York: Basic Books, 1969); Henry Kariel, *The Decline of American Pluralism* (Stanford: Stanford University Press, 1961); Theodore Lowi, "The Public Philosophy: Interest-Group Liberalism," *American Political Science Review*, 61 (March 1967), 5–24; Philip Green, "Science, Government and the Case of RAND," *World Politics*, 20 (January 1968), 301–326. For a collection of the best analytic critiques of pluralism, see the articles reprinted in *Apolitical Politics: A Critique of Behavioralism*, ed. by Charles McCoy and John Playford (New York: Thomas Y. Crowell, 1967).

5. See Peter Bachrach, *The Theory of Democratic Elitism* (Boston: Little, Brown, 1967), 37. Some anti-pluralists such as G. William Domhoff, *Who Rules America?* (Englewood Cliffs, N.J.: Prentice-Hall, 1967) conclude that a power elite rules at the national level even if there may be more pluralistic elites at the community levels.

6. See Kariel, *Decline of American Pluralism*, especially chs. 5 and 6 for a development of this point; also Lowi, "Interest-Group Liberalism."

7. Even the pluralist Banfield seems to support the above idea. In *Political Influence* he observes (251): "When Mayor Daley took office, he immediately wrote to three or four of the city's most prominent businessmen asking them to list the things they thought most needed doing. . . . He may be impressed by the intrinsic merit of a proposal . . . but he will be even more impressed at the prospect of being well regarded by the highly respectable people whose proposal it is."

8. Peter Bachrach and Morton Baratz, "Two Faces of Power," *American Political Science Review*, 56 (December 1962), 1950, reprinted in McCoy and Playford, *Apolitical Politics*. For a detailed development of the effects of myth and ritual in political life, see Murray Edelman, *The Symbolic Uses of Power* (Urbana, Ill.: University of Illinois Press, 1964); also Thurman Arnold, *The Symbols of Government* (New Haven: Yale University Press, 1935). For a detailed analysis of the structure and content of a prevalent belief system, see Francis X. Sutton *et al.*, *The American Business Creed* (Cambridge: Harvard University Press, 1956).

9. Polsby, *Community Power*, 88–89. Yet Polsby goes on to say, "Mayor Lee's achievement in generating support from New Haven's economic and social elite should not be underestimated. . . . Economic and social leaders, who had originally been reluctant to support the urban redevelopment program, became so firmly committed to the program and to Lee that many of these lifelong Republicans found themselves actively supporting Lee for the U. S. Senate and contributing heavily to his re-election campaign against the Republican candidate. At least one businessman even suggested that the *Republican* party nominate Lee for Mayor." (emphasis in the original) It seems not to have occurred to Polsby that Lee's unusual popularity with businessmen was due less to his personal seductiveness than to his having proven himself so repeatedly responsive to business interests. For a more critical study of Mayor Lee's urban renewal program and his dealings with the economic elite, see John Wilhelm, "The Success and Tragedy of Richard Lee," *The New Journal*, 1 (October 15, 1967), 5–9.

10. Polsby, *Community Power*, 60. By this approach, considerations of historical, class, cultural, and structural factors are relegated to an incidental or even non-scientific status. Here indeed is "behaviorism" in its Pavlovian-Watsonian sense.

11. Dahl, *Who Governs?*, 180–181. Other community studies similarly find that active participants are almost invariably drawn from professional, business, and better-income strata.

12. *Ibid.*, 164 and 100–103.

13. *Ibid.*, 164; the italics are mine.

14. *Ibid.*, 270 ff.

15. Polsby, *Community Power*, 116–117; see the critical comments in Jack L. Walker, "A Critique of the Elitist Theory of Democracy," *American Political Science Review*, 60 (June 1966), 289.

16. Polsby, *Community Power*, 134.

17. Actually, political activities involving the dispossessed occur more frequently than we have assumed. In recent years migrant workers, sharecroppers, ghetto blacks, rural whites, American Indians, indigent elderly, and others have made scores of attempts to effect specific changes in various communities and institutions. Most of these activities have yet to be studied systematically as situations that tell us something about the dynamics and distributions of power in America. Most studies of conflict and discontent within the political system are written from the perspective of those concerned with channelizing or reducing the challenges of competing groups; see, for example, Neil J. Smelser, *Theory of Collective Behavior* (New York: Free Press, 1963). Note the discussion in William Gamson's *Power and Discontent* (Homewood, Ill.: Dorsey Press, 1968), 11–19.

18. Todd Gitlin, "Local Pluralism as Theory and Ideology," *Studies on the Left*, 5 (Summer 1965), reprinted in McCoy and Playford, *Apolitical Politics*, 143.

19. More than one-half of Newark's 400,000 residents are black. A third of the city's housing is substandard. Unemployment in the ghetto is "officially set at 12 per cent, unofficially as high as 20 per cent"; some 17,000 households try to exist on annual incomes of less than $3,000. See Paul Goldberg in the *New York Times Magazine*, September 29, 1968, 117. The conditions in Newark are bad but hardly atypical. In municipal governmental structure, political-party system, racial makeup, population density, housing conditions, occupational and income distributions, and the incidence of riot and civil disturbances Newark is fairly representative of most good-sized American cities in the Northeast.

20. Many of the events described herein occurred before I began my research. My information is based on protracted interviews and less structured conversations conducted in the autumn of 1965, the winter of 1966, and the spring of 1968 with black activists and whites involved in NCUP, and with other Newark residents. In most instances the information reported here has been corroborated by two or more respondents. A less detailed but helpful history of the events described above has been recorded in the documentary film, "The Troublemakers," produced and distributed by Newsreel, Inc. New York, N.Y. The direct quotations in these case studies are from my interviews and field observations, except for a few taken from the documentary film.

21. One of the black leaders, Jesse Allen, a former union shop steward, exhausted his life savings in order to support himself while working for NCUP. Other black activists included youths, welfare mothers, housewives, and working and unemployed men.

22. In a number of instances it was difficult to determine who owned what building. Some owners found it advantageous to use "fronts." Occasionally a

building might change hands several times in quick succession only to return to the hands of the original owner.

23. The detectives charged that Mrs. Brown threw one of them down a flight of stairs. Eyewitnesses gave a contrary account, testifying that it was Mrs. Brown who was thrown down the stairs. The jury chose to believe the police and Mrs. Brown was convicted and given three years probation. A subsequent grand-jury investigation of her countersuit led to the conviction of one of the detectives for assault and battery. The conviction against Mrs. Brown, however, was never repealed.

24. This also seems to be the case in other communities. In Mount Vernon, N.Y., in 1965, 15 welfare mothers submitted a petition to housing authorities protesting conditions in their apartment building. Within a week all had been served eviction notices. In New York and other cities, rent strikes when "successful" often produce results of dubious value to the tenants. After laborious legal proceedings on the tenants' parts and after the numerous delaying tactics and appeals available to the landlord have been exhausted, the city usually takes the building into receivership, uses the rent money to make repairs and then returns the building to the landlord while allowing him to charge substantial rent increases because of the improved conditions. Frequently, the repairs are so extensive that the tenants are evicted by the city only to be relocated in slums elsewhere, far from their neighborhood friends, their jobs and their children's schools. Today most community organizers have few illusions about the efficacy of rent strikes. See Stanley Aronowitz, "New York City: After the Rent Strikes," *Studies on the Left,* 5 (Winter 1965), 85–89.

25. The South Ward might be considered as having a "modified two-party system": the Republicans are always strong enough to raise a serious electoral challenge but seldom strong enough to win.

26. Compare with Howard Swearer's explanation of the electoral participation in the Soviet Union in his "The Functions of Soviet Local Elections," *Midwest Journal of Political Science,* 5 (May 1961), 149.

27. Those who insist that more militant protest tactics should not be employed until all legitimate legislative and administrative channels for redressing grievances have been exhausted, might consider whether such channels are not, by their very nature, inexhaustible.

28. Kenneth Keniston, *Young Radicals. Notes on Committed Youth* (New York: Harcourt, Brace and World, 1968), 127.

29. Christian Bay, "Politics are Pseudopolitics: A Critical Evaluation of Some Behavioral Literature," *The American Political Science Review,* 59 (March 1965), 39–51; reprinted in McCoy and Playford, *Apolitical Politics.*

30. Banfield, *Political Influence,* 272; Robert Dahl, *A Preface to Democratic Theory* (Chicago: University of Chicago Press, 1956), 137, but see the qualification Dahl offers on 138. Another pluralist, Merelman, goes so far as to argue that those who are defeated nevertheless share in power because they have been able to induce the prevailing group to expend the effort needed to vanquish them! "Even if those planning to initiate policies hostile to an 'elite' become subject to its power and are constrained to desist, they still have exerted power of their own. The elite has been forced to anticipate them and exert power in return." Richard Merelman, "On the Neo-Elitist Critique of Community Power," *The American Political Science Review,* 62 (June 1968), 455. It is impossible using Merelman's model to imagine any

situation, even a suppressive one, as not being somewhat pluralistic: both conqueror and conquered, victimizer and victim, share in power. In contrast, the model offered by Dahl and Polsby defines power as the ability to prevail in a given issue conflict.

31. Polsby, *Community Power*, 118.

32. See Edelman, *Symbolic Uses of Power*, 2 and *passim*; and Michael Lipsky, "Protest as a Political Resource," *American Political Science Review*, 62, (December 1968) , 1148 and 1155.

33. Lipsky, "Protest," 1156–1157.

34. Here I am not referring to that category of nondecisions that Bachrach and Baratz see contained in the norms and beliefs of the socio-political culture and that are less frequently or less obviously the objects of deliberate manipulation. But even such "unconscious," "implicit" belief systems are not inaccessible to analysis. See Sutton *et al.*, *American Business Creed* and Edelman, *Symbolic Uses of Power*. Few political scientists have begun to think of belief systems as resources of power comparable to the other resources commonly identified in decision conflicts.

35. Harold Lasswell, *Psychopathology and Politics* (Chicago: University of Chicago Press, 1930) , 196–197; also the critical comments in Kariel, *Decline of American Pluralism*, 117 ff., and Bachrach, *Democratic Elitism*, 66–67.

36. Compare with E. E. Schattschneider's remark: "People are not likely to start a fight if they are certain that they are going to be severely penalized for their efforts. In this situation repression may assume the guise of a false unanimity." *The Semi-Sovereign People* (New York: Holt, Rinehart and Winston, 1960) , 8.

37. Painstaking field work may no longer be necessary if one simply wishes to establish the fact that lower-class grievances exist. Expressions of ills have become so explosive and riotous as to have won even the glaze-eyed attention of the mass media. In the summer of 1967 there were 75 major outbreaks of disorder and in the spring of 1968 over 100 cities suffered some kind of riot and disorder.

38. Non-participation can also be ascribed in part to conditions that are hardly exclusive to the poor. Thus it may not be clearly within the interest of individual members of large groups to make the kinds of personal expenditures needed to win goals beneficial to the entire group unless there are more particularized rewards or coercions that act as personal incentives. To some extent this is a problem confronting all collective action. See Mancur Olsen, Jr., *The Logic of Collective Action* (New York: Schocken Books, 1965) . One might still observe that economically deprived groups are unusually wanting in the resources that allow for particularized incentives and hence they suffer unusually severe difficulties of organization and leadership.

39. Kenneth Clark, *Dark Ghetto* (New York: Harper and Row, 1965) , 156.

40. Contrary to an accepted notion, the great majority of the poor families of Newark, New York, New Haven, Chicago, Washington, D.C., and Watts—to mention a few of the places that have been studied—are stable, self-respecting, and hard-working, headed by fathers, or in the absence of a male, by working mothers who care deeply and labor hard for their children, but they face substandard housing, inhumane hospitals and schools, poor work conditions, low pay, high rents, overpriced stores, etc. They find themselves trapped not by "a matriarchal slave-family cultural heritage" but by the socio-economic system. See Studs Terkel, *Division Street: America* (New York: Pantheon Books,

1967) ; Paul Jacobs, *Prelude to Riot* (New York: Random House, 1966) ; Charles Willie's "Two Men and their Families." in *Among the People*, ed. by Irwin Deutscher and Elizabeth Thomson (New York: Basic Books, 1968) , 53–66; and Clark, *Dark Ghetto*.

41. Many of the black poor of Newark fit Robert Lane's description of the "alienation syndrome": "I am the object, not the subject of political life. . . . The government is not run in my interest; they do not care about me; in this sense it is not my government. . . ." *Political Ideology* (New York: Free Press, 1962) , 162.

42. A similar conclusion is drawn by Terkel, *Division Street*, after extensive interviews with whites and blacks in Chicago. See also the findings on black attitudes concerning the 1964 riots and the comparison to white responses in J. R. Feagin and P. B. Sheatsley, "Ghetto Resident Appraisals of a Riot," *Public Opinion Quarterly*, 32 (Fall 1968) , 352–362; and the "Kerner Report" on the 1967 riots: *Report of the National Advisory Commission on Civil Disorders* (New York: Bantam Books, 1968) , ch. 5 and *passim*.

43. Thus neither Dahl nor Polsby have much to say about the reactions of slum dwellers displaced by the New Haven urban renewal program. Polsby observes: "Who wanted urban redevelopment? By 1957, practically everyone who had anything to say in public strongly favored this program." *Community Power*, 71. Dahl makes a passing reference to those who did not have "anything to say in public": "several hundred slum dwellers without much political influence" and a handful of small businessmen. Nothing more is heard about those who suffered from urban redevelopment. *Who Governs?*, 244. (See comments by Gitlin, "Local Pluralism," 141–142.) Polsby (*Community Power*, 96–97) further assures us that in regard to goals that are "in some way explicitly pursued by people in the community, the method of study in New Haven has a reasonable chance of capturing them." Whether that claim is true or not, his method of study will tell us nothing about those goals desired by large segments of the population but not "explicitly pursued," or goals that, if pursued, fail to achieve political visibility because of the organizational weakness of the deprived group or the unresponsiveness of community leaders. Similarly, Harold Lasswell's contention that "it is impossible to locate the few without considering the many" is highly questionable. Lasswell's own work repeatedly demonstrates that a student of power can focus on the activities of the few without finding it imperative to consider the well-being of the many. See his *Politics: Who Gets What, When, How* (New York: World Publishing Co., 1936) , 309 and comments by Bachrach, *Democratic Elitism*, 66.

44. McCoy in the introduction to McCoy and Playford, *Apolitical Politics*, 5.

45. Dahl, *Who Governs?*, 85; italics in the original.

46. In fairness to Dahl it should be said that his view of "potential power" is not as simple as that held by other students. In *Who Governs?*, 275, he notes that there are important "objective differences" among constituents that limit their potential power: ". . . being poor or rich, well-educated or uneducated, a professional man or an unskilled laborer, living in a slum area or a middle-class neighborhood—these are differences in objective situations of a most persistent and general sort that are likely to show up in a variety of different ways over a long period of time." It is our loss that Dahl did not see fit to develop these observations.

47. *Ibid.*, 97.

48. See the analysis in James Q. Wilson, "The Strategy of Protest: Problems of Negro Civic Action," *Journal of Conflict Resolution*, 3 (September 1961), 291–303; and Lipsky, "Protest," 1145–1146.

49. Newark is not the only city in which the party regulars manifest either indifference or antipathy toward the issues raised by reformers. Describing Negro politicians in Chicago, Banfield notes: "Like all politicians, they had to consider their political futures. Only one or two were 'race men.' The others had accommodated themselves to a situation in which whites held the upper hand." The man who dominated Negro political life for so many years, Congressman Dawson, is described as one who does small favors for constituents, "takes care" of his precinct workers, and remains "indifferent to issues and principles including those of special importance to the race." Banfield, *Political Influence*, 41, 260. A year as participant-observer in New Haven politics (1967–68) leads me to the same conclusions about the Negro ward leaders in that city; they say and do nothing that might earn the disapproval of Democratic Town Committee Chairman Barbieri, raise no issues of racial or economic content, and oppose those white reformers and black activists who do— as on the issue of the black boycott in the spring of 1968.

50. Truman, *Governmental Process*, 513.

51. See Michael Walzer, "Civil Disobedience and Corporate Authority," forthcoming in a book of readings edited by Philip Green and Sanford Levinson.

52. Thus Truman notes that the rules of the game are part of "the substance of prevailing values without which the political system could not exist." *Governmental Process*, 348; and James D. Barber writes: "To a large degree, a successful democracy depends on agreement as to how the system is to be used, on the rules of the game." *Citizens Politics* (Chicago: Markham Publishing Company, 1969), 93–94.

ARTICLE 16

Mayoral Leadership by a Modern Boss-Politician

Alan Shank

Over the last decade, the pivotal role of big-city mayors in the urban crisis has brought increasing attention to their leadership qualities. With the intensified urban malaise, the mayors have attempted to save their cities from impending disaster. The nationwide impact of urban

This essay, appearing here for the first time, is part of the author's larger study of big-city mayoral leadership roles and styles.

problems has brought together many big-city mayors to testify before congressional committees and to seek mutual aid and assistance from the White House. Many mayors have called for a reordering of national priorities by opposing the Vietnam War and unnecessary defense spending.

While mayoral leadership (or the lack of it) is generally considered an integral feature of effective municipal government, the roles and styles of big-city chief executives have been conspicuously ignored by social scientists. In fact, the mayor's office has usually been considered a political dead end. As long as the mayor's position lacked prestige, visibility, and upward mobility, politically ambitious men were not attracted to City Hall. In 1963 Marilyn Gittell found that only ten of ninety-six mayors in the nation's twenty-four largest cities were elected to higher office during the preceding two decades.[1] She observed that "mayors throughout the United States have little in common but the lack of a political future—that they are, as a profession, predestined to political oblivion is a historical fact."[2]

Today, big-city mayors face one of the toughest public jobs in America. Political scientist James Q. Wilson argues that the key dilemma of the mayors has been "a simultaneous growth in the problems of the central cities and a decline in the authority of the mayor to handle those problems."[3] The men in City Hall often find it difficult to resolve the conflicting demands of a fragmented, hostile, and politically polarized constituency. Their capacity to develop effective solutions to urban problems depends largely on public support, available resources, and authority to get things done—all of which are frequently lacking.

What are some of the major challenges to vigorous and effective mayoral authority and leadership?

Riots, crime, lawlessness, community fear: The massive city riots of 1967 focused nationwide attention on the urban crisis as expressed by frustrated and alienated ghetto residents. Continuing public protests and mass demonstrations against a variety of grievances place constant pressure on the police to maintain order and to protect the rights of demonstrators. Additionally, the cities are faced with an upward spiral in serious crime. Fear in the streets intensifies demands for "law and order." Hostility between working-class ethnic groups and blacks produces daily tensions in various city neighborhoods. All of these factors mean that mayors cannot develop effective, long-range solutions to the underlying causes of social disorder: They are constantly involved with the crisis management of daily problems.

Racial polarization, poverty, high taxes, low-quality public services: Many central cities have become large-scale black ghettoes as the middle class flees to the suburbs and residential integration is vigorously resisted in the remaining white neighborhoods. The loss of industry and the white middle class erodes the city's tax base. Extensive poverty in the slums brings great pressure on city hall to provide more and better social welfare services for broken families, the unemployed, and the poorly educated. But the poor are unable to pay the high costs of public assistance. The burden falls largely on taxpayers who complain that the mayors give too much attention to the needs of the poor and neglect white neighborhoods which suffer from declining public services.

Bureaucratic unresponsiveness, public employee strikes, lack of budgetary control: The mayors cannot control city government and make it responsive to the needs of the people. The vast and impersonal bureaucratic agencies are not accustomed to responding quickly to social crises. Public employee unions have become more militant in demanding higher wages and fringe benefits for their members. When policemen, firemen, sanitation workers, and public school teachers refuse to work, the entire functioning of city government is threatened. Mayoral authority is limited by the city's fiscal dependence on the state. Mayors have less authority than presidents and governors to control their own budgets. Cities cannot control their own budgetary priorities to meet pressing social demands for urgent public programs.

To respond to the urban crisis, big-city mayors should be able to mobilize politically effective *constituencies,* seek out and maximize available *fiscal* and *program resources,* and overcome formal restraints on *executive* and *municipal* powers in dealing with local problems. To achieve these objectives, local chief executives may employ one of several distinctive leadership roles and styles. These include the modern boss-politicians, the program-politicians, the politically independent mavericks, the cosmopolitan innovators, and the "law and order" advocates. If these various leadership approaches are to be analyzed, two cautions should be mentioned. First, mayoral roles and styles often reflect the actions of particular individuals with distinctive personalities functioning in specific cities. Second, the various leader-ship categories are not mutually exclusive. Some big-city executives may combine several leadership qualities found in the different classifications.

MODERN BOSS-POLITICIANS

Many observers have noted that the classic model of boss rule and machine politics has largely disappeared from American cities.[4] How-ever, there are still a few mayors whose formal authority is less important than their skillful centralization of influence as party lead-ers. Such boss-politicians may provide the appearance and even the substance of modern, efficient executive management, but their real power is based upon ironclad control of the local party apparatus. As described by Professors Edward C. Banfield and James Q. Wilson, such boss-politicians assume the role of "brokers" to enhance and maintain their party influence:

> As a rule, the boss gets his initial stock of influence by virtue of holding a party or public office. He uses the authority of the office to acquire power, and then he uses the power to acquire more power and ultimately more authority. By "buying" bits of authority here and there . . . the boss accumulates a "working capital" of influence. Those who "sell" it to him receive in return jobs, party preferment, police protection, other bits of influence, and other considerations of value. The boss, like any investor, has to increase his influence if he is to maintain and increase it.[5]

Mayor Richard J. Daley of Chicago is not only the single best example of an incumbent boss-politician leader but also perhaps the most powerful Democratic party mayor in the United States. Daley has served longer than any other mayor in Chicago's 134-year-old his-tory.[6] In 1971, he was elected to his fifth four-year term with 70 per cent of the popular vote, a victory margin that was only slightly below his 74 per cent plurality in 1967.

What is the source of Daley's considerable political power and influence? A casual observer examining the formal governmental structure of Chicago might well conclude that the mayor is only one relatively unimportant actor in an extremely fragmented and decentralized system. In theory, the "weak" mayor shares power with a host of elected and appointed city and Cook County officials, none of whom are responsible to each other: the 50-member city board of aldermen (councilmen elected from individual wards), the county board, the city and county clerks, the city and county treasurers, the city school board, housing authority, and transit commission, and the county sheriff and coroner.

However, Mayor Daley has overcome the formal limits on vigorous executive leadership. His substantial power and influence come from his unchallenged supremacy as chairman of the Cook County Democratic Party Committee. As the party leader, Daley has imposed extensive centralization on the extremely decentralized governmental system. By skillfully building his influence as the master party "broker," Daley "slates" (designates) all Democratic party candidates for city and county elective offices, controls a sizeable bloc of state legislators (which all Illinois governors must reckon with), and leads the Illinois delegation to the quadrennial national Democratic party conventions (where Daley frequently plays the role of "king-maker" for aspiring presidential hopefuls).

The Cook County party organization, which consists of fifty city and thirty suburban township committeemen, mobilizes the necessary votes to elect Daley's handpicked candidates in the primaries and the general elections. If the expected voting margins for these candidates are not delivered, not only do the party leaders face Daley's wrath, but even more important, the mayor can withhold favors and patronage jobs, which include some 12,000 city and 30,000 county government positions. Thus Daley maintains close scrutiny of the party rank-and-file, a fact which can often prove to be intimidating for laggards:

> . . . One of the most withering experiences in a ward boss's life comes on election night. . . Somewhat in the manner of a school-boy presenting his report card to a stern father, each of the 50 meets alone with Daley to submit his precinct-by-precinct vote. According to one insider who has observed the ritual, Daley sits at a desk and silently studies the tallies. If they please him, he rises and vigorously pumps both of the successful committeeman's hands. If they displease him, Daley gives the miscreant a blistering tongue-lashing. On one such occasion, the mayor was so incensed with a non-producer that he reached across his desk and began shaking him by his necktie.*

* "Chicago's Daley: How to Run a City," *Newsweek* (April 5, 1971), p. 82. Copyright Newsweek, Inc. 1971, reprinted by permission.

Daley's *role* as party boss should be distinguished from his mayoral leadership *style*, which has encompassed the urban renewal objectives of the program-politician mayors and the efficiency and economy goals of the municipal reform movement. Chicago's governing coalition includes the Democratic party machine, organized labor, the downtown business community, and suburban voters in Cook County. In return for non-interference in party affairs (other than backing the mayor for re-election), Mayor Daley provides each part of the coalition with enthusiastic endorsement for their particular objectives. Labor union leaders, many of whom are Daley's boyhood friends, are rewarded with high city construction wage rates, generous overtime pay, and appointments to prestigious boards and commissions. The predominantly Republican commercial, banking, and real estate interests support Daley's massive downtown urban renewal projects and multilane expressways, programs which have restored confidence in the city's economic base. Finally, Daley has catered to the "good government" reformers and the Cook County suburban constituency by preventing corruption in city hall, providing efficient municipal services with balanced budgets, and establishing an informal metropolitian system of government which offers the suburbs planning and technical assistance to help solve region-wide problems.

Thus, the boss-politician's ruling coalition has considerable strength when it includes one-man party omnipotence, "good government" reform administration, and urban renewal goals which attract business and labor support. Does all of this imply that Mayor Daley is immune from criticisms and attacks by dissatisfied groups? Can he withstand challenges by reformers, liberals, party dissidents, black militants, and other minority group activists? Can he continue to keep these interests from exercising any kind of meaningful influence within the governing coalition? Are such groups even considered vital to the city's future?

Even though Mayor Daley is assured of remaining in office until 1975, there are several danger signs threatening the city's political and economic stability. The governing coalition has generally refused to yield to demands for racial justice and minority group participation in the political process. Chicago's black community, which comprises about one-third of the population, is nearly totally isolated from the white power structure. With 77 per cent of the blacks living in neighborhoods that are 90 per cent or more Negro, Chicago's black population is perhaps the most segregated minority group of any large city in the country.[7] The blacks suffer from inadequate social welfare services, high unemployment rates, and poor public schools. The most impoverished blacks are forced to live in high-rise fortress-like public housing projects. Negro voters continue to support the Democratic party machine as a result of threats by ward committee-men to cut off public welfare payments and to evict residents from public housing. While the ruling coalition and the white working-class ethnics generally support Daley's policies of racial isolation and segregation, the city's white middle class continues to flee to the suburbs at a rate of 50,000 per year. Widespread community fear has made Chicago a repressive city, as the police try to prevent the politically powerless blacks from changing the *status quo*.

Thus Daley's "law and order" stance in the black ghettoes tells the black community that they cannot participate in the political system unless they accept the old-style machine rules of the game and that they cannot influence the governing coalition without becoming a part of it. However, the boss-politician and the ruling elite pay a price for perpetuating the blacks' sense of powerlessness and the white opposition's sense of political alienation. By fostering distrust, hostility, and despair among his political opponents, Daley and the ruling coalition actually help extremist and radical leaders to gain support for their revolutionary assaults on the political and social structure. Thus, while Chicago's political future under Mayor Daley's leadership is undebatable, there are key questions to be asked about the future. Can the hard line on social and political change be maintained indefinitely? And what happens to Chicago's political life after Mayor Daley leaves office?

NOTES

1. Marilyn Gittell, "Metropolitan Mayors: Dead End," *Public Administration Review*, Vol. 23, No. 1 (March 1963), pp. 20–21.
2. *Ibid.*, p. 20.
3. James Q. Wilson, "The Mayors vs. The Cities," *The Public Interest*, No. 16 (Summer 1969), p. 36.
4. See, for example, Fred I. Greenstein, "The Changing Pattern of Urban Party Politics," *The Annals*, Vol. 353 (May 1964), pp. 7–8.

5. Edward C. Banfield and James Q. Wilson, *City Politics* (New York: Random House, Inc., Vintage Books, 1963), pp. 104–105. For a more thorough analysis of decision making and political power in Chicago's formally decentralized system, see Edward C. Banfield, *Political Influence* (New York: The Free Press, 1961), Ch. 8, "The Structure of Influence."

6. *The New York Times* (April 7, 1971), p. 22, col. 1.

7. *The New York Times* (May 16, 1971), p. 50, col. 4.

ARTICLE 17

Los Angeles Liberalism

Richard L. Maullin

In November 1970, California voters elected Wilson Riles, a black man, superintendent of public instruction, ousting one of California's leading arch-conservatives, Max Rafferty. Riles' election came as a great surprise because it followed by 17 months the defeat of another black political figure, Los Angeles City Councilman Thomas Bradley, whose inability to turn a primary election lead into a final victory for mayor of Los Angeles, has been attributed to the rejection by white voters of even moderate black candidates. Riles won slightly more than half the votes in suburban white neighborhoods of the city of Los Angeles where Bradley gained barely 30 percent.

In many respects, the Los Angeles mayoral election that Bradley lost was a primer for the 1970 electoral campaigns. Bradley's opponent, two-term Mayor Samuel W. Yorty, seized upon the "radical liberals" long before the vice-president succeeded in making them his principal bogeymen this past year. And for black candidate Wilson Riles, Tom Bradley's campaign provided many precedents to follow and some important ones to avoid in his attempt to become the first black man elected to a major constitutional or executive office in California history. Greatest of the lessons provided by the Bradley

Reprinted from Richard L. Maullin, "Los Angeles Liberalism," *Trans-Action*, Vol. 8, No. 7 (May 1971), pp. 40–51. Copyright © May, 1971, by Transaction, Inc., New Brunswick, New Jersey. Reprinted by permission.

campaign of 1969 was the need "to finesse" the "social issue," which is to say tensions created by changing racial and moral values. The Bradley election showed that the electorate could be frightened by a conscious attempt to conjure up a radical threat with racial undertones. That possibility existed in 1970 as in 1969—as a strategy, as the vice-president's and Max Rafferty's campaigns showed, fear was again to be animated against liberals and blacks. Survey research conducted privately in the California gubernatorial contest indicates that the "social issue," while important as a background factor, may have lost some of the saliency it had in 1969. Yet for Riles, running against an incumbent known for vicious attack precisely on the social issue, the precedents and problems of the Tom Bradley-Sam Yorty election were highly meaningful. The story of Riles' campaign and other seeming reversals of social conservatism in 1970 is in itself fascinating. As a prelude, however, the story of Los Angeles' 1969 mayoral election needs to be examined to highlight the relationships between social attitudes, social science research and the conduct of political campaigns.

The two candidates for mayor of Los Angeles in the spring of 1969 epitomized in their persons and campaign followings important conflicting forces in American society. The incumbent mayor, Samuel William Yorty, a white man with a flamboyant style and a conservative political stance, was strongly challenged by Councilman Thomas Bradley, a black man with liberal support and a cool and dignified manner who had amassed 42 percent of the vote to Yorty's 26 in the primary election earlier.

Yet certain similarities between the two adversaries are also important. Unlike the contrasts, which seemed to mirror national tensions, the similarities between the two candidates derived from the peculiar political world spawned by the ethnic and social character of Los Angeles. Both Yorty, age 60, and Bradley, age 51, were born in the American midlands, Yorty in Nebraska and Bradley in Texas, and both migrated to Los Angeles in the 1920s. Both men came from broken-home, lower-middle-class families; and both men relied on local public education to become men of the law, Yorty as a lawyer and Bradley first as a policeman and later as a lawyer. Both men started their careers as public servants at an early age.

Even their positions on major issues bear some resemblance to each other when viewed in historical perspective. Sam Yorty in the 1930s spoke for Los Angeles' social underdogs, the rural-to-urban

migrant, the unionizing worker, the low-paid consumer. His elec-
torates were composed of the little men disdained by the big forces
controlling national wealth and claiming social deference. Today,
however, as his supporters have become political and social advocates
of a status quo in which they are relatively well off, Yorty has moved
away from fighting to get things for his clientele to fighting to keep
things for it.

By the same token, today Tom Bradley has emerged as an advocate of social justice and equality for those who only marginally
benefited from Sam Yorty's earlier political struggles. Bradley's principal following, the black migrants and sons of migrants to Los
Angeles, are just beginning to make it. But instead of pushing against
a thin line of early pioneers not so unlike the newcomers themselves,
they are challenging the white new middle class, a bulky mass of
people spread over large homogeneous tracts of single family residences many freeways away, while disputing the nearly white Mexican-Americans of neighboring ghettos for jobs and higher social status.
But in a historical and comparative sense, Bradley's and Yorty's public
goals have been similar: social and economic opportunity for those
who are denied it on the basis of family background and economic
status, and an America made strong because of liberty and justice
for all.

The special social characteristics of Los Angeles are important as
factors in the political conflict of forces represented by Mayor Yorty
and Councilman Bradley. The ethnic heterogeneity of the Los Angeles electorate is not by itself especially great. The ethnic breakdown
in the city is approximately as follows: Mexican-Americans, 8 percent; Negroes, 18 percent; Jews, 10 percent; Orientals, 3 percent;
white Anglo-Saxon gentiles (of predominantly midwestern and
border state origin, but with enclaves of Italians, Latin Americans,
Slavs and Central Europeans), 61 percent. As a result, the dominant
ethnic tone of Los Angeles is that of the Anglo-Saxon small-town
midwestern and border states.

More important in designing the peculiar social configuration of
Los Angeles have been the high rates of migration—the metropolitan
area population increased 54 percent between 1950 and 1960—and
the continuing creation of new wealth in different social strata of the
population.

Continuous migration has also prevented uniformly strong ties
from developing in Los Angeles. Many people, it seems, continue to

move about the area, especially if they are not constrained by racial barriers, in a continuous search for the economic and social goals that prompted them to move there in the first place. For many, Los Angeles is where they live, but it is not "home." Even for the more stable, loyalty to place is focused on the homogeneous neighborhood, many of which, in a city of 451 square miles, are five to 25 miles distant from the civic center or other neighborhoods peopled by different ethnic and social types.

AMERICAN SUCCESS STORIES

Los Angeles also lacks a commonly acknowledged structure of social deference. Because the city's economy and land resources have absorbed so many migrants successfully, Los Angeles has a large middle-income, high school educated sector living comfortably within the city limits. These tens of thousands of American success stories feel that they owe their well-being to their own efforts. Therefore, they appear less willing to be led in political and social matters by "civic leaders" and "high society" to whom (even if they could identify them) they owe nothing and who are certainly irrelevant to their general life style.

The growth of southern California's population in the early part of the twentieth century led the state's then rather clubby sociopolitical elite to guard the electoral process against ethnic and populist politics thought to be conducive to corruption and mob influence. Partisan political machines in older eastern cities were judged to be a contributing evil, so partisan elections were replaced by nonpartisan contests in many California cities, including Los Angeles.

The nonpartisan nature of Los Angeles elections now seems to encourage local candidacies reflecting the complexity of the city's 1.1 million-person electorate. These elections deny political parties their important function of coalescing the city's diverse social, ethnic and ideological currents behind a limited number of candidate choices. With lessened constraints from organized partisan politics, many groups venture their champion into the mayoral arena. Yet the possibility of victory is held out only to those adept at massaging the moods and opinions of the social majority, a combination of groups likely to change by the issue and over time.

The structure of government also inhibits the formation of a potential power elite of political figures. Legal authority over the social and economic issues affecting Los Angeles is widely dispersed among a welter of jurisdictions. The city and county of Los Angeles have separate police and fire services. Welfare is a state-county concern, and education is controlled by an independent school district whose boundaries are not coterminous with the city's. Smog, largely generated on the freeways and streets of the city, is the problem of state and county agencies. For the vast majority of the Los Angeles electorate, therefore, local political figures, aside from the mayor, have low visibility. They have no publicly displayed partisan labels, and they are not grouped in a coherent body to deal with the multi-faceted situations affecting life in Los Angeles.

In short, no effective local power structure of political, business or social elites exists in Los Angeles with sufficient self-assurance, public acknowledgement and legitimacy to operate effectively as a mobilizer of votes in a mass electoral situation. As a result, candidates for major office must face the voter without strong middlemen and mediating institutions that identify the candidate or confer a meaningful endorsement. In this context, the media of mass communication, which deliver the image of the candidates directly to the people, assume great importance. Candidates must rely primarily on skill in the use of mass media, especially television and radio, and on a capacity to sense both what issues are important to the public mood and what is the position of the popular majority on those issues.

PHASE AND TACTICS

To understand the Los Angeles election fully, the campaign must be viewed as a public event of six months' duration. There were three distinct phases of the campaign: the period prior to filing for candidacy when initial financial support was sought and long-range planning begun, then the primary campaign in which four serious contenders prevented any one person from winning with an early majority and finally the Yorty-Bradley runoff two months later. Each phase required a somewhat different strategy and set of tactics by the candidates. In the entire period, however, to quote the California state legislature's annual *Report to the People*, "No single public issue . . . so alarmed and perplexed the people of California as the disorder and lawlessness on [the state's] public campuses."

No matter what other issues were raised about Los Angeles, its leadership and its problems, they inevitably had to compete with student militancy and other law and order issues for the attention of the public. By mid-April, six weeks before the election, in response to the open-ended question, "What is the major problem facing the city of Los Angeles?" carried in a private poll commissioned by the Bradley forces, 39 percent of the replies, the largest grouping of responses in the survey, named an issue related to the campus militancy problem.

Mayor Yorty did not stage an aggressive primary campaign, expecting the opposition candidates to destroy each other. In comparison to Bradley and another contendent, moderate Republican Congressman Alphonzo Bell, who spent $408,000 and $522,000 respectively, Yorty spent relatively little—$285,000. Through February and March, billboards proclaimed him to be "America's Best Mayor," and in his speeches and half-hour TV specials, the mayor concentrated on his "support for the police" and on answering the attacks on his administration by the *Los Angeles Times* and Bradley. For these efforts, Yorty won 26 percent of the vote, about equal to what opinion polls taken by potential opposition from mid-1968 indicated to be his minimum popular following.

Bradley and his managers began the campaign in January with a strategy based on justifiable expectations of a massive black support, as well as several ideological assumptions about the fittingness of a coalition incorporating blacks and Jews, liberal gentiles and Mexican-Americans. Bradley's speeches, charged with reformist rhetoric, accused Yorty of a "total lack of leadership" and referred in vague terms to reforms, which would include the police department. The black-brown aspect of a reformist coalition assumed particular importance for Bradley. But ideological assumptions about the common cause of oppressed minorities could not forever screen out evidence of growing group animosity between Mexican-Americans and blacks as well as abrasive competition for jobs and scarce fruits of social reform. Later, the imperfect fit between the rhetoric of coalition and fact of conflict was to torment Bradley in his relations with the important Mexican-American voting bloc, and Bradley's campaign managers spent countless hours attempting to heal fights among Bradley's squabbling coalition supporters.

Nevertheless, the flaws in Bradley's strategy were slow to appear, and approximately three weeks before the 1 April primary, his campaign seemed to jell. Borrowing a tactic and a line from a primary opponent who had dropped out, Bradley advertised himself as *the* Democratic candidate in an attempt to coalesce Democrats and to overcome the frustrating obstacle of nonpartisanship in the election. (Democratic registration in Los Angeles was roughly 651,000 out of 1.1 million voters.) Fund raising began to pick up as many Democratic party, union and civic leaders began to view Bradley as having some chance for success. Two preprimary polls showing Bradley gaining and taking the lead aided this process.

BRADLEY AT THE PEAK

Bradley, in fact, was probably at his apogee on 1 April. Solidly backed by white Democratic liberals, as well as by the black voters, the primary that day gave Bradley 294,000 votes (42 percent), Yorty 183,000 (26 percent) and the remainder to the others. Voter turnout was equal to the turnout in the 1965 final mayoral election, approximately 65 percent.

To Bradley's benefit the campaign had been fairly free of open racial innuendos. (Some observers felt, in fact, that only half the voters on 1 April knew Bradley was black, but this was never substantiated through public opinion polling.) The press had taken Bradley's rather detached and cool manner as a virtue, and they played it up in contrast to Yorty's perpetual accusatory brashness. Just enough of the total electorate disliked Yorty and were convinced by Bradley to give him a real chance.

Nevertheless, as Table 1 shows, the distribution of Bradley's vote according to social and ethnic group provided a bad augury for the runoff, if anyone in his camp had been inclined to read it that way. Bradley emerged from the 1 April primary a national (liberal) hero, apparently riding the crest of a powerful wave of voter support. But the makeup of the support reflected only partial success for his basic strategy of coalition. He successfully monopolized the black vote and raised their turnout. But expectations had been much higher for the Jewish and Mexican-American votes, and a strong black and Mexican-American voters' coalition failed to materialize. Mayor Yorty commented in an interview that if Bradley had done a little better with the brown component of the hoped-for black-brown coalition, Bradley would have been elected in the primary. This might have suggested to Bradley's people that if Mexican-Americans were to support him in the final election it would have to be for reasons other than a desire for a common front with blacks.

As if these signs weren't ominous enough, the last weeks of the primary campaign coincided with a decided worsening of the campus militancy situation, and for the first time during the election campaign, campus incidents with racial content occurred in Los Angeles.

Disturbances by students and black militant organizations continued nationally and locally for the remainder of the campaign, and they succeeded admirably in unsettling the Los Angeles electorate. As mentioned before, private polls taken by Bradley and Yorty indicated that the most important issues for voters in Los Angeles were school disturbances and "law and order." In addition, they showed almost overwhelming support for the Los Angeles police.

Mayor Yorty's counterattack for the third and final stage of the campaign began even as the adverse primary returns were still being counted. Obviously infuriated by his poor showing, Yorty stormed into the city council chamber, where the returns were being reported for the public media, and immediately accused Bradley of being anti-police and of waging a racist campaign to capitalize on the black bloc vote.

Yorty's tone against Bradley was direct and quite virulent, and it was quickly echoed by some of his supporters who distributed leaflets purporting to show synagogues being bombed by black militants and suggesting that a Bradley victory would bring the same to Los Angeles. Bumper stickers bloomed with the words "Bradley power" and a picture of a black fist raised in the black power gesture. There were newspaper ads that showed Bradley, obviously very black, with the copy asking, "Will your city be safe with this man?" The basic objective, of course, was to discredit the image of Councilman Thomas Bradley by a racist frontal assault.

Nevertheless, as Bradley's private mid-April opinion polling indicated, these tactics had no immediate effect. Some of Yorty's backers, shocked by his poor showing and continuing defensiveness, began to have second thoughts about letting their man shoot from the hip quite as much as his nature prompted him to.

A complete reorganization of the Yorty campaign took place in mid-April. Yorty's campaign committee, co-chaired by conservative

Republican party financial leaders Henry Salvatori and Preston Hotchkiss, hired the political management firm of Haig and Associates. Fresh from managing Barry Goldwater, Jr.'s election to Congress, Haig and Associates, led by conservative Republican lawyer Haig Kehaiyan, argued that a more affirmative message from the mayor and tighter control on the various advertising and public relations activities of his campaign were essential. Instead of answering Bradley's charges of incompetence in city government, Kehaiyan's group insisted that the mayor emphasize his commitment to law and order and support for the police and attack Bradley as a tool of radical forces.

To control the public face and voice of the mayor's campaign, Haig and Associates attempted to coordinate the presentation of a "positive" image. As a result, Yorty's theatrics took on a new cast. His speeches satisfied those seeking to hear his view of things in more reasoned tones, while he continued to titillate audiences during question periods with his flamboyant off-the-cuff remarks. In Yorty's words, all this was necessary to keep the press from distorting his position by reporting only his more colorful remarks.

Yorty's campaign managers formed a law enforcement officers' committee, headed by a regular police officer on leave of absence. The committee charged that 90 percent of the police force would resign if Bradley were elected, and to skeptics Yorty urged that they just go up to any policeman and ask if it wasn't true. This group also ran ads in the metropolitan press linking Bradley with several liberal political organizations and these in turn to various militant and Communist groups. Revelations about alleged militants on Bradley's staff were first handled by others, with Yorty echoing the charges like a Greek chorus.

In addition, Kehaiyan, a strong believer in the utility of door-to-door precinct canvassing in areas of potential strength, analyzed the past voting behavior of Los Angeles neighborhoods and then organized numerous Republican volunteers and other conservative groups into a field force to carry personally the new "positive" message. In contrast to Bradley's volunteers, who were more at home with highly verbal "do your thing" politics, Kehaiyan's volunteers seemed like Christian soldiers grimly marching as to war.

Yorty's campaign objective remained the same—to discredit Bradley—but the means were now quite different from the earlier frontal assault. One was to link Bradley to extremist and militant forces so prominent in the news and to cast doubt on Bradley's record as a policeman. The second was to tone down Sam Yorty to make him acceptable to those who had voted against him, *but not for Bradley*, in the primary, or those who did not vote at all.

To some Yorty watchers, his toning down probably seemed the more difficult task. A master of innuendo and the political ad-lib, the mayor has also more than a usual share of irrepressible gall. Yet Yorty has a fantastic survival instinct as well. When pressed, as he was after the primary, he has the capacity to organize all ideas and information in close relation to their possible effect on his basic political goals: survival and new upward chances. Moreover, the message Haig and Associates developed really implied no radical change from what Yorty himself was inclined to say; it just organized it better. Yorty is, after all, a hawk on Vietnam, a propolice hardliner on student militants and a believer in an internal threat posed by American communists. Haig and Associates' concept was as ideological (to the Right) as it was instrumental. Yorty's critics say that his use of Kehaiyan strategy demonstrated a cynical willingness to exploit popular fears and prejudices. His supporters claim Yorty believes what he said. But whatever the truth, the important fact is that he became credible to a majority of the voters.

Bradley's campaign managers, exhilarated by the primary election results, decided to follow a safe and orthodox strategy of not changing what appeared to be a winning campaign unless a serious crisis developed. However, when indications of trouble did show themselves in late April and early May, the Bradley campaign organization proved too inflexible in concept and too amorphous in organization to make needed adjustments in the themes of the campaign or the image of the candidate. Bradley, therefore, continued to emphasize vague liberal reformist slogans while promising to provide Los Angeles with "leadership and integrity." He also hammered away at the corruption for which certain Yorty-appointed city commissioners, but not Yorty, had been indicted. Yet, listening to some of Bradley's followers talk of the mayor, it often seemed that it was Mayor Sam's crass style rather than his supposed misdeeds that really bothered these nouveau cosmopolites who wanted a clean, sophisticated mayor to preside over urbane Los Angeles.

Perceiving Bradley to be in the lead, his campaign managers— with some exceptions—rejected the idea that the two candidates should debate. When local TV offered to carry a Bradley-Yorty encounter,

Bradley appointed a committee of six lawyers to negotiate (and evade) the conditions under which the two might meet. Yorty, immediately assuming the pose of the brave sheriff standing nearly alone at the far end of the bar, responded that he would debate anywhere, any time. Later, toward the middle of May, Bradley's managers aborted a chance meeting with Yorty on the rostrum of a local chamber of commerce, even though two previous chance encounters had been judged in Bradley's favor by professional newsmen.

The decision not to debate Sam Yorty was more than a simple tactical one. The arguments over the debate illustrated important differences within Bradley's camp. One position was simply that the front runner never debates a challenger, and since Bradley had done so well in the primary and in published public opinion polls, his views were well supported and there was no need to run the risks of a bad performance. Another participant argued that Bradley would be no match for Yorty's ability to put out faster and better abuse. A third view, argued by a black member of the candidate's inner sanctum, asserted that Bradley would lose even if he won because the public would not tolerate a black man showing up a white man in a face-to-face encounter. Finally, some former Kennedyites, remembering Bob Kennedy's confrontation with Eugene McCarthy more than the 1960 debates, argued that debates are essentially opportunities to project an image directly to the voters and not a contest of wit and intelligence. These people also argued that no matter what the polls or the primary showed, Bradley, a nonincumbent and a black, should always act the hungry challenger eager for opportunities to prove himself.

These arguments carried over into other aspects of the campaign. So long as the campaign tasks were the articulation of liberal social ideas and the projection of Bradley as a man of quiet reason, the previous political experiences and collective liberal assumptions of Bradley's campaign advisers were sufficient to provide direction. But as Yorty's counterattack began to build steam, *using Bradley's liberal supporters and preference for "rational discussion" as arguments against Bradley*, precedents from other liberal campaigns often failed to indicate what to do next. Bradley's campaign had underlying moral assumptions. It argued that Yorty was an opportunistic and corrupt boor and promised to install a regime of personal integrity. These themes, so much a part of a liberal reformer's perspective, actually contributed to the worsening of a key incident signaling Bradley's decline.

THE ROTHENBERG AFFAIR

On 23 April, a Yorty "truth squad" composed of three Los Angeles city councilmen revealed that Don Rothenberg, a campaign coordinator for Tom Bradley, was an ex-Communist who had been a party member as recently as 1956. Bradley strategists, including Maury Weiner, his campaign manager, and Steven Reinhardt, national Democratic committeeman, knew the Rothenberg story would be released, yet they waited for the attack before making any statement or taking any action; they dealt with the problem only after it became a major news story. Then, when first questioned about Don Rothenberg, Tom Bradley did not have a convincing reply. Eventually, a rather weak statement was issued in which Bradley disclaimed knowledge of Rothenberg's past when he was hired but added that he would not fire him. He said, "A man must not be cast aside. He has paid for his mistake . . . he plays no role in deciding issues."

Seizing an opportunity, Yorty began to hammer on the theme that while Tom Bradley might not be a bad guy he was naive and could be manipulated by radical forces. Reporters, even those friendly to Tom Bradley, continued to question him about Rothenberg because, as they indicated later, the question was never really resolved.

The Rothenberg explosion in a national and local environment rife with fear and concern over student disturbances and militant demands marked the point when the Bradley campaign began to sour. Bradley himself agrees that the Rothenberg affair hurt him badly, and he implied that were he to face that issue again he would probably handle it differently. But, Bradley added, if it hadn't been the Rothenberg case, then some other means would have been found to link him maliciously and unjustifiably to extremism. Other key Bradley supporters, while admitting to the harm the incident caused, still maintain that Bradley did the right thing in keeping Rothenberg in spite of Yorty's exploitation of the issue.

Yorty, in a private interview, argued that Rothenberg's presence was just one manifestation of radical and Communist support for Bradley, Yorty was quick to point out that in addition to Rothenberg, whose renunciation of communism Yorty implied was not credible, Gus Hall, leader of the American Communist party, also endorsed Bradley and "even held a meeting of the Western region to instruct the Communists to work for Bradley." For the mayor, nevertheless, Rothenberg was the key to making his point about radical influences over Bradley. It is hard to escape the conclusion of one political reporter that Bradley's handling of the Rothenberg affair was "humanitarian, but politically stupid."

As the contest neared the final four weeks and the pace became exhausting for the candidates, Yorty's campaign seemed to take on the character of Bradley's primary campaign. Fence sitters and their money fell into line, and a winning theme was hit upon.

Some of Bradley's supporters, including staff people lent by other local political figures and leaders of the United Auto Workers, became increasingly uneasy about Bradley's ability to hold his lead after the Rothenberg story broke and Yorty began to exploit it. In their view Bradley needed more stimulating material for his public appearances to make his assertions of energetic leadership more credible. Accordingly, the United Auto Workers brought in both Robert Kennedy's and Eugene McCarthy's principal speech writers to generate a key set of speeches that projected a Kennedy-like forcefulness in the place of Bradley's heretofore unimpassioned, if dedicated tone. Their presence, while ostensibly welcomed by older Bradley hands, in the end added yet more voices to the constant tug and pull between the more optimistic believers in continuity and the more aggressive among Bradley's advisers who wished to change the tone of the campaign.

By deciding to hold the line after the development of the Rothenberg affair, Bradley's campaign managers also seemed to be overlooking many of the implications of the public opinion survey they commissioned for their private use from Opinion Research of California. This survey was conducted one day prior to the breaking of the Rothenberg affair. Even so, the study indicated that a more direct and assertive position by Bradley was needed to answer Yorty's already heavy attacks on the issue of radicalism.

More importantly, the detailed, 66-page Opinion Research study gave Bradley a set of conclusions with potentially broad-reaching and disturbing conclusions:

Bradley's lead was based primarily upon his ability to attract virtually all Negro votes.

Mayor Yorty held a substantial lead among Republican voters and Councilman Bradley held a very strong lead among Democratic voters, but that lead was slight if Negro voters were excluded.

Mayor Yorty would benefit by a high voter turnout.

Although widespread concern existed over the activities of Yorty appointees, most voters did not think that Yorty himself was dishonest or corrupt.

Opinions about Yorty centered on his personality rather than his actions or stands on issues.

Bradley had a favorable image, although most voters did not know much about him or his record and philosophy. At the time of the study, not many voters had formed *strong* opinions about Bradley, pro or con.

Not many voters were inclined to believe Bradley was antipolice, indicating an opportunity to counteract Yorty's charges.

Most voters were satisfied with the level of services in the city of Los Angeles. No single service was universally condemned.

The public image of the Los Angeles Police Department was good, with unfavorable opinions restricted to a small portion of the Negro community.

Moreover, well over a third of the responses to this opinion study cited school problems and law and order as the major local concerns. Only 3.6 percent of the responses of those who said they would vote pointed to corruption and lack of leadership in government—Bradley's theme about Yorty—as an important issue.

Most of these conclusions conflicted with what Bradley thought were the real issues in the campaign so far and with where Bradley thought his support lay. Corruption, concern about police misbehavior, dissatisfaction about the uglification of *arriviste* Los Angeles were notably absent as major public concerns; yet this is what Bradley talked about most. As soon as the opinion survey was received, Bradley's advisers began grappling with its implications. Although an effort was made to beef up Bradley's image as a leader and to reach out to groups in the white majority, the study's implications for a strategy change towards emphasizing Tom Bradley of the Los Angeles Police Department, a hardnose on militant demonstrators, were overwhelmed by the argument that the liberal reformist campaign waged so far was a winner and, the study notwithstanding, no major changes or new efforts were necessary.

In the final analysis, the results of the Opinion Research survey and their interpretation and use by the Bradley campaign underscored the tension that seems to exist between ideological preference and the application of social science techniques and their results. Bradley's people, like other political liberals and like Yorty's men, were not innocent or simple-minded when it came to testing the public's mood. Bradley's staff used all the devices of modern opinion polling, played games of strategy and looked at their candidate in terms of the image he would project over the mass media. Yet when the result of this social science research began to materialize, some of the information was highly disturbing.

One approach to the electorate implied by the Opinion Research survey was to be better than Yorty at his own game. Bradley's team looked at these results, were shocked by this implication and looked away. Their eyes shifted to the page of the report that told them who was ahead on the day of the survey: Bradley, 44 to 37 percent, the rest refusing to answer.

Bradley's men, like most men, did not go into politics simply to merchandize a product; they are political. That is, they are concerned with the use of power to affect values—public and private, material and spiritual. They did not support Bradley only to have his campaigning sanction a rigid, authoritarian approach to police-community problems or student activism. Bradley, undoubtedly, would have rejected such an approach anyway.

Thus, faced with a scientific revelation of public indifference to what they thought were the real issues at stake, they turned back with even greater fervor to the crusade for reform. New position papers, press releases and speeches came out in an unfocused mass telling of corruption, bad police-community relations, pollution and the other standards of a reform campaign today.

But was there only a single implication of the Opinion Research poll's results? The same survey implied other things about potential directions for the remaining weeks of the Bradley campaign, and perhaps about future campaign styles for liberals in the difficult final Vietnam years ahead as well. If Bradley was not a radical, he could take them on strongly, this pool seemed to say, perhaps neutralize Yorty's biggest issue. If Bradley was a policeman and supported true law and order, which he did and which most political liberals do, then he could emphasize that fact clearly, as this poll seemed to invite him to do, without providing distractions about a hard-to-believe corruption he was going to eliminate anyway, once he got in.

In short, this poll told Bradley, as it tells liberals elsewhere, that there are only a few areas where the beliefs, anxieties and concerns of the white middle-class electorate are open for manipulation by liberal candidates. But there are these few. The question might have been asked, "If a fair number of people do not share our view, are there things we can share with them? If there are, will it alienate the *voters* who have so far given us their support?" In Bradley's case, since so much of his strength rested on a unanimous bloc of black votes it was logical to ask if they had any alternative.

As the final weeks wore on, Yorty found the correct optical language for the nightly television news coverage. At the same time, Bradley became increasingly tired, and his rather stiff television manner turned wooden.

A review of the candidates' public activities and the news for the day for 20 and 21 May highlight the differences in the two candidates' tactical style and basic strategy.

On a day one week before the election, University of California students and demonstrators were dispersed by the National Guard and police using tear gas and shotguns. News stories and film clips showed an American city turned into a battleground under siege; buildings were barricaded by students at the University of California at Santa Cruz, and 250 youths were dispersed near Stanford.

And in the campaign? Yorty reiterated forcefully that Governor Ronald Reagan was right in calling the National Guard to Berkeley. Tom Bradley released his income tax returns for the last five years.

News for the following day, 21 May: draft records were set afire in Los Angeles; Oregon saboteurs dynamited a church, a bank and other buildings; mobs were teargassed at Berkeley; hundreds of students battled police at San Fernando High School in a Los Angeles neighborhood.

And in the campaign? Bradley said that city government corruption was still the main issue while Yorty for the first time in his campaign read a prepared speech in its entirety. In it Yorty said that he could deal with militants better than Bradley and linked the Students for a Democratic Society (SDS) threat with "forces" on Bradley's campaign staff. Whether Yorty and his backers were conscious of this or not, most serious studies of public attitudes towards riot, protest demonstrations and other types of physically assertive political behavior by minorities with grievances (reported best in *Public Opinion Quarterly*) have indicated that roughly between 45 and 60 percent of American whites believe that there is some sort of conspiracy coordinating as well as stimulating protest behavior.

LINKING BRADLEY UP

On the crucial issues of militancy and race, Yorty constantly attempted to link Bradley to the troubles prominent in the news. For example, at a Rotary Club meeting in a predominantly Mexican-American business district, shortly after black militants invaded a Gary, Indiana city council meeting, Yorty said that if Tom Bradley became mayor "the militants could come down and intimidate the City Council . . . I don't want to see that happen in the City of Los Angeles . . . And this could happen, couldn't it? If Bradley got elected, we could have that . . . So I hope that our people will wake up. I'm doing my best to tell them and I need your help in doing it because it's not just my city, it's our city and I think we want to . . . keep the kind of investment climate we've got here now, where people are encouraged to come and where they feel the government is stable and the Police Department will operate and protect them in their rights."

Bradley never ducked the issue of campus unrest and militancy, but his quiet tone and preference for a "reasonable" answer were pale next to Yorty's demagoguery. Bradley would say, "The first step to be taken to solve this problem [campus disorders] is to begin an examination of the fundamental lack of communication and dialogue. Once we do this, we can resolve our difficulties in a proper atmosphere." Yorty's message was simpler: smash them if they show up, and in any case keep their spokesman out of City Hall.

In the end Yorty received 447,000 votes (53.25 percent, and Bradley 392,000 votes (46.74 percent).

There can be little doubt that a backlash factor was at play in public opinion during Los Angeles' election. This attitude, a focused public reaction to a political or social object, was ultimately the most crucial one for determining the vote. It would be a mistake, however, to conclude that backlash was simply and solely rejection of Tom Bradley because of his race. Certainly the national implications of Bradley's defeat and Yorty's victory go beyond simple rejection or vindictiveness on the grounds of race. The election presaged much of 1970's betterness about "radical liberals" and vice-presidential rhetoric.

Many of Bradley's campaign staff and personal supporters, as well as Bradley himself, explain the defeat by reference to Yorty's successful appeal to racial prejudice and to fear of the unknown consequences that could flow from being governed by a black man. Still Bradley would not have made his bid if he had believed race would be an a priori factor against him. After the campaign Bradley said, "We should have taken on the racial issue frontally, as John Kennedy faced the Catholic issue in 1960, rather than insisting that race was irrelevant, as it most likely is, to being a good mayor." Yet some Bradley supporters, even those who are now quite critical of certain tactical moves in the campaign, feel that even a better-run campaign would have failed in the end.

Yorty's more moderate backers argue that Bradley's blunders, such as the Rothenberg affair, and his poor TV manner allowed Yorty to take the initiative. Race alone, they say, would not have defeated Tom Bradley.

The truth of the matter probably lies somewhere between. Undoubtedly, being black was a drawback for Bradley in dealing with some of the white population. A trade-off could, it is true, exist between the number of real bigots among the whites and the ethnic bloc loyalty of the blacks. Nevertheless, Bradley's race put him at a distinct disadvantage among the white population, which was becoming greatly·disturbed by increased social protest in the United States. Even so, it is important that one remember that Bradley was not overwhelmed in the election even though Sam Yorty mounted what has to have been one of the most effective exploitations of daily events, underlying suspicions of minorities and beliefs in conspiracies against the well-being of the American people. In many respects, the Los Angeles election resembled the Carl Stokes election in Cleveland in 1967. The blacks gave their candidate a solid vote, while roughly a third of the whites joined in. The difference, of course—apart from the nature of the campaigns—was that Cleveland is over 40 percent black, while Los Angeles' black community is less than 20 percent of the total population. One national implication raised by Cleveland and Los Angeles is that black candidates in big cities don't lose all white

TABLE 1. Percentage of Voters by Social Groups in the Primary and Final Election

Group	% Bradley		% Yorty		% Gain-Loss From Primary To Final Election		% Turnout	
	Primary	Final	Primary	Final	Bradley	Yorty	Primary	Final
Middle- to Upper-Middle-Class Whites	27	32	32	68	+5	+36	63	77
Middle-Class Blacks	85	89	7	10	+4	+3	77	85
Laboring and Lower-Middle-Class Blacks	94	99	4	1	+5	−1	70	79
Laboring and Lower-Middle-Class Mexican-Americans	34	33	30	67	−1	+37	56	70
Lower-Middle to Upper-Middle-Class Jews	52	52	18	48	0	+30	62	78

support simply by race alone. Other factors, not always present even in racially troubled United States cities, must be at hand.

Three factors combined to produce the backlash sentiment in Los Angeles, and each of these factors depended in some crucial way on mass media to shape the public expression of backlash.

First, the challenge to established values manifest in the often violent confrontations between students (mostly) and public authorities sensitized a large part of the public, not so much to the points the protesters were raising but to the behavior of the protesters. This is a national phenomenon just as television itself is nationwide. The mass media, by routinely and daily showing protest events, succeeded in proving with visual evidence that the students were running amok instead of studying and that someone—the person the news would fall upon to interview—was "leading" the protest. The fact that local news brought incidents from all over the United States into Los Angeles homes in a regular fashion probably served to intensify concern over the militancy issue. No one in Los Angeles, or Seattle or Mineola for that matter, missed the photograph of black student militants seizing a Cornell University building with rifles and crossed bandoliers. As regards the Los Angeles election, it is important to remember that mass media exposure of these militant student protests began long before the campaign occupied time on television and radio and space in the press. Thus, when candidates came into public focus, really not until shortly before the primary and final elections, the issue most preoccupying the public's mind was the perplexing character of student protest. Students and mass media, in effect, prepared the principal issue for the public and the candidates.

Bradley's argument that other things besides student militancy were important for Los Angeles was evidently unheeded by the voters. The people apparently wanted answers from public officials, regardless of what the city charter or state constitution said about their actual responsibilities. This is probably true nationwide. Paradoxically, being sophisticated enough to distinguish local from national issues may hurt you with the "folks at home" who are wired into a national circuit several hours each night. Yorty, however, was quick to seize upon the public's questioning mood and produced a set of answers to the student protest issue, thus providing the second factor contributing to the backlash sentiment. Ignoring completely the substantive issues raised by the protesters, Yorty assured the public that they were "radicals," "SDS," "anarchists" and "communists" and that the purpose of the protests was to destroy "America," a concept often used by Yorty in its most mythic nationalist connotation.

To convey these "answers" to the greater public—essentially telling the noninvolved "silent majority" who the protesters were and what they were up to—Yorty and his campaign staff relied on the mass media's desire to report his election campaign, a public service paid for by their business, the sale of advertising space and time. Carefully coordinating the free and paid media, Yorty organized public opinion around the problem that local and national opinion polls showed to be a crucial public issue. Once organized, public perplexity and malaise over student military protest were more readily available for conscious expression by the electorate. What the public needed was some object on which they could focus their hostility and fear. That object was Tom Bradley and his followers, the third factor in the creation of a backlash in Los Angeles.

But Bradley alone, or the simple fact of his race, is not a sufficient explanation of why he could become the object of that focus. Bradley and his campaigning had to contribute certain acts and statements in order to link himself negatively to the turbulent public mood. Yorty's role, while catalyzing, was, by itself, insufficient to produce the backlash.

Bradley gave a lot of ground to Yorty. He allowed him to work the issue of militancy—student and racial—at will. It was Yorty who captured the initiative on the police issue in spite of Bradley's 21-year record of service in the Los Angeles Police Department. When Yorty formed an aggressive policeman's committee, only then, and in haste, did Bradley form one. Even then, it lacked strong representation from rank and file policemen. Bradley's campaign spent tens of thousands of dollars on computerized mailing, yet one of its simplest and most effective pieces of literature, a brochure with a picture of Bradley in his police lieutenant's uniform, was developed and mailed only in the twilight of the six-month campaign effort.

Bradley allowed many accusations to go ineffectively answered, though of course he always tried to respond. The Yorty charge of militants in Bradley's campaign is a case in point. There were no white radical New Leftists in the Bradley camp nor any black militants, because both of these groups considered Bradley an Uncle Tom. Indeed, Bradley is a personally conservative person, the antithesis of the radical stereotype. Perhaps the old-time liberals (ironically champions of a new Democratic coalition of Kennedy and McCarthy activists) who were running Bradley's campaign could not bring themselves for ideological-moral reasons to generate the words and the campaign activities necessary to distinguish Bradley *in the public's mind* from forces much further to his left.

Liberal ideological beliefs were, in fact, an important factor in the development of Bradley's candidacy and subsequent campaign. For example, among Bradley's strongest supporters, white and black, a firm belief in rational cooperation for the common good, in which all of America's social groups share on a basis of justice and equality, was the basis for a rejection of the revolutionary rhetoric and occasional violence of the New Left. A deep commitment to individual dignity and to the intrinsic cultural worth of all groups in plural America lay behind the acceptance of Bradley on his merits and the selection of the black-brown-liberal (Jewish) strategy as a key component of the campaign.

Two themes particular in the liberal American credo widely held by Bradley's campaigners seem to have contributed significantly to Bradley's demise. First, the belief in justice and equality led to a reformist view of the police as the front line of justice in America. Los Angeles police had had their brutal and brutalizing moments, apart from the 1965 Watts riot. On 23 June 1967, when President Lyndon B. Johnson visited Los Angeles for a political dinner, the Los Angeles Police Department restrained a large crowd of middle-class war protesters. Excesses occurred, and in hearings before the city council, former policeman Bradley took the police chief and his force to task.

Later, in the Chicago Democratic convention of 1968, other police participated in a many-sided riot as rioters and many of the people who directed Bradley's effort had seen it happen as McCarthy-Kennedy delegates. As a result, reforming the police—not destroying them—became a driving purpose for Bradley's supporters and, one may assume, for Bradley himself. That the police were seemingly expressive of a majority's mood, and had therefore become a politically sensitive subject indicative of dominant social trends, was lost in the impulse to reform them to a more liberal image of public service. The liberal impulse, in other words, contributed purely and simply to the Bradley's camp missing the political point raised by all sides in the disturbances: more fundamental issues were felt to be at stake than forms and reforms.

Second, the growing assertion of intrinsic worth in the peculiarities and differences among the immigrant, religious and racial groups in

America overtly determined Bradley's strategy toward two pivotal social groups in the Los Angeles electorate: the approximately 110,000 Mexican-American voters and the slightly larger number of Jews.

Bradley and his white and black supporters tended to view the Mexican-Americans as a natural ally in the struggle for equality and justice. And to be sure, among the group as a whole, political advocates can be found who champion a sort of romantic cultural nationalism with solidarity toward other colored peoples, but there is also in this group a variety of assimilationist positions as well as a conservative cultural nationalism that rejects contact with outsiders.

Bradley's campaign, however, tended to impose the perspective of the solidarity-oriented cultural nationalists among the Mexican-American population. The black-brown coalition in effect was telling Mexican-American voters that their social and economic goals would only really be achieved when the blacks also received justice. This message negated much of the experience of thousands of Mexican-Americans, who, by virtue of not being black, had greater access to nonghetto housing, higher income and less social hostility from whites than blacks experienced. It is true that Mexican-Americans as a whole have a lower level of educational attainment than blacks, and no one in the Mexican-American community is oblivious to the difficulties of getting a good education in insensitive English-speaking schools. But Bradley's approach to the Mexican-Americans went beyond recognizing the problems. It suggested a means of solution—a black-brown coalition and an emphasis on *chicanismo* (the ambivalent status of being Mexican in an Anglo-American world). To a majority of Mexican-Americans, such a separatist solution was less acceptable than the assimilation implicitly offered by the Yorty forces.

Where Bradley said wait until we are all free, Yorty said, you Mexicans are fine people, "got all the street names in Los Angeles" and I am offering you a chance to get a little closer to good things—jobs, suburbia, a preferred station in the local caste system without having to deal with those aggressive *mayatas* (blacks).

Bradley, in effect, tried to gain Mexican-American support by playing to the brown, poor, equality-demanding—Mexican—side of the Mexican-American group personality. Yorty won his support by appealing to the lower-middle-class, upward-focused, status-oriented and assimilative—American—trend in Mexican-American group behaviors. Yorty said in an interview that he treated Mexican-Americans like anyone else. "I gave them jobs, go to their fiestas and try to provide what they are looking for in Los Angeles. Mexicans don't like to be called Brown." Tom Bradley offered the distant prospect of expanding the Los Angeles City Council so that a Mexican-American would have an easier time in getting elected. Bradley said, "I tried to work with Mexican-American leadership, but their conflicts over who was going to get what finally were more than we could handle."

Bradley had more success in his approach to the Jewish population. The liberal creed is widely held among Jews who in Los Angeles, like other major American cities, tend to fall into middle-income professional life or commerce and live in homogeneous clusters. Newspapers, high culture, the manipulation of life by intelligence rather than by force—these are Jewish-liberal things, especially for the highly educated professionals. For these Jewish voters, this is what Tom Bradley tried to identify himself with, and many listened.

But fear of being squeezed between the black and the white *goyim*, while not so liberal an attitude, exists in varying degrees among Jews of all economic brackets. Sam Yorty, for all his demagoguery, is no George Wallace. He said repeatedly that he couldn't understand why everyone was against him in the black community; after all, he integrated city government in 1961. For half the Jews, this was liberal enough. Bradley was all right, it might be said, but recalling the New York school mess and all the charges of black anti-Semitism, these were not normal times. Small groups who have made it in some ways can't afford to take chances in others.

In essence, Tom Bradley contributed to the blacklash sentiment by being black in a de facto segregated society, by espousing liberal political views easily interpreted as being soft on militant protesters and in any case less relevant to the immediate interests of potential allies and by employing a person whose previous Communist party connection seemed to back up Yorty's claim that Bradley was in league with campus and racial militants.

No doubt it was easier to convince the white electorate that Bradley was a threat simply because he was black. By and large white people have very little contact with blacks, and too often those they do see are either cleaning the floor or raising a black gloved fist on television. Consequently, as a black candidate, Bradley automatically faced a lower threshold of public suspicion than his white opponent. But Bradley's outspoken liberalism helped push the white electorate over that threshold. Espousing the liberal slant on justice, championing as it does minority causes, Bradley lent himself to the accusation that he would be "their" mayor. Undoubtedly for liberals it is a vile business to be constantly on guard against speaking out on dearly held principles, for fear of adverse voter reaction. But under the reign of one man-one vote, the nonliberals have a majority nationally and in the national microcosm, Los Angeles.

APOCRYPHA

Every campaign generates apocryphal stories: One of Bradley's white field deputies has a six-year-old daughter who marched up and down her block handing out literature and pitching hard for Tom Bradley. Stopped on the street by a middle-aged woman of Italian descent, the little girl handed her a piece of literature. The woman said, "I hear if Bradley wins all the blacks will take over Los Angeles." Thinking about it for a monent, the little girl replied, "If it's all right with Mr. Bradley, it's all right with me."

ARTICLE 18

The Mayors vs. the Cities

James Q. Wilson

So accustomed have we become to the daily dispatches from the urban battlefront—reports of perpetual crisis, the descriptions of mayors struggling in vain against seemingly hopeless odds, the ominous warnings of growing frustrations and anger—that we are in danger of taking for granted, as though they were part of the natural

Reprinted from James Q. Wilson, "The Mayors vs. The Cities," *The Public Interest*, No. 16 (Summer 1969), pp. 25–37. © 1969 by National Affairs, Inc. Reprinted by permission of *The Public Interest* and James Q. Wilson.

order, some rather remarkable developments. By the standards of any other era, what is happening today—or more precisely, what is *not* happening—needs to be explained.

Consider: Despite the fact that ghetto riots have torn scores of cities and that rising rates of violent crime have afflicted even more, and despite the fact that George Wallace revealed by his campaign that there are millions of Americans ready for a hard-line, get-tough policy on civil disorder, there are few big-city mayors—Los Angeles in this, as in other respects, is an exception—who publicly endorse this approach or who act as if they thought there was any political mileage in it. In New York, Boston, Detroit, San Francisco, Atlanta, and many other cities, the mayors, far from trying to put together a political base out of white "law-and-order" sentiments, are repudiating this strategy and continuing to argue for meliorative measures designed to better the lot of the poor and the black. Though every public opinion poll shows Americans, especially but not wholly white Americans, to be deeply troubled and angered by crime and disorder, and though every group of organized police officers are demanding that the mayors "unleash" them; and though there is usually a primary opponent in the wings, waiting to run against "crime in the streets"— nevertheless the standard reply of the mayors has been to deplore violence, to call for renewed efforts to eliminate its causes, and to attack overzealousness about this issue as a form of disguised racism. Finally, a "law-and-order" candidate in office rarely maintains the "hard line" that got him there; Sam Yorty, since reelection, has been speaking far more softly and sociologically than he campaigned. So, it can be predicted, will Marchi or Procaccino, if either of these gentlemen is elected Mayor of New York.

Consider also: Whenever a clear choice confronts a mayor, he tends (again, especially in the big cities) to side with the liberal (though rarely the radical) side even when the liberal side appears to be widely unpopular. John Lindsay favored a civilian review board for the police, though any sounding of opinion would have shown that the vast majority of New York voters were strongly opposed to the board. Joseph Alioto became, as mayor, a backer of the police-community relations unit of the San Francisco police department even though the unit was detested by many, probably most, San Francisco officers and criticized by many civilians for allegedly "siding with the criminals" against the police. The response of Jerome Cavanagh to the fearful riot in Detroit was to appoint and actively support a "New

Detroit Committee" that consulted with (though did not satisfy) the most militant blacks and urged programs and patience rather than tanks and toughness. And he did this though he was facing an organized campaign among white voters to recall him from office for alleged failures to curb rising crime (by which the petitioners meant, of course, rising *Negro* crime).

Consider finally: Though municipal tax rates have been steadily rising and though the "revolt of the taxpayers" is often predicted and indeed sometimes occurs, the "new breed" mayors are rarely, if ever, fiscal conservatives. Instead, they launch new programs and raise property and other taxes to new highs, despite the fact that one reason they defeated their predecessor may have been that he seemed to be responsible for a tax level the voters found unacceptable. Of course, many of the subsequent increases result from forces over which no mayor has any control—legislatively mandated pay raises for city workers, for example—but some substantial part of the boost is caused by the fact the mayor is innovative and program-oriented rather than single-mindedly tax-conscious.

FINDING EXPLANATIONS

One possible explanation for these apparent paradoxes is that acting other than as the mayors do would be politically risky. A tough law-and-order posture would alienate Negro voters and a failure to improve services (even at the cost of higher taxes) would alienate white homeowners. But in many of these cities with the most conspicuously "new breed" mayors—Boston, New York, San Francisco—the black vote is but a small fraction of the total (in Boston, for example, it is probably less than 10 per cent of the whole and in New York and San Francisco, it could not be much more). And in some of these cities, as well as in cities (such as Detroit) where Negroes are a much larger fraction of the population, persons get elected to the city councils on the basis of much more conservative images, even though they run at large and thus have exactly the same constituencies as does the mayor.

Nor can it be said that the present strategy of the more progressive mayors confers any obvious political rewards. At this writing, the probability of Lindsay's reelection hardly seems overwhelming. The common complaint of (white) New York voters seems to be that he "gives too much to the Negroes" (though, naturally, Negroes may feel that they have in fact received very little). And Cavanagh in Detroit did not appear to enhance his shaky political position with the steps he took after the riot—indeed, for many voters he probably worsened it. By contrast, Mayor Richard Daley in Chicago won a great deal of support by his tough line during and after the police clashes with demonstrators at the Democratic National Convention.

Of course, chance may play some part in deciding who gets to be mayor. Afer all, Louise Day Hicks campaigned in Boston in a way that attracted strong support from the police, from opponents of measures designed to further school integration, and from many victims of the city's chronically high tax rate. She led the field in the preliminary election and ran a quite respectable second in the elimination round. If she had not been a woman and if some campaign breaks had gone her way, she might well be the mayor of Boston. But what is striking is not that she lost, but that Kevin White, who won, did not operate the mayor's office in a way obviously calculated to win over to him the voters who opposed him. One of his first acts was an effort (aborted by premature publicity) to replace the police commissioner; subsequently, he announced some of the largest tax increases any Boston mayor has ever had to take responsibility for. And other measures intended to help the lot of Boston Negroes have earned for him, in certain neighborhoods, the unflattering nickname of "Mayor Black."

To some persons, finding explanations for why mayors act as they do is unnecessary, or rather the explanation is obvious—these officials are courageous, right-thinking persons who deeply believe in what they are doing and are willing to take the blame for having done it. There is no doubt a good deal of truth in this view, but it does not seem adequate. These mayors are also intelligent, and they would have little to lose by deciding that discretion is the better part of valor. Given the heavy law-and-order majorities in many cities, one would expect even the most forward-looking chief executive to at least talk tough if only to win breathing space for himself and perhaps some consent for the programs he seeks to carry out. Most liberal mayors face no threat from the left (the Negroes have no realistic alternative), but they do face serious threats from the right. Yet the center-seeking tendencies of state and national candidates seems not to be duplicated at the big-city level. Hubert Humphrey as well as

Richard Nixon found it important to have firm law-and-order (or "order-and-justice") positions; anybody running against Ronald Reagan in California would be foolish indeed to assume that he would improve his chances of election by departing radically from Reagan's position on student unrest, welfare programs, or crime in the streets. The best he could hope for would be to display a difference in emphasis sufficient to acquire votes on the left while keeping his losses in the center and on the right to a minimum.

A NEW ERA IN CITY POLITICS?

I would suggest that there is a general, structural reason for the behavior of many big-city mayors, a reason that, if correct, implies the arrival of a new era in city politics, one unlike either the era of the political machine or that of conventional political reform. For many mayors today, and perhaps for some time to come, their *audience* is increasingly different from their *constituency*. By "audience" I mean those persons whose favorable attitudes and responses the mayor is most interested in, those persons from whom he receives his most welcome applause and his most needed resources and opportunities. By "constituency" I mean those people who can vote for or against him in an election.

At one time, audience and constituency were very nearly the same thing. The mayor was reelected if he pleased his party and the city's voters, or at least a substantial number of the wards and factions making up these voters. The only resources he needed (money to finance his campaign and taxes with which to run the city) were available from city interests. The only help he needed was from party workers who not only staffed his campaign but his government as well. From time to time, the highly partisan, machine-style mayor would be replaced by a nonpartisan or reform mayor, but for him, too, audience and constituency were similar. His constituents were those voters (temporarily a majority) who were disgusted by scandal or bored by sameness; his audiences were essentially *local* reformers —business groups, good government or "municipal research bureau" organizations, and crusading big-city newspapers.

With the decline of the urban political party and with the decline in the vitality and money resources of the central city, postwar mayors began to look to new sources for both support and issues. Many found them in urban redevelopment. Business and planning groups were concerned about the fate of the downtown business district and willing to back mayors who promised to do something. But many, if not most, of these supporters had themselves moved outside the city limits, and a large part of the bill for the new improvements was to be paid by the federal government with grants directly to the cities (and not, as with traditional programs, funnelled through the states). In this period, the separation between audience and constituency began. The mayor was elected by city residents, but he campaigned through the help of—and in part with the intention of influencing—businessmen, planners, and federal agencies.

In the 1960's, the primarily physical emphasis of the urban renewal program fell under strong criticism, and new needs, chiefly involving problems of poverty and racial isolation, came to the fore. The new concerns were nonbusiness, and to a degree antibusiness, though businessmen later joined in some of the programs created, especially those having to do with employment. But this shift in substantive focus to social issues was not so much a reassertion of the concerns of constituents as it was a change in the composition of the audience. To be sure, the riots were chiefly the acts of a certain group of constituents, but these disturbances, though they imparted a special sense of urgency to urban concerns, did not create them. The model cities program, the war on poverty, most civil rights bills, the aid of education programs, and the various pilot projects of both the government and private foundations were largely devised, promoted, and staffed by groups who were becoming the mayor's audience though they were not among his constituents.

This audience consists principally of various federal agencies, especially those that give grants directly to cities; the large foundations, and in particular the Ford Foundation, that can favor the mayor with grants, advice, and future prospects; the mass media, or at least that part of the media—national news magazines and network television—that can give the mayor access to the suburbs, the state, and the nation as a whole; and the affluent (and often liberal) suburban voters who will pass on the mayor's fitness for higher office.

No mayor can afford to cater to this audience to the exclusion of constituency interests nor is the audience always in agreement as to what it will applaud. But to a growing degree, the audience is the source of important cues and rewards that tend, however much they may conflict in detail, to be on the whole consistent. First of all, the audience sets the tone and provides much of the rhetoric for the discussion of urban issues. Indeed, it often decides what *is* an urban issue. At one time, taxes and the fate of the central business district were the issues; then housing became more important; juvenile delinquency enjoyed a brief vogue and now seems to be coming back for an encore; poverty and race have been the most recent issues, though while the "race problem" was once thought to require removing the barriers to integration, it is now more likely to be seen in terms of "community control" and "neighborhood action" (neither of which will do much at all for integration). "Talking the language" of the audience is an important way for a mayor to win esteem and to become a state or even national figure.

THE AUDIENCE HAS POWER

But more than esteem is at stake. The audience also controls much of the free resources that a mayor needs so urgently, given his pinched tax base, the rising demand for services, and the shortage of able people to staff city hall. The great bulk of any city's budget is, in effect, a fixed charge the mayor is powerless to alter more than trivially. He must pay the policemen, firemen, and sanitation workers; he must service the municipal debt; and he must meet his share of welfare and educational costs. After he does these things, there is not much left over to play around with. If he is to be "innovative," or even if he is to respond to any new demands, he must find new money and, equally important, more staff people. The federal government is obviously one source of new money, but is not always available—at least in large amounts—just for the asking. If the mayor wants his city to be a "model city" or if he wants a generously funded poverty program, it helps if he is thought, by the relevant agency, to be a "good mayor" with "ideas" and the "right approach." Such decisions are not made so much in traditional political terms—Congress, for example, may have little collective influence on these allocations though substantial influence in particular cases involving particular members—but in terms of bureaucratic politics in which most of the persons involved do not think of themselves as politicians at all. Undersecretaries and assistant secretaries and bureau administrators and (often of greatest importance) the personal assistants to department heads decide whom among the mayors they can "talk to."

Nor is the money always used wholly for the stated purposes. Cities such as Boston and New Haven that had vigorous urban renewal programs had them in part to get federal funds for the city but also in part to create within the city, but outside the normal departmental structure, a large staff of professional talent that could be used for any number of purposes. The best local renewal authorities become generalized sources of innovation and policy staffing, and their directors become in effect deputy mayors (and sometimes more than that).

Foundations and private organizations can also provide free resources that, though small in amount compared to federal largesse, can often make the difference between running an "ordinary" administration and running one that is newsworthy, exciting, or "different." The Ford Foundation "Gray Areas" program was for a while a systematic effort at serving, however unintentionally, just this function. (Many mayors later decided that what they really wanted was the attention that came from *announcing* the program, not the often less flattering attention that came from trying to *run* it. The ideal "pilot project" from the mayor's point of view is one that puts some money into the city treasury, gets some good headlines, provides a few more staff assistants, and then promptly vanishes without a trace before anyone can start quarreling about what purpose it is to serve or who should control it.)

The audience is just as important as a source of skills. For all the talk about cities being "where it's at," very few able administrators seek out employment in the low-prestige, low-paying jobs that city hall has to offer. There are such people, but they are small in number and young in age. To get the best of them, or even to get any at all, every big-city mayor is in competition with every other one. The mayor that runs (however well advised) a "business-as-usual" administration is at a profound disadvantage in this competition. Indeed, the would-be mayor must often start seeking them out when he decides to run for office so that they can give him the speeches, the position papers, and the "task force reports" that increasingly are the hallmark of a campaign that wins the sympathy of the media. The process of tuning the mayor to be responsive to the audience begins, therefore, even before he becomes mayor. And if he should ever entertain any thoughts about taking a "tough line" or going after the "backlash vote" (however rational such a strategy might be), he would immediately face a rebellion among his younger campaign and staff assistants.

THE NEW UPWARD MOBILITY

Finally, the audience is increasingly able to reward and thus shape the career aspirations of the big-city mayor. There was a time when being mayor was a dead-end street, and in terms of advancing to higher elective office, it may still be. Cavanagh could not win his own party's nomination, to say nothing of the Senate seat, even when he was still enjoying the unstinting praise of the media and the tranquility of preriot Detroit. Kevin White of Boston appears eager to run for governor in 1970, but many are skeptical that he can get either the nomination or the office. (His predecessor, John Collins, tried for the Democratic nomination for United States Senator but in the primary election failed even to carry his own city, Boston.) This may be changing, however, as more public attention is focused on cities, and if the mayor is adroit enough to get out of city hall and into a safer office before criticisms begin to mount up.

But higher elective office is no longer the only place for an ex-mayor to go. Today he can reasonably hope—*if* he is in good standing with the audience—to be offered an important Washington assignment, to join a private organization or foundation working in the urban field, or at least to acquire some sort of professorship that will sustain him, offer him a chance to gather his thoughts, and provide a base from which he can seek consulting opportunities (and fees). If he had his choice, of course, almost any mayor would prefer public office to the relative obscurity of private action; one must have a powerful love of politics even to think seriously of running for mayor in the first place. But whereas former mayors once had a choice among higher elective office (sometimes shabby), idleness, or at best a low-paying judgeship or post as recorder of deeds, now they can be fairly sure that they can join the board of a corporation doing business in cities or the ranks of the nonprofit (but not necessarily unrewarding) foundations, alliances, coalitions, institutes, and centers. Sure, that is, if their credentials are in order with the audience that has created and sustains such enterprises.

OPPOSED PERSPECTIVES

It is important not to overstate the point. "New-style" mayors are no more engaged in the single-minded pursuit of audience acclaim than "old-style" mayors were preoccupied with winning constituency votes. The former clearly need votes, too, and the latter were at least partially concerned with "respectability." And in either case, no one theory can possibly explain all the actions undertaken at city hall— every mayor of any style responds to a complex set of external pressures and personal judgments that cannot be summarized as mere self-interest, however conceived.

Furthermore, the behavior rewarded by the audience changes from time to time. Once, urban renewal was the favored policy, but that is no longer the case. Today, influential parts of the audience are concerned about neighborhood representation, community control, and governmental decentralization. Many mayors are hoping that there is now a substantial overlap between audience concerns and constituency interests and accordingly are betting heavily on "little city halls," neighborhood service centers, and school decentralization. The audience is now reacting against the excesses of urban renewal —its orientation to the central business district and to land clearance —and is developing a concern for neighborhood integrity and local public services that can reinforce the obvious interest constituents have in just such matters.

The congruence of interest may be real; at the very least, it tends to obscure the differences, described in exaggerated terms earlier in this article, between audience and constituency. Obscures, but does not eliminate, for the two groups act out of fundamentally different motives and with quite opposed perspectives on what a "neighborhood orientation" is supposed to achieve. The audience, though it may give lip service to neighborhood benefits and decentralization in general, is primarily interested in such things for the poor and the black, especially the latter; the constituency, or at least its white majority, sees a neighborhood orientation as meaning getting help from city hall to hold down taxes, provide more police, and keep black children from being "forcibly" (i.e., by busing or redistricting) brought into their schools. "Community control" to many elements of the audience means Negro control; to many central-city white constituents, it means anti-Negro control. In the reaction against the disadvantages of the era of mayor-backed urban renewal and high-way projects, some of the compensating advantages of a city-wide perspective were lost sight of. Taking influence over decisions away from neighborhoods meant preventing them from acquiring governmental power to use against one another, admittedly at a price in decreased responsiveness to local interests.

Managing a city government so that it is receptive to legitimate neighborhood concerns and unreceptive to illegitimate ones is difficult under the best of circumstances, but especially trying when the consensus as to what is legitimate has begun to disintegrate. In New York City, Jewish voters, who are normally warm supporters of any mayor who seems forward-looking, liberal, and honest, have been plunged into a state hovering between confusion and fury by the discovery that school decentralization seemed to mean allowing black militants to harass Jewish teachers and a Jewish-led teachers' union. As a result, a part of the audience that might ordinarily think decentralization is a good idea has defected from its ranks. (It is interesting to speculate what their attitude might have been if community control had come first to the police instead of the schools. They might have regarded it—as they did the civilian review board—as a threat to "law and order" or they might have ignored it as a threat only to Irish police and an Irish policeman's union.)

In short, though present mayors seem to be neighborhood-oriented and thus constituency-oriented, the style and to a degree the substance of that orientation is heavily influenced by audience rather than constituency concerns: it favors social experimentation and innovation, it gives special attention to the interests of black citizens, and it treats gingerly (if at all) local demands for a strong law-enforcement policy. It does not follow, of course, that the supposed beneficiaries of this policy, the blacks, see themselves as having benefited. They are no doubt likely to give strong political support to the present mayors in New York, Boston, and elsewhere, but many of their leaders feel that the neighborhood orientation, though in general desirable, has delivered rather little in the way of concrete gains and that it may in fact have raised neighborhood expectations unrealistically.

BENEFITS AND COSTS

The advantages of the growing influence of the mayor's audience should not be underestimated. The reasons for the importance of the audience—its control of important resources in money and talent —are directly related to the needs of the cities. At a time when new funds are hard to find and able people hard to entice, one is prepared to look kindly on almost any strategy that will provide more of either. Indeed, the role of the audience may be important in getting some men to run for mayor in the first place. When city hall seems to be both a political dead end and an institutionalized nightmare, audience support and interest may be critical as an inducement for attracting at least certain kinds of talent to mayoral elections. (I do not wish to exaggerate this point. With no audience interest whatsoever, there would still be a surprising number of candidates for the special purgatory that is city hall. Ambition has probably led to the ruination of more men than lust.)

Above all, the audience has played a critical role in preventing (or since history is yet to run its course, slowing) the emergence of an urban nativism that would exploit base emotions and encourage vindictive sentiments. Without the increase in the number of big-city Negro voters as well as the increased salience of a liberal, city-oriented audience, there would surely have been a large number of candidates and officials making racist (in the strict sense) appeals to white voters.

But the advantages should not blind us to the costs of audience involvement. Its members, because they rarely have anything personally at stake in big-city politics, attach rather little value to stability and order and a high value to experimentation and change. Furthermore, because they have little direct experience with the results of programs, they are likely to be relatively uncritical of what is new (newness suggests initiative, concern, action) but highly critical of what exists (oldness suggests the status quo, passivity, and indifference). And since few members of audience need take (in the usual case) responsibility for any programs, the audience as a whole is generally unaware of, or unconcerned with, the failure of earlier ideas it had once endorsed. If a bold new program falls flat on its face, that fact is either unremarked or taken as a sign that what is needed next time is a program that is even newer and bolder.

There is also a tendency for the mayors, in responding to audience concerns, to accelerate the rate of increase in unrealizable expectations. The new mayors are under considerable pressure to out-promise each other (at least initially, but, because they can rarely deliver on these promises, they may leave a legacy of frustration and cynicism. This would be true, of course, even if the audience did not exist—candidates always tell voters what they want to hear, even if what they want is utterly impossible. But the audience exacerbates this tendency. By making mayors rival claimants for media attention and federal largesse, it induces a mayor to bid against mayors in other cities as well as opponents in his own. Mayors must now not only out-promise challengers with respect to what the constituents want, but out-promise them with respect to what the audience wants as well.

To be sure, the audience-oriented mayors occasionally succeed. A riot may (apparently) be prevented, or a public agency usefully reorganized, or a new service installed. When that happens, it is often as much the result of luck and particular circumstances as of style and skill. But a success in one place, and for reasons unique to that place, encourages others to believe that similar successes are possible in other places. The audience generalizes the example of the single mayor and makes him the model for all mayors. Everywhere, one hears of persons who are running or acting in the "Lindsay style" as if that style were both an unqualified blessing and an exportable commodity. Television commentators, who are especially prone to conceptualize public events in stylistic terms, owing in great part to their own needs to attract audience interest with one- or two-minute film clips, are particularly likely to seize on a "good style" (good, they believe, for both their entertainment needs as well as for public problems) and measure other persons by that standard.

One group of mayors may be exempt from the dilemmas of pleasing both constituency and audience. The black mayors, at least for the time being, enjoy a guaranteed audience with instinctively favorable reactions. Being black, they attract the sympathetic attention of the media, the foundations, the federal agencies, and most liberal voters. Grants for special purposes and designations as "model cities" are likely to come fairly easily for such mayors. To the extent they can take audience support for granted, they are free to turn their attention to constituency problems, and, in dealing with these constituents, can afford to promise less. (Partially offsetting their freedom is the greater criticism from white voters and the higher expectations of black ones within their cities.)

DEMOGRAPHY AND AUTHORITY

All the foregoing is said, not in criticism of mayors, but in sympathy for their plight. The audience, after all, is almost as ready as the constituency to criticize a mayor who fails to conform to their expectations. When a man is elected with an audience-acclaimed style and then, within a few weeks, begins speaking prosaically about the tax rate and the demands of the organized city employees, he begins to disenchant his audience who thought that he was somehow "above that sort of thing." And he, in turn, can be pardoned for becoming exasperated at the unreasonable demands of his vicarious voters, the unfranchised audience.

At the root of his difficulties are demography and authority: the liberal voters have moved out of the city without relinquishing their claim to share in its governance, and the process of governing has been made immeasurably more difficult by the inability of the mayor to acquire enough power to manage an increasingly intense conflict. There has been a simultaneous growth in the problems of central cities and a decline in the authority of the mayor to handle those problems. Among the many crises, real and imagined, that are the lot of cities these days, should be numbered the crisis of authority.

The mayor is increasingly unable to control his own bureaucracy owing to the growth both in its size and in the strength of its protective devices (civil service and employee organizations). He increasingly finds that there are no political parties capable of producing stable governing majorities on the city councils. And he increasingly confronts issues that are of such fundamental importance or laden with such symbolic significance that they cannot be resolved by the normal processes of bargaining and modest revenue reallocations—crime, racial conflict, and civil disorder. It is not surprising that, faced with these difficulties, he should seek allies and help wherever he can find them. Thus, when a national commission blames urban riots on "white racism," the mayors of the cities where those riots occurred hastened to agree with this diagnosis—partly because they may think it is right, but more importantly because they see the acceptance of this verdict as a useful means for placing a moral obligation on the federal government to send more financial aid to the cities.

The situation that results is inherently unstable. If the resources to govern can only be obtained by the mayor joining his audience in characterizing white big-city voters in terms the latter reject as untrue and unfair, these constituents are likely quickly to lose patience. If, on the other hand, no resources are to be had from any source, black voters are also likely to lose patience. Newsworthy "happenings," theatrical events, and walking tours of the slums may divert attention from these dilemmas, but they are unlikely to resolve them. (There is something to be said for even a diversion, of course. The vitriolic mayorality campaign in Boston in 1967 was less divisive than otherwise owing, I believe, to the preoccupation of the voters with the dramatic Red Sox pennant race, and the tense Detroit summer of 1968 did not become explosive partly because the Tigers, by winning the pennant and the World Series, were a unifying influence. Unfortunately, only two teams can win pennants each year.)

There is little comfort and even less guidance to be drawn from these somber reflections. If there were a better way to do things, no doubt some mayor would by now have found it. What seems clear, however, is that the "new breed" mayors—of whom John Lindsay is perhaps the archetype—are new in more senses than one. They are not simply new personalities or new styles, they are responses to important underlying shifts in the distribution of influence in American urban politics—shifts that have brought new sources of power to bear on cities as, indeed, they have brought such sources to bear on the country generally. Urban politics have become, in significant degree, nationalized.

The "Liberation" of Gary, Indiana

Edward Greer

In silhouette, the skyline of Gary, Indiana, could serve as the perfect emblem of America's industrial might—or its industrial pollution. In the half-century since they were built, the great mills of the United States Steel Corporation—once the largest steel complex on earth—have produced more than a quarter-trillion tons of steel. They have also produced one of the highest air pollution rates on earth. Day and night the tall stacks belch out a ruddy smoke that newcomers to the city find almost intolerable.

Apart from its appalling physical presence, the most striking thing about Gary is the very narrow compass in which the people of the city lead their lives. Three-quarters of the total work force is directly employed by the United States Steel Corporation. About 75 percent of all male employment is in durable goods manufacture and in the wholesale-retail trades, and a majority of this labor force is blue-collar. This means that the cultural tone of the city is solidly working-class.

But not poor. Most Gary workers own their own homes, and the city's median income is 10 percent above the national average. The lives of these people, however, are parochial, circumscribed, on a tight focus. With the exception of the ethnic clubs, the union and the Catholic church, the outstanding social edifices in Gary are its bars, gambling joints and whorehouses.

Reprinted from Edward Greer, "The 'Liberation' of Gary, Indiana," *Trans-Action*, Vol. 8, No. 3 (January 1971), pp. 30–39, 63. Copyright © January, 1971, by Transaction, Inc., New Brunswick, New Jersey. Reprinted by permission.

COMPANY TOWN

The city of Gary was the largest of all company towns in America. The United States Steel Corporation began construction in 1905, after assembling the necessary parcel of land on the Lake Michigan shore front. Within two years, over $40 million had been invested in the project; by now the figure must be well into the billions.

Gary was built practically from scratch. Swamps had to be dredged and dunes leveled; a belt-line railroad to Chicago had to be constructed, as well as a port for ore ships and of course a vast complex of manufacturing facilities including coke ovens, blast furnaces and an independent electrical power plant. The city was laid out by corporation architects and engineers and largely developed by the corporation-owned Gary Land Company, which did not sell off most of its holdings until the thirties. Even though the original city plan included locations for a variety of civic, cultural and commercial uses (though woefully little for park land), an eminent critic, John W. Reps, points out that it "failed sadly in its attempt to produce a community pattern noticeably different or better than elsewhere."

The corporation planned more than the physical nature of the city. It also had agents advertise in Europe and the South to bring in workers from as many different backgrounds as possible to build the mills and work in them. Today over 50 ethnic groups are represented in the population.

This imported labor was cheap, and it was hoped that cultural differences and language barriers would curtail the growth of a socialist labor movement. The tough, pioneer character of the city and the fact that many of the immigrant workers' families had not yet joined them in this country combined to create a lawless and vice-ridden atmosphere which the corporation did little to curtail. In much more than its genesis and name, then, Gary is indelibly stamped in the mold of its corporate creators.

LABOR AND THE LEFT

During the course of the First World War, government and vigilante repression broke the back of the Socialist party in small-town America, though it was not very strong to begin with. Simultaneously, however, the Left grew rapidly as a political force among the foreign-born in large urban centers. As the war continued, labor peace was kept by a combination of prosperity (full employment and overtime), pressures for production in the "national interest," and Wilsonian and corporate promises of an extension of democracy in the workplace after the war was over. The promises of a change in priorities proved empty, and in 1919 the long-suppressed grievances of the steelworkers broke forth. Especially among the unskilled immigrant workers, demands for an industrial union, a reduction of the workday from 12 to eight hours and better pay and working conditions sparked a spontaneous movement for an industry-wide strike.

For a time it appeared that the workers would win the Great Steel Strike of 1919, but despite the capable leadership of William Z. Foster the strike was broken. The native white skilled labor aristocracy refused to support it, and the corporation imported blacks from the South to scab in the mills. This defeat helped set back the prospect of militant industrial trade unionism for almost a generation. And meanwhile, racism, a consumer-oriented culture (especially the automobile and relaxed sexual mores) and reforms from above (by the mid-twenties the eight-hour day had been voluntarily granted in the mills) combined to prevent the Left from recovering as a significant social force.

It was in this period between World War I and the depression that a substantial black population came to Gary. Before the war only a handful of black families lived there, and few of them worked in the mills. During World War I, when immigration from abroad was choked off, blacks were encouraged to move to Gary to make up for the labor shortage caused by expanding production. After the war this policy was continued, most spectacularly during the strike, but rather consistently throughout the twenties. In 1920 blacks made up 9.6 percent of the population; in 1930 they were 17.8 percent—and they were proportionately represented in the steel industry work force.

When the CIO was organized during the depression, an interracial alliance was absolutely essential to the task. In Gary a disproportionate number of the union organizers were black; the Communist party's slogan of "black and white unite and fight" proved useful as an organizing tactic. Nevertheless, it was only during World War II (and not as the result of the radicals' efforts) that black workers made a substantial structural advance in the economy.

317

Demography, wartime full employment and labor shortages proved more important to the lot of black workers than their own efforts and those of their allies.

As after the First World War, so after the second, there came a repression to counter the growth of the Left. The Communist component of the trade union movement was wiped out, and in the general atmosphere of the early cold war black people, too, found themselves on the defensive. At the local level in Gary, the remaining trade union leaders made their peace with the corporation (as well as the local racketeers and Democratic party politicians), while various campaigns in the forties to racially integrate the schools and parks failed utterly.

Finally, in the early fifties, the inherently limited nature of the trade union when organized as a purely defensive institution of the working class—and one moreover that fully accepts capitalist property and legal norms—stood fully revealed. The Steelworkers Union gave up its right to strike over local grievances, which the Left had made a key part of its organizing policy, in return for binding arbitration, which better suited the needs and tempers of the emerging labor bureaucrats.

CORPORATE RACISM

The corporation thus regained effective full control over the work process. As a result, the corporation could increase the amount of profit realized per worker. It could also intensify the special oppression of the black workers; foremen could now assign them discriminatorily to the worst tasks without real union opposition. This corporate racism had the additional benefit of weakening the workers' solidarity. For its part, the union abolished shop stewards, replacing them with one full-time elected "griever." This of course further attenuated rank-and-file control over the union bureaucracy, aided in depoliticizing the workers and gave further rein to the union's inclination to mediate worker/employer differences at the point of production, rather than sharpen the lines of struggle in the political economy as a whole.

The corporate and union elites justified this process by substantial wage increases, together with other benefits such as improved pension and welfare plans. For these gains a price was paid. Higher product prices, inflation and a rising tax burden on the workers all ensued from the union's passive acceptance of corporate priorities.

There were extremely important racial consequences as well. For as the union leadership was drawn further and further into complicity with corporate goals, a large segment of the industrial working class found itself in the apparently contradictory position of opposing the needs of the poorest workers for increased social welfare services. A large part of the material basis for white working-class racism originates here. Gary steelworkers, struggling to meet their home mortgage payments, are loath to permit increased assessments for additional municipal services which they view as mostly benefitting black people.

UNITED STATES STEEL

Needless to say, the corporation helped to develop, promote and protect the Gary working class's new ways of viewing itself and its world.

In the mill, the corporation systematically gave the black workers the dirtiest jobs (in the coke plants, for example) and bypassed them for promotion—especially for the key skilled jobs and as foremen. Nor has that policy changed. Although about a third of the employees in the Gary Works are black, and many of them have high seniority, and although virtually all the foremen are promoted directly from the ranks without needing any special qualifications, there are almost no black (or Spanish-speaking) foremen. According to figures submitted by the United States Steel Corporation to the Gary Human Relations Commission, as of 31 March 1968, out of a total of 1,011 first-line supervisors (foremen) only 22 were black.

The corporation not only practices racism directly, it also encourages it indirectly by supporting other discriminatory institutions in Gary. Except for some free professionals and small business, the entire business community is a de facto fief of the corporation. The Gary Chamber of Commerce has never to my knowledge differed from the corporation on any matter of substance, though it was often in its economic self-interest to do so. This has been true even with regard to raising the corporation's property assessment, which would directly benefit local business financially. And in its hiring and sales practices, as well as in its social roles, this group is a leading force for both institutional racism and racist attitudes in the community. For instance, it is well known that the local banks are very reluctant to advance mortgage money in black areas of town, thus assuring their physical decline. White workers then draw the reasonable conclusion that the movement of blacks into their neighborhoods will be at the expense of the value of their homes and react accordingly. The local media, completely dependent financially on the local business community, can fairly be described as overtly racist. The story of the voting fraud conspiracy to prevent the election of the present mayor, Richard Hatcher, a black man, didn't get into the local paper until days after it made the front page of the *New York Times*.

The newspaper publisher is very close to the national Catholic hierarchy and the local bishop, who in turn is closely linked to the local banks. The church is rhetorically moderately liberal at the diocesan level, but among the ethnic parishes the clergy are often overtly racist.

POLITICAL CONSIDERATIONS

While the United States Steel Corporation has an annual budget of $5 billion, the city of Gary operates on some $10 million annually. (This figure applies only to municipal government functions; it excludes expenditures by the schools, welfare authorities, the Sanitary Board and the Redevelopment Commission.)

And the power of the city government, as is usually the case in this country, is highly fragmented. Its legal and financial authority is inadequate to carry out the public functions for which it bears responsibility. The power of the mayor is particularly limited. State civil service laws insulate school, welfare, fire and police personnel from the control of City Hall. Administrative agencies control key functions such as urban renewal, the low income housing authority, sanitation, the park system and the board of health. Appointive boards, with long and staggered terms of tenure, hire the administrators of these agencies; and although in the long run a skillful mayor can obtain substantial control over their operations, in the short run (especially if there are sharp policy differences) his power may well be marginal.

Two other structural factors set the context in which local government in Gary—and in America generally—is forced to operate.

First, key municipal functions increasingly depend upon federal aid; such is the case with the poverty program, urban renewal, low income housing and, to a substantial degree, welfare, education and even police and sanitation. Thus, the priorities of the federal government increasingly shape the alternatives and options open to local officials, and their real independence is attenuated.

Second, the tax resources of local governments—resting for the most part on comparatively static real estate levies—are less and less able to meet the sharply rising costs of municipal services and operations. These costs reflect the increased social costs of production and welfare, costs that corporations are able to pass on to the general public.

This problem is particularly acute in Gary because of the ability of the corporation to remain grossly underassessed. As a result, there are implacable pressures to resist expansion of municipal services, even if the need for them is critical. In particular, since funds go to maintain existing services, it is virtually impossible for a local government to initiate any substantive innovations unless prior funding is assured. In this context, a sustained response to the urban crisis is prevented not only by a fragmentation of power but also by a lack of economic resources on a scale necessary to obtain significant results.

For the city of Gary, until the election of Mayor Hatcher, it was academic to talk about such considerations as the limits of local government as an instrument of social change and improvement of the general welfare. Before him, municipal government had been more or less content simply to mediate between the rackets on the one hand and the ethnic groups and business community on the other.

The Democratic party, structured through the Lake County machine, was the mechanism for accomplishing a division of spoils and for maintaining at least a formal legitimacy for a government that provided a minimum return to its citizenry. Left alone by the corporation, which subscribed to an inspired policy of live and let live where municipal politics were concerned, this political coalition governed Gary as it saw fit.

In return for the benevolent neutrality of the corporation toward its junior partner, the governing coalition refrained from attempting to raise the corporation's tax assessments or to otherwise insinuate itself into the absolute sovereignty of the corporation over the Gary Works. Air pollution activities were subjected only to token inspection and control, and in the entire history of the city the Building Department never sent an inspector into the mill. (These and other assertions about illegal or shady activities are based on reports from reliable informants and were usually verified by a second source. I served under Mayor Hatcher as director of the Office of Program Coordination until February 1969.)

In this setting—particularly in the absence of a large middle class interested in "good government" reform—politics was little more than a racket, with the city government as the chief spoils. An informal custom grew up that representatives of different ethnic minorities would each hold the mayor's office for one term. The mayor then, in association with the county officials, would supervise the organized crime (mostly gambling, liquor and prostitution) within the community. In effect, the police force and the prosecutor's office were used to erect and centralize a protection racket with the mayor as its director and organized crime as its client. Very large sums of money were involved, as indicated by the fact that one recent mayor was described by Internal Revenue officials as having an estimated annual income while in office of $1.5 million.

Besides the racket of protecting criminal activity, other sources of funds contributed to the large illicit incomes of city officials. There were almost 1,000 patronage jobs to distribute to supporters or sell to friends. There were proceeds from a myriad of business transactions and contracts carried out under municipal authority. Every aspect of municipal activity was drawn into the cash nexus.

For instance, by local ordinance one had to pass an examination and pay a $150 fee for a contractor's license to do repair or construction work within city limits. The licensing statute was enacted to maintain reasonable standards of performance and thus protect the public. In reality, as late as 1967, passing the exam required few skills, except the ability to come up with $1,200 for the relevant officials, or $1,500 if the applicant was unfortunate enough to have black skin.

Gary municipal affairs also had a racist quality. The black population continued to rise until in the early sixties it composed an absolute majority. Yet the benefits of the system just outlined were restricted to the less scrupulous of the leaders of other ethnic groups, which constituted altogether only 40 percent of the population. The spoils came from all; they were distributed only among whites.

And this was true not only for illegal spoils and patronage but also for legitimate municipal services. As one example, after Hatcher became mayor, one of the major complaints of the white citizenry concerned the sharp decline in the frequency of garbage collection.

This resulted, not from a drop in efficiency of the General Services division, as was often charged, but from the fact that the garbage routes were finally equalized between white and black areas.

In short, the city government was itself just another aspect of the institutionalized structure of racism in Gary. To assure the acquiescence of Gary's blacks to the system, traditional mechanisms of repression were used: bought black politicians and ward leaders, token jobs, the threat of violence against rebels and the spreading of a sense of impotence and despair. For instance, it was a Gary tradition for the Democratic machine to contribute $1,500 each week to a black ministers' alliance for them to distribute to needy parishioners—with the tacit understanding that when elections came around they would help deliver the vote.

HATCHER'S CAMPAIGN

The successful insurgency of Richard Gordon Hatcher destroyed the core of this entire relationship.

Hatcher developed what can best be described as a black united front, inasmuch as it embraced all sectors of the black community by social class, occupation, ideology and temperament. The basis of this united front was a commonly held view that black people as a racial group were discriminated against by the politically dominant forces. Creating it required that Hatcher bridge existing divisions in the black community, which he did by refusing to be drawn into a disavowal of any sector of the black movement either to his left or right— except for those local black politicians who were lackeys of the Democratic machine. Despite immense public pressure, for example, Hatcher refused to condemn Stokely Carmichael, even though scurrilous right-wing literature was widely circulated calling him a tool of Carmichael and Fidel Castro. Actually, the rumor that hurt Hatcher the most was the false assertion that he was secretly engaged to a white campaign worker—and it was so damaging in the black community that special pains had to be taken to overcome it.

Muhammad Ali was brought to the city to campaign for Hatcher, but Hubert Humphrey was not invited because of the bitter opposition of white antiwar elements within his campaign committee. It is worth noting that a substantial portion of Hatcher's financial and technical assistance came from a very small group of white liberals and radicals, who, while they played a role disproportionate to their numbers, suffered significant hostility from their white neighbors for involving themselves openly with Hatcher. Their support, however, made it possible for the campaign to appeal, at least rhetorically, to all the citizens on an interracial basis.

Of course, this support in the white community did not translate into votes. When the count was complete in the general election, only 13 percent of Gary's overwhelmingly Democratic white voters failed to bolt to the Republicans; and if one omits the Jewish professional and business section of town, that percentage falls to 6 percent (in blue-collar Glen Park)—a figure more explicable by polling booth error than goodwill.

Even in the Democratic primary against the incumbent mayor, Hatcher barely won, although he had the support of a large majority of the Spanish-speaking vote and overwhelming support (over 90 percent) of the black vote. His victory was possible, moreover, only because the white vote was split almost down the middle due to the entry of an insurgent and popular "backlash" candidate.

Hatcher's primary victory was particularly impressive given the obstacles he had to face. First, his entire primary campaign was run on less than $50,000, while the machine spent an estimated $500,000 in cash on buying black votes alone. Second, the media was openly hostile to Hatcher. And third, efforts were made to physically intimidate the candidate and his supporters. Death threats were common, and many beatings occurred. Without a doubt, the unprecedented action of the Hatcher organization in forming its own self-defense squads was essential in preventing mass intimidation. It was even necessary on primary day for armed groups to force open polls in black areas that would otherwise have remained inoperative.

These extraordinary methods demonstrated both how tenuous are the democratic rights of black people and what amazing organization and determination are necessary to enforce them when real shifts of power appear to be at stake. When the primary results came in, thousands of black citizens in Gary literally danced in the streets with joy; and everyone believed that the old Gary was gone forever.

HATCHER'S TEMPTATIONS

Immediately after the primary victory, the local alignment of forces was to some degree overshadowed by the rapid interposition of national ones. Until Hatcher won the primary, he was left to sink or swim by himself; after he established his own independent base of power, a new and more complex political process began: his reintegration into the national political system.

The county Democratic machine offered Hatcher a bargain: its support and $100,000 for the general election campaign in return for naming the chief of police, corporation counsel and controller. Naturally, Hatcher refused to accept a deal that would have made him a puppet of the corrupt elements he was determined to oust from power. Thereupon the county machine (and the subdistrict director of the Steelworkers Union) declared itself for, and campaigned for, the Republican.

But the question was not left there. To allow the Democratic party to desert a candidate solely because he was black would make a shambles of its appeal to black America. And dominant liberal forces within the Democratic party clearly had other positive interests in seeing Hatcher elected. Most dramatically, the Kennedy wing of the Democratic party moved rapidly to adopt Hatcher, offering him sorely needed political support, financial backing and technical assistance, without any strings attached. By doing this, it both solidified its already strong support from the black community and made it more reasonable for blacks to continue to place their faith in the Democratic party and in the political system as a whole.

As a necessary response to this development (although it might have happened anyway), the Johnson-Humphrey wing of the Democratic party also offered support. And this meant that the governor of Indiana and the Indiana State Democratic party endorsed Hatcher as well—despite the opposition of the powerful Lake County machine. Thus Hatcher achieved legitimacy within the political system —a legitimacy that he would need when it came to blocking a serious voting fraud plot to prevent his winning the election.

Despite clear evidence of what was happening, the Justice Department nevertheless refused to intervene against this plot until Hatcher's campaign committee sent telegrams to key federal officials warning them that failure to do so would result in a massive race riot for which the federal officials would be held publicly responsible. Only by this unorthodox maneuver, whose credibility rested on Hatcher's known independent appeal and constituency, was the federal executive branch persuaded to enforce the law. Its intervention, striking 5,000 phony names from the voters rolls, guaranteed a Hatcher victory instead of a Hatcher defeat.

The refusal of the Justice Department to move except under what amounted to blackmail indicated that the Johnson-Humphrey wing of the party was not enthusiastic about Hatcher, whose iconoclastic and often radical behavior did not assure that he would behave appropriately after he was in power. But its decision finally to act, together with the readiness of the Kennedy forces to fully back Hatcher, suggests that there was a national strategy into which the Hatcher insurgency could perhaps be fitted.

My own view of that national strategy is that the federal government and the Democratic party were attempting to accommodate themselves to rising black insurgency, and especially electoral insurgency, so as to contain it within the two-party system. This strategy necessitated sacrificing, at least to a degree, vested parochial interests such as entrenched and corrupt machines.

Furthermore, black insurgence from below is potentially a force to rationalize obsolete local governments. The long-term crisis of the cities, itself reflecting a contradiction between public gain and private interest, has called forth the best reform efforts of the corporate liberal elite. Centered in the federal government, with its penumbra of foundations, law firms and universities, the political forces associated with this rationalizing process were most clearly predominant in the Kennedy wing of the Democratic party.

The economic forces whose interests are served by this process are first the banks, insurance companies and other sections of large capital heavily invested in urban property and, more generally, the interests of corporate capital as a whole—whose continued long-range profit and security rest on a stable, integrated and loyal population.

Thus the support given to Hatcher was rational to the system as a whole and not at all peculiar, even though it potentially implied economic and political loss for the corporation, United States Steel, whose operations on the spot might become more difficult. The interests of the governing class as a whole and of particular parts of it often diverge; this gap made it possible for Hatcher to achieve some power within the system. How these national factors would shape the amount and forms of power Hatcher actually obtained became quite evident within his first year of office.

MOSAIC OF BLACK POWER

When I arrived in the city five months after the inauguration, my first task was to aid in the process of bringing a semblance of order out of what can fairly be described as administrative chaos.

When the new administration took over City Hall in January 1968 it found itself without the keys to offices, with many vital records missing (for example, the file on the United States Steel Corporation in the controller's office) and with a large part of the city government's movable equipment stolen. The police force, for example, had so scavenged the patrol cars for tires and batteries that about 90 percent of them were inoperable. This sort of thing is hardly what one thinks of as a normal process of American government. It seems more appropriate to a bitter ex-colonial power. It is, in fact, exactly what happened as the French left Sekou Toure's Guinea.

There were no funds available. This was because the city council had sharply cut the municipal budget the previous summer in anticipation of a Hatcher victory. It intended, if he lost, to legislate a supplemental appropriation. But when he won without bringing in a council majority with him, its action assured that he would be especially badly crippled in his efforts to run the city government with a modicum of efficiency. Moreover, whenever something went wrong, the media could and did blame the mayor for his lack of concern or ability.

Not only did Richard Hatcher find his position sabotaged by the previous administration even before he arrived, but holdovers, until they were removed from their positions, continued to circumvent his authority by design or accident. And this comparatively unfavorable situation extended to every possible sphere of municipal activities.

Another problem was that the new administrators had to take over the management of a large, unwieldly and obsolete municipal system without the slightest prior executive experience. That there were no black people in Gary with such experience in spite of the high degree of education and intelligence in the black community is explicable only in terms of institutionalized racism—blacks in Gary were never permitted such experiences and occupational roles. Hatcher staffed his key positions with black men who had been schoolteachers, the professional role most closely analogous to running a government bureaucracy. Although several of these men were, in my

327

view, of outstanding ability, they still had to learn everything by trial and error, an arduous and painful way to maintain a complex institution.

Furthermore, this learning process was not made any easier by the unusually heavy demands placed on the time of the mayor and his top aides by the national news media, maneuvering factions of the Democratic party, a multiplicity of civil rights organizations, universities and voluntary associations and others who viewed the mayor as a celebrity to be importuned, exploited or displayed. This outpouring of national interest in a small, parochial city came on top of and was almost equal to, the already heavy work load of the mayor.

Nor were there even clerical personnel to answer the mail and phone calls, let alone rationally respond to the deluge. The municipal budget provided the mayor with a single secretary; it took most of the first summer to make the necessary arrangements to pay for another two secretaries for the mayor's own needs. One result was that as late as June 1968 there was still a two-month backlog of personal mail, which was finally answered by much overtime work.

In addition to these problems there were others, not as common to American politics, such as the threat of violence, which had to be faced as an aspect of daily life. The problem of security was debilitating, especially after the King and Kennedy assassinations. In view of the mayor's aggressive drive against local organized crime, the race hatred whipped up during and after the campaign by the right wing and the history of violence in the steel town, this concern with security was not excessive, and maintaining it was a problem. Since the police were closely linked with the local Right, it was necessary to provide the mayor with private bodyguards. The presence of this armed and foreboding staff impaired efficiency without improving safety, especially since the mayor shrugged off the danger and refused to cooperate with these security efforts.

In addition, the tremendous amounts of aid we were offered by foundations, universities and federal officials proved to be a mixed blessing. The time needed to oversee existing processes was preempted by the complex negotiations surrounding the development and implementation of a panoply of new federal programs. There had never been a Concentrated Employment Program in Gary, nor a Model Cities Program, nor had the poverty program been locally controlled. Some of these programs weren't only new to Gary, they hadn't been implemented anywhere else either. The municipal bureaucracy, which under previous administrations had deliberately spared itself the embarrassment of federal audits, didn't have the slightest idea as to how to utilize or run these complex federal programs. Moreover, none of the experts who brought this largesse to Gary had a clear understanding of how it was to be integrated into the existing municipal system and social structure. These new federal programs sprang up overnight—new bureaucracies, ossified at birth—and their actual purposes and effects bore little relation to the legislative purposes of the congressional statutes that authorized them.

Needless to say, ordinary municipal employees experienced this outside assistance as a source of confusion and additional demoralization, and their efficiency declined further. Even the new leadership was often overwhelmed by, and defensive before, the sophisticated eastern federal bureaucrats and private consultants who clearly wanted only to help out America's first black mayor. The gifts, in other words, carried a fearful price.

BUREAUCRATIC ENEMIES

Except for the uniformed officials and the schools, which were largely outside the mayor's control, the standing city bureaucracy was a key dilemma for Mayor Hatcher.

The mayor had run on a reform program. His official campaign platform placed "good government" first, ahead of even tax reform and civil rights. Hatcher was deeply committed to eliminating graft and corruption, improving the efficiency of municipal government—especially the delivery of services to those sectors of the citizenry that had been most deprived—and he did not view his regime as merely the substitution of black faces for white ones in positions of power.

But he also had a particular historic injustice to rectify: the gross underrepresentation of blacks in the city government, and their complete exclusion from policy-making positions. Moreover, implicit in his campaign was a promise to reward his followers, who were mostly black. (At least most participants in the campaign assumed such a promise; Hatcher himself never spoke about the matter.)

Consequently, there was tremendous pressure from below to kick out everyone not covered by civil service protection and substitute all black personnel in their places. But to do so would have deepened the hostility of the white population and probably weakened Hatcher's potential leverage in the national Democratic party. He resisted this pressure, asserting that he believed in an interracial administration. However, in addition to this belief (which, as far as I could determine, was genuine), there were other circumstances that dictated his course of action in this matter.

To begin with, it was always a premise of the administration that vital municipal services (police and fire protection, garbage collection, education, public health measures) had to be continued—both because the people of Gary absolutely needed them and because the failure to maintain them would represent a setback for black struggles throughout the country.

It also appeared that with a wholesale and abrupt transition to a totally new work force it would be impossible to continue these services, particularly because of a lack of the necessary skills and experiences among the black population—especially at the level of administration and skilled technical personnel. In this respect Hatcher faced the classic problem faced by all social revolutions and nationalist movements of recent times: after the seizure of power, how is it possible to run a complex society when those who traditionally ran it are now enemies?

The strategy Hatcher employed to meet this problem was the following. The bulk of the old personnel was retained. At the top level of the administration (personal staff, corporation counsel, chief of police, controller) new, trustworthy individuals were brought in. Then, gradually, new department heads were chosen, and new rank-and-file people included. If they had the skill already, they came at the beginning; if they didn't, they were brought in at a rate slow enough to provide for on-the-job training from the holdovers, without disrupting the ongoing functions of the particular department.

The main weakness of this gradualist strategy was that it permitted the old bureaucracy to survive—its institutional base was not destroyed.

The result was that the new political priorities of the administration could not be implemented with any degree of effectiveness in a new municipal political practice. City government remained remarkably like what it had been in the past, at least from the perspective of the average citizen in the community. While the political leadership was tied up with the kinds of problems I noted earlier, the bureaucracy proceeded on its own course, which was basically one of passive resistance. There were two aspects to this: bureaucratic inertia, a sullen rejection of any changes in established routine that might cause conflicts and difficulties for the employees; and active opposition based on politics and racism, to new methods and goals advocated by the mayor.

To cite just one example, the mayor decided to give a very high priority to enforcement of the housing codes, which had never been seriously implemented by preceding administrations. After much hard work, the Building Department was revamped to engage in aggressive inspection work. Cases stopped being "lost," and the number of inspections was increased by 4,000 percent while their quality was improved and standardized. Then it was discovered that cases prepared for legal enforcement were being tabled by the Legal Department on grounds of technical defects.

I personally ascertained that the alleged legal defects were simply untrue. I then assumed that the reason for the legal staff's behavior was that they were overburdened with work. Conferences were held to explain to them the mayor's priorities so they could rearrange their work schedule. Instead, a series of bitter personal fights resulted, culminating in my removal from that area of work since the staff attorneys threatened to resign if there were continued interference with their professional responsibility. In the course of these disputes, both black and white attorneys expressed the opinion that they did not consider themselves a legal aid bureau for Gary's poor, and furthermore the root of the city's housing problem was the indolent and malicious behavior of the tenants. In their view, it was therefore unjust to vigorously enforce the existing statutes against the landlords. Thus, despite the administration's pledge, black ghetto residents did not find their lives ameliorated in this respect.

Gradually, then, the promise of vast change after the new mayor took office came to be seen as illusory. Indeed, what actually occured was much like an African neocolonial entity: new faces, new rhetoric and people whose lives were scarcely affected except in their feelings towards their government.

This outcome was not due to a failure of good faith on the part of the Hatcher administration. Nor does it prove the fallacious maximalist proposition that no amelioration of the people's conditions of life is possible prior to a revolution. Instead, it was due to the decline of the local mass base of the Hatcher administration and the array of national political forces confronting it.

Most black people in Gary were neither prepared nor able to take upon themselves the functions performed for them by specialized bureaucracies. They relied upon the government for education, welfare, public health, police and fire protection, enforcement of the building codes and other standards, maintenance of the public roads and the like. Unable to develop alternative popularly based community institutions to carry on these functions by democratic self-government, the new administration was forced to rely upon the city bureaucracy—forced to pursue the option that could only result in minor changes.

ABORTED LIBERATION

The most significant consequence of the Hatcher administration's failure to transcend the structural terrain on which it functioned was political, the erosion of popular support after the successful mobilization of energies involved in the campaign. The decline of mass participation in the political process contributed in turn to the tendency of the new regime to solve its dilemmas by bureaucratic means or by relying on outside support from the federal government.

The decline in mass support ought not to be confused with a loss of votes in an election. Indeed, Hatcher is now probably as secure politically as the average big city mayor. The point is that the mass of the black population is not actively involved in helping to run the city. Thus, their political experiences are not enlarged, their understanding of the larger society and how it functions has not improved, and they are not being trained to better organize for their own interests. In short, the liberating process of the struggle for office was aborted after the initial goal was achieved—and before it could even begin to confront the profound problems faced by the mass of urban black Americans.

For example, after the inauguration, old supporters found themselves on the outside looking in. For the most part, since there was no organized effort to continue to involve them (and indeed to do so could not but conflict with the dominant strategy of the administration), they had to be content to remain passive onlookers. Moreover, the average citizen put a lot of faith in the mayor and wanted to give him an opportunity to do his job without intruding on the process.

Even among the most politicized rank-and-file elements there was a fear of interfering. Painfully conscious of their lack of training and experience, they were afraid of "blowing it." Instead they maintained a benevolent watchfulness, an attitude reinforced by the sense that Hatcher was unique, that his performance was some kind of test of black people as a race. (Whites were not the only people encouraged by the media to think in these terms.) There were of course some old supporters who were frankly disillusioned: they did not receive the patronage or other assistance they had expected: they were treated rudely by a bureaucratic holdover or were merely unable to reach the ear of a leader who was once accessible as a friend.

The ebbing away of popular participation could be seen most markedly in the Spanish-speaking community, which could not reassure itself with the symbolic satisfaction of having a member of its group in the national spotlight. With even less education and prior opportunity than the blacks, they found that the qualifications barrier to municipal government left them with even less patronage than they felt to be their due reward. This feeling of betrayal was actively supported by the former machine politicians and criminal elements, who consciously evoked ethnic prejudices to isolate the mayor and weaken his popular support.

What happened in the first year of the new administration, then, was a contradiction between efficiency and ethnic solidarity. At each point the mayor felt he had to rely upon the expert bureaucracy, even at the cost of increasing his distance from his mass base. And this conflict manifested itself in a series of inexorable political events (the appointment of outside advisors, for example), each of which further contributed to eroding the popular base of the still new leadership.

As Antonio Gramsci pointed out, beneath this contradiction lies a deeper one: a historic class deprivation—inflicted on the oppressed by the very structure of the existing society—which barred the underclass from access to the skills necessary for it to run the society directly in its own interests and according to its own standard of civilization. Unless an oppressed social group is able to constitute itself as what Gramsci characterizes as a counterhegemonic social bloc, its conquest of state power cannot be much more than a change in leaders. Given the overall relation of forces in the country at large, such an undertaking was beyond the power of the black community in Gary in 1968. Therefore, dominant national political forces were able quickly to reconstitute their overall control.

NATIONAL POWER

What happened to Richard Hatcher in Gary in his first year as mayor raises important questions—questions that might be of only theoretical interest if he were indeed in a unique position. He is not. Carl Stokes, a black, is mayor of Cleveland. Charles Evers, a black, is mayor of Fayette, Mississippi. Thomas Bradley, a black, very nearly became mayor of Los Angeles. Kenneth Gibson, a black, is now mayor of Newark. The list will grow, and with it the question of how we are to understand the mass participation of blacks in electoral politics in this country and the future of their movement.

I believe that until new concepts are worked out, the best way of understanding this process is by analogy with certain national liberation movements in colonial or neocolonial countries. Of course, the participants—in Gary as in Newark—are Americans, and they aren't calling for a UN plebiscite. But they were clearly conscious of themselves as using elections as a tool, as a step toward a much larger (though admittedly ill-defined) ultimate goal—a goal whose key elements of economic change, political power, dignity, defense of a "new" culture and so forth are very close to those of colonial peoples. It is because Hatcher embraced these larger objectives (without, of course, using precisely the rhetoric) that his campaign can be thought of as part of a nationalist process that has a trajectory quite similar to that of anticolonial liberation movements.

In its weakened local posture, the Hatcher administration was unable to resist successfully a large degree of cooptation by the national political authorities. Despite a brave vote at the Democratic National Convention for Reverend Channing Philips, Hatcher was essentially forced to cooperate with the national government and Democratic party—even to the extent of calling on the sheriff of Cook County to send deputies to reinforce the local police when a "mini-riot" occurred in the black ghetto.

Without either a national coordinated movement or an autonomous base of local insurgency—one capable of carrying out on a mass scale government functions outside the official structure—Hatcher's insurgency was contained within the existing national political system. Or, to express it somewhat differently, the attempt by black forces to use the electoral process to further their national liberation was aborted by a countervailing process of neocolonialism carried out by the federal government. Bluntly speaking, the piecemeal achievement of power through parliamentary means is a fraud—at least as far as black Americans are concerned.

The process by which the national power maintained itself, and even forced the new administration to aid it in doing so, was relatively simple. As the gap between the popular constituency and the new government widened, like many another administration, Hatcher's found itself increasingly forced to rely upon its "accomplishments" to maintain its popularity and to fulfill its deeply held obligation to aid the community.

Lacking adequate autonomous financial resources—the mill remained in private hands, and it still proved impossible to assess it for tax purposes at its true value—accomplishments were necessarily dependent upon obtaining outside funds. In this case, the funds had to come from the federal government, preferably in the form of quick performance projects to maintain popular support and to enable everyone to appear to be doing something to improve matters.

These new programs injected a flow of cash into the community, and they created many new jobs. In his first year of office, the mayor obtained in cash or pledges more federal funds than his entire local budget. Hopes began to be engendered that these programs were the key to solving local problems, while the time spent on preparing them completed the isolation of the leadership from the people.

Then, too, the stress of this forced and artificial growth created endless opportunities for nepotism and even thievery. Men who had never earned a decent living before found themselves as high-paid executives under no requirement to produce any tangible results. Indeed, federal authorities seemed glad to dispense the funds without exercising adequate controls over their expenditures. A situation arose in which those who boasted of how they were hustling the system became prisoners of its largesse.

Even the most honest and courageous leader, such as Mayor Hatcher, could not help but be trapped by the aid offered him by the federal authorities. After all, how can any elected local executive turn down millions of dollars to dispense with as he sees fit to help precisely those people he was elected to aid: The acceptance of the help guaranteed the continuation of bonds of dependence. For without any real autonomous power base, and with new vested interests and expectations created by the flow of funds into the community, and with no available alternate path of development, the relation of power between the local leader and the national state was necessarily and decisively weighted toward the latter.

In Gary, Indiana, within one year after the most prodigious feat in the history of its black population—the conquest of local political power—their insurgency has been almost totally contained. It is indeed difficult to see how the existing administration can extricate itself from its comparative impasse in the absence of fresh national developments, or of a new, more politically coherent popular upsurge from below.

There is, however, no doubt that the struggle waged by the black people of Gary, Indiana, is a landmark on their road to freedom; for the experiences of life and struggle have become another part of their heritage—and thus a promise for us all.

ARTICLE 20

If Nixon Were Mayor

Russell Baker

The trouble with New York is that Richard Nixon decided to run for President instead of Mayor. Some will say that this is also the trouble with the United States, but never mind that just now; we are on to bigger intellectual exercise than President-baiting. The purpose here is to illustrate how the positive thinking of a Mayor Nixon could again make New York a genuine "Fun City," or even a Baghdad-on-Hudson, and for that purpose we take you now, through the miracle of human imagination, to Mayor Nixon's citywide televised news conference.

Mayor Nixon: I have a few announcements, ladies and gentlemen. First of all, I have just signed a mayoral order directing all city officials hereafter to refer to our city—and by that, I mean your

Reprinted from *The New York Times* (May 4, 1971), p. 45, col. 1–2. © 1971 by The New York Times Company. Reprinted by permission.

city and my city and Spiro's city and the city of which all America is so proud—to refer to this great city of ours on all occasions hereafter as "Gotham." Second, I am requesting all teachers in the public school system to begin classes each day with group singing of "The Sidewalks of New York," "Give My Regards to Broadway" and any other appropriate old favorites we can find in the archives which will remind us that we live in a city that has inspired men to write songs that stir men's blood. And third, my wife, Pat, has suggested that we fly the New York Yankees and the New York Mets' pennants over Gracie Mansion 24 hours a day. I am proud to announce that those great old pennants will so fly, starting at midnight tonight. Are there any questions?

Question: Your Honor, you may recall that in the campaign you promised to bring us all together—.

Answer: Just a minute, Bob. You will recall—and of course you, Bob, were there at the Grand Concourse rally when I said this—that I had a plan for bringing us all together again, but couldn't divulge it until I was elected. That plan, of course, is now in operation and is being carried out. I have already brought together more than 300,000 of us, and more will be brought together as my plan unfolds. Now, your question.

Q. My question, Mister Mayor, is, when will the last New Yorkers be brought together?

A. I want to make one thing clear, and that is that New Yorkers are being brought together after years in which they were split apart by previous administrations. To reveal a date on which the last New Yorkers would be brought together, however, would obviously play into the hands of those who want to pry us apart, and that, ladies and gentlemen, I will never be intimidated into doing, no matter how unpopular it may make me with that noisy minority who fill the streets with their shouts and give the false impression in Philadelphia, Chicago and faraway Los Angeles that there is weakness and division and lack of resolution in this great Gotham of ours.

Q. In that connection, Mayor Nixon, what answer do you have for your critics who say the city is going bankrupt in spite of this latest huge tax increase of yours?

A. First of all, Mr. Burks—and you will remember this, because you were in my office when I first said it to a group of cab drivers— what I have done cannot be called a tax increase, and it would be wrong to so look at it. This is merely a fiscal readjustment. As you know, fiscal readjustments can just as easily be made in a downwards direction as in an upwards direction, and I see many, many signs that within six months the greatest corporations in America will be fighting to move their headquarters back into Gotham, as the result of the rate at which we are being brought together again, and that revenue will rise at a rate of which all Gothamites will be proud.

Q. Sir, do you have any comment on the Deputy Mayor's statement that the people in Queens complaining about not having their garbage collected are, and I quote, "queasy and querulous quibblers of Queens"?

A. As you know, Pete, I don't believe in calling it garbage, and if we all stopped thinking of it as garbage we would be brought together much faster. Because you see, Pete, a city as great as Gotham just can't create garbage. There is no way it can be done, Pete. You heard me say that yourself to David and Julie while I was riding along Eighth Avenue last winter, because you were there with us. You may remember I said, "David, in a city as great as Gotham there can never be any garbage. In Gotham, what we have is effluvium, effluvium of the good life."

Q. Your Honor, the number of people on welfare is still increasing in spite of your Give-a-Bum-a-Bedpan campaign to put more of these people to work. Would you—.

A. Just a minute, Bill, I've never used the word "bum" in connection with the welfare problem, as you know, of course, Bill, because you were there at the Plaza when I resisted the temptation to use it. With these bedpans we are giving people to empty, we are conferring human dignity on our less fortunate Gothamites, the dignity that comes with honest work. That is why every indicator my Council of Happiness Advisers has shown me indicates that within six months we will be entering a period of booming joy, when cab drivers will open doors for their passengers and men will yield their seats to the aged blind in subways and armed robberies in the classroom will almost cease, and . . .

Imagination begins to fail.

SUGGESTIONS FOR FURTHER READING

I. Historical Overview

Bryce, James. *The American Commonwealth.* Volume I, chapter LI, "The Working of City Governments," pp. 606–619. New York: Macmillan and Company, 1889. (A classic indictment of city problems and suggested structural remedies.)

Glaab, Charles N., and A. Theodore Brown. *A History of Urban America.* Pp. 211–220. New York: The Macmillan Company, 1967. (A historical account of reformer attacks on political machines and lack of mass base of voter support as party reformers were "mornin' glories.")

Hofstadter, Richard. *The Age of Reform.* Pp. 3–22, 174–214, 257–271. New York: Random House, Inc., Vintage Books, 1955. (An excellent analysis of Progressive reform attitudes toward the cities.)

Howe, Frederick C. *The City: The Hope of Democracy.* Seattle: University of Washington Press, Americana Library Paperback, 1967. (A classic attack on the excesses of economic self-interest in the cities at the turn of the twentieth century.)

Low, Seth. "An American View of Municipal Government in the United States." In *The American Commonwealth,* Volume I, edited by James Bryce. Pp. 620–635. New York: Macmillan and Company, 1889. (New York reform mayor's discussion of inadequacies of immigrants to govern themselves and the poor quality of city services together with the duties and responsibilities of a big-city chief executive.)

Mowry, George E. *The Era of Theodore Roosevelt and the Birth of Modern America: 1900–1912.* Pp. 59–84. New York: Harper & Row, Publishers, Harper Torchbooks, 1962. (Social democracy in the cities during the Progressive era.)

Richards, Allan R. "Half of Our Century." In *The 50 States and Their Local Governments,* edited by James W. Fesler. Pp. 71–103. New York: Alfred A. Knopf, Inc., 1967. (A review of democratic and structural reforms in American cities.)

Sayre, Wallace S., and Nelson W. Polsby. "American Political Science and the Study of Urbanization." In *The Study of Urbanization,* edited by Philip M. Hauser and Leo F. Schnore. Pp. 115–156. New York: John Wiley and Sons, Inc., 1965. (A comprehensive overview of political science analysis and prescriptions for change in American cities.)

Steffens, Lincoln. *The Shame of the Cities.* American Century Series Paperback. New York: Hill and Wang, 1966. (The classic muckraker attack on graft and corruption in the cities.)

II. The "Public Regarding" Ethos

Banfield, Edward C., and James Q. Wilson. "Public Regardingness as a Value Promise in Voting Behavior." *American Political Science Review* 58 (1964):876–887. (The application of the "public regarding" view in local bond issues in Cleveland.)

Hays, Samuel P. "The Politics of Reform in Municipal Government in the Progressive Era." In *American Urban History*, edited by Alexander B. Callow, Jr. Pp. 421–439. (An argument that the middle-class basis for municipal reform is largely a myth, since Progressive reformers were primarily upper-class members who wanted to shift power in the cities from bosses to themselves.)

Lineberry, Robert L., and Edmund P. Fowler. "Reformism and Public Policies in American Cities." *American Political Science Review* 61 (1967):701–716. (An examination of reformed institutions, nonpartisan ballots, and at-large elections which uncovers less responsiveness to community cleavages at this level than in cities with unreformed institutions.)

Wolfinger, Raymond E., and John O. Field. "Political Ethos and the Structure of City Government." *American Political Science Review* 60 (1966): 306–326. (A test of "public regardingness" wherein the authors do not find sufficient evidence to support a relationship between attitudes of city residents and form of local government.)

III. Political Party Reform

Banfield, Edward C. *Big City Politics*. Pp. 107–120. Studies in Political Science. New York: Random House, Inc., 1965. (A discussion of reform mayor accommodation with party bosses in Philadelphia, 1947–1962.)

Banfield, Edward C., and James Q. Wilson. *City Politics*. Pp. 138–150. New York: Random House, Inc., Vintage Books, 1963. (An analysis of extraparty and intraparty reform efforts.)

Costikyan, Edward N. *Behind Closed Doors*. New York: Harcourt, Brace & World, Inc., Harvest Books, 1966. (An evaluation of intraparty reform in New York City by a former Tammany Hall "reform" leader.)

Lowi, Theodore J. *At the Pleasure of the Mayor*. Chapter 8, "The Reform Cycle," pp. 175–214. New York: The Free Press, 1964. (Very useful analysis of party reform v. professional politician efforts in New York City. Questioning of the long-range effectiveness of party reform.)

Ostrogorski, Moisei. *Democracy and the Organization of Political Parties*. Volume II: *The United States*, pp. 238–252. New York: Doubleday & Company, Inc., Anchor Books, 1964. (Criticism of party reform ineffectiveness in building an effective base of voter support to combat the machines at the turn of the twentieth century.)

Reeves, Richard. "The Six-Party System." *The New York Times* (September 29, 1969):41, cols. 1–2. (An argument that major parties in New York City were splintering as a result of conflict over Mayor Lindsay's 1967 re-election campaign.)

Reichley, James. *The Art of Government: Reform and Organization Politics in Philadelphia.* New York: The Fund for the Republic, 1958. (Discussion of Democratic party reform efforts to oust entrenched Republicans and elect "blue ribbon" mayors Clark and Dilworth to city hall in the late 1940's and early 1950's.)

Wilson, James Q. *The Amateur Democrat.* Chicago: The University of Chicago Press, Phoenix Books, 1966. (Intraparty reform efforts in New York, Chicago, and Los Angeles during the 1950's.)

Wilson, James Q. "Politics and Reform in American Cities." In *American Government Annual, 1962–1963.* Pp. 37–52. New York: Holt, Rinehart and Winston, Inc., 1963. (Classification and evaluation of various intraparty and extraparty municipal reform efforts.)

IV. Nonpartisan Elections

Adrian, Charles R. "A Typology for Nonpartisan Elections." *Western Political Quarterly* 12 (1959):449–458. (Fourfold classification of nonpartisan systems where party activity is more or less influential.)

Adrian, Charles R. "Some General Characteristics of Nonpartisan Elections." In *Democracy in Urban America*, edited by Oliver P. Williams and Charles Press. Pp. 251–262. Chicago: Rand McNally & Company, 1961. (Analysis of nonpartisan state legislatures in Nebraska and Minnesota and city councils of Minneapolis and Detroit which reveals eleven specific consequences of nonpartisan elections.)

Alford, Robert R., and Eugene C. Lee. "Voting Turnout in American Cities." *American Political Science Review* 62 (1968):796–813. (An exposition of how cities with "unreformed" structures and partisan elections have higher voting turnouts than cities with "reformed" structures and nonpartisan elections.)

Banfield, Edward C., and James Q. Wilson. *City Politics.* Chapter 12, "Nonpartisanship," pp. 151–167. New York: Random House, Inc., Vintage Books, 1963. (Relationship of nonpartisan elections to politicians, voters, parties, and government.)

Cutright, Phillips. "Nonpartisan Electoral Systems in American Cities." In *Politics in the Metropolis*, edited by Thomas R. Dye and Brett W. Hawkins. Pp. 298–314. Columbus, Ohio: Charles E. Merrill Books,

Inc., 1967. (Relationship of nonpartisan elections to community cleavages.)

Gilbert, Charles E. "Some Aspects of Nonpartisan Elections in Large Cities." *Midwest Journal of Political Science* 6 (1962):345–362. (A discussion of the fact that nonpartisanship normally favors Republicans over Democrats in local communities.)

Gilbert, Charles E., and Christopher Clague. "Electoral Competition and Electoral Systems in Large Cities." *Journal of Politics* 24 (1962):323–349. (Exposition of how nonpartisan elections generally favor incumbents on city councils.)

Greenstein, Fred I. *The American Party System and the American People.* Pp. 57–60. Englewood Cliffs, N. J.: Prentice-Hall, Inc., 1963. (A discussion of irrelevant influences which affect voter choices in communities where neither parties nor slate-making groups are active in nonpartisan contests.)

Lee, Eugene C. "City Elections: A Statistical Profile." In *The Municipal Year Book, 1963.* Pp. 74–84. Chicago: The International City Managers' Association, 1963. (A determination of the fact that voter participation in cities with nonpartisan elections is substantially lower than in cities with partisan elections.)

Lee, Eugene C. *The Politics of Nonpartisanship: A Study of California Elections.* Berkeley: University of California Press, 1960. (A comprehensive analysis of nonpartisanship after which the author challenges the principles of nonpartisanship in terms of actual performance.)

Lockard, Duane. *The Politics of State and Local Government.* 2d ed. Pp. 214–224. New York: The Macmillan Company, 1969. (A challenge of the premises of nonpartisanship by comparing it with results.)

Pomper, Gerald. "Ethnic and Group Voting in Nonpartisan Municipal Elections." *Public Opinion Quarterly* 30 (Spring 1966): 79–97. (Analysis of Newark, New Jersey, nonpartisan city contests in comparison with partisan elections for New Jersey legislature which finds that ethnic cleavages replace party cues in absence of party labels.)

Salisbury, Robert H., and Gordon Black. "Class and Party in Partisan and Non-partisan Elections: The Case of Des Moines." *American Political Science Review* 57 (1963):584–592. (Discovery of a persistence of party divisions in nonpartisan local elections.)

Williams, Oliver P., and Charles R. Adrian. "The Insulation of Local Politics Under the Nonpartisan Ballot." *American Political Science Review* 53 (1959):1052–1063. (Analysis of voting in four Michigan cities which discloses the persistence of party influences in local nonpartisan contests.)

V. Direct Democracy: Initiative, Referendum, and Recall

Adrian, Charles R., and Charles Press. *Governing Urban America*. 3d ed. Pp. 81–83, 106–113. New York: McGraw-Hill Book Company, 1968. (Historical review of municipal reform and appraisal of instruments of direct democracy.)

Baker, Benjamin. *Urban Government*. Pp. 199–208. Princeton, N. J.: D. Van Nostrand Company, Inc., 1957. (Procedures and evaluation of direct democracy.)

Crouch, Winston W. "The Initiative and Referendum in Action." In *Capitol, Courthouse and City Hall*, edited by Robert L. Morlan. 3d ed. Pp. 308–312. Boston: Houghton Mifflin Company, 1966. (Discussion of direct democracy in California.)

Lockard, Duane. *The Politics of State and Local Government*. 2d ed. Pp. 247–254. New York: The Macmillan Company, 1969. (Evaluation of direct democracy and referendum campaigns.)

VI. At-Large Representation

Banfield, Edward C., and James Q. Wilson. *City Politics*. Chapter 7, "Electoral Systems," pp. 87–100. New York: Random House, Inc., Vintage Books, 1963. (Comparison of at-large and ward representation together with consequences in terms of representing particular groups on city councils.)

Berkley, George E. "Flaws in At-Large Voting." *National Civic Review* 55 (1966):370–373, 379. (Criticism of at-large systems in Boston.)

VII. Proportional Representation

Banfield, Edward C., and James Q. Wilson. *City Politics*. Pp. 96–98. New York: Random House, Inc., Vintage Books, 1963. (The effects of P.R. in American cities.)

Childs, Richard S. *The First 50 Years of the Council-Manager Plan of Municipal Government*. Pp. 65–68. New York: National Municipal League, 1965. (A history of development and attacks on P.R.)

Dixon, Robert G., Jr. *Democratic Representation: Reapportionment in Law and Politics*. Pp. 525–527. New York: Oxford University Press, Inc., 1968. (An analysis of techniques of P.R. elections.)

Hechinger, Fred M. "New York's School Vote Is a Start, But Toward What?" *The New York Times* (March 29, 1970):Section 4, p. 1, cols. 1–3. (The use of P.R. in New York City school decentralization plan which has mixed results for representation of blacks and Puerto Ricans on community school boards.)

Straetz, Ralph A. *PR Politics in Cincinnati*. New York: New York University Press, 1958. (A history of 32 years of P.R. elections in Cincinnati together with its demise in 1957.)

Zeller, Belle, and Hugh A. Bone. "The Repeal of P.R. in New York City— Ten Years in Retrospect." *American Political Science Review* 42 (1948): 1127–1148. (An argument that P.R. was repealed in the nation's largest city because of the representation of the wrong kinds of minorities on the city council, particularly communists.)

Zimmerman, Joseph F. "Electoral Reform Needed to End Political Alienation." *National Civic Review* 60 (1971):6–11, 21. (A discussion of how P.R., while not a panacea, can assist disadvantaged minorities if they take full advantage of it in city elections.)

VIII. City Government Structure and Political Environment

Adrian, Charles R., and Charles Press. *Governing Urban America*. 3d ed. Chapter 8, "Forms of Government," pp. 183–216. New York: McGraw-Hill Book Company, 1968. (A comparison of major structural plans for American cities.)

Alford, Robert R., and Harry M. Scoble. "Political and Socioeconomic Characteristics of American Cities." In *The Municipal Year Book, 1965*. Pp. 82–97. Chicago: The International City Managers' Association, 1965. (An examination of the fact that the council-manager cities are likely to have upwardly-mobile white middle-class populations.)

Childs, Richard S. *Civic Victories*. Chapters 14 and 15. New York: Harper & Brothers, Publishers, 1952. (The development of strong mayor-council, commission, and council-manager plans.)

Childs, Richard S. *The First 50 Years of the Council-Manager Plan of Municipal Government*. New York: National Municipal League, 1965. (Progress of the council-manager plan as explained by its founder.)

East, John P. *Council-Manager Government: The Political Thought of Its Founder, Richard S. Childs*. Chapel Hill: The University of North Carolina Press, 1965. (A comprehensive political analysis of municipal reformer Childs in developing the council-manager plan.)

Kessel, John H. "Governmental Structure and Political Environment: A Statistical Note About American Cities." *American Political Science Review* 56 (1962):615–620. (A discussion of the fact that the council-manager plan is associated with weak party competition, an absence of ethnic diversity, and a predominance of local businessmen.)

Sayre, Wallace S. "The General Manager Idea for Large Cities." *Public Administration Review* 14 (1954):253–258. (The development of strong mayor-CAO plans in large cities.)

Stone, Harold A., Don K. Price, and Kathryn H. Stone. *City Manager Government in the United States*. Chicago: Public Administration Service, 1940. (The rationale and development of a council-manager plan after twenty-five years of existence.)

IX. Big City Mayors

Allen, Ivan, Jr. "Growing Up Liberal In Atlanta." *The New York Times Magazine* (December 27, 1970):4–5, 32–33. (Discussion of his political career by the program-politician leader of Atlanta.)

Asbell, Bernard. "Dick Lee Discovers How Much Is Not Enough." *The New York Times Magazine* (September 3, 1967):6–7, 31, 40–44. (Discussion of the fact that although Mayor Lee of New Haven, Connecticut, supported urban renewal and anti-poverty programs, the city had three days of major riots in the summer of 1967.)

Banfield, Edward C. *Political Influence*. New York: The Free Press, 1961. (Six case studies of civic projects in Chicago which show how the mayor centralizes influence over a decentralized local governmental system.)

Dahl, Robert A. *Who Governs?* New Haven: Yale University Press, 1961. (An analysis of community power in New Haven, Connecticut, indicating the executive-centered coalition developed by Mayor Richard Lee in political nominations, urban redevelopment, and public education.)

Gittell, Marilyn. "Metropolitan Mayors: Dead End." *Public Administration Review* 23 (March 1963):20–25. (A description of how in the past, most mayors have been predestined to political oblivion.)

Higdon, Hal. "A Minority Objects, But Daley Is Chicago." *The New York Times Magazine* (September 11, 1966):85, 182–195. (A description of Mayor Daley's rise to power and his opposition to present-day civil rights activists.)

Langguth, Jack. "Yorty Has His Eye On The Big Apple." *The New York Times Magazine* (September 17, 1967):32, 114–128. (A description of the colorful and controversial maverick mayor of Los Angeles.)

Lindsay, John V. *The City*. New York: The New American Library, Inc., Signet Books, 1969. (A discussion by the mayor of the nation's largest city of its problems and prospects.)

Lowe, Jeanne R. *Cities In A Race With Time*. New York: Random House, Inc., Vintage Books, 1967. (Big-city mayoral leadership in urban renewal and anti-poverty programs.)

Maier, Henry W. *Challenge To The Cities*. New York: Random House, Inc., 1966. (The Mayor of Milwaukee's unique view of his problems and a model of executive decision making.)

Ruchelman, Leonard I., ed., *Big City Mayors*. Bloomington: Indiana University Press, 1969. (Selected essays on political and administrative roles of city chief executives.)

Serrin, William. "How One Big City Defeated Its Mayor." *The New York Times Magazine* (October 27, 1968):39, 134–139. (The rise and fall of Detroit mayor Jerome P. Cavanagh.)

Talbot, Allan R. *The Mayor's Game*. New York: Harper & Row, Publishers, Inc., 1967. (The politics and urban renewal and anti-poverty programs of Mayor Richard Lee in New Haven, Connecticut.)

X. Black Political Power

Bailey, Harry A. Jr., ed. *Negro Politics In America*. Columbus, Ohio: Charles E. Merrill Books, Inc., 1967. (Selected readings on comparative black politics.)

Barbour, Floyd B., ed. *The Black Power Revolt*. Boston: Porter Sargent Publisher, Extending Horizons Books, 1968. (Selected readings on black power.)

Carmichael, Stokely, and Charles V. Hamilton. *Black Power: The Politics of Liberation in America*. New York: Random House, Inc., Vintage Books, 1967. (Development of the causes and reasons for black power. Particularly recommended for discussion on coalition politics.)

Dymally, Mervyn M., ed. *The Black Politician: His Struggle for Power*. Belmont, California: Duxbury Press, A Division of Wadsworth Publishing Co., Inc., 1971. (An important collection of original essays, articles, and speeches by leading black politicians.)

Foner, Philip S., ed. *The Black Panthers Speak*. Philadelphia: J. B. Lippincott Co., 1970. (Selected article on the politics and programs advocated by the Panthers.)

Greenberg, Edward S., Neal Milner, and David J. Olson, eds. *Black Politics: The Inevitability of Conflict*. New York: Holt, Rinehart and Winston, Inc., 1971. (Selected articles on black politics, the police, conflict, violence, and protest.)

Greer, Edward, ed. *Black Liberation Politics*. Boston: Allyn and Bacon, Inc., 1971. (Selected articles on black politics, including a case study section on Gary, Indiana.)

Hadden, Jeffrey K., Lewis H. Masotti, and Victor Thiessen. "The Making of the Negro Mayors 1967." *Trans-Action* 5 (1968):21–30. (An interesting analysis of Mayor Carl Stokes' 1967 electoral victory in Cleveland.)

Marine, Gene. *The Black Panthers*. New York: The New American Library, Inc., Signet Books, 1969. (A history of the rise of the militant Black Panther party in California.)

Naughton, James M. "Mayor Stokes: The First Hundred Days." *The New York Times Magazine* (February 25, 1968):26–27, 48–62. (A critical review of initial problems and prospects of Cleveland's first black mayor.)

Piven, Frances Fox, and Richard A. Cloward. "Dissensus Politics: A Strategy For Winning Economic Rights." *The New Republic* 158 (April 28, 1968):20–24. (An argument that a dissensus strategy within the Democratic party will achieve long-term economic gains for urban blacks.)

Rustin, Bayard. " 'Black Power' and Coalition Politics." *Commentary* 42 (September 1966):35:40. (The major hope for urban blacks: to form new and effective coalitions with sympathetic and influential whites.)

————. "From Protest to Politics: The Future of the Civil Rights Movement," *Commentary* 39 (February 1965):25–31. (Emphasis on the fact that blacks will achieve political power and influence by establishing a grand coalition with whites.)

Stone, Chuck. *Black Political Power In America*, Rev. ed. New York: Dell Publishing Co., Inc., Delta Books, 1970. (In-depth analysis of black politics through 1969.)

Van Der Slik, Jack R., ed. *Black Conflict With White America*. Columbus, Ohio: Charles E. Merrill Publishing Co., 1970. (Selected articles on black politics.)

Weinberg, Kenneth G. *Black Victory*. Chicago: Quadrangle Books, Inc., 1968. (An analysis of Carl Stokes' political career which culminated in his election as mayor of Cleveland in 1967.)

Wilson, James Q. *Negro Politics: The Search For Leadership*. New York: The Free Press, 1960. (An analysis of black political and civic leadership in Chicago.)

Chapter 4

Metropolitics

Is Intergovernmental Cooperation Possible?

Metropolitan cooperation is essential to solving the urban crisis, particularly since the population trends of the last two decades have enlarged the metropolis, placed tremendous demands on local governments for quality public services, and indicated that existing rivalries frequently leave local governments incapable of solving regional problems. Central cities cannot eradicate poverty, pay for the public assistance burdens, or provide adequate housing or public education without substantial new sources of public funds. Cities and suburbs cannot fight environmental pollution when dirty air and water refuse to recognize artificial governmental jurisdictions. Planning is ineffective without an area-wide approach to regional problems. The movement of jobs and industry further emphasizes the archaic structure of dispersed local governments in the metropolis.

When these and other problems are considered, an analysis of metropolitan patterns of decision making raises the following questions: How are decisions presently made in most metropolitan areas? What factors have promoted reform demands for alternative approaches to governmental reorganization? What are the distinguishing characteristics of several of the alternatives which are most often debated? What are the political constraints, particularly those imposed by vocal minorities, which effectively limit the range of metropolitan choices? What differences in the relationships of cities to states have resulted from the reapportionment of state legislatures? Can modern varieties of home rule promote greater local government responsiveness to urban, suburban, and regional problems? What are the implications of metropolitan reform in response to financial pressures and the need for improved coordination in the federal system? What are the pros and cons of revenue sharing as a reform proposal promoted as a way of improving intergovernmental cooperation?

Our nation's metropolitan areas presently contain numerous extremely decentralized and fragmented local governments. Local government dispersion stands in direct contrast to the extensive metropolitan economic interdependence of the private sector. Even though most people accept without question the necessity to commute to work, travel long distances for shopping and recreation, and belong to a wide variety of organizations that cross local jurisdictional lines, local governments continue to operate on a relatively small scale within a fixed territory. In particular, suburban residents have idealized the principles of "grass roots" democracy, a heritage of America's rural past. Suburbanites favor government that is close to the people; they place a high value on civic participation. In seeking to be free from the allegedly corrupting influences of the central cities, suburbanites consistently disavow social and political responsibility for inner-city problems. While much can be said for the proximity of government to the voters—minorities in city ghettos are also demanding community control, a form of neighborhood democracy (see Article 11)—it is equally clear that such public problems as transportation, planning, pollution, and housing have taken on regional implications far beyond the political and administrative scope of small local governments.

Over the years, reformers have advocated that city-suburban cooperation can be improved by various forms of metropolitan government. In Article 21, Joseph F. Zimmerman presents a useful review of these structural reforms, particularly the consolidation and semiconsolidation proposals. Metropolitan government has been more successful in the South than in other regions, since the county could be adapted to burgeoning urban problems. In particular, the Nashville and Jacksonville areas had worsening area-wide problems that could not be solved by existing local governments: duplication of services, fragmentation of powers and responsibilities, and alienation of citizens from their local governments. Professor Zimmerman argues that the creation of special tax and service zones facilitated acceptance of metropolitan government in both city-suburban areas.

However, Lee Sloan and Robert M. French (Article 22) take issue with Zimmerman's view on the financial imperatives of metro government. They argue that racial crisis provided the central reason for reform, particularly in Jacksonville-Duval County. As the white population flees to the suburbs, it has become increasingly apparent that blacks and other minorities will gain more political power in the central cities. The Sloan-French thesis is that metropolitan government becomes one means for redefining political boundaries to reduce the proportion of blacks in the new unit. In other words, white suburbanites will back metropolitan government as an obstacle to black control of central cities. At the same time, blacks do not necessarily oppose metro government, especially when they recognize the lack of central city resources to deal with the urban crisis. As long as the new metro proposal is presented to them in a spirit of cooperation and particularly when blacks are guaranteed their fair share of representation in the newly structured government, they will generally support city-county consolidation in voter referendums.

Another obstacle to intergovernmental cooperation has been the antagonistic attitude of state legislatures toward the cities. In the past, rurally gerrymandered state legislatures often directly interfered in city affairs by directing state government toward rural values and placing the cities in financial straitjackets. Unfortunately for the cities, the reapportionment revolution of the 1960's came too late. The Supreme Court's "one man, one vote" ruling largely benefited the rapidly expanding suburbs, as the inner cities either remained static or lost population.

Moreover, the huge population shifts from cities to suburbs have resulted in a suburban-rural coalition in many state legislatures.[1] In most states outside the South and the Southwest, city legislative delegations are usually Democratic, while suburban and rural representatives are likely to be Republican. Thus suburban legislators are probably more susceptible to the political influence of rural members in Republican party caucuses than they are to the pressing social welfare arguments made by Democratic city delegations. The political imperatives of this suburban-rural legislative coalition will probably prevent city-suburban cooperation, even though both will continue to share many common functional problems, such as transportation, environmental pollution, housing, etc.

State legislative hostility toward the cities might be reduced by altering local government charters, those documents which establish the legal relationship between the state and its municipalities. More particularly, states may grant cities home rule. Home rule charters permit cities to control distinctly local functions, such as public safety, health, assessment and collection of taxes, location and maintenance of streets, responsibility for municipal indebtedness, and slum clearance. Second, such charters permit localities to select their own governing structure, including the mayor-council, commission, and council-manager forms of organization. Third, home rule usually implies that local governments will be able to administer local programs, without direct state interference or state establishment of independent boards and commissions.

On the other hand, home rule does not grant complete autonomy to local governments. Such charters are still subject to general state authority and to interpretation by state courts, which have the final say in distinguishing between local powers and statewide power. Also, home rule does not modify state supremacy in taxation and control over state aid to local governments.

A more serious limitation of home rule relates to the metropolitan tangle of uncoordinated governments. Instead of promoting common solutions to area-wide problems, home rule charters may in fact result in separatism and narrow provincial outlooks. For these reasons the two proposals by Mayor John V. Lindsay (Article 23) and Richard P. Burton (Article 24) merit close examination.

To strengthen the nation's largest cities, free them from hostile state governments, and alleviate the inequitable burdens they are now forced to assume, Mayor Lindsay proposes that the federal government charter a number of "national cities," granting them special powers in areas such as trade, finance, and social welfare. They would receive broader financial support in order to ensure functions of national responsibility. Ideally, these "national cities" would include entire metropolitan areas, particularly for the country's 25 largest cities.

Richard Burton carries Mayor Lindsay's incorporation plan one step further by developing a rationale for new "metropolitan states." He argues that the creation of these states would redress the present imbalance of political power in state legislatures, would provide functionally meaningful boundaries for comprehensive planning, and would protect the local political gains of blacks and other minorities.

He feels their creation would also force greater state responsiveness to the urban crisis by significantly altering the federal city-aid programs which currently bypass state participation. Burton's plan would grant statehood to every consolidated metropolitan region that reaches a population of one million. He argues that if the metropolitan roles and functions of urban counties are increased, these units of government might eventually develop into metropolitan states.

Metropolitan reform proposals must take into account the huge financial resources required by local governments to deal effectively with the burgeoning costs of public services. Today there are real questions about the ability of cities and states to meet their financial obligations. Since the 1930's, the federal government has provided cities and states with a wide range of grants-in-aid to finance specific programs. The Nixon administration has proposed to alter these arrangements by instituting a revenue sharing system (Articles 25 and 26). Originally proposed by economist Walter W. Heller, revenue sharing seeks to strengthen the federal aid system in two ways: (1) by eliminating many of the restrictions imposed in categorical grants and (2) by giving a fixed percentage of the federal income tax revenues to the states and the cities on a "no-strings-attached" basis. Under the Nixon Plan, many of the categorical grants would be consolidated into block grants to be used at the discretion of state and local governments. In the two selections, the Advisory Commission on Intergovernmental Relations and Max Frankel debate the pros and cons of revenue sharing. The ACIR defends the plan by emphasizing the superior tax position of the national government and the political liabilities incurred by state and local officials who seek new taxes and higher tax rates. Such a program would also replace the managerial chaos of the presently uncoordinated system of categorical grants, which have proliferated into more than 500 programs costing more than $25 billion per year. In contrast, Mr. Frankel attacks revenue sharing as a counterrevolution in the federal system. In his view, Mr. Nixon's plan ignores the need for metropolitan reform and the problems to be overcome before revenues can be shared when the burdens are distributed so unequally in the federal system. If urban problems have assumed nationwide proportions, how can the cities do more than maintain their present programs, even with increased federal revenues? Thus Frankel concludes that the federal government should assume more responsibility for solving urban problems rather than merely funding possible solutions.

The critical issue is which level of government is in the best position to establish national priorities.

Future metropolitan cooperation must take into account the increasing inability of local governments to cope with area-wide problems. Whether the future will bring voluntary interlocal cooperation, integrated metropolitan government, new "national cities," "metropolitan states," or reformed federal-state-local financial arrangements is difficult to forecast. But one thing is certain: Comprehensive metropolitan solutions will not be possible until a new consensus is established to erase city-suburban hostilities and to unite the divergent goals of different political constituencies.

NOTES

1. For a good discussion of urban, suburban, and rural political alignments in state legislatures, see A. James Reichley, "The Political Containment of the Cities," pp. 169–195, in Alan K. Campbell, ed., *The States and the Urban Crisis* (Englewood Cliffs, N.J.: Prentice-Hall, Inc., 1970) .

QUESTIONS FOR DISCUSSION AND DEBATE

1. Compare and contrast the major objectives of consolidation and semiconsolidation efforts to restructure government in metropolitan areas. Why have metro government proposals been more successful in the South than in other regions? Do you agree or disagree with Professor Zimmerman's observation that "it is unlikely that the 1970's will be a decade of metropolitan reform"?

2. Black leaders and voters generally supported metro government in Nashville and Jacksonville but opposed it in St. Louis and Cleveland. How do you evaluate the reasons given by Professors Sloan and French for this situation? Also, what are the strongest arguments possible for defending metro consolidation on the basis of tax and financial issues rather than race issues? How do you stand on this problem?

3. If the cities do not have either the votes or the influence to build effective coalitions in state legislatures, what would you suggest as the next best set of alternatives to achieve state responsiveness

to urban problems? Do you foresee any possibilities for closer city-suburban cooperation in state legislatures?

4. Compare and contrast the major strengths and weaknesses of the Lindsay city-state and the Burton metropolitan state proposals. Do you think that there is any chance that either of these proposals will ever be put into effect? Why? Are Burton's arguments for an incremental approach via the urban county worth considering?

5. Compare and contrast the major arguments for revenue sharing made by the ACIR. Which position would you defend: Revenue sharing strengthens intergovernmental relations in the federal system, or revenue sharing results in abdication of domestic responsibilities by the federal government? Are there any alternatives to revenue sharing that might alleviate the fiscal crisis of state and local governments?

Metropolitan Reform in the U.S.: An Overview

Joseph F. Zimmerman

The metropolitan problem, variously defined, has been accorded recognition since the early part of the 20th century, and numerous proposals have been advanced for a restructuring of the system of local government to solve the problem. With relatively few exceptions, reorganization proposals have been rejected by voters who apparently have been influenced more by arguments promising to keep the tax rate low and the government close to the people and free of corruption than by arguments stressing the correction of service inadequacies and the economical and efficient provision of services.

Interest in the structural reform of the local government system appeared to reach its peak in the 1950's. Frank C. Moore wrote in 1958 "that more surveys have been initiated in the last five years than in the previous thirty."[1] Seventy-nine of the 112 surveys initiated between 1923 and 1957 were launched between 1948 and 1957, compared to one or two per year from 1923 to 1948.[2]

The number and nature of surveys underwent a significant change in the 1960's, primarily as the result of requirements in various federal grant-in-aid programs. A sharp rise in transportation and comprehensive land-use studies occurred. The number of transportation studies rose from 15 to 1960 to 118 in 1966, 154 in 1967, and 198 in 1968.[3] Comprehensive land-use studies increased from 15 in 1960 to 48 in 1966 and 73 in 1967, but decreased to 71 in 1968. Studies concerned with governmental organization declined from 40

Reprinted from Joseph F. Zimmerman, "Metropolitan Reform in the U.S.: An Overview," *Public Administration Review*, Vol. 36, No. 5 (September-October 1970), pp. 531–543. © 1970 by the American Society for Public Administration. Reprinted by permission of the publisher and author.

in 1960 to 34 in 1966 and 29 in 1967. Thirty-six such studies were launched in 1968. Although the results of a comprehensive canvass of metropolitan studies are not currently available, it appears that there has been a vast upsurge since 1968 in the number of governmental organization studies, particularly in the South.

THE CONSOLIDATIONISTS

Nineteenth century metropolitan reorganization took the form of city-county consolidation without referenda in Boston, Philadelphia, New Orleans, and New York City. In addition, entire towns were consolidated by legislative edict with the central city; Charlestown, Dorchester, and Roxbury were consolidated with Boston. And annexation also commonly was used by the central city to keep pace with urbanization.

The leading consolidation advocate in recent years has been the Committee for Economic Development (CED), composed of 200 prominent businessmen and educators, which maintains there is a great need for a revolutionary restructuring of what is labelled an anachronistic system of local government. In 1966 CED urged an 80 per cent reduction in the number of units to no more than 16,000, with increased reliance being placed upon reconstituted county governments everywhere except in New England, where the proposal was advanced that towns should be consolidated or closely federated to form metropolitan governments.[5] Interestingly, CED in February 1970 recommended "as an ultimate solution a governmental system at two levels."[6]

The National Commission on Urban Problems (Douglas Commission) in 1968 accepted the CED's basic consolidation recommendation. The Commission was convinced that the solution of housing and other problems was seriously impeded by a multiplicity of local governments, many of which have restrictive codes designed to discourage low-income persons from migrating to these communities. A major recommended solution was the use of federal revenue sharing as a catalyst to encourage local governments with a population under 50,000 to consolidate.[7] Units with a population of less than 50,000 would be ineligible to share in the revenue, and units with a population between 50,000 and 100,000 would share in the revenue based on the percentage by which their populations exceed 50,000. No action has been taken by Congress on this proposal, and it is improbable that any action will be taken until the federal budgetary situation improves substantially and inflationary pressures are sharply curtailed.

When we speak of consolidation we may refer either to the consolidation of functions which occurs when a function is shifted to a higher level of government—this is labelled centralization by some—or to a consolidation of units of government. The creation of a metropolitan federation also may be referred to as a type of consolidation in view of the fact certain functions are taken away from municipalities and assigned to the newly created upper-tier unit.

City-county consolidation may be complete or partial. In a complete consolidation, a new government is formed by the amalgamation of the county and municipal governments. Partial consolidation may involve the merger of most county functions with the cities to form a new consolidated government, but the county continues to exist for the performance of a few functions required by the state constitution. A second form of partial consolidation involves the merger of several but not all municipalities with the county.

Twentieth-Century Consolidations

Prior to 1947 there was relatively little 20th-century interest in city-county consolidation. The Hawaiian Territorial Legislature did merge the City and County of Honolulu in 1907 without a referendum, but only three proposals for consolidation in other areas reached the ballot and each of the proposals was defeated.

Louisiana voters in 1946 approved a constitutional amendment permitting a home rule charter to be drafted for the Baton Rouge area. Voters in 1947 approved a charter providing for the partial consolidation of the City of Baton Rouge and East Baton Rouge Parish effective in 1949. The city, parish, and two small municipal governments were continued and a city-parish council was created. It is composed of the seven-member city council and two members from the remainder of the parish.

After rejecting a consolidation charter in 1958, voters approved a similar charter in 1962 creating the Metropolitan Government of Nashville and Davidson County. The charter created an urban services district and a general services district, and authorized a separate tax rate for each district based upon services provided. Six small cities were exempted from the consolidation, but may disincorporate and join the urban services district when it is expanded to their area.

The next major partial consolidation occurred in the Jacksonville area as the result of a 1967 referendum when a charter consolidating the City of Jacksonville and Duval County was approved. The voters of three small cities and a town voted to retain their separate corporate status. Patterned largely upon the Nashville model, the new city has a general and an urban services district.

A minor consolidation—Carson City and Ormsby County, Nevada—received voter approval in 1969. A more major consolidation occurred in the Indianapolis area on January 1, 1970, as the result of the passage of an act by the Indiana Legislature consolidating the city and Marion County.[8] This consolidation is particularly noteworthy in that it is the first one in the northern United States, as well as the first one implemented without a popular referendum since 1898 when New York City was formed by a five-county consolidation.

UNIGOV, the popular name for the new government, is a misnomer in that the existing 58 units of government in the county are only partially consolidated. Two small cities and a town are excluded from the consolidation, as are 16 townships, school corporations, Marion County Health and Hospital Corporation, and Indianapolis Airport Authority. The latter two units are subject to budget review by the city-county council.

The elective county constitutional officers are continued, and there is no change in the County Welfare Board, County Assessors, and County Tax Adjustment Board. Police and fire protection services remain unchanged as the office of sheriff continues and a police special service district was created within the old city. Furthermore, a fire special service district was created within the old city and volunteer firemen continue to serve the remaining area.

After a ten-month study in 1969, the Charlottesville, Virginia, City Council and the Albemarle County Board of Supervisors prepared a charter consolidating the city, county, Town of Scottsville, and Crozet Sanitary District.[9] The charter, on March 3, 1970, met with voter disapprobation by negative margins of two to one in the city and four to one in the county. As a result of the charter defeat, the city has decided to initiate annexation proceedings.

A proposed consolidation of the City of Roanoke, Roanoke County, and the Town of Vinton in Virginia was rejected by voters in November 1969. Approval required a concurrent majority in the city, county, and town; city voters approved the proposal but it was rejected by county voters.

Consolidation Studies Underway

In 1969 the North Carolina Legislature created an 18-member Charlotte-Mecklenburg Charter Commission charged with the duty of creating a single government charter for the county and presenting it to the voters no sooner than December 1, 1970.[10] The charter must contain a provision allowing Cornelius, Davidson, Huntersville, Matthews, and Pineville voters to decide whether they want to merger their governments with the city and county.

The South Carolina General Assembly, in January 1969, created a 25-member commission to prepare a charter consolidating the governments in Charleston County. In November the commission released the first six articles of a proposed charter consolidating all governments into a new City of Charleston.

A 15-member council would govern the new city, with 12 members elected by single-member districts and three members elected at-large. The chief executive would be a mayor elected for a four-year term, but limited to two consecutive terms. He would possess the veto power and would be authorized to appoint department heads with approval of the council. Two service districts would be established—an urban services district and a general services district. A separate tax rate would be established for each district and the council would be authorized to extend the urban services district whenever the consolidated government is able to provide the necessary services.

Local governments in the Atlanta area have been under pressure from the Georgia Legislature to reorganize. In 1969 the House of Representatives voted 89 to 61 to consolidate Atlanta and Fulton County without a referendum, but the bill lacked the constitutionally required majority of the entire house. Although the 1970 Legislature did not pass a bill consolidating the city and county, a bill was enacted authorizing the creation of a commission to study the proposed consolidation of Macon and Bibb County.

The Institute of Public Administration prepared for Atlanta and Fulton County a report which recommends the consolidation of the two governments.[11] The proposed merger would be a partial one, as

the report indicates there is no need to include the smaller municipalities in the merger, but recommends that enabling legislation
should provide these units with the option of joining the amalga-
mated government at any time by means of a referendum.

Consolidation of governments is complicated by the fact that 8.0
per cent of Atlanta's population and 6.3 per cent of its land area are
in DeKalb County. Since the Institute's polls reveal that only 32 per
cent of De Kalb County voters favor merging the county with the
consolidated government, the Institute came to the conclusion that it
is politically infeasible to include the county in the merger.

Recognizing the need for a governmental mechanism to handle
problems transcending Fulton County, the report recommends the
creation of a limited-purpose regional council to be responsible for
water supply, aviation, sewage and solid waste disposal, recreation,
and a few other functions. The suggestion was advanced that the
proposed council might incorporate the functions of the Metropolitan Atlanta Council of Local Governments, Atlanta Region Metropolitan Planning Commission, and Metropolitan Atlanta Rapid
Transit Authority.

Although the precise structure of the proposed government
would be determined by a charter commission, the report recommends a mayor-council plan with 10 councilmen elected by districts
and seven elected at-large with a requirement that each of the seven
live in a different area.

A 10-member Metropolitan Charter Commission for Chattanooga
and Hamilton County, Tennessee, was elected on September 18,
1969, to prepare a charter for submission to the voters. The state
constitution stipulates that approval of a charter is contingent upon
a concurrent majority of votes in the city and the remainder of the
county.

A Local Government Consolidation Study Committee was
appointed in Chatham County, Georgia, in 1969 by the elected
officials of the county, City of Savannah, four small cities, and the
county legislative delegation. In January 1970 consulting firms were
invited to submit proposals for the preparation of a report "on the
feasibility of consolidation and the alternative forms of consolidation
of governments and/or services."

The Hillsborough County Home Rule Charter Commission has
prepared a charter providing for the consolidation of the City of
Tampa and Hillsborough County. Currently, the county legislative

delegation is considering the charter, subject to amendment, for introduction as a local bill. If approved by the legislature, the proposed charter will be placed on the November 3, 1970, ballot for voter action.

The proposed charter provides for city-county consolidation and the consolidation into the new government of all "boards, districts, authorities, agencies and councils other than the public school system, the Junior College System, the Tampa Port Authority, the Hillsborough County Aviation Authority, [and] the Tampa-Hillsborough Expressway Authority."

The municipalities of Plant City and Temple Terrace would be allowed to continue their separate corporate existence, but their ordinances, with the exception of zoning, could not conflict with the ordinances of the consolidated government.

The unified government would be governed by a 21-member council. Twenty members would be elected by districts and the chairman—the vice-mayor—would be elected at-large. A popularly elected mayor would be the chief executive officer and his appointments would be subject to council confirmation. The charter also provides for the initiative, referendum, and recall.

Earlier, the Hillsborough County Local Government Study Commission issued a report in 1964, and the voters on June 27, 1967, rejected a charter creating a unified government of Tampa and Hillsborough County.

In a related action, the Escambia County Legislative Delegation is drafting for introduction in the legislature the final version of a bill providing for the consolidation of the City of Pensacola, Town of Flomaton, and Escambia County.

In Niagara County, New York, the Local Governments Improvement Commission—LOGIC—released in January 1970 the first draft of a charter creating a consolidated government by the amalgamation of three cities, 12 towns, five villages, and the county.

In January 1970 a 14-member task force, appointed by the Louisville, Kentucky, Area Chamber of Commerce, proposed that the city be enlarged to include all unincorporated areas of Jefferson County. The 65 fourth-, fifth-, and sixth-class cities would be given the option to join the enlarged city, but would not be forced to do so. Several city and county functions would be merged, but county constitutional officers would continue to perform functions such as health and welfare. As authorized by a constitutional amendment ratified by voters in November 1969, the city would be empowered to establish separate tax rates for each area based upon services provided. Under the task force's proposal, the plan would become effective upon approval by a simple majority of all voters in Louisville and the unincorporated areas of the county.

An attempt was made in 1955 to reorganize the government system in the area when a six-member Local Government Improvement Committee, appointed by the mayor, recommended that the city annex 46 square miles of urbanized land containing approximately 68,000 residents and 31 suburban cities. The proposal was approved by city voters, but rejected by suburban voters by more than a two-to-one margin.

At the request of the Salt Lake City and Salt Lake County Commissions, the University of Utah undertook a local government modernization study. In January 1970 a report was released recommending city-county consolidation, exemption of smaller municipalities from the consolidation, and the use of service and tax districts by the consolidated government.

Consolidation in the South

With the exception of the Indianapolis-Marion County merger, all 20th-century city-county consolidations and a major semiconsolidation, Dade County, have occurred in the South. Furthermore, a three-judge annexation court in Virginia in 1969 allowed Richmond to annex 23 square miles of territory and 44,000 residents; the largest annexation in terms of population and area in the state's history.[12] The city had sought to annex 51 square miles of territory and 72,000 residents. And indications, as reflected by the creation of charter commissions, are that most consolidations in the next few years will occur in the South.

What factors, other than general geographical location, are common to each area or to each reorganization plan where consolidation has occurred or current interest in consolidation is strong? Even a superficial analysis of the areas indicate that they possess a number of similarities with each other and dissimilarities with metropolitan areas in other sections of the United States.

Number of units. There were relatively few units of local government in each metropolitan area prior to consolidation, and each unit had a small population with the exception of the central city.

The partial consolidation in the Baton Rouge area involved only four units, and the partial consolidation in the Nashville area involved only seven municipalities, six of which are small and were exempted from the consolidation. In Duval County there were only five municipalities and six special districts; only four of the special districts had property-taxing powers. Aside from Jacksonville, the largest municipality had a population of 16,000. And the four small municipalities were given the option of remaining out of the consolidation.

In the Charlotte area there are only six municipalities and one special district with property-taxing powers. Other than Charlotte, the largest municipality has a population under 5,000. We find a somewhat similar situation in the Savannah area where there are six small municipalities, four of which have a population under 5,000. In the Chattanooga area, three of the six municipalities have a population under 5,000, and in the Charleston area six of the eight municipalities have a population under 5,000.

Dade County with 27 municipalities is the exception, and the fact that there were such a large number of municipalities may account at least partially for the fact the two-tier approach was adopted. Proposals were made in 1945, 1947, and 1953 to consolidate the county and the City of Miami, but were defeated.

Partial consolidations. The Nashville and Jacksonville reorganizations were partial consolidations in that the few existing small municipalities were given the option, by referendum, to remain out of the consolidation, and all chose to do so. The Baton Rouge consolidation retained the city, the parish, and two small municipalities. The Dade County reorganization provided only for functional consolidation and not for the merger of governments. And most of the proposed consolidations in the South offer the smaller municipalities the option of continuing their separate corporate existence.

Use of the county. An established government, the county, was utilized as the base to build the new metropolitan government. This strategy improves the prospects of creating an areawide government with sufficient powers since it usually is easier, under state enabling legislation, to restructure the county government than to create a new regional unit. In the South, the county traditionally has been a stronger unit of government than in the Northeast. In North Carolina, for example, the county can perform nearly all urban-type functions.

Irving G. McNayr, the second manager of Dade County, in a 1964 speech, stated:

> Realizing that the county's inadequate tax structure and lack of long-range plans for operating special districts held little hope for expansion of urban services throughout the county, the citizens of the unincorporated area began supporting the new concept for an area-wide government with broad powers.[13]

Incremental consolidation. City-county consolidation is not entirely new in most southern areas, as partial consolidation has occurred incrementally over the years and citizens, consequently, were accustomed to look to the county for solutions to areawide problems.

In the 1940's the Dade County school system was created by the consolidation of 10 school districts, a county health department was created by the consolidation of all municipal health departments, and a county port authority was created to operate all airports and terminals. In 1948 Miami turned its hospital over to the county.

In the Jacksonville area health, tax assessing, tax collecting, voter registration, and planning and zoning had been consolidated prior to 1967.

Charlotte-Mecklenburg County currently have consolidated school, public health, and public welfare systems, and jointly finance a single agency responsible for elections, a second agency responsible for planning, and a third agency responsible for property tax administration. According to a recent report, "only thirty per cent of combined city and county expenditures are in areas where further consolidation or joint financing arrangements would appear to deserve consideration."[14]

Special service zones. The consolidations, starting with the Baton Rouge one in 1947, rely upon special service and taxing zones. A separate tax rate is established for each zone based upon the number and level of services provided. The use of service zones has made consolidation more appealing to residents of unincorporated territory, and proposed southern consolidations provide for the use of service zones.

Dade County is not allowed by the Florida constitution to utilize tax and service zones. This means that residents of unincorporated territory receive urban services from the county and pay *ad valorem* property taxes to the county at the same rate as residents of the 27 municipalities who do not receive these services from the county.

Lack of a competitive political system. The political system in southern metropolitan areas is, in general, not highly competitive. In 1957 Edward C. Banfield wrote, "it will be difficult or impossible to integrate local governments where the two-party system operates. . . . In effect, advocates of consolidation schemes are asking the Democrats to give up their control of the central cities or, at least, to place it in jeopardy."[15]

The term "No-party system" has been used by Edward Sofen to describe the absence of powerful political parties in Dade County.[16] In Charlotte, elections are nonpartisan, but all councilmen are Democrats. Partisan elections are used in Mecklenburg County, and two of the five county board members currently are Republicans; the system, however, is not highly competitive.

Scandals. Scandals in Nashville and Jacksonville worked in favor of the consolidationists. In Nashville prior to the referendum there were charges of police scandals. Jacksonville was plagued by a high crime rate and insurance and police scandals. In November 1966 the grand jury indicted two city commissioners, four councilmen, the recreation director, and the city auditor. In addition, the tax assessor resigned and the city's 15 senior high schools were disaccredited shortly before the referendum.

Racial overtones. There were racial overtones attached to the Nashville and Jacksonville referenda campaigns, as it was charged in each case that consolidation was designed to dilute the growing black voting strength in the central city. It has been suggested that Richmond's 1969 annexation of 44,000 persons, most of whom are white, would help to offset black political strength in the city. Prior to annexation, an estimated 55 per cent of the population was black. It must be pointed out, however, that City Manager Alan F. Kiepper testified at the annexation trial the city's need was for land for new industry and housing. Only 6.4 per cent of the city's land prior to annexation was vacant, whereas 27.7 per cent is now vacant. The city maintains that the annexation will strengthen the economy of the metropolitan area by providing a more realistic economic base for the central city.

State Senator LeRoy Johnson of Atlanta has charged that the 1969 bill providing for the consolidation of Atlanta and Fulton County was designed not as "an effort of extending the tax base of the City but from an effort of curtailing and limiting the Negro voting strength."[17] Mr. Johnson pointed out that nearly 50 per cent of Atlanta's population is black and that a black vice-mayor, five black aldermen, and two black school board members were elected in the fall of 1969. Nevertheless, a black has never been elected to a county office.

Motivations for consolidation are many and varied. Although the growing political power of blacks in central cities may predispose a number of whites to favor consolidation, it must not be overlooked that the deep and growing fiscal crisis of many central cities is a major reason why certain groups favor consolidation. If conditions in the central city, which increasingly is becoming black, are to be improved, new financial resources must be found. A metropolitan government would be in a position to mobilize considerably larger resources than a central city to solve the most pressing problems in the area.

The Nashville consolidation was endorsed by a number of prominent blacks, even though black voting strength would be decreased from approximately 40 per cent in the city to 25 per cent countywide. According to 1960 census data, 37.9 per cent of Nashville's population was black and 19.2 per cent of the county's population was black. Currently, approximately 19.3 per cent of the population of the consolidated government is black.

Professor Brett W. Hawkins analyzed the 1962 Nashville referendum and pointed out that "both whites and nonwhites in the old city voted against Metro, and by very similar percentages."[18] He concluded that the racial factor was relatively unimportant and that blacks and whites may have voted in the same manner for different reasons.

Prior to consolidation there were two blacks serving on the 31-member Nashville City Council and none on the 55-member county court or in any other local office. Currently, five members of the metropolitan council are black; 35 of the 40 members are elected by districts. All other elective offices are held by whites. There is a black attorney in the Metropolitan Department of Law, a second black attorney in the Office of Public Defender, and one black has been appointed a judge of the Court of General Sessions.

Jacksonville had a population which was 42 per cent black in 1967, yet black areas voted in favor of the consolidation which was endorsed by civil rights groups and resulted in black population dropping to approximately 23 per cent of the total population. Fourteen members of the 19-member Jacksonville City Council are elected by districts, and blacks felt that this system would guarantee them increased representation. L. A. Hester, former executive director of the Local Government Study Commission of Duval County, has testified that the most popular aspect of the proposed consolidation was district elections.[19] The proposed electoral system was designed to guarantee blacks three seats immediately, with prospects of two or more additional seats in the future. Whites favored district elections because they felt that blacks had been exercising the balance of power in the at-large city elections. There is some evidence that suburban whites favored consolidation to prevent the blacks from capturing control of the core city.

Two blacks were elected to the nine-member city council shortly before the referendum creating the consolidated government was held; the first time a black had been elected to local office. Currently, there are four blacks on the 19-member council, three elected by districts and one at-large. Furthermore, a black has been elected to the school board and another black has been elected to the Civil Service Board. A black has been appointed head of the Motor Pool Division, a second black has been appointed a legislative aide to the mayor, and several blacks have been appointed to the Community Relations Commission and other advisory boards.

The black population in Dade County in 1957 was approximately 15 per cent, but no black had ever been elected to the Board of County Commissioners or any other elective county office. The nine-member county board presently has one black member, and the black population has increased to 18 per cent of the total population. Blacks have been appointed to a number of top offices, including the director and assistant director of the Housing and Urban Development Department, director and assistant director of the Welfare Department, director and assistant director of the Community Relations Board, executive director of the Fair Housing and Employment Commission, head of the Waste Division of the Public Works Department, and head of the Children's Home in the Youth Services Department.

Other factors. The fact there is less industry in southern metropolitan areas compared to northern areas is of some significance, as it may indicate a lesser role played by manufacturing interest groups in the areas' politics. Table 1 clearly indicates that white-collar employment is of much greater importance than manufacturing. Although no hard evidence has been produced, it is possible that northern industrial firms which have found a haven in suburbia from central-city woes may be opposed to consolidation or the creation of a federation if it appears that their taxes will be increased substantially to help solve central-city problems. Conversely, central-city industry may favor creation of a metropolitan government because of the tax relief it would afford.

TABLE 1. Manufacturing and White-Collar Employment in Selected Metropolitan Areas   1960

Area	Per Cent of Employed in Manufacturing Occupations	Per Cent of Employed in White-Collar Occupations
East Baton Rouge Parish, La.	24.4	41.0
Davidson County, Tenn.	23.1	45.9
Dade County, Fla.	11.6	46.3
Duval County, Fla.	13.2	45.4
Mecklenburg County, N.C.	22.8	45.7
Hamilton County, Tenn.	31.1	40.0
Charleston County, S.C.	23.2	39.0
Charlottesville, Va.	15.1	49.1
Fulton County, Ga.	19.3	44.3
Cook County, Ill.	34.1	45.3
Erie County, N.Y.	36.9	43.3
Genesee County, Mich.	50.7	33.4
Lehigh County, Penn.	45.1	38.9
Mahoning County, O.	41.9	37.4
Monroe County, N.Y.	42.8	45.8
Summit County, O.	44.7	42.1

Source: United States Bureau of the Census, *U.S. Census Population: 1960*, Vol. I, "Characteristics of the Population." Tables 33 and 36 (Washington, D.C.: U.S. Government Printing Office, 1963) .

Finally, Nashville annexed 49.46 square miles of territory and 82,000 citizens subsequent to the defeat of the proposed consolidation charter in 1958, and the threat of further annexations helped to persuade outlying areas to vote in favor of consolidation. Voter rejection of two proposed Virginia mergers—Winchester and Frederick County in December 1969 and Charlottesville and Albemarle County in March 1970—have led to the initiation of annexation proceedings. The threat of continued annexation in time may make county voters more receptive to a merger.

THE SEMICONSOLIDATIONISTS

The semiconsolidationists advocate a two-tier system of local government in metropolitan areas, the upper tier to handle areawide functions and the lower tier of municipalities to handle local functions. The metropolitan county, federation, and metropolitan special district are the three varieties of two-tier systems which have been employed. Each may be viewed as a type of semiconsolidation in that certain functions are consolidated at the upper-tier level. A new unit of local government, the upper tier, is formed by a decision to create a federation or a special district, whereas an existing unit is utilized in the case of the metropolitan county. Under federation, of course, a number of lower-tier governments could be consolidated as they were in the Toronto area in 1966.

A metropolitan county may be developed either by the incremental approach or the revolutionary approach. Los Angeles County, which developed as a major provider of urban services since the turn of the century, represents the first, and Dade County, Florida, which adopted a home rule charter in 1957, represents the second. It must be pointed out that Metropolitan Dade County simultaneously is a two-tier and a single-tier system. There is a two-tier system in the 27 areas of the county where there are municipalities, but there is only one local government in unincorporated areas—the county.

Opponents of metropolitan Dade County challenged its constitutionality and entered a total of 155 suits affecting aspects of the new government during its first three years; the courts ruled in favor of the county. Attempts were made to emasculate the government by charter amendment in 1958 and 1961, but each was defeated. However, two amendments weakening the power of the county manager were approved in 1962; his administrative orders creating or combining departments and his appointments of department heads were made subject to the approval of the county commissioners.

In 1963 voters approved amendments providing for the at-large election of one commissioner from each of eight districts. More recently, voters in November 1968 defeated a proposed amendment consolidating all police and fire-fighting functions on the county level.

In spite of the fact the Dade County League of Municipalities has led a strong fight against metro, city-county cooperation has been common and the county provides services to a number of cities on a contract basis. In addition, cities gradually have turned functions over to the county under the charter provision authorizing a city council, by a two-thirds vote, to turn over functions. To cite two recent examples, Florida City and North Miami turned their fire departments over to the county in 1968 and 1969 respectively.

Pressure for the creation of a regional government for the San Francisco area has been growing for a number of years. In March 1969 the legislature's Joint Committee on Bay Area Regional Organization (BARO) introduced a bill creating a 36-member board to be in charge of a nine-county regional government which, in terms of functions, would be limited to reviewing applications for state and federal grants, signing joint agreements with local governments, and preparing and adopting a regional general plan.

The Association of Bay Area Governments (ABAG) has recommended since 1966 that it be converted into a regional government, and a bill was introduced in the 1969 legislature creating a 14-member Bay Area Transportation Authority to prepare a plan for highways and mass transportation facilities. However, no action was taken by the legislature prior to its adjournment.

Addressing a meeting of the Council on Regional Issues in Concord, Massachusetts, on November 25, 1969, Mayor Kevin H. White of Boston proposed the creation of the Eastern Massachusetts Council of Governments consisting of a general council of 200 representatives —two from each of the 100 cities and towns in the region—and an executive committee of 18 members chosen by nine districts of approximately equal population.

Mayor White did not propose the creation of a traditional council of governments, a voluntary association of elected officials, but rather an upper-tier metropolitan government which would be the governing body of the Metropolitan Area Planning Council, Massachusetts Bay Transportation Authority, Massachusetts Port Authority, Metropolitan District Commission, and Metropolitan Boston Air Pollution Control District, all of which are state-controlled agencies.[20] The Task Force on Regional Legislation of the Council on Regional Issues in January 1970 prepared a draft enabling bill for introduction in the General Court.

On March 26, 1970, the Volusia County Charter and Study Commission presented the legislative delegation a proposed charter providing for the consolidation with the county government of 38 boards, districts, authorities, and agencies; Daytona Beach and other municipalities would not be consolidated with the county.

Under provisions of the charter, a seven-member county council would be chosen in nonpartisan elections. The five members elected by districts would serve two-year terms and be limited to three consecutive terms. The two at-large members would serve four-year terms and be limited to two consecutive terms. By a two-thirds vote, the council would be authorized to hire and fire a county manager. Ten departments would be created to receive the powers of former constitutional officers.

The new county would "have all powers and duties prescribed by the Constitution, laws of Florida, and this charter," and may establish service and tax districts. Furthermore, municipalities and special districts are authorized to transfer functions to the county.

The charter stipulates that a:

> county ordinance in conflict with a municipal ordinance shall not be effective within the municipality to the extent of such conflict . . . provided that county ordinances shall prevail over municipal ordinances whenever the county shall set minimum standards protecting the environment by prohibiting or regulating air or water pollution or the destruction of the resources of the county belonging to the general public.

THE STATISTS

The creation of state authorities has been a third major organizational response to metropolitan exigencies. Massachusetts in the late 19th century created three state agencies, a metropolitan water district, a metropolitan sewer district, and metropolitan parks district in the Boston area; they later were merged to form the Metropolitan District Commission. In more recent years, other state authorities were created in eastern Massachusetts.

New York State, under Governor Nelson A. Rockefeller, decided in the 1960's to use its plenary authority to directly solve areawide problems and adopted the authority approach. Both statewide and regional authorities have been created for special purposes: Urban Development Corporation (UDC), Environmental Facilities Corporation, Job Development Authority, Metropolitan Transportation Authority, Niagara Frontier Transportation Authority, Capital District Transportation Authority, Central New York Regional Transportation Authority, and Rochester-Genesee Transportation Authority. UDC, for example, may override local codes and laws by a two-thirds vote of its nine-member board of directors.

The rationale for the creation of state authorities is a simple one: only the state has the authority and resources to solve critical metropolitan problems. Other reasons for the use of authorities in New York State include a desire to avoid the constitutional debt limit and civil service, and to remove items from the state budget and annual appropriation processes.

A different state approach has been adopted by Minnesota whose legislature created in 1967 a 15-member Metropolitan Council for the seven-county Twin Cities area. Fourteen members are selected from equal population districts by the governor who also appoints the chairman at-large.

The Council assumed the functions of the abolished Metropolitan Planning Commission, and was granted authority to review and suspend plans of special districts in conflict with the Council's development guidelines. The Council initially also was authorized to appoint a nonvoting member to the board of each special district, conduct research, operate a data center, and intervene before the Minnesota Municipal Commission in annexation and incorporation proceedings. Contracts subsequently signed with the Metropolitan Transit Commission and the Minnesota Highway Department provide that the Council is responsible for metropolitan transportation planning. And the Governor's Crime Commission designated the Council as the criminal justice planning agency.

The Council's principal function is the establishment of policy and not its execution. In December 1968 the Council proposed that the legislature create three, seven-member service boards; one to operate a metropolitan zoo, one to operate a sewage collection and treatment system, and one to operate an open space system. The legislature responded by creating a sewer service board and a metropolitan park board and authorizing the Council to appoint their members. The Council is responsible for determining policies and priorities in these two functional areas, and each board is responsible for carrying out the Council's policies relative to the service.

Debate in the legislature on the creation of the Council centered on the question of whether it should be popularly elected. An amendment providing for the popular election of members in 1970 failed to pass by three votes in the House of Representatives and by a tie vote in the Senate. This issue is not dead and it is possible that legislation will be enacted in the foreseeable future transforming the Council from a state agency to a popularly elected metropolitan government.

THE ECUMENICISTS

Coming into prominence during the 1960's primarily as the result of conditional federal grants-in-aid, the ecumenicists hold that metropolitan exigencies can be solved by inter-local cooperation within the existing governmental framework. In particular, ecumenicists maintain that conjoint action will be stimulated by the development of areawide plans identifying problems and mechanisms for their solution.

Comprehensive metropolitan planning is a form of intergovernmental cooperation which may be traced in origin to the Regional Plan for New York and Its Environs completed in 1929 under the sponsorship of the Russell Sage Foundation. By 1961 it was generally concluded that areawide planning had been ineffective because of a schism between the planners and the decision makers. In that year, the Advisory Commission on Intergovernmental Relations suggested that planning should be the responsibility of an organization composed of local elected officials and private citizens, and indicated its opposition to the creation of commissions "comprised solely of part-time commissioners, and dominated by professional planning staff."[21]

The sharp increase in the number of metropolitan planning agencies since 1963 resulted from a conclusion reached by the federal government that areawide planning is the most feasible method of guaranteeing coordinated development of metropolitan areas. A decision was made by Congress in 1965 to involve local elected officials in the planning process, and was implemented by the Housing and Urban Development Act of 1965, which made organizations of local elected officials—councils of governments (COG's)—eligible for the receipt of grants for the preparation of comprehensive metropolitan plans.[22] The following year Congress provided an additional stimulus for the formation of commissions by enacting a requirement that all local government applications for federal grants and loans for 30 specified projects must be submitted for review to an organization responsible for areawide planning "which is, to the greatest practicable extent, composed of or responsible to the elected officials of a unit of areawide government or of the units of general local government."[23] This requirement promoted the formation of a COG or planning commission in each of the 233 standard metropolitan statistical areas.

Until 1965 most commissions were composed of nonelected officials and COG's generally were composed only of elected officials.[24] The 18 COG's active in the spring of 1966 were strictly voluntary associations of governments seeking to identify problems and develop a consensus for coordinated remedial action.[25] The 1966 act led a number of planning commissions to convert themselves into COG's while retaining their original names and others to change their membership and names. Furthermore, several COG's assumed responsibility for planning. As a consequence, it no longer is possible to make a clear distinction between the two types of organizations.

Several early appraisals of the COG movement were relatively optimistic regarding its future potential. One study concluded that ABAG "is a quasi-governmental agency. It is an agency of government which administers governmental programs and functions at a regional level. It is no longer a narrowly oriented discussion group."[26] A similar conclusion was reached by another organization which concluded ABAG was "transforming itself from one of the myriad discussion forums into a vigorous and potent governmental force."[27] And the executive secretary of the Metropolitan Washington Council of Governments wrote that COG's "may show the way toward finding a new and better means of coordinating the governing of the metropolis."[28]

During the past three years, however, there has been a growing consensus that the potential of COG's, a form of voluntarism, is limited in view of the increasing magnitude of metropolitan exigencies.[29] Any organization built upon cooperation between local governments with widely differing socioeconomic makeups and aspirations is predestined to experience serious difficulty in attempting to develop a program, based upon conjoint action, to solve major problems. The fact that a COG member from a given community ratifies a proposed plan of action does not necessarily mean that his community will take steps to initiate the plan. COG's have developed and helped to implement programs to solve minor problems, but no COG has successfully implemented a program to solve a highly controversial problem such as housing in the metropolis.

Furthermore, COG officials are beginning to question whether regional organizations are becoming "arms of the federal government."[30] Board Chairman Joseph L. Fisher of the Metropolitan Washington COG maintains that most federal grants-in-aid received by his COG are dedicated to specific purposes and "virtually all of the one-quarter of our total funds that come from the contributions of local jurisdictions is used in matching and otherwise accommodating the specific activities that federal and state agencies would like us to undertake."[31]

CONCLUSIONS

The continued existence of a fractionated local government system is attributable to political inertia, strong opposition to reorganization, and the failure of the federal and state governments to promote a rationalization of the government of metropolitan areas. The constitution and statutes in most states inhibit or prevent a reorganization of the local government system, and federal and state grants-in-aid have strengthened the ability of smaller units of government to survive. Should the ecumenical approach succeed in solving major area-wide problems, the pressure for a major overhaul of the governmental system will be reduced.

Barring a dramatic reversal of federal policy, it is unlikely that the 1970's will be a decade of metropolitan reform. The current interest in consolidation in the South may prove to be transitory, and it is unlikely that interest in consolidation will become widespread elsewhere without federal or state encouragement.

If either the federal or state government decides to promote a rationalization of the local government system, it is probable that the prescription will call for the use of revenue sharing and grants-in-aid to encourage the creation of a two-tier system, as it is less disruptive to the existing system, allows for uniformity in certain functional areas and diversity in other areas, and would not be as susceptible as consolidation to promoting alienation between citizens and their governments. If a federation is not formed, a number of urban states probably will follow New York State's lead and create authorities to solve problems transcending local political boundaries.

The formation of a megalopolis as metropolitan areas grow and amalgamate with each other has effectively limited the use of the ecumenical, single- and two-tier approaches to smaller areas. The only governments able to cope with the major problems of an interstate megalopolis are the state and federal governments, and this means that greater reliance will be placed upon direct federal and state action, interstate compacts, and federal-state compacts.

NOTES

1. *Metropolitan Surveys: A Digest* (Chicago: Public Administration Service. 1958), p. vii.

2. Daniel R. Grant, "General Metropolitan Surveys: A Summary," in *Metropolitan Surveys: A Digest, op. cit.*, p. 3.

3. See *Metropolitan Surveys* (Albany: Graduate School of Public Affairs, State University of New York, published annually.)

4. John C. Bollens and Henry J. Schmandt, *The Metropolis* (New York: Harper and Row, Publishers, 1965), p. 438.

5. *Modernizing Local Government* (New York: Committee for Economic Development, July 1966).

6. *Reshaping Government in Metropolitan Areas* (New York: Committee for Economic Development, February 1970), p. 19.

7. National Commission on Urban Problems, *Building the American City* (Washington, D.C.: U.S. Government Printing Office, 1968), pp. 376–382.

8. *Indiana Acts of 1969*, chapter 173.

9. *Charter for the Consolidated City* (Charlottesville, Va.: City of Charlottesville and Albemarle County, 1969).

10. *North Carolina Acts of 1969*, chapter 67.

11. *Partnership for Progress* (New York: Institute of Public Administration, November 1969).
12. "Virginia Capital Wins Big Annexation," *National Civic Review* (October 1969), p. 436.
13. Irving G. McNayr, "The Promise of Metropolitan Government," paper delivered at a Boston College Conference, May 26, 1964 (mimeographed), p. 2.
14. *Single Government* (Charlotte, N.C.: Charlotte Chamber of Commerce, 1968), p. 12.
15. Edward C. Banfield, "The Politics of Metropolitan Area Organization," *Midwest Journal of Political Science* (May 1957), p. 86.
16. Edward Sofen, *The Miami Metropolitan Experiment* (Bloomington: Indiana University Press, 1963), pp. 74, 86, and 212.
17. "Abolish Atlanta Gains in Georgia," *The New York Times*, November 9, 1969, p. 65.
18. Brett W. Hawkins, *Nashville Metro* (Nashville: Vanderbilt University Press, 1966), p. 133.
19. "Statement by L. A. Hester," *Hearings Before the National Commission on Urban Problems*, Vol. 3 (Washington, D.C.: U.S. Government Printing Office, February 1968), p. 272.
20. Joseph F. Zimmerman, "An Areawide Federation," *National Civic Review* (June 1969), pp. 248–252.
21. *Governmental Structure, Organization, and Planning in Metropolitan Areas* (Washington, D.C.: Advisory Commission on Intergovernmental Relations, 1961), p. 34.
22. Housing and Urban Development Act of 1965, 75 STAT. 502, 20 U.S.C. §§ 461 (g) (1965).
23. Demonstration Cities and Metropolitan Development Act of 1966, 80 STAT. 1255, 42 U.S.C. §§ 3301–14 (1966).
24. Royce Hanson, *Metropolitan Councils of Governments* (Washington, D.C.: Advisory Commission on Intergovernmental Relations, August 1966).
25. Joseph F. Zimmerman (ed.), *1966 Metropolitan Area Annual* (Albany: Graduate School of Public Affairs, State University of New York, 1966), pp. 5–6.
26. *ABAG Appraised* (Berkeley, Calif.: Institute for Local Self Government, December 1965), p. 19.
27. "The Association of Bay Area Government—A Gathering Force," *Bulletin* (San Francisco Bureau of Governmental Research, April 1, 1965), pp. 1–2.
28. Samuel Humes, "Organization for Metropolitan Cooperation," *Public Management* (May 1962), p. 107.
29. Joseph F. Zimmerman, "Metropolitan Ecumenism: The Road to the Promised Land?" *Journal of Urban Law* (Spring 1967), pp. 433–457.
30. "Chairman Urges Assessment of COG's Future Status," *National Civic Review* (March 1970), p. 158.
31. *Ibid.*

Black Rule in the Urban South?

Lee Sloan
Robert M. French

Jacksonville is a major commercial and financial city in northeast Florida, a regional center for banking and insurance. As a port city with access to the Atlantic, it serves as a major transfer point. But, like many cities, Jacksonville was caught in the familiar cycle of urban decay and suburban exodus. For Jacksonville this has meant racial transition as well. As affluent whites fled to suburban Duval County, low-income blacks crowded Jacksonville's central city. As the non-white population of Jacksonville approached the 50 percent mark, area whites saw a need for change. Whether racial imbalance was seen as a problem in itself or as an indicator of deeper troubles is unclear. In any case, a group of reformers proposed a solution to the city's problems—to consolidate the government of Jacksonville with that of Duval County.

City-County consolidation or "Metrogovernment" has often been proposed, but has rarely been achieved. Prior to the 1967 merger in Jacksonville-Duval, the most prominent recent instance involving major governmental reorganization was the 1962 merger of Nashville and Davidson County in Tennessee.

Those supporting consolidation have always presented their case in terms of "good government" reform. The reformers stress that consolidation will result in the establishment of a "rational" government which will provide increased governmental efficiency, greater economy, expanded and improved services, greater accountability of public officials, the elimination of overlapping jurisdictions and the duplication of services, the elimination of corruption, and so forth.

Further, reformers claim that consolidation facilitates the expression of a "public interest" thus guaranteeing, as Michael Danielson has expressed it, that "the metropolis will be governed in the interest of the whole rather than in the conflicting interests of its many parts."

Yet conflicting interests, and particularly racial interests, may be crucial in determining whether or not consolidation is achieved and, if so, its specific form. Racial transition in metropolitan areas concentrating blacks in the central core of the city and whites in the surrounding suburbs may lead to a point in time when tolerance for existing governmental arrangements is drastically reduced—a kind of political "tip point." Though the political tip point is analogous to neighborhood or school tip points, its accompanying problems are less easily resolved. Many whites cope with racial transition in both neighborhoods and schools by simply moving out. It may be, however, that simple evasion does not truly resolve racial problems centered in residential neighborhoods and the schools, but simply buys some time before the problems must be confronted in the political realm. It is becoming increasingly evident that whites moving out may be forfeiting political control to the blacks who are left behind. Already black mayors have been elected in Cleveland, in Gary, and most recently, in Newark. Furthermore, in Los Angeles, Tom Bradley ran first in the primary election for mayor in 1969, though he failed to obtain an absolute majority. He subsequently lost in the run-off election to the incumbent mayor, Sam Yorty.

Holding the line against black power seems to be a growing problem for metropolitan white America. Resolving it will often involve *redefining political boundaries so that the proportion of blacks within the new political unit is drastically decreased.* This can assume the forms of gerrymandering or annexation, and the at-large election is a variation of the theme. Gerrymandering is a time honored means of limiting or controlling such minority-group political power. But in recent years, court decisions regarding compliance with the one man —one vote principle have undermined the effectiveness of the gerrymander.

Annexation, the formal addition of new territory to an existing governmental unit, too has provided a means of coping with the concentration of blacks in urban centers. Though race is surely not the only motivating force behind annexation movements, the addition of outlying areas to the city oftentimes reduces the relative size of the black population, for those areas annexed are often predominantly white. The white doughnut, then, becomes a formal part of the black center, thus reducing the relative power of the center's black citizens over their destiny. Though those whites who moved to the suburbs to escape the problems of the city will not see annexation as a panacea, the risk of forfeiting the city's government to blacks may well be sufficient to swing many white suburbanites to a pro-annexation position.

The at-large electoral system also may be used to limit or control black political power. In cities where blacks still constitute a numerical minority, an at-large (as opposed to a ward or district) electoral system offers assurance that the black community will either be unable to elect a black representative, or white leaders will see to it that blacks have but token conservative representation. Under an at-large system, black candidates cannot expect to win election without the financial support of white leaders and the endorsement of civic associations. Of course, if blacks become a numerical majority of the electorate, then the at-large system could work to their advantage.

Now in metropolitan areas, governmental consolidation may be emerging as a new means of dealing with the growing black threat to the existing political structure. While accomplishing the same racial goal as other techniques, it holds the promise of coping with other problems related to interdependency. Our argument should not be interpreted to imply that race is the only factor leading the residents of metropolitan areas (in Jacksonville or elsewhere) to contemplate or actually adopt a metropolitan area-wide government. There are other reasons, many of which we ourselves would recognize as valid. Still we are convinced that local political elites may be deceiving themselves as well as others in failing to face the racial realities behind governmental reorganization.

JACKSONVILLE AND DUVAL—THE SETTING

At the time of consolidation, the citizens of Jacksonville and of Duval County were beset with many governmental problems, some related to governmental structure and others to governmental inaction in the past. The city charter was 50 years old, and provided for a uniquely inefficient governmental structure. An elected five-member city commission was the major administrative body, although additional elected officials and independent boards shared administrative functions. The elected mayor, who sat on the commission, had relatively little power. Theoretically, an elected city council served as the city's legislative body. But in actuality, the commission, other elected officials and the various independent boards all encroached upon the policy-making authority of the council. Under this complex arrangement, power and authority were so diffused that it was difficult, if not impossible, to establish governmental responsibilities.

Jacksonville's history provides a dismal record of governmental corruption. The citizens of the city have spoken for years of a machine government. Richard Martin reports that for a city of its size in 1966, Jacksonville had the largest number of full-time employees and the highest monthly payroll in the nation.

The governmental structure of Duval County provided even greater problems. The elected five-member county commission was really an administrative arm of the state government. Legislative authority rested not with the commission nor with the other 69 elected county officials, but rather with the state legislature which meant, in effect, the Duval County legislative delegation. Until Florida's new constitution went into effect in 1969, local bills pertaining to Duval could be passed only during a 60-day period every other year. Because of the tradition of "local bill courtesy" and the fact that for many years Duval County had only one state senator, that one person actually possessed veto power over all legislative matters. In brief, the county government was without the power and authority to meet the problems of an essentially urban and suburban population.

Not only were city and county governments unable to handle their own respective problems, but city-county cooperation was nearly impossible. As Martin points out, as many as four governmental bodies were required to have a say in any city-county project: the city council and city commission, the Duval legislative delegation and the county commission.

Population growth was at the root of many problems in Jacksonville and Duval. Total county population doubled between 1930 and 1950, but the increase was very uneven. The growth rate in the decade of the forties, for example, was only 18.2 percent in Jacksonville but 168.4 percent in the remainder of the county. Comparable figures for the decade of the fifties were —1.7 percent and 155.6 percent. By the mid-sixties Jacksonville had an estimated population of 196,000, while the county population outside the city was estimated at 327,000.

As in most large metropolitan areas, a rapidly growing nonwhite population was centered in the core of the city. According to the 1966 Local Government Study Commission, Jacksonville ranked third in the nation in percentage of total population nonwhite for cities of over 100,000. But nonwhite population outside the city limits in Duval was only 9.2 percent of the total.

The area was also plagued by economic problems. Within the city, 31 percent of all families earned less than $3,000 according to the 1960 census. The same source classified over 30 percent of Jacksonville's housing units as in either deteriorating or dilapidated condition. The schools were similarly rundown and their condition, combined with a tradition of political meddling in educational affairs, led to disaccreditation of every senior high school in the county in 1964. Adding to the list of area problems were pollution of air and water, lack of adequate county police and fire protection, soaring taxes, a rising crime rate and an economic slowdown. As Martin points out, concern over these conditions made the move to consolidation more popular.

By the mid-sixties, both blacks and whites were aware that approximately 44 percent of the city's population was black. *The Report of the National Advisory Commission on Civil Disorders* estimated that if current trends continued, a majority of Jacksonville's citizens would be black by 1972. Martin writes that:

> The specter of a Negro mayor and of a government dominated by Negroes became a subject of growing concern for all citizens whose thoughts ran in such directions, and there were many. In 1966 the Community Development Action Committee . . . noted tactfully that the movement of the young and higher income groups out of the city was putting Jacksonville "under the potential control of lower income groups who may not have a feeling of responsibility toward local government."

This racial transition was surely one of the more crucial factors leading to popular referenda to annex in both 1963 and 1964. In both instances, voters in the outlying areas voted against their being annexed.

A few black leaders in Jacksonville argued that these trends would lead inevitably to the day when black voters would outnumber whites and it would be possible to elect a black mayor and a black council. From the perspective of these persons, consolidation would lead to the dilution of the black vote just when the establishment of black political power was a distinct possibility. One black leader argued that under the old city government, all candidates for the council had to appeal to the black electorate. He argued that black voters, representing approximately 42 percent of the total, would be foolish to support consolidation which would reduce their share of the total electorate to approximately 19 percent. As the most vocal black leader opposing consolidation, he charged that the black leaders supporting consolidation "sold out" the black community. This individual was generally identified as the old line, traditional Negro leader, and he had been tied to the political machine in Jacksonville for years. Other blacks believed that he opposed consolidation because the machine opposed it and because he reaped economic benefits from his promises to deliver the Negro vote, despite the widespread belief that he could no longer, in fact, deliver it.

Very few black leaders openly opposed consolidation, but the dilution argument was the basis of their opposition. These persons also argued that consolidation would not lead to governmental economy, but this was a minor theme. Several of those who originally opposed consolidation were eventually neutralized or converted during the course of the consolidation movement. At any rate, only two black leaders of stature took strong positions opposing consolidation, and the other opponent was also considered to be tied to the old machine government.

Most of Jacksonville's black leaders recognized well that dilution would indeed be a consequence of consolidation, but they still found reasons to support consolidation. Foremost among those black leaders supporting consolidation was a lawyer viewed by others as moderate even though his office was noted for playing a strong role in civil rights cases. He had made a very favorable impression on both blacks and white liberals in a losing campaign for a seat in the state legislature. Even though he probably had the best chance of becoming Jacksonville's first black mayor, he expressed his position as follows:

> I argued that such a town as Jacksonville was becoming couldn't hope to attract industry or new blood. And that if that was the case, the black man obviously had more to lose than anybody else. All of the wealth in the community was outside the corporate limits. The young folks—black and white—were pretty much outside the corporate limits. All of the innovators and the creators were moving into the suburbs. That's where the industry and business was, except for a few little stores—and Main Street was declining. Main Street was a

street of black faces and store windows, shop windows. The educated were in the suburbs and not in the corporate limits. Jacksonville was being run from! It would do me no good to be mayor of such a town as Jacksonville was becoming. There would certainly be no interest on the part of the people sitting out there in the suburbs if they were fighting coming in all the while.

Jacksonville's black leaders were convinced that whites were not going to allow the day to come when they would have to accept a black mayor. One embittered black leader said that whites "would have resorted to any means to prevent black control of the city." Most black leaders were convinced that the future held either consolidation or annexation, either of which would have diluted Negro voting strength. Many, though not all black leaders, were aware that the Duval legislative delegation could have annexed by merely passing a local bill, thus bypassing a popular referendum. And most were fairly certain that if consolidation failed, the delegation indeed would have passed annexation by decree.

Most black leaders, then, saw consolidation as the lesser of two evils. Recognizing that white pro-consolidation leaders felt they needed to prevent a heavy negative vote in the black community, black leaders sought the best deal they could get. From the perspective of these individuals, the most important feature of the proposed charter was the provision for a council with 14 of 19 members elected by district. District lines were drawn to assure the election of three blacks to the council, and it was argued that blacks could also be elected to the five at-large seats. Some black leaders even felt they had promises from white leaders to support black candidates in the at-large elections. A charter requirements for regular reapportionment and compliance with the principle of one man—one vote representation also reassured black leaders.

The significance of the districting provision lies in the fact that the entire council under the old Jacksonville government had been elected at large. Nearly twenty years earlier, Jacksonville had moved from district to at-large council elections, and most observers are convinced that the rapid increase of black voters was a crucial factor in that change. It was only in the last election held under the old government that the black community succeeded in placing the first blacks on the council (in this century). Two black women, with vastly different kinds of appeal within the black community, were elected to the council as a part of a reform government. But many black leaders were quick to observe that there was no guarantee that black candidates could continue to win at-large elections.

One might be tempted to label the districting under consolidation as "benign gerrymandering" since lines were drawn so as to assure representation of blacks in proportion to their county population, at least so far as district seats were concerned. White leaders who wrote the charter were of the opinion that this was a major step toward justifying the support of consolidation by black leaders. However, the authors were also aware of an ideological commitment to local representation among whites which also favored district seats on the council. Since the provision of black seats on the council may also be viewed as a concession made to assure continued white political control, however, the gerrymandering was not totally benign.

The major argument used by black leaders to support consolidation, then, stressed the assurance of black representation on the new council. These leaders discounted the election of the two Negro councilwomen under the old Jacksonville government, emphasizing that there was no guarantee that black candidates could win again at large. Parris N. Glendening and John Wesley White expressed well the rationale of those black leaders supporting consolidation: "A possibility of future Negro political power of undetermined strength was, apparently, traded for immediate power of limited strength in Duval County." From their perspective, the black community stood to gain a voice in government where they had had none in the past. This argument was strengthened by black leaders' certainty that Jacksonville and Duval County whites would not have allowed a black takeover of Jacksonville government.

Representation was not the only factor leading black leaders to support consolidation. These leaders also advanced the general argument that they had not fared well under the old governmental system. Many felt that in years past, white political leaders had maintained a machine government largely on the strength of black votes purchased cheaply at election time. One leader respected by the rank-and-file within the black community observed that consolidation would eliminate a lot of the problems blacks had lived under. "This city has suffered from political boondoggling, financial irresponsibility and a high crime rate," he said, "and when the city suffers, the black man suffers the most."

CLEAN GOVERNMENT CAMPAIGN

Pro-consolidation blacks argued that the old government was corrupt through and through, and they had plenty of evidence to back them up. Since 1965 a local TV station, through documentaries and editorials, had exposed local governmental corruption. As a result of the station's efforts a grand jury called in 1966 indicted two of five city commissioners, four of nine city councilmen, the city auditor and the recreation chief. Charges included larceny, grand larceny, conspiracy, perjury and the acceptance of bribes. Media reports of the trial proceedings led the public to believe that other officials avoided indictments merely because they had more cleverly covered their tracks. Thus pro-consolidationists could turn the movement into a "throw the rascals out" kind of campaign, and blacks as well as whites were influenced by this appeal.

In addition to the issues of representation and governmental corruption, black pro-consolidationists stressed the minor themes that the new system would yield: 1) greater employment opportunities for blacks in government, 2) tax resources from affluent suburban whites, 3) elimination of duplication of services and the overlapping of jurisdictions, 4) improved municipal services at greater economy, and 5) solutions for problems related to disaccreditation and segregation in the schools.

The arguments of the pro-consolidation forces proved convincing. In August of 1967, 63.9 percent of the more than 86,000 Duval County voters who voted approved governmental consolidation. This was indeed an impressive victory. In the Nashville consolidation in 1962, only 56.8 percent of the voters favored Metro, and the reformers there had lost the first referendum in 1958. And just two months prior to the victory in Jacksonville, voters in Tampa and Hillsborough County had soundly defeated a consolidation proposal.

Aggregate voting statistics in previous consolidation referenda show Negro precincts returning heavier anti-consolidation votes than white precincts. This pattern held also in Duval, but *a healthy majority of black voters still approved consolidation.* The Jacksonville data conflict with Grubbs' study of the 1958 Nashville referendum which concluded that "the Negroes on the whole did not favor the charter and that the higher the proportion of Negroes the less the support for the charter." (See Table 1.)

TABLE 1.   Anti-Consolidation Vote by Race—Jacksonville

Precincts by Racial Composition	Total County Vote %
Less than 5% Negro (122)*	36.3
5—24% Negro (21)	41.6
25—49% Negro (9)	46.9
50—94% Negro (7)	43.8
95—100% Negro (28)	40.1

* Figures in parentheses indicate the number of precincts in each category.
Source: P. N. Glendening and J. W. White, "Local Governmental Reorganization Referenda in Florida: An Acceptance and a Rejection," *Governmental Research Bulletin*, Fla. State U., Vol. V, No. 2, Mar. 1968:3.

The difference notwithstanding, there are some striking similarities in the two successful consolidation movements in Jacksonville and Nashville. Both metropolitan areas were confronted with a rapidly growing Negro population. The threat of growing black political power, as we have seen, was a crucial factor leading Jacksonville and Duval County influentials to push for a consolidated government. Nashville whites felt similarly threatened. During the decade of the fifties, the percentage of nonwhites in the city grew from 31.4 percent to 38.1 percent. Though the first consolidation referendum was defeated in 1958, the city council passed annexation bills in 1958 and 1960 without referenda. Annexation reduced the percentage of nonwhites within the city to 27.6 percent, a figure actually lower than that in the 1940 census.

A second major similarity between Nashville and Jacksonville is that in both cities, black leaders perceived themselves to be confronted with the dilemma of choosing between consolidation and annexation. We have just observed that the defeated '58 referendum in Nashville led to hasty annexation which diluted black voting strength. In Jacksonville, two annexation referenda were voted down in the years immediately prior to the consolidation movement. But most Jacksonville black leaders were convinced that a defeat of consolidation would be followed by annexation, perhaps accomplished by the Duval legislative delegation without a referendum. Especially in Jacksonville, but also in Nashville, many black leaders reached the judgment that the probabilities of maximizing gains and minimizing losses lay in support of consolidation. It is especially interesting to note that in Nashville, the 1958 charter assured blacks of only two of 21 seats on the new council, but the 1962 charter assured blacks of six of 40 seats. In Jacksonville also, there is reason to believe that blacks were assured seats on the new council in the hope of preventing a heavy anti-consolidation vote among blacks.

A third similarity between the two cities shows the success reformers had in using consolidation as an anti-status quo movement. This strategy was employed in both cities. Apparently in Jacksonville, both black and white citizens—and perhaps especially whites in the suburbs—were influenced by the timely exposure of extensive governmental corruption. In Nashville, most observers felt that white suburbanites threw their support to Metro because they were opposed to accomplished and anticipated annexations, and because they opposed the city government's tax upon cars operated in the city by suburban residents. Nashville's mayor Ben West provided a convenient scapegoat for the frustrations of suburban residents. For many, a vote for Metro was a vote against the city machine and the referendum served as a purification rite.

The reform theme was missing in both the unsuccessful movements in St. Louis and Cleveland. Scott Greer concluded that "The decision not to attack incumbent officials and existing governments for their incompetence and inability weakened the hands of the crusaders." Greer also notes that there had been some "extreme dissatisfaction" with the government of Miami, which in 1957 adopted a "federalized" form of consolidation (and thus a much weaker form of consolidation than in either Jacksonville or Nashville).

There were further dissimilarities between Jacksonville and the unsuccessful efforts to consolidate in St. Louis and Cleveland where, according to Greer, Negro wards voted almost solidly against reform. Greer cites three major reasons for black opposition to consolidation in those cities. Probably of most importance, in both St. Louis and Cleveland, blacks were fearful of losing representation in the central city councils. A black leader in Cleveland argued that Negroes could elect two and only two represenatives under the proposed system, while in Jacksonville, blacks were guaranteed greater representation under consolidation.

Greer also reported that reformers in St. Louis neglected to consult leaders from the black community. As a result black leaders made a pact *not to support anything they had had nothing to do with formulating.*

In Cleveland, black leaders were approached, but the nature of the approach led black leaders to oppose reform. Greer quotes one black leader's sentiments:

> We have just got to stop this business of the white people treating us without any respect. Lindseth (leader of the charter campaign) came down to us, to the assembled Negro community political leaders, and he said: 'Gentlemen, what is this going to cost us?'

In Jacksonville, on the other hand, white leaders supporting consolidation worked with and through black leaders in their attempt to win black pro-consolidation votes. The Duval County legislative delegation saw to it that four Negroes were appointed to the study commission which was responsible for drafting the new charter. One of those four, the prominent and respected attorney discussed above (who was later to be elected at-large to the new Jacksonville council), was appointed secretary of the commission and served as the major voice of the black community.

Another successful tactic used by Jacksonville reformers was to provide civil service job protection under consolidation. Greer notes that the failure of Cleveland to make such a guarantee led to fears such as those expressed by one black leader:

> The charter would write the protection out of civil service and you know how important civil service is to my people. They have a better shake there than in industry. They have better jobs and if you put those jobs into a county government without civil service, the chances are that a lot of people will lose their jobs.

These differences between Jacksonville's approach to reform versus that of St. Louis and Cleveland go far in explaining the differences in the extent of black support for consolidation. Blacks in Jacksonville perceived potential gains under consolidation because they had so little under the old system of government, and thus a majority of them supported consolidation. Blacks in St. Louis and Cleveland perceived potential losses under consolidation because they had something to lose, and thus they cast heavy votes against consolidation.

The history of governmental reorganization through consolidation is largely one of failure—there are few success stories. But perhaps the next few decades will change that. Since the first writing of this article, Indianapolis and Marion County in Indiana were consolidated (by state legislation, by passing a referendum).

There are indications that governmental consolidation is currently being discussed in the following southern cities: Atlanta, Macon, Savannah, and Brunswick (all in Georgia); Charlottesville, Richmond and Roanoke, in Virginia; Charleston, South Carolina; Charlotte, North Carolina; Tampa, Pensacola, and Tallahassee in Florida; and Chattanooga, Tennessee.

If consolidation does become more widespread in the near future, we suspect that racial conflict will play a crucial role in the change. We would hypothesize that consolidation movements will be likely to emerge in those metropolitan areas where the proportion of blacks within the corporate limits of the city 1) is growing rapidly, and especially where it is 2) approaching 40 or 50 percent.

This may well be a movement which initially will be restricted to southern cities. In most northern cities, a proposal of consolidation would pit the Democratic central city against the Republican suburbs. As Edward C. Banfield observed over a decade ago, "advocates of consolidation schemes are asking the Democrats to give up their control of the central cities or, at least, to place it in jeopardy." Furthermore, as Glendening and White observed, "all of the post-1945 reorganization plans for area-wide government that have been accepted by the voters have been in the one-party South."

The "urge to merge" through consolidation can also be expected as a response to the election of black mayors in a number of cities and to the continuing development of Black Power with its emphasis on community control. Consolidated metropolitan government may well become a part of the backlash to the ideology and potential reality of Black Power. The major dilemma for black leaders faced with a consolidation movement becomes that stated by the black attorney in Jacksonville: to fight consolidation in the hopes of capturing the government of a dying city or to support consolidation and bring the taxes of white suburbanites back into the city. It is reported by Michael Lipsky and David J. Olson that this was also the major divisive issue in the deliberations on Newark by the Governor's Select Commission on Civil Disorders of New Jersey:

> One-half of the commissioners argued that political consolidation was the only means of establishing a tax base that would allow Newark to solve its problems. They argued that in the long run this would

yield the greatest benefit to Negroes in Newark. Other commissioners argued against political consolidation on the grounds that this would, in effect, disenfranchise black people in Newark precisely at the time when their numbers had grown to constitute a majority of the city electorate. The first argument risked disturbing white suburbanites upon whom the commission felt dependent for implementation of recommendations directed at the state government. The second argument risked assuring Negroes of electoral success without the resources to provide basic services.

Newark did not consolidate, and Newark now has Kenneth Gibson as its own black mayor. No doubt some black leaders in Jacksonville still feel that one of their own could be the mayor of their city some day soon had they fought consolidation. But most of Jacksonville's black leaders were convinced that whites would not have allowed such a development under any conditions, and they cast their lot with consolidation knowing that it destroyed any chance of their electing a black mayor—though it may have guaranteed black representation on the commission. Whether blacks should have supported consolidation or whether they got enough in return for their support are difficult judgments.

MIDDLE-CLASS POLITICAL STYLE

The rhetoric of the middle-class political style, of course, avoids the nastiness of racial conflict. A review of the public record of the consolidation movement in Jacksonville would not lead one to suspect that race was a crucial factor. Jacksonville's white elite used the good government reform rhetoric, thus avoiding the mention of race, and still got their message of the significance of race across to those who were attuned. This was beautifully illustrated in the Community Development Action Committee's warning that Jacksonville could come "under the potential control of lower income groups who may not have a feeling of responsibility toward local government." Anyone clever enough to know what "law and order" says of contemporary race relations is also clever enough to know the identity of the lower-income groups under discussion.

What happened in Jacksonville is an old story. At precisely that point in time when blacks threatened to wrest their share of political power from others, the rules of the game were changed. Black Americans may well be justified in concluding that the history of urban governmental reform reveals ever-changing attempts to conform to good government while at the same time avoiding what white Americans see as the detrimental consequences of democracy.

ARTICLE 23

For New National Cities

John V. Lindsay

I welcome this opportunity to talk to you at the first conference on cities attended by representatives of the NATO countries.

The significance of urban growth in international relations is not often recognized. Yet it may be the central issue of civilization in the 1970's. I do not mean to suggest that the security of our people depends on anything less than the delicate balance among nations. But military balance alone is not enough. The tensions and divisions inside nations are as critical to peace and security as those among nations. We have all too often seen how wars between nations are spawned from internal dissension and civil strife. And now, more than ever, we have little hope of achieving peace in the world unless we manage to create something approaching peace in our own countries. . . .

Since 1964, we have witnessed a series of deadly urban disorders that have posed a fundamental threat to our domestic stability. This urban violence has brought the problems of the cities to the forefront of national concern. For the first time in our history, Presidential commissions have focused on the urban scene.

Excerpts from a speech delivered by the Hon. John V. Lindsay, Mayor of New York City, before the International Conference on Cities, Indianapolis, Indiana, May 27, 1971.

But cities have remained at the bottom of the American governmental structure. Cities have no formal existence under the United States Constitution—not even a single reference. They have no basic grant of national power or authority. Our central government is a compact of 50 states. And our cities, as creations of the states, remain totally at their mercy. That might have made sound Constitutional theory 200 years ago when the Founding Fathers built a new federal system. But today it defies the facts of Urban America.

One can no longer think of America without thinking of its major cities. New York and Chicago, Boston and Los Angeles, New Orleans and Indianapolis form a national commercial and industrial network. And yet, virtually every American city remains in servitude to its state government. Cities cannot levy taxes without state approval; cities cannot modernize management without state approval; cities cannot set work rules without state approval. The cities have absorbed staggering national burdens. But they remain hamstrung by state governments dominated by rural and suburban interests. They are treated as children of the state—an inferior form of government with less authority, less judgment, and less maturity.

It is no longer reasonable to say that under our federal system cities must continue only as supplicants to their states. Cities like Houston and Detroit and Philadelphia are each larger than fifteen of the 50 states. And the budget of my own city is larger than the budget of New York State.

It is time that we rethought the role of these cities in the American governmental system. It is time for us to recognize that they are "national cities," with a unique role to play in our national life and deserving a prominent status in our political structure.

The Federal Government should charter a number of "national cities" with a grant of special powers.

Under their charter, national cities could deal directly with Washington on matters of trade, finance and social welfare. They could receive broader federal financial support in order to ensure functions of national responsibility. They could have independent authority on issues of local concern and urban development.

There are parallels in federal law for a national cities charter.

In the area of corporate law and finance, the Federal Government has responded to high-priority needs with the creation of federal corporations and nationally chartered banks. The Federal Deposit Insurance Corporation was set up across state and local lines to guarantee bank deposits at a time of economic crisis. T.V.A.—the Tennessee Valley Authority—was established to generate the power for the development of an important region. Amtrak has just moved to operate our declining railroads.

These are different from a "national cities" charter, which would probably require a constitutional amendment to authorize this change in our federal structure. But evolution and change have been the strength of our constitutional system.

The charter for national cities would fill the unique need of great urban centers for that measure of independence and stability so desperately lacking at the present time.

Our cities are already corporate entities—but chartered by the states. They perform services for the states, but far more importantly, they fulfill vital federal functions. Their claim to national status is strong and clear. The 25 American cities with over 500,000 population certainly qualify as national cities. Perhaps others would, too.

I know this would confirm the sense of many of us in these great cities that our futures are linked to one another far more than to the governments of our states. We have only recently discovered that Seattle and Baltimore, Atlanta and Milwaukee, San Francisco and Pittsburgh have inherited a common national legacy. Despite state differences—despite a long history of regional competition for national resources, we have learned, as the NATO countries have, that the things that unite us are more important than the things that divide us.

A national cities charter would free these cities from the restraints imposed by unresponsive state governments. It would lift the inequitable burdens and restrictions imposed by state legislatures under the domination of anticity interests. And it would formalize the Federal responsibility for the national scope of urban development.

This is not to suggest that we can "solve" our urban problems by a mere change in structure. The needs of the working man denied marginal security, the jobless veteran, the pressured pensioner, the welfare mother, and the harried commuter in our cities involve the whole range of vital urban services—police, fire, sanitation, health, education, jobs, and recreation. Obviously, a new structure is only a beginning.

This is not to suggest, either, that the three-tiered concept of American federalism is not relevant to the issues of the seventies. It is, and should remain the basic pattern of American government.

But a national cities charter does suggest that after nearly 200 years of the American experience, we have understood the changes that have occurred not only in our own country, but in world civilization.

There are, of course, other fundamental defects in the present structure of our cities. Looking outward to the suburbs, we see the irrationality of present city boundaries as a tax base and a service area. The move toward metropolitan and regional government is spreading. Looking inward, we find that city governments with a million citizens can be remote and unresponsive to their residents. We need a more compact unit of government at the neighborhood level to rebuild a sense of urban community.

Ideally, we might dream of redrawing the map of America so that each national city becomes a metropolitan government which incorporates smaller neighborhood government units. That would be a new metropolitan federalism—with a national, regional and neighborhood government. Some of us have looked longingly at the structure of London for such a model.

But American history, geography and law make that dream unreal for most of our cities. Instead, we will respond to the need for metropolitan and neighborhood government in our own local ways. There will be a mix of structures and arrangements. But we can meet the overriding need for national commitment with a new national cities policy.

Recently, I toured the Brownsville section of my own city with a group of twelve other big-city mayors. Seeing the empty shells of abandoned buildings and the ruins of a once thriving community of 170,000 people, the Mayor of Seattle, Wes Uhlman, said to me: "God, it looks like Dresden after World War II."

I could not help but think that if it were Dresden, it would have long since been rebuilt with substantial American support. Indeed, I have sometimes wondered, if Brownsville had been discovered in Burma, whether our national Government would not have responded far faster and with greater generosity that it has, so far, here at home.

America's $135 billion commitment to foreign aid, including the Marshall Plan, was not only an act of generosity. It also marked the real end of American isolationism. A commitment to a national cities policy would be no less significant—for it would signal the end of America's bias against its own cities.

The Metropolitan State

Richard P. Burton

The alternative proposed here is that any consolidated metropolitan region in the United States whose population reaches one million be admitted to statehood.

Basically, the Metropolitan State would be an attempt to reconcile the jurisdictional boundaries of state governments with the geographical distribution of the population.

As such, the concept parallels that of reapportionment of legislative districts. Both are in direct response to the successive waves of rural-urban and urban-suburban migration, i.e., the metropolitanization of the population.

The Metropolitan State must be distinguished from the city-state of Plato, Norman Mailer, Rep. Bella Abzug, and others. By excluding the suburban sector of the metropolitan area, the city-state would cast the present artificial separation of city and suburbs into institutional concrete.

A word of definition: The term *consolidated metropolitan region* in the proposal draws upon the work of urban economists and geographers in refining the Census Bureau's Standard Metropolitan Statistical Area (SMSA). The basic building blocks of the SMSAs are atavistic county boundaries. Consolidated metropolitan regions additionally take into account commutation and other economic relationships between counties.

The following can only be an introduction of the idea of Metropolitan States, holding it up for comparison with other forms of metropolitanism in relation to needs and functions. Thus:

In the first place, Metropolitan States would keep intact local governments within their consolidated metropolitan regions. Cities, coun-

Reprinted from Richard P. Burton, "The Metropolitan State," *City*, Vol. 5, No. 5 (Fall 1971), pp. 44–48. Copyright 1971 by The National Urban Coalition. Reprinted by permission.

ties, and special districts would continue to function as before, the only differences being that a new Metropolitan State government would be established whose legislative body would consist of the same state representatives that had previously served the population of the area, and that a new governor would be elected. Thus it would retain the efficiency characteristics of general-purpose local government, and it would meet the test of political acceptability. The second advantage obviously requires some clarification.

Many proposals for metropolitan reorganization fail, not necessarily because of the lack of popular support, but because a vote for reorganization on the part of a local official would very often be a vote for political extinction. Hence, it is not altogether surprising that local officials rarely form the vanguard of metropolitan reform movements. Under a Metropolitan State reorganization plan, however, the vested interests of local officials and governmental personnel in the metropolitan area are not at stake, as the entire structure of local government is held intact.

But many reorganization bills are tabled or defeated in state legislatures, and it might be asked: What about resistance on behalf of state representatives? This is a more difficult question, to be sure, but it should be kept in mind that conversion to smaller legislatures would have the effect of strengthening the relative political influence of the individual representative. For example, a representative in a nine-county San Francisco state legislature would possess a much larger voice in the conduct of affairs than he has at the present time.

Second, Metropolitan States would provide metropolitan-wide areas with a fiscally and constitutionally viable form of government. Dean Alan Campbell of Syracuse University has observed: "State governments have been described as the 'keystones of the American governmental arch.' They sit midway between the local governments on the one hand, which are their creatures, and the federal government on the other, which constitutionally possesses only delegated powers. By virtue of their position, state governments possess the power, and theoretically the responsibility, for attacking practically all those problems which in sum equal the urban crisis."

Thus, Metropolitan States would be constitutionally and fiscally superior to any of the alternative forms of metropolitan reorganization.

Third, Metropolitan States would redress the city-suburban imbalance of political power that presently exists in state legislatures. It is now rather widely accepted among students of state and local government that most of our state legislatures are dominated by the existence of 'rural-suburban coalitions,' and that, among the many causes of state unresponsiveness to city problems, this is singularly the most important.

By elimination of nonmetropolitan representation, Metropolitan States would automatically sever the ties of the rural-suburban coalition and, although suburban domination of central cities would still be maintained in most cases, the relative political interests of the central cities within the new metropolitan legislatures would be enhanced. As a basis for illustration, let us turn to California, our most metropolitanized state. According to my calculations the composition of the 1970 California state legislature is as follows:

	Assembly	Senate
Central City	24 (30%)	13 (33%)
Suburban	32 (41%)	13 (33%)
Rest of State	23 (29%)	14 (34%)

Hence, it can be observed easily that the suburban/rest-of-state block constitutes 70 percent of the membership in the assembly, as opposed to the central city's 30 percent. Approximately the same conditions prevail in the senate. But if we eliminate the influence of the rest of the state's representation and isolate the Metropolitan States of Los Angeles and San Francisco, a substantial redress in the balance of suburban/central-city political power emerges:

	Assembly	Senate
Los Angeles		
Central City	15 (37%)	9 (53%)
Suburban	25 (63%)	8 (47%)
San Francisco		
Central City	9 (56%)	4 (46%)
Suburban	7 (44%)	5 (54%)

Fourth, Metropolitan States would provide functionally meaningful state boundaries within which comprehensive planning finally could realize its promise.

Fifth, Metropolitan States would preserve the local political gains of blacks and other minority groups. It is well-known that central-city blacks have been highly suspicious of most reorganization proposals because their gerrymandering potential could lead to loss of local political control.

A reorganizational plan along the lines of Metropolitan States would not constitute a threat to the political life of *any* locality in the metropolitan community, and the political gains of central-city blacks would be effectively safeguarded, if not enhanced.

Sixth, Metropolitan States would also force state responsiveness to the problems of the urban crisis and would obviate the need for 'direct federalism.' Perhaps the most vivid testimony to Campbell's "fallen arch" description of state government's emerging new role in the federal system is to be found in the phenomenon of "direct federalism," a federal-city relationship in which states are bypassed.

Unspecialized and unresponsive, state government as presently constituted does not qualify as an appropriate link between federal government and locality—either by federal *or* by local standards. But the jurisdictions of Metropolitan States would furnish the comprehensive regional domain that the federal government demands of councils of government—the servants of direct federalism. In contrast with any of the alternative forms of metropolitan organization, only the Metropolitan State would be capable of restoring state government to its former "keystone" status.

The proposal for Metropolitan States requires a fundamental change in the territorial structure of state government, one that has far-reaching consequences for the federal system.

A prescription for converting to Metropolitan States would be highly negligent if it were not assumed that metropolitan society was here to stay. Indeed, if there were any indications of a return to a nonmetropolitan, agrarian way of life, the present pattern of state boundaries would become increasingly efficient, as they were long ago —*and as they still are in many of the agricultural sections of the nation.* But, if anything, we know that there is a distinct tendency toward increased metropolitanization, and that the future geographical requirements of metropolitan areas are very likely to increase. How then would a system of Metropolitan States be in a position to accommodate such growth? The system could adjust to further metropolitanization in a manner similar to reapportionment. Whenever any territory (functional economic area) adjacent to an existing

Metropolitan State had become functionally integrated, as conceivably determined by the decennial census, it would automatically become annexed. Thus, the system would be characterized by constitutionally sanctioned *boundary flexibility* and would adjust to future changes in territorial specialization either through the creation of new state boundaries or by the expansion of existing ones.

The thought of altering state boundaries, which have served the nation so well—at least until some 25 years ago—veers sharply in the direction of irreverence. Therefore, let us grant (for the moment) that the Metropolitan State concept may be somewhat premature, and turn to the question that doggedly persists: If not political decentralization, what alternative course of action is open to the states? Can a more incremental option be identified that is perhaps capable of restoring the fallen arch and adapting the powerful decision-making authority of the states to metropolitan-area governance?

We hope to show that:

1. In those metropolitan areas where the single county is able to take on the tasks of metropolitanwide governance, and has elected to do so, administrative decentralization has recently begun to proceed in an orderly fashion consistent with the original concept of the county in our federal system.
2. Where metropolitan governance requires multicounty jurisdictions, administrative decentralization continues to founder, continues to act as the major contributor to fragmented governmental organization in the metropolitan area.

County government has only recently undergone some changes that may well transform its status from "the dark continent of American politics" (as described by H. S. Gilbertson at the turn of the century) to a "fourth tier" of general-purpose government which would respond to the regionwide service requirements in many of our metropolitan areas. In "California Government and Politics," William W. Crouch reviews the original concept of counties:

> This territorial inclusiveness of counties resulted from the decision of the original constitution-makers that some type of governmental unit was needed for the purpose of helping the state government carry out its statewide programs in local areas. Each of these statewide programs was usually placed in charge of specially elected officials specified in the state constitution [judge, district attorney, clerk and recorder, etc.]. . . . Thus, at the inception of statehood, counties

were largely regarded as agents of the state government, designed to facilitate the performance of state services.

Hence, we have the original concept of the county as an administrative subdivision of the state. But county government has never functioned purely as an agent of the state nor exclusively as a unit of local government.

In response to the service requirements of urbanization and the need for regionwide government, the states have seen fit to decentralize, not by strengthening and widening the scope of their traditional general-purpose agents, but instead by formally sanctioning the creation of a host of special-purpose districts and authorities. As the institutional inadequacies of this tack became more and more apparent over time, the *county* modernization movement has gradually become a powerful force from below in reaction to the steadfast reluctance of the states to step in and provide effective organizational solutions in the metropolitan areas. The movement, which has actually been under way for more than 20 years, has focused primarily on acquisition of home-rule powers, administrative and fiscal reform, and functional expansion into the provision of areawide services.

The results of this movement have culminated in the emergence of the "Urban County," a fourth layer of general-purpose government intended to supplant (or avoid) the fragmentation that results from ad hoc multiplication of special districts. What has been the impact on the range of county services? Herbert Duncombe writes in "County Government in America":

> Many of the services provided by county government are those in which the county is acting, to some extent, as an administrative arm of the state. . . . However, many of the services performed by county governments in densely populated areas are not services that the county performs as an arm of the state but are the same type of urban services provided by cities. These include construction and maintenance of expressways, operation of airports, operation of park and recreation systems, air pollution control, establishment of fire and police departments, provision of water and sewage lines, street construction, street lighting, garbage collection, and operation of bus systems.

On precedent set in such counties as Dade (Miami), Los Angeles, Westchester, Duval (Jacksonville), Milwaukee, San Diego, and

Jackson (Kansas City), states and localities are now giving serious attention to the Urban County's potential as a promising alternative for combining areawide governance with retention of the polycentric (third tier) system of local government. For example, the County and Municipal Government Study Commission of New Jersey, after concluding that "county government can play an increasingly important role in a revitalized and strengthened local government system," recognized the need for a "middle" level of government that can:

1. "Move to meet problems which individual municipalities or groups of municipalities *cannot* meet unaided, and yet which *should not* be met by the state and federal governments."
2. Perform areawide and interlocal functions which municipal and other local leaders believe must be met by such a middle-level or middle-tier government.
3. Coordinate state and federal programs affecting local government to make sure that local needs are met with a minimum of confusion, delay, waste, and overlapping.
4. Serve as a rallying point for local leadership so that the leaders "can unite to provide needed services and solve pressing problems, decide on the area's goals and policies, and, through this middle-level government, make their desires known both to their citizens and to state and federal officials."

Unlike annexation or city-county consolidation, the Urban County preserves intact the polycentric system of local government. Unlike regional government, it does not superimpose an additional— a fifth—layer of government on the metropolitan area. Unlike special districts, it has political visibility and does not fragment areawide governance. And, as Norman Beckman has noted, the county *exists*. Therefore, the usual fears of new governmental units are not aroused.

Yet, even with all of these unique advantages, the Urban County is still institutionally deficient for dealing with the complexities of our large metropolitan areas. In places such as New York City, Los Angeles, Chicago, Philadelphia, etc., the crucial shortcoming is one of geographical extent, a limitation which we shall turn to next.

Thus far we have seen that county government has begun to emerge as the logical metropolitanwide agent of the state. This holds great promise for the 133 metropolitan areas that are contained within a single county, but falls considerably short of the mark in those 79 metropolitan areas that spread into two or more counties. To be sure, these larger areas present organizational difficulties of extraordinary complexity, not to mention the intricacies of the 24 areas that are interstate. Even with reduction of special-purpose fragmentation through strengthening of county government, the governance of the multiple-county metropolitan area becomes fractionalized along Urban County lines, and to a degree that varies positively with their numbers. Urban County advocates are rarely distracted by this crucially important issue, but when an occasional solution is forthcoming, it is usually through one of three casually discussed methods: intergovernmental cooperation, federation, or county consolidation.

"Where a metropolitan area exceeds in extent the jurisdiction of one county, voluntary multicounty cooperative arrangements using existing city-county structure have been and will be created," declares Bernard Hillenbrand, executive director of the National Association of Counties. However, in the wake of a lengthy record of local government's inability to reach and to sustain both formal and informal agreements, the "voluntarists" have more recently turned to somewhat more structured alternatives, such as COGs (councils of government) and the so-called A-95 process which authorizes the COGs to review and comment on local grant applications. But the effectiveness of this kind of forum has been questioned already. Melvin Mogulof of the Urban Institute, although granting that the COG has generally helped to create a metropolitan point of view and fostered regional leadership, criticizes its structural quality in the following terms:

> (1) [The COG] receives the bulk of its financial support from federal sources to engage in 'areawide' planning, and these federal sources seem increasingly skeptical of planning which does not have its 'payoffs' in implementation; (2) it receives its aura of authority from the A-95 circular [of the Office of Management and Budget] which seems to call for a structure which can coordinate regional activities but which can also evaluate these activities against the goals of regional planning; (3) it receives its legitmacy from its member governments. But these governments do not seem to want the COG to emerge as a force different and distinct from the sum of its governmental parts. Member governments do not generally see the COG structure as an independent source of regional influence but rather as a service giver, a coordinator, a communications forum, and an insurance device for the continued flow of federal funds to local governments.

These concerns have led the Committee for Economic Development and others to propose federation as an alternative to voluntary cooperation. In its impressive statement in "Reshaping Government in Metropolitan Areas," CED has recently recommended conversion to a "two level" system of government in the metropolitan area, a conversion that combines both the qualities of "decentralization" (polycentrism) and "centralization" (areawide government): "To gain the advantages of both centralization and decentralization, we recommend as an ultimate solution a governmental system of two levels. Some functions should be assigned in their entirety to the areawide government, others to the local level, but most will be assigned in part to each level. In those situations where the metropolitan area is contained within one county, a *reconstituted* county government should be used as the basic framework for a new areawide government."

The term *reconstituted* is quite critical; virtually all fourth-tier proposals regard modernization as a prerequisite to turning over areawide governance to the Urban County. The prototype of CED's two-level model evolved from two successive reorganizational experiences in metropolitan Toronto.

In 1954, the Ontario legislature authorized creation of a 13-city federation known as the Municipality of Metropolitan Toronto, an organization which took possession of responsibility for areawide functions, shared certain powers with the cities, while the latter retained certain powers over local activities. However, in what was presumably a response to representational inequities, a "stronger form" of government—the borough plan—was introduced in 1967. This plan maintained the principal of a two-level federated system, but involved the consolidation of "constituent municipalities" at the third tier, i.e., the 13 original municipalities were merged into six municipalities—five boroughs plus the city of Toronto. Therefore, by elimination of seven municipalities, the reorganization, in effect, created a federation of six jurisdictional units each quite similar in nature to the Urban County.

CED's report said that "although a federation of existing counties and towns might be considerably easier to implement, it is clear that rapid metropolitan growth makes a stronger jurisdiction considerably more appropriate, especially for the purpose of long-range planning."

The two-level system could be maintained within a "stronger jurisdiction" through consolidation. However, in the context of American government, the municipality as the vehicle of consolidation is singularly inappropriate. This would restrict the choice set of general-purpose government at the third tier. The proper target for metropolitan government consolidation in the United States is the county—the administrative agent of the state in matters of areawide concern.

The Advisory Commission on Intergovernmental Relations has developed a draft bill to implement county consolidation "in those states desiring to allow local initiative and determination on consolidation proposals."

The same area-classification system under which we delineated the appropriate boundaries for the Metropolitan State may be used to define, as the real domain of the Metropolitan County, the "consolidated metropolitan region" (CMR). Thus, all counties within the CMR would be eligible for consolidation. For example, the nine counties in the San Francisco Bay Area CMR would be merged into a single Metropolitan County.

How does the Metropolitan County compare as a governmental structure with what we have already defined as the optimal institutional form—the Metropolitan State? The best test might be to consider the Metropolitan County's capacity to respond to the urban crisis. For example, like the Metropolitan State, we find that:

1. Metropolitan Counties would preserve intact the current polycentric system of local government within their jurisdictional space.
2. Metropolitan Counties would provide functionally meaningful boundaries within which "comprehensive planning" would have the opportunity to finally realize its promise.
3. Metropolitan Counties would preserve the local political gains of blacks and other minority groups.
4. Metropolitan Counties, as an exercise in administrative decentralization, would represent state responsiveness to the problems of the urban crisis and would obviate the need for "direct federalism."

However, unlike the Metropolitan State, it is equally evident that:

1. Metropolitan Counties would not provide metropolitanwide areas with a fiscally and constitutionally viable form of government.
2. Metropolitan Counties would not redress the city-suburban imbalance of political power that presently exists in state legislatures.

3. Metropolitan Counties would not respond to the governmental problems created by fragmentation of the metropolitan area along interstate lines.

Although the Metropolitan County falls short of the optimum, it represents the most responsible form of administrative decentralization of the state for purposes of large-area metropolitan governance and, perhaps most important of all, *it could easily supply the necessary catalyst for political decentralization and emerge as a forerunner of the Metropolitan State.*

The plausibility of such an outcome derives from a recognition of the fact that installation of the Metropolitan County would require the replacement of several small (and unrepresentative) county boards with a single legislative body representative of the entire metropolitan area. In combination with other modernization requirements, including election of the Metropolitan County executive officer, this would create a sufficiently large bloc of political power that would begin to alter the essential character of the county from that of administrative agent to one of middle-tier partnership. And then, as predicted by Paul Ylvisaker over a decade ago:

> In this coming era of the powerful metropolis, becoming politically self-conscious and economically more self-sufficient, state governments will come under heavy competitive pressures . . . unless they overcome the inflexibilities and social lag which are now characteristic, *unless, in short, they themselves develop as effective general instruments of government,* governors will be taking backseats to the new metro-mayors, legislatures will dance to the pipes of metropolitan political blocs, and the states may well suffer in full the lurking fate of all 'middle levels.'

When this prediction is fully realized, and the cult of incrementalism fades somewhat, perhaps the Metropolitan State will come to be regarded as a far less fanciful prescription for institutional reform.

Revenue Sharing: An Idea Whose Time Has Come

Advisory Commission on Intergovernmental Relations

Federal revenue sharing with State and local governments stands out as the next logical development in our system of shared power.

Barring a sharp rise in the Nation's foreign commitments, the revenue sharing idea has a fairly good chance of being translated into the law of the land. This optimistic assessment is underpinned by an impressive array of favorable developments that have occurred since the idea was broached seriously to the Johnson Administration in 1964 by Walter Heller, then Chairman of the Council of Economic Advisors and Joseph Pechman, Director of Economic Studies at Brookings Institution.

1. The revenue sharing idea now enjoys widespread public support— 71 percent of the American people favor this proposition according to a recent Gallup poll. Revenue sharing enjoys overwhelming support across the entire political spectrum—76 percent of the Republicans, 71 percent of the Democrats, 68 percent of the Independents—believe that revenue sharing is a good idea.
2. Representatives of State and local governments give revenue sharing top priority billing and agree on the basic outline of the plan for the distribution of revenue sharing funds.
3. The Nixon Administration assigns high legislative priority to revenue sharing.
4. Notwithstanding its power sharing characteristics, revenue sharing also enjoys strong Congressional backing. Over 30 percent of the members of Congress have either introduced or co-sponsored revenue sharing bills.

Reprinted from Advisory Commission on Intergovernmental Relations, *Revenue Sharing—An Idea Whose Time Has Come*, pp. 1–21. Washington: U.S. Government Printing Office, December 1970.

To be sure, several major obstacles must be overcome before revenue sharing can be enacted. It must compete for Congressional attention and support with some dramatic specific problems—cleaning up the environment, speeding the development of urban mass transit, enlarging Federal support for education and restructuring public assistance programs. In addition, because to some Federal revenue sharing seems to imply Federal power sharing, the depth of support for and understanding of the concept must be demonstrated forcefully before favorable action can be expected.

For reasons that will be made apparent in the following pages, this Commission favors early Congressional enactment of the revenue sharing principle. To focus public attention on this issue and to rally both public and Congressional support for the adoption of revenue sharing we seek to answer three questions about it.

What is the basic idea behind revenue sharing?
What are the major arguments in its favor?
What are the major objections to it and how can they be answered?

The Idea

The basic idea behind revenue sharing is quite simple—to strengthen the fiscal capabilities of State and local governments by requiring the National Government to share with them a designated portion of the Federal personal income tax revenue *on a no expenditure strings basis.* In essence, revenue sharing would establish the principle that State and local governments should have a guaranteed, albeit limited, access to the Nation's prime power source—the Federal personal income tax. Then, and only then, will they be able more effectively to carry out their assigned task of delivering the bulk of domestic public services.

The abiding American belief in the positive virtues of "grass roots" government underpins any effort to strengthen the fiscal independence of State and local governments. This preference for decentralized government reflects the widespread recognition that the National Government lacks the perspective to heal all the Nation's domestic ills. More importantly, it recognizes the great strength of decentralized government—a flexibility that stimulates individual response to diverse local conditions and needs.

This concern for strengthening the position of State and local governments also reflects the powerful attraction that the concept of "balance" exerts within our federal system. We are still receptive to the idea of "leaning against the wind," of resisting those tendencies and forces in our system that if unchecked would result in lodging a disproportionate amount of political power at one level of government. During the days of the Confederation, the federalists sought ways of strengthening the National Government without undue sacrifice of the powers of the State. Contemporary "federalists" are now searching for ways to strengthen the States and localities without undue sacrifice of National goals. Because money and political power are so inexorably intertwined, this search concentrates on developing fiscal mechanisms such as revenue sharing—a means best calculated to use the unquestioned revenue superiority of the National Government to reinforce the advantages of decentralized government.

Revenue Sharing—Redressing the Power Imbalance

Federal revenue sharing is needed to check the steady centralization of power in Washington—an imbalance situation that can be traced to the growing Federal revenue superiority and increasing Federal control over State and local expenditure decisions.

Growing Federal revenue superiority. An increasingly interdependent economy, a vastly superior jurisdictional reach and a near monopoly of the income tax enable the Congress to raise far more revenue at far less political risk than can all of the State and local officials combined. While the careers of many State and local officials have been wrecked by courageous decisions to increase taxes, similar action at the Federal level is seldom necessary and rarely if ever fatal to a political career.

It is not surprising therefore that power gravitates to the place (Washington) that can command resources more readily. To put the matter in more philosophical terms, the growing revenue superiority of the Federal Government undercuts a basic premise that supports our federal system—that officials at each level of government will experience about the same degree of resistance when making demands on the taxpayer's pocketbook.

The dominant income tax position enjoyed by the Federal Government helps to insulate Federal policymakers from irate taxpayers. Because the National Government now collects about 90 percent of all personal income tax revenue, it has virtually "cornered" the revenue producer that is most sensitive to economic growth. For every one percent of growth in the Nation's economy, individual income tax receipts automatically rise by about 1.5 percent. In contrast, most of the State and local tax levies behave rather sluggishly—their "automatic" growth performance lags somewhat behind economic growth.

While the National Government can count on automatic higher revenue yields generated by economic growth to accommodate most of its growing expenditure needs, almost every year State and local policymakers are forced to take the politically risky course of imposing new taxes and raising the rates of existing taxes to meet the rising expenditure requirements of an urbanized society. In 1960, nineteen States were imposing both general sales and personal income taxes. Ten years later the number had climbed to thirty-three. Over this same time span, the growth in State and local tax collections outpaced national economic growth. State and local taxes rose from the equivalent of 7.3 percent of the Gross National Product in 1960 to 8.6 percent of GNP at the close of the decade. A study by the Commission staff revealed that between 1950 and 1967 only 47 percent of the increase in major State taxes—income, and general and selective sales taxes—was the result of economic growth while 53 percent resulted from legislative enactment.

In addition to this automatic growth superiority, the National Government enjoys another revenue raising advantage—its freedom from the hobbling fears of interlocal and interstate tax competition. The more limited a government's jurisdictional tax reach, the more apprehensive the government becomes about its relative tax climate. Two great forces are heightening this sensitivity to intergovernmental tax competition—the growing desire of State and local policymakers to promote economic development and the increasing interdependence of our economy.

Growing Federal control of State and local programs. The lopsided Congressional reliance on the narrow categorical or conditional aid tips the power scales even further toward the Federal Government.

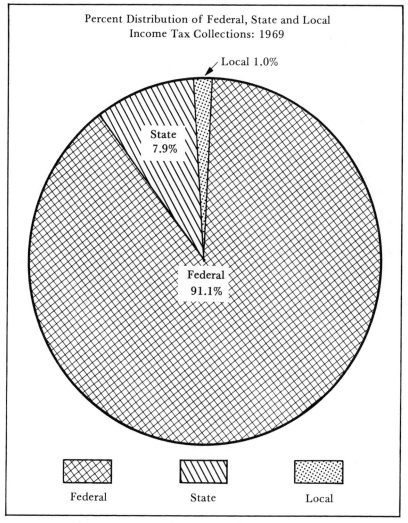

Source: U.S. Bureau of the Census, *Governmental Finances in 1968-69.*

FIGURE 1. Federal Government dominates income tax field.

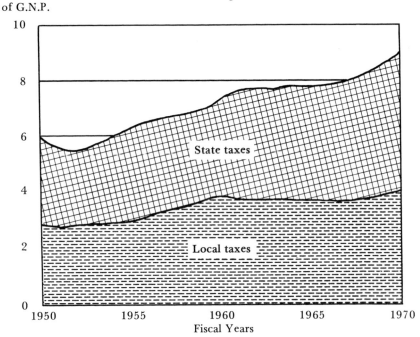

State and Local Taxes As A Percentage of Gross National Product, 1950 through 1970

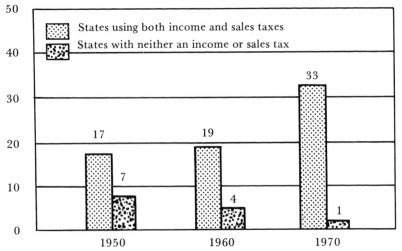

Number of States With General Sales and Broad-Based Personal Income Taxes, As of January 1, 1950, 1960 and 1970

FIGURE 2. State and local governments continue to increase their tax effort.

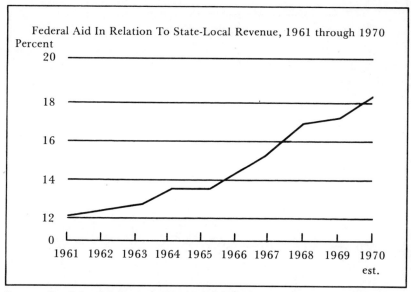

Federal Aid In Relation To State-Local Revenue, 1961 through 1970

Source: Special Analysis O, Budget of the United States, Fiscal Year 1971.

FIGURE 3. State and local governments are becoming increasingly dependent on Federal conditional aids.

The Congress is now dangling almost 500 large and small conditional aid carrots collectively worth more than $25 billion a year before State and local governments. The hope was that each conditional aid would provide sufficient financial incentive to spur the States and localities on to greater action in some more or less narrowly defined field of "National interest." But there is overwhelming evidence that State and local governments cannot readily absorb such a large number of diverse programs over restricted periods of time. The sheer number of these Federal incentives, each designed to accomplish a different objective, has produced managerial apoplexy if not financial exhaustion for those jurisdictions not able to devote the time and resources necessary to track down and match every available Federal aid dollar.

Progressive loss of freedom of choice, therefore, is an additional price that must be paid by all State and local jurisdictions for categorical aid dollars. Professor Walter Heller, both a keen student of

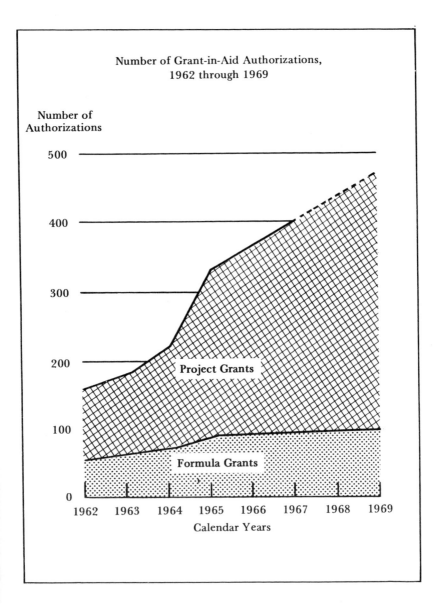

Source: Advisory Commission on Intergovernmental Relations, *Fiscal Balance in the American Federal System, Vol. 1;* and Library of Congress, Legislative Reference service.

FIGURE 4.   Federal conditional aids are proliferating.

our intergovernmental fiscal system and a prominent member of the liberal establishment, has pointed up the dangers of this trend toward centralized power. "Unless this trend is reversed," he wrote, "Federal aids may weave a web of particularism, complexity, and Federal direction which will significantly inhibit a State's freedom of movement."[1] The illusion of Congressional "control" has in reality disappeared into the dark jungles of bureaucratic red-tape.

Because Federal revenue sharing is "power sharing" in the very best tradition of equal partners in a joint governmental endeavor, this Federal aid approach stands out as the most direct and the most effective method to redress the fiscal and power imbalance caused by both the growing revenue raising superiority of the National Government and the lopsided and increasing Federal reliance on conditional aids with its inevitable loss of responsible "control."

Revenue Sharing—A Versatile Fiscal Tool

Another outstanding strength of revenue sharing is its versatility —the capacity to achieve many different objectives.

Accords with federalism. Revenue sharing harmonizes with one of the strengths of the American system—its diversity. States and localities must take different approaches to problems and all benefit by their experimentation. The National Government has a clear-cut interest in creating a fiscal environment that is conducive to experimentation. If the benefits of diversity are to be exploited, and indeed enhanced, the National Government must help create a fiscal environment that will enable its federal partners to exercise wide latitude in determining their budgetary priorities.

Revenue sharing would promote the use of State-local funds in a manner that accords best with National political priorities. Because this form of financial aid could be free of expenditure strings, each State and locality would have complete freedom to use these funds, as it would those raised by its own taxes, on items of greatest urgency in accordance with the jurisdiction's peculiar needs. As State-local expenditures go, this suggests that at least 40 percent of the revenue sharing funds might be spent on education, another 20 percent, on welfare and health programs, with substantial portions for police and fire protection and the provision of sanitation services.

Helps ease State and local fiscal tensions. A well-financed Federal revenue sharing plan is needed to ease a growing fiscal squeeze at the State and local levels. On the revenue side, these governments, already hobbled by fears of intergovernmental tax competition, are meeting increasing taxpayer resistance as they push property, sales, and income tax rates ever higher. On the expenditure side, the unremitting demand for safer streets, better schools, a cleaner environment, and rapid urban transit, all combine to place massive expenditure pressures on these jurisdictions. If State and local governments are to continue to provide the bulk of the Nation's domestic services, they must be placed in a stronger revenue position. Revenue sharing will accomplish that objective by guaranteeing them a designated proportion of the Nation's prime revenue source—the personal income tax.

Responds to need for equalization. Revenue sharing would operate in the right direction from the standpoint of interstate equalization and could be adjusted to serve as a powerful equalization instrument below the State level. A per capita distribution formula alone produces a moderate degree of equalization between wealthy and poor States, at the same time providing the most aid to the most populous States. Still more equalization can be built in with sophisticated tax effort and fiscal capacity measures.

Strengthens the Federal aid system. The present Federal aid system results in fiscal rigidity at the State and local level. By providing unconditional aid, revenue sharing will correct this major deficiency. Along with the present efforts to consolidate and simplify categorical aids, revenue sharing would provide State and local governments the added financial flexibility needed to package the many narrow Federal categorical aids into well-rounded public service programs.

Introduces greater equity into the Nation's intergovernmental tax system. The sharing of Federal personal income tax revenue would enable State and local governments to make somewhat less intensive use of local property and State sales taxes—levies that are most burdensome for low-income families. Indeed, some States may use revenue sharing funds to build greater equity into their tax systems by shielding basic family income from undue burdens of sales and property taxes. The Commission has recommended that the States finance property tax relief for low-income families and pull the regressive

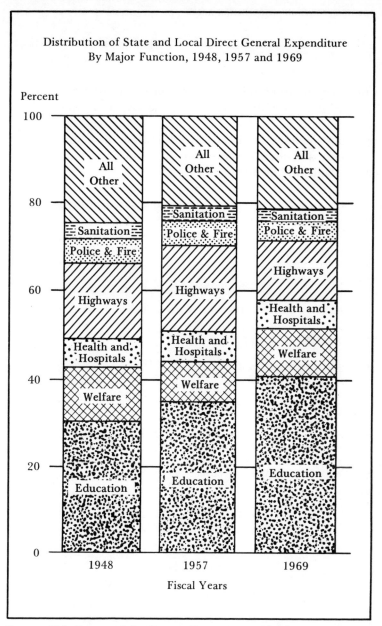

Distribution of State and Local Direct General Expenditure
By Major Function, 1948, 1957 and 1969

Source: U.S. Bureau of the Census, Governments Division.

FIGURE 5. State and local governments put their money where the needs are.

stinger from the sales tax by means of a food exemption or tax credits.

Protects the domestic front. The emergence of this Nation as a super power with massive foreign commitments makes it all the more necessary to develop new safeguards designed to prevent the short-changing of our domestic needs in general and our domestic instrumentalities (State and local governments) in particular. Witness this assessment by Daniel P. Moynihan:

> As far as I can see, an American national government in this age will always give priority to foreign affairs. A system has to be developed, therefore, under which domestic programs go forward regardless of what international crisis is preoccupying Washington at the moment. This in effect means decentralizing the initiative and the resources for such programs.[2]

The sharing of Federal revenue with State and local governments in good times and bad times is responsive to this need to decentralize both initiative and resources.

NOTES

1. Walter W. Heller, *New Dimensions of Political Economy.* (Cambridge: Harvard University Press, 1966) p. 142.
2. *Congressional Record,* September 26, 1967, p. H. 12499. Speech to meeting of Americans for Democratic Action, September 23, 1967.

ARTICLE 26

Revenue Sharing Is a Counterrevolution

Max Frankel

> *Happy it is when the interest which the Government has in
> the preservation of its own power coincides with a proper
> distribution of the public burdens and tends to guard the
> least wealthy part of the community from oppression!*
>
> Publius, The Federalist, No. 36, 1788

Poor Publius, operating under the name of Alexander Hamilton,
had only $4.2-million of the public burden to distribute in his first
three years as Secretary of the Treasury. Most of it came from customs
collections, and after he paid interest on the public debt and the costs
of the Army and its veterans there wasn't very much left for guarding
the least wealthy part of the community from anything. But Publius
was richly endowed with an idea, a Federal idea whose meaning and
power seem to have escaped the notice of his successors as they plot a
"New American Revolution."

The Revolution, if you haven't heard, is to be President Nixon's
bloodless execution of the Federal monster by a technique called
Revenue Sharing. Its promise is "cash and freedom" for the states
and cities. Its slogan is "power to people." Its goal, a "new Federalism."

The governors, mayors and people need more money, right? Too
much of their money now gets shipped off to Washington, right? Too
many Congressmen and bureaucrats try to tell them how to run their
affairs, right? Well, step right up and let us help yourselves: one
pot for "general" revenue sharing—let's say $25 a head to start, half
to the states, half to the cities, no strings attached, no serious questions asked; a second pot for "special" revenue sharing, using moneys

Reprinted from *The New York Times Magazine* (April 25, 1971), pp. 28–29,
87–91. © 1971 by The New York Times Company. Reprinted by permission.

hitherto earmarked for definite projects—about $50 a head, to be spent almost as freely, though with a little more guidance and accounting. Right? Right on!

Like all revolutionary doctrine, this is heady stuff. A good many governors and mayors are rushing headlong for this dole, duly reciting the selfless doctrines of the revolution—that revenue sharing will not only rescue local government from financial collapse but also bring decision-making "closer to the people," eliminate waste and tyranny along the Potomac and generally breathe new life into our democracy.

The only trouble is that like all simplistic formulas, revenue sharing ignores a good many political facts of life. It dangles cash before some hard-pressed communities without really defining the object of such a costly "reform." Indeed, it proposes to commit an open-ended portion of our jointly owned treasure without achieving any significant reform. And it gives virtually no thought to the desired purposes of our Federal system, old or new. Publius, where are you?

The fact is we need not a new Federalism but some clear thought about our neglect of the old. For the very purpose of our hierarchy of Federal, state and local governments was to have been a careful pooling (sharing!) of their revenues to provide for the common defense and to promote the general welfare. Many states and cities are in trouble now for the simple reason that we have failed to use the Federal power to insure either the fair raising of revenues or the rational sharing of costs. It is no answer to give away the money and the power that could correct these failures. The revenue-sharing revolution is, in essence, an abdication.

The President, Congress and their bureaucracies were never meant to be merely tax collectors. They were meant to govern, to attain a wider reach and a broader view of the national interest than any local regime, and indeed they have until now progressively done so. They were meant to preside over a system of multiple tax collection and spending that allows money to pass up the ladder of governments for services best managed by a higher authority and to be redistributed down the chain for services best administered at the state, city, county, village or school-district level.

The central flaw in the President's revenue-sharing scheme is that it would ignore this system in the name of reforming it. It would begin to turn the Federal Government into little more than a tax collector and dispenser. It would leave the states and cities saddled

with costs—welfare, for instance—that ought to be shared by the population as a whole. It would leave them free to tax their citizens in
wildly unequal patterns. It would give them portions of the common
national treasure with only negligible concern for their capacity to
spend it effectively. A program that does not address the ways in
which governments raise their revenues hardly deserves the name
revenue sharing. A program that does not relieve local governments
of obligations they neither created nor sought should not be palmed
off as burden sharing. The Nixon program is revolutionary only in
the sense that it is antigovernment, hostile to the very idea that the
Federal moneys and powers should be used to achieve desirable and
necessary ends.

The most clearly stated purpose of the President's plan is to
relieve the money shortage of state and local governments. But it is
bound to fail because it has not faced the basic questions: Who needs
more money? Why? How could it best be provided to achieve the
Federalist goal of truly sharing revenues and obligations?

Some states and localities need money because they have been
forced to assume burdens that are excessive. Still others need money
because, though they have tried hard to meet their obligations, they
remain poor. And some, being rich, energetic and lucky, don't need
any relief. Mr. Nixon would just kick back money to all of them.

The President favors such a wholesale distribution because he
believes it would simultaneously unravel a good deal of Federal red
tape, enhance the power of local governments to choose their own
priorities and revive the authority (and presumably the accountability) of state and local office holders. These are worthy objectives but
dubious assumptions. The nearer our elections get to the local level,
the less adequate the public discussion and the smaller the participation. In any case, the President's objectives are not likely to be
realized by a program that fails to deal with the structure of local
administrations, with their unequal tax systems and their uneven
burdens.

SHARING THE WORK

The President's judgment that the Federal edifice is buckling under
the weight of a top-heavy steeple tends to ignore the fact that the
rest of the American structure of government is in no condition to

support anything. At the middle levels are the state and county administrations, mostly weak, outmoded or corrupt, even when they are not broke. At the lowest level, the foundation of local government can be described only as jerrybuilt.

The problem goes far beyond local officials who stash public funds in unmarked shoe boxes, as in Illinois, or squander them on luxury suites for the poor, as in New York. Money alone has never fostered honesty or intelligence, and there is no reason to believe that the infusion of Federal money will increase the supply of either. The Federal dollar is money, not manna.

And even a shortage of money has not induced the states and localities to streamline their administrations. It is the illogical and complex structure of local governments, not their poverty, that has placed them beyond the reach and comprehension of the citizenry.

There are more than 80,000 units of local government in the United States—21,000 of them juggling the affairs of the major metropolitan areas that house 70 per cent of the population. That works out to an average of 91 governments for the typical metropolitan area, or 48 for each metropolitan county, including—besides the county government itself—12 school districts, 12 municipalities, 7 townships and 16 special districts that run the water supply, treat the sewage or provide some other service.

Only about 20 of the nation's 247 metropolitan areas are managed by fewer than 10 local governments. The Chicago area embraces 1,113, Philadelphia and environs 871, metropolitan New York 551. The average metropolitan citizen is the subject of at least four levels of local government. The average metropolitan county provides work for 350 *elected* officials.

Counties and school districts in this tangle exercise powers delegated to them by the states and therefore dovetail across the map in jigsaw pattern. All the other units of local government have sprung up in random and overlapping profusion, for purposes of exclusion (we'll fend for ourselves, Jack, and let the rest of the region go hang) or evasion (if state law says no more borrowing by county or city, we'll just make us up a new government, Guv).

Whatever is not hopelessly hobbled by quadruplication in this structure is ludicrously hampered by miniaturization. Two-thirds of our municipalities and townships have populations of less than 5,000. Among 5,000 metropolitan school districts, about one-fourth educate fewer than 300 pupils and about one-third operate no more than a single school. All but 200 of 5,000 metropolitan municipalities govern less than 25 square miles, the majority of them less than two square miles.

To exercise "control" over these local governments, the citizen must pick his way through laundry-list ballots of nonentities. And controlled or not, local office holders can rarely find enough money or authority in their slender jurisdictions to fill even the most elementary needs of the citizens. Most of the thousands of local governments can neither attract nor afford the expertise and administrative skills that they so plainly lack.

Whoever presumes to talk of invigorating these local governments and their state counterparts is talking about many governors condemned to serve only one brief term, often alongside independently chosen, unresponsive, perhaps even disloyal, cabinet officials. He is talking about state legislatures, a number of which may still meet only in alternate years and most of which are ill-paid, ill-staffed and ill-housed. He is talking about multiple systems of state justice in which judges are often subject to partisan election without regard for their professional qualification. He is talking about mayors, managers, executives, councils, school boards, directors, commissioners, assessors and the Lord knows who else with wholly uncoordinated mandates, all scrambling for taxes and loans and subsidies and carving out their own areas of sovereignty and authority.

Custom, confusion, regulation and debt seem to have petrified this overgrown forest. The states themselves have been passive about reorganization. The public has been apathetic, turning out no more than 25 per cent of the electorate for the few occasions when local reform has come to a vote. President Nixon grandly asserts his "trust" in the people and local office holders to reorder their affairs once they are given a little more money. Revenue sharing is being pushed on them with all the promise of the quick fix.

It is much more likely that the hasty injection of miscellaneous moneys into this structure will only reinforce its worst habits. And the very worst are the tendency to keep enlarging the tax burden of those least able to pay while sparing those who could afford to pay more and the toleration of scattered administrations that neatly wall off the people with the most money from the people with the greatest problems.

There is much to be said for the claim of governors and mayors that they usually know better than horse-trading members of Congress or rule-writing bureaucrats where their communities can most profitably invest new revenues. But that does not relieve the Federal Government of its obligation to direct the spending of its function that national priorities, too, will be served. In devising the great G.I. Bill program after World War II, the Federal Government did not force every returning veteran into college or tell those who went what they should study. But it did assert the national will. It spent billions to encourage the training and education of the postwar generation and to keep it from overwhelming the job market during the postwar demobilization. It required the veterans to account for their expenditures and it set standards for the schools that wished to compete for their tuition.

So, too, the help that is given states and cities from the common treasury can be used to promote the national purpose. Instead of being distributed at random, as Mr. Nixon proposes, the Federal dollar could be used to induce structural reform at all levels of government, above all, reforms that would produce a genuine and democratic sharing of revenues and burdens.

SHARING THE REVENUE

There is little doubt that state and local governments, in the aggregate, need more money. Their expenses have increased more than twelvefold since World War II—to an estimated $132-billion—more than three times as fast as spending by the Federal Government or individual citizens. By 1975, presuming roughly the present range of obligations, the state and community budgets will total about $200-billion, and between $6-billion and $10-billion of that amount will be lacking.

But none of this tells us anything about who actually needs money, or how much. And only by the crudest possible standards of accounting do these figures alone justify a massive Federal dole. To define the "needs" of state and local governments we ought to have some idea of how much and how fairly they tax their own citizens. We ought also to have some common standards to suggest which level of government should properly pay for different kinds of services.

Over the last 10 years, without waiting for such a rational division of labor, the Federal Government has increased its aid to local governments from $7-billion to about $30-billion a year. Though these expanded programs failed to meet many of the high goals set for them, they were born of the proper impulse to spend Federal funds for the benefit of the poorest portions of the population. The main purpose was to produce, in effect, a redistribution of the national treasure by taxing those best able to pay to support programs that would benefit those in greatest need. Title I of the Elementary and Secondary Education Act, for instance, tried to pump out about $1-billion for additional, compensatory schooling for the children of the poor; in fact, most of that money has been used merely to equalize the schooling of the poor at standards that the states were supposed have been meeting in the first place.

There have been other Federal failures, which Mr. Nixon and his aides have been most eager to advertise. Many of the regulations written into Federal programs have turned out to be unsettling and restrictive—for example, the ones requiring states and cities to divert money from their own favored projects to "match" Federal expenditures on Federal priorities. Many Federal programs have been drawn so narrowly that they strangle decision-making at lower levels; others have been so complex that only administrative geniuses can learn to qualify for their benefits.

It is a long leap backward, however, from the idea that regulations and restrictions on Federal spending need to be changed to the proposition that national purpose must be abandoned in the very design of the programs. Surely the *minimal* concern of a Federal program to give the states and cities more money should be the adequacy and fairness with which those states and cities levy taxes. President Nixon shuffled the deck awfully fast when he came to this point in his pitch for revenue sharing. Nothing better demonstrates his eager flight from Federal purpose and his lack of interest in genuine reform or, if you will, revolution.

In his political haste and anti-Federal fervor, Mr. Nixon argued that the Federal Government had "pre-empted and monopolized" the personal income tax as a source of revenue, leaving the states and cities to depend upon inferior and unfair taxes on property and sales. He noted, rightly enough, that the Federal income tax was a far more equitable way of raising revenue and that some of the local levies were becoming an almost intolerable burden on many citizens, notably those least able to pay. But these were crocodile tears, shed for a system that the President treated as a state of nature, as if it were beyond the capacity of men and governments to change. Far from advocating local tax reform or making Federal aid contingent upon constructive change, he offered revenue sharing to the perpetrators of inequity. Instead of changing the deplored system, he proposed to underwrite it indefinitely.

Some of the most flagrant inequities in our national tax system result not from the Federal "surplus" and local "shortages" that allegedly trouble Mr. Nixon. They result from the disparities of wealth and need among the states, cities and communities, often within just a few miles of each other.

Throughout the country, groups of citizens have fled the central cities with their wealth, walled themselves off behind "local" governments and ordinances and left the inner cities and neighboring counties to cope with their growing problems and diminishing sources of revenue. Some of the local governments we hold so dear for being "close" to the people are in fact little more than fiscal sanctuaries erected to prevent genuine revenue sharing. For reasons of state and liberty, we may not be able to reorder things by telling people where they should live and work. But we can certainly push their money around to spread the burdens and the wealth.

Even more disturbing is the evidence that many states and communities simply refuse to raise the revenues they so manifestly need for the services they crave and that the majority of local governments persist in rigging the taxes they collect so that they fall cruelly upon those least able to pay.

For all its imperfections, the Federal income tax stands as the most progressive levy yet devised to spread the burdens of government. It draws relatively more from the most fortunate and little or nothing from the unfortunate. No Federal edict prevents any state or locality from adopting an identical or similar tax system. They could even save themselves the collection costs and ride piggyback on the Federal tax structure by laying claim to any add-on percentage they wish, as they have been invited to do by the members of Congress most influential in these matters.

Some taxes on property and sales are obviously desirable at the lower levels to pay for facilities of direct benefit to local businessmen and residents. But as a principal source of general revenue for states and localities, which these taxes have become, they are viciously unfair. They produce such practical and theoretical absurdities as the requirement that a region's public education system be roughly commensurate with the market value of its real estate.

It is such unfair local taxes that have been rising the fastest and feeding the frustrations of taxpayers. The property tax has been a special favorite, largely, it is thought, because it can be adjusted and manipulated by administrative fiat, usually without legislative action.

Ten states, including New Jersey, Connecticut and Texas, have thus far refused to impose any income tax on their residents. Pennsylvania and Ohio are just getting around to thinking about one. Three other states tax only dividend income. Four large states, including Illinois and Michigan, tax only at a flat rate, to the obvious advantage of the wealthy. Of the remaining 34 states with nominally "progressive" income taxes, only 17 bother to vary the rates on earnings beyond $10,000, and most of the other progressive scales don't go beyond $5,000. One consequence of this pattern of taxation is that citizens earning $15,000 or more, who pay 33 per cent of all taxes collected by the Federal Government, pay only 8 per cent of those collected by state and local governments.

The inequalities are horizontal as well as vertical. There is no precise way to compare the taxes paid in different parts of the country or the quality of services they buy. But there exist some estimates of the state and local tax burden borne by an average family of four with a gross income of $10,000 in the largest city of each state. That burden ranges from $1,121 in Baltimore to $387 in Charleston, W. Va. It is $816 in New York City; $610 in Hartford; $507 in Cleveland; $414 in Houston, and $398 in Seattle.

Many local governments simply do not tax as much as they should, and the vast majority of them burden the poor and middle classes while they spare the rich. Although most of them need more money, the extent of their real "need" and the character of that need cannot be judged from their budget deficits. Some poor states need a lot more help. Some rich ones need relatively little. Poor communities and cities in wealthy regions probably need the most help, but the quirks of political boundaries and aggregate statistical tables hide the evidence.

To bail out and subsidize such a tax system, as the President proposes, would not only reinforce the unfairness of it all. It would also pass up what may be a rare opportunity to use the power of the Federal dollar to coerce—or, if the ideologues prefer, to induce—real reform. For there exist dozens of formulas by which Federal aid could be used to promote local tax reform so that the burdens would fall more equally on all citizens.

SHARING THE BURDEN

Even a fair revenue system, however, would work unfairly unless we also arrange a logical and equitable distribution of governmental burdens.

Obviously, sending out checks to a million welfare recipients in New York City is a burden for City Hall. It is in fact a burden twice over, for these million people must also be provided with public services to which they contribute next to nothing in taxes. But why should this be the exclusive burden of other New Yorkers? We wouldn't dream of asking Alaska to bear a heavier share of the national defense budget because it happens to border on the Soviet Union. We don't expect St. Petersburg, Fla., to pay a larger share of Social Security taxes just because the elderly like to settle there. We don't ask Kansans to assume a bigger responsibility for subsidizing agriculture because the farmers are their neighbors. Yet we let Mississippi or Louisiana or Puerto Rico or Appalachia export its poorest citizens to New York or Chicago or Detroit and, if they cannot earn their keep, throw much of the responsibility for their support on the states and cities in which the poor happen to congregate.

Underwriting that kind of isolationism may strike some as a "new Federalism," but it is not the kind Founder Publius had in mind or the kind any thoughtful person would wish to perpetuate. Yet that is precisely what President Nixon's revenue sharing envisions—alleviating the burden a little, but doing nothing whatever to shift its horrendous weight from the localities to the entire country, where it belongs. Welfare costs represent a redistribution of income, and that can be accomplished fairly only through the national treasury. Indeed, the assumption of welfare costs by the Federal Government should be accompanied by a subsidy to the communities in which the recipients reside to compensate for the services they require.

Pegging the burdens of social service to the appropriate level of government is what genuine Federalism is all about. And only when we get a system that fairly distributes the costs among states and localities can we determine which of them truly need special help from the rest of us.

All this involves much more than administrative tidiness. Of the $9-billion spent on relief programs for 14 million people unable to support themselves, more than $6-billion comes out of the Federal budget. But the confusions of purpose and administration at all levels of government impose severe hardships on the recipients as well as the taxpayers.

As Gilbert Y. Steiner demonstrates in a brilliant new study of relief programs, the "lucky" poor family can have its welfare income doubled through food stamps and public housing while a comparable but "unlucky" family must put its name on waiting lists for both of the added benefits. The reason is that some states and communities participate in food-stamp and public-housing programs while others don't. There are the Mississippis of the nation, already taxing themselves fairly hard, which cannot afford the payments of New York or California, and there are the Delawares, which simply won't.

At the moment, the Federal Government pays out almost as much in relief to the families of poor veterans (not in any way disabled in war) as it does to families with dependent children. But the dependent children program is tied into so many state and local variations that the payments change from place to place. The relief to veterans is fair across the board and fairly shared by all the nation's tax-payers, and it has become the very model of tidy administration. Notwithstanding Mr. Nixon's dragon portrait of the Federal bureaucracy, the program for aid to former soldiers and their families provides uniform Federal standards and payments and simple access to the system by potential beneficiaries and by nongovernmental groups, such as the American Legion, that lobby on their behalf. The benefiting veterans are, in fact, a privileged group among the unequal poor, and it has been argued that their program ought to be merged with all other relief measures. But such reform, like others, could be achieved only if all major relief projects were placed under Federal control. Revenue sharing, as conceived by the President, would simply give away the money with which this could be accomplished.

The President's other big proposal, for "welfare reform," would offer some valuable new assistance to the working poor and it would give some financial relief to some states—without, however, assuring that the benefits would be passed on to the needy. And it would do very little for most of the seven million recipients of aid to families with dependent children.

It is simply absurd to regard relief as a local responsibility. Just as veterans are helped from a sense of national obligation, so should the poor, and especially the poor descendents of slaves, be treated out of a sense of national duty. If they are deemed worthy of help they should not have to shop around for the counties and cities that offer more than others. And if they are deemed to be a common obligation, their support should not depend on local or state budgets.

Nor is welfare the only item on the agenda of intelligent Federalism. State laws requiring children to attend school and setting minimum standards for schools—even while the schools are administered "locally"—were among the earliest expressions of the doctrine that higher levels of government must protect the common interest in lower-level administration. Now the time has come for an even broader Federal standard and subsidy of education.

We have become a highly mobile country. A hundred communities may benefit from the schooling provided by one, and a hundred may suffer for the educational neglect of another. Yet many state governments have failed to assure at least minimum patterns of equal spending on education in their jurisdictions. And the Federal Government, now bearing only 7 per cent of the cost of public education, has not even begun the search for common minimal standards.

It seems that we have been federalizing the interstate highway system for nearly two decades with very little thought about the caliber of person we wish thus to turn loose in the land.

The financial crisis afflicting state and local governments has been laid to many causes, including the wage clamors of newly militant unions of public employes, the soaring costs of construction, the slowdown in aid from the states to cities and the slumping economy that simultaneously reduced tax collections and raised welfare costs. By far the greatest surge in local expenditures over the last decade is traceable to the soaring costs of education and assistance to the poor. Genuine reform, therefore, promises not only fairness and neatness but the very financial relief that Mr. Nixon says he seeks.

The Federal Government cannot and should not prescribe the *maximum* service that local citizens may wish to support. If some villagers want more traffic lights, they can organize to get them and pay the cost. Many local requirements are peculiar or particular and of little importance to higher levels of government. But we can and should work toward *minimum* standards of life throughout the nation.

The Federal Government has a right and duty to establish minimum standards of relief, education and health, as it does in setting minimum benefits under Social Security. It has the right and duty to use its power and money to adjust for the spread of problems from one region to another, as it does in attacking air and water pollution. It has a right and duty to equalize the burdens on its citizens, as it does by taking relatively more tax money from wealthy communities and individuals and giving relatively more to poorer ones. It has a right and duty to induce and coerce the states to work toward the sharing of revenues and burdens within their jurisdictions, as well as without.

It would be refreshing if such ardent advocates of the needs and rights of the states as Mr. Nixon would occasionally speak to the obligations of the states and localities. For the failures of the Federal Government become quickly apparent to everyone, but the failures of local administration are never really rectified or even noticed until they become an oppressive burden on the country at large.

The President's "New American Revolution" would not only fail to remedy these shortcomings. It does not even recognize them. If we followed his advice, what is deceptively called revenue sharing would become a constant flow of money out of the Federal treasury that would not buy anything for the national interest. The new revolution is in fact a counterrevolution. Publius, where are you?

SUGGESTIONS FOR FURTHER READING

I. Government and Politics of Metropolitan Areas

Advisory Commission on Intergovernmental Relations. *Alternative Approaches to Governmental Reorganization in Metropolitan Areas.* Washington: U.S. Government Printing Office, June, 1962. (Institutional alternatives for metropolitan government.)

————. *Factors Affecting Voter Reactions to Governmental Reorganization in Metropolitan Areas.* Washington: U.S. Government Printing Office, May, 1962. (The record of consistent rejection of metropolitan government.)

————. *Metropolitan America: Challenge To Federalism.* A Study submitted to the Intergovernmental Relations Subcommittee of the Committee on Government Operations. U.S. House of Representatives, 89th Congress, 2d Session. Washington: U.S. Government Printing Office, October, 1966. (A useful analysis of metropolitan area-wide problems and prospects.)

————. *Metropolitan Councils of Government.* Washington: U.S. Government Printing Office, August, 1966. (An analysis of a voluntary approach to interlocal cooperation.)

————. *Urban America and the Federal System.* Washington: U.S. Government Printing Office, August, 1966. (An analysis of a voluntary approach to interlocal cooperation.)

————. *Urban America and the Federal System.* Washington: U.S. Government Printing Office, October, 1969. (An analysis of metropolitan-area-wide governmental, fiscal, and planning problems together with the commission's recommendations for solutions.)

Banovetz, James M. *Perspectives on the Future of Government in Metropolitan Areas.* Chicago: Center For Research In Urban Government, Loyola University, April, 1968. (The thesis that governmental changes in metropolitan areas are gradual rather than dramatic.)

Bish, Robert L. *The Public Economy of Metropolitan Areas.* Chicago: Markham Publishing Co., 1971. (An attempt to explain the structure and functioning of the public economy of metropolitan areas.)

Bollens, John C., and Henry J. Schmandt. *The Metropolis.* 2d ed. Chapters 11–14. New York: Harper & Row, Publishers, Inc., 1970. (A comprehensive analysis of metro government proposals.)

Campbell, Alan K., ed. *The States and the Urban Crisis.* Englewood Cliffs, New Jersey: Prentice-Hall, Inc., Spectrum Books, The American Assembly, 1970. (Original essays on the state response to urban fiscal, governmental, and planning problems.)

Committee for Economic Development. *Reshaping Government in Metropolitan Areas.* New York: Committee for Economic Development, 1970. (Proposals for metro governments plus a useful essay on the Metropolitan Toronto (Canada) experience.)

Coulter, Philip B., ed. *Politics of Metropolitan Areas.* New York: Thomas Y. Crowell Co., 1967. (Essays on government and politics of cities, suburbs, and metropolitan areas.)

Danielson, Michael N., ed. *Metropolitan Politics*. Boston: Little, Brown and Co., 1966. (Selected essays on the government and politics of the metropolis.)

Downes, Bryan T., ed. *Cities and Suburbs*. Belmont, California: Wadsworth Publishing Co., Inc., 1971. (A useful collection of essays and articles on the politics and public policy of cities and suburbs together with the editor's own interpretive introductory comments.)

Dye, Thomas R., and Brett W. Hawkins. *Politics in the Metropolis*, 2d ed. Columbus, Ohio: Charles E. Merrill Publishing Co., 1971. (Selected essays on metropolitan government, politics, and public policy conflicts.)

Friesma, H. P. "The Metropolis and the Maze of Local Government." *Urban Affairs Quarterly* 2 (December 1966:68–90. (Criticism of metro government reform proposals.)

Grant, Daniel R. "Metro's Three Faces." *National Civic Review* 55 (1966): 317–324. (A discussion of the fact that while Miami-Dade County, Florida, Nashville-Davidson County, Tennessee, and Toronto, Canada, have had some success in attacking area-wide problems, their solutions may not be applicable to other parts of the U.S.)

———. "The Metropolitan Government Approach: Should, Can, and Will It Prevail?" *Urban Affairs Quarterly* 3 (March 1968): 103–110. (Intergovernmental cooperation rather than metro government as the norm for the future.)

Rehfuss, John A. "Metropolitan Government: Four Views." *Urban Affairs Quarterly* 3 (June 1968): 91–111. (An analysis of various justifications for metro government and how to achieve it.)

Reining, Henry, Jr., symposium ed. "Governing Megacentropolis." *Public Administration Review* 30 (1970):473–520. (Six essays on the crisis of the central cities.)

Smallwood, Frank. *Greater London*. Indianapolis: The Bobbs-Merrill Co., 1965. (An account of the political struggle to create the Greater London Council, a metro form of government.)

Sofen, Edward. *The Miami Metropolitan Experiment*, 2d ed. Garden City, New York: Doubleday & Co., Inc., Anchor Books, 1966. (Problems and prospects of Miami-Dade County, Florida, metro government.)

Wood, Robert. *1400 Governments*. Garden City, New York: Doubleday & Co., Inc., Anchor Books, 1964. (The maze of local governments in the New York City metropolitan region.)

———. *Suburbia*. Boston: Houghton Mifflin Co., 1958. (Still one of the best studies of the people, politics, and political philosophy of suburban America.)

Zimmerman, Joseph F., ed. *Government of the Metropolis.* New York: Holt, Rinehart and Winston, Inc., 1968. (Essays and articles on the government and politics of metropolitan areas.)

II. Intergovernmental Relations: Fiscal and Planning

Aleshire, Robert A. "The Metropolitan Desk: A New Technique In Program Development." *Public Administration Review* 26 (June 1966): 87–95. (A description of how the Department of Housing and Urban Development tries to coordinate state and local programs.)

Beckman, Norman. "How Metropolitan Are Federal and State Policies?" *Public Administration Review* 26 (June 1966): 96–106. (A discussion of how to encourage state participation in solving urban problems, the federal government can require minimum adequate standards to be met by the states in channeling funds to metropolitan areas.)

Chinitz, Benjamin, ed. *City and Suburb.* Englewood Cliffs, New Jersey: Prentice-Hall, Inc., Spectrum Books, 1964. (Selected essays on economic problems of metropolitan areas.)

Heller, Walter W. *New Dimensions of Political Economy.* Chapter III. New York: W. W. Norton & Co., Inc., 1967. (Discussion of tax-sharing plan by its originator.)

Levin, Melvin R. *Community and Regional Planning: Issues in Public Policy.* Special Studies in U.S. Economic and Social Development. New York: Frederick A. Praeger, Publishers, 1969. (Original essays on urban planning and related public policy issues.)

Martin, Roscoe C. *The Cities and the Federal System.* New York: Atherton Press, 1965. (Problems and programs of intergovernmental and metropolitan development.)

Ranney, David C. *Planning and Politics in the Metropolis.* Columbus, Ohio: Charles E. Merrill Publishing Co., 1969. (A short text on planning and politics in the metropolis.)

Reuss, Henry S. *Revenue-Sharing.* New York: Praeger Publishers, 1970. (The urging of the Democratic Congressman from Wisconsin for enactment of revenue sharing together with tax reforms and administrative reorganization.)

Rodwin, Lloyd. *Nations and Cities.* Boston: Houghton Mifflin Co., 1970. (Urban growth and planning strategies in selected foreign nations and the United States.)

PART 3

The Urban Crisis

Chapter 5

Urban Problems and Policies
of the 1960's

Riots, Police, Poverty, Employment, Education, Housing, and Environment

The urban crisis involves fundamental questions of public policy. Is discrimination against blacks and other minorities the basic source of urban unrest? Should ghetto riots be met by massive displays of police force? Should "law and order" be restored to make our city streets safe? Are inadequate public education, unemployment, and slum housing results of unequal distribution of economic resources and inadequate government effort in metropolitan areas? Must our affluent society produce so much that the environment is destroyed for future generations?

The crisis of urban America is a nationwide problem of epidemic proportions. If the urban problem is viewed as primarily one of black-white hostility, then most public programs will probably fall short of changing the discriminatory attitudes that have long persisted. More likely, the white majority will support armed encirclement of city ghettoes and massive police repression of black unrest. On the other hand, if solving the basic urban problem involves eradicating the underlying causes of both ghetto tensions and hostile black-white relations, then the government may be able to mobilize the tremendous resources of our economy to overcome the disadvantages of distressed minority groups. The choice is clear: Either government shows that it *is* capable of responding to the needs of *all* the people, or those unaided may respond to inaction with revolution.

The urban riots of the 1960's focused nationwide attention on the unbearable social and economic conditions of ghetto residents. Following the explosive disruptions during the summer months of 1967, President Lyndon B. Johnson appointed the National Advisory Commission on Civil Disorders to discover the causes of riots and to propose comprehensive solutions to prevent them in the future. In Article 27, Ralph W. Conant analyzes and compares the underlying causes and processes of recent ghetto protests. He finds that city riots stem largely from two factors: (1) black grievances against symbols of hated white authority, such as the police, and (2) economic oppression, including exploitation by white-owned neighborhood businesses. No one can predict exactly when a specific "triggering" incident will lead to a riot, and the violence will almost inevitably result in more destruction of black property and homes than of white-owned real estate. More blacks than whites are arrested by the police, and the disorder is confined to the ghetto, leaving white neighborhoods untouched. Thus the riots of the 1960's were not interracial in the sense that blacks directly battled whites.

Furthermore, in contrast to the more popularly held view that only a few outside agitators were involved, the anatomy of a "typical" riot indicates that many ghetto residents participated. Widespread involvement, particularly in looting activities, was commonplace because most blacks felt that the benefits of material gain exceeded the costs of punishment or arrest. Rioting was perceived as a legitimate protest to white injustices. Essentially, the riots were primitive efforts at income redistribution which white society would not support in a lawful manner. Since rioting was controlled only by massive displays of counterforce, it seems crucial to deal with the underlying causes of black discontent.

Many of the major riots were sparked by precipitating incidents between the police and ghetto residents. The individual policeman was often the target of hostility, not only because of his actions but also because he was an easily identifiable lightning rod. The smoldering rage of the ghetto flashed out at white police officers who were readily accessible substitutes for the white Establishment. Minority groups often view the local police presence negatively: The police are not considered to be pillars of strength within the community but puppets from outside to insure that the Establishment's social and economic interests in the ghetto are protected.

What are some central problems of our big-city police forces? In Article 28 David P. Stang, writing for the Violence Commission, discloses that many policemen consider themselves to be members of a misunderstood minority group who are often blamed for creating social conditions over which they have no control. The individual policeman reasons that he is not responsible for slum problems. He might even favor equal opportunity for all. But in enforcing the law, he is often accused of prejudice or incitement to riot by detached "outsiders" who engage in social theorizing about the proper role of the police. He also believes that citizen disrespect for law and order is harmful and undermines his effectiveness as a law enforcement officer. He often finds the behavior of ghetto residents personally offensive to his values. With all of these tensions, it is necessary to develop programs that will promote better understanding between the police and minority groups. Aside from the explosive and damaging 1967 riots, the ghettoes seethe with daily violence: high crime rates, illegal drug traffic, and considerable community fear. It may well be the case that ghetto residents favor more effective police protection than they have right now.

Massive unemployment and extensive poverty are two of the root causes of ghetto discontent. In 1968, there were 25.4 million poor in the United States, a rather shocking statistic when one considers the tremendous affluence of American society. It is clear that absolute poverty must soon be ended because its very existence condemns our citizens to death or lives of misery. Also greater access to opportunity must be provided for all Americans.

The Johnson Administration's War on Poverty represented the first full-scale attack on the underlying causes of urban misery. One of the key elements of the 1964 Equal Opportunity Act was the "maximum feasible participation" of the poor in local community action programs. Sanford Kravitz and Ferne K. Kolodner (Article 29) credit these community action programs with bringing about major changes in the social welfare structure of American communities. Some of the more notable achievements were spreading service programs to previously unorganized areas, reaching downward into the poor and nearly poor groups for additional sources of leadership, training new black leaders, and developing the concept of subprofessional employment. On the local level, community action programs have been plagued by several problems: a constant search for appropriate levels for decentralizing power and programs, departure from traditional patterns of delivering services, and management of large-grant programs. While the CAP has made tremendous contributions, it needs better planning capability, improved management, and greater fiscal responsibility. On the national level, the Nixon Administration has de-escalated the War on Poverty with a corresponding reduction of federal financial support. Thus the hopes of the urban poor that were uplifted by the OEO-CAP programs are no longer a central concern of the national government.

Unemployment in many central city ghettoes exceeds the 1930's depression levels. Blacks and other minorities generally have higher unemployment rates, hold worse jobs, receive less pay, work fewer hours, have fewer members in the working force, and suffer higher disability rates than whites. Within the black community, unemployment is especially severe for men, and teenagers have unbelievably high jobless rates.

The Job Corps, originally a part of the War on Poverty, was conceived as a program to assist high school dropouts (particularly among minority groups from urban slums) who lacked sufficient employment skills to get jobs in the private economy. By establishing rural conservation and urban residential centers, the Job Corps took these young people from their homes and provided them with vocational training and basic literacy skills. While many of the graduates benefitted from their experiences with Job Corps, Comptroller General Elmer B. Staats (Article 30) concluded that because of excessively high training costs (estimated at more than $8,000 per trainee), poor screening and counseling services, high dropout rates, and generally poor placement of graduates, the entire Job Corps program required drastic overhauling. Mr. Staats doubted whether Job Corps graduates were any more employable than disadvantaged youth who chose not to enter the program. In his view, the subsequent employment opportunities were probably more related to "the process of growing up and to higher employment and wage levels . . ." Subsequently, the Department of Labor announced the closing of 59 Job Corps centers together with a considerable reduction in the number of trainees and budgetary commitments.

Inadequate education is closely related to the problems of poverty and unemployment. The persistence of *de facto* segregation in the public schools has resulted in alarmingly high levels of racial isolation and underachievement among minority group students. What are the effects of segregated education on the learning capabilities of disadvantaged pupils? In 1966, the U.S. Office of Education commissioned a team of researchers to conduct one of the most complete investigations ever made of American public schools. Among other things, the Coleman Report (Article 31) attempted to evaluate the differences in achievement levels between whites and blacks. Test scores to measure verbal, mathematics, and general information skills indicated that "the average minority pupil scores distinctly lower than the average white pupil." Furthermore, "the deficiency is progressively greater for minority pupils at progressively higher grade levels." In attempting to explain these findings, the Coleman Report did *not* discover strong correlations between lower achievement and the conditions of ghetto schools, the quality of teachers, the kinds of curricula, or the level of expenditures. Rather the key factor was the attitude of the student toward learning. The motivation to learn was strongly influenced by children attending the same school; therefore, "if a minority pupil from a home without much educational strength is put with schoolmates with strong educational backgrounds, his achievement is likely to increase."

In effect the Coleman Report endorsed a public policy of massive integration of the public schools as the only path to improving the quality of education for blacks and other disadvantaged minorities. Integration is necessary because compensatory programs to upgrade the quality of education in ghetto schools will not result in significant benefits for the masses of disadvantaged students.

School busing is one alternative for achieving racially balanced education in the nation's metropolitan areas. The objective is to eliminate dual school systems created by segregated housing patterns in cities and suburbs. In the *Swann* case (Article 32), the United States Supreme Court upheld the constitutionality of busing in the South. Busing could be a tool of integration for the school district of Charlotte-Mecklenburg, North Carolina, unless "the time or distance is so great as to risk either the health of the children or significantly impinge on the educational process."

As a consequence of the *Swann* decision, many Southern communities felt they were unfairly treated because metropolitan areas of the North also had a considerable number of racially imbalanced schools resulting from *de facto* segregated housing patterns. Governor George Wallace of Alabama took a strong position against massive busing in his 1972 bid for the Democratic presidential nomination and attracted considerable support for his views in several northern states, including Michigan and Indiana. Additionally, President Nixon urged Congress to support "neighborhood schools" and to oppose busing. On March 17, 1972, he requested that Congress "impose a temporary freeze on new busing orders by the Federal courts." In contrast to the findings of the Coleman Report, Mr. Nixon favored a policy of upgrading ghetto schools by increased governmental expenditures. It is clear that busing will remain a politically controversial issue in the public arena.

Ghetto housing facilities are often run-down, poorly maintained, deteriorating, and dilapidated. Such slum conditions have prevailed for many years, and they aggravate the persistent social problems of poverty, unemployment, and inadequate education. However, recent findings suggest that many inner-city residents are abandoning their homes and apartments. Ironically, this movement is occurring simultaneously with a serious shortage of low-income housing for the blacks and other minority groups. As a result of financial and administrative deficiencies in federal programs, the Department of Housing and Urban Development has become the owner of many vacated slum properties. In Article 33, George Sternlieb finds that abandonments result from vandalism, scarcity of capital for rehabilitation and simple repairs, and landlords who refuse to maintain buildings that are no longer profitable. He suggests several constructive remedies to halt this deterioration.

What has the federal government done to provide decent housing for all Americans? Three of the most important national housing policies to appear during the last twenty years include urban renewal, Model Cities, and the 1968 Housing Act. The 1966 Model Cities program was intended to be a coordinated and comprehensive approach to neighborhood renewal. It offered great hope for transforming the inner-city slums to livable communities. The 1968 Housing Act established, among other things, the goal of eliminating all substandard housing in the country.

In addition to urban problems connected with poverty, unemployment, education, and housing, many Americans have become increasingly concerned with environmental and ecological problems. This new public awareness raises a whole series of public policy considerations affecting all people, regardless of where they live. If the nation's air and water become totally unfit for human use, what happens to the quality of life to which we have become accustomed? The environmental crisis, as discussed by Harvey Lieber in Article 34, goes to the heart of America's post-industrial economy. In our zeal to create an affluent society, we run the risk of destroying our natural resources.

The portrait of urban problems presented in this chapter is certainly grim and foreboding.[1] The urban crisis, in all of its dimensions, is one of the greatest challenges America has faced since the Civil War. Recognition of this fact is a good starting point to solving our critical domestic problems. It *is* possible to change the current picture of urban poverty, despair, and hopelessness. The difficulties associated with education, employment, housing, and the environment can be effectively attacked with massive amounts of federal funds, coordinated and comprehensive intergovernmental efforts, and effective leadership at all levels of government. Nothing less than a total effort, coupled with a reordering of national priorities, will be required to solve the urban crisis.

NOTES

1. For further material on this subject, please consult "Suggestions for Further Reading" at the end of Chapter 6.

QUESTIONS FOR DISCUSSION AND DEBATE

1. What do you think accounts for the discrepancies between the widely held view that urban riots are caused by militants or "riff-raff" and social science findings that a rather large number of ghetto residents participated? Do you think that urban riots are caused basically by racial or economic class factors? What evidence is there to suggest that the large-scale riots of the 1960's will not occur in the future? Do you agree or disagree with optimistic interpretations of this evidence?

2. Assume the roles of a slum resident and a police patrolman. Assess, to the best of your ability, the perceptions of these two people in terms of "law and order." What do you consider the necessary ingredients for developing an effective police-com-

munity relations program? Should more efforts be made in this
direction, or would you suggest alternative programs for the
police in relation to slum problems?

3. Do you consider the persistence of poverty as an American paradox, or are there fundamental inequities in our system of income distribution which cannot be eliminated? Do you think
that most Americans are aware of the poverty problem? Why?
Is the "cycle of poverty" primarily caused by personal deficiencies, or are there enough meaningful jobs for all able-bodied
Americans?

4. How do you account for the federal government's encouraging
"maximum feasible participation" of the poor in the 1964 EOA?
Do you consider this clause a radical approach to community
self-help programs? What happens when the political perception
of the poor reaches levels of awareness about their social, economic, and political conditions?

5. Compare and contrast a set of arguments that defend and criticize employment programs for the poor on the basis of efficiency
and economy criteria and on the basis of social welfare criteria.
Considering the GAO report on the Job Corps, which set of
arguments is most compelling, and which set of arguments has
the greatest political feasibility in Congress?

6. Since 1967, has the level of racial isolation in the public schools
(particularly in the North) increased or decreased? What do you
consider the strongest arguments against widespread bussing of
public school pupils? Do you agree or disagree with these arguments?

7. What accounts for the abandonment of housing in the nation's
cities? What governmental policies could reverse abandonment?
Would you favor an increase in demolition of slums, low-interest
loans for rehabilitation, or direct subsidies to individuals to purchase housing available in the private real estate market?

8. Assuming the role of a governmental administrator, how would
you go about developing an environmental control program that
requires large-scale industry to comply with your regulations?

Patterns of Civil Protest: Ghetto Riots

Ralph W. Conant

Riots stem from conflicts in society similar to those that inspire civil disobedience, but riots do not ordinarily develop directly from specific acts of civil disobedience. Repeated failure of civil disobedience to achieve sought-after goals, however, can and often does produce frustrations that result in rioting.

Rioting is a spontaneous outburst of group violence characterized by excitement mixed with rage. Riots are usually directed against alleged perpetrators of injustice or gross misusers of political power. The typical rioter has no premeditated purpose, plan, or direction, although systematic looting, arson, and attack on persons usually occur once a riot is under way. Also criminals and conspirators may expand their routine activities in the wake of the riot chaos.

Although riots are unpremediated outbursts, they are not as a rule *senseless* outbursts. The rage behind riots, like the frustration behind other forms of protest, is a shared anger growing out of specific rage-inducing experiences. In the United States, the anger felt by blacks (manifested in ghetto riots) initially was based on centuries of slavery and oppression and, in latter times, on discriminatory practices that frustrated access to social, economic, and political opportunities.

Large, heterogeneous societies are likely to experience internal violence during periods of rapid social change, a situation compounded, as in the United States, for example, where ethnic groups are forced to live in ghettos. As long as subordinate groups accept their status, violent conflict is minimized; but when a subordinated

From pp. 21–40 in *The Prospects For Revolution: A Study of Riots, Civil Disobedience, and Insurrection in Contemporary America*, by Ralph W. Conant. Copyright © 1971 by Ralph W. Conant. Reprinted by permission of Harper & Row, Publishers, Inc.

group lashes out at the structure (or when the dominant group perceives a threat of assault), violence is likely to occur. In the history of black-white relationships in the United States, dominant whites have, upon occasion, responded to such threats by direct attacks on the minority.

The period of race riots between the turn of the century and 1950 was one in which whites responded to black aggression and "insubordination" by mob assault (Springfield, Ohio, 1906; Atlanta, 1906; Springfield, Illinois, 1908; East St. Louis, 1917; Washington, D.C., and Chicago, 1919; Detroit and Los Angeles, 1934). The riots of the 1960's, however, were characterized by blacks reacting to real or perceived threats (or harassment) by agents of the dominant whites, especially local police (Harlem, 1965; Watts, 1965; Newark, 1967; Detroit, 1967).

All riots stem from intense conflicts within the value systems that stabilize the social and political processes of a community. The ghetto riots of the 1960's in the United States are a concrete example of a group attempt to restructure values and to clarify social relationships in a short time by extraordinary methods.

There are two classes of value conflicts, each of which gives rise to a different kind of struggle. The first calls for a normative readjustment because the dominant values of the society are being applied inequitably. The aggrieved group ordinarily calls attention to the inequity by petition for redress; if this method fails, aggressive protest may follow. If the protest fails to attain readjustment, the aggrieved may riot provided certain other conditions are also present.

The antidraft rioters at the time of the Civil War were protesting the plight of the common man who could not, like his wealthier compatriots, buy his way out of the draft: American egalitarian values were not being applied across the board. The readjustment came only after the intensity of the riots stimulated public concern to force a change in an unfair national policy. The draft card burners of the 1960's were as much protesting what they saw as inequities in the contemporary selective service system as they were the war in Vietnam.

The ghetto riots of the 1960's grew out of the failure of the civil rights movement to achieve normative readjustment for black people through nonviolent protest. The failure produced lines of cleavage which, if intensified, could result in the second type of value conflict, namely value readjustment. In this case, the dominant values of the society are brought under severe pressure for revolutionary change. The organizers of the aggrieved, having given up hope of benefiting from the existing value system, offer a new configuration of values, its objective being the establishment of a new political system to replace the old. A protest movement that reaches this point is revolutionary.

When the American colonists gave up hope of benefiting from the English institutions of the monarchy and the colonial system, they set up their own egalitarian value system, established the framework of a national government, and staged a revolution. In the present day, some blacks and some youth groups are moving toward value readjustment. The blacks talk about organizing "their people" on the basis of separatist and collectivist values and reject the "melting-pot" individualistic values of the American society, which they are convinced are not working for them.

An aggrieved population can erupt into violence on the basis of a pre-existing set of hostile beliefs about adversaries in the dominant community. During anti-Catholic riots in the United States in the nineteenth century, Protestant rioters believed that the pope in Rome was trying to take over the country. The anti-Negro rioters in Chicago, East St. Louis, and Detroit during World War II believed that new black immigrants from the rural South were trying to appropriate their jobs, rape their women, and attack their men.

Today, many rioters in urban ghettos believe in the malevolence and duplicity of whites and in their basic commitment to oppressing blacks. An important component of a hostile belief system is that the expected behavior of the identified adversary is seen as extraordinary, that is, beyond accepted norms. In urban ghettos, people are convinced, for example, that police will behave toward them with verbal incivility and physical brutality far beyond any incivility and brutality displayed toward whites in similar circumstances.

The hostile belief system is connected on the one hand with the value conflict and on the other with an incident that precipitates a riot: it embodies the value conflict—giving it form, substance, and energy—and sets the stage for an incident to become a concrete illustration of the hostile beliefs. Thus, a police officer who shoots and kills a young black suspected car thief (San Francisco, September 1966) or beats and bloodies a black taxi driver (Newark, July 1967) tragically dramatizes and seems to confirm the hostile belief. An ensuing melee, however violent and destructive, is wholly justified in the minds of the rioters who share the hostile belief. Rumors of further brutalities are seized upon to bolster feelings of justification, and any provocations by adversary police are utilized to create still more of the type of behavior the aggrieved want to see enacted to support their angry behavior.

Hostile beliefs bear varying relations to "reality." In some aspects they are exaggerations; in others, they are very close to the truth. In the 1830's the Catholic church actually wanted more power and influence locally in America, but it was not out to take over the country. Today, large numbers of whites want to keep blacks where they are by allowing them to advance only gradually; but they do not consciously want to oppress and harass them.

As stated earlier, an important and perhaps universal causal factor in riots is perception of real or imagined deprivation. The aggrieved see a gap between the conditions in which they find themselves and what could be their situation, given the opportunity. Ghetto residents in U.S. cities use middle-class white suburban living standards as a comparative point, and they feel acutely deprived, not so much of goods and services associated with the standard of suburban living, but of access to the jobs and salaries which put the desired goods and services within reach. The areas of relative deprivation for black Americans are political and social as well as economic. Blacks are not adequately represented in governing councils at the local or national levels, and they are excluded from social opportunities.

Another causal factor behind riots is the lack of effective channels for bringing about change. Stanley Lieberson and Arnold Silverman, in their study of riots in U.S. cities between 1910 and 1961, note that those cities in which riots have occurred were cities where officials were elected at large rather than by district or wards. In citywide voting, blacks and other minority groups are not likely to get adequate representation, if any. As a result, these groups feel deprived of a political voice and a potential channel through which to air grievances. A case in point is the American Revolution: the American colonists suffered "taxation without representation" and in the end rebelled when they felt their case was not being forcefully pressed in the British Parliament. An aggrieved population with no access to grievance channels is bound to resort to rioting or rebellion, especially if some of its grievances are dramatized in a precipitating incident.

Although rioters do not have much of a chance to think about the consequences of a riot, those who participate do harbor hopes, however vague, that extreme and violent behavior may bring about desired changes. Certainly the contagion effect had a significant role in the crescendo of ghetto riots in the United States in 1967 and 1968. Ghetto residents were known to feel that things could not be made worse by rioting and that riots might achieve concessions from influential whites (which indeed they did). As the disturbances spread, the riot became an important threat weapon in the hands of black militant leaders in cities everywhere in the nation, whether riots had actually occurred there or not. Although no one could claim the ability to start a riot or guarantee to stop one once it was started, the fear that rioters would attack white neighborhoods was sometimes enough of a threat (though unspoken) to give ghetto leaders a temporary advantage in negotiations on ghetto problems. Any hard-pressed people are riot prone, especially if they see others in similar conditions making gains from rioting. What happens to start a riot is spontaneous, but hope for change raises the combustion potential.

One of the characteristics of the conflict between blacks and whites in America is that communication between the two has been largely blocked by white denial and black intransigence. This condition intensifies the hostile belief systems of each group toward the other and, among black citizens, sets the stage for rumor to amplify a potential incident into a riot trigger.

A communications gap between an aggrieved community and local civil authorities is symptomatic of the distrust, bitterness, and hatred which intensified between whites and blacks in American cities during the 1960's. In many cities, relations between minority-group communities and city hall were damaged almost beyond repair by hostile outbursts in the aggrieved community and unsympathetic or repressive reaction from local authorities.

The condition of relations between city authorities and the black community in Omaha, Nebraska, in 1969 illustrates the point. Despite years of apparently sincere but ineffective efforts by city officials to deal with ghetto issues—a police recruiting program to attract officers, a store-front community relations office in the ghetto, a police-youth athletic program—police relations in the black community were deteriorating. Indeed, by the summer of 1969 the police department had become the focal point of tense racial divisions. In June, a riot followed the fatal shooting of Vivian Strong, a black teen-age girl, by a white police officer. The riot, which resulted in scores of fires and nearly a million dollars in property damage, was a protest against a brutal police act and a substitute means of communicating an acute grievance in the absence of open or trustworthy channels.

Black spokesmen in Omaha complained at the time of the 1969 disturbance that they had no effective way of having grievances heard in the white community. With the exception of one weekly newspaper, all communications media were white owned and white staffed. Communications with city officials, in conferences and working sessions, were said to be sporadic and infrequent. A community spokesman accused police and city officials of deliberately trying to arrest key black leaders on framed charges. (This spokesman was arrested during the disturbance and then released on bond, allegedly for carrying concealed weapons.)

A moderate black spokesman who ran unsuccessfully for the Omaha city council in 1965 and 1969, told a reporter that bitterness toward the police was spreading in the ghetto community. A black grocer told how the police had once arrested his teen-age son for a minor infraction that the youth had not committed. Eventually the boy was cleared in court but only at great cost to the father. "And that's how it is here . . . like a continuing war," he said.[1]

In interviews with the police chief, the mayor, the assistant county attorney, and black spokesmen, I learned that the police had killed four black youths within a period of 18 months before the June 1969 incident. In each case, the policemen involved were able to claim successfully that a felony had been or was about to be committed, and in each case the county attorney ruled justifiable homicide. These killings and other incidents of prejudicial police behavior in the Omaha ghetto community had fed a hostile belief system among blacks that created an atmosphere ripe for riot.

Until Vivian Strong was killed, Omaha authorities had been able to defend police killings and complaints about police behavior in the black community. However, at the time no city or county official claimed justifiable homicide in the case of Vivian Strong, for there was no evidence or indications of the dead girl's involvement in a felony. She just happened to be present when police officers arrived to investigate a complaint from a housing development manager that a group of teen-agers were using a vacant apartment for partying. When the two policemen arrived, the teen-agers had fled the apartment. The teen-agers who were at the scene, except for Vivian Strong, were standing around watching the developing action. Vivian Strong ran, but neither the policemen nor bystanders saw her leave the apartment. Indeed, there is no evidence at all that she had been in the apartment. As she ran, one of the policemen fired a shot which struck the girl in the back of the head, killing her instantly.

On the following day the officer was arraigned, charged with manslaughter, and released on a $500 bond, one-half the amount that had been suggested by the county attorney. The presiding judge in the public arraignment praised the officer for his past service. (The officer had served on the force for two years prior to the incident.) The charge of manslaughter, the amount of the bail bond, and the judge's sympathetic comments to the accused officer impelled leaders in the black community to call a mass meeting that same evening in a local park. Community leaders who had been in discussions that day with the mayor and the county attorney's staff urged the crowd (estimated at 1000 persons) to protest the killing of Vivian Strong and the action of the arraigning judge. They did not suggest violent action, according to police observers.

Near the end of the mass meeting small groups of youths began rampaging through nearby streets breaking windows and tossing fire bombs into stores, although no one could trace a direct connection between the mass meeting and the start of the rioting. Disorders were spasmodic and scattered on three successive nights. The targets were almost exclusively white business establishments, several of which were destroyed totally. City police were out in full force in continuous efforts to deal directly with breaking and burning incidents as they occurred. The National Guard was alerted, but no major siege strategies were applied.

Ironically, the quick action to arraign the officer who killed Vivian Strong prevented detailed coverage of the precipitating incident. Thus, few people in the white community were informed of the circumstances surrounding the girl's death. Most whites heard that the incident had involved an attempted burglary by teen-agers, that one youth had been arrested and another had been shot trying to escape. This misunderstanding may have accounted for strong reactions among whites against the manslaughter charge. The mayor received many provocative calls protesting the charge against the officer and his suspension from duty. A few months after the event, the police officer charged with Vivian Strong's death was acquitted.

The Omaha case is a classic illustration of the noncommunication, misunderstanding, bitterness, and tension which have characterized the relations between the black and white communities in American cities in the period preceding a riot. Actually, efforts had been made in Omaha at communication and understanding by representatives of both communities. A police community-relations office was established to take complaints in the community about police behavior. There were other efforts too. The mayor and the county attorney were accessible to black leaders. Once the precipitating incident occurred, officials immediately made plain their recognition that a wrong had been done. Once the rioting started, police officials invoked a "no shooting" policy. (There were a few shots fired during the riot but no casualties.) More than 80 persons were arrested; but the county attorney's office screened arrestees and charged only 23 of them. All of those were released on $500 bonds or on their own signatures. These actions by the county attorney were designed to minimize the appearance of a repressive response and to communicate this policy to the black community. Unfortunately, the arrest of a militant leader and a colleague discredited this policy in the eyes of other angry militants.

The black community had made similar efforts to develop effective communication with city and county officials. Ghetto leaders had had repeated informal conferences with officials about a variety of grievances, including specific complaints about the police, the schools, employment discrimination, community improvement, and other matters. The mass meeting preceding the June riot was an attempt to demonstrate the black community's reaction to the Vivian Strong killing. The riot itself was a message of admonition to white businessmen in the ghetto community and to the white community at large; but militant spokesmen expressed the view that rioters struck at white property within the black community only because they did not want to risk leaving the relative protection of the ghetto.

For all the efforts at communication, the white and black communities of Omaha were more polarized than ever when the riot subsided. Resentments hardened into hatreds. What blacks believed about whites became fearful reality, and what whites believed about blacks seemed abundantly confirmed. In such a situation, the role of the communications media is crucially important.

To get the facts in a period of intense community conflict is extremely difficult if reporters have had no experience with ghetto and street leaders. Black people naturally resent getting attention only when trouble breaks out, for they are then made to appear violent. Policy guidelines for the media should emphasize reporting during quiet periods—on value conflicts, on hostile beliefs, and especially on day-to-day events in the black community. Other ethnic groups in the United States are regularly mentioned in the media. Much is made of their religious holidays, appointments to positions of prominence, and cultural affairs in general. Until recently, in fact until the riots of the 1964–1968 period, blacks got no such treatment or they received only token attention.

Since a riot is a dynamic process, it goes through different phases of development. Given the preconditions described earlier—a value conflict intensifies short of a settlement; hostile beliefs flourish; an incident occurs which exemplifies them; communications between the adversaries are inadequate; and rumors drive feelings of resentment to a fever pitch—the process will get started. How far it will go depends upon the success or failure of a further process of interaction between the local authorities and the aroused community.[2]

There are four stages in the full-scale riot: (1) the precipitating incident; (2) the confrontation; (3) the "Roman holiday"; and (4) the siege or war. Few local riots go through all four stages; most do not reach Stage 3. Moreover, it is by no means certain at what point in a disturbance the term "riot" appropriately describes the event.

Stage 1: The precipitating incident. All riots begin with a precipitating incident, usually a gesture or act by a member or agent of the dominant community which the aggrieved community sees as concrete evidence of the injustice or deprivation that is the substance of their hostility or rage. The incident is inflammatory if it typifies the adversary's behavior toward the aggrieved and symbolizes the conditions suffered by the aggrieved. The incident becomes an excuse for striking back with "justified" violence in behavior akin to rage.

The event may be distorted by rumor and made to seem more inflammatory than it actually is. In communities where the level of grievance is high, a seemingly minor incident may set off a riot; conversely, where grievance levels are low, a more dramatic event may be required to touch off a disturbance.

A significant aspect of the precipitating event, besides its inflammatory nature, is the fact that it draws together large numbers of people. Some persons come out of curiosity; others, because they have heard rumors about the precipitating event; and still others, because they happen to be in the vicinity. Some of the converging crowd are instigators or agitators who attempt to get a riot started; others come to exploit the ensuing chaos and use the crowd as a cover for criminal activities. Local officials, civic leaders, and community organizers from church and social service agencies come because they feel a duty to try to control the violent outburst.

Stage 2: The confrontation. Following the instigating incident, the local population swarms to the scene. A process of "keynoting" takes place. Potential riot promoters begin to articulate the rage accumulating in the crowd, and they vie with each other in suggesting violent courses of action. Recognized community leaders suggest that the crowd disband to let tempers cool and allow time for a more considered course of action. Law-enforcement officers appear and try to disrupt the keynoting process by ordering and forcing the crowd to disperse. Often the behavior of the police at this critical stage serves to elevate one or another of the hostile keynoters to a position of dominance, thus flipping the riot process into the next phase.

The outcome of the confrontation is of crucial importance in the development of a full-blown disturbance. The temper of the crowd may dissipate or escalate explosively. The response of civil authorities may tip the scales in either direction. If representatives of local authority appear, listen with sympathy to complaints, and suggest some immediate and practical methods for dealing with them, the agitators lose ground and the fury of the crowd tends to subside. A "wait and see" attitude takes over. If local authorities fail to show up and are represented only by the police, the level of agitation tends to rise, especially if the police use indiscriminately harsh or brutal measures to disperse and subdue the crowd.

How the news media handle the confrontation has a direct and critical effect on the course of a riot. During the sensationalizing era of earlier years in the United States, almost any street confrontation was likely to be reported as a "riot." In the policy of "restraint" adopted by many big city news media during the riots of the 1960's, a street confrontation was sometimes not reported at all. Indeed, some news media blacked out coverage of local race-related disturbances. For a time, these news media gave minimum local coverage to serious disturbances in other cities.

Neither policy is appropriate. Instead of the extremes of sensationalism or blackout, a policy of adequate communications is required. The grievances stemming from the precipitating incident and crowd agitation should be identified. The response of local authorities should be described. The adversary relations and their possible resolutions, violent or nonviolent, should be laid out insofar as is possible.

Stage 3: "Roman holiday." If hostile keynoting reaches a sufficient crescendo in urban ghetto riots, a quantum jump in the disturbance process occurs and the threshold of Stage 3 is crossed. Usually the crowd leaves the scene of the street confrontation, and groups of rioters reassemble elsewhere. Older persons drop out for the time being, and young people take over the action; displaying an angry intoxication indistinguishable from glee, they may hurl rocks, bricks, and bottles at white-owned stores and at cars containing whites or police, wildly cheering every "hit." They taunt law-enforcement officers, risk capture, and generally act out routine scenarios featuring the sortie, the ambush, and the escape—the classic triad of violent action they have seen whites go through endlessly on television.

They set the stage for looting but at this stage are too involved in the "chase" and too excited for systematic plunder. That action comes later in Stage 3 when first younger, then older adults, caught up in a "Roman holiday" atmosphere and angered by tales of police brutality toward the youngsters, join in a spirit of righting ancient wrongs.

Stage 3 has a game structure. It is like a sport somehow gone astray but still subject to correction. Partly this openness derives from the "king-for-a-day" carnival climate. Partly it is based on the intense ambivalence of black people toward the white-dominated system and its symbolic representatives: its hated stores and their beloved contents, its despised police and their admired weaponry, its unregenerate bigots and its exemplary civil rights advocates. Because of the ambivalence, motive and action are unstable. Middle-class or upward-mobile blacks can become militant overnight. In some cities gripped in riot during the 1960's, youths on the rampage one day put on white hats (or red vests) and armbands to "cool the neighborhood" the next. Because of the ambivalence felt by blacks, not only toward whites but toward violence itself, few Stage 3 disturbances in the 1960's passed over into Stage 4.

Stage 4: War. If a city's value conflict continues to be expressed by admonishment from local authorities and violent suppression of the "Roman holiday" behavior in the ghetto, the riot process may develop into a state of war employing fire bombs, selected targets, harassing tactics, and sniping. The adversary relations between ghetto dwellers and civil authorities have often reached such a degree of polarization that no direct communications of any effective kind could be established. In this situation, communications, such as they are, consist of symbolic, warlike acts: state and federal troops are summoned; a curfew is declared; the ghetto community is subjected to a state of siege. Citizens can no longer move freely into and out of their neighborhoods. Forces within the ghetto, now increasingly composed of adults, throw fire bombs into white establishments, disrupt fire fighters, overturn and burn automobiles of whites caught in the area. Snipers attack invading paramilitary forces. Once Stage 4 is reached, the rioting runs its course like a Greek tragedy until both sides tire of the conflict and devastation.

Studies of past and contemporary riots show that the collective hostility of a community breaks out as a result of inattention by community leaders to value conflicts and as a result of failures in social control. The failures of social control are of two sorts: undercontrol and overcontrol.

The condition of undercontrol exists when the normal forces for social control in the community are ineffective or inactive. These forces include law-enforcement personnel, the family structure, and both formal and informal community-neighborhood leaders. Although a condition of undercontrol may occur in various ways, the effect is always the same. The dissident groups, noting the weakness of authorities or the ambivalence of leaders within the aggrieved community, seize the opportunity of a spontaneous precipitating incident to express hostility and anger. Inactivity of law-enforcement personnel functions as a further stimulation for the aggrieved to act out long-suppressed feelings, free of the social or legal consequences of unlawful behavior.

In some situations—for example in the 1967 Detroit riot—undercontrol during early Stage 3 produced a rapid spread of looting and was then suddenly replaced with overcontrol, which frequently produces brutal acts of suppression. One cannot expect police officers to be ordered to stand by while looting is going on and then act with restraint when they are turned loose to put a stop to it.

In other communities overcontrol is instituted early during Stage 2. Local and state police are rushed to the scene of the confrontation and begin to manhandle everyone in sight. Since such action at this stage is out of proportion to the event, it can generate an intense reaction. If overcontrol is sufficiently repressive, as in the 1967 Milwaukee disturbance (where a 24-hour curfew was ordered early in Stage 3 and the National Guard summoned to occupy and seal off the ghetto community), the eruption is quieted. In Milwaukee the black community was placed under a state of siege as the "Roman holiday" behavior was beginning to spread in the community. No catharsis occurred, and there was no improvement in communications between city hall and the black community.

The consequences of such repression are hard to discern. Short of the use of sustained and overwhelming force (which is the principal characteristic of a police state), overcontrol usually leads to increased frustration and conflict. People in the ghetto see the police as violent and strike back with increasing intensity which leads eventually to insurrectionist activities. Studies conducted at the Lemberg Center for the Study of Violence at Brandeis University in the 1960's showed that in a majority of cases police violence toward ghetto residents preceded violence by ghetto residents, although police and news media accounts of events have often made it seem the opposite.

An adequate law-enforcement response requires an effective but nonprovocative police presence when illegal activities, such as looting, take place. Arrests can and should be made, without brutality. It is not necessary that all offenders be caught and arrested to show that authorities intend to maintain order. Crowds can be broken up or contained through a variety of techniques not based on clubbing or shooting.

The avoidance of both undercontrol and overcontrol is a matter of appropriate police training. The results of such training were demonstrated in the deliberate policies of firmness and restraint adopted by police in several cities (notably Pittsburgh and New York) in response to the disturbances following the assassination of Dr. Martin Luther King, Jr., in April 1968.

Several conclusions may be drawn from studying the interaction between rioters and social control agencies: (1) the presence of the police tends to create an event, provide a focal point, and draw people together for easy rumor transmittal; (2) the result of too few police is likely to be uncontrolled deviant behavior; (3) a legitimate police activity (from the standpoint of riot participants) will not escalate the event, but even if the original police activity is seen as legitimate, policemen observed being rude, unfair, or brutal at the scene may touch off a riot; (4) in some situations success of a police withdrawal during a riot depends upon officials contacting recognized community leaders and allowing them to exert social control; (5) when officials do not know community leaders (or no effective ones are available), withdrawal of law-enforcement personnel is a mistake for it allows the instigators and exploiters to create or continue the riot; and (6) the presence of police who do not exert control encourages the acceptance of deviant behavior as normal. In the Newark riot of 1967, scores of ordinarily law-abiding citizens in the black community were observed participating in looting during a period when law-enforcement personnel had reduced their control to containment of riot action to the devastated area.

Further, the sooner help comes from outside control agencies, the sooner the riot stops. And the sooner the dominant community seeks out recognized ghetto leaders and moves to satisfy their grievances, the sooner the riot stops. The sooner the audience ceases watching the riot activity, the sooner the disturbance simmers down. The greater the degree of normality maintained in the daily routine of the community during the disturbance, the more likely it is that the riot will be limited or cease.

What is the responsibility of the press and other media toward deficiencies in social control? At minimum, they should function to seek out and report the truth, to recognize the public's right to know how civil authorities are functioning. It is not necessary to defend or to attack but simply "to tell it as it is," so that behavior can be corrected if in error or reinforced if appropriate. Reporters must dig for hard-to-get facts, penetrate political defensiveness and evasiveness of special interest groups, and capture the missing information to explain what is taking place and overcome the "Rashomon effect."[3]

The public media are, of course, part of the apparatus of social control in the community; therefore it is extremely important that they establish guidelines that will help avoid oscillation between overcontrol and undercontrol. Rumors of impending disorder should never be published for their own sake in the style of playing for the sensational story. If treated as a prediction, a rumor serves only to arouse useless anxiety in the public mind. If dealt with at all, rumors should be used to document unrest and grievance levels in the ghetto.

Radical leaders should not be given a public forum simply because they make good headlines (again the sensational). The spotlight on such spokesmen gives them an unrealistic sense of power far beyond their actual influence in the community and presents a fear-inducing threat in the larger community. Fear produces overreaction and plays into the hands of the backlash element.

The events of the different riot phases are too chaotic to be covered and digested by a few reporters acting alone. Reporters should function in intermedia teams, with two-way radios to communicate with each other and to listen in on police broadcasts. News media ordinarily in competition should combine resources in a prearranged pooling operation to secure maximum coverage of the riot process without influencing the course of events by their presence.

In formulating editorial policy, the criteria should be completeness, truth, and fairness to all sides of the conflict. There should be no concern about the contagion effect under these terms. After all, news of a riot will spread as quickly, or nearly so, by word of mouth as by any other means. A serious problem associated with the role of the news media in reporting on civil disturbances is the matter of emphasis: the action versus the issues. News reporting that focuses on the issues can play a very constructive role in controlling the spread of destructive action. Conversely, reporting that focuses primarily on the action of a disturbance can obscure the grievance issues and leave the public with the impression of chaos and unjustified violence. If the underlying issues become obscured in the heat of an escalated protest or violent outburst, the distorted perspective almost always serves the interest of recalcitrant authorities who can then condemn the protesters for "inappropriate (or criminal) behavior."

Inadvertently, news media are often the most effective instruments for those who would deflect attention away from the real issues. Reporters, trained to the "deadline," tend to emphasize the action and the salable headline. Keeping the real issues in the forefront is difficult even when the conscientious reporter deliberately and carefully spells them out in his story. Of course, reporters and editors are only too well aware that the reading public prefers the action story and tends to skip over substantive analysis. Often, another reason the news media underplay issues is that some media corporations are in sympathy with those institutional and governmental authorities under attack. The proper responsibility of the media is to search through the complexities of the issues and without oversimplification translate them compellingly and as objectively as possible to an often ignorant and evasive public.

NOTES

1. Guy Halverson, *Christian Science Monitor* (Boston) , July 5, 1969, p. 12.
2. The following description is based on concepts developed by Dr. John P. Spiegel, director of the Lemberg Center for the Study of Violence at Brandeis University.
3. This term derives from Garson Kanin's play *Rashomon*, based on a classic Japanese legend in which an event is recounted differently by each participant.

ARTICLE 28

The Police and Their Problems

David P. Stang

In society's day-to-day efforts to protect its citizens from the suffering, fear, and property loss produced by crime and the threat of crime, the policeman occupies the front line. It is he who directly confronts criminal situations, and it is to him that the public looks for personal safety. The freedom of Americans to walk their streets and be secure in their homes—in fact, to do what they want when they want—depends to a great extent on their policemen.[1]

There is little question that during the past decade of turbulent social change, our nation's policemen have not been able to escape from the front lines. More than that, they are called upon to fight against one side one day and then for it the next day. The same policeman who on a Wednesday is mobilized to help control a blazing ghetto riot and arrest throngs of looters may by week's end find himself assigned to keep traffic clear from the parade route being followed by hundreds of blacks conducting an anti-poverty march.

Reprinted from David P. Stang, "The Police and Their Problems," in *Law and Order Reconsidered*, co-directors James S. Campbell, Joseph R. Sahid, and David P. Stang. Vol. 10, National Commission on the Causes and Prevention of Violence Staff Study Series. Washington, D.C.: U.S. Government Printing Office, 1969. Pp. 285–308.

In fact, the very same policeman may on a Saturday rescue a hippie college student victimized by a gang of motorcyclists, and by the next Monday be summoned to the campus to assist university officials in re-capturing a building held by stone-throwing, epithet-screaming student dissidents. The same policeman in the morning may be called "soft and ineffective" by our "forgotten man" and "fascist pig" by a young revolutionary in the afternoon. How our nation's police are able to fulfill such drastically conflicting roles without lapsing into an anomic stupor[2] is perhaps the best measure of the degree to which the policeman is in fact a professional.

What is the policeman's job? Who and what is he supposed to protect? How can he most effectively execute his responsibilities? What are his problems and how can these problems be solved? These are the questions we address in this chapter.

DUTIES OF THE POLICE

Police responsibilities fall into three broad categories.[3] First, they are called upon to "keep the peace." This peacekeeping duty is a broad and most important mandate which involves the protection of lives and rights ranging from handling street corner brawls to the settlement of violent family disputes. In a word, it means maintaining public safety.

Secondly, the police have a duty to provide services which range from bestowing menial courtesies to the protection of public and private property. This responsibility is the one that many police officers complain about the most but, nevertheless, are called upon to perform the most frequently. In fulfilling these obligations, a policeman "recovers stolen property, directs traffic, provides emergency medical aid, gets cats out of trees, checks on the homes of families on vacation, and helps little old ladies who have locked themselves out of their apartments."[4]

The third major police responsibility, which many policemen and a considerable segment of the public feel should be the exclusive police responsibility, is that of combating crime by enforcing the rule of law. Execution of this task involves what is called police operations and this ranges from preparing stakeouts to arresting suspects.

That policemen have difficulty assigning priorities to these some-times conflicting responsibilities is one major operating limitation the police have recently had to endure.[5] There are, however, other important limitations imposed on the police to which we shall briefly refer before returning to the crucial subject of conflicting police roles.

Among these, special attention must be given to manpower deficiencies, inadequate financing, and frictions with courts and other governmental agencies.

MANPOWER LIMITATIONS

According to the President's Crime Commission, there are approxi-mately 420,000 policemen in the United States today.[6] Yet most police departments are under-manned, thus spreading the existing complement of police personnel much too thin. This manpower sup-ply has been further depleted by more generous holiday, vacation and sick-leave policies, reduced weekly work-hours, increased speciali-zation, continued use of police personnel to perform a heavier burden of clerical, technical and service activities more suitable for civilian employees.[7] The manpower problem is further exacerbated by diffi-culties in recruiting, especially recruitment among minority groups; resignations of experienced police officers; early retirements; overly rigid restrictions on manpower distribution and assignment; and the dissipation of police-man-hours in nonproductive or minimally pro-ductive activity. This latter category involves, in part, hours spent waiting to be called as a witness, writing out multiple copies of reports, assignment to fixed posts of questionable utility, being forced to provide special escort services, and other irritating and time consuming chores. Nor is the available manpower scientifically allo-cated either in terms of ratios of police to population (which range from fewer than 1:1000 to more than 4:1000) or in terms of crime incidence, traffic volume, calls for police services or other meaningful indices of demands for more effective policing.

This inadequacy is magnified by reports that newly recruited officers are less well-educated than veteran officers,[8] that they are being assigned to full police patrol duty without completing the pre-scribed training;[9] that morale is low and supervision lax;[10] and that advanced in-service and refresher training to keep them abreast of legal, social, and technological changes is inadequate.[11]

FINANCIAL LIMITATIONS

In 1968, in the most affluent nation in world history, our total expenditures for police (Federal, state, and local, including sheriffs and such *ad hoc* police agencies as the New York City Transit Police, Port of New York Authority Police, park police, Capitol Police, and other full-time enforcement personnel) approximated $3 billion. Most commentators consider this amount inadequate in light of current recruitment problems, resignations, early retirement difficulties, and widespread police "moonlighting" with its negative effects on police alertness and departmental sick-leave rates.

Inadequate police budgets, too, have made it difficult or impossible in many jurisdictions to construct needed modern headquarters facilities, to provide decentralized substations in areas of demonstrated need, to modernize communications systems, to install improved traffic control devices, to acquire computers and other advanced management and operations control "hardware," to finance pilot projects and demonstrations and to recruit at highly-paid specialist levels the qualified personnel, all of which are essential to the implementation of the recommendations of the President's Commission on Law Enforcement and Administration of Justice and of the National Advisory Commission on Civil Disorders.

Police costs in the United States have been traditionally a local burden . . . a burden which many local jurisdictions are no longer able to support if fully effective law enforcement is to be achieved. Certainly the funds now being provided by Congress through the Law Enforcement Assistance Administration of the Department of Justice to support police planning, training, and research will prove of some assistance in easing the budgetary limitations under which many law enforcement units are presently operating.

POLICE CONFLICTS WITH OTHER
CRIMINAL JUSTICE AGENCIES

The police establishment is only one of the agencies constituting the criminal justice system. By the very nature of the criminal justice system, the police are required to cooperate with the other agencies, including the prosecutors, the courts, the jails and correctional institutions. In many locations, however, there is neither formal nor informal machinery for cross-professional dialogue between the police and the representatives of the other agencies involved in criminal justice administration or policy-making, so that minor irritations and misunderstandings often cumulate into major bureaucratic conflicts. The failure to involve the courts, prosecutors, and corrections officials in the training of police, the failure to involve police in the orientation of newly-chosen judges and prosecutors and in the training curricula for newly appointed probation and parole officers, and the even more general failure to consult police in the planning stages of executive and legislative decision-making in areas which may directly or indirectly affect their responsibilities or operations—all further compound this already difficult situation.

In recent years the courts in particular have become more and more the target of severe police criticism. Police problems involving the courts arise at three levels: (1) Procedural requirements which result in the loss of many hundreds of thousands of police man-hours annually because of inefficient or uncooperative court administration and resistance to changes in traditional practices (*e.g.*, central booking, computerized dockets, the impanelling of additional grand juries, and such apparently simple courtesies as moving cases involving police witnesses to the top of the calendar or the taking of police testimony in pre-trial proceedings);[12] (2) allegedly improper dispositions of cases both at preliminary hearings and arraignments and after trial (*e.g.*, dismissal of charges and release of persons arrested for serious crimes, speedy setting of low bail or release on personal recognizance of offenders police believe dangerous and likely to commit additional crimes or granting probation to dangerous and persistent offenders where probation supervision is inadequate); and (3) constitutional limitations on police tactics and procedures both in general law enforcement and specifically in the area of criminal investigation (e.g., the decisions of the Supreme Court which have forced the police to be more careful in the conduct of searches and seizures, and in warning suspects of their constitutional rights against compulsory self-incrimination).

The question of court-imposed constitutional limitations on police practices is especially sensitive. Whether these restrictions on traditional police practices have actually reduced police effectiveness is a matter of some controversy even among police and prosecutors; but a significant consensus among police officers of all ranks in every part of the country interprets these decisions as favoring the criminal and as deliberately and perversely hampering, indeed punishing, the police.

One police spokesman has stated:

> It would appear that the primary purpose of the police establishment has been overlooked in the tendency of our courts and the other officers of the judicial process to free the most heinous of criminals because of legalistic errors by law enforcement officers. . . . To allow criminals to go free because of legalistic error turns our judicial process into a game and makes mockery of our supposedly sophisticated society. . . . From the police standpoint, one of the very real dangers is that decisions from the courts are breeding indecision and uncertainty in the individual police officer. The inevitable result is that the policeman's duty has become so diffused that it is difficult for him to carry out his responsibilities.[13]

Another observer stated even more dramatically that, "The Courts must not terrorize peace officers by putting them in fear of violating the law themselves."[14] Views of this kind are set forth repeatedly in articles and comments in such respected police professional periodicals as *The Police Chief, Law and Order* and *Police*.[15]

Police in general also have little confidence in the ability of jails and prisons to reform or rehabilitate convicted offenders. This is not surprising, of course, for this view is shared, if perhaps for different reasons, by the great majority of American criminologists and even by residents of our so-called "correctional system." This lack of confidence in institutional rehabilitation programs underlies the strong police opposition to the parole system and the somewhat less aggressive opposition to work release, school release, and prisoner furlough programs, open institutions, and halfway houses. There is a rather generalized feeling among large segments of the police that potentially dangerous offenders are released far too often on low bail, or their own recognizance or following conviction far too soon by parole boards; that these paroled offenders are frequently inadequately supervised by unqualified parole officers with excessive case-load responsibilities; and that they commit new and serious crimes thus adding additional burdens of investigation and apprehension to already overburdened police agencies.

Police in some jurisdictions have encountered difficulties in their relationships with the executive and legislative branches of government. These difficulties range from the irritation of requests for special treatment for favored traffic offenders and detail of police personnel to jobs as chauffeur and doorman in the Mayor's office to outside interference in internal personnel matters such as assignments and promotions and in general policy matters such as enforcement strategies and operational tactics.

Legislatures too have been criticized by police for failure to appropriate sufficient funds to provide adequate law enforcement for repeated investigations and inquiries which contribute to a negative police image; for penal law and criminal procedure changes which reduce penalties, make parole easier, or impose new restrictions on police efforts; and for failure to protect the police from changes in their working conditions which police feel deleterious to their welfare.[16]

POLICE ROLE CONFLICTS

As we stated earlier, perhaps the most important source of police frustration, and the most severe limitation under which they operate, is the conflicting roles and demands involved in the order maintenance, community service, and crime-fighting responsibilities of the police. Here both the individual police officer and the police community as a whole find not only inconsistent public expectations and public reactions, but also inner conflict growing out of the interaction of the policeman's values, customs, and traditions with his intimate experience with the criminal element of the population. The policeman lives on the grinding edge of social conflict, without a well-defined, well-understood notion of what he is supposed to be doing there.

Police involvement in order maintenance situations such as family disputes, tavern brawls, disorderly teenagers loitering in the streets, quarrels between neighbors, and the like inevitably produces role conflict. One party is likely to feel harassed, outraged or neglected. The police officer quite frequently has no clear legal standard to apply—or one that, if applied, would produce an obviously unjust result.[17] The victim is often as blameworthy as the perpetrator, often the parties really want him only to "do something" that will "settle things" rather than make an arrest. Should an arrest be demanded, he is in many jurisdictions foreclosed from complying since the misdemeanor complained of was not committed in his presence, and the vociferously complaining victim or witness is unwilling to sign a complaint.[18] Thus, he must devise a solution based almost entirely on his own discretion and judgement.[19]

Oftentimes the policeman is forced to arrest persons for violations of laws he does not believe are fair. But more often, he sees the fear and the pain and the damage that crime causes, and he feels that criminals are getting away with too much. This frustration mounts each time he arrives at the scene of a recently-reported crime to discover the offender has escaped. He finds justification for his contempt for the "criminal element" when he reads of public approval of night-stick justice techniques.[20]

Police in the United States are for the most part white, upwardly mobile lower middle-class, conservative in ideology and resistant to change. In most areas of the country, even where segregation has been legally eliminated for long periods, they are likely to have grown up without any significant contact with minority and lower socioeconomic class life styles—and certainly with little or no experience of the realities of ghetto life. They tend to share the attitudes, biases and prejudices of the larger community, among which is likely to be a fear and distrust of Negroes and other minority groups.

Appointed to the police force and brought into day-to-day contact with what is to him an alien way of life, the young police officer experiences what behavioral scientists refer to as "cultural shock." His latent negative attitudes are reinforced by the aggressive and militant hostility which greets him even when he is attempting to perform, to the best of his ability, a community service or order maintenance function, or is attempting to apprehend a criminal whose victim has been a member of the minority community.

Negative responses to minorities and to non-conforming groups such as "hippies," campus militants, antiwar demonstrators, and the new breed of "revolutionaries," are also reinforced by the socialization process which transforms the new recruit into a member of the police community. Not only during the formal training process but in the everyday contacts with his fellow officers and his participation with them in both on-duty activity and off-duty socializing tend to mutually reinforce the police ideology, the closed-ranks defensiveness, which separates "we" who are on the side of law, order, morality and right from "they" who are immoral, criminal, delinquent, idle, lazy, dirty, shiftless or different.

Efforts to bridge the gap between the police and some segments of the community have proved only minimally successful.[21] The realities of police confrontation with these "undesirable elements," whether on occasions of episodic violence or, more importantly, when a police officer is killed or seriously injured as a result of minority group militance, tend to offset the gains made by efforts directed toward improving police attitudes and police-community relationships.

POLICE INEFFECTIVENESS

The cumulative result of the many limitations and frustrations described above is an evident inability of the police, as presently organized, manned, financed, equipped and led, to meet effectively all of the demands and expectations placed on them by the public. These inadequacies are evidenced in their inability to prevent crime, their declining record in solving crimes known to them; their sluggish response to and indifferent investigation of all but major crimes or those involving important persons, businesses, or institutions.[22] Particularly evident is an inability to deal effectively with crime in minority-populated ghettoes—for reasons which involve minority group attitudes and noncooperation as importantly as police attitudes, facilities and efficiency.

Various analyses of police confrontations with minority and protest groups have identified 'over-response,' inadequate crowd control training, poor planning, failures in supervision and leadership, as well as the residual hostility of the police to the minorities and nonconformists involved, their suspicion of dissent, and their disagreement with the demonstrators on the substantive issues as causative factors.[23] Nor have these analyses neglected to underline the difficult conditions to which the police have been subjected: the provocations, verbal and physical, to which they were subjected by participants in demonstrations;[24] and at least in some instances the distorted or at least unbalanced coverage by news media.[25] That at least some participants in many of these conflict episodes wanted to provoke a police over-response may be true—but that individual police officers, and sometimes apparently whole police units, cooperated enthusiastically with their plans is equally obvious.[26]

That the police and major elements of the public are becoming more polarized is well established.[27] This polarization is intensified by police frustrations growing out of what they perceive as the public's unreasonable expectations of them and even more unreasonable limitations imposed on them, the growing militancy of minority and dissident groups, their strategy of confrontation, and the vicious cycle of police overresponse. These factors often are aggravated by new and highly publicized charges of police brutality and derogatory attitudes toward minority groups, which attract new sympathizers from previously moderate or non-activist segments of the population and often tend to encourage reactive ghetto counter-violence.

POLICE POLITICIZATION

Recently, the police have begun to realize that acting exclusively as individuals in attempting to deal with their role, conflicts, frustrations and limitations has failed to pay dividends. Thus, as is the case with other newly self-aware special interest groups in our society, the police have begun to enter active politics on a much larger scale.

Police participation in the political process in America has traditionally been limited and local: limited to securing favorable legislation as to pensions, working conditions and pay rates,[28] with occasional lobbying for or against proposals to abolish the death penalty, legalize gambling, or raise the age of juvenile court jurisdiction —and local in the sense that it invariably involved approaches by the locally organized police to municipal authorities or at most to the state legislator representing the district. Occasionally charges would be made of more active police involvement in local campaigns, but there was a consensus even among the police that they, like the military, should abstain from active, overt participation in politics. Various police departments incorporated in their police regulations stringent rules prohibiting political activity other than voting.

In the past decade, largely as a result of efforts to raise police pay scales to a parity with those of skilled workmen, more militant police associations—some trade-union affiliated, others in loose state and national affiliations—escalated their pressure tactics so that job action, "blue-flu," and even threatened police strikes became common-place in police-municipality salary disputes.[29]

The major impetus to police politicization, however, was without doubt the attempt to impose a civilian review apparatus to adjudicate complaints against police officers by aggrieved citizens and attempts of citizen groups to restrict police use of firearms.[30] The proposals for civilian review boards were fought in the communications media, in the courts, in the legislature, and finally in a popular referendum in New York City in which the police won a resounding victory after a campaign which did much to further polarize the dissident minorities.[31] The victory[32] convinced many in the police community of the desirability of abandoning the internecine battles which had divided them and reduced their political effectiveness in the past.

The future of expanded police participation in politics is not entirely clear at present. Certainly there has been important police support for conservative, even radical right, candidates in recent national and local elections, and there are signs that police officials are finding increasing opportunities as successful political candidates.

But the police have not had an unbroken record of political successes. In the 1969 legislative session in Albany, a bill abolishing the fifty-eight year old three-platoon system passed by a near unanimous vote, despite strong opposition by the united police pressure groups. Whether activities such as aroused police officers seeking the removal of a judge in Detroit, or an equally aggressive organization (the Law Enforcement group in New York City) seeking to monitor the conduct of judges and their case dispositions, will be widely and successfully imitated cannot be predicted at this time.[33]

What is clear, however, is that a politicized police force united and well financed and perhaps closely allied to conservative political and social forces in the community poses a problem for those interested in preserving internal democracy and insuring domestic tranquility. As the only lawfully armed force within the community, and possessed by the nature of their duties and responsibilities of unique authority and powers over their fellow citizens (including access to derogatory information, potential for discriminatory enforcement of the laws against their opponents, licensing and inspection functions), the united incursion of the police into active politics must be regarded with some trepidation.

More and more, the police community perceives itself as a minority group, disadvantaged and discriminated against, surrounded by, servicing, and protecting a public, which is at best apathetic or unaware of the frustrations and limitations imposed on the police; and at worst, unsympathetic or hostile. The dynamics of this self-perception, assuming a continuation or possible escalation of the external aggravants (verbal and physical abuse of the police; more stringent judicial and legislative restrictions; budgetary difficulties), involve reinforced defensive group solidarity, intensified feelings of alienation and polarization, and a magnified and increasingly aggressive militancy in reaction and response to those individuals, groups and institutions (social and governmental) perceived as inimical—an action-reaction pattern which, unfortunately, will inevitably be replicated within the aggrieved and dissident communities.

SOME SUGGESTED SOLUTIONS

There are two areas of police-public confrontations in which changes in police policy and practice can lead to a reduction of friction and restoration of public respect for the police which the police themselves feel to be so sorely lacking. The first involves highly visible police relationships with the public, often involving the combined presence of great numbers of police and the public at the same time and place. The second is the less visible contact of the police with the public and usually involves ordinary relationships between individual police officers and individual members of the public.

THE POLICE AND POLITICAL VIOLENCE

The police often believe that ideological and political conflicts like the Chicago convention demonstrations involve clashes between good, upright and honest groups of citizens on the one hand and bad, lawless and deceitful troublemakers on the other. In fact, however, these great struggles between large groups of the public more clearly involve political difference than they do questions of criminal behavior. Often the "good, upright and honest" citizens are better characterized simply as conservative elements of the population who are resisting the demands of other factions seeking social, political, or economic benefits at the direct expense of the conservative groups.

Unfortunately, these conflicts involving demonstrations, mass protests, and strikes by the dissidents often involve violence and the call-up of the police for front-line duty. The police, instead of taking a neutral position in attempting to restore order during these primarily political clashes, often tend to become participants in the clash on the side of the conservative elements and against the dissident elements.[34] The dissidents quickly recognize the active participation of the police in siding with the "enemy" and then begin to concentrate their attacks, both verbal and physical, more directly on the police than on the groups whose interests the police are supposedly protecting. The cycle becomes vicious and the ultimate loser is always the police.

This recurring phenomenon has been discussed quite extensively in the Task Force report on *Violence in America: Historical and Comparative Perspectives*. Thus, we refer only for example to the conservative-reformist clashes, entailing the victimization of the police, between management and labor of the 1930's; between the landowners and the migrant farm workers in California of the late 1930's and early 1940's; between the small town or rural white Southern population—and the civil rights workers and Southern blacks of the early 1960's; between the urban governments, employers, landlords, and business establishments—and the anti-poverty and black power advocates of the middle to late 1960's. On each of these battlefields some of the police have unnecessarily taken sides and have become the target of violence.

In *Rights In Concord*, this Task Force's investigative report on the Washington counter-inaugural demonstration, we have shown that when the police, through disciplined supervision, refrain from taking sides and steadfastly remain neutral in the face of a political demonstration that is perhaps distasteful to most of them personally, physical injuries and the destruction of property are minimized and the police emerge as widely respected umpires and peace-keepers. Thus, with respect to political differences between elements of the population in these socially troubled times, police leadership must decline invitations to take sides and to refrain from engaging in unnecessary fights. Only in this way can the police surely reemerge as the respected keepers of the peace—the principal duty of their worthy profession.[35]

THE PATROLMAN AND THE PEOPLE

The second area of police-public confrontation in which there has been a loss of respect for the police is the routine day-to-day encounters between individual police officers and members of minority groups. These encounters form the crux of what is commonly referred to as the "police-community relations problem." The problem manifests itself particularly in the inner city.

> The crowded center city is where crime rates are the highest, where the black minority has experienced the catharsis of bloody, blazing riots, and is now struggling to develop a new and proud identity. The people no longer doubt that they are entitled to be treated with respect and dignity, and often militantly demand it. They are aspiring for the social and material benefits that they have been so long without. Hopes are high, but the results have not yet begun to materialize substantially. Houses and apartments are still over-crowded, too cold in the winter, and unbearably hot in the summer. Homes still are often without fathers. Mothers still are searching for the where-withal to purchase the next meal. Children of all ages are out on the street and in the alleys.
>
> They see the very visible white man who, for years, has owned the corner grocery stores. He still tells them to get out if they are not going to buy anything. But he's scared of them now and they know it. So they goad him, throw his merchandise around and sometimes steal it if they think they can do so without getting caught. The grocer calls the police.
>
> The police arrive in a radio-dispatched squad car with red lights flashing. The young candy thieves have made a clean getaway. Their friends, however, are still on the street. The policemen talk with the grocer then return to the street to question the kids. The kids are amused and enjoy the excitement. "No," they did not see anybody leave the store. The policemen know otherwise and in frustration they ask, "What are you kids doing here?" "Nothing," is the answer. "Then you better move on or we're gonna lock you up," the kids are told. Reluctantly they make feeble efforts to obey. The police get back into their squad car and start to drive off. Ten seconds later they hear the kids' jeers and laughter.
>
> Night falls. More of the older kids are now seen on the street corners "shucking and jiving." Some bounce basketballs. Some listen to portable radios. Others dance or feign boxing matches.
>
> In the homes the fights begin. Sometimes it is between man and

woman; sometimes between teenage child and an aunt or grandmother. The police are called again. The people on the street watch as the squad car arrives. The police go inside; they hear shouting. The accusations begin. The police explain that in order for them to arrest anybody, the complainant is going to have to go down to the D.A.'s office and sign a complaint. "Just lock the 'so and so' up," is the response. The police do the best they can to quiet things down, then leave. Nobody is satisfied. As the squad car pulls away from the curb, the kids jeer again.

Later in the evening the same policemen see a loud street corner disturbance involving about a dozen young men. The policemen are now a little more weary. In another half hour their tour will be finished.

They get out of the car and ask, "What's going on?" Two of the young men continue to swing at one another. "Alright, break it up!", a policeman orders. One of the two stops swinging. The other, apparently intoxicated, continues to brawl. The policemen get gruff. "I said, 'knock it off'!," barks the policeman. The young fighter utters a profane epithet followed by, "Honky cop." More people gather around.

One of the policemen responds, "Buddy, you're coming down to the stationhouse. We're gonna lock you up." The policemen reach for his arms. He kicks, swings his fists, and continues to yell "Honky cop!" The two policemen slam him up against the squad car, handcuff him, pat him down and shove him into the back seat. The crowd is sullen. Fists are clenched and teeth are gritted. One of the policemen says, "Move on. We don't want any more trouble out of you people tonight." The policemen get back into the squad car and drive off. The still undispersed crowd mutters words of hatred.

These are ordinary events in the average day of a policeman assigned a squad car beat in the center city. There is no love lost between the police and the center city residents. The residents, whether they be black, Puerto Rican, Mexican, of any other minority group, or just plain hippies, see the police as bullies, unfair, stupid, rude, and brutal—a symbol of "Whitey's power." The police, in turn, see the minority groups as hostile, dirty, lazy, undisciplined, dishonest, immoral, and worst of all, disrespectful of the "badge" they try to represent.

> "In the old days," the police say, "colored people would move on if you told them to. Now they don't. They just give you a bunch of crap."

On a wooden fence in the center city there are new epigrams scrawled in crayon. They read "Black Power!," "Say it now and say it loud—I am black and I am proud!," "Kill a pig."

IMPROVING POLICE COMMUNITY RELATIONS

The police are, indeed, prejudiced against minorities. And the minority groups are equally prejudiced against the police. The prejudice on both sides is not without some foundation. The views of each side toward the other are constantly being reinforced and have become self-fulfilling prophesies. Doing something about this problem is what is called "improving police-community relations."

The need to improve police-community relations has existed and been recognized for decades. Local, state and federal commissions have written hundreds of pages about it. Police experts and academics have written books about it.[36] Public officials, including police chiefs, have made speeches about it. Civil rights leaders have conducted demonstrations concerning it. All agree that something should be done. Recommendations have been made by the score. The most frequently made suggestions—many of them worthwhile—include:

Extending human-relations training of recruits and officers;
Creating or enlarging police-community relations units within police departments;
Starting precinct and city-wide citizen advisory committees, including minority leaders, to meet with the police;
Developing programs to educate the public about the police, such as visits of school children to precinct stations, lectures by police officers to adults or youth groups, and school courses concerning police work;
Running recruitment campaigns aimed at members of minority groups.
Ending discrimination within police departments, such as that relating to promotions, and integration of patrols;
Issuing orders banning use of abusive words or excessive force by police officers; and
Developing procedures to handle citizen complaints within the police department which are fair and designed to impose real discipline.[37]

Other recommendations have included the suggestion that the police be disarmed or at least that each police department adopt a strict firearms use policy.[38] Some have suggested that the police discontinue wearing military-type uniforms and instead don more friendly working garb, such as blazers and slacks.[39] Still others have encouraged the adoption of psychological pre- and post-recruitment tests designed to identify for "weeding-out" purposes the bullies and misfits. More extreme suggestions have been made to the effect that all the "bully cops" be fired or retired and that college graduate, social science majors be hired to replace them. Some have suggested either neighborhood control of the police, or that neighborhoods desiring it police themselves and that regular policemen not be permitted to enter such areas.[40]

Although some of these ideas have been adopted by some police departments in whole, or in part, in even the most progressive police departments the problem of police-community relations remains a sore spot. The reason is that most of the efforts at improving police-community relations have been undertaken merely as "programs," minor changes in the police department's organizational structure, or as public relations efforts.

To produce effective results, efforts at improving police-community relations require modification of the underlying context of attitudes stemming from the everyday contacts between the policeman on the beat and the people he normally deals with. The individual patrolman must recognize that for some time to come he will be viewed by members of the center city community not as an individual but as an oppressive symbol of the dominant white society. Of course, no community believes that "all cops are bad," and when a police officer treats people with consistent fairness, he will tend to gain a reputation for being "a good cop." But the depth of hostility between the police and the ghetto resident means that the policeman will have to persist in his efforts to be "a good cop" without any significant rewards in terms of appreciation from the community he serves.

On the other hand, the inner-city community, and particularly its leaders, must recognize that policemen cannot be converted into social workers who operate on the assumption that felons are morally innocent products of a criminogenic environment. More importantly, members of the center city community must recognize not only the inevitability, but the desirability, of the policeman's primary identity as a member of the "thin blue line." A policeman's over identity with the community and a non-identity with "the force" tends to destroy a policeman's effectiveness both in the eyes of the community, and of his peers and superiors on the force. Just as members of the military think of themselves as "the military" as opposed to "the civilians," police officers, too, will continue to think of themselves primarily as policemen. Thus, instead of attempting to destroy this "we-they" identity it should, be capitalized upon and used to maximum advantage.

It is true that the "we-they" identity of the police has undesirable aspects to it, especially an apparent need to be tougher than "they." It is also true, however, that this toughness, or at least a confidence in a superior toughness, lies at the very foundation of a policeman's ability to arrest a violently resisting suspect who is 6 inches taller and 75 pounds heavier than he, or to calm an unruly group of aggressive teenagers. The problem is how to shape the "we-they" identity so that the end result will not lessen the policeman's ability to apprehend criminals and maintain order, yet at the same time not destroy the policeman's desire or ability to interact on a humane, civil basis with the community.

We do not accept the views of some critics that the problem is a dilemma, the solution to which is impossible without changing the very nature of the policeman's role. Scores of interviews with the police themselves have convinced us otherwise (although we do believe that the present service-providing function of the police can be shifted in part to civilians and citizen auxiliaries).

When we asked various policemen what they thought the main advantage was in being police officers as contrasted to most other occupations, most replied, first, that it was the superior ability to understand people and how they behave that was afforded them by constant exposure to all segments of the public. Secondly, the majority answered that it was the ability to "keep a cool head" under stress, danger, and provocation. A black policeman, asked why he decided to become a police officer, gave us this answer:

> Man, when I was a little kid I thought cops were God. I lived in the ghetto and I saw drunks, addicts, cuttings, shooting, and husbands hitting wives and kids fighting on street corners and other bad scenes everyday.
>
> Somebody always called the police. The police arrived in the middle of the hassle and were always cool and always got on top of the problem fast. If they could break it up by quiet mouthing it they would. If they had to bust somebody they did it quick and were gone.

477

> Whatever it was, they arrived on the scene, got with it fast, stopped the trouble and split—always with a cool head. I figured that was smooth and so I decided when I was a kid I wanted to be a policeman and do the same thing.[41]

Understanding and coolheadedness—these qualities represent the very essence of a "good cop." These are the traits most required by the patrolman in the performance of his peace-keeping function. If these two qualities can be developed in more of our policemen, it will do much to alleviate tensions between the police and the community.

The breeding ground of community resentment of the police is principally at the patrolman level, not at the command level. When patrolmen fail to show understanding, i.e., act insensitively, and fail to maintain coolheadedness, i.e., loose control and act intemperately, the community becomes incensed. The state of police-community relations is basically the result of everyday contacts of the community with the patrolmen, not the chiefs. The problem of police-community relations is thus one of ascertaining how to encourage understanding and discourage insensitivity in the patrolman, how to encourage cool-headedness and discourage losing control or "blowing one's cool."

The yardstick for testing the application of a mature, sensitive understanding and coolheadedness is often (once deciding that intervention is necessary)[42] how quickly and quietly a patrolman can restore calm without having to make an arrest. This is what 'good cops' are made of. This is what constitutes "good police work." This is what breeds community respect for the police.

One of the major problems with the present system of policing is that of convincing patrolmen that when they perform their *peace-keeping* duties well, they are rendering a service no less valuable to the community than when they perform their *law-enforcement* function. Presently the rewards to a patrolman who is an effective peace-keeper at best, are slight. His promotion in rank is seldom the result of a good record at peace-keeping. This situation should be changed and greater recognition accorded to the effective peace-keeper as well as to the effective crime-fighter. (Properly trained sergeants and lieutenants who demand compliance with departmental policy can also ensure remarkable results.)

As Professor Wilson has noted:

The central problem of the patrolman, and thus the police, is to maintain order and to reduce, to the limited extent possible, the opportunities for crime."[43]

A police department that places order maintenance uppermost in its priorities will judge patrolmen . . . by their ability to keep the peace on their beat. This will require, in turn, that sergeants and other supervisory personnel concern themselves more with how the patrolmen function in family fights, teenage disturbances, street corner brawls, and civil disorders, and less with how well they take reports at the scene of burglary or how many traffic tickets they issue during a tour of duty. Order maintenance also requires that the police have available a wider range of options for handling disorder than is afforded by the choice between making an arrest and doing nothing. Detoxification centers should be available as an alternative to jail for drunks. Family-service units should be formed which can immediately assist patrolmen handling domestic quarrels, provide community-service information, answer complaints, and deal with neighborhood tensions and rumors.[44]

Some police departments are already making notable progress along these lines. Under a federal grant, the New York City Police Department has formed a "Family Crisis Intervention Unit" consisting of 18 highly trained officers to handle interfamily assaults and violence in West Harlem. Although it is estimated that as much as 40 percent of police injuries stem from family complaint calls, these crisis unit officers have not received any injuries in 15 months. Moreover, in the 1,120 family crises in which they have intervened, there has not been a single homicide among the families.[45] At the root of this project is a recognition that specialized peacekeeping training pays off.

Police departments throughout the country are beginning to conduct what is referred to as "provocation training." These projects range from training involving crowd control to handling of street corner disturbances. Provocation training entails, in part, staging the kind of provocation which police offenders may expect to face on the job. The trainees are taunted by instructors who call them names, use obscene gestures, and generally imitate the kinds of abuse policemen may expect to face in the conduct of their assigned responsibilities. The purpose of this specialized training is to develop and maintain coolheadedness under extreme provocation.

Other projects being conducted by large city police departments involve efforts to establish closer links between patrolmen and the neighborhoods or communities they serve. The advantage of establishing firmer ties with the community is that it increases a police officer's capacity to make reliable judgments about the character, motives, intentions and future actions of those among whom they keep the peace. As Professor Wilson has suggested, "The officer's ability to make such judgments is improved by increasing his familiarity with and involvement in the neighborhood he patrols, even to the extent of having him live there. The better he knows his beat, the more he can rely on judgments of character. . . ."[46] One method being used by several police departments in achieving this end is through a return to the foot-beat policeman. Most cities which have increased the number of foot-beat patrolmen have used them as a supplement to squad-car or motorcycle beats, thus preserving the mobility inherent in the latter technique. Other police departments have been experimenting with motorscooters in combination with foot-beat patrols.

Another notable example of a department's attempt to bridge the gap between the police and the community is the model precinct project being conducted by the Washington, D.C., Metropolitan Police. This project involves the creation of neighborhood centers which are staffed around the clock by resident civilians as well as police officers. The police teams working out of the centers are assigned for long periods of time to work in the neighborhoods covered by the centers' jurisdiction. Instead of being spread thin, they have an opportunity to get to know families, youth on the street, householders, and proprietors of businesses much more intimately. With a narrower area of patrol responsibility, the possibilities for positive, interested, and friendly contact among police and citizens is greatly improved.

The resident civilian workers, employed and trained by agencies such as welfare and legal aid, provide assistance to citizens referred by police on patrol, as well as to those who walk in off the street. These civilian positions help relate police peacekeeping to other activities of a positive help-giving nature, and to provide avenues by which civilians from the neighborhood can formally assist in keeping the peace (and perhaps later enter into careers in law enforcement or allied fields).

MINORITY RECRUITMENT

One fundamentally important method by which the police can improve their relations with the public is through increased recruitment of minority group policemen. The absence of many minority group policemen in our Nation's center city areas has been a source of community hostility for many years.

This Task Force surveyed minority recruitment efforts by police departments in several large cities. Although we found a rising percentage of minority policemen being recruited each year, the ratio of white to minority group policemen on any force never approximated the ratio of white to minority citizens in any given city's total population.

Many of the cities reported stepped up recruiting campaigns for minority group policemen. We inquired about the relative lack of success of such campaigns. One police chief answered:

> The problem as we see it is twofold: (1) in today's labor market there is full employment and special efforts are being directed toward the Negro community by private industry in an effort to attract qualified applicants. These companies are able to offer outstanding starting salaries and numerous fringe benefits that place police departments in a competitive disadvantage; (2) several of our Negro applicants have expressed the opinion that many segments of the Negro community regard Negro officers as "Uncle Toms" and enforcers of a white man's justice and are therefore hesitant to apply with a police department. Also we have not been entirely pleased with our efforts in the Negro community. Organizations such as the Urban League and the NAACP have not been able to refer many applicants to the Department.

There are other problems too. Although we found that in terms of percentages more minority group recruits succeeded in graduating from police training school than did white policemen, more minority applicants failed the original entrance examination than did whites. We do not feel that these failures were "arranged" by prejudiced police officials. The failures seem to us to reflect the tragedy of the ghetto schools' failure to educate its students.

The police are caught in a bind. Law enforcement consultants, Presidential and State crime commissions constantly urge that recruitment standards be upgraded. The result is that many applicants for police work who have attended ghetto schools simply are not intellectually equipped to pass the entrance examinations. If more minority policemen are to be recruited, accommodations must be found for the disparities in public school education.

Some police departments have been making commendable efforts at achieving such an accommodation. The Atlanta Police Department reported to us that during the summer months it employed 50 "Community Service Officers" between the ages of 17 and 21. These young men are recruited from the heart of the ghetto and are furnished police uniforms and equipment (except firearms). Their work is largely in the ghetto and has resulted in a betterment of police community relations. The Chief of Police reported to us that, most of them returned to school in October to finish their education and "we are convinced that eventually we will get at least 40 good patrolmen out of this group."

Other cities have shown similar good faith through special recruitment campaigns by sound truck, neighborhood centers, newspaper, TV, radio and billboard advertisements. More efforts of these kinds are needed if minority group policemen are to have an equal opportunity to demonstrate an ability to serve the community in the interest of keeping the peace.

CONCLUSION

That the policemen of our country are both criticized and misunderstood by large and diverse elements of the population is becoming increasingly clear. That these diverse elements make inconsistent and contradictory demands on the police is also clear. As a result of being thus criticized and misunderstood, and being called upon to perform inconsistent and contradictory services in the front lines of our disturbed and often violent urban society, the policeman is becoming more confused not only about what his function is, but also about what it should be.

Besides lacking the financial, manpower and technological resources necessary to respond adequately to the many demands made of them, the police also lack a coherent sense of what direction their changing mission must take. Our police consequently are becoming more alienated from many factions of the pluralistic society which it is their duty to protect. The police have thus begun to fight back, not only as individuals with threats and counterviolence, but also as an increasingly organized group doing combat in the political arena.

How are we to bring the police and the diverse groups they serve back together again? With regard to the police taking sides in primarily political struggles, bitter past experience, at least, dictates that the abstention of the professional is the wisest choice. As to day-to-day contact between the police and the citizenry, there must be renewed attention to the peace-keeping role of the patrolman on the beat, which entails in part increased efforts to develop in the patrolman the understanding and coolheadedness which that vital role demands. Despite the depth of the hostility which exists between the police and some of the communities they serve, we believe that a "good cop" can still be a good friend to all of our people. Better training, supervision, and recognition, together with more effective minority group recruitment, are needed if our hopes of producing police excellence are to materialize.

NOTES

1. President's Commission on Law Enforcement and Administration of Justice (hereinafter cited as Crime Commission), *Challenge of Crime in a Free Society* (Washington, D.C.: Government Printing Office, 1967), at 92.

2. See Arthur Niederhoffer, *Beyond the Shield: The Police in Urban Society* (Garden City, N.Y.: Doubleday, 1967), at 95–108.

3. See, generally, O. W. Wilson, *Municipal Police Administration* (1961); Bruce J. Terris, "The Role of the Police," 374 *Annals* 58–69 (1967); Crime Commission, *supra* note 1, *Task Force Report: The Police*; Schwartz and Goldstein, *Police Guidance Manuals* (1968); and James Q. Wilson, *Varieties of Police Behavior* (Cambridge: Harvard University Press, 1968).

4. Wilson, *Varieties of Police Behavior, id.*, at 4.

5. See generally, Paul Chevigny, *Police Power; Police Abuses in New York City* (New York: Pantheon Books, 1969); *The Police: Six Sociological Essays*, David Bordua, ed. (New York: John Wiley & Sons, 1967); Jerome H. Skolnick, *The Police and the Urban Ghetto* (1968); Niederhoffer, *supra* note 2.

6. Crime Commission, *supra* note 1, *The Challenge of Crime in a Free Society*, at 91. More recent reports indicate that the number of policemen in the United States has climbed to nearly 500,000, yet most departments are still undermanned.

7. In ch. 17, *infra*, we discuss the possibilities for alleviating police manpower shortages through the use of citizen volunteers to perform some police functions.

8. Not only are far fewer college graduates (or men with some college training) found among recruit classes but large numbers have only a high school equivalency diploma and still others are from the lower quarters of their high school classes. *Time*, Oct. 4, 1968, at 26, reports this true of recent Detroit police recruits; Chief William Beall of the Berkeley, California, Police Department calls it "a sharp decline in the educational level of recent police recruits; and in Oakland, California, police captain with twenty-seven years service states: "We are not getting the type of college people in the department that we were before." See also Niederhoffer, *supra* note 2, at 16–17, 209–210. Part of the reason for this failure is that college graduates do not wish to begin a police career at the bottom of the ladder. Few police departments have adopted the Crime and Kerner recommendations for lateral entry for college graduates.

9. Staff interviews with a New York patrolman recently graduated from the Police Academy and with a police sergeant-instructor. See also memorandum from Prof. George D. Eastman to the Commission, dated Sept. 30, 1968, especially at 3–4.

10. This Commission's Task Force Report entitled *The Politics of Protest* at 192–194 and *Municipal Yearbook* (Washington, D.C.: International City Managers Association, 1968), at 339–350. Klein, *The Police: Damned If They Do—Damned If They Don't* (1968).

11. Crime Commission, *supra* note 1, *Challenge of Crime in a Free Society*, at 113. See also James Q. Wilson, "Police Morale, Reform and Citizen Respect: The Chicago Case," in *The Police: Six Sociological Essays, supra* note 5, at 137–162.

12. See discussion in ch. 21, *infra*.

13. Quinn Tamm, "Police Must Be More Free," in *Violence In The Streets*, Shalom Endelman, ed. (Chicago: Quadrangle Books, 1968).

14. *Id.*

15. See ch. 20, *infra*.

16. E.g., the almost unanimous approval of the so-called "Fourth Platoon" Bill by the New York State legislature in the face of strong opposition by police organizations is a recent example of the complaints falling within the latter category.

17. Schwartz and Goldstein, *supra* note 3, at Nos. 4, 7, and 9. And see our discussion of "over-criminalization" in ch. 23, *infra*.

18. *Id.*

19. See Wilson, *Varieties of Police Behavior, supra* note 3 at 83–139.

20. 56 percent of the American public expressed approval of the Chicago police handling of unruly demonstrators at the Democratic National Convention last summer. *New York Times*, Sept. 18, 1968, at 25.

21. Such efforts include human relations courses, police-community councils, recruitment of minority group policemen, advanced educational opportunities, and civilian complaint mechanisms.

22. John Guidici, "Police Response to Crimes of Violence," a paper submitted to this Task Force, at 1–14.

23. See *Report of the National Advisory Commission on Civil Disorders* (Washington, D.C.: Government Printing Office, 1968) and Chevigny, *supra* note 5, at 161–179.

24. See, *e.g.*, *Rights in Conflict*, a special report to this Commission by Daniel Walker, Director of the Chicago Study Team.

25. Guidici, *supra* note 22, at 7–8.

26. See *Rights in Conflict, supra* note 24.

27. See, *e.g., The Politics of Protest,* supra note 10; and *Shoot-Out in Cleveland* and *Miami Report,* two investigative reports submitted to the Commission.

28. Wilson, *Varieties of Police Behavior, supra* note 3, at 248.

29. Chevigny, *supra* note 5, at 51–83.

30. *Id.* See also Chapman and Crockett, *Gun Fight Dilemma: Police Firearms Policy* (1963) ; *Washington Post,* Sept. 18, 1968, at A–1.

31. *Id.*

32. "The Administration of Complaints by Civilians Against the Police," 77 *Harv. L. Rev.* 499, Jan. 1964. See also Thomas R. Brooks, " 'No!' Sayth the P.B.A.," *New York Times Magazine,* Oct. 16, 1966, at 37; Ralph G. Murdy, "Civilian Review Boards in Review," and Aryeh Neier, "Civilian Review Boards— Another View," *Criminal Law Bulletin* vol. 21, No. 8 (1966) at 3 and 10; Kenneth Gross and Alan Reitman, *Police Power and Citizens' Rights* (New York: American Civil Liberties Union, 1966) ; "Civilian Complaints Against the Police," 22 *Bar Bulletin* 228 (New York County Lawyers Association) (1964) .

33. See ch. 7 of *The Politics of Protest, supra* note 10.

34. See *Rights in Conflict, supra* note 24.

35. The proper role of the police in mass political confrontations is dealt with more extensively in ch. 16, *infra.*

36. See, generally, Edwards, *The Police On The Urban Frontier* (1967) ; *One Year Later* (Washington, D.C.: Urban America, Inc., and The Urban Coalition, 1969) ; Reiss, "Police Brutality—Answer to Key Questions," *Transaction,* July/Aug. 1, 1968, at 10.

37. Terris, *supra* note 3, at 58 and 64.

38. See any of several articles on this subject by Prof. Samuel G. Chapman.

39. "Training Cops in Covina," *Capital East Gazette,* Feb. 1969, vol. 3, No. 2, at 10, 12.

40. E.g., the proposal of Washington, D.C., Black United Front concerning neighborhood control of police.

41. These remarks were recorded during a staff interview.

42. Not infrequently a decision by the policeman not to intervene is the wiser choice, particularly in situations where the police have not been called and where upon arriving at the scene the policeman sees that there is no real trouble brewing.

43. Wilson, *Varieties of Police Behavior, supra* note 3, at 291.

44. James Q. Wilson, "Dilemmas of Police Administration," *Public Administration Review,* Sept./Oct. 1 1968, at 407, 412, 413.

45. See testimony of Patrick V. Murphy, before the Violence Commission, Oct. 30, 1968; Sullivan, "Violence, Like Charity Begins at Home," *New York Times Magazine,* Nov. 24, 1968; and Bard, "Iatrogenic Violence," statement submitted to this Task Force, Oct. 4, 1968.

46. Wilson, *Varieties of Police Behavior, supra* note 3, at 291.

ARTICLE 29

Community Action: Where Has It Been?
Where Will It Go?

Sanford Kravitz
Ferne K. Kolodner

The idea of co-ordinated community action to relieve human distress and poverty has been present in America for almost a hundred years. For the past five years, it has been a subject of widespread public discussion. The focus of the discussion has been the Community Action Program of the Office of Economic Opportunity.

THE BACKGROUND OF COMMUNITY ACTION

The growth of a variety of local forms of community action began to take real shape in the first decade of this century as social-service organizations struggled with the tasks of co-ordinating the services to the poor of sixty years ago.

The movement received an impetus during World War I when community "war fund" campaigns urged unity and co-ordination. From this grew the "Community Chest," and close upon its heels came the "Community Welfare Council." Councils were formed to evaluate and co-ordinate the efforts of agencies which the Community Chest was supporting, and thus community-service co-ordination was wedded to the voluntary social-service sector and to fund-raising.

The "movement," as members of the welfare councils called their efforts (despite the fact that it lacked the attributes of a social movement), spread to about 450 cities over the United States in the next forty years.

The rapid growth of governmental services after 1930 placed strains on the welfare councils to become more inclusive in membership and to widen their concern with social problems. Until the 1960's, the councils appeared to be unable to make any major break from the form and function that had governed their early beginnings. Some large councils struggled to find scientific means to determine community needs and priorities. Some attempted to engage public agencies and to plan for public services. Others had only modest funds for planning. Their research efforts were largely the gathering of statistics on utilization of services which would be helpful to the Community Chest in its campaign. To be sure, discussions were held among the professional workers and the council members concerning their role in generating social action, but fear of jeopardizing tax-exempt status generally put a damper on most council efforts to enter the public arena. For most of this forty-year period, the main concern of councils was to balance community resources to meet the capacity of the Community Chest to raise money in the community. They had little or no influence on the allocation of public health and welfare resources, and their impact on public social programs was minimal. Its coordinating-structure mode of organization and its reliance on the business and social elites for key leadership gave the council a stance that was directed at social services and their refinement, not at social problems and their causes. Social-welfare-planning councils, the major community vehicle present in American communities for collective attention to social problems, were mainly concerned with co-ordination and efficiency, not with innovation or with structural deficiencies in the social-service-delivery system. In 1960, no American city had an organization fully prepared to engage the critical problems of poverty in urban America.

THE EMERGENCE OF NEW FORMS

American communities had passed through the 1950's with only mild awareness of the growing numbers of problems that were soon to confront them. Little or no attention was given to the alarming rise in unemployment. In 1953 unemployment stood at 3.5 percent; it rose to

3.8 percent in 1956 and to 5.5 percent in 1959. In 1940 Negro unemployment was 20 percent higher than that of whites. In 1953 it had risen to 71 percent higher than white unemployment. By 1963 it had risen to 112 percent. During the 1950's, 1,400,000 Negroes left the South and migrated north and west to the urban and industrial centers to replace the two million whites who had fled to the suburbs. Planning agencies faced suburbia, or talked about regional problems or metropolitan government.

The lack of action or direction in local communities was mirrored in the inaction of a conservative administration in Washington. The Housing Act of 1949's grand promise of decent housing for all had been converted to tokenism by the action of congressional appropriations committees. The amendments to the Social Security Act of 1956 authorized social services for families on welfare, but, once again, Congress failed to appropriate funds. The Civil Rights Act of 1957 was another dismal disappointment. The elementary and secondary education systems of the nation were beset with the Sputnik challenge, with demands for improved education of the talented, and with a growing concern for academic excellence. Most school systems, as well as their critics and supporters, seemed unaware of the growing crisis in the inner-city schools.

Public welfare programs for the very poor had expanded greatly since the passage of the Social Security Act. The degree of skill and enlightenment with which they were operated, however, varied across the country. Attitudes toward public welfare were particularly characterized by a harsh and punitive attitude on the part of the public, reflecting a more general feeling that, indeed, the poor make their own poverty.

THE FORD FOUNDATION GRAY AREAS PROGRAM

The first substantial departure from the drift which had characterized the 1950's came with the development of the Ford Foundation Gray Areas Program in 1961. In the late 1950's, the Foundation had invested in a series of experimental programs in metropolitan planning, aid to education in the inner city, and urban renewal. The Public Affairs Department of the Foundation sought a bolder and more comprehensive approach—an approach which would be broader than efforts to affect one subsystem, the inner-city school, but smaller, more manageable, more capable of producing action than efforts to achieve metropolitan governmental and regional planning. The Foundation started this new program with the establishment of what were considered, for that time, to be enormous development funds allocated to selected cities to be used for co-ordinated programs in such areas as youth-employment, education, and expanded social and community services. Grants ranging from one to two million dollars per year were made to five cities and to a statewide organization. In the cities, the Foundation pressed for the establishment of new community agencies, which were intended to be uncommitted to the existing service structure. It was believed that such new agencies would be more readily prepared to experiment and to use the new funds for leverage for change.

THE PRESIDENT'S COMMITTEE ON JUVENILE DELINQUENCY

In September of 1961, almost coincidentally with the development of the new Ford Foundation program, the Congress passed the Juvenile Delinquency and Youth Offenses Control Act of 1961. The act provided funds for demonstration projects and training efforts in order to launch a new national and comprehensive attack on the problem of juvenile delinquency and youth crime. The language of the act, which had been prepared by the new President's Committee on Juvenile Delinquency, under Robert Kennedy, specifically focused attention on the social antecedents of juvenile crime, youth-unemployment, poor housing, poor health, inadequate education, and the alienation of lower-class communities and neighborhoods.

The President's Committee viewed the conventions of institutional practice as their principal reform targets. The new program was characterized by a requirement for innovation, by its intellectual and theoretical underpinnings, and by its general antibureaucratic stance. Criteria for effective programs stressed certain critical elements:

1. The recognition of the strong interrelationship of social problems.
2. Remedies that would focus on change in the opportunity structure, rather than on changes in the behavior of an individual or on redirection of personality.

3. The requirement that communities undertake a rational analysis of their social problems and propose solutions consistent with the problem-definition. The solutions were assumed to be capable of integration.
4. The recognition of the necessity for substantial participation of public agencies and the political executive arm of government in the efforts to be undertaken.

Seventeen demonstration projects were chosen in sixteen cities.

The programs of the Ford Foundation and the President's Committee on Juvenile Delinquency emerged at a critical moment in American social history. Along with the civil rights revolution, the worsening problem of youth-unemployment, and concern over automation and its impact on the unskilled, they highlighted the failures of existing planning mechanisms and educational and welfare institutions. They talked in terms of problems, not organizations; they acknowledged the power of professional politicians; they called for public responsibility in addressing the problems of the inner city, and they called for rededication to serving the poor.

The contribution of these two demonstration efforts to each community was mixed, but the fact of their development—and even the criticism and attacks they sustained—brought long festering problems into wide public view, so that discussion of them as critical national issues could no longer be evaded. Thus, a seedbed, however imperfect, was provided for the central conceptual elements in the Community Action Program, the program that was to become a major pillar in the Economic Opportunity Act of 1964.

THE CONCEPT OF COMMUNITY ACTION AS IT EMERGED IN THE ECONOMIC OPPORTUNITY ACT

The history as well as the conflicts in the emergence of the Community Action Program are currently being well documented. Those who were actually engaged in the design of the program, and who had either worked in or watched the experience of the Gray Areas Program and the Juvenile Delinquency Program, were pursuing a line of thinking that went something like this: Any set of proposed solutions to the central problem of poverty must deal with the individual problems that are faced by the poor in their own communities—

problems that are beyond the provision of direct financial assistance and beyond the provision of employment through the usual market place. The Social Security Act of the 1930's and its subsequent amendments had been relatively effective in dealing with a part of the problem, but it was clear that there were still great deficiencies in both national and local agencies' capacities to serve the poor effectively.

The problem confronting the planners of the war on poverty in the winter and spring of 1964 might be described thus: Poverty is a complex social and economic issue; it is rooted in an extensive array of social and individual causes. What kind of program could be developed that would permit a counterattack across the total spectrum of need, at the local community level as well as at the national policy level?

The designers of the war-on-poverty program were clearly thinking of the local community—in part because of distrust of the states and the antiurban bias of the state grant-in-aid programs and in part because these planners represented the vanguard of the later, and now current, advocates of local control and local power. They believed that the existing and emerging welfare, education, and manpower-retraining programs would be unable to achieve their full potential unless effective ways could be found (1) to diagnose the problem of poverty within a local community and (2) to apply the specific remedies in a co-ordinated and rational program.

The planners of the CAP also believed that redistribution of power and resources and the humanizing of social institutions were basic to the creation of a decent nation. They did not believe that this could come solely through welfare-state policies which would perpetuate impersonal bureaucracies and caste and class relationships.

It is important to recognize that the planners had great, almost naïve faith in the capacity of local communities to take coherent and rational action. They felt that, given the incentive of ever increasing federal funds, local communities could apply these remedies. They argued that the availability of new, large sums of money for planning and for program-assistance would reform the existing institutions, or would create new agencies that would assume the necessary responsibility.

The conceptual model of a community-action effort called for careful diagnosis of needs and subsequent application of all appropriate programmatic and organizational solutions. It implied the existence of a central local authority to exert influence on, and make decisions about, the critical program components, the involvement of major institutions, and, above all, the power to control allocation of resources. With some modest (and some major) concessions that were contrary to the original model—for example (1) de-emphasis on planning and (2) increased emphasis on the development of a con-sensus-co-ordinating structure—the Community Action Program emerged as a major weapon in the war on poverty.

The willingness of the early programs to confront the major in-stititutions directly, and to be prepared to engage in combat over principle, was sidetracked in favor of a consensus structure for policy-making, in which the relevant actors were (1) the political structure, (2) the structure of the social agency or civic organization, and (3) the residents of the areas to be served. It should be explicitly noted that community action, critics to the contrary, was not seen as a replacement for large-scale national efforts in the areas of housing, income-maintenance, and employment, but was specifically aimed at developing responsive local community structures in order to reach the poor more effectively with relevant programs. The issue of the relevance of the programs which emerged is a critical one and will be discussed below.

PROBLEMS AND CONTRIBUTIONS OF COMMUNITY ACTION

In the four and a half years since the program's inception, the CAP has contributed, substantially in some communities and modestly in others, to power realignments, to the formation of new leadership groups, and to new social welfare programs. Over a thousand com-munities have been organized, including urban, rural, Indian-reserva-tion, and migrant-labor areas. This accomplishment might be compared with the 45 years that it took to organize about 450 welfare-planning councils. For many of these communities, the goal of a truly comprehensive poverty program is not even in sight, even if under-stood. The tasks of ascertaining needs, planning programs, co-ordin-ating services, and maximizing all relevant resources are well beyond the present capabilities of most of these programs. For a few com-munities with skill and competence, the process is well under way. Many areas are embarked on a handful of useful programs. But the range of these programs is limited, and whether they are capable of providing basic long-range solutions to the problems of poverty is a gnawing question.

Almost all of the local community-action agencies were pressed into the operation or co-ordination of the programs of their delegate agency operations, and few, if any, CAA's ever developed a special planning capability. OEO recently has experimented with grants to 100 CAA's for planning, but the results of these efforts have yet to be evaluated. The capacity of the CAA to co-ordinate effectively beyond the range of programs for which it was currently receiving funds was initially jeopardized by the hostility toward the organization of a new agency which pervaded local communities. The idea that one agency would be *the* agency that was to have the planning and co-ordinating capability was hard for local officials to accept, particularly when the attempt to develop this role was accompanied by attacks on existing institutions and pejorative comments concerning established professional workers' insensitivity to the poor. The past four-and-a-half years has brought about a narrowing of sights in almost all CAA's, which has resulted in a much tighter range of programs, sometimes dealing almost exclusively with manpower problems.

This tightening in range is the result, in part, perhaps in large part, of the severe limitations in funds which CAA's have faced and of the commitments that they have had to make to the so-called national-emphasis programs. However, another cause is the increasing recognition of the enormous difficulty, particularly in the larger urban areas, for any one agency to perform the dual functions of planning and operating in fields so diverse as employment, housing, education, and social services. The CAA's have adjusted to the pluralism of the American community. Comprehensive planning is an elusive goal.

The emergence of the Model Cities program has created problems for CAA's in those cities which have both programs. The administrators have not been able to reconcile the fact that essentially the same task has been assigned to two programs for the same turf. The White House may mandate co-operation, but the struggle for hegemony rages at the federal, regional, and local levels. Many local CAA's have lost early friends as a result of creation of rising expectations by the grand promises of the Congress and the administration, with insufficient dollars allocated to follow through. The war on poverty has literally become a skirmish.

CAA programs have encountered difficulty in reaching, to any significant degree, the so-called hard-core poor. While CAA programs cut far below the creaming level of other agencies, most CAA programs only reach the top of the low-income group: the most aggressive, the most competitive, the most highly motivated. No program, despite relatively favorable comparative funding, is capable of meeting true need. Head Start meets about 25 percent of the universe of need, according to OEO officials.

Administration, particularly financial management and personnel, has been among the most serious local problems. Local CAA's have had serious problems in attracting and holding first-class executives after the first-year honeymoon period. The senior management positions are fraught with frustrations, irritations, and an almost certain sense of being doomed to fail. The effective operation of a CAA in a medium- to large-sized city with serious problems of poverty, racial unrest, a limited local tax base, a problem school system, and hostile political leadership requires the qualities of a Renaissance diplomat, a Chinese warlord and a saint, embodied in one person. It is clear that there is no well-operated CAA in which the executive director is a poor leader, although there are some CAA's with good leadership that are having serious problems.

The problems of management of the large amounts of money flowing through many hands and over many programs has been an enormous headache. Inexperienced management, poor fiscal procedures, and, in a few cases, flagrant dishonesty have brought about the institution of stringent fiscal control procedures from Washington which are far more severe than those demanded in any other federal program. Increasingly elaborate reporting systems have been built in as a protection. The shortage of competent fiscal personnel at the local level has been met by the institution of procedures that require a certified public accountant to interpret. But fiscal mismanagement is an important source for the loss of credibility that the program has suffered.[1]

The vagaries of the Congress in approving the OEO budget, as well as problems with the program-review mechanism at the federal and regional levels, forced all programs into a pattern of hand-to-mouth programming which has had a debilitating effect on participant and staff morale—often impelling irrational temporary closing of a program or forcing trained staff to seek employment elsewhere. Failures in communication or in understanding or simply stupid budgetary cuts in which a certain program might be allowed a secretary but no typewriter are examples of the problems encountered by administration.

The most controversial aspect of the CAP has been the growth and development of the concept of maximum feasible participation. Here again, its history is being written, but, it may suffice to say, it has certainly been an evolutionary history, almost with a life of its own. It emerged initially with a heavy emphasis on the employment of the poor as subprofessionals, and was soon interpreted to mean that poor people should be placed on the managing boards of CAA's. By 1965, this was standard doctrine at OEO. This doctrine received a setback when big-city mayors began to complain to the White House, but it was an idea which could not be constrained, even by Mayor Daley. Even the Green Amendment to the Economic Opportunity Act of 1967, giving city halls the opportunity to recapture control, has failed to halt the demand for greater participation of the poor and of neighborhood residents in the control and management of programs. Following the passage of the Green Amendment, only 26 CAA's, or 7 percent of the total, shifted from private to public control.

The issue of who is in control, the poor or the mayor, may be moot, inasmuch as so much of the CAA effort is already locked into earmarked funds or national-emphasis programs. The current OEO national leadership is dedicated to the proposition that quality programs and protection are obtained by earmarking funds and establishing rigid federal guidelines. In addition, local boards-of-directors of CAA's, whether public or private, are, because of limited discretionary funds, locked into patterns that are firmly set at the federal level.

DECENTRALIZATION

The Community Action Program has been one of the potent forces contributing to the current thrust toward decentralization. Enormous CAP effort has gone into the organization of local communities and the building of neighborhood organizations. A large number of the new black leaders of the ghetto received their training and experience as employees of CAA's and delegate agencies.

Sanction was given by CAP to organization, and funds were made available. These ghetto organizations, some strong, some weak, have developed lives and identities of their own. They are a *key* element in the politicalization of the ghetto that is currently underway. Although CAP has generally encouraged these developments, policy and direction are still vague. Decentralization is currently supported by a strange assortment of bedfellows—for instance, the Congress of Racial Equality (CORE), the Southern Christian Leadership Conference (SCLC), the National Association of Manufacturers (NAM), the United States Chamber of Commerce, the Urban Coalition, and the National Council of Churches of Christ, as well as intellectuals in government and the universities. The CAP is well aware that decentralization is a controversial item, but is, as yet, unclear about how to shift to decentralized programs. This movement is a major one for American communities and is fraught with unanswered questions: What is to be gained and lost from particular schemes? Who will gain or lose? What processes for reallocation of powers, resources, and functions will produce what results? Some forms of decentralization are inimical to the interests of the CAA. Many OEO officials are aware of the mass of evaluative documents which indicate many of the failures of the CAA's. They believe that reorganizing CAA's may be a way to get the job done. Some argue that reorganization toward decentralization may speed the redistribution of power, functions, and resources. Others argue that decentralization would make CAA's more responsive to citizens' needs. It is believed by some that devolution is a cure for restlessness, and, thus, an antiriot device, and, finally, it is argued that many CAA's have become large and ineffective downtown bureaucracies, and need to be fragmented. The future of CAA's in regard to decentralization is grossly uncertain, and is tied dually to the will of Congress and to the emerging patterns that will become either fashionable or imbedded in law.

DELIVERY OF SERVICES AND PROGRAM-RELEVANCE

A major criticism of the local CAA is that it has become simply another variety of the standard social-service agency. It is argued that the programs are palliative and residual, and that they accept, without substantial challenge, current institutional arrangements. Many of the CAA programs of direct service are, in fact, some form of rehabilitation, an approach which concentrates on changing people to restore or improve their social functioning. Rehabilitation hopes to overcome poverty by overcoming personal or family disorganization and deviance. The essential thesis of its advocates is that those reclaimed will become more acceptable, more employable, and more competent.

This approach is derided by those who believe that only more fundamental changes in the system will really affect poverty. They would argue that income-transfer or investment in training programs or community control would have a more profound effect than case services. OEO-CAP has invested, to some degree, in a variety of strategies, but a large portion of its resources are going into the delivery of standard social services. If services are needed, and will be required, by the poor as well as by many others, for a long time, what has been the CAP impact?

The Community Action Program has made strategic improvements in the delivery of services to the poor. These have come in three major areas. The first is the promotion of the concept of unified service systems to address the needs of individuals, families, and neighborhoods in an interdisciplinary and interagency context. Socond, in the promotion of decentralization of services to the neighborhood level, the CAP reversed the flight to centralized locations of many of the traditional agencies. It made detached, neighborhood service fashionable again. Third, it has been the major force in the exhaustive and continuing movement for promotion of paraprofessionals, subprofessionals, and new careerists. (*This* effort is really becoming a social movement.)

Several issues confront CAP in these areas where it has, in fact, made enormous contributions. The decentralized-multiservice-center concept still merits testing and evaluation as an effective vehicle for service-delivery. Unfortunately, it is being widely promoted as a panacea. The issues of service-delivery encompass concerns about control, location, manpower, and relevance. OEO-CAP has not really been prepared to examine totally new approaches to services, except in the neighborhood health centers, and even here the tendency is to harden and limit the experimentation. While recognizing the advances that have been made, it is important to realize that most CAP programs are quite conventional, and function well within the norms established by the controlling professional groups.

There is still substantial reluctance among professionals to consider the wider use of service aides. Some professionals do see the subprofessional as a welcome agent of change, but the enormous resistance to this idea should not be underestimated. The new career programs are still trapped in deep-seated problems concerning professional domain. Any effort to deal with manpower for service-delivery must confront these issues directly. Neither the CAP nor any other federal program has really confronted these issues.

THE FUTURE

The CAP program cannot be evaluated out of the context of the times and the constraints under which it has been operating.

It is now abundantly clear, and no longer needs to be argued, that the most fundamental poverty issue which we face is income-redistribution. We must raise income levels for millions of families living below the poverty levels. There is, additionally, general acceptance of the fact that the free operation of the economy does not currently engage the productive capacity of those members of the society willing and capable to do work. This implies a program in which the government is the employer of last resort. There is also the requirement that we produce a sufficient supply of housing at costs that will enable every family to live in decent surroundings.

Within the parameters of such prerequisites the CAP has filled very vital tasks in the war on poverty:

It has:

1. Linked low-income people to critical resources, for example, education, manpower-training, counseling, housing, and health.
2. Increased the accessibility of available critical services that the poor still often find beyond their reach or blocked off from them by the manner in which their need has been defined.
3. Contributed to the creation of competent communities by developing in and among the poor the capacity for leadership, problem-solving, and participation in the decision-making councils which affect their lives.
4. Contributed in some degree to the restructuring of community service institutions to assure flexibility, responsiveness, respect, and true relatedness to the problems faced by the poor.

There is no organizational model currently available or proposed that can replace the CAP and fulfill these functions in American communities. If the CAP is terminated, a new model will have to be invented, and one has yet to be proposed. We desperately need either to build improvements into our present model or to invent a new one.

All programs to address poverty at the local level of government must, first of all, be matched by several major national commitments.

The first of these is a national income-redistribution program which would bring new dollar resources directly into the hands of poor people. Such financial relief would very directly remove from program and service concern those among the poor who are perfectly able to cope with life except for the absence of money.

The second program is a large-scale, public, subsidized employment program, locally administered, that would assure employment at a decent wage for all those willing and capable of working.

The third effort must be in the area of housing. It has been recognized that the nation requires at least six million new low-income dwelling units as soon as it can get them, if it is to meet the current housing needs of the poor. Such a program must be nationally organized even though it can be effectively administered locally. Major efforts in this direction would remove the presence of the most ubiquitous environmental hazard that the poor face: the place in which they live. Every person needs a livable physical environment if he is to thrive and be productive.

Given these national efforts, the concepts of concerned community action has a chance of surviving and making a significant contribution toward the reduction of poverty and poverty-producing conditions. To carry on this task, four conditions will be required:

1. The community-action agency must strengthen its central planning capability. It must gain increased technical capacity for diagnosing need and in applying the appropriate programmatic interventions. Some way must be devised to allocate scarce resources more effectively among the gamut of needs at the local community level. CAA's have not been able to do this, and yet, without this, planning becomes an intellectual exercise.
2. Experimentation with decentralization of power must continue but with the full awareness that there is no panacea in "neighborhood control." Advocates must be prepared to confront a troubling assumption that is in vogue: that is, if neighborhood people are in control, they will be able to handle previously insoluble problems, problems that the federal government, the states, and the city halls have been unable to handle. Yet, the

assumption persists that local people, with a limited amount of education, limited information, and few chances to participate in decision-making, will be able to deal with them. Local neighborhoods cannot be expected, unaided, to put in order the mess which confronts so many of the urban areas.

3. The problems of management and fiscal accountability of these large-scale programs must be solved if public support is to be maintained. This may appear to be of less moment to some, but it is clear that problems in this area have severely damaged credibility.

4. Trained and skilled personnel are essential. No program can survive without cadres of well-trained, well-paid, and dedicated personnel. The nation has not been willing to make the investments in developing the people to work at these problems at all levels of skill. Such investments are absolutely essential.

The curse of the Community Action Program has been "maximum feasible public relations" in the face of limited resources and many critics and enemies. On balance, the contribution has been enormous and the investment worthwhile. Let us take the next steps, even though the way is not wholly clear.

NOTES

1. It should be noted that the federal government has little—or no—recent experience in turning over large sums of money to newly organized and inexperienced groups, and the planners had not spent much time worrying about this problem. The elaborate procedures emerged as the field problems developed.

ARTICLE 30

The Closing of Job Corps Centers

Elmer B. Staats

We are pleased to appear here today to report on one aspect of a review that we have been involved in at the request of the Congress over the past year or so in an effort to evaluate the effectiveness of the programs authorized under the Economic Opportunity Act. . . . Our review included examinations of recruiting and screening activities at selected locations, detailed examinations at nine Job Corps Centers, and analyses of post Job Corps experience of terminated corps members (those whose enrollment was terminated) on a sample basis.

Through Job Corps institutionalized training, corps members have had an opportunity to develop, in varying degrees, work skills, improved work habits, and an opportunity to further their academic education. These corps members have also received benefits in a number of areas, such as health and social and psychological development, which are generally not subject to precise measurement. Also, after Job Corps experience, some corps members have obtained good employment, returned to school, or joined the Armed Forces.

On an overall basis, however, it appears that the Job Corps had achieved only limited success in fulfilling its primary purpose of assisting young persons who need and can benefit from an unusually intensive program, operated in a group setting, to develop their capacities for work and social responsibilities. Our views are based in large part on our findings with respect to post-Job Corps employment experience and related economic benefits of corps members, the

Reprinted from Statement of Hon. Elmer B. Staats, Comptroller General of the United States, in *Closing of Job Corps Centers*, pp. 343–348, 354–365. Hearings before the Subcommittee on Employment, Manpower, and Poverty of the Committee on Labor and Public Welfare. U.S. Senate, 91st Congress, 1st Session, April 18, 25, and May 2, 1969. Washington, D.C.: U.S. Government Printing Office.

unfavorable retention rate of corps members, and problems relating to program content and administration which have existed.

On the basis of studies by our contractor and ourselves relating to post-Job Corps experience, it is questionable whether Job Corps training has resulted in substantial economic benefit thus far for those youths who participated in the program, although our tests showed that employment and earning power were somewhat greater after Job Corps experience than before. We believe that the increased employment and earning power among those included in our sample can be attributable, for the most part, to the greater employability of youths due to the process of growing up and to higher employment and wage levels. This increased employability and earning power also appeared to be associated with the length-of-stay of corps members at the centers, those who graduated being the most successful. It also appeared that Job Corps terminees had not done materially better than the other eligible youths who had applied to enter the program and then chose not to participate.

Factors limiting the success of Job Corps are many and vary in degrees of importance. One of the most significant factors was the short length-of-stay by corps members. Given the limited achievement level of the entering youths, no program can be expected to have dramatic results if the youths cannot be induced to remain at the centers long enough to benefit from the training. The effectiveness of the program in meeting its objectives of assisting young persons who need and can benefit from an intensive training program is highly questionable for the large number of youths who remained at the centers for only short periods of time.

Weaknesses in the policies and procedures under which the program has been administered have detracted significantly from program success. According to Job Corps estimates, direct costs per enrollee man-year were $6,600 for fiscal year 1968. Considering both the direct and indirect costs for those centers in operation as of June 30, 1968, enrollee man-year costs for fiscal year 1968 were $8,300. Although the program had been in existence for over 4 years, our study identified a number of major problems of administration including:

1. A need for improving the recruiting and screening procedures. A significant portion of corps members have not met the qualifications generally considered necessary or desirable for participation in the program and the alternatives of enrolling applicants

in other less costly, and possibly more suitable, training programs apparently were not always considered.

2. A need for improving the administration of the vocational and academic training programs and for establishing minimum graduation criteria which would provide assurance that graduates possess the minimum requisites for successful employment.

3. A need for strengthening the counseling system at each of the centers to more fully assist corps members in making the social, educational, and vocational adjustments necessary to become self-supporting members of society and to provide a means by which corps members could be encouraged to remain at the centers for a sufficient period of time to acquire the skills necessary to obtain and hold jobs.

4. A need for the centers to improve their records and reporting systems in order to obtain accurate and meaningful information about individual corps members and program operations as a tool for evaluating the effectiveness of the centers' various activities.

We have considerable doubt as to whether conservation centers can be expected to provide the intensive training contemplated in the act, at least without substantially upgrading the vocational training program which we believe would be quite costly. Conservation centers generally provide vocational training through the performance of conservation work projects, with little or no related vocational classroom instruction. We recognize the value of conservation work in itself. We also recognize that most of the centers have some work projects which permit exposure to certain occupational skills and that, generally, work projects are a good vehicle for instilling proper work habits in corps members. However, the size and complexity of the work projects coming to our attention at the centers we reviewed generally, were not of a nature to serve as a basis for intensive vocational training. It does not appear to us that the use of work projects as the primary vehicle for providing vocational training would permit the centers to establish and operate an effective training program directed toward skill development in occupational areas above the helper or laborer categories. Job Corps and the administering departments of conservation centers, Agriculture and Interior, recognized that weaknesses and deficiencies had existed in training programs at the centers and, in a joint effort, considered means for improvement. However, our perusal of the requirements prescribed in May 1968 by Job Corps, in conjunction with the departments, for improvements in the training program indicated that, in order for

Corps members to accomplish the minimum requirements for program completion in the various occupational areas, Corps members would need an opportunity to take part in extensive classroom and work-experience programs directed specifically toward development of the knowledge and technical skills needed beyond the helper and laborer categories. To establish intensive vocational training programs at each of the 82 centers in a number of vocational areas for the 100 to 250 corpsmen enrolled at each of the centers would appear to be quite costly. Moreover, it is questionable whether a sufficient number of qualified instructors could be obtained to provide such training at the generally remote and isolated conservation center locations. In summary, we believe that a valid need can be documented for residential training of the type envisioned in Job Corps for a certain number of youths whose needs, because of environmental characteristics or because of geographic location, cannot be well served through other programs operating in or near their home communities. We have doubt, however, that, in light of our findings and the cost of this type of training, the resources now being applied to the Job Corps program can be fully justified. Our doubt in this regard is especially applicable to the conservation center component of the program, particularly in consideration of the significant changes which appear necessary in this component to upgrade its effectiveness in achieving training program objectives. In accordance with the foregoing conclusions, we recommended in our report that the Congress consider whether the Job Corps program, particularly with respect to conservation centers, is sufficiently achieving the purposes for which it was created to justify its retention at present levels.

I would like now to discuss in more specific terms the review we made of Job Corps and the findings upon which we base our conclusions.

RECRUITING AND SCREENING ACTIVITIES

Recruiting and screening activities are carried out for the Job Corps by the U.S. Employment Service (USES), Women in Community Service, Inc., community action agencies, and other private recruiters and screeners on the basis of quotas established by Job Corps. For fiscal year 1968, the Job Corps reported that recruiting and screening costs amounted to about $8 million. We examined recruiting and screening activities at six of the seven OEO regional offices and at 17 local agencies. Although the Job Corps has carried out a widespread advertising campaign and has estimated that about 900,000 youths are eligible for the program, we found that recruiting and screening organizations generally were unable to meet quotas during fiscal year 1968. The Job Corps established a quota of about 117,000 youths for the fiscal year which, after allowing for an anticipated no-show rate of 30 percent, was to insure that about 82,000 youths would enter the program. The recruiting organizations were able to recruit and screen about 90,000 youths of which about 73,000 entered the program and the remaining 17,000 were classified as no-shows. The recruiting agencies provided us with a number of reasons for their inability to meet quotas. These reasons included (1) the existence of available jobs in certain areas, (2) disinterest of eligible youths in the program, and (3) discouraging reports on the Job Corps program made to potential enrollees by returning terminated corps members.

It appeared that the lack of an active and direct recruiting activity by the organizations also contributed to the inability to meet quotas. Generally, we found that the organizations waited for applicants to appear rather than to actively solicit youths in the hard-core poverty areas. Also, of 638 terminated corps members which were interviewed in August 1968, as part of our review, less than 15 percent stated that they became aware of the program directly from the recruiting organizations. The inability to meet established quotas may have resulted in eligibility requirements being waived for a considerable number of enrollees. It appears that screeners have requested waivers on a significant number of cases, because of the difficulty in recruiting applicants. Although responsibility for approving waivers of eligibility requirements rests with officials of the OEO regional offices, we noted that they relied heavily on the recommendations of the screeners in these cases. Waivers of important eligibility criteria were granted for about 33 percent of the 1,000 enrollees included in our test. A subsequent study by the Job Corps revealed that, of the 73,000 Job Corps enrollees during fiscal year 1968, information on eligibility criteria was available on about 46,000 enrollees. The remaining 27,000 enrollee applications were not properly completed at the screening levels so that the eligibility status could be determined. Waivers had been granted for about 10,000 or 22 percent, of the 46,000 enrollees. Among the more important criteria frequently waived were—

1. The minimum period that an applicant had to be out of school, a requirement designed to discourage youths from dropping out of school to join the program;
2. The requirement that an applicant meet certain behavior standards; and
3. The requirement that an applicant not be a high school graduate.

In addition, we noted that in many cases there was not adequate verification by the screening agencies of data supplied by applicants and their parents, a factor which raises additional questions as to the extent to which youths may not have met the eligibility criteria for acceptance in the program.

Also, we noted instances where screening organizations apparently accepted youths without first determining whether the Job Corps was the most appropriate available training program to meet the applicants' needs. This condition existed primarily because (1) emphasis was on meeting quotas, (2) screeners were not familiar with other available programs, and (3) screening personnel did not question the wisdom of the applicants' choice to participate in the program. Job Corps agreed that such instances occur but informed us that it relies primarily on USES affiliated State employment service offices which screen about 70 percent of Job Corps applicants to make proper selections of applicants.

We also found that the Job Corps did not conduct periodic reviews designed to permit an overall evaluation of the effectiveness and efficiency of the activities of recruiting and screening organizations. We were advised by the Job Corps that the OEO-Job Corps-Labor-USES agreement places the responsibility of monitoring the performance of the affiliated States agencies on the USES. However, USES advised us that they did not have the funds or manpower capability to perform evaluation reviews at each employment service office and that all such reviews conducted were done on an exception basis. We believe that the absence of periodic reviews, at least to some extent, may have contributed to the conditions noted above.

CENTER OPERATIONS

We made detailed reviews of the operations at nine centers—two men's urban centers—Kilmer Job Corps Center in New Jersey and the

Atterbury Center in Indiana; five conservation centers—the Eight Canyon Center in New Mexico, the Collbran Center in Colorado, the Cispus Center in Washington, the Acadia Center in Maine, and the Wellfleet Center in Massachusetts: and two women's centers—the Keystone Center in Pennsylvania and the Albuquerque Center in New Mexico. . . . During fiscal year 1968, direct operating costs for these centers amounted to about $32 million and about 55,000 man-months of training were provided to about 13,000 youths who were in attendance at the centers for varying periods of time.

Originally, young men were assigned to the conservation centers to increase their basic academic skills to a point where they could undertake vocational training at the urban centers. Subsequently, a determination was made to offer sufficient training at the conservation centers for employment. The urban centers offered the more advanced training for young men in Job Corps programs. Young men participating at these centers were selected primarily because of their higher achievement on tests given by recruiting and screening agencies. Separate urban centers were used for training young women. Late in fiscal year 1968, Job Corps, in consultation with the Departments of the Interior and of Agriculture who operated conservation centers, made a decision to materially strengthen the training program available at these centers. Also, in November 1968, achievement test results were discontinued as a determinant factor for the initial assignment of an enrollee to the two types of centers, primarily to assign youths to centers close to their homes.

RETENTION OF CORPS MEMBERS

A factor critical to the success of the Job Corps program is the need to retain Corps members for a sufficient period of time for them to attain the attributes necessary for responsible, productive citizenship. Job Corps, on the basis of its experience, believes that a Corps member must remain in the program for at least 6 months to develop such attributes and, during its existence, has taken a number of actions designed to encourage Corps members to remain in the program.

Although we found that Job Corps had achieved only limited success in assisting youths to become more responsible, productive citizens, we did find that the longer a Corps member stayed in the program the better his post-Job Corps experience was.

Of 73,500 Corps members who left Job Corps in fiscal year 1968, 26,300 were classified as graduates. Of the remaining 47,200 youths, 18,200 had remained over 90 days and 29,000 less than 90 days at the centers. Overall, the length of stay of Corps members averaged 6 months. We found that, at the centers we reviewed, the majority of Corps members left the program in less than 6 months.

The reasons most readily identified by the centers we reviewed and most frequently expressed by the terminees that we interviewed regarding the failure of Corps members to stay at the centers until completing a program were (1) dissatisfaction with the center or Job Corps as a whole, (2) homesickness, (3) the inability to obtain desired vocational training, and (4) the fear of bodily harm. The reported overall average length of stay of those corpsmen who terminated from the conservation center program during fiscal year 1968 was 6.3 months, and at the centers we reviewed the average ranged from 3.9 to 6.1 months. We found that the percentage of youth terminating in less than 6 months at the five centers ranged from 52 to 74 percent.

It should be noted that a corpsman's time at a conservation center is generally equally divided between academic classes and vocational training. Consequently, with the prevailing average retention period, the time available for Corps member training in each field would, in effect, be limited to an average of 2 or 3 months. Our review showed that, because of variations and weaknesses in the development and use of graduating criteria at conservation centers, classification of a Corps member as a graduate would not in itself provide reasonable assurance that the Corps member had satisfactorily attained the academic, vocational, and behavioral levels required for entrance into employment in his selected vocational field.

The percentage of Corps members who left urban centers and who failed to complete a defined program (nongraduates) at the four centers we reviewed varied from center to center; however, during fiscal year 1968, this percentage was about 60 percent of all terminees from the two men's centers and about 65 percent of all terminees from the two women's centers.

Nearly 65 percent of the nongraduate corpsmen and about 60 percent of the nongraduate corpswomen left Job Corps in 3 months or less. The length of stay for Corps members who terminated during fiscal year 1968 averaged 6.2 months and 5.7 months for urban women's and men's centers, respectively. For the centers included in our review, the average length of stay for Corps members who terminated during fiscal year 1968 ranged from 4.5 to 5.4 months.

VOCATIONAL AND ACADEMIC TRAINING— CONSERVATION CENTERS

The conservation centers generally provided vocational training through on-the-job training in performing conservation work projects with little or no classroom instruction related to the on-the-job training. Generally, conservation center work projects consist of projects for the development and improvement of public lands under the supervision of the Department of Agriculture and/or the Department of the Interior. The agencies plan the work, and corpsmen are assigned to work crews. Specific work projects may include such things as landscaping, forest culture and protection, water control, irrigation, drainage, erosion control, construction and repair of buildings and recreation facilities, and construction and repair of roads and trails. Training at the centers we reviewed was provided to corpsmen primarily within the context of the goals of such projects. If youths were induced to remain at a center for a reasonable period of time, such projects could provide an opportunity to instill good work habits in the youths and to contribute to their social and psychological development.

On the other hand, the nature of the projects limited the opportunity for intensive vocational training. Projects such as cleaning debris from beaches and parks, clearing out undergrowth in forests, and seeding barren areas call primarily for common labor. Projects such as building and road construction, while providing greater potential for skills training, were not required to the extent necessary to allow the centers to provide intensive and progressive vocational training to the many corpsmen entering training at various times during the year. We noted that the training program at the centers generally lacked precise, detailed curriculums and lesson plans, and the performance records showing achievements of corpsmen generally were not maintained. Further, at some centers, the emphasis placed on the need to accomplish conservation work projects appeared to have adversely affected in varying degrees the training program and resulted in the instructors' performing the role of foremen rather than teachers.

Job Corps and the administering departments of conservation centers, Agriculture and Interior, recognized that weaknesses and deficiencies existed in training programs at the centers and, in a joint effort, considered means for improvement. On May 2, 1968, a Job Corps civilian conservation centers program task force report was issued containing, in part, a number of new program concepts and policies for future operations of academic and vocational training programs at the centers. Our perusal of the various occupational standards issued by Job Corps as a result of the task force report indicates that, in order for Corps members to accomplish the minimum requirements for program completion in these occupational areas, Corps members will need an opportunity to take part in intensive classroom and work-experience programs directed specifically toward development of the knowledge and technical skills needed beyond the helper and laborer categories. In our opinion, implementation of the requirements of the task force report, as they relate to vocational training, would have a beneficial effect on the training program at the centers. However, these requirements are to be established within the context of the goals of the work projects.

We believe that, to provide programs of maximum benefit to the Corps members, it is necessary to emphasize skill-developing vocational programs through intensive classroom training and related work experience and, through the development of work projects of sufficient complexity, to provide training of the caliber which would lead to skill training necessary to obtain worthwhile employment. More importantly, a sufficient number of such tasks should be developed to provide continuous and progressive training so that each Corps member may develop his capabilities at a pace appropriate to this readiness to move forward. Generally, the size and complexity of the work projects coming to our attention were not of a nature to serve as a basis for intensive vocational training.

Job Corps has recently enlisted the assistance of certain labor unions in training and placing conservation center corpsmen as carpenters, heavy equipment operators, cooks, and painters, and in other skills. As of January 1969, union assistance programs were being operated at 11 centers and, according to OEO, its plans provided that such programs would be implemented at 41 additional centers during

calendar year 1969. In our opinion, implementation of the requirements for satisfactory completion of these programs would require
Job Corps to develop training programs specifically designed to be in
consonance with such requirements, which may not be possible within
the context of available conservation work projects at the centers. For
example, the carpentry program calls for the use of five instructors
and a coordinator, all supplied by the union, to provide 52 weeks of
training for participating corpsmen, half of which time is to be spent
in general classroom instruction and half in practical carpentry-
related work experience.

Regarding the academic program, we found that few corpsmen
achieved the program goals established by Job Corps for conservation
centers that were equivalent to about a seventh grade public school
level. The enrollees' generally low academic achievement level upon
entering the program and their short length-of-stay at the centers,
along with the centers' practice of generally dividing corpsmen time
equally between academic and vocational training, precluded them
from advancing to the desired grade level. In one instance there
were indications that academic training was not emphasized because
of the importance attached by the center to completing work projects.
The need for intensive academic training is apparent from Job Corps
data showing that enrollees who entered conservation centers during
fiscal year 1968 had average grade levels of 3.7 in reading and 4.1 in
mathematics.

We found that graduation criteria varied among centers, that
they usually were minimal, and that frequently they were not adhered
to. We found instances where terminees were classified as graduates,
without regard to their length-of-stay, on such basis as their having
obtained employment or having entered the armed services after
termination. Some terminees were classified as graduates although
they apparently had not made measurable progress in vocational or
academic training areas. In May 1968, Job Corps prescribed minimum criteria for graduation from conservation centers under which
corpsmen would be required to demonstrate proficiency in certain
vocational and academic areas and to meet certain social and emotional standards. Few of the graduates from the conservation centers
we reviewed would have met the new Job Corps criteria.

VOCATIONAL AND ACADEMIC TRAINING—URBAN CENTERS

The vocational programs at the urban centers were structured to provide vocational training in a number of areas. Although at the time of our review Job Corps was in the process of establishing uniform training objectives for vocational areas at men's urban centers, it had not prescribed uniform criteria for graduation from either men's or women's urban centers and, therefore, such criteria were established by each of the centers.

There was no assurance that the criteria established by the various centers were comparable or were always met. A number of Corps members were classified as graduates, although it did not appear that they had developed the necessary attributes required for employment in the area of their vocational training.

The academic programs at the centers were structured to provide the Corps members with the reading and mathematical skills necessary for employment in the area of their vocational training. In recognition that certain levels of academic achievement were essential to successful performance in various occupational areas, the centers generally established minimum academic requirements that were to be attained either prior to entering a specific vocational training program or by the time of completion of that program. Most of the centers we reviewed generally did not enforce the requirements however, and as a result, many Corps members had not reached these academic levels by the time they had graduated from Job Corps. Also, although on-the-job training was a final objective for completing certain of the courses, such training was not being provided for many Corps members at the centers we reviewed.

Classification of a Corps member as a graduate even though he or she has not adequately demonstrated successful completion of all areas deemed necessary may initially increase a Corps member's chance to obtain employment because of Job Corps policy to place greater emphasis on obtaining employment for those terminees classified as graduates. However, in our opinion, such circumstances may also increase the possibility of losing the job obtained because of his or her inability to perform satisfactorily and may have an adverse effect on attempts to place future graduates. . . .

Generally, centers' placement efforts were limited to their immediate geographic area. OEO regional offices have overall placement responsibility for all Corps members not placed by the centers. Since conservation centers are located on public lands in isolated areas, they have very limited responsibility in this area. The urban centers we reviewed had varying degrees of success in placing terminated Corps members. The highest rate of success was in placing center graduates as contrasted with nongraduates. Although some confirmations of initial placements were made by all centers, we found that reports of placements were not fully accurate. One center reported placements solely on the basis of confirmations that interviews were scheduled between terminees and prospective employers, and two other centers lacked adequate documentation on center placements.

Generally, Job Corps did not require the centers to obtain periodic followup information on terminated Corps members but, instead relied on followup data on a sampling of terminated Corps members obtained by an independent firm under contract to Job Corps. The resulting data, although useful to Job Corps in considering its overall program, generally were not of a nature to provide meaningful data on specific centers. It appeared that a periodic followup system for each of the centers would provide both the centers and the Job Corps with useful data for evaluating the effectiveness of programs at specific centers and for providing a basis for determining whether further assistance might be needed by terminees.

In addition to the matters just discussed concerning center operations, we found a need to improve the counseling provided Corps members and a need to place more emphasis on encouraging Corps members to participate in the high school equivalency program. Also, we found that various methods of assigning appraised values to completed work projects were being used at the centers we reviewed, which in some cases did not provide assurance that the assigned values were realistic.

POST-PROGRAM EXPERIENCE OF ENROLLEES

As part of our review of program results, in August 1968, we made inquiries of first employers of record for all those Corps members who had terminated in August and September 1967 from the nine centers where we made detailed examinations and who were reported to have been employed immediately after termination. Also, in August

1968, our contractor interviewed 638 youths out of about 1,850 who in August and September 1967 had terminated from the nine centers and 145 youths out of about 550 who had been selected to begin training at these centers during August and September 1967 but who had decided not to participate in the program (no-shows). To the extent practicable, the youths selected for interview were selected at random. However, certain limits were placed on the sample because some youths were not readily available or could not be located. In September 1968, we made inquiries of the named employers of those youths who, during the interviews, had stated that they were then currently employed. Also, another of our contractors made an analysis of the reported employment and earnings of a group consisting primarily of calendar year 1966 trainees and no-shows selected on a national basis. We recognize that in such tests the possibility exists that terminated Corps members selected in a sample may not be fully indicative of all terminated Corps members. Also, the development of fully comparable control groups is not possible to achieve, and we recognize that some differences must exist between applicants who take part in Job Corps and applicants who, although scheduled to attend, decide not to take part. We believe, however, that the data developed in our review do provide an indication of the relative extent to which Job Corps training assisted participants toward self-sufficiency.

EMPLOYMENT AND EARNINGS

Post-Job Corps data concerning the 638 August and September 1967 trainees from the various types of centers and the corresponding 145 no-shows are summarized as follows: For the terminees, the percentage of the youths engaged in gainful employment was greater after Job Corps experience than before such experience and earning power among those working had increased. Also, we found that a number of youths were, after terminating from Job Corps, engaged in such useful pursuits as serving in the Armed Forces or continuing their education. It appeared that the increased employment and earning power among those included in our sample can be attributable, for the most part, to the greater employability of youths due to the aging process and to higher employment and wage levels. This increased employability and earning power also appeared to be associated with the length of stay of Corps members at the centers; those who were graduated were the most successful.

Among the indications which are shown by the data are that, for men who had Job Corps experience and were working, earning power increased over a period of time but unemployment was relatively greater for terminees from the conservation centers than for male terminees from the urban centers. At the time of interview, about 26 percent of those men terminating from urban centers were unemployed compared with 36 percent of those terminating from conservation centers. A comparison between conservation center and urban center male terminees at the time of interview also showed that the urban center terminees were earning 10 cents an hour more than conservation center terminees. It should be noted that on the average the terminees from the conservation centers had a lower achievement level than those from the urban centers.

Percentagewise, employment at the time of interview, among terminated corpsmen was greater and unemployment was less than among no-shows. Among those working, however, earning power was substantially the same for both groups. An average of wages for employed terminated corpsmen—$1.90 an hour for urban center terminees and $1.80 an hour for conservation center terminees—would amount to about $1.87 an hour compared with $1.90 an hour reported by no-shows. Comparable figures for corpswomen and women no-shows, developed from a relatively small sample, indicate a greater variation: $1.60 for corpswomen and $1.41 for women no-shows.

Although we believe that such comparisons provide worthwhile information as to the circumstances of the youths at the time of interview, the projection of uncertain program results over an extended period of time would require a number of arbitrary assumptions which we believe cannot reasonably be made. Also, we believe that conclusions drawn from comparisons of the extent of change among the terminees and no-shows included in our test need to take into consideration that the no-shows were persons who failed to report to Job Corps during the same months in which the participants terminated rather than at dates, about 6 months earlier, corresponding to the time of enrollment of the participants. As a result, the beginning wage and employment data for no-shows more closely correspond to similar data on Corps members immediately after they terminated from the program.

As a further part of our review, another one of our contractors made an analysis of the reported employment and earnings of a group of August 1966 terminees and a sample of no-shows from the last quarter of 1965 and the first three-quarters of 1966, corresponding approximately to the time that terminees entered the Job Corps. This analysis was based on the findings of, and data available from, an opinion research organization which had been making a continuing study of post-Job Corps experience of a sampling of terminees and no-shows during calendar year 1966 under a Job Corps contract. The research group interviewed about 900 terminees from all three types of centers and about 500 no-shows; both groups consisted of more than 85 percent males. Our contractor concluded on the basis of its analysis that in the employment area the terminees had not shown any major improvement clearly attributable to the program. The contractor found that Job Corps males had an employment rate of 56 percent when they entered the program and 58 to 60 percent measured at various periods ranging from immediately to 18 months after the program. The contractor was unable to ascribe even the small increase in employment to the program because the control groups showed even larger increases going from 47 percent at entry to 49 to 58 percent at various periods.

Our contractor found also that the average wage for male terminees increased from $1.22 at entry to $1.55 at 6 months and $1.91 at 18 months after termination. Female wages increased from $1.05 at entry to $1.56 at 18 months. No-show males earned $1.17 at time of sign up and $1.46 at 6 months. Data on no-shows were not available for later periods, but short-term (0–3 months) enrollees, with wage rates at entry and 6 months later that were closely similar to those of the no-shows, were used as a substitute control group. The latter had wage rates of $1.81 at 18 months—that is, 10 cents less than the average for male terminees. Based on the difference between wage increments from pre-entry to 18 months after termination, however, the net average wage increment attributed to the program was estimated at 7 cents.

The contractor did find that individuals who spent more than 6 months in the program appeared to improve their employment chances, and those who spent 12 months or more had a considerable additional wage advantage. Retention rates, however, were such that the weight of these groups in the average terminee performance was relatively small.

There are a number of variations between the data as to employment, earnings, and so forth, found by our contractor and ourselves.

The data generally indicate the same tendencies, however, and the differences could be expected in view of the differences between the groups which were used for the analyses.

CONTINUING EMPLOYMENT PROBLEMS OF TERMINEES

Our tests directed toward identifying measurable economic gains revealed evidence of continued employment problems for a significant portion of those samples. Of all the terminees interviewed, 14 percent informed us that they had held no jobs and 13 percent informed us that they had held four or more jobs during the 1 year since their termination. In August 1968, we received responses from the initial employer of record of 362 of the Corps members who had terminated from the nine centers during August and September 1967 and were reported to have been employed immediately after termination. Eighty, or 22 percent, of the employers of the 362 terminees indicated that the terminees had never worked for them. Of the 282 remaining terminees who had worked for the reported employers, 211, or 75 percent, had left their jobs and 71, or 25 percent, were still working at the time of our inquiry.

Of the 211 terminees who were no longer working at their first job, 75 percent left during the first 4 months. Of the 211 who left their jobs, 59, or 28 percent, were discharged and an additional 59, or 28 percent, left but gave no reason for leaving. Most employers gave multiple reasons for discharging the 59 youths. With respect to responses received from 166 employers identified by the terminees we interviewed as their current employer, 18 employers, or 11 percent, had no record that the terminees ever worked for them. Of the 148 who had worked, 81 were still working at the time of our inquiry. Of the 67 who had left their jobs, 19, or 28 percent, were discharged and 14, or 21 percent, left but gave no reason for leaving. Some of the employers gave multiple reasons for discharging the 19 youths.

EFFECT OF TRAINING; AGE, AND LENGTH OF STAY

We compared the type of occupational endeavors that the terminees were engaged in at the time of our interview with the type of occupational training received by the terminees while in Job Corps. We found that 25 percent of the working terminees included in our sample for whom training information was available were working in areas in which they had received training and 75 percent were working in other areas. Our analysis of data obtained from the interviews showed that the percentage of those working and the wages earned had increased with the age of those included in the sample. About 46 percent of those under 18 years of age at the time of interview were working and earning an average wage of $1.79 an hour. In comparison, about 55 percent of those 18 years of age and older were working and earning an average wage of $1.90 an hour. Our analysis showed also that both the wage rate and the employment rate had increased in relation to the time spent in the program. The average hourly wage rate was, at the time of interview, for Corps members who stayed in the program for 6 months or less, $1.78; for those who stayed 7 through 12 months, $1.87; and for those who stayed more than 1 year, $2.03. Further, the employment percentages for those who had corresponding lengths of stay in the program were 43 percent, 59 percent, and 60 percent, respectively.

ARTICLE 31

Equality of Educational Opportunity

James S. Coleman

SEGREGATION IN THE PUBLIC SCHOOLS

The great majority of American children attend schools that are largely segregated—that is, where almost all of their fellow students

Reprinted from *Equality Of Educational Opportunity, Summary Report.* U.S. Department of Health, Education, and Welfare, Office Of Education. Pp. 3, 8, 9, 14, 20–22, 28, 31. Washington, D.C.: U.S. Government Printing Office, 1966.

are of the same racial background as they are. Among minority groups, Negroes are by far the most segregated. Taking all groups, however, white children are most segregated. Almost 80 percent of all white pupils in 1st grade and 12th grade attend schools that are from 90 percent to 100 percent white. And 97 percent at grade 1, and 99 percent at grade 12, attend schools that are 50 percent or more white.

For Negro pupils, segregation is more nearly complete in the South (as it is for whites also), but it is extensive also in all the other regions where the Negro population is concentrated: the urban North, Midwest, and West.

More than 65 percent of all Negro pupils in the 1st grade attend schools that are between 90 and 100 percent Negro. And 87 percent at grade 1, and 66 percent at grade 12, attend schools that are 50 percent or more Negro. In the South, most students attend schools that are 100 percent white or Negro.

The same pattern of segregation holds, though not quite so strongly, for the teachers of Negro and white students. For the Nation as a whole the average Negro elementary pupil attends a school in which 65 percent of the teachers are Negro; the average white elementary pupil attends a school in which 97 percent of the teachers are white. White teachers are more predominant at the secondary level, where the corresponding figures are 59 and 97 percent. The racial matching of teachers is most pronounced in the South, where by tradition it has been complete. On a nationwide basis, in cases where the races of pupils and teachers are not matched, the trend is all in one direction: white teachers teach Negro children but Negro teachers seldom teach white children; just as, in the schools, integration consists primarily of a minority of Negro pupils in predominantly white schools but almost never of a few whites in largely Negro schools.

In its desegregation decision of 1954, the Supreme Court held that separate schools for Negro and white children are inherently unequal. This survey finds that, when measured by that yardstick, American public education remains largely unequal in most regions of the country, including all those where Negroes form any significant proportion of the population. Obviously, however, that is not the only yardstick. The next section of the summary describes other characteristics by means of which equality of educational opportunity may be appraised.

THE SCHOOLS AND THEIR CHARACTERISTICS

The school environment of a child consists of many elements, ranging from the desk he sits at to the child who sits next to him, and including the teacher who stands at the front of his class. A statistical survey can give only fragmentary evidence of this environment.

Great collections of numbers such as are found in these pages—totals and averages and percentages—blur and obscure rather than sharpen and illuminate the range of variation they represent. If one reads, for example, that the average annual income per person in the State of Maryland is $3,000, there is a tendency to picture an average person living in moderate circumstances in a middle-class neighborhood holding an ordinary job. But that number represents at the upper end millionaires, and at the lower end the unemployed, the pensioners, the charwomen. Thus the $3,000 average income should somehow bring to mind the tycoon and the tramp, the showcase and the shack, as well as the average man in the average house.

So, too, in reading these statistics on education, one must picture the child whose school has every conceivable facility that is believed to enhance the educational process, whose teachers may be particularly gifted and well educated, and whose home and total neighborhood are themselves powerful contributors to his education and growth. And one must picture the child in a dismal tenement area who may come hungry to an ancient, dirty building that is badly ventilated, poorly lighted, overcrowded, understaffed, and without sufficient textbooks.

Statistics, too, must deal with one thing at a time, and cumulative effects tend to be lost in them. Having a teacher without a college degree indicates an element of disadvantage, but in the concrete situation, a child may be taught by a teacher who is not only without a degree but who has grown up and received his schooling in the local community, who has never been out of the State, who has a 10th grade vocabulary, and who shares the local community's attitudes.

One must also be aware of the relative importance of a certain kind of thing to a certain kind of person. Just as a loaf of bread means more to a starving man than to a sated one, so one very fine textbook or, better, one very able teacher, may mean far more to a deprived child than to one who already has several of both.

Finally, it should be borne in mind that in cases where Negroes in the South receive unequal treatment, the significance in terms of actual numbers of individuals involved is very great, since 54 percent of the Negro population of schoolgoing age, or approximately 3,200,-000 children, live in that region.

All of the findings reported in this section of the summary are based on responses to questionnaires filled out by public school teachers, principals, district school superintendents, and pupils. The data were gathered in September and October of 1965 from 4,000 public schools. All teachers, principals, and district superintendents in these schools participated, as did all pupils in the 3d, 6th, 9th, and 12th grades. First grade pupils in half the schools participated. More than 645,000 pupils in all were involved in the survey. About 30 percent of the schools selected for the survey did not participate; an analysis of the nonparticipating schools indicated that their inclusion would not have significantly altered the results of the survey. The participation rates were: in the metropolitan North and West 72 percent, metropolitan South and Southwest 65 percent, nonmetropolitan North and West 82 percent, nonmetropolitan South and Southwest 61 percent.

All the statistics on the physical facilities of the schools and the academic and extracurricular programs are based on information provided by the teachers and administrators. They also provided information about their own education, experience, and philosophy of education, and described as they see them the socioeconomic characteristics of the neighborhoods served by their schools.

The statistics having to do with the pupils' personal socioeconomic background, level of education of their parents, and certain items in their homes (such as encyclopedias, daily newspapers, etc.) are based on pupil responses to questionnaires. The pupils also answered questions about their academic aspirations and their attitudes toward staying in school.

All personal and school data were confidential and for statistical purposes only; the questionnaires were collected without the names or other personal identification of the respondents.

Data for Negro and white children are classified by whether the schools are in metropolitan areas or not. The definition of a metropolitan area is the one commonly used by Government agencies: a city of over 50,000 inhabitants including its suburbs. All other schools in small cities, towns, or rural areas are referred to as nonmetropolitan schools.

Finally, for most tables, data for Negro and white children are classified by geographical regions. For metropolitan schools there are usually five regions defined as follows:

Northeast—Connecticut, Maine, Massachusetts, New Hampshire, Rhode Island, Vermont, Delaware, Maryland, New Jersey, New York, Pennsylvania, District of Columbia. (Using 1960 census data, this region contains about 16 percent of all Negro children in the Nation and 20 percent of all white children age 5 to 19.)

Midwest—Illinois, Indiana, Michigan, Ohio, Wisconsin, Iowa, Kansas, Minnesota, Missouri, Nebraska, North Dakota, South Dakota (containing 16 percent of Negro and 19 percent of white children age 5 to 19).

South—Alabama, Arkansas, Florida, Georgia, Kentucky, Louisiana, Mississippi, North Carolina, South Carolina, Tennessee, Virginia, West Virginia (containing 27 percent of Negro and 14 percent of white children age 5 to 19).

Southwest—Arizona, New Mexico, Oklahoma, Texas (containing 4 percent of Negro and 3 percent of white children age 5 to 19).

West—Alaska, California, Colorado, Hawaii, Idaho, Montana, Nevada, Oregon, Utah, Washington, Wyoming (containing 4 percent of Negro and 11 percent of white children age 5 to 19).

The nonmetropolitan schools are usually classified into only three regions:

South—as above (containing 27 percent of Negro and 14 percent of white children age 5 to 19).

Southwest—as above (containing 4 percent of Negro and 2 percent of white children age 5 to 19).

North and West—all States not in the South and Southwest (containing 2 percent of Negro and 17 percent of white children age 5 to 19).

Data for minority groups other than Negroes are presented only on a nationwide basis because there were not sufficient cases to warrant a breakdown by regions. . . .

ACHIEVEMENT IN THE PUBLIC SCHOOLS

The schools bear many responsibilities. Among the most important is the teaching of certain intellectual skills such as reading, writing, calculating, and problem-solving. One way of assessing the educational opportunity offered by the schools is to measure how well they perform this task. Standard achievement tests are available to measure these skills, and several such tests were administered in this survey to pupils at grades 1, 3, 6, 9, and 12.

These tests do not measure intelligence, nor attitudes, nor qualities of character. Furthermore, they are not, nor are they intended to be, "culture-free." Quite the reverse: they are culture-bound. What they measure are the skills which are among the most important in our society for getting a good job and moving up to a better one, and for full participation in an increasingly technical world. Consequently, a pupil's test results at the end of public school provide a good measure of the range of opportunities open to him as he finishes school—a wide range of choice of jobs or colleges if these skills are very high; a very narrow range that includes only the most menial jobs if these skills are very low.

Table 1 gives an overall illustration of the test results for the various groups by tabulating nationwide median scores (the score which divides the group in half) for 1st-grade and 12th-grade pupils on the tests used in those grades. For example, half of the white 12th-grade pupils had scores above 52 on the nonverbal test and half had scores below 52. (Scores on each test at each grade level were standardized so that the average over the national sample equaled 50 and the standard deviation equaled 10. This means that for all pupils in the Nation, about 16 percent would score below 40 and about 16 percent above 60.)

With some exceptions—notably Oriental Americans—the average minority pupil scores distinctly lower on these tests at every level than the average white pupil. The minority pupils' scores are as much as one standard deviation below the majority pupils' scores in the first grade. At the 12th grade, results of tests in the same verbal and nonverbal skills show that, in every case, the minority scores are *farther below* the majority than are the 1st graders. For some groups, the relative decline is negligible; for others, it is large.

Furthermore, a constant difference in standard deviations over the various grades represents an increasing difference in grade level gap. For example, Negroes in the metropolitan Northeast are about 1.1 standard deviations below whites in the same region at grades 6, 9, and 12. But at grade 6 this represents 1.6 years behind, at grade 9, 2.4 years, and at grade 12, 3.3 years. Thus, by this measure, the

TABLE 1.   Nationwide median test scores for first- and twelfth-grade pupils

Test	Racial or ethnic group					
	Puerto Ricans	Indian-Americans	Mexican-Americans	Oriental-Americans	Negro	Majority
First grade:						
Nonverbal	45.8	53.0	50.1	56.6	48.4	54.1
Verbal	44.9	47.8	46.5	51.6	45.4	53.2
Twelfth grade:						
Nonverbal	43.3	47.1	45.0	51.6	40.9	52.0
Verbal	43.1	43.7	43.8	49.6	40.9	52.1
Reading	42.6	44.3	44.2	48.8	42.2	51.9
Mathematics	43.7	45.9	45.5	51.3	41.8	51.8
General information	41.7	44.7	43.3	49.0	40.6	52.2
Average of the 5 tests	43.1	45.1	44.4	50.1	41.1	52.0

deficiency in achievement is progressively greater for the minority pupils at progressively higher grade levels.

For most minority groups, then, and most particularly the Negro, schools provide no opportunity at all for them to overcome this initial deficiency; in fact, they fall farther behind the white majority in the development of several skills which are critical to making a living and participating fully in modern society. Whatever may be the combination of nonschool factors—poverty, community attitudes, low educational level of parents—which put minority children at a disadvantage in verbal and nonverbal skills when they enter the first grade, the fact is the schools have not overcome it.

Some points should be borne in mind in reading the table. First, the differences shown should not obscure the fact that some minority children perform better than many white children. A difference of one standard deviation in median scores means that about 84 percent of the children in the lower group are below the median of the majority students—but 50 percent of the white children are themselves below that median as well.

A second point of qualification concerns regional differences. By grade 12, both white and Negro students in the South score below their counterparts—white and Negro—in the North. In addition, Southern Negroes score farther below Southern whites than Northern Negroes score below Northern whites. The consequences of this pattern can be illustrated by the fact that the 12th grade Negro in the nonmetropolitan South is 0.8 standard deviation below—or in terms of years, 1.9 years behind—the Negro in the metropolitan Northeast, though at grade 1 there is no such regional difference.

Finally, the test scores at grade 12 obviously do not take account of those pupils who have left school before reaching the senior year. In the metropolitan North and West, 20 percent of the Negroes of ages 16 and 17 are not enrolled in school, a higher dropout percentage than in either the metropolitan or nonmetropolitan South. If it is the case that some or many of the Northern dropouts performed poorly when they were in school, the Negro achievement in the North may be artificially elevated because some of those who achieved more poorly have left school.

RELATION OF ACHIEVEMENT TO SCHOOL CHARACTERISTICS

If 100 students within a school take a certain test, there is likely to be great variation in their scores. One student may score 97 percent, another 13; several may score 78 percent. This represents variability in achievement *within* the particular school.

It is possible, however, to compute the average of the scores made by the students within that school and to compare it with the average score, or achievement, of pupils within another school, or many other schools. These comparisons then represent variations *between schools*.

When one sees that the average score on a verbal achievement test in School X is 55 and in School Y is 72, the natural question to ask is: What accounts for the difference?

There are many factors that in combination account for the difference. This analysis concentrates on one cluster of those factors. It attempts to describe what relationship the school's characteristics themselves (libraries, for example, and teachers and laboratories and so on) seem to have to the achievement of majority and minority groups (separately for each group on a nationwide basis, and also for Negro and white pupils in the North and South).

The first finding is that the schools are remarkably similar in the effect they have on the achievement of their pupils when the socio-economic background of the students is taken into account. It is known that socioeconomic factors bear a strong relation to academic achievement. When these factors are statistically controlled, however, it appears that differences between schools account for only a small fraction of differences in pupil achievement.

The schools *do* differ, however, in the degree of impact they have on the various racial and ethnic groups. The average white student's achievement is less affected by the strength or weakness of his school's facilities, curricula, and teachers than is the average minority pupil's. To put it another way, the achievement of minority pupils depends more on the schools they attend than does the achievement of majority pupils. Thus, 20 percent of the achievement of Negroes in the South is associated with the particular schools they go to, whereas only 10 percent of the achievement of whites in the South is. Except for Oriental Americans, this general result is found for all minorities.

The conclusion can then be drawn that improving the school of a minority pupil will increase his achievement more than will improving the school of a white child increase his. Similarly, the average minority pupil's achievement will suffer more in a school of low quality than will the average white pupil's. In short, whites, and to a lesser extent Oriental Americans, are less affected one way or the other by the quality of their schools than are minority pupils. This indicates that it is for the most disadvantaged children that improvements in school quality will make the most difference in achievement.

All of these results suggest the next question: What are the school characteristics that account for most variation in achievement? In other words, what factors in the school are most important in affecting achievement?

It appears that variations in the facilities and curriculums of the schools account for relatively little variation in pupil achievement insofar as this is measured by standard tests. Again, it is for majority whites that the variations make the least difference; for minorities, they make somewhat more difference. Among the facilities that show some relationship to achievement are several for which minority pupils' schools are less well equipped relative to whites. For example, the existence of science laboratories showed a small but consistent relationship to achievement. And minorities, especially Negroes, are in schools with fewer of these laboratories.

The quality of teachers shows a stronger relationship to pupil achievement. Furthermore, it is progressively greater at higher grades, indicating a cumulative impact of the qualities of teachers in a school on the pupils' achievement. Again, teacher quality is more important for minority pupil achievement than for that of the majority.

It should be noted that many characteristics of teachers were not measured in this survey; therefore, the results are not at all conclusive regarding the specific characteristics of teachers that are most important. Among those measured in the survey, however, those that bear the highest relationship to pupil achievement are first, the teacher's score on the verbal skills test, and then his educational background—both his own level of education and that of his parents. On both of these measures, the level of teachers of minority students, especially Negroes, is lower.

Finally, it appears that a pupil's achievement is strongly related to the educational backgrounds and aspirations of the other students in the school. Only crude measures of these variables were used (principally the proportion of pupils with encyclopedias in the home and the proportion planning to go to college). Analysis indicates, however, that children from a given family background, when put in schools of different social composition, will achieve at quite different levels. This effect is again less for white pupils than for any minority group other than Orientals. Thus, if a white pupil from a home that is strongly and effectively supportive of education is put in a school where most pupils do not come from such homes, his achievement will be little different than if he were in a school composed of others like himself. But if a minority pupil from a home without much educational strength is put with schoolmates with strong educational backgrounds, his achievement is likely to increase.

This general result, taken together with the earlier examinations of school differences, has important implications for equality of educational opportunity. For the earlier tables show that the principal way in which the school environments of Negroes and whites differ is in the composition of their student bodies, and it turns out that the composition of the student bodies has a strong relationship to the achievement of Negro and other minority pupils. . . .

Effects of integration on achievement

An education in integrated schools can be expected to have major effects on attitudes toward members of other racial groups. At its best, it can develop attitudes appropriate to the integrated society these students will live in; at its worst, it can create hostile camps of Negroes and whites in the same school. Thus there is more to "school integration" than merely putting Negroes and whites in the same building, and there may be more important consequences of integration than its effect on achievement.

Yet the analysis of school effects described earlier suggests that in the long run, integration should be expected to have a positive effect on Negro achievement as well. An analysis was carried out to examine the effects on achievement which might appear in the short run. This analysis of the test performance of Negro children in integrated schools indicates positive effects of integration, though rather small ones. Results for grades 6, 9, and 12 are given in table 2 for Negro pupils classified by the proportion of their classmates the previous year who were white. Comparing the averages in each row, in every

TABLE 2.   Average test scores of Negro pupils

Grade	Region	First grade with majority pupils	Proportion of majority classmates last year				
			None	Less than half	Half	More than half	Total
9	Metropolitan Northeast	1, 2 or 3	45.9	46.7	46.9	48.1	46.8
		4, 5 or 6	45.2	43.3	44.4	44.4	44.8
		7, 8 or 9	43.5	42.9	44.6	45.0	44.0
		Never	43.2	—	—	—	43.2
9	Metropolitan Midwest	1, 2 or 3	45.4	46.6	46.4	48.6	46.7
		4, 5 or 6	44.4	44.1	45.3	46.7	44.5
		7, 8 or 9	44.4	43.4	43.3	45.2	43.7
		Never	46.5	—	—	—	46.5
12	Metropolitan Northeast	1, 2 or 3	40.8	48.6	45.2	48.6	46.2
		4, 5 or 6	46.7	45.1	44.9	46.7	45.6
		7, 8 or 9	42.2	43.5	43.8	49.7	48.2
		10, 11 or 12	42.2	41.1	43.2	46.6	44.1
		Never	40.9	—	—	—	40.9
12	Metropolitan Midwest	1, 2 or 3	47.4	44.3	45.6	48.3	46.7
		4, 5 or 6	46.1	43.0	43.5	46.4	45.4
		7, 8 or 9	46.6	40.8	42.3	45.6	45.3
		10, 11 or 12	44.8	39.5	43.5	44.9	44.3
		Never	47.2	—	—	—	47.2

case but one the highest average score is recorded for the Negro pupils where more than half of their classmates were white. But in reading the rows from left to right, the increase is small and often those Negro pupils in classes with only a few whites score lower than those in totally segregated classes.

Table 2 was constructed to observe whether there is any tendency for Negro pupils who have spent more years in integrated schools to exhibit higher average achievement. Those pupils who first entered integrated schools in the early grades record consistently higher scores than the other groups, although the differences are again small.

No account is taken in these tabulations of the fact that the various groups of pupils may have come from different backgrounds. When such account is taken by simple cross-tabulations on indicators of socioeconomic status, the performance in integrated schools and in schools integrated longer remains higher. Thus although the differences are small, and although the degree of integration within the school is not known, there is evident even in the short run an effect of school integration on the reading and mathematics achievement of Negro pupils.

Tabulations of this kind are, of course, the simplest possible devices for seeking such effects. It is possible that more elaborate analyses looking more carefully at the special characteristics of the Negro pupils, and at different degrees of integration within schools that have similar racial composition, may reveal a more definite effect. Such analyses are among those that will be presented in subsequent reports.

School Busing: Swann v. Board of Education

United States Supreme Court

Mr. Chief Justice Burger delivered the opinion of the Court, saying in part:

We granted certiorari in this case to review important issues as to the duties of school authorities and the scope of powers of federal courts under this Court's mandates to eliminate racially separate public schools established and maintained by state action. *Brown* v. *Board of Education* (1954) (*Brown I*).

This case and those argued with it arose in States having a long history of maintaining two sets of schools in a single school system deliberately operated to carry out a governmental policy to separate pupils in schools solely on the basis of race. That was what *Brown* v. *Board of Education* was all about. These cases present us with the problem of defining in more precise terms than heretofore the scope of the duty of school authorities and district courts in implementing *Brown I* and the mandate to eliminate dual systems and establish unitary systems at once. Meanwhile district courts and courts of appeals have struggled in hundreds of cases with a multitude and variety of problems under this Court's general directive. Understandably, in an area of evolving remedies, those courts had to improvise and experiment without detailed or specific guidelines. This Court, in *Brown I*, appropriately dealt with the large constitutional principles; other federal courts had to grapple with the flinty, intractable realities of day-to-day implementation of those constitutional commands. Their efforts, of necessity, embraced a process of "trial and error," and our effort to formulate guidelines must take into account their experience.

Reprinted from *United States Supreme Court Reports, Swann, et. al.* v. *Charlotte-Mecklenburg Board Of Education, et. al.*, 402 U.S. 1 (1971). Washington, D.C.: U.S. Government Printing Office, 1972.

I

The Charlotte-Mecklenburg school system, the 43d largest in the Nation, encompasses the city of Charlotte and surrounding Mecklenburg County, North Carolina. The area is large—550 square miles—spanning roughly 22 miles east-west and 36 miles north-south. During the 1968–1969 school year the system served more than 84,000 pupils in 107 schools. Approximately 71% of the pupils were found to be white and 29% Negro. As of June 1969 there were approximately 24,000 Negro students in the system, of whom 21,000 attended schools within the city of Charlotte. Two-thirds of those 21,000—approximately 14,000 Negro students—attended 21 schools which were either totally Negro or more than 99% Negro.

This situation came about under a desegregation plan approved by the District Court at the commencement of the present litigation in 1965, based upon geographic zoning with a free-transfer provision. The present proceedings were initiated in September 1968 by petitioner Swann's motion for further relief based on *Green* v. *County School Board* (1968), and its companion cases. All parties now agree that in 1969 the system fell short of achieving the unitary school system that those cases require.

The District Court held numerous hearings and received voluminous evidence. In addition to finding certain actions of the school board to be discriminatory, the court also found that residential patterns in the city and county resulted in part from federal, state, and local government action other than school board decisions. School board action based on these patterns, for example, by locating schools in Negro residential areas and fixing the size of the schools to accommodate the needs of immediate neighborhoods, resulted in segregated education. These findings were subsquently accepted by the Court of Appeals.

II

Nearly 17 years ago this Court held, in explicit terms, that state-imposed segregation by race in public schools denies equal protection of the laws. At no time has the Court deviated in the slightest degree from that holding or its constitutional underpinnings. None of the parties before us challenges the Court's decision of May 17, 1954, that

> in the field of public education the doctrine of 'separate but equal' has no place. Separate educational facilities are inherently unequal. Therefore, we hold that the plaintiffs and others similarly situated . . . are, by reason of the segregation complained of, deprived of the equal protection of the laws guaranteed by the Fourteenth Amendment. . . .
>
> Because these are class actions, because of the wide applicability of this decision, and because of the great variety of local conditions, the formulation of decrees in these cases presents problems of considerable complexity. (*Brown* v. *Board of Education*).

None of the parties before us questions the Court's 1955 holding in *Brown II* . . .

Over the 16 years since *Brown II*, many difficulties were encountered in implementation of the basic constitutional requirement that the State not discriminate between public school children on the basis of their race. Nothing in our national experience prior to 1955 prepared anyone for dealing with changes and adjustments of the magnitude and complexity encountered since then. Deliberate resistance of some to the Court's mandates has impeded the good-faith efforts of others to bring school systems into compliance. The detail and nature of these dilatory tactics have been noted frequently by this Court and other courts.

By the time the Court considered *Green* v. *County School Board* in 1968, very little progress had been made in many areas where dual school systems had historically been maintained by operation of state laws. In *Green*, the Court was confronted with a record of a freedom-of-choice program that the District Court had found to operate in fact to preserve a dual system more than a decade after *Brown II*. While acknowledging that a freedom-of-choice concept could be a valid remedial measure in some circumstances, its failure to be effective in *Green* required that:

> The burden on a school board today is to come forward with a plan that promises realistically to work . . . *now* . . . until it is clear that state-imposed segregation has been completely removed.

This was plain language, yet the 1969 Term of Court brought fresh evidence of the dilatory tactics of many school authorities. . . .

The problems encountered by the district courts and courts of appeals make plain that we should now try to amplify guidelines, however incomplete and imperfect, for the assistance of school authorities and courts. The failure of local authorities to meet their constitutional obligations aggravated the massive problem of converting from the state-enforced discrimination of racially separate school systems. This process has been rendered more difficult by changes since 1954 in the structure and patterns of communities, the growth of student population, movement of families, and other changes, some of which had marked impact on school planning, sometimes neutralizing or negating remedial action before it was fully implemented. Rural areas accustomed for half a century to the consolidated school systems implemented by bus transportation could make adjustments more readily than metropolitan areas with dense and shifting population, numerous schools, congested and complex traffic patterns. . . .

V

The central issue in this case is that of student assignment, and there are essentially four problem areas:

1. to what extent racial balance or racial quotas may be used as an implement in a remedial order to correct a previously segregated system;
2. whether every all-Negro and all-white school must be eliminated as an indispensable part of a remedial process of desegregation;
3. what the limits are, if any, on the rearrangement of school districts and attendance zones, as a remedial measure; and
4. what the limits are, if any, on the use of transportation facilities to correct state-enforced racial school segregation.

1. **Racial balances or racial quotas.** The constant theme and thrust of every holding from *Brown I* to date is that state-enforced separation of races in public schools is discrimination that violates the Equal Protection Clause. The remedy commanded was to dismantle dual school systems.

We are concerned in these cases with the elimination of the discrimination inherent in the dual school systems, not with myriad factors of human existence which can cause discrimination in a multitude of ways on racial, religious, or ethnic grounds. The target of the cases from *Brown I* to the present was the dual school system. . . .

Our objective in dealing with the issues presented by these cases is to see that school authorities exclude no pupil of a racial minority from any school, directly or indirectly, on account of race; it does not and cannot embrace all the problems of racial prejudice, even when those problems contribute to disproportionate racial concentrations in some schools.

In this case it is urged that the District Court has imposed a racial balance requirement of 71%–29% on individual schools. The fact that no such objective was actually achieved—and would appear to be impossible—tends to blunt that claim, yet in the opinion and order of the District Court of December 1, 1969, we find that court directing

> that efforts should be made to reach a 71–29 ratio in the various schools so that there will be no basis for contending that one school is racially different from the others . . ., [t]hat no school [should] be operated with an all-black or predominantly black student body, [and] [t]hat pupils of all grades [should] be assigned in such a way that as nearly as practicable the various schools at various grade levels have about the same proportion of black and white students.

The District Judge went on to acknowledge that variation "from that norm may be unavoidable." This contains intimations that the "norm" is a fixed mathematical racial balance reflecting the pupil constituency of the system. If we were to read the holding of the District Court to require, as a matter of substantive constitutional right, any particular degree of racial balance or mixing, that approach would be disapproved and we would be obliged to reverse. The constitutional command to desegregate schools does not mean that every school in every community must always reflect the racial composition of the school system as a whole.

As the voluminous record in this case shows, the predicate for the District Court's use of the 71%–29% ratio was twofold: first, its express finding, approved by the Court of Appeals and not challenged here, that a dual school system had been maintained by the school authorities at least until 1969; second, its finding, also approved by the Court of Appeals, that the school board had totally defaulted in its acknowledged duty to come forward with an acceptable plan of its own, notwithstanding the patient efforts of the District Judge who, on at least three occasions, urged the board to submit plans. As the statement of facts shows, these findings are abundantly supported by the record. It was because of this total failure of the school board that the District Court was obliged to turn to other qualified sources, and Dr. Finger was designated to assist the District Court to do what the board should have done.

We see therefore that the use made of mathematical ratios was no more than a starting point in the process of shaping a remedy, rather than an inflexible requirement. From that starting point the District Court proceeded to frame a decree that was within its discretionary powers, as an equitable remedy for the particular circumstances. . . .

2. **One-race schools.** The record in this case reveals the familiar phenomenon that in metropolitan areas minority groups are often found concentrated in one part of the city. In some circumstances certain schools may remain all or largely of one race until new schools can be provided or neighborhood patterns change. Schools all or predominately of one race in a district of mixed population will require close scrutiny to determine that school assignments are not part of state-enforced segregation.

In light of the above, it should be clear that the existence of some small number of one-race, or virtually one-race, schools within a district is not in and of itself the mark of a system that still practices segregation by law. The district judge or school authorities should make every effort to achieve the greatest possible degree of actual desegregation and will thus necessarily be concerned with the elimination of one-race schools. No *per se* rule can adequately embrace all the difficulties of reconciling the competing interests involved; but in a system with a history of segregation the need for remedial criteria of sufficient specificity to assure a school authority's compliance with its constitutional duty warrants a presumption against schools that are substantially disproportionate in their racial composition. Where the school authority's proposed plan for conversion from a dual to a unitary system contemplates the continued existence of some schools that are all or predominately of one race, they have the burden of showing that such school assignments are genuinely nondiscriminatory. The court should scrutinize such schools, and the burden upon the school authorities will be to satisfy the court that their racial composition is not the result of present or past discriminatory action on their part.

An optional majority-to-minority transfer provision has long been recognized as a useful part of every desegregation plan. Provision for optional transfer of those in the majority racial group of a particular school to other schools where they will be in the minority is an indispensable remedy for those students willing to transfer to other schools in order to lessen the impact on them of the state-imposed stigma of segregation. In order to be effective, such a transfer arrangement must grant the transferring student free transportation and space must be made available in the school to which he desires to move. . . . The court orders in this and the companion *Davis* case now provide such an option.

3. **Remedial altering of attendance zones.** The maps submitted in these cases graphically demonstrate that one of the principal tools employed by school planners and by courts to break up the dual school system has been a frank—and sometimes drastic—gerrymandering of school districts and attendance zones. An additional step was pairing, "clustering," or "grouping" of schools with attendance assignments made deliberately to accomplish the transfer of Negro students out of formerly segregated Negro schools and transfer of white students to formerly all-Negro schools. More often than not, these zones are neither compact nor contiguous; indeed they may be on opposite ends of the city. As an interim corrective measure, this cannot be said to be beyond the broad remedial powers of a court. . . .

No fixed or even substantially fixed guidelines can be established as to how far a court can go, but it must be recognized that there are limits. The objective is to dismantle the dual school system. "Racially neutral" assignment plans proposed by school authorities to a district court may be inadequate; such plans may fail to counteract the continuing effects of past school segregation resulting from discriminatory location of school sites or distortion of school size in order to achieve or maintain an artificial racial separation. When school authorities present a district court with a "loaded game board," affirmative action in the form of remedial altering of attendance zones is proper to achieve truly nondiscriminatory assignments. In short, an assignment plan is not acceptable simply because it appears to be neutral. . . .

We hold that the pairing and grouping of noncontiguous school zones is a permissible tool and such action is to be considered in light of the objectives sought. . . .

4. **Transportation of students.** The scope of permissible transportation of students as an implement of a remedial decree has never been defined by this Court and by the very nature of the problem it cannot be defined with precision. No rigid guidelines as to student transportation can be given for application to the infinite variety of problems presented in thousands of situations. Bus transportation has been an integral part of the public education system for years, and was perhaps the single most important factor in the transition from the one-room schoolhouse to the consolidated school. Eighteen million of the Nation's public school children, approximately 39%, were transported to their schools by bus in 1969–1970 in all parts of the country.

The importance of bus transportation as a normal and accepted tool of educational policy is readily discernible in this and the companion case. The Charlotte school authorities did not purport to assign students on the basis of geographically drawn zones until 1965 and then they allowed almost unlimited transfer privileges. The District Court's conclusion that assignment of children to the school nearest their home serving their grade would not produce an effective dismantling of the dual system is supported by the record.

Thus the remedial techniques used in the District Court's order were within that court's power to provide equitable relief; implementation of the decree is well within the capacity of the school authority.

The decree provided that the buses used to implement the plan would operate on direct routes. Students would be picked up at schools near their homes and transported to the schools they were to attend. The trips for elementary school pupils average about seven miles and the District Court found that they would take "not over 35 minutes at the most." This system compares favorable with the transportation plan previously operated in Charlotte under which each day 23,600 students on all grade levels were transported an average of 15 miles one way for an average trip requiring over an hour. In these circumstances, we find no basis for holding that the local school authorities may not be required to employ bus transportation as one tool of school desegregation. Desegregation plans cannot be limited to the walk-in school.

An objection to transportation of students may have validity when the time or distance of travel is so great as to either risk the health of the children or significantly impinge on the educational process. . . .

VI

The Court of Appeals, searching for a term to define the equitable remedial power of the district courts, used the term "reasonableness." In *Green, supra,* this Court used the term "feasible" and by implication, "workable," "effective," and "realistic" in the mandate to develop "a plan that promises realistically to work, and . . . to work *now*." On the facts of this case, we are unable to conclude that the order of the District Court is not reasonable, feasible and workable. However, in seeking to define the scope of remedial power or the limits on remedial power of courts in an area as sensitive as we deal with here, words are poor instruments to convey the sense of basic fairness inherent in equity. Substance, not semantics, must govern, and we have sought to suggest the nature of limitations without frustrating the appropriate scope of equity.

At some point, these school authorities and others like them should have achieved full compliance with this Court's decision in *Brown I*. The systems would then be "unitary" in the sense required by our decisions in *Green* and *Alexander*.

It does not follow that the communities served by such systems will remain demographically stable, for in a growing, mobile society, few will do so. Neither school authorities nor district courts are constitutionally required to make year-by-year adjustments of the racial composition of student bodies once the affirmative duty to desegregate has been accomplished and racial discrimination through official action is eliminated from the system. This does not mean that federal courts are without power to deal with future problems; but in the absence of a showing that either the school authorities or some other agency of the State has deliberately attempted to fix or alter demographic patterns to affect the racial composition of the schools, further intervention by a district court should not be necessary.

For the reasons herein set forth, the judgment of the Court of Appeals is affirmed as to those parts in which it affirmed the judgment of the District Court. The order of the District Court, dated August 7, 1970, is also affirmed.

It is so ordered.

ARTICLE 33

Housing Abandonment: What Is to Be Done?

George Sternlieb

INTRODUCTION

We know very little about the phenomenon of abandoned structures. The reality has outrun the scholarly apparatus. There has been little research done on this situation, and even the very definition of the phenomenon is far from precise. Typically, the phrase refers to buildings which are vacant of tenantry. Commonly this is coupled with the virtual disappearance of the owner either de jure or de facto. *But abandonment is a process*, a reflection of a much deeper seated and extensive phenomenon—the disinvestment of private capital in core cities. The absolute number of abandoned structures is much less important than the process—and the state of mind which has produced them.

It results in a series of actions in which the properties in question in question are permitted to degenerate until despite the need for housing they are essentially unlivable. As we will note later in more detail in this paper, by the time the process reaches its terminus

Reprinted from George Sternlieb, "Abandonment and Rehabilitation: What Is To Be Done?" pp. 315–320; 325–331 in *Papers submitted to Subcommittee on Housing Panels on Housing Production, Housing Demand, and Developing a Suitable Living Environment*, Part I. Committee on Banking and Currency, House of Representatives, 92d Congress, First Session. Washington, D.C.: U.S. Government Printing Office, June 1971.

there is little that can be done with the shell. For the purposes of policy making therefore, it is essential that the process be reversed before its conclusion. Why is this process occurring?

THEORIES OF THE CAUSES FOR ABANDONMENT

An Evolution of the Market

When this writer first studied the abandonment problem in Newark, N.J. in 1965, there was approximately a five to six percent vacancy rate in the community as a whole, and much more than that in the core area where most of the abandonments were localized.[1] The vacant structures which dotted the core area could be viewed as a positive sign that the filtering down process, i.e., the development of new and better housing occasioning a series of shifts of families with each successive shift moving the particular household into better accommodations, was leaving behind it a residue of structures which were no longer competitive within the market. The abandoned structures, therefore, could be viewed as a very positive token of housing betterment.

True their effects in blighting a neighborhood, in providing a club house for the less reputable elements within the area and of serving as easy available tinder for fires, posed a challenge. But this essentially was a challenge of a rehabilitation or replacement procedure which at worst could easily be resolved through the process of demolition. The buildings could be viewed as no longer needed, serving only as a tribute to the fact that at long last housing was partaking, if only in a very minor degree, in the phenomenon so familiar in automobiles, i.e., a basic level of scrappage after a number of years of usage.

This orientation is no longer satisfactory. *What is becoming very clear in a number of cities is that the phenomenon has a life force of its own. Good housing and substantial shells which are much needed are being swept away by abandonment. The process currently is something much more than the "normal market" forces could engender.*

The Area and Infra-structure Decline

In a study currently being conducted by the author, *The Housing of Welfare Recipients* (Rutgers 1971), the question of whether welfarites would be interested in measures leading to the owning of their present apartments was asked of a probability sampling of 400 of them. Of those who answered in the affirmative, however, more than half answered that they would not be interested in any apartment or home ownership that involved staying in the same neighborhood.

Similarly, in a later context the respondents were asked a series of questions about housing problems. The great majority of volunteered responses involved area problems, particularly those of crime and drugs.

Does the abandoned structure therefore represent more than the abandonment of bricks and mortar, but rather the decay of the whole area?—with the building merely an eruption above a plain of desolation?

Certainly there is considerable truth in this statement. To use it as a complete denial of the efficacy of physical rehabilitation, however, is probably a drastic oversimplification.

While we wait for that halcyon day in which the state of the art, both in terms of the social sciences as well as the administrative effort, permits a complete integration of the social service and governmental intervention, we better keep moving. One of the things prevalent in the "zone of abandonment" is a failure of confidence in the future. The belief, voiced by some academics as well as administrators, that there is no point in putting money into poor areas becomes a self-fulfilling prophecy.

Housing rehabilitation and investment must be viewed as much as a psychological mechanism as a plumbing improvement approach.

The importance of improved housing from the viewpoint of the family needs little elaboration. Of equal importance, however, is the fact that of all governmental dollar inputs, it is probably housing investment which has the greatest degree of visual impact. As such its psychological value should not be underestimated.

Weakness in Property Holding Mechanism

One of the most satisfying figments of folk lore in our time is the portrait of the slum landlord. A typical vision is that of the central city slums essentially being the fiefdom of a small group of large owners. The latter in turn grow very fat indeed on the high rents and low input which their tenants and buildings are subjected to.

I have called it a satisfying illusion because it has in turn permitted us the belief that all that is required in low income housing was a repartitioning of an already adequate rent pie. Whether through code enforcement, rent controls, or any of a host of other mechanisms, the problem of good maintenance could be resolved by squeezing some of the excess profits out of the landlord's hands. This process would still leave enough of a residue to maintain his self-interests in the longevity and satisfactory quality of the structure in question.

This bit of folklore may have had considerable validity a decade or two ago. It has little relationship to the realities currently. A strong thesis can be made that much of the problems of the low income private housing stock in the central core stem from the disappearance of the large scale operator who, if nothing more, at least had the professional and technical capacity to maintain—whether the willingness was there or not. In our own investigations of housing economics the process of abandonment is more a tribute to the inadequacies of scale and professionalism of owners than it is of a merciless professionalism.[2]

The Elderly

Perhaps the weakest of the core housing owners are the typically elderly, white, remnants of earlier immigrant groups left behind in the core; the Italian widow, the Jew who didn't make it to the suburbs, the elderly Polish social security recipient. Their capacity and interest in reinvestment is minimal. Frequently structures which are well on the road to abandonment are actually owned free and clear by such individuals. Their horror at the very thought of assuming a mortgage even if one were available for the purposes of rehabilitation is a tribute to the fact that one of their major life goals is finally to own a building without a drain of funds going "to the bank."

The Small Scale Absentees

Many of the absentee owners particularly in minority tenanted areas are relatively small holders, owning perhaps two to a half dozen parcels. Their early dreams of substantial profits have disappeared, some of them indeed are owners by inheritance rather than by design. They have little confidence and decreasing interests in the maintenance and upkeep of the parcels. What is required is a take-out mechanism, i.e., a purchase or resale methodology which will permit such structures to move into more interested and/or perhaps stronger ownership patterns.

Ethnic Minority Owners

The third category of owner that I would refer to are the increasing number of ethnic minority, resident-owners. The problem here is that typically their acquisition procedures, because of weaknesses in the financing structures, involve an intermediary speculator who purchases a structure for cash at perhaps the 10 or 12 thousand dollar level. Because he has good credit, this may involve no more than a two or three thousand dollar down payment with the balance being secured through institutional financing. The speculator in turn resells to a local resident interested in a purchase of a home. A pattern which is fairly common is one in which the new purchaser makes a very nominal cash down payment, sometimes less than 1,000 dollars. In turn, however, he becomes involved in a very substantial purchase money mortgage to the seller.

In some of the cases which we have observed, these purchase money mortgages on parcels which initially cost no more than 12,000 dollars, to the seller involve as much as 18 to 20 thousand dollars. The cash flow burdens involved in this kind of pattern need little elaboration. Suffice it to say they frequently end up in abandonment.

Financing

The age of the structure, the decaying area characteristics, the generally low income, to say nothing of ethnic characteristics of local inhabitants, all conspire against the securing of institutionalized financing. In Appendix 2 is a study of financing patterns of tenement structures in New York City. It is evident from these findings that even without red line areas—areas in which no bank financing is available—that the belief in the value of collateral results in a number of areas and housing types being regarded as ineligible for investment. This in turn means that new buyers are involved in the pattern described earlier of high cost, short term purchase money mortgages. Those owners who are interested in and willing to make reinvestments in their parcels are not able to do so through conventional mortgaging channels:

> Note that the great bulk of multiple family residential structure rehabilitation has been done by the recasting of the mortgage. Under normal circumstances, assume a mortgage of X dollars which has been paid down to half of X, the owner in most areas can return to his bank and recast the mortgage for the original amount or perhaps even more than that particularly in the context of investing the additional proceeds in rehabilitating his premises. This provides long-term relatively low interest rate resources for the owner. Contrast this with the situation in core areas. Most banks, if they have mortgage outstanding on the parcels, as noted in the appendix, are most anxious to get out from under. Rather than permitting the recasting of the mortgage in an increased amount for rehabilitation, they are rather interested in its termination.[3]

Even given owner willingness therefore, the resources frequently are not at hand. While as will be noted later, there have been a number of governmental interventions both proposed and implemented in this area, much requires to be done.

WHAT IS TO BE DONE?

The abandoned structure is symbolic of the decay of the low income private housing market. Of all of the symptoms of urban blight, it is perhaps the most acute. As such, it must be viewed not as a phenomenon in and of itself rather as the epitome of a national urban housing problem. There are three basic targets that are required:

1. *Old housing plus new money is adequate housing; old housing without new money must decay.* It will decay more slowly if it is

occupied by elderly childless individuals. Its pace of degeneration will be accelerated if more youthful people particularly with many children utilize it, but regardless of the pace, it will ultimately end up on the discard heap unless fresh money is brought in.

The process of abandonment must be halted at its inception. This means that in areas peripheral to hard core blight, confidence in the market, confidence in the area, and confidence in the style of life possible within the city must be restored. These are major undertakings. They are what urban renewal and model cities and all the other elements of federal urban policy are about. Our assignment here is, however, focused on one of the several facets, but far from the least, of physical inputs. These must be secured, otherwise the process of abandonment will accelerate.

In order to insure the slowing down of abandonment, there must be the following:

a. Generous termed and generously implemented funding for cosmetic rehabilitation.
b. An improved financing and take-out mechanism for property transfers between owners who want out and potential owners, particularly resident owners, who are interested in staying in.
c. The development of operating and maintenance expertise and infra-structure in these areas. One of the very real problems of genuinely interested owners is not only the high cost, but the lack of availability of qualified repair people.
d. The provision of a total level of municipal services which will preserve the area. Not least of these is a much more intensive crime prevention activity. While in this paper little additional reference will be made on this point since it is covered in some of the other assignments, its absence here should not be seen in any way as indicative of its lack of importance.

2. *The development of an early warning system.* This is the most difficult and perhaps the most essential element if we wish to halt the process of decay and abandonment before it has proceeded so far as to lead to the demise of the structure. Current knowledge of social indicators is dreadfully limited. Intensive research on the dynamics of area degeneration, of what causes slums, and the epitome of slums —the abandoned structure—require intensive study. Much of the activity in this sector has essentially been a snapshot at a moment of time: a census, a model cities' application, an urban renewal induced

inspection of housing and the like. What has been lacking is something in the nature of a dynamic on-going continuous re-evaluation of high risk areas.

More on this point will be included later. Certainly, however, one easily implemented though far from perfect tool is very tight observation of tax delinquency rolls. These are engendered as part of the city's financing structures, and as such they involve little in the way of additional labor and costs. In many cases they serve as an early warning of parcels that are "in trouble."

3. *A demolition program that makes sense.* In the words of a housing official in Philadelphia who was contacted in the cause of this research, "the problem with demolition is that we take down a dirty old building and generate a dirty old vacant lot."

We have yet to develop the state of the art competent to deal with this very clear cut problem. Demolition of structures which are beyond rehabilitation is absolutely essential. Federal funding of the demolition program is quite adequate now.

The problem, however, is what do we do with a 20′ by a 100′ lot in the middle of the core area? The answer currently within the state of the art is "very little."

In Baltimore, for example, where the typical structure pattern is one of two-story, masonry row housing, the impact of demolishing a structure within the row has had disastrous consequences on its immediate abutters. The vacant lot becomes a garage heap and source of decay for the entire neighborhood. Any stroller in New York's East Side where a number of Old Law tenements have been demolished will observe the same phenomenon. There does not seem to be any fence so high as to inhibit this kind of development.

The Philadelphia vest pocket park program has made some headway in this regard, and certainly it should be looked into in more detail. The costs of operating small scale recreational areas in most cities, however, has precluded their development. I would think that this is an area that should fall within the aegis of the research and development end of HUD and that a number of modular formats should and *must* be evolved. . . .

A REVIEW OF SOME OF THE PROPOSED REMEDIES IN THE CONTEXT OF MARKET REALITIES

The basic concept of low income housing market is one in which the incomes derived from properties are adequate both to service those properties and to keep the owners in business. This has in turn engendered a variety of punitive measures to insure maintenance. Unfortunately, in many cases these have backfired.

The impacts of code enforcement without a realistic view of the market has been touched on before. It may be appropriate here, however, to indicate some of the experiences in Chicago along this line. According to Judge Kral of Chicago's Housing Court, as part of the Model Cities, a program of concentrated code enforcement was instituted. This involved the owner being presented with a choice of either fixing up the parcel in question or having it demolished. The economics of the situation are illustrated by the fact that as many as 4000 units in a single year were demolished under the program before it was halted.[4]

Emergency Repair Program

New York City has pioneered a program of having the city provide emergency repairs. If a tenant reports a health impairing violation the city makes efforts to make the landlord remedy the situation. If suitable action is not forthcoming from this source, the city undertakes the responsibility for the repairs and in turn presents the landlord with a lien against the structure. The logic and need of such a program is undeniable. The results, however, in a great many cases have been the landlord walking away from the parcel in question and its subsequent demise.

Rent Escrow Programs

Rent escrow programs have been instituted in a number of cities for parcels which do not meet code standard. In this program, rents are collected from the tenants, and held by the municipality or a subsidiary authority. The rents in turn serve as the basis for rehabilitation financing. The concept is that when the structure again meets standard its rents revert to the owner. Unfortunately, again the flow of funds typically are not found adequate to service the costs of required repairs. The results frequently have been the abandonment of the structure by the private owner and the inheritance by the city of yet another parcel.

The City as the Owner of Last Resort

As the result of these punitive acts against the private market, cities are inheriting increasing numbers of parcels. Unfortunately, there is little in the way of a track record to indicate that municipalities are very much better operators than private owners. The cost of maintenance in the structures which have been examined under this program, particularly in New York are very high, the delivery of housing services are far from adequate. A new administrative apparatus obviously is going to be required; again it may behoove HUD to provide something in the nature of pilot programs with which to explore alternatives.

SECURING LOCAL INVOLVEMENT

The action areas discussed below are important in themselves. They may be even more so in insuring the survival both of improvements and area. This requires local involvement. It is much more important then merely as an opportunity for "make work." A building's survival is dependent on good will and attention by owners, operators, tenants and neighbors.

The Development of Repair and Maintenance Services

Frequently, owners even with the best of good intentions, find it most difficult to secure adequate repair and services in core areas. The faulty heating system, which might have been repaired for a trifling expenditure, if not cured, may lead to the abandonment of yet another building. Lack of adequate repair facilities is far from confined to the central city—it is the backbone of much suburban conversation.

The common reality is accentuated, however, in the central city by the typical age of structure which is so prevalent there. Older structures suffer from all of the geriatric diseases: faulty plumbing, heating and roofing requirements. In the New York study, mentioned earlier for example, expenditures upon these areas were far higher as a proportion of rents and even in terms of absolute dollars for older, poorer structures than they were for newer, more substantially built ones.

The difficulties in securing repair action in slum areas are caused by a complex of reasons. Not the least of them is fear of crime. An example of this was a wildcat strike carried out several years ago by the installation and repair men of a major New York City utility company. The purpose of the strike was to protest the practice of dispatching single installers to certain core areas. The installers and repairmen felt that, based on experience with mugging and other forms of violence, this was too dangerous. The ultimate resolution of the strike has involved the company in sending out two-men teams to such areas with concomitant doubling of labor costs. This same type of affliction and cost increment obviously affects other repair provisions in the central city.[5]

The Need for Keeping Parcels Occupied

In a series of interviews with municipal housing authorities in major cities there was one constant observation: the need to keep tenants in structures or else run the risk of them being vandalized beyond repair. This was confirmed by core area landlords in New York City who expressed a similar fear. The statement is frequently made by the latter that if a parcel is vacant for more than a week, all too commonly, the owner will discover that the heating apparatus has disappeared, pipes may have been removed from the wall, and the level of rehabilitation required will be well beyond the scope of the market.

One of the necessities, therefore, is the development of renovation proceedings which involve a minimal dislocation of present tenants. The fiasco of instant rehabilitation in New York should not detract from the necessity of developing more adequate mechanisms.

Rehabilitation

The Department of Housing and Urban Development is presently funding Project Rehabilitation. This is an effort to develop a large scale rehabilitation industry, to secure know-how on the problems of feasibility of rehabilitation and to provide a model for future activity in this sphere. It is very clear that this type of large scale activity is an absolute requirement. In many areas, however, it must and should be coupled with the involvement of local community groups in the rehabilitation procedures. It is far from easy.

In some ways rehabilitation requires much more in the way of skilled jack-of-all-trades input in order for it to be economically viable than is true of new construction. Fitting to extant structures which, as a function of their age are askew and out of square, requires much more in the way of manual input and skill than is true of new construction. The utilization, therefore, of such activity as a training ground for large numbers of central cityites is a very expensive one.

There has been some experience in this regard in terms of the Roxbury rehabilitation effort in the Boston area, and as well in Newark.

In the Newark experience, the costs of rehabilitation were increased by approximately 2,000 dollars per unit through the use of local workers in housing units which averaged approximately $13,000 in costs. (This includes approximately $5,000 in acquisition costs.) The figure is far from a horrendous one, and it may be a relatively modest contribution toward generating the kinds of ongoing expertise which will be required in the future as well as providing core employment opportunity. The use of local residents in rehabilitation is closely connected with the next factor whose importance it is difficult to exaggerate.

The Maintenance and Operating Problem

The financial difficulties of public housing have brought to the fore the problems of maintenance and operating costs. Public housing units typically are built to very, very high standards. As such, the maintenance and operating costs they must endure are minimized. The federal government assumes all of the capital costs. Local taxes are minimized through the requirement of the host municipality charging no more than 10 percent of the shelter rent in lieu of taxes.

Contrast this with the typical, relatively small structure which must be rehabilitated. Unless the heating plant is completely revived it tends to be relatively archaic and an inefficient one with much higher fuel costs. The very age of the structure as earlier pointed out generates much higher costs of operating. Typically full real estate taxes are involved. (In the New York study pointed to earlier, real estate taxes are approximately, depending upon the calibre of the structure, anywhere from 15 to 25 percent of contract rent or approximately 17 to 28 percent of gross shelter rent—from nearly two times to over three times the equivalent for the public housing unit.)

It is little wonder then that, given limited rent paying capacity on the part of tenants in core areas where abandonments are localized, there is considerable difficulty in making both ends meet much less in generating the wherewithal for additional investment. Older, smaller structures are very frail vehicles regardless of the level of rehabilitation which they may have enjoyed. As such, adequate maintenance is an ongoing necessity.

If this level of service is to be provided, something in the nature of centralized repair and maintenance facilities must be secured. Again, an appropriate demonstration program on the part of HUD involving the development of alternative approaches might be advisable.

I cannot stress too strongly here that we must broaden the state of the art. The phenomenon of abandonment is not a transient. It will deepen and increase. What will be required to deal with it are a whole armory of weapons and they must be developed. Abandonment is an immediate emergency, and it should not be forgotten, but that emergency will be us for many years. Unless we make the investment in securing added know-how now, we will be no better equipped in the future than we are presently.

Tenurial Forms

What is the future of private entrepreneurs in the low income housing market? This is a very pertinent question for the future of the structures. The entrepreneurial function: the optimization between the resources available to a parcel and investments in that parcel, should not be forgotten. Similarly, the screening of tenantry and management control of the building as a whole, are very important functions which must be at hand even given the provision of enabling activity on maintenance and financing.

There are two forms of ownership which should be discussed here. The first is the question of absentee owners substantially involved through the hope of profitable investment. The situation obviously varies very considerably from city to city. There are a significant number of places, however, with New York and perhaps Chicago leading where absentee owners are essentially withdrawing their investments.

Indeed the statement can be made quite strongly that if the market was somewhat stronger, so much so that there were alternative buyers in the scene, this march would become a race. The problems of the variance in tenant and landlord ethnicity, of poor versus rich, of area decay, obviously shadow the shape of the housing market to come. It is future expectation as much as present yield that determines landlord behavior. When the former becomes highly questionable, even though current yields may be adequate, there is little incentive for long term investment.

What is required, therefore, is alternative forms of ownership for those absentee owners who want to get out of the area; in essence a take-out mechanism.

Resident Ownership

For many Americans of modest income, the only housing purchase which makes economic sense is that of an older property in the central city such as a Boston three-decker or a Newark six-family house. This involves much too high a level of investment for the return potential. This form of ownership is growing rapidly. Unfortunately it grows within a market context which typically involves high purchase money mortgages, the exploitation of relatively innocent owners by high pressure repair services, and a concomitant high failure rate. Would it be possible for the government to facilitate these transfers by providing an appropriate financing mechanism? The recent criticisms of some of the 235–236 exploitations should not be permitted to cloak both the potential and the necessity for such transfer approaches. In Appendix III is a memorandum on an Urban Homestead Act which I think might meet some of these problems.

Low-Income Cooperatives or Non-Profit Corporation Holdings

Both of these approaches have been espoused quite vigorously in the housing literature in the last several years. Unfortunately, neither of them has an adequate track record, particularly in terms of older parcels, which permit any generalization of the success or failure that is incumbent within the form. There is no question, however, that older parcels, which permits any generalization of the success or failure that insure their survival. To the degree that a local group can provide this, such ownership has considerable promise. Again, HUD should attempt a number of demonstration approaches to test the feasibility of these forms of tenure.

Summary

The problem of abandonment of structures is a reflection of the decline in the private housing market in core areas. The problem must be attacked both in its inception and in terms of its results. The former requires a revitalization of the private housing market such as to provide both stimulus and wherewithal for owner investment. The 312 program and the grant in aid program are most successful first steps in this procedure. In order to meet the challenge they must be broadened in terms of their funding and in terms of the qualification requirements.

The results of abandonment, the vacant boarded up structures which are beginning to dot our cities in increasing numbers, must be attacked through much more rigorous action. The combination of the public housing turnkey approach plus 235–236 funding provides the wherewithal for massive rehabilitation. The costs are high; this should not be underestimated. The costs of do-nothingness are even higher.

Once a parcel is rehabilitated we have the problem of its ownership and management. For this a variety of alternative forms of tenure are going to be required. These will involve the fostering of resident landlords, the development of alternative ownership methods such as low income co-ops and local community groups as owner-operators, coupled with the provision of efficient maintenance services.

Pervading this entire area is the question of what is the function of core residential areas. The great waves of migration from the South and from Puerto Rico have slowed down and are substantially bypassing many of their historical focal points. Middle class oriented minority group members, within the limitations of their pockets, are moving out of the older core areas. At the same time the relative youth of central city inhabitants, coupled with a high rate of household formation, is generating a nearly equivalent demand. This demand function is fostered by the lack of new housing construction and with it the slowing down of the filtering process.

When there is an acceleration of new housing development and with it a rejuvenation of the filtering down process, more in the way of partial vacuums—in need and demand—for core housing will be engendered. But this is a long time off. The great gap between present housing demands and needs augmented by household formation, as against the level of housing construction, indicates that the time is far distant when the abandoned structure can be seen as a tribute to the appropriate workings of the supply/demand nexus. Until that time, the buildings are needed. There is no alternative. In addition, the process of abandonment, while in part caused by area characteristics, in turn engenders a degeneration of the same area. It is difficult to envision any definition of appropriate environment which could include proximity of a shell of a house vacated by all but intruders.

The question of municipal provision of services touched on earlier is obviously a question that is even broader than the problem of abandonments. Several years ago, for example, in conducting a study of Newark, we had occasion to contrast garbage collection procedures in core residential areas as against those in suburban garden apartment developments. The latter, for which developers must typically secure variances, not uncommonly involve garbage pick-up as much as five times a week for dwelling units occupied by at most 20 small families to the acre. Contrast this with the Newark core scene where garbage collection is conducted only twice a week,[6] and too frequently in areas which have 60 large families to the acre. The situation in terms of schools, policing, and the like parallels this imbalance.

The largest single expenditure by owners typically are local taxes. And certainly one of the most significant *growth* areas in expenditures are these very same taxes. Despite this absolute level of costs and its growth, the provision of services is faltering.

In order to provide adequate housing at relatively low rentals typically some form of tax concession must be made. We have the sad example of the bankrupt attempting to bootstrap themselves. The utilization of the local public housing authority as the rehabilitator of abandoned structures utilizing the 235–236 mechanism as well as the turnkey provisions of the law is a most encouraging development. It flies in the face, however, of the local municipality's need for resources. As such in the older city, one of the principal objections to public housing is the fiscal imbalance that it tends to generate.

The need for increased protection services in core areas, voiced by core residents and reported earlier in the study of welfare recipients in turn can only be met by more in the way of expenditures.

Where is the money to come from? We must have an improved physical housing shell. Unless, however, this is coupled with an improved infra-structure, at best it can only serve as a momentary inspiration for the better life.

NOTES

1. See G. Sternlieb, *Tenement Landlord* (Rutgers, 1969).

2. See G. Sternlieb, *The Urban Housing Dilemma* (N.Y.C. 1971).

3. *Ibid.*

4. Communication from Judge Kral, December 30, 1970.

5. Examples in New York City involved a plumber using a two man crew within the building *plus* another man to "watch the truck." And all this on a simple one man job!

6. For more on this point see G. Sternlieb, *Social Needs and Social Resources,* (Rutgers 1967).

Public Administration and Environmental Quality

Harvey Lieber

Environment, ecology, and quality of life are currently fashionable words. A recent Gallup poll found that more than 85 per cent of the population is concerned about environmental pollution and that three out of four people said they would be willing to pay some additional taxes to improve our natural surroundings.[1] Auto stickers urge us to ban DDT. Walter Hickel wins confirmation from a concerned Senate only after pledging to have the Department of Interior zealously fight for environmental enhancement. The United Nations calls a conference on the worldwide problems of the human environment.

Yet despite the rising national and international concern over the deterioration of the environment there has been an institutional and political lag. Public administration theory and practice has hardly faced up to the problem of environmental management, except for repeating the traditional dogmas. Few middle-level theories or administrative models which would be of aid in the control and abatement of pollution, for example, have been proposed.[2] This article is a brief survey or situation paper on the environmental crisis and an analysis of the slow response of public policy and institutions to the challenge.

In the year since the *Public Administration Review* devoted an entire issue to environmental policy[3] we have experienced (to use only water pollution cases) an oil spill in Santa Barbara, a Rhine River fish kill, a fire on the oily Cuyahoga River, and seizure by the Food and Drug Administration of 22,000 pounds of Lake Michigan salmon with dangerous levels of DDT. In addition, controversy is

Reprinted from Harvey Lieber, "Public Administration and Environmental Quality," *Public Administration Review*, Vol. 30, No. 3 (May-June 1970), pp. 277–286. © 1970 by the American Society for Public Administration. Reprinted by permission of the author and publisher.

growing over ocean disposal of nerve gas, deep well storage of toxic wastes, the construction of a giant jetport bordering Everglades National Park, and thermal pollution from nuclear power plants. At the same time Congress has taken more than two years to reach agreement on a bill controlling oil, vessel, thermal, lake, and acid mine pollution while a proposal for long-term financing of sewage treatment works is stalled. Also, articles have recently appeared exposing the severe administrative and political difficulties the Federal Water Pollution Control Administration is experiencing in trying to carry out its water quality mission.[4] Thus it appears that in this "transitional stage of complexity and uncertainty" public administration has so far failed to act "with the intelligence, vigor, and self-consciousness that the situation demands."[5]

ENVIRONMENTAL PROBLEMS

A wide and diffuse range of concerns is subsumed under the subject heading of environmental problems. Besides air, water, noise, and solid waste pollution, this term often is expanded to include other amenities of life such as beautification, reacreation, and at times urban structure and stress, transportation, food and drugs, even population problems.[6]

Environmental disasters such as acute air pollution "episodes," hepatitis outbreaks from eating polluted clams, or the accidental death of 6,000 sheep by nerve gas attract headlines. Less prominent but no less threatening are the quiet crises: the gradual disappearance of San Francisco Bay, the death of Lake Erie from eutrophication, or the water supply courses that are declining in quality and purity.

Consider the following possible harmful environmental effects, chosen at random from this year's scientific and popular literature:

A slow heating up of the earth's atmosphere and climate through a steady increase of carbon dioxide, released by burning oil and coal. Or, conversely:

A gradually colder climate, through the cooling effects of accelerating quantities of smoke and dust.

Increased incidence of lung cancer caused by asbestos in mining, building, and construction materials.

Teenage deafness as a result of the sonic boom of loud rock music.

A proposed sea-level canal to join the Atlantic and Pacific Oceans near Panama, to be created by nuclear detonation which may have distastrous effects on the climate, currents, food industries, species, and general bioecology of 10,000 miles of coastline.

Earthquakes and ground water contamination caused by the deep well storage of toxic chemical wastes.

Migrant workers poisoned by continual contact with parathion, a chemical pesticide.

Acid wastes, surface subsidence, and fires in the accumulation of solid wastes and debris of underground mining.

The Mediterranean as a fished-out, typhoid laden, dying body of water from overloading by untreated sewage and industrial wastes.

Irrigated crops adversely affected by boron contained in the new presoak detergents.

Nitrate poisoning of babies from children's food containing traces of artificial nitrogen fertilizers.

Mutagenesis, or chromosome changes in body and germinal cells caused by ingesting hallucinogenic drugs, pesticides, food ingredients (caffeine) and additives (cyclamates), industrial chemicals, and solvents.

Most of these asserted threats are still open to verification and are the subject of intense scientific controversy. Nevertheless they offer us some idea of the "unanticipated environmental hazards resulting from technological intrusions."[7] And they also raise the possibility that we may have to plan and manage our environment in such a manner as to prevent or at least minimize some of these irreversible effects.

Aside from these more exotic cases, few can today doubt that "normal" air, water, and land pollution is increasing or that our general biophysical environment is deteriorating. Our mounting waste disposal problems can be quickly described and documented:

As long as our population size, density, and industrialization were low, our environment—our air, land and water—could absorb these wastes and no great problems arose.

We now face a new situation: Rapid population growth, predicted to double in 50 to 60 years; demand for water tripling while population doubles; increasing output of wastes and increasing pollution of our air, land, and water from all sources, municipal, industrial, agricultural, recreational; new types of wastes from industry, new chemicals which are more difficult to manage and control; increasing urbanization, industrialization, and use of technology, rising levels of income and increased outdoor recreation, all of which help to increase demand for clean water, pure air, and unlittered land.[8]

. . . the pollution problems will probably increase as the economy grows. If, for example, industrial production tends to grow 4½ percent per year, it will have increased fourfold by the year 2000 and and almost tenfold by 2020. Unless there are changes in technology or the composition of output, the total weight of the materials going through the economy, and the wastes generated, will have increased by a like amount. . . .[9]

If all municipal wastes were treated and if the effectiveness of treatment were raised to 85 percent, on average, actual municipal discharges into rivers would still be greater in 1980 than they were in 1962, and would have doubled by 2020. If on the other hand, we raised the effectiveness of all treatment to 95 percent, municipal waste discharges into rivers would probably decline over the next 60 years. But 95 percent goes to the outer limits of present technology, and would perhaps triple or quadruple treatment costs.

One estimate puts the costs of building and operating treatment plants that would remove at least 85 percent of the organic wastes from both municipal and industrial effluents by 1973 at over $20 billion, or $4 or $6 billion a year.[10]

Within twenty years life on our planet will be showing the first signs of succumbing to pollution. The atmosphere will later become unbreathable for men and animals; life will cease in rivers and lakes and plants will wither from poisoning.[11]

This last "alarmist" prediction comes from UNESCO! Adding it all up, there is reason to believe that the recent American Museum of Natural History exhibition, "Can Man Survive?" was not entirely mistitled.

TECHNOLOGY UNDER FIRE

When New York City mayoral candidate Norman Mailer was asked what he would do about the smoke blowing over from New Jersey, he replied, perhaps only partly in jest, that he would blow up the factories which were causing the air pollution.

This perceptive writer's remark expressed some of the current second thoughts about the blessings of modern technology, which many now view as an uncontrolled 20th century Frankenstein monster which threatens to poison nature and contaminate our planet. Rather than a revolt against technology, it would be more accurate to speak of a backlash, against the unforeseen and harmful byproducts of our machine age. Factories, power plants, automobiles, and jets, once considered signs of progress, now also symbolize major environmental threats. This is a recent but nevertheless widespread, even worldwide, phenomenon.

The Taylorites and other scientific managers applauded the introduction of time-saving devices and attempted to devise more efficient means of utilizing such machines. Later students of administration recognized that successful production rates and outputs made it necessary that attention be given to worker morale and interpersonal behavior. However, until recently few questioned the goals and products of the organization, its ends or its priorities; efficiency and growth were accepted as the highest good.

We are now living in what has variously been called a post-industrial, a new industrial, or a technetronic society. A generation which has been shaped by the impact of technology and is aware of its perils can question the purpose and priority of even such a fabulous technological feat as Apollo 11. It wryly notes that man's first act on the moon was to pollute it with chemicals from his engine exhaust while later jettisoning behind him a sizeable accumulation of solid wastes.

Similarly other probably technological successes such as our chemical and bacteriological warfare program and the supersonic transport plane are being increasingly attacked for their unplanned but extremely harmful environmental byproducts. You cannot stop progress—yet an expressway that would impair the historic quality of the New Orleans French Quarter has just been vetoed and a moratorium is in effect on building or annexation proceedings in New Jersey communities that have inadequate sewage treatment facilities. We have not yet reached the point where we are ready to seriously consider W. H. Ferry's proposal of a two-year ban on technological innovation to give us time to catch up on its side effects.[12] However, we are beginning to pause before embarking on projects that are advanced in the name of progress and modernization and justified solely on the basis of immediate economic benefits.[13]

THE SCIENTIFIC RESPONSE TO THE CHALLENGE

The realization that "we have become victims of our own techno-logical genius"[14] has spurred initial scientific and governmental responses. The scientific community, especially biologists, has been among the most concerned and active in environmental controversies. This involvement may be due to immediate research interests or per-haps it arises from guilt feelings. In any case, three basic ideas which have been advanced by scientists—pollution as a system, spaceship earth, and recycling—are becoming part of the basic theoretical frame-work of environmental management policy, and so will be discussed before turning to public administration theory in a strict sense.

Under the concept of environmental systems, pollution is viewed as one total system, whose outward manifestations may differ in form. Thus air, water, and solid waste pollution are all interdependent. For example, straw was found to be the most effective beach cleanup material at Santa Barbara. Useful for oil pollution removal, its dis-posal by burning could have posed a serious air pollution problem. The final solution, however, was to bury the straw, which brings us to the third part of our interrelated pollution system—solid waste disposal or land pollution.

Awareness of the finite resources and the very limited assimila-tive capacity of our planet has given rise to the simile of "spaceship earth,"[15] a closed production system whose wastes must be repurified for the sake of survival. Thus the concept of recycling rather than disposal is gaining widespread acceptance. If one views pollution as "a resource out of place"[16] then reuse rather than throw away becomes a guiding commandment and conservation rather than exploitation acquires a newer and more sophisticated meaning.

Technology, the application of science to practical tasks, is a two-edged sword. It concentrates on immediate economic benefits and often ignores long-range environmental impact. Yet at the same time its inventions promise to reverse the trend towards environmental degradation. Besides those scientists and engineers manning the bar-ricades, such as Barry Commoner, there are others at work developing technological alternatives. A breakthrough in pest control, new energy sources, or alternatives to the internal combustion engine would be of obvious benefit in eliminating some of the present technologically caused problems. Less spectacular ideas, such as easily degradable beer cans, would also help. Other scientists are beginning to concentrate on utilizing waste for beneficial purposes, such as warm water irrigation from thermal pollution to stimulate plant growth and to protect fruit trees from killing frost; converting dairy whey into saleable food products; using domestic sewage as compost; and deriving protein from petroleum wastes, yeast from industrial wastes, and sugars from pulp wastes.

The accelerating pace of technological innovation has also spurred scientific interest in futurism, which looks toward the year 2000 and beyond.[17] Alarmed by the hazards, conflicts, and crises which may be caused by uncontrolled social and technological change, physical and social scientists are joining forces in systematic long-range forecasting. The President has recently formed a National Goals Research Staff in the White House which will assess the long-range consequences of present social trends and evaluate alternative courses of action.[18] This too is an indication of the rapid acceptance of the need for planning and preparing for the hidden environmental costs of such changes through environmental early warning systems.

CONGRESSIONAL INITIATIVE

Congress, rather than the Executive Branch, has historically been the most responsive to demands for stepped-up air and water pollution control.[19] Similarly recent congressional initiatives for a recognition of the seriousness of present ecological trends and the need for a reassessment of general environmental policies have been followed by the Nixon Administration's present emphasis on this problem.

In particular, Senators Jackson, Muskie, and Nelson, and Congressman Daddario have performed a valuable educational function by alerting the public to environmental threats. The 91st Congress has been blessed with an abundance of legislative proposals on the environment, to the point where individual competition for legislative honors and intercommittee jurisdictional rivalries at one time threatened the passage of any bill.

The most significant recent legislative accomplishment has been passage of S 1075, Senator Jackson's National Environmental Policy Act of 1969. It contains a declaration of national environmental policy and goals, establishes a Council on Environmental Quality, and provides for review of federal programs for their impact on environmental quality.

S 1075 recognizes "that each person should enjoy a healthful environment" along with "a responsibility to contribute to the preservation and enhancement of the environment." It declares a national policy to prevent and eliminate damage to the environment and "to create and maintain conditions under which man and nature can exist in productive harmony." PL 91–190 also seeks to:

> assure for all Americans safe, healthful, productive, and esthetically and culturally pleasing surroundings;
>
> attain the widest range of beneficial uses of the environment without degradation, risk to health or safety, or other undesirable and unintended consequences;
>
> preserve important historic, cultural, and natural aspects of our national heritages, and maintain, wherever possible, an environment which supports diversity and variety of individual choice;
>
> achieve a balance between population and resource use which will permit high standards of living and a wide sharing of life's amenities; and
>
> enhance the quality of renewable resources and approach the maximum attainable recycling of depletable resources.[20]

S 1075 established a three-member independent advisory group in the Executive Office of the President which is modeled after the Council of Economic Advisers. This is the Council on Environmental Quality which is to study environmental trends and federally related programs and submit an annual report to the President on the state and condition of the environment.

Under Title II of S 7, sponsored by Senator Muskie, a White House Office of Environmental Quality is to be established to give the Council an operating staff and professional expertise. The chairman of the Council would be the director of this high-level office which would have an annual authorization of more than one million dollars and which would be directed to send its annual report to all standing congressional committees with jurisdictional involvement in environmental matters.[21]

The most controversial part of the National Environmental Policy Act directs every government agency to adjust its policies and carry out its functions in conformance with the stated congressional policy on the environment. A finding on environmental impact and effects would be required by the responsible agency official in every recommendation or report on proposals for legislation and other major federal actions which significantly affect the quality of the environment.

In addition to this Act, other more far-reaching legislative proposals in the 91st Congress would create a Department of Conservation and Environment (S 2312), a Department of Natural Resources (S 1446) or a Department of Resources, Environment, and Population (HR 12000). This reorganized department would generally be made up of most of the established Interior Department bureaus and other related agencies (e.g., National Air Pollution Control Administration, Consumer Protection and Environmental Health Service, Forest Service, Environmental Science Services Administration). In any case, the Congress clearly intends to upgrade and stress the need to take environmental considerations into federal programs and actions.

EXECUTIVE ACTION

During its first year in office the Nixon Administration was as unable as its predecessors to make its performance match its environmental quality promises. The sole innovation was the creation by Executive Order of an advisory Cabinet-level body, paralleling the National Security and Urban Affairs Councils, to review environmental policies and programs and suggest improvements. This interdepartmental coordinating body rarely met and failed to live up to its stated function to serve as "the focal point for this Administration's efforts to protect all of our natural resources."[22]

However, a series of presidential statements and messages indicate that environmental problems now have top priority, to the point where the Administration has almost preempted pollution as a political issue. Although initially unenthusiastic about the National Environmental Policy Bill, President Nixon upon signing it on January 1, 1970, strongly praised the new legislation, saying that it was a "particularly fitting" first act of the new decade. He then followed up his statement that "it is literally now or never" by selecting three distinguished conservationists for the Council and by proposing in his first State of the Union Message a national growth policy which would stress qualitative improvements rather than quantitative growth.

An ambitious presidential message of February 10 proposed a 51-point program of legislative and executive actions concerning water and air pollution, solid waste management, parklands and recreation, and organizing for action. Succeeding presidential statements and a study of possible consolidation and reorganization of environmental agencies also show a continuing awareness of the immensity of these problems and a willingness to tackle them.

Nevertheless, the effectiveness of the government's environmental policy will in the final analysis be judged not by the organizational mechanisms it establishes but on the basis of the specific actions and priorities it imposes. Also, as Sundquist has pointed out, environmental quality is not a single issue to be resolved like medicare or social security;[23] rather it is a series of continuing fights and use conflicts, with entrenched interests, such as oil companies, waging a series of strong rearguard actions.

At present expectations are high but the possibility of delivery is debatable. For example, the technology is generally well in hand (although not without some very troublesome exceptions) for the control of pollution. The cost of control, however, is quite high—for water pollution alone, 20 to 30 billion dollars over the next five years and perhaps 100 billion dollars over the next 20 years. And the gap between promise and performance is most striking when one compares the difference between money authorized and funds actually appropriated for air and water pollution control and for water and sewer grants.[24]

The government is lagging administratively as well. Air pollution standards are several years from completion and the water pollution control program is also faltering from lack of sewage treatment plant construction funds. Less than half of the states have water quality standards that are fully acceptable to the Secretary of the Interior.

The phenomenon of commitment far outstripping resources is of course not unique to this area. Despite Vietnam, inflation, and hard-core city problems, the Administration now pledges to fully devote itself to upgrading the quality of our life. However even when money is available it will be difficult to change direction—the classic example of distorted priorities being the billions of government subsidies for the construction of the SST with its unresolved sonic boom problems and the meagre amount spent by the government for research on alternatives to the smoggy internal combustion engine.

ENVIRONMENTAL QUALITY AND ADMINISTRATION

Until the 1960's, environmental quality was an issue of little public or academic interest, despite the rising levels of contamination. In this decade it has emerged as a major concern and political problem. With the advent of prosperity and economic security for most Americans, quantitative "bread and butter" issues have declined in importance. However, certain intangible aspects of living—beautification, air, water, noise, the quality of life—have become increasingly significant.

We are now in the middle stage of tentative actions and gropings toward solutions. Environmental quality activities have not broken fresh ground in terms of innovative policics and new institutional arrangements. Programs have generally been undertaken on an ad hoc basis without the benefit of much elucidation from public administration theory. Confronted with a wide range of emerging environmental problems, administrative theory's answer to the litany of doom has been an antiquated catechism whose key phrases—regional and coordination—fail to reflect political reality.

Consider the following syllogism:

1. Air pollution does not respect political boundary lines.
2. Existing local and state agencies deal with air pollution on a limited, piecemeal, and uncoordinated basis.
Therefore—3. An areawide agency covering the entire problem-shed would be the most effective unit to deal with the problem.

But whether through interstate compact, council of government, or special district, there is hardly a single effective regional air pollution agency founctioning today. With the possible exception of the Delaware River Basin Commission, the same could be said for water pollution control. As in the case of metro governments, the immense political difficulties in organizing areawide control operations vitiate the apparent administrative advantages attributed to such regional agencies.[25]

Similarly the Johnson Administration's "Creative Federalism" has left a legacy of extremely limited regional governments, such as the federal-state river basin commissions, devoted largely to planning along with some new programs of federal interstate compacts and other cooperative regional arrangements.[26] These have failed to stem the increasing assumption of responsibility for environmental quality management by the federal government. And we will have to see, in the area of environmental programs, if the "New Federalism" becomes anything more than a new slogan.

"Coordination" instead of "fragmentation" is often advocated for environmental policy disputes in the hope that an optimal solution can be reached.[27] Such overoptimistic attitudes only succeed in masking genuine clashes of interests which are not easily reconciled, such as the preservation vs. development fights that occur in many of our estuarine zones. In this search for harmony some are reluctant to recognize the basic economic and interagency conflicts that are present in most environmental policy issues.

It remains to be seen how well a Cabinet body or a White House staff will be able to "coordinate" conflicting uses and interests such as the differing attitudes of the Department of Agriculture and Health, Education, and Welfare over the use of pesticides, or the dissimilar views of the Atomic Energy Commission and the Department of the Interior over the efforts of nuclear detonations.

Similarly, the stress on finding alternatives that are feasible often overlooks the catalytic role that "unrealistic" threats of outright banning play in eliminating environmental threats. We already know that bills banning over-sudsy detergents spurred the industry into developing biodegradable detergents; one may wonder what effect recent legislation passed by the California Senate banning the use of DDT or the sale of internal combustion engines by 1975 will have on manufacturers.

Finally, "reorganization" is often used in conjunction with coordination by advocates of superenvironment departments. If the lessons of the Federal Water Pollution Control Administration are in any way instructive, they show that transfer from the Department of Health, Education, and Welfare to the Interior Department has had a traumatic effect in terms of personnel turnover without any appreciable benefits; further although FWPCA, the Fish and Wildlife Service, and the U.S. Geological Survey were all under one departmental umbrella, there was still insufficient consideration of environmental impact by the Department of the Interior in awarding Santa Barbara oil drilling and production leases.

FUTURE AVENUES OF RESEARCH AND POLICY

Instead of relying on the perennial administrative dogmas and proposing utopian (literally: no place) solutions or purported panaceas, there are several fruitful areas of inquiry for students of administration in present decisional mechanisms:

1. Analysis and evaluation of the performance of existing agencies and arrangements, their strong points and short-comings. Especially useful would be appraisals of the present regional mechanism for areawide control of pollution and of the effectiveness of the carrots and sticks by which the federal government is attempting to induce state and local governments to upgrade their environmental efforts.

2. Studies of the innovative and status quo forces, in particular the role that interest groups have played in the establishment and administration of environmental programs. For example, the shift of many conservationist organizations from a wildlife preservation mission to environmental concerns and their more sophisticated methods of operation should help to explain some of the recent policy initiatives in this area.[28] On the other side of the fence, a study of the influence of the power companies with their air pollution, thermal pollution, and scenic preservation problems or the powerful oil and automobile industries would also yield considerable insight into environmental quality administration.

3. The courts have been a long-neglected arena, yet the use of legal tools in the struggle against environmental degradation is growing. The successful efforts of the Environmental Defense Fund against the use of DDT, or the Scenic Hudson Preservation Conference's fight against the Con Ed Storm King project, and the recent suit by the American Civil Liberties Union against the resumption of Santa Barbara drilling all suggest that considerable changes in the rules of the game are being accomplished through legal and judicial avenues.

While public administration has been singularly barren of new ideas on environmental management, economists have been offering various intriguing proposals, such as effluent charges, environmental contamination taxes, and waste disposal charges on manufacturers.[29] One such approach is already being employed in the Virgin Islands where the Hess Oil Company pays a royalty of 50 cents a barrel on the oil it refines into a special conservation fund where it is utilized for the control of air and water pollution, urban beautification, and other conservation projects.[30]

It would therefore be particularly rewarding if economists and public administrators joined forces in devising workable and equitable systems and laws which would offer incentives to closed production systems which internalize external costs by reprocessing wastes, such as encouraging the recovery of sulfur from power stack gases, or discouraging the production of no deposit, no return bottles. Also needed are means to build environmental constraints into design specifications and industrial site locations. Hopefully, once these initial studies are accomplished, we can tackle the larger question—organizing total management systems which would include anticipatory assessment of technological impact, costs, and consequences.

Concern over the biophysical environment may merely be a broadening of previous conservation interests. However, the new conservation has also been transformed to stress not just preserving nature, but managing the entire environment, man-made as well as natural. Pinchot and Muir led us to the realization that our natural resources were limited; today we recognize that our ability to absorb our wastes is equally restricted. Not only are our traditional physical resources diminishing, but our air, open space, and natural beauty is equally threatened. As a result of increasing, possibly catastrophic, levels of pollution, man himself is an endangered species.

The early conservationists stressed multiple use; the ecologists now urge reuse. From an earlier interest in U.S. forests, soil, and water, our concerns have expanded to include the global effects of the complex interaction of society, environment, and technology.

One observer has attributed the generation gap to the horrendous threats of the future—nuclear war, overpopulation, and pollution—being built into the flesh and blood of the young.[31] Indeed, college students are now seizing upon quality of life issues and channelling their idealism into crusades for cleaner air and water. Concern over threats to coastal zones, rivers, and mountains has resulted in "ecological activism," a union of old-line conservationists and youthful militants employing political pressure and communications techniques, staging confrontations and demonstrations. This environmental mobilization is symbolized by the April 22 "Earth Day" or the national teach-in and day of protest on high school and college campuses. On the more academic side, there has been a dramatic rise in the number of environmental law and conservation courses being taught on the campuses[32] as well as the mushrooming number of environmental studies centers and pollution symposia. These events sparked by those who will inherit our polluted planet have served to highlight the environmental crisis to a growing conservation constituency.

As a result we are beginning to develop an ecological conscience or "the emergence of a concept of public responsibility for the environmental welfare of the American people"[33] and for the long-range consequences of our technological actions. This ethic values a livable environment over economic expansion and recognizes an individual's right to live in a pleasant environment "free from improvident destruction or pollution."[34]

With our higher standard of living we have broadened our concerns to include qualitative social and moral questions as well as economic issues. From preventing diseases and death we are now equally interested in reaching an optimal state of well being and in enjoying the amenities of life. These enlarged areas of interest may be indicated by the gradual shift of terminology from "sewage" to "water pollution" to "water resources" to "water quality." Yet the gap between private consumption and public needs is still one of the basic characteristics of the Effluent Society.

We have reached an awareness of the seriousness of these problems, but our political structures are still not keeping up with changes in the biophysical environment. The challenge of the 1970's will be to confront the difficult policy problems of institutional arrangements and establish effective systems for environmental management and enhancement.

NOTES

1. See U.S. Congress, House Committee on Merchant Marine and Fisheries, *Environmental Quality, Hearings,* before the Fisheries and Wildlife Conservation Subcommittee of the Committee on Merchant Marine and Fisheries, on H.R. 6750, *et. al.,* 91st Congress, First Session, 1969, pp. 59–92. Lou Harris also finds that, next to aid to education, Americans are most opposed to cutting federal spending for pollution control (*Life,* August 15, 1969, p. 23).

2. One significant exception is the monograph by Matthew Holden, Jr., *Pollution Control as a Bargaining Process: An Essay on Regulatory Decision Making* (Ithaca: Cornell University Water Resources Center, October 1966).

3. PUBLIC ADMINISTRATION REVIEW, Vol. XXVIII, No. 4 (July/August 1968).

4. Luther J. Carter, "Water Pollution Control: Trouble at Headquarters," *Science,* Vol. 165, pp. 573–575, and Anonymous, "Carl Klein: A Tough Boss Who Promises To Run a Taut Ship at FWPCA," *Air & Water News,* August 11, 1969, p. 3.

5. Lynton K. Caldwell, "Restructuring for Coordinative Policy and Action," PUBLIC ADMINISTRATION REVIEW, *op. cit.,* p. 303, and Dwight Waldo, "Public Administration in a Time of Revolutions," PAR, *op. cit.,* p. 299.

6. For a broad classification of activities within the scope of environmental policy, see U.S. Congress, Senate Committee on Interior and Insular Affairs, *A Definition of the Scope of Environmental Management,* 91st Congress, Second Session, 1970.

7. The December 1968 meeting of the American Association for the Advancement of Science had a panel with this title as well as several other sessions dealing with the global effects of environmental pollution.

8. U. S. Congress, Senate Committee on Appropriations, *Public Works and Atomic Energy Commission Appropriations for the Fiscal Year 1968, Hearings,* before a subcommittee of the Committee on Appropriations, Senate, on H.R. 11641, 90th Congress, First Session, 1967, p. 1170.

9. U. S. Department of Health, Education, and Welfare, *Toward a Social Report,* (Washington, D.C.: U.S. Government Printing Office, 1969), p. 28.

10. *Ibid.,* pp. 32–33.

11. Tom Davey, "Industrial Pollution: The Macabre Legacy," *Water and Pollution Control,* July 1969, p. 14. This statement was made after 200 experts from 50 countries met in Paris for the Inter-Governmental Conference of Experts of the Scientific Bases for the Rational Utilization and Conservation of Biospheric Resources.

12. See U. S. Congress, Senate Committee on Government Operations, *Establish a Select Senate Committee on Technology and the Human Environment, Hearings,* before a subcommittee on Intergovernmental Relations, Senate, on on S. Res. 78, 91st Congress, First Session, 1969, p. 252.

13. A special task force has just submitted a report on revising procedures for evaluating water and related land resource projects which attempts to take into consideration environmental enhancement and well-being of people as well as the traditional benefit/cost indices of national income and regional development. See Report by the Special Task Force, *Procedures for the Evaluation of Water and Related Land Resource Projects* (Washington, D.C.: U.S. Water Resources Council, 1969).

14. Statement by the President Upon Creating the Environmental Quality Council, May 29, 1969, *Weekly Compilation of Presidential Documents,* June 2, 1969, p. 771.

15. This simile was used by Adlai Stevenson and amplified by Kenneth Boulding, "The Economics of the Coming Spaceship Earth," in *Environmental Quality in a Growing Economy,* Henry Jarrett (ed.), (Baltimore: The Johns Hopkins Press, 1966), pp. 9–12.

16. Committee on Pollution, National Academy of Sciences-National Research Council, Report of the Committee to the Federal Council for Science and

Technology, *Waste Management and Control* (Washington, D.C.: National Academy of Sciences-National Research Council, Publication 1400, 1966), p. 35.

17. See Herman Kahn and Anthony J. Wiener, *The Year 2000* (New York: Macmillan Company, 1967), and Burnham P. Beckwith, *The Next 500 Years* (New York: Exposition Press, 1967).

18. See *Weekly Compilation of Presidential Documents*, July 21, 1969, pp. 982–988.

19. Frederic N. Cleaveland cites the 1961 Water Pollution Control Act and the 1963 Clean Air Act as examples of legislative initiative where "Congressional leadership was clearly decisive . . . despite executive branch reluctance," "Congress and Urban Problems: Legislating for Urban Areas," *Journal of Politics*, Vol. XXVIII (May 1966), pp. 289–307.

20. Section 101, S. 1075, Public Law 91–190, 83 Stat. 852. S. 1075 as originally introduced stated that each person "has a fundamental and inalienable right" to a healthy environment. However, this wording was dropped from the final bill because of possible legal entanglements. See U.S. Congress, Senate Committee on Interior and Insular Affairs, *National Environmental Policy Act of 1969*, Report 91–296 to accompany S. 1075, 91st Congress, First Session 1969.

21. Senator Muskie has also sponsored S. Res. 78, to establish a select Senate committee on technology and the human environment, which would be composed of three members each from the Agriculture and Forestry, Banking and Currency, Commerce, Interior and Insular Affairs, Labor and Public Welfare, Public Works, and Government Operations Committees, which would assess the benefits and hazards of technology.

22. *Congressional Quarterly*, June 6, 1969, p. 958, text of President Nixon's May 29 statement. See note 14.

23. James L. Sundquist, *Politics and Policy* (Washington, D.C.: The Brookings Institution, 1968), p. 375.

24. See U. S., Senate, *Establish a Select Senate Committee, op. cit.*, p. 143.

25. See the author's "Controlling Metropolitan Pollution Through Regional Airsheds: Administrative Requirements and Political Problems," *Journal of the Air Pollution Control Association*, Vol. XVIII, No. 2 (February 1968), pp. 86–94.

26. See Gary Warren Hart, "Creative Federalism: Recent Trends in Regional Water Resources Planning and Development," *University of Colorado Law Review*, Vol. 39 (1966), pp. 29–47.

27. For an insightful paper on this subject see Norman Wengert, "Perennial Problems of Federal Coordination," in *Political Dynamics of Environmental Control*, Vol. I of *Environmental Studies: Papers on the Politics and Public Administration of Man-Environment Relationships*, Lynton K. Caldwell (ed), (Bloomington: Institute of Public Administration, Indiana University, 1967).

28. A poll of National Wildlife Federation members, for example, revealed that 58 per cent considered air and water pollution as the nation's most pressing conservation problems, while only 12 per cent named "preservation of natural wilderness areas," and only 10 per cent chose "destruction of wildlife and resources," *Conservation News*, Vol. 33, No. 24 (December 15, 1968), p. 8.

29. See Allen V. Kneese, *The Economics of Regional Water Quality Management* (Baltimore: Johns Hopkins Press, 1964), and *New York Times*, July 20, 1969, p. 42. Also see *Select Committee, op. cit.*, p. 65.

30. The funds amounts to about $2.7 million a year (*Washington Post*, December 29, 1968, p. B1).

31. Stephen Spender, *The Year of the Young Rebels* (New York: Random House, 1969).

32. See the *New York Times*, November 30, 1969, "Environment May Eclipse Vietnam as College Issue," pp. 1, 57, and *Washington Post*, November 20, 1969, "New Militancy Pumps Life Into Conservation Fight," p. 117.

33. Caldwell, *op. cit.*, p. 302.

34. This is from the ACLU suit against resuming oil drilling in Santa Barbara (*The New York Times*, July 11, 1969). New York State has also recently adopted a constitutional amendment embodying a Conservation Bill of Rights guaranteeing the right to an unimpaired environment.

Chapter 6

The Cities and the Federal System
Public Policies for the 1970's

A massive effort by government, private enterprise, and the white majority is required to solve the urban crisis. Instead of blaming the disadvantaged victims of urban poverty and other debilitating social conditions for their own plight, we must mobilize the full energies of our political and economic resources behind comprehensive programs to improve the urban situation. These are the major questions facing us: Do we have the *will* to act? And *when* will we act? Once we have recognized the serious dangers of domestic decay, we will be able to answer these questions when our leaders give as much attention to the nation's internal problems as they do to foreign affairs, defense, and America's international policeman role.

In Article 35, Daniel P. Moynihan, one of the nation's leading urban affairs experts and former counselor to President Nixon, outlines ten specific proposals for a national urban policy. If the federal government becomes forthrightly committed to Moynihan's recommendations, our nation will be well on its way to developing the necessary solutions to the urban malaise. However, as a former advisor to a Republican Administration, Moynihan does not tell us how urban problems are related to defense and foreign affairs. Surely, a national urban policy must outline how billions of dollars in the federal budget can be diverted to crucial domestic programs.

One of Professor Moynihan's leading contributions to the Nixon Administration was developing a reform proposal to eradicate the nation's welfare dependency problem. In Article 36 President Nixon outlines this reform to the Congress in his message of August 11, 1969. Essentially, the Nixon Administration sought to substitute a family assistance plan (or income support) for the Aid to Dependent Children provisions of the Social Security Act. It is important to note that this revolutionary idea came from a Republican president, even though social welfare assistance for the poor is more frequently associated with Democratic leaders.

However, Dr. George A. Wiley (Article 37), Executive Director of the National Welfare Rights Organization, criticizes President Nixon's Family Assistance Plan as an inadequate solution to the welfare crisis. In his testimony before the House Ways and Means Committee, Dr. Wiley rejects the punitive features of public assistance, particularly governmental actions that attempt to reduce the welfare rolls and impose forced work requirements when meaningful jobs are not available. He argues that the poor need a minimum level of income to guarantee them access to basic living necessities. The NWRO program calls for a "guaranteed adequate income" of $5,500 per year for a family of four, which is based on figures determined by the Bureau of Labor Statistics. Dr. Wiley concludes that until such a plan is adopted by the federal government, poverty will persist, together with millions of welfare recipients who are thereby denied the opportunity to a decent education and employment. Others have suggested that the best way to end the welfare problem is for the federal government to take it over completely in order to relieve the states and the cities from the unbearably high costs of maintaining a system that nobody likes.

Racial and economic segregation in the metropolis is in part a result of those suburban governmental practices which exclude moderate and low-income groups. According to urban planners Linda and Paul Davidoff and Neil N. Gold (Article 38), the suburbs have consciously prevented blacks and other minorities from leaving the central city slums by establishing restrictive zoning, taxation, and housing construction regulations. This situation results in an "Ivy League socialism": Suburban governments perpetuate the interests of the rich by acting directly in their behalf. As an alternative, these urban planners present a series of proposals to open the suburban housing market. They argue that these programs would result in more jobs, more construction, and less racial tension in the metropolis.

On June 11, 1971, President Nixon issued a major policy statement on federal equal housing policies (Article 39). After reviewing past civil rights efforts, Mr. Nixon made a crucial distinction between "racial" and "economic" segregation. He argued that racial barriers in housing are unconstitutional and "will not be tolerated." The full strength of federal enforcement powers would be used to prevent such unlawful restrictions by local communities. On the other hand, the president would not use his executive powers to prohibit "economic" segregation, a prevention which he defined as the imposition of federal authority on local communities to accept low- and moderate-income housing. Thus, the President appeared to establish a somewhat questionable distinction between racially restrictive local zoning laws (which he condemned) and local voter referenda opposing federally supported low-income housing projects (with which he would not interfere). Several civil rights observers found it difficult to distinguish between Mr. Nixon's two categories. Apparently, blacks and other minorities who wish to leave the central cities and move to the suburbs cannot be discriminated against in the private housing market or by specific kinds of locally restrictive laws, but the federal government will only obey court orders and will not take positive steps to promote racial dispersion in metropolitan areas.

In the final selection (Article 40), Demetrios Caraley raises a serious and fundamental question underlying nearly all of the specific policy problems discussed in Chapters 5 and 6: Can the nation's large cities be governed at all when they must operate under such adverse social, economic, and political constraints? More emphatically, do most Americans believe there *is* an urban crisis, and, if so, what are they willing to do about it? Professor Caraley observes that the greatest obstacles in the future will be political rather than administrative or programmatic. Until effective leaders and a majority of Americans agree that massive commitments of funds, energies, and resources are needed for the cities, our urban centers will probably become "black tinderboxes" of violence, repression, and fear. Caraley believes that urban governance is possible, but it must be coupled with a significant and meaningful reordering of national priorities.

As this book concludes, we are not left with attitudes of hopelessness, despair, and bewilderment. True, the urban crisis has assumed proportions of seemingly complex magnitude. But our urban problems can be solved. Comprehensive solutions do not need to be utopian in order to succeed. What is required now is a firm commitment to overall efforts to deal with the urban crisis. As we move forward in the decade of the 1970's, we await the realization of this hope. The 1970's can be the time when America begins to build the "good city."

QUESTIONS FOR DISCUSSION AND DEBATE

1. Assume that you are president of the United States and you have received Professor Moynihan's ten-point program for a national urban policy. How, specifically, would you go about convincing Congress that such a policy could be put into effect? What specific programs would you support that would implement such a policy?

2. In this problem you are requested to respond to the following proposition as a federal government administrator and a resident of a poverty area: "Public welfare in the United States is a waste of the taxpayer's money, does not eliminate poverty, does not encourage work, and is poorly administered. Therefore, President Nixon's Family Assistance Plan is the best alternative solution at the present time."

3. Test the following hypothesis by referring to specific urban policies in this chapter: The only way of achieving a substantial re-ordering of national domestic priorities is to improve federal-state-local administrative relationships within the federal system.

4. What are the differences and/or similarities between racial and economic segregation in metropolitan housing patterns? What are the strongest possible arguments to support President Nixon's distinctions between these two categories? What are the strongest possible rebuttals to his views?

5. Big-city mayors are faced with a host of problems relating to the urban crisis. In the past, efforts have been made at local, state, and federal levels to deal with city problems. Considering both the programs developed in the past and the programs now in effect, do you think that city problems are manageable? Which level(s) of government are best suited to institute effective and long-range solutions?

6. If, as Professor Caraley observes, urban governance is a critical problem, how would you go about building an effective and politically viable electoral coalition that would respond positively to urban problems?

Toward a National Urban Policy

Daniel P. Moynihan

In the spring of 1969, President Nixon met in the Cabinet room with ten mayors of American cities. They were nothing if not a variegated lot, mixing party, religion, race, region in the fine confusion of American politics. They had been chosen to be representative in this respect, and were unrepresentative only in qualities of energy and intelligence that would have set them apart in any company. What was more notable about them, however, was that in the interval between the invitation from the White House and the meeting with the President, four had announced they would not run again. The mayor of Detroit who, at the last minute, could not attend, announced *his* noncandidacy in June.

Their decisions were not a complete surprise. More and more, for the men charged with governance of our cities, politics has become the art of the impossible. It is not to be wondered that they flee. But we, in a sense, are left behind. And are in trouble.

At a time of great anxiety—a time that one of the nation's leading news magazines now routinely describes as "the most serious domestic crisis since the Civil War," a time when Richard Rovere, writing of the 1972 elections, can add parenthetically, "assuming that democracy in America survives that long"—these personal decisions may seem of small consequence; yet one suspects they are not.

All agree that the tumult of the time arises, in essence, from a crisis of authority. The institutions that shaped conduct and behavior in the past are being challenged or, worse, ignored. It is in the nature of authority, as Robert A. Nisbet continues to remind us, that it is consensual, that it is not coercive. When authority systems collapse, they are replaced by power systems that *are* coercive.[1] Our vocabulary rather fails us here: the term "authority" is an unloved one, with its connotations of "authoritarianism," but there appears to be no substitute. Happily, public opinion is not so dependent on political vocabulary, certainly not on the vocabulary of political science, as some assume. For all the ambiguity of the public rhetoric of the moment, the desire of the great mass of our people is clear. They sense the advent of a power-based society and they fear it. They seek peace. They look to the restoration of legitimacy, if not in existing institutions, then in new or modified ones. They look for a lessening of violent confrontations at home, and, in great numbers, for an end to war abroad. Concern for personal safety on the party of city dwellers has become a live *political* fact, while the reappearance— what, praise God, did we do to bring this upon ourselves?—of a Stalinoid rhetoric of apocalyptic abuse on the left, and its echoes on the right, have created a public atmosphere of anxiety and portent that would seem to have touched us all. It is with every good reason that the nation gropes for some means to weather the storm of unreason that has broken upon us.

It would also seem that Americans at this moment are much preoccupied with the issue of freedom—or, rather, with new, meaningful ways in which freedom is seen to be expanded or constrained. We are, for example, beginning to evolve some sense of the meaning of group freedom. This comes after a century of preoccupation with individual rights of a kind which were seen as somehow opposed to, and even threatened by, group identities and anything so dubious in conception as *group* rights.

The Civil Rights Act of 1964 was the culmination of the political energies generated by that earlier period. The provisions which forbade employers, universities, governments, or whatever to have any knowledge of the race, religion, or national origin of individuals with which they dealt marked in some ways the high-water mark of Social Darwinism in America; its assumption that "equality" meant *only* equal opportunity did not long stand unopposed. Indeed, by 1965 the federal government had already, as best one can tell, begun to require ethnic and racial census of its own employees, and also of federal contractors and research grant recipients. To do so violated the spirit if not the letter of the Civil Rights Act, with its implicit model of the lone individual locked in equal—and remorseless—competition in the market place, but very much in harmony with the emerging sense of the 1960's that groups have identities and entitlements as well as do individuals. This view is diffusing rapidly. In Massachusetts, for example, legislation of the Civil Rights Act period, which declared any public school with more than 50 per cent black pupils to be racially "imbalanced" and in consequence illegal, is already being challenged—by precisely those who supported it in the first instance. In so far as these demands have been most in evidence among black Americans, there is not the least reason to doubt that they will now diffuse to other groups, defined in various ways, and that new institutions will arise to respond to this new understanding of the nature of community.

In sum, two tendencies would appear to dominate the period. The *sense of general community is eroding*, and with it the authority of existing relationships; simultaneously, a powerful *quest for specific community is emerging* in the form of ever more intensive assertions of racial and ethnic identities. Although this is reported in the media largely in terms of black nationalism, it is just as reasonable to identify emergent attitudes in the "white working class," as part of the same phenomenon. The singular quality of these two tendencies is that they are at once complementary and opposed. While the ideas are harmonious, the practices that would seem to support one interest are typically seen as opposing the other. Thus, one need not be a moral philosopher or a social psychologist to see that much of the "crisis of the cities" arises from the interaction of these intense new demands, and the relative inability of the urban social system to respond to them.

PROGRAMS DO NOT A POLICY MAKE

Rightly or otherwise—and one is no longer sure of this—it is our tradition in such circumstances to look to government. Social responses to changed social requirements take the form, in industrial democracies, of changed government policies. This had led, in the present situation, to a reasonably inventive spate of program proposals of the kind the New Deal more or less began and which flourished most notably in the period between the presidential elections of 1960 and 1968, when the number of domestic programs of the federal government increased from 45 to 435. Understandably, however, there has been a diminution of the confidence with which such proposals were formerly regarded. To say the least, there has been a certain nonlinearity in the relationship between the number of categorical aid programs issuing forth from Washington and the degree of social satisfaction that has ensued.

Hence the issue arises as to whether the demands of the time are not to be met in terms of *policy*, as well as program. It has been said of urban planners that they have been traumatized by the realization that everything relates to everything. But this is so, and need paralyze no one; the perception of this truth can provide a powerful analytic tool.

Our problems in the area of social peace and individual or group freedom occur in urban settings. Can it be that our difficulties in coping with these problems originate, in some measure, from the inadequacies of the setting in which they arise? Crime on the streets and campus violence may mark the onset of a native nihilism: but in the first instance they represent nothing more complex than the failure of law enforcement. Black rage and white resistance, "Third World" separatism, and restricted neighborhoods all may define a collapse in the integuments of the social contract: but, again, in the first instance they represent for the most part simply the failure of urban arrangements to meet the expectations of the urban population in the areas of jobs, schools, housing, transportation, public health, administrative responsiveness, and political flexibility. If all these are related, one to the other, and if in combination they do not seem to be working well, the question arises whether the society ought not to attempt a more coherent response. In a word: ought not a national urban crisis to be met with something like a national urban policy? Ought not the vast efforts to control the situation of the present be at least informed by some sense of goals for the future?

The United States does not now have an urban policy. The idea that there might be such is new. So also is the Urban Affairs Council, established by President Nixon on January 23, 1969, as the first official act of his administration, to "advise and assist" with respect to urban affairs, specifically "in the development of a national urban policy, having regard both to immediate and to long-range concerns, and to priorities among them."

WHAT HAPPENED

The central circumstance, as stated, is that America is an urban nation, and has been for half a century.

This is not to say Americans live in *big* cities. They do not. In 1960 only 9.8 per cent of the population lived in cities of 1 million or more. Ninety-eight per cent of the units of local government have fewer than 50,000 persons. In terms of the 1960 census, only somewhat more than a quarter of congressmen represented districts in which a majority of residents lived in central city areas. The 1970 census will show that the majority of Americans in metropolitan areas in fact live in suburbs, while a great many more live in urban settlements of quite modest size. But they are not the less urban for that reason, providing conditions of living and problems of government profoundly different from that of the agricultural, small town past.

The essentials of the present "urban crisis" are simple enough to relate. Until about World War II, the growth of the city, as Otto Eckstein argues, was "a logical, economic development." At least it was such in the northeastern quadrant of the United States, where most urban troubles are supposed to exist. The political jurisdiction of the city more or less defined the area of intensive economic development, that in turn more or less defined the area of intensive settlement. Thereafter, however, economic incentives and social desires combined to produce a fractionating process that made it ever more difficult to collect enough power in any one place to provide the rudiments of effective government. As a result of or as a part of this process, the central areas ceased to grow and began to decline. The core began to rot.

Two special circumstances compounded this problem. First, the extraordinary migration of the rural southern Negro to the northern city. Second, a postwar population explosion (90 million babies were born between 1946 and 1968) that placed immense pressures on municipal services, and drove many whites to the suburbs seeking relief. (Both these influences are now somewhat attenuating, but their effects will be present for at least several decades, and indeed a new baby boom may be in the offing.) As a result, the problems of economic stagnation of the central city became desperately exacerbated by those of racial tension. In the course of the 1960's tension turned into open racial strife.

City governments began to respond to the onset of economic obsolescence and social rigidity a generation or more ago, but quickly found their fiscal resources strained near to the limit. State governments became involved, and much the same process ensued. Starting in the postwar period, the federal government itself became increasingly caught up with urban problems. In recent years resources on a fairly considerable scale have flowed from Washington to the cities of the land, and will clearly continue to do so. However, in the evolution of a national urban policy, more is involved than merely the question of programs and their funding. Too many programs have produced too few results simply to accept a more or less straightforward extrapolation of past and present practices into an oversized but familiar future. *The question of method has become as salient as that of goals themselves.*

As yet, the federal government, no more than state or local government, has not found an effective *incentive* system—comparable to profit in private enterprise, prestige in intellectual activity, rank in military organization—whereby to shape the forces at work in urban areas in such a way that urban goals, whatever they may be, are in fact attained. This search for incentives, and the realization that present procedures such as categorical grant-in-aid programs do not seem to provide sufficiently powerful ones, must accompany and suffuse the effort to establish goals as such. We must seek, not just policy, but policy allied to a vigorous strategy for obtaining results from it.

Finally, the federal establishment must develop a much heightened sensitivity to its "hidden" urban policies. There is hardly a department or agency of the national government whose programs do not in some way have important consequences for the life of cities, and those who live in them. Frequently—one is tempted to say normally!—the political appointees and career executives concerned do *not* see themselves as involved with, much less responsible for the urban consequences of their programs and policies. They are, to their minds, simply building highways, guaranteeing mortgages, advancing agriculture, or whatever. No one has made clear to them that they are simultaneously redistributing employment opportunities, segregating or desegregating neighborhoods, depopulating the countryside and filling up the slums, etc.: all these things as second and third order consequences of nominally unrelated programs. Already this institutional naivete has become cause for suspicion; in the future it simply must not be tolerated. Indeed, in the future, a primary mark of competence in a federal official should be the ability to see the interconnections between programs immediately at hand and the urban problems that pervade the larger society.

THE FUNDAMENTALS OF URBAN POLICY

It having been long established that, with respect to general codes of behavior, eleven precepts are too many and nine too few, ten points of urban policy may be set forth, scaled roughly to correspond to a combined measure of urgency and importance.

1. *The poverty and social isolation of minority groups in central cities is the single most serious problem of the American city today. It must be attacked with urgency, with a greater commitment of resources than has heretofore been the case, and with programs designed especially for this purpose.*

The 1960's have seen enormous economic advances among minority groups, especially Negroes. Outside the south, 37 per cent of Negro families earn $8,000 per year or more, that being approximately the national median income. In cities in the largest metropolitan areas, 20 per cent of Negro families in 1967 reported family incomes of $10,000 or over. The earnings of *young* married black couples are approaching parity with whites.

Nonetheless, certain forms of social disorganization and dependency appear to be increasing among the urban poor. Recently, Conrad Taeuber, Associate Director of the Bureau of the Census, reported that in the largest metropolitan areas—those with 1 million or more inhabitants—"the number of black families with a woman as head increased by 83 per cent since 1960; the number of black families with a man as head increased by only 15 per cent during the same period." Disorganization, isolation, and discrimination seemingly have led to violence, and this violence has in turn been increasingly politicized by those seeking a "confrontation" with "white" society.

Urban policy must have as its first goal the transformation of the urban lower class into a stable community based on dependable and adequate income flows, social equality, and social mobility. Efforts to improve the conditions of life in the present caste-created slums must never take precedence over efforts to enable the slum population to disperse throughout the metropolitan areas involved. Urban policy accepts the reality of ethnic neighborhoods based on free choice, but asserts that the active intervention of government is called for to enable free choice to include integrated living as a normal option.

It is impossible to comprehend the situation of the black urban poor without first seeing that they have experienced not merely a major migration in the past generation, but also that they now live in a state almost of demographic seige as a result of population growth. What demographers call the "dependency ratio"—the number of children per thousand adult males—for blacks is nearly twice that for whites, and the gap widened sharply in the 1960's.

TABLE 1.   Children per 1000 adult males

	1960	1966
White	1,365	1,406
Negro	1,922	2,216

It is this factor, surely, that accounts for much of the present distress of the black urban slums. At the same time, it is fairly clear that the sharp escalation in the number of births that characterized the past twenty-five years has more or less come to an end. The number of Negro females under age five is now exactly the number aged five to nine. Thus the 1980's will see a slackening of the present severe demands on the earning power of adult Negroes, and also on the public institutions that provide services for children. But for the decade immediately ahead, those demands will continue to rise—especially for central city blacks, whose median age is a bit more than ten years below that for whites—and will clearly have a priority claim on public resources.

2. *Economic and social forces in urban areas are not self-balancing. Imbalances in industry, transportation, housing, social services, and similar elements of urban life frequently tend to become more rather than less pronounced, and this tendency is often abetted by public policies. A concept of urban balance may be tentatively set forth: a social condition in which forces tending to produce imbal-*

ance induce counterforces that simultaneously admit change while maintaining equilibrium. It must be the constant object of federal officials whose programs affect urban areas—and there are few whose do not—to seek such equilibrium.

The evidence is considerable that many federal programs have induced sharp imbalances in the "ecology" of urban areas—the highway program, for example, is frequently charged with this, and there is wide agreement that other, specifically city-oriented programs such as urban renewal have frequently accomplished just the opposite of their nominal objectives. The reasons are increasingly evident. Cities are complex social systems. Interventions that, intentionally or not, affect one component of the system almost invariably affect second, third, and fourth components as well, and these in turn affect the first component, often in ways quite opposite to the direction of the initial intervention. Most federal urban programs have assumed fairly simple cause and effect relationships that do not exist in the complex real world. Moreover, they have typically been based on "common sense" rather than research in an area where common sense can be notoriously misleading. In the words of Jay W. Forrester, "With a high degree of confidence we can say that the intuitive solution to the problems of complex social systems will be wrong most of the time."

This doubtless is true, but it need not be a traumatizing truth. As Lee Rainwater argues, the logic of multivariate analysis, and experience with it, suggest that some components of a complex system are always vastly more important than others, so that when (if) these are accurately identified a process of analysis that begins with the assertion of chaos can in fact end by producing quite concise and purposeful social strategies.

3. At least part of the relative ineffectiveness of the efforts of urban government to respond to urban problems derives from the fragmented and obsolescent structure of urban government itself. The federal government should constantly encourage and provide incentives for the reorganization of local government in response to the reality of metropolitan conditions. The objective of the federal government should be that local government be stronger and more effective, more visible, accessible, and meaningful to local inhabitants. To this end the federal government should discourage the creation of paragovernments designed to deal with special problems by evading or avoiding the jurisdiction of established local authorities, and should encourage effective decentralization.

Although the "quality" of local government, especially in large cities, has been seen to improve of late, there appears to have been a decline in the vitality of local political systems, and an almost total disappearance of serious effort to reorganize metropolitan areas into new and more rational governmental jurisdictions. Federal efforts to recreate the ethnic-neighborhood-based community organization, as in the poverty program, or to induce metropolitan area planning as in various urban development programs, have had a measure of success, but nothing like that hoped for. Meanwhile the middle class norm of "participation" has diffused downward and outward, so that federal urban programs now routinely require citizen participation in the planning process and beyond; yet somehow this does not seem to have led to more competent communities. In some instances it appears rather to have escalated the level of stalemate.

It may be we have not been entirely candid with ourselves in this area. Citizen participation, as Elliott A. Krause has pointed out, is in practice a "bureaucratic ideology," a device whereby public officials induce nonpublic individuals to act in a way the officials desire. Although the putative object may be, indeed almost always is, to improve the lot of the citizen, it is not settled that the actual consequences are anything like that. The ways of the officials, of course, are often not those of the elected representatives of the people, and the "citizens" may become a rope in the tug-of-war between bureaucrat and representative. Especially in a federal system, "citizen participation" easily becomes a device whereby the far-off federal bureaucracy acquires a weapon with which to battle the elected officials of local government. Whatever the nominal intent, the normal outcome is federal support for those who would diminish the legitimacy of local government. But it is not clear that the federal purposes are typically advanced through this process. To the contrary, an all round diminishment rather than enhancement of energies seems to occur.

This would appear especially true when "citizen participation" has in effect meant putting indignant citizens on the payroll. However much these citizens may continue to "protest," the action acquires a certain hollow ring. Something like this has already happened to groups that have been openly or covertly supported by the federal government, seeking to influence public opinion on matters of public policy. This stratagem is a new practice in American democracy. It began in the field of foreign affairs, and has now spread to the domestic area. To a quite astonishing degree it will be found that those groups that nominally are pressing for social change and development in the poverty field, for example, are in fact subsidized by federal funds. This occurs in protean ways—research grants, training contracts, or whatever—and is done with the best of intentions. But, again, with what results is far from clear. Can this development, for example, account for the curious fact that there seems to be so much protest in the streets of the nation, but so little, as it were, in its legislatures? Is it the case, in other words, that the process of public subsidy is subtly debilitating?

Whatever the truth of this judgment, it is nevertheless clear that a national urban policy must look first to the vitality of the elected governments of the urban areas, and must seek to increase their capacity for independent, effective, and creative action. This suggests an effort to find some way out of the present fragmentation, and a certain restraint on the creation of federally-financed "competitive governments."

Nathan Glazer has made the useful observation that in London and Tokyo comprehensive metropolitan government is combined with a complex system of "subgovernments"—the London Boroughs —representing units of 200,000–250,000 persons. These are "real" governments, with important powers in areas such as education, welfare, and housing. In England, at all events, they are governed through an electoral system involving the national political parties in essentially their national postures. (Indeed, the boroughs make up the basic units of the parties' urban structure.) It may well be there is need for social inventions of this kind in the great American cities, especially with respect to power over matters such as welfare, education, and housing that are now subject to intense debates concerning "local control." The demand for "local control" is altogether to be welcomed. In some degree it can be seen to arise from the bureaucratic barbarities of the highway programs of the 1950's, for example. But in the largest degree it reflects the processes of democracy catching up with the content of contemporary government. As government more and more involves itself in matters that very much touch on the lives of individual citizens, those individuals seek a greater voice in the programs concerned. In the hands of ideologues or dimwits, this demand can lead to an utter paralysis of government. It has already done so in dozens of urban development situations. But approached with a measure of sensitivity—and patience—it can lead to a considerable revitalization of urban government.

4. *A primary object of federal urban policy must be to restore the fiscal vitality of urban government, with the particular object of ensuring that local governments normally have enough resources on hand or available to make local initiative in public affairs a reality.*

For all the rise in actual amounts, federal aid to state and local government has increased only from 12 per cent of state-local revenue in 1958 to 17 per cent in 1967. Increasingly, state and local governments that try to meet their responsibilities lurch from one fiscal crisis to another. In such circumstances, the capacity for creative local government becomes least in precisely those jurisdictions where it might most be expected. As much as any other single factor, this condition may be judged to account for the malaise of city government, and especially for the reluctance of the more self-sufficient suburbs to associate themselves with the nearly bankrupt central cities. Surviving from one fiscal deadline to another, the central cities commonly adopt policies which only compound their ultimate difficulties. Yet their options are so few. As James Q. Wilson writes, "The great bulk of any city's budget is, in effect, a fixed charge the mayor is powerless to alter more than trivially." The basic equation, as it were, of American political economy is that for each one per cent increase in the Gross National Product the income of the federal government increases one and one-half per cent while the normal income of city governments rises half to three-quarters of a point at most. Hence both a clear opportunity and a no less manifest necessity exist for the federal government to adopt as a deliberate policy an increase in its aid to urban governments. This should be done in part through revenue sharing, in part through an increase in categorical assistance, hopefully in much more consolidated forms than now exist, and through credit assistance.

It may not be expected that this process will occur rapidly. The prospects for an enormous "peace and growth dividend" to follow the cessation of hostilities in Vietnam are far less bright than they were painted. But the fact is that as a nation we grow steadily richer, not poorer, and we can afford the government we need. This means, among our very first priorities, an increase in the resources available to city governments.

A clear opportunity exists for the federal government to adopt as a deliberate policy an increase in its aid to state and local governments in the aftermath of the Vietnam war. Much analysis is in order, but in approximate terms it may be argued that the present proportion of aid should be about doubled, with the immediate objective that the federal government contribution constitute one-third of state and local revenue.

5. *Federal urban policy should seek to equalize the provision of public services as among different jurisdictions in metropolitan areas.*

Although the standard depiction of the (black) residents of central cities as grossly deprived with respect to schools and other social services, when compared with their suburban (white) neighbors, requires endless qualification, the essential truth is that life for the well-to-do is better than life for the poor, and that these populations tend to be separated by artificial government boundaries within metropolitan areas. (The people in between may live on either side of the boundaries, and are typically overlooked altogether.) At a minimum, federal policy should seek a dollar-for-dollar equivalence in the provision of social services having most to do with economic and social opportunity. This includes, at the top of the list, public education and public safety. (Obviously there will always be some relatively small jurisdictions—"the Scarsdale school system"—that spend a great deal more than others, being richer; but there can be national or regional norms and no central city should be allowed to operate below them.)

Beyond the provision of equal resources lies the troubled and elusive question of equal results. Should equality of educational opportunity extend to equality of educational achievement (as between one group of children and another)? Should equality of police protection extend to equality of risks of criminal victimization? That is to say, should there be not only as many police, but also as few crimes in one area of the city as in another? These are hardly simple questions, but as they are increasingly posed it is increasingly evident that we shall have to try to find answers.

The area of housing is one of special and immediate urgency. In America, housing is not regarded as a public utility (and a scarce one!) as it is in many of the industrial democracies of Europe, but there can hardly be any remaining doubt that the strong and regular production of housing is nearly a public necessity. We shall not solve the problem of racial isolation without it. Housing must not only be open, *it must be available.* The process of filtration out from dense center city slums can only take place if the housing perimeter, as it were, is sufficiently porous. For too long now the production of housing has been a function, not of the need for housing as such, but rather of the need to increase or decrease the money supply, or whatever. Somehow a greater regularity of effective demand must be provided the housing industry, and its level of production must be increased.

6. *The federal government must assert a specific interest in the movement of people, displaced by technology or driven by poverty, from rural to urban areas, and also in the movement from densely populated central cities to suburban areas.*

Much of the present urban crisis derives from the almost total absence of any provision for an orderly movement of persons off the countryside and into the city. The federal government made extraordinary, and extraordinarily successful, efforts to provide for the resettlement of Hungarian refugees in the 1950's and Cuban refugees in the 1960's. But almost nothing has been done for Americans driven from their homes by forces no less imperious.

Rural to urban migration has not stopped, and will not for some time. Increasingly, it is possible to predict where it will occur, and in what time sequence. (In 1968, for example, testing of mechanical tobacco harvesting began on the east coast and the first mechanical grape pickers were used on the west coast.) Hence, it is possible to prepare for it, both by training those who leave, and providing for them where they arrive. Doubtless the United States will remain a nation of exceptionally mobile persons, but the completely unassisted processes of the past need not continue with respect to the migration of impoverished rural populations.

There are increasing indications that the dramatic movement of Negro Americans to central city areas may be slackening, and that a counter movement to surrounding suburban areas may have begun. This process is to be encouraged in every way, especially by the maintenance of a flexible and open housing market. But it remains the case that in the next thirty years we shall add 100 million persons to our population. Knowing that, it is impossible to have no policy with respect to where they will be located. *For to let nature take its course is a policy.* To consider what might be best for all concerned and to seek to provide it is surely a more acceptable goal.

7. *State government has an indispensible role in the management of urban affairs, and must be supported and encouraged by the federal government in the performance of this role.*

This fact, being all but self-evident, tends to be overlooked. Indeed, the trend of recent legislative measures, almost invariably prompted by executive initiatives, has been to establish a direct federal-city relationship. States have been bypassed, and doubtless some have used this as an excuse to avoid their responsibilities of providing the legal and governmental conditions under which urban problems can be effectively confronted.

It has, of course, been a tradition of social reform in America that city government is bad and that, if anything, state government is worse. This is neither true as a generalization nor useful as a principle. But it is true that, by and large, state governments (with an occasional exception such as New York) have *not* involved themselves with urban problems, and are readily enough seen by mayors as the real enemy. But this helps neither. States *must* become involved. City governments, without exception, are creatures of state governments. City boundaries, jurisdictions, and powers are given and taken away by state governments. It is surely time the federal establishment sought to lend a sense of coherence and a measure of progressivism to this fundamental process.

The role of state government in urban affairs cannot easily be overlooked (though it may be deliberately ignored on political or ideological grounds). By contrast, it is relatively easy to overlook county government, and possibly an even more serious mistake to do so. In a steadily increasing number of metropolitan areas, it is the county rather than the original core city that has become the only unit of government which makes any geographical sense. That is to say, the only unit whose boundaries contain most or all of the actual urban settlement. The powers of county government have typically lagged well behind its potential, but it may also be noted that in the few—the very few—instances of urban reorganization to take place since World War II, county government has assumed a principal, even primary role in the new arrangement.

8. *The federal government must develop and put into practice far more effective incentive systems than now exist whereby state and local governments, and private interests too, can be led to achieve the goals of federal programs.*

The typical federal grant-in-aid program provides its recipients with an immediate reward for promising to work toward some specified goal—raising the education achievement of minority children, providing medical care for the poor, cleaning up the air, reviving the downtown business district. But there is almost no reward for actually achieving such goals—and rarely any punishment for failing to do so.

There is a growing consensus that the federal government should provide market competition for public programs, or devise ways to imitate market conditions. In particular, it is increasingly agreed that federal aid should be given directly to the consumers of the programs concerned—individuals included—thus enabling them to choose among competing suppliers of the goods or services that the program is designed to provide. Probably no single development would more enliven and energize the role of government in urban affairs than a move from the *monopoly service* strategy of the grant-in-aid programs to a *market* strategy of providing the most reward to those suppliers that survive competition.

In this precise sense, it is evident that federal programs designed to assist those city-dwelling groups that are least well off, least mobile, and least able to fend for themselves must in many areas move beyond a *services* strategy to an approach that provides inducements to move from a dependent and deficient status to one of independence and sufficiency. Essentially, this is an *income* strategy, based fundamentally on the provision of incentives to increase the earnings and to expand the property base of the poorest groups.

Urban policy should in general be directed to raising the level of political activity and concentrating it in the electoral process. It is nonetheless possible and useful to be alert for areas of intense but unproductive political conflict and to devise ways to avoid such conflict through market strategies. Thus conflicts over "control" of public education systems have frequently of late taken on the aspect of disputes over control of a monopoly service, a sole source of a needed good. Clearly some of the ferocity that ensues can be avoided through free choice arrangements that, in effect, eliminate monopoly control. If we move in this direction, difficult "minimum standard" regulation problems will almost certainly arise, and must be anticipated. No arrangement meets every need, and a good deal of change is primarily to be justified on grounds that certain systems need change for their own sake. (Small school districts, controlled by locally elected boards may be just the thing for New York City. However, in Phoenix, Arizona, where they have just that, consolidation and centralization would appear to be the desire of educational reformers.) But either way, a measure of market competition can surely improve the provision of public services, much as it has proved an efficient way to obtain various public paraphernalia, from bolt-action rifles to lunar landing vehicles.

Here, as elsewhere, it is essential to pursue and to identify the *hidden* urban policies of government. These are nowhere more central to the issue than in the matter of incentives. Thus, for better than half a century now, city governments with the encouragement of state and federal authorities have been seeking to direct urban investment and development in accordance with principles embodied in zoning codes, and not infrequently in accord with precise city plans. However, during this same time the tax laws have provided the utmost incentive to pursue just the opposite objectives of those incorporated in the codes and the plans. It has, for example, been estimated that returns from land speculation based on zoning code changes on average incur half the tax load of returns from investment in physical improvements. Inevitably, energy and capital have diverted *away* from pursuing the plan and *toward* subverting it. It little avails for government to deplore the evasion of its purposes in such areas. Government has in fact established two sets of purposes, and provided vastly greater inducements to pursue the implicit rather than the avowed ones. Until public authorities, and the public itself, learn to be much more alert to these situations, and far more open in discussing and managing them, we must expect the present pattern of self-defeating contradictions to continue.

9. *The federal government must provide more and better information concerning urban affairs, and should sponsor extensive and sustained research into urban problems.*

Much of the social progress of recent years derives from the increasing quality and quantity of government-generated statistics and government-supported research. However, there is general agreement that the time is at hand when a general consolidation is in order, bringing a measure of symmetry to the now widely dispersed (and somewhat uneven) data-collecting and research-supporting activities. Such consolidation should not be limited to urban problems, but it must surely include attention to urban questions.

The federal government should, in particular, recognize that most of the issues that appear most critical just now do so in large measure because they are so little understood. This is perhaps especially so with respect to issues of minority group education, but generally applies to all the truly difficult and elusive issues of the moment. More and better inquiry is called for. In particular, the federal government must begin to sponsor longitudinal research—i.e., research designed to follow individual and communal development over long periods of time. It should also consider providing demographic and economic projections for political subdivisions as a routine service, much as the weather and the economy are forecast. Thus, Karl Taeuber has shown how seemingly unrelated policies of local governments can increase the degree of racial and economic differentiation between political jurisdictions, especially between cities and suburbs.

Similarly, the extraordinary inquiry into the educational system begun by the U.S. Office of Education under the direction of James S. Coleman should somehow be established on an on-going basis. It is now perfectly clear that little is known about the processes whereby publicly-provided resources affect educational outcomes. The great mass of those involved in education, and of that portion of the public that interests itself in educational matters, continue undisturbed in its old beliefs. But the bases of their beliefs are already thoroughly undermined and the whole structure is likely to collapse in a panic of disillusion and despair unless something like new knowledge is developed to replace the old. Here again, longitudinal inquiries are essential. And here also, it should be insisted that however little the new understandings may have diffused beyond the academic research centers in which they originated, the American public is accustomed to the idea that understandings do change and, especially in the field of education, is quite open to experimentation and innovation.

Much of the methodology of contemporary social science originated in clinical psychology, and perhaps for that reason tends to be "deficiency-oriented." Social scientists raise social *problems*, the study of which can become a social problem in its own right if it is never balanced by the identification and analysis of social *successes*. We are not an unsuccessful country. To the contrary, few societies work as hard at their problems, solve as many, and in the process stumble on more unexpected and fulsome opportunities. The cry of the decent householder who asks why the social science profession (and the news media which increasingly follow the profession) must be ever preoccupied with juvenile delinquency and never with juvenile decency deserves to be heard. Social science like medical science has been preoccupied with pathology, with pain. A measure of inquiry into the sources of health and pleasure is overdue, and is properly a subject of federal support.

10. *The federal government, by its own example, and by incentives, should seek the development of a far heightened sense of the finite resources of the natural environment, and the fundamental importance of aesthetics in successful urban growth.*

The process of "uglification" may first have developed in Europe; but, as with much else, the technological breakthroughs have taken place in the United States. American cities have grown to be as ugly as they are, not as a consequence of the failure of design, but rather because of the success of a certain interaction of economic, technological, and cultural forces. It is economically efficient to exploit the natural resources of land, and air, and water by technological means that the culture does not reject, albeit that the result is an increasingly despoiled, debilitated, and now even dangerous urban environment.

It is not clear how this is to change, and so the matter which the twenty-second century, say, will almost certainly see as having been the primary urban issue of the twentieth century is ranked last in the public priorities of the moment. But there *are* signs that the culture is changing, that the frontier sense of a natural environment of unlimited resources, all but impervious to human harm, is being replaced by an acute awareness that serious, possibly irreparable harm is being done to the environment, and that somehow the process must be reversed. This *could* lead to a new, nonexploitive technology, and thence to a new structure of economic incentives.

The federal establishment is showing signs that this cultural change is affecting its actions, and so do state and city governments. But the process needs to be raised to the level of a conscious pursuit of policy. The quality of the urban environment, a measure deriving from a humane and understanding use of the natural resources, together with the creative use of design in architecture and in the distribution of activities and people, must become a proclaimed concern of government. And here the federal government can lead. It must seek out its hidden policies. (The design of public housing projects, for example, surely has had the consequence of manipulating the lives of those who inhabit them. By and large the federal government set the conditions that have determined the disastrous designs of the past two decades. It is thus responsible for the results, and should force itself to realize that.) And it must be acutely aware of the force of its own example. If scientists (as we are told) in the Manhattan Project were prepared to dismiss the problem of long-lived radioactive wastes as one that could be solved merely by ocean dumping, there are few grounds for amazement that business executives in Detroit for so long manufactured automobiles that emitted poison gases into the atmosphere. Both patterns of decision evolved from the primacy of economic concerns in the context of the exploitation of the natural environment in ways the culture did not forbid. There are, however, increasing signs that we are beginning to change in this respect. We may before long evolve into a society in which the understanding of and concern about environmental pollution, and the general uglification of American life, will be both culturally vibrant and politically potent.

Social peace is a primary objective of social policy. To the extent that this derives from a shared sense of the aesthetic value and historical significance of the public places of the city, the federal government has a direct interest in encouraging such qualities.

Daniel J. Elazar has observed that while Americans have been willing to become urbanized, they have adamantly resisted becoming "citified." Yet a measure of "citification" is needed. There are perhaps half a dozen cities in America whose disappearance would, apart from the inconvenience, cause any real regret. To lose one of those six would plunge much of the nation and almost all the immediate inhabitants into genuine grief. Something of value in our lives would have been lost, and we would know it. The difference between these cities that would be missed and the rest that would not, resides fundamentally in the combination of architectural beauty, social amenity, and cultural vigor that sets them apart. It has ever been such. To create such a city and to preserve it was the great ideal of the Greek civilization, and it may yet become ours as we step back ever so cautiously from the worship of the nation-state with its barbarous modernity and impotent might. We might well consider the claims for a different life asserted in the oath of the Athenian city-state:

We will ever strive for the ideals and sacred things of the city, both alone and with many;

We will unceasingly seek to quicken the sense of public duty;

We will revere and obey the city's laws;

We will transmit this city not only not less, but greater, better and more beautiful than it was transmitted to us.

NOTES

1. "The Twilight of Authority," *The Public Interest*, no. 15, Spring 1969.

ARTICLE 36

Presidential Message on Welfare Reform

Richard M. Nixon

TO THE CONGRESS OF THE UNITED STATES:

A measure of the greatness of a powerful nation is the character of the life it creates for those who are powerless to make ends meet.

If we do not find the way to become a working nation that properly cares for the dependent, we shall become a welfare state that undermines the incentive of the working man.

Reprinted from *The President's Proposals for Welfare Reform and Social Security Amendments 1969*, pp. 93–99. Committee on Ways and Means. U.S. House of Representatives, 91st Congress, 1st Session. Washington: U.S. Government Printing Office, October 1969.

599

The present welfare system has failed us—it has fostered family breakup, has provided very little help in many States and has even deepened dependency by all too often making it more attractive to go on welfare than to go to work.

I propose a new approach that will make it more attractive to go to work than to go on welfare, and will establish a nationwide minimum payment to dependent families with children.

I propose that the Federal Government pay a basic income to those American families who cannot care for themselves in whichever State they live.

I propose that dependent families receiving such income be given good reason to go to work *by making the first $60 a month they earn completely their own, with no deductions from their benefits.*

I propose that we *make available an addition to the incomes of the "working poor,"* to encourage them to go on working and to eliminate the possibility of making more from welfare than from wages.

I propose that these payments be made upon certification of income, with demeaning and costly investigations replaced by simplified reviews and spot checks and with *no eligibility requirement that the household be without a father.* That present requirement in many States has the effect of breaking up families and contributes to delinquency and violence.

I propose that all employable persons who choose to accept these payments be required to register for work or job training and *be required to accept that work or training,* provided suitable jobs are available either locally or if transportation is provided. Adequate and convenient day care would be provided children wherever necessary to enable a parent to train or work. The only exception to this work requirement would be mothers of preschool children.

I propose *a major expansion of job training and day care facilities,* so that current welfare recipients able to work can be set on the road to self-reliance.

I propose that we also *provide uniform Federal payment minimums for the present three categories of welfare aid to adults*—the aged, the blind, and the disabled.

This would be total welfare reform—the transformation of a system frozen in failure and frustration into a system that would work and would encourage people to work.

Accordingly, we have stopped considering human welfare in isolation. The new plan is part of an overall approach which includes a comprehensive new Manpower Training Act, and a plan for a system of revenue sharing with the States to help provide all of them with necessary budget relief. Messages on manpower training and revenue sharing will follow this message tomorrow and the next day, and the three should be considered as parts of a whole approach to what is clearly a national problem.

Need for New Departures

A welfare system is a success when it takes care of people who cannot take care of themselves and when it helps employable people climb toward independence.

A welfare system is a failure when it takes care of those who *can* take care of themselves, when it drastically varies payments in different areas, when it breaks up families, when it perpetuates a vicious cycle of dependency, when it strips human beings of their dignity.

America's welfare system is a failure that grows worse every day.

First, it fails the recipient: In many areas, benefits are so low that we have hardly begun to take care of the dependent. And there has been no light at the end of poverty's tunnel. After 4 years of inflation, the poor have generally become poorer.

Second, it fails the taxpayer: Since 1960, welfare costs have doubled and the number on the rolls has risen from 5.8 million to over 9 million, all in a time when unemployment was low. The taxpayer is entitled to expect government to devise a system that will help people lift themselves out of poverty.

Finally, it fails American society: By breaking up homes, the present welfare system has added to social unrest and robbed millions of children of the joy of childhood; by widely varying payments among regions, it has helped to draw millions into the slums of our cities.

The situation has become intolerable. Let us examine the alternatives available:

We could permit the welfare momentum to continue to gather speed by our inertia; by 1975 this would result in 4 million more Americans on welfare rolls at a cost of close to $11 billion a year, with both recipients and taxpayers shortchanged.

We could tinker with the system as it is, adding to the patchwork of modifications and exceptions. That has been the approach of the past, and it has failed.

We could adopt a "guaranteed minimum income for everyone," which would appear to wipe out poverty overnight. It would also wipe out the basic economic motivation for work, and place an enormous strain on the industrious to pay for the leisure of the lazy.

Or, we could adopt a totally new approach to welfare, designed to assist those left far behind the national norm, and provide all with the motivation to work and a fair share of the opportunity to train.

This administration, after a careful analysis of all the alternatives, is committed to a new departure that will find a solution for the welfare problem. The time for denouncing the old is over; the time for devising the new is now.

Recognizing the Practicalities

People usually follow their self-interest.

This stark fact is distressing to many social planners who like to look at problems from the top down. Let us abandon the ivory tower and consider the real world in all we do.

In most States, welfare is provided only when there is no father at home to provide support. If a man's children would be better off on welfare than with the low wage he is able to bring home, wouldn't he be tempted to leave home?

If a person spent a great deal of time and effort to get on the welfare rolls, wouldn't he think twice about risking his eligibility by taking a job that might not last long?

In each case, welfare policy was intended to limit the spread of dependency; in practice, however, the effect has been to increase dependency and remove the incentive to work.

We fully expect people to follow their self-interest in their business dealings; why should we be surprised when people follow their self-interest in their welfare dealings? That is why we propose a plan in which it is in the interest of every employable person to do his fair share of work.

The Operation of the New Approach

1. *We would assure an income foundation throughout every section of America for all parents who cannot adequately support themselves and their children.* For a family of four with income of $720 or less, this payment would be $1,600 a year; for a family of four with $2,000 income, this payment would supplement that income by $960 a year.

Under the present welfare system, each State provides "Aid to families with dependent children," a program we propose to replace. The Federal Government shares the cost, but each State establishes key eligibility rules and determines how much income support will be provided to poor families. The result has been an uneven and unequal system. The 1969 benefits average for a family of four is $171 a month across the Nation, but individual State averages range from $263 down to $39 a month.

A new Federal minimum of $1,600 a year cannot claim to provide comfort to a family of four, but the present low of $468 a year cannot claim to provide even the basic necessities.

The new system would do away with the inequity of very low benefit levels in some States, and of State-by-State variations in eligibility tests, by establishing a federally financed income floor with a national definition of basic eligibility.

States will continue to carry an important responsibility. In 30 States the Federal basic payment will be less than the present levels of combined Federal and State payments. These States will be required to maintain the current level of benefits, but in no case will a State be required to spend more than 90 percent of its present welfare cost. The Federal Government will not only provide the "floor," but it will assume 10 percent of the benefits now being paid by the States as their part of welfare costs.

In 20 States, the new payment would exceed the present average benefit payments, in some cases by a wide margin. In 10 of these States, where benefits are lowest and poverty often the most severe, the payments will raise benefit levels substantially. For 5 years, every State will be required to continue to spend at least half of what they are now spending on welfare, to supplement the Federal base.

For the *typical "welfare family"*—a mother with dependent children and no outside income—the new system would provide a basic national minimum payment. A mother with three small children would be assured an annual income of at least $1,600.

For the *family headed by an employed father or working mother*, the same basic benefits would be received, but $60 per month of earnings would be "disregarded" in order to make up the costs of working and provide a strong advantage in holding a job. The wage earner could also keep 50 percent of his benefits as his earnings rise above that $60 per month. A family of four, in which the father earns $2,000 in a year, would receive payments of $960, for a total income of $2,960.

For the *aged, the blind, and the disabled*, the present system varies benefit levels from $40 per month for an aged person in one State to $145 per month for the blind in another. The new system would establish a minimum payment of $65 per month for all three of these adult categories, with the Federal Government contributing the first $50 and sharing in payments above that amount. This will raise the share of the financial burden borne by the Federal Government for payments to these adults who cannot support themselves, and should pave the way for benefit increases in many States.

For the *single adult* who is not handicapped or aged, or for the *married couple without children*, the new system would not apply. Food stamps would continue to be available up to $300 per year per person, according to the plan I outlined last May in my message to the Congress on the food and nutrition needs of the population in poverty. For dependent families there will be an orderly substitution of food stamps by the new direct monetary payments.

2. *The new approach would end the blatant unfairness of the welfare system.* In over half the States, families headed by unemployed men do not qualify for public assistance. In no State does a family headed by a father working full time receive help in the current welfare system, no matter how little he earns. As we have seen, this approach to dependency has itself been a cause of dependency. It results in a policy that tends to force the father out of the house.

The new plan rejects a policy that undermines family life. It would end the substantial financial incentives to desertion. It would extend eligibility to *all* dependent families with children, without regard to whether the family is headed by a man or a woman. The effects of these changes upon human behavior would be an increased will to work, the survival of more marriages, the greater stability of families. We are determined to stop passing the cycle of dependency from generation to generation.

The most glaring inequity in the old welfare system is the exclusion of families who are working to pull themselves out of poverty. Families headed by a nonworker often receive more from welfare than families headed by a husband working full time at very low wages. This has been rightly resented by the working poor, for the rewards are just the opposite of what they should be.

3. The new plan would create a much stronger incentive to work. For people now on the welfare rolls, the present system discourages the move from welfare to work by cutting benefits too fast and too much as earnings begin. *The new system would encourage work by allowing the new worker to retain the first $720 of his yearly earnings without any benefit reduction.*

For people already working, but at poverty wages, the present system often encourages nothing but resentment and an incentive to quit and go on relief where that would pay more than work. The new plan, on the contrary, would provide a supplement that will help a low-wage worker—struggling to make ends meet—achieve a higher standard of living.

For an employable person who just chooses not to work, neither the present system nor the one we propose would support him, though both would continue to support other dependent members in his family.

However, a welfare mother with preschool children should not face benefit reductions if she decides to stay home. It is not our intent that mothers of preschool children must accept work. Those who can work and desire to do so, however, should have the opportunity for jobs and job training and access to day-care centers for their children; this will enable them to support themselves after their children are grown.

A family with a member who gets a job would be permitted to retain all of the *first $60 monthly income*, amounting to $720 per year for a regular worker, *with no reduction of Federal payments.* The incentive to work in this provision is obvious. But there is another practical reason: Going to work costs money. Expenses such as clothes, transportation, personal care, social security taxes and loss of income from odd jobs amount to substantial costs for the average family. Since a family does not begin to *add* to its net income until it surpasses the cost of working, in fairness this amount should not be subtracted from the new payment.

After the first $720 of income, the *rest* of the earnings will result in a systematic reduction in payments.

I believe the vast majority of poor people in the United States prefer to work rather than have the Government support their families. In 1968, 600,000 families left the welfare rolls out of an average caseload of 1,400,000 during the year, showing a considerable turnover, much of it voluntary.

However, there may be some who fail to seek or accept work, even with the strong incentives and training opportunities that will be provided. It would not be fair to those who willingly work, or to all taxpayers, to allow others to choose idleness when opportunity is available. Thus, they must accept training opportunities and jobs when offered, or give up their right to the new payments for themselves. No ablebodied person will have a "free ride" in a nation that provides opportunity for training and work.

4. *The bridge from welfare to work shall be buttressed by training and child care programs.* For many, the incentives to work in this plan would be all that is necessary. However, there are other situations where these incentives need to be supported by measures that will overcome other barriers to employment.

I propose that *funds be provided for expanded training and job development programs* so that an additional 150,000 welfare recipients can become jobworthy during the first year.

Manpower training is a basic bridge to work for poor people, especially people with limited education, low skills and limited job experience. Manpower training programs can provide this bridge for many of our poor. In the new manpower training proposal to be sent to the Congress this week, the interrelationship with his new approach to welfare will be apparent.

I am also requesting authority, as a part of the new system, to provide child care for the 450,000 children of the 150,000 current welfare recipients to be trained.

The child care I propose is more than custodial. This Administration is committed to a new emphasis on child development in the first 5 years of life. The day care that would be part of this plan would be of a quality that will help in the development of the child and provide for its health and safety, and would break the poverty cycle for this new generation.

The expanded child care program would bring new opportunities along several lines: opportunities for the further involvement of private enterprise in providing high quality child care service: opportunities for volunteers; and opportunities for *training and employment in child care centers of many of the welfare mothers themselves.*

I am requesting a total of $600 million addition to fund these expanded training programs and child care centers.

5. *The new system will lessen welfare redtape and provide administrative cost savings.* To cut out the costly investigations so bitterly resented as "welfare snooping," the Federal payment will be based upon a certification of income, with spot checks sufficient to prevent abuses. The program will be administered on an automated basis, using the information and technical experience of the Social Security Administration, but, of course, will be entirely separate from the administration of the social security trust fund.

The States would be given the option of having the Federal Government handle the payment of the State supplemental benefits on a reimbursable basis, so that they would be spared their present administrative burdens and so a single check could be sent to the recipient. These simplifications will save money and eliminate indignities; at the same time, welfare fraud will be detected and lawbreakers prosecuted.

6. *This new departure would require a substantial initial investment, but will yield future returns to the Nation.* This transformation of the welfare system will set in motion forces that will lessen dependency rather than perpetuate and enlarge it. A more productive population adds to real economic growth without inflation. The initial investment is needed now to stop the momentum of work to welfare, and to start a new momentum in the opposite direction.

The costs of welfare benefits for families with dependent children have been rising alarmingly the past several years, increasing from $1 billion in 1960 to an estimated $3.3 billion in 1969, of which $1.8 billion is paid by the Federal Government, and $1.5 billion is paid by the States. Based on current population and income data, the proposals I am making today will increase Federal costs during the first year by an estimated $4 billion, which includes $600 million for job training and child care centers.

The startup costs of lifting many people out of dependency will ultimately cost the taxpayer far less than the chronic costs—in dollars and in national values—of creating a permanent underclass in America.

From Welfare to Work

Since this administration took office, members of the Urban Affairs Council, including officials of the Department of Health, Education, and Welfare, the Department of Labor, the Office of Economic Opportunity, the Bureau of the Budget, and other key advisers, have been working to develop a coherent, fresh approach to welfare, manpower, training, and revenue sharing.

I have outlined our conclusions about an important component of this approach in this message; the Secretary of HEW will transmit to the Congress the proposed legislation after the summer recess.

I urge the Congress to begin its study of these proposals promptly so that laws can be enacted and funds authorized to begin the new system as soon as possible. Sound budgetary policy must be maintained in order to put this plan into effect—especially the portion supplementing the wages of the working poor.

With the establishment of the new approach, the Office of Economic Opportunity will concentrate on the important task of finding new ways of opening economic opportunity for those who are able to work. Rather than focusing on income support activities, it must find means of providing opportunities for individuals to contribute to the full extent of their capabilities, and of developing and improving those capabilities.

This would be the effect of the transformation of welfare into "workfare," a new work-rewarding system:

For the first time, all dependent families with children in America, regardless of where they live, would be assured of minimum standard payments based upon uniform and single eligibility standards.

For the first time, the more than 2 million families who make up the working poor would be helped toward self-sufficiency and away from future welfare dependency.

For the first time, training and work opportunity with effective incentives would be given millions of families who would otherwise be locked into a welfare system for generations.

For the first time, the Federal Government would make a strong contribution toward relieving the financial burden of welfare payments from State governments.

For the first time, every dependent family in America would be encouraged to stay together, free from economic pressure to split apart.

These are far-reaching effects. They cannot be purchased cheaply, or by piecemeal efforts. This total reform looks in a new direction; it requires new thinking, a new spirit and a fresh dedication to reverse the downhill course of welfare. In its first year, more than half the families participating in the program will have one member working or training.

We have it in our power to raise the standard of living and the realizable hopes of millions of our fellow citizens. By providing an equal chance at the starting line, we can reinforce the traditional American spirit of self-reliance and self-respect.

ARTICLE 37

NWRO Proposals for a Guaranteed Adequate Income

George A. Wiley

I would like to speak to those issues. One is the question of the welfare crisis that has so captured the concern of the President and the Nation and has led to the proposals for welfare reform and to the

Reprinted from Statement of Dr. George A. Wiley, Executive Director, National Welfare Rights Organization and "NWRO Proposals for a Guaranteed Adequate Income," in *Social Security and Welfare Proposals*, Part 3 of 7, pp. 1014–1015, 1018–1023. Hearings before the Committee on Ways and Means. U.S. House of Representatives, 91st Congress, 1st Session, October 22, 23, 24, and 27, 1969. Washington, D.C.: U.S. Government Printing Office.

problem of the inadequacy of the solutions that have been offered by the President and by the present administration.

I want to preface that by saying that the solutions offered are indeed, in major respects, in the right direction, but fail to go to the heart of the matter, which is the inadequacy of the income which is provided and available to poor people to raise and nurture their families.

The welfare crisis has bothered people basically apparently for two reasons. One is that it costs too much money. The administration in its proposing H.R. 14174 said directly that "The growth of the welfare rolls threatens the fiscal stability of the States and the Federal-State partnership."

It also alluded to the harm that the present welfare system does to the recipients and the fact that it is destructive of human dignity and of human initiative. It is true that many more people are receiving welfare today and we are aware that this committee has been concerned about these problems for many years.

In fact, in 1962, when social welfare experts told you that the problem was that poor people needed more social services, you responded by recommending and having passed the 1962 amendments to the Social Security Act which provided additional rehabilitative services to welfare recipients under the assumption that this would help to reduce the welfare caseload.

The fact is, of course, that this did not work, that the welfare caseload and the welfare rolls continued to rise. In 1967 many experts pointed out the possibilities of supplying a new answer through the work incentive programs and the result was the proposal of the very harsh and punitive measures designed to force welfare recipients into work and training programs and to try to cut the welfare rolls by this kind of device.

The fact is, I think, that many of you will now recognize that this also failed, that it was not responsive to the basic issues and the basic needs of welfare recipients and poor people, and that we are now in the situation in 1969 where the President has offered proposals that he describes as "workfare" and which again raise in part some of the old solutions of trying to get welfare recipients off the rolls by getting them into job programs and training, while at the same time not providing the adequate income so necessary for people to grow and to develop and to have any kind of opportunity.

We think that it is time that somebody told this committee the truth about the problems of welfare and the rise in the welfare rolls. The welfare rolls are not growing because welfare recipients are having more children. They are not growing because there is something wrong with poor people and they need rehabilitation.

They are growing because millions of Americans have been denied adequate education, have been denied access to decent employment and equal opportunities, and in increasing numbers these people are turning to welfare as a basic source of support.

Indeed, in the last few years our organization has engaged in vigorous campaigns to get poor people together to help them organize, to press to get the benefits, to find out their legal rights and entitlements and to press for the things that they need to meet the basic food, clothing, shelter, and other needs of their families.

Indeed, we have been assisted in this process by local poverty programs and by legal services that for the first time have been helping poor people know their rights and entitlements, and the promises under Federal laws and regulations and have been challenging some of the unconstitutional and arbitrary practices of welfare agencies which deny poor people even the meager benefits that are offered by our present public welfare system.

NWRO believes that welfare should not be viewed as a problem for this country, but should be viewed as a solution, that welfare is a way that the country can invest money in human beings, that welfare is a way that we can begin to subsidize life in this country, the way that we can begin to subsidize opportunities for all Americans.

At the heart of the matter is adequate income.

NWRO believes that in order for welfare to begin to solve the problem of poverty, every American must be assured an adequate income to meet the basic necessities of life.

Government studies by the highly respected Bureau of Labor Statistics of the U.S. Department of Labor show that the minimum necessity for a family of four in order to get the minimum standards for health and decency, is around $5,500 per year.

Contrast this with the present average welfare payments, somewhere around $2,000 a year, and the family assistance plan, which would only give a Federal insurance of $1,600 a year for a family of four, and you see that we are not even in the right ballpark.

Finally, I would like to say that one of the basic things that needs to be done is that the Congress and the Government begin at least to set a goal of adequate income for every American citizen and that the Federal Government begin contributing toward that goal with the idea that a real partnership between Federal and State Governments would supply as much of the resources as they possibly can to meet the actual needs that poor people have. . . .

NWRO PROPOSALS FOR A GUARANTEED ADEQUATE INCOME

The National Welfare Rights Organization is a nationwide grassroots organization of welfare recipients and other poor people. It has 250 affiliates in 46 states and more than 100 cities. NWRO is launching a nationwide compaign for a *guaranteed adequate income* for every American citizen. NWRO is challenging the country to change its priorities from an emphasis on death and destruction to an emphasis on life and peace. We believe that every man, woman, and child has the right to live. We call upon our country to begin subsidizing life!

The Bureau of Labor Statistics of the U.S. Department of Labor says that a family of four needs at least $5,500 a year for the basic necessities of life, not counting medical care. We call upon the Federal Government to guarantee every American this minimum income.

This income should be automatically adjusted for variations in size of family, costs of living in various parts of the country, and changes in cost-of-living as they occur.

Eligibility should be based solely on need, and should be based on a person's declaration of what his needs are, with spot checks as is done under our income tax system.

The system should provide a work incentive by permitting recipients to keep 50% of earned income, up to 25% of their grant level.

Recipients should be entitled to a fair hearing prior to the termination or reduction of benefits. The hearing should take place within fifteen (15) days of the application for appeal. Special grants should be provided for recipients to obtain lawyers or other advocates.

The regulations pertaining to rights and entitlements under this system should be public information. Simplified versions should be distributed to every recipient and potential recipient.

Persons eligible for these benefits should be entitled to *free medical care, legal services,* and *day care* facilities of a high quality in the neighborhoods where they live.

Other services to the recipients should be on a completely voluntary basis, administered by agencies separate from those administering the guaranteed income payments. Example of these are: family planning, homemaker services, family counseling, child welfare, etc.

Special grants should be available to take care of all special or unusual situations. These would include grants for clothing and furniture to bring the recipients household up to minimum standards of health and decency at the time they come under the program. Replacement costs should be provided in case of fire, flood, or substantial change in circumstance.

A recipient should have the right to choose between a flat grant or an itemized assessment of his needs, taking into account actual cost of housing, transportation, clothing, and other special requirements he might have. This would be similar to the income tax system where an individual may either itemize his deductions or take a standard deduction, depending on which method of benefits suits him more.

Table 1 outlines the guaranteed adequate income. It is based on the Bureau of Labor Statistics "Lower Living Standard Budget." This is the Labor Department's "minimum standard for the maintenance of health and social well being, the nurture of children and participation in community activities."

The so-called "poverty line" is not an adequate income budget, but a level below which everyone is desperately poor. It is based upon the U.S. Department of Agriculture's "economy food plan" on which it is only possible to survive with adequate nutrition for "short emergency periods of time" and only under very special circumstances, (Poverty Line income is $3335 for a family of four). The so-called "low income poverty line," is based on the USDA's "low-cost food plan." It sets an income of approximately $4400 a year for a family of four. Government surveys show however, that only 23% of the families with food budgets equivalent to the low-cost food plan actually have nutritionally adequate diets.

The NWRO adequate income budget therefore uses the USDA "moderate food plan" which would insure the average family an adequate diet. NWRO contends that providing adequate income is the only sure way to combatting hunger in America.

The adjusted budget excludes the basic costs of hospital and doctors care since it is assumed that free medical care would be available through national health insurance or Medicaid or some other

TABLE 1. NWRO Proposed Guaranteed Adequate Income, Spring 1969, Detailed Budget for Family of 4

Category	Cost per—		
	Year	Month	Week
Food	$2,237	$186	$43
This allowance is a total of the BLS moderate budget cost for food at home ($1,999 per year, $166 per month, $38 per week) and the BLS lower standard for food away from home ($238 per year, $18 per month, $5 per week). The latter includes snacks, school lunches, etc.			
Housing	1,402	117	27
These costs represent the BLS lower standard costs updated. They are meant to cover all supplies and furnishings for the home and its operations including telephone and postage. Rental costs ($1,108 per year, $92 per month) include all items like gas, electricity, and water.			
Clothing and personal care	784	65	15
The items in this budget, shampoo and yard goods, as well as clothing and clothing care, are unchanged from the BLS lower standard. The cost has simply been updated.			
Medical care	312	26	6
Dental, eye care, and nonprescription drugs are included here. BLS consideration of doctor and hospital care has been omitted as explained in the text. There is no provision for appliances and supplies.			
Transportation	484	40	9
Includes school bus rides and all other use of public transportation by noncar owners.			
Other	442	37	9
Reading, recreation, and education comprise about ½ of this category. Life insurance is also included. There is no provision according to the BLS study for club membership dues, hobby expenses, or the acquisition of musical instruments.			
Total	5,541	462	106

program. It should also be noted that this budget includes no money for cigarettes (regarded by BLS as a health hazard), non-prescription drugs or medical supplies, out-of-town travel, long-distance telephone calls, dry cleaning, or use of a laundromat.

The budget is based on statistical averages and is subject to 10% to 20% per variations depending on the locality. The range runs from $5209 in most nonmetropolitan areas to $6649 for Honolulu. The budgets for several cities are estimated in Table 2.

Inflation has caused a 9.4% increase in the cost of living since BLS computed the cost of living in 1967. The NWRO budget has been updated to Spring 1969 prices.

TABLE 2.   1969 Minimum Adequacy Budget—Comparison of Major Cities[1]

City	Index	Adjusted BLS budget
United States:		
Urban average	100	$5,541
Metropolitan	101	5,596
Nonmetropolitan	94	5,209
Atlanta, Georgia	96	5,300
Austin, Texas	90	5,000
Baltimore, Maryland	98	5,400
Boston, Massachusetts	105	5,800
Cincinnati, Ohio, Kentucky, Indiana	96	5,300
Chicago, Illinois, Indiana	103	5,700
Cleveland, Ohio	100	5,500
Dallas, Texas	96	5,300
Detroit, Michigan	100	5,500
Honolulu, Hawaii	120	6,600
Kansas City, Missouri, Kansas	101	5,600
Los Angeles-Long Beach, California	107	5,900
New York City, New York, New Jersey	101	5,600
Orlando, Florida	93	5,200
Philadelphia, Pennsylvania, New Jersey	99	5,400
St. Louis, Missouri, Illinois	101	5,600
San Francisco-Oakland, California	110	6,100
Seattle-Everett, Washington	111	6,200
Washington, D.C., Maryland, Virginia	103	5,700

Computed from the Bureau of Labor Statistics "Lower Standard Budget," as described in the text.

The importance of continued recognition of special needs and of providing alternate ways of meeting needs, either through the adequate income (flat grant) or through individual considerations (computations), is important for two reasons:

1. BLS assumed in establishing the budget that the family had been established for fifteen (15) years and had accumulated stock of clothing and furniture. The budget was intended only to cover replacements. This assumption does not apply to the average family in poverty. Thus, special grants for wardrobe and furnishings to bring persons up to minimum standards for health and decency.
2. The budget is based on statistical averaging formulas which do not necessarily apply to real people or real situations. For example, an individual family of four may or may not be able to obtain adequate housing in good condition at the $92 a month rent that the budget allows, even if that happens to be the average for the city in which he lives.

Similar arguments can be applied to transportation costs, where the transportation quantity for school children in the BLS budget was less than the number of days in the school year! This is because it was an average among children who rode to school and those who walked. It can be assumed that some families would be over in one category and under in another. These statistical differences may not always average out in any given family. If a family has greater need in a number of categories, they should have the option of itemizing their family budget, and applying for a grant that meets the actual needs that they have.

Table 3 gives the minimum adequacy budget for various family sizes.

Hunger

The elimination of hunger in the United States requires that adequate income be provided to every citizen. Poor people know better than anyone else that the hodge-podge of programs set up by the Department of Agriculture are welfare programs for farmers and the food processing and distribution industry. They are not designed to serve the needs of poor people. Welfare programs which exclude people for reasons other than need and which do not provide adequate income are a basic source of hunger and malnutrition.

TABLE 3.   1969 Minimum Adequacy Budget (Adjusted BLS Budget[1]), by Family Size

Family size	Budget		
	Year	Month	Week
1	$ 1,900	$ 160	$ 40
2	3,100	260	60
3	4,300	360	80
4	5,500	460	100
5	6,200	520	110
6	7,200	600	140
7	8,200	680	160
8	9,200	770	180
9	10,200	850	200
10	11,100	930	210
11	12,100	1,000	230
12	13,100	1,100	250
13	14,100	1,200	270

[1] Computed from the Bureau of Labor Statistics, "Lower Standard Budget," as described in the text, and from the BLS "Revised Equivalence Scale" "for estimating equivalent incomes or budget costs by family types."

Food stamp programs in which recipients cannot afford to participate only perpetuate that condition. Surplus commodity programs which cannot provide enough of the right kinds of food and which are cumbersome and inefficient do not meet the basic needs either. The food stamp program does not provide enough stamps for a nutritionally adequate diet, even if a recipient can afford to participate. The Nixon Administration's recent proposal for improving these programs provides only a one hundred dollar ($100) per month worth of stamps. This is equivalent to the USDA's "economy food plan." USDA itself points out that "this plan is not a reasonable measure of basic money needs for a good diet;" it is a plan "designed for temporary emergency use." The "low cost food plan" (See Table 4) which is the basis for the so-called "low income poverty line," and the BLS "lower standard budget." BLS recognizes the inadequacy of the low-cost plan in the following statement: "Although families can achieve nutritional adequacy from it, it has been estimated that only about a fourth—(23%) of those who spend amounts equivalent to the cost of the plan actually have nutritionally adequate diets. Menus

TABLE 4. Comparison of Food Budgets, Family of 4, December 1968

	Per year	Per month	Per week	Budget based on this food plan	Annual budget for plan
USDA moderate food plan	$2,235	$186	$43	BLS moderate standard budget	$7,398
				NWRO minimum adequacy budget	5,353
USDA low-cost food plan	1,744	145	34	BLS lower standard budget	4,922
				Social Security Administration low-income line	4,400
USDA economy food plan	1,197	100	23	Social Security Administration poverty line	3,335
				Nixon administration proposed food stamp program	—
Present food stamp program	700–1,488	60–124	14–30	Food stamp recipients	—
AFDC	864	72	17	AFDC recipients	2,592

based upon this plan will include food requiring a considerable amount of home preparation as well as skill in cooking to make varied and appetizing meals."

It is for these reasons that the USDA "moderate food plan" used by BLS in developing its "moderate budget," was adopted by NWRO in establishing a minimum adequacy budget.

The solution to the problem of hunger and malnutrition is for every citizen to be guaranteed an adequate income to meet his basic food and other needs. Therefore, the money directed toward giving bonuses in food stamps could better be redirected toward providing more adequate basic income for poor people.

Until this change can be brought about the Federal subsidy in the food stamp program should be given in the form of free bonus food stamps to supplement the inadequate food budgets that poor people have. These bonuses should be large enough to bring the food budget up to the USDA's "moderate food plan" to insure adequate diets.

A less desirable alternative to free bonus stamps is to allow poor people to buy whatever amounts of food stamps they feel they can afford, based on a range of prices to be set by the Department of Agriculture for their income category.

Poor people should be allowed to trade-in stamps for money to meet emergency needs and be allowed to apply unused stamps against next month's stamp purchases.

There should be no minimum amount of stamps to buy. (People with no money should receive free stamps—people with almost no money should be able to buy very small amounts of stamps.)

Stamps should be sold at more frequent intervals (at least weekly) and recipients should set their own buying pattern (weekly, monthly, etc.).

A fair hearing process should be established for recipients to appeal the decisions of the local administering agencies' procedure that are at least equivalent to the procedures now in force to protect stores which participate in the program.

Recipients' concerns and interests should be given consideration equal to that given farmers in the regulation and administration of this program.

Welfare

Much has been said and written of the inadequacies of our present welfare system. As we press toward a guaranteed adequate income much can be done to improve the welfare system NOW! The following should be implemented immediately.

1. Repeal the compulsory work provisions of the Work Incentive Program.
2. Repeal the Federal freeze on AFDC payments.
3. Repeal the 1967 restrictions on the AFD–IP program and make AFDC–UP mandatory on all states.
4. The principal costs of welfare should be borne by the Federal Government.
5. The Federal Government should set standards of eligibility using financial need as the basic requirement.

6. *The Federal Government should require states to provide special grants for clothing, household furnishing, other basic needs to insure that recipients have the minimum standards for health and decency.*
7. Retain Medicaid standards and provisions as originally provided in Title 19 of the Social Security Act.
8. Make welfare payments retroactive to the date of application.
9. Make the declaration methods universal to all categories.
10. Permit recipients access to their own case records.
11. Provide special grants for legal services for appeals and for conduct of fair hearings.
12. Provide for participation of WRO's in rule making, enforcement of regulations at Federal, state and local levels.

Finally, I want to say that this proposal for adequate income is in contrast to the Nixon proposal of $1,600 and only maintaining welfare payments at their present level, which is totally inadequate and second, to even the use of the poverty line as a measure of who is poor and who is not poor.

The poverty line uses formulas [described above] . . . which the Government itself identifies as being inadequate, particularly in the area of the food budget, as meeting the basic needs of families.

Where you use our figures or not, which are based on the Bureau of Labor Statistics, we believe it is vital that the Nation identify what is an adequate income at least as the goal. We recognize that this committee and the Congress, because of other priorities are not prepared to embark on a very costly program of the nature that we would outline, but it couldn't cost anything to at least identify the goal and the objective, so that the country can begin building and working toward a system that provides adequately for all of its citizens. Indeed, in working toward this goal, we believe it is particularly important to recognize the need that there be a flexible program which provides for special grants for emergency needs, for the special problems which arise in the winter where high utility bills occur, which arise around school time when children have to be clothed to go back to school, and around needs such as when there is a breakdown of a refrigerator or stove or something like that in the home, where there is an emergency in the family.

I might mention that the response in many of the States to the fact of their increased financial pressure is to cut out many of the emergency provisions within their programs and it is very basic that the Federal Government begin providing both money and incentive to the States to provide for emergency needs that families have.

I want to again point out that a system which is unresponsive to the needs of the people, a system that provides a flat and inadequate grant is a system that invites disaster, is a system that invites people to go outside the processes of Government, to go outside the processes of legal redress, and to go outside the channels established within our democracy for people to be able to move for change.

I think that the welfare rights organizations have demonstrated by their organization, by their attempt to come to the Congress, to the committee, to the courts and to use the avenues provided by the Constitution for redress of the grievance of inadequate income, that so many of our people have that by using that we offer a hope and a lifeline to this country and we hope that this committee and this Congress would assist in the process of helping poor people to participate in the country, to participate in the process by providing the goal of adequate income for all Americans, and providing ways through a flexible system and through establishing legal rights and legal avenues for welfare recipients to aid recipients in being able to move to use the institutions provided by the Government, the laws and the Constitution, for getting the minimal benefits they need to sustain life in this country.

ARTICLE 38

The Suburbs Have to Open Their Gates

Linda and Paul Davidoff
Neil N. Gold

A few years ago, socially conscious residents of the New York suburbs joined in a project that occupied several spring weekends: they

Reprinted from Linda and Paul Davidoff and Neil N. Gold, "The Suburbs Have To Open Their Gates," *The New York Times Magazine* (November 7, 1971), pp. 40–44, 46, 48, 50, 55, 58, 60. © 1971 by The New York Times Company. Reprinted by permission.

chose blocks in the East Harlem and Bedford-Stuyvesant ghettos and traveled to them in teams, equipped with paint, brushes, buckets and mops, for cooperative clean-up, fix-up sessions with the residents. This was a way for middle-class people to experience and, at the same time, try to help solve the neighborhood problems of the ghettos.

A few weekends and some paint had little effect on the crumbling structures and festering economic and social problems of the ghetto neighborhoods. But these efforts, worthy enough in themselves, skirted the reality: that it is the exclusionary practices of the suburbs themselves that help create the poverty and ugliness of the slums, and that well-motivated suburbanites could do more for poor and working-class people trapped in the inner cities by opening up their land, job markets and tax resources to them.

The 1970 Census revealed what had begun to dawn on urbanists in the nineteen-sixties: that the suburbs contain the largest share of America's population. In 1970, 36 per cent of the people lived in suburban parts of metropolitan regions, 30 per cent in the central cities and 34 per cent in rural areas. Some time in the current decade, more people will be employed in the suburbs than in either the cities or rural areas. And according to all predictions, the suburbs will continue to have the largest number of Americans for a long time.

Although the suburbs have provided housing and jobs for millions of new families since 1950, many suburban communities have maintained controls over the kinds of families who can live in them. Suburban values have been formed by reaction against crowded, harassed city life and fear of threatening, alien city people. As the population, the taxable income and the jobs have left the cities for the suburbs, the "urban crisis" of substandard housing, declining levels of education and public services, and dried-up employment opportunities has been created. The crisis is not urban at all, but national, and in part a product of the walls that have been built by the suburbs to discourage outward movement by the poor and blacks in the cities.

Opening the suburbs will not only reduce race and class tensions in our society but bring economic gains to all our people—through better use of the resources these communities have to offer: *land* for housing (and with it the opportunity for a decent public education), *jobs* and *tax revenues*. To bring this about, we need *action* to convince the communities—as well as Federal and state courts and legislators —that change must come, plus imaginative *planning* for an era of housing construction that will meet the needs of an expanding suburban population.

LAND

The new ecological consciousness in America and the cityward movement of our population have led to a widespread belief that we are exhausting our most precious resource: the land. Nothing could be further from the truth. America is land rich. "Megalopolis," the concentration of population along the Eastern seaboard from Boston south to Washington, consists largely of unbroken expanses of open space. Settlements along the Boston-Washington corridor are mostly thin strips along major roads and railroads; off the beaten path, woods and farms predominate. Outside the great metropolitan complexes, the land is open and unused, and places that once were farm land or villages are losing their populations and returning to the wilds. Out of 3,000 counties in the U.S., 1,000 have had a net loss in population during the last 30 years; the move from country to city, and the mechanization of agricultural production, are leaving larger and larger portions of the continent's land to open space.

Within metropolitan areas, population growth has exhausted the supply of developable open land only within the older inner cities. Vacant land is plentiful within 20 to 30 miles of the centers of every major city in the nation. Without restrictive laws, it would be possible to develop commercial and industrial properties at relatively low land costs in the outer suburbs of metropolitan regions. Moreover, only restrictive zoning, building codes and other antidevelopment legislation prevent the construction of a large number of housing units in these same areas.

The zoning laws cover a large proporation of vacant developable land in the suburbs. In the New York region, 90 per cent of all such land is zoned for single-family residential use; in eight counties of New Jersey, 82 per cent of it is zoned for lots of a half-acre or more; in the portion of Connecticut closest to New York City, three-fourths of the open residential land is zoned for an acre or more. While many older suburban towns either have no significant tracts of vacant land or already have a large population of working-class and minority families, the communities that control the bulk of the vacant land have enacted exclusionary laws.

If housing could be built in an open-market situation in the suburbs, the structure of the housing market in metropolitan America would change sharply. It would be possible to build many more houses on quarter- and half-acre lots, the accepted pattern of construction in the nation since World War II. And it would be possible to build row houses and garden apartments, the least expensive form of housing for families of moderate means.

The land supply in metropolitan areas is being kept off the market not by private acts, but by public enactment. In creating private preserves for the wealthy, law has become the instrument of those who want to keep out moderate- and low-income families. This leads to a paradox that has been called "Ivy League Socialism": excessive government intervention, on behalf of not the poor but the rich. The protected property owners are precisely those most able to protect themselves from undesired neighbors by their own wealth. They can buy large tracts of land, build high fences around them and put their houses in the middle of their estates at the end of long driveways. They do not need the help of the law.

The exclusionary laws are not completely explicit: there are no zoning maps divided into racially or economically restricted areas, so labeled. But there are thousands of zoning maps which say, in effect: "Upper Income Here"; "Middle-to-Upper Income Here"; "No Lower-Income Permitted Except as Household Employees"; "No Blacks Permitted." The practical effect of the maps and codes is to prohibit all but the most costly forms of housing development.

Why do we call the result *de jure* segregation? Because the racial consequences have been understood for a decade or more by anyone familiar with patterns of a population movement. *It is a certainty that the planners and public officials who draft and enact zoning ordinances restricting land development to single-family, detached structures on plots of an acre or more do so in full awareness that, as a consequence, almost all blacks will be excluded from such zones.*

In many areas, acreage zoning is the preferred exclusionary device. The bulk of the land in a municipality is held off the market except for purchasers who are able to afford a house on a tract of one, two, three or more acres of land. Since a single-family home on an acre or more of land cannot be constructed in most suburban areas for less than $35,000, including the lot, families with incomes under $17,000 cannot afford to buy a house built on this land (under the generally accepted rule of thumb that a family can afford to buy a house that costs twice the annual household income). Thus the housing market in the community is effectively closed to the 80 per cent of the population which earns under $17,000—and to 90 per cent of the blacks.

In other areas—and in some communities that also have acreage-zoning regulations—housing-construction codes have been devised which require extremely expensive forms of residential development: wide lot frontages, costly materials and equipment, square-footage requirements for house interiors—all beyond what is needed for health and safety.

In almost all suburban municipalities tax laws undergird the structure of land-use controls and provide a rationale for exclusion. The real-property tax pays the bulk of local costs for public education, the biggest item in the budget and a major factor in maintaining the status of the community. If a dozen houses are built at costs within the reach of low-income or moderate-income families, the entire community suffers because the taxes realized from the new houses will tend to be below the additional expense to the school system of educating the children from the new families.

(In New Castle, a Northern Westchester community, a 1968 League of Women Voters study showed that local school costs were so high that a new house would have to cost $58,500 in order to yield enough taxes to educate the average number of children per household—$1,688 in taxes for 1.6 children.)

As expenses for education have become the last straw on the suburban taxpayer's back, the impetus toward ever-higher barriers to moderate-cost housing construction has been almost irresistible. Even if motivated by the best and most democratic public instincts, a community must finance its schools; and the easiest way to make the burden bearable is to keep the community costly and exclusive.

What would happen if the exclusionary land-use controls were eliminated? In the private market, the effect would be to dramatically increase the supply of building lots, both for single-family homes and for garden apartments and row houses. The increase in supply would lower the price per lot; the result would be a sharp reduction in the cost of a new home and an increase in the number of families that could afford one. The construction industry would boom, and lower-cost housing could be produced as the market demands.

Putting aside for the moment the moral questions raised by suburban exclusion, another argument against the regulations adopted over the past decade or more by suburban communities is that they have stifled the natural development of the home-building industry. Today, most of the vacant residential land around New York and in other metropolitan areas is zoned for homes on lots 5 to 10 times larger than Levittown's. Zoning has operated to slow down and spread out development. In a nation that has highly valued growth, it is strange to find growth disdained as a matter of policy. Particularly at a time of recession, the multiplier effect of a sustained form of new community development—which would require large capital investment—cannot be ignored. A reinvigorated residential building industry would not only create jobs for unemployed construction workers but lead to enlarged investment in all industries required to serve new suburban developments—and to other urgently needed jobs.

Even if a construction boom produced mostly middle-class or luxury housing, it would help to ease the pressures throughout the housing market that keep moderate-income housing consumers bottled up in city neighborhoods. This is because the "filtering" process—lower-income consumers moving into housing left behind by more affluent consumers moving into bigger and better homes—could begin to operate again. The result would be some improvement in the housing situation for low-income families. The favorite argument of real-estate operators against Government housing subsidies to the poor used to be that "filtering" would satisfy this group's needs. In fact, filtering alone will never provide enough used housing to meet the needs of the lowest-income families. But the current virtual halt in the construction of new, moderately priced housing in suburbia has made the absence of a normal used-house, or "filtered," market acutely noticeable to moderate-income families who would normally be able to afford such homes.

When, in the late nineteen-forties and fifties, it was possible for a family earning a moderate income to buy a new small house in Levittown or its equivalent, the houses and apartments these families vacated went on the market at reduced prices to families earning below the median level. Now that no Levittowns are being built, mobility in the housing market has been sharply reduced and families that should have been able to move are staying put. Obsolescent housing that should have been torn down decades ago is still in use, often at exorbitant prices; city neighborhoods that should have been torn down for urban renewal are still desperately needed for families that have nowhere else to go. It is as true as it ever was that the private market in housing, whether in new or used units, cannot provide housing for the families at the bottom of the income ladder. Subsidies, either in the form of cash to families or Government outlays for housing construction, must be provided. But the costs of such programs has become exorbitant because the private construction market for new housing has been closed off in the suburbs by artificial means.

Since the Industrial Revolution began dumping rural families into big-city slums, housing planners have recognized that public subsidy is needed to enable working-class families to live decently. Every industrial nation provides some form of subsidy for workers' housing; the United States has been in the housing business on a large scale since the thirties.

The 19th-century English garden-city movement laid down the principle that the cheapest—and most wholesome—form of housing for working-class families was the attached cottage, or row house, built so that each unit would have access to common open space. But in America, housing built for low-income and moderate-income families has generally been "projects" in the central cities: massive apartment towers built on the sites of destroyed ghettos, on land that is close to the city's hub and therefore so expensive that building at lower densities is not possible. In the nineteen-thirties the housing pioneers Henry Wright and Lewis Mumford decried the trend to housing for the poor in the inner cities; they pointed out that cheap housing at livable densities requires cheap land, and they urged public-housing authorities to build at the city's fringes. Urban-Renewal experts in the Federal Government and city authorities ignored the experts. Suburban land was locked up, and housing for the poor built at choking densities on the sites of the old ghettos.

Opening up suburban land would mean that Federal money, rather than being used to build absurdly expensive high-rise structures in inner cities, could be spread to a far larger number of units. In New York City, it costs more than $30,000 per unit in Federal and local funds to build public housing. Row houses and garden apartments could be built in the suburbs for well under $20,000 per dwelling unit, if the land costs were reasonable and if lot-size and square-footage requirements were not excessive. Not the least of the savings in time and money would come from working through the manageable governments of the towns, instead of the tangled and near-paralyzed bureaucracies of the cities.

JOBS

If the growth of the suburbs in sheer numbers of people has not yet been fully recognized as a fact of national life, suburban dominance of the metropolitan—and national—job markets has been barely noticed. Yet in "bedroom" suburbs like Westchester County in New York, as many workers now commute into the county each day as travel to the city in the customary pattern.

The service sectors of the job market—the shopping centers and colleges, for instance—have followed the roads and the population. One example is the Cherry Hill Mall shopping center in Philadelphia, which employs 2,000 workers and occupies 80 acres of land about eight miles from the center of the city (accessible via three major highway bridges).

The demand for cheaper land for single-floor assembly-line and warehousing operations has brought more companies—and jobs—to the suburbs. The long, low building requires land; parking lots for employes' cars and for truck storage require land; and land that is far from the streets of the central city costs less. In Mahwah, N. J., for example, the Ford Motor Company purchased about 200 acres just off a New York State Thruway interchange, about 25 miles from the center of New York City and about the same distance from downtown Newark, for a plant which now employs 4,200 workers.

Traditionally, companies that are prestige-conscious or need a communications network near their headquarters have occupied space in downtown skyscrapers. Increasingly, however, they have been able to enhance their prestige and satisfy the residential preferences of their executives by moves to long, low buildings in parklike settings in far-out suburbia. For instance, Pepsico, Inc., has just completed a corporate headquarters in Purchase, N. Y., which employs 1,250 people on a 112-acre site.

The decentralization of the metropolitan job market means that the working population must be permitted to decentralize too, if workers are to be matched with jobs. The unemployment rate in this recession period may be hovering around 6 per cent for the society at large, but inside the urban ghettos it has been at the Depression level of 12 per cent for years. To end the acute problem of unemployment and underemployment, ghetto workers must be permitted to follow the blue-collar jobs out of the central cities.

The remoteness of the job market for relatively low-skilled workers from the ghetto areas aggravates the employment problem. So does the lack of coordination between job-finding agencies in the cities and the suburbs, which makes it difficult for the low-skilled worker living in the ghettos to find out about and apply for low-skilled but decently paid jobs in suburban manufacturing plants. The United States Employment Service and other job-finding agencies must be reorganized along metropolitan lines, so that information about openings can be transmitted to the unemployed in the ghettos. But this will not be enough. Workers must be able to travel to the jobs, which means in the case of blue-collar jobs that they must be permitted to find homes near enough to the jobs so that commuting does not take an excessive bite out of their incomes.

If the ghettos are viewed as underdeveloped areas—an approach that became fashionable in the sixties—the need for movement of workers to jobs in suburbia is even more sharply evident. Economists who were once captivated by the notion of pouring capital investment into depressed regions in order to create new factory jobs are now beginning to recognize that by far the cheapest solution to the problem is to give unemployed workers information about jobs in thriving industrial areas, help them to learn about the unfamiliar customs and housing patterns of the new area, pay them resettlement allowances and get them moved. Only in rare cases does it pay to invest heavily in declining areas rather than help families left behind by changing patterns of industrialization to move into the economic mainstream.

TAXES

Of the 4,200 workers employed at the Ford plant in Mahwah, many live in Newark and New York, and only 88, or 2 per cent, in the town where they work. Despite the important role that this factory plays in the metropolitan economy, the local property taxes paid by Ford benefit only Mahwah residents. Taxes on industrial and commercial property that are paid to suburban communities are another example of a metropolitan resource that could be—but is not—used to help solve inner city problems.

The tax rate on business property reflects the needs only of the suburban jurisdiction that levies it. If the suburb has a relatively small public-school enrollment, and few low- and moderate-income families, its local tax rate will be much lower than the rate that would be necessary if the business property were situated in a poverty-ridden central city. The tax rate is further reduced when, as in the case of Mahwah the suburb uses its zoning powers to keep out children and to exclude low- and moderate-income households, including those whose breadwinners work in the plant.

Mahwah's successful effort to lure new companies and to exclude the companies' employes has resulted in a 1970 tax rate on industrial and commercial property of 1.55 per cent of full value. By comparison, the city of Newark, which houses and educates nearly 1,000 of Ford's black workers and their families, is compelled to tax business property at the rate of 7.14 per cent of full value.

Mahwah's tax base included $104,000,000 of business property and yielded $1,612,000 in revenues. If this $104,000,000 were taxed at the rate levied on similar property in Newark, it would bring $7,426,000 in added funds to the city. The comparison, of course, is a rough one, since a bigger tax base in Newark might permit the city to lower its rate somewhat. But it does demonstrate the fiscal gains that induce corporations to relocate from poverty-ridden central cities to restrictively zoned suburbs.

Suburban towns and cities use the taxes generated by the coming of large new business properties to reduce residential property taxes or to increase the quality of public services, or both. On the other side of the coin, the movement of industry to the suburbs weakens the tax bases of central cities, requires an increase in their tax rate and cripples their capacity to respond to the social and educational needs of the disadvantaged groups, many of whose members are forced to commute at great cost in money and time to the very suburban plants which are no longer on the city's tax rolls.

ACTION

The movement to open the suburbs has begun. The thorny legal, financial and moral questions will be settled not only by debate but by legislative and court action and by economic pressure.

The first step may well be the establishment of a clear connection, in the public mind and in public law, between jobs and housing for workers. The decentralization of the job market is, as we have noted, one of the least appreciated phenomena of metropolitan life; it is time that voters and public officials became aware of it and acted accordingly. Rather than assuming that a corporation moving its plant or offices from the central city to the suburbs is a tax bonanza for the lucky municipality that succeeds in attracting it, we must require that the company have a clear policy of relating jobs to workers' housing and commuting patterns. The rule must therefore be: no corporation hiring a significant number of workers can move to a location in a suburban community where the housing market is closed to families earning what the workers in the plant will earn.

In effect, this will mean that the tax benefits to a town which welcomes new industry will be balanced by the costs to that community of educating the workers' children, policing their neighborhoods, providing them with municipal services. If a community has all its vacant land zoned for single-family houses on five acres of land, then if it permits a zoning variance for the construction of Jones Corporation's new international headquarters, it must also rezone land for sufficient new garden apartments to house Jones's 300 janitorial, service and lower-level clerical workers; create sufficient quarter-acre plots so that Jones's 250 executive secretaries and junior managerial personnel have a chance of buying homes, and make sure that land and construction costs do not make housing prohibitively expensive in the five-acre zones for its 100 middle-management people.

Both state and Federal action will be needed to promote the rule. In Washington, Senator Abraham Ribicoff is working for just such an approach by reintroducing the proposed Government Facilities Location Act of 1970, which provides that no Federal installation may move to a community which refuses to provide land for workers' housing. Though it does not cover private industry, the bill would have significant impact on communities bidding for Federal largess in the form of shipyards, research facilities and other economic jackpots. (The bill did not emerge from committee last year; this year hearings are scheduled for late fall.)

If a community enforces zoning laws which in effect keep out blacks, can the Federal Government continue to provide water and sewer grants, open-space acquisition loans and other forms of aid to them? Does not such aid violate the antidiscrimination guidelines imposed by the Civil Rights Act of 1964? The clamor against suburban exclusion has led to sharp questioning of the President on this point, and a now-famous statement issued by the Administration last June was meant to answer the questions by establishing a distinction between economic and racial discrimination. A community cannot be punished, in the Administration's view, for keeping out the poor, only for overtly keeping out the black. This distinction is, to say the least, far from firmly established; and lawsuits will soon be brought to challenge the point. The suits will argue that the racial discrimination in the suburbs is the direct and calculated result of zoning laws.

In New York State, Assemblyman Franz Leichter has introduced a package of anti-exclusionary bills which include a prohibition against establishing state facilities in exclusionary communities. Such a prohibition would affect the location plans of state university branches, hospitals, state schools and other major service installations, as well as—under some interpretations of the bill—state-assisted elementary and secondary schools (meaning all schools, now that the barriers to state aid to parochial schools have largely fallen).

Massachusetts enacted in 1969 its "antisnob zoning law," which provided that at least 0.3 per cent of every community's vacant land must be made available for the construction of low- and moderate-cost housing in each of five years. Other states, including New York, New Jersey and Connecticut, are considering similar legislation to exempt at least a portion of suburban land from the exclusionary regulations.

Our own organization, Suburban Action Institute, is seeking to induce Federal regulatory agencies to act against corporations planning moves to exclusionary suburbs. We have filed complaints with three agencies—the Federal Equal Employment Opportunity Commission, the Federal Communications Commission and the Office of Federal Contract Compliance—against R.C.A., American Telephone and Telegraph and General Electric, for taking steps to relocate to the acreage-zoned communities of New Canaan, Conn., Bernards Township, N. J., and Fairfield, Conn.

By moving to communities within which their minority-group

employes cannot find housing, we charge, these corporations are creating conditions of employment discrimination. We believe that they are not simply acquiescing in a discriminatory situation, but affirmatively aiding the creation of segregated employment. (Because of the complaint against RCA before the Equal Employment Opportunity Commission, the company has temporarily withdrawn its proposal to build offices in New Canaan for 1,000 people.)

Making laws to restrict corporations from moving jobs to exclusionary communities will not remove the basic incentive for such moves: the tax laws. As long as the costs of educating suburban children are borne by the local real property tax, a community will try to enhance its tax base by luring industry, and will try to keep out housing developments that attract families with children. A radical restructuring of the tax system for financing education is needed, both to end exclusion and to assure every child, whether born in a rich or a poor community, equal educational opportunity.

A statewide income tax for education is the remedy now advocated by the Regional Plan Association of New York, by the Lindsay administration, and even by suburban taxpayers who can no longer pay educational costs in newly developing communities. Gov. William G. Milliken of Michigan, a Republican, has moved to establish a statewide tax for education. New York State's Fleischman Commission is about to conclude a study of school financing by calling for "full state assumption" of the cost of educating children. Political pressure to relieve local property owners of the burden of school costs is building up around the country as record numbers of local school budgets are defeated.

A recent decision in the California Supreme Court may signal the beginning of the end of the present system of financing local schools. In *Serrano v. Priest*, the court said that the local property tax "invidiously discriminates against the poor because it makes the quality of a child's education a function of the wealth of his parents and neighbors. Recognizing, as we must, that the right to an education in our public schools is a fundamental interest which cannot be conditioned on wealth, we can discern no compelling state purpose necessitating the present method of financing."

The Supreme Court has not ruled on the fundamental issues raised by zoning since 1926 when, in the case of *Euclid v. Ambler*, it declared that comprehensive zoning ordinances are a reasonable and constitutional method of controlling land use. But the lower courts have begun to rule on the contention that the zoning frequently denies racial minorities the equal protection of the law guaranteed by the 14th Amendment. In one recent Pennsylvania Supreme Court case, the justices declared:

"We fully realize that the over-all solution to [housing and growth] problems lies with greater regional planning; but until the time comes that we have such a system, we must confront the situation as it is. The power currently resides in the hands of each local governing unit, and we will not tolerate their abusing that power in attempting to zone out growth at the expense of neighboring communities."

The Justice Department and the American Civil Liberties Union have raised questions of suburban-exclusion with their suit against Black Jack, Mo., on behalf of a group of black residents in St. Louis who wanted to build housing in the town. The group charged that Black Jack incorporated itself into a municipality for the purpose of denying the needed zoning change.

Court cases challenging exclusionary laws are in preparation against a number of suburban communities around the nation and the biggest initial victory has just been won in New Jersey. Judge David Furman of the Middlesex County Supreme Court 10 days ago declared invalid an ordinance in Madison Township, N.J., that called for one- and two-acre lots, required a minimum floor-area that was excessive and placed limitations on multifamily dwellings. The ordinance, the judge said, had the effect of preventing 90 per cent of the people in the area from living in the township, and directly contributed to the ghettoization of neighboring cities. (The suit was brought in behalf of a group of black and Spanish-speaking residents of Elizabeth, Plainfield and New Brunswick.)

The judge did not reach the constitutional questions, basing his ruling instead on the state zoning law, which says that localities must zone for the public welfare. Under this law, he said, a community when it passes land-use regulations must in the future take into account not only its own needs but those of the region.

The direction the U.S. Supreme Court may take has been hinted at in recent rulings on the need for school busing to achieve integration. Despite the negative decision in the recent Valtierra case in California, which dealt with a referendum that was designed to prevent construction of housing for an *economic* minority, the record of the court on matters relating to *racial* discrimination has been quite uncompromising. It is fair to expect that proof of the racially discriminatory effects of exclusionary zoning will carry great weight with the court.

PLANNING

The massive spurt in suburban housing construction which followed World War II occurred at a time when new young families were desperate for homes—in a full-employment economy and following the end of war-related restraints on building. The decade of the seventies has brought the beginnings of another market of this kind (as those born in the postwar baby boom come into their own child-rearing years), but without the economic conditions which made the housing surge possible after the war.

Housing construction is now at a low ebb. Even if the vise of exclusionary zoning is removed, government subsidies and controls will be required to see to it that the combined public-private housing market actually produces the needed housing. The Kaiser Commission has called for the construction of 600,000 units of Federally-assisted housing each year for the next decade, at a cost of $2.8-billion per year. Aid to the housing market of this magnitude, *combined with* the opening up of vast acreages of suburban land, can insure the construction of the housing that is needed to eliminate the slums and ghettos of the central cities and to permit rebuilding on their land at decent densities.

If suburban land resources do become available, new residential development can be of a far higher quality than that of the nineteen-fifties, which gave rise to fears about "urban sprawl," Levittowns and endless identical rows of shoddily built bungalows. Critics of America's suburbs have led us to fear the terrible sterility of look-alike suburbs. But the suburbs have offered a very satisfactory form of life to those who live in developments that do look alike in many respects. Suburbanites in Levittown and Scarsdale have found that despite the similarities of dwellings and ways of life in their communities, they still like to live there. Of course, suburbs have many problems; what form of human community does not?

We should not prohibit development because it may have some undesirable aspects, unless we develop alternatives that provide suitable housing for all classes of the population.

The garden-city movement and the new towns of Europe as well as the best examples of new development in this country—Columbia, Md., and Reston, Va.—have demonstrated that amenable communities open to all classes can be constructed at far higher standards than those of today's expensive suburban developments, in which each house sits on a plot of one, two or more acres. Present acreage development saves no open space for the public. It calls for cookie-cutter development writ large. It demands that every inch of space be devoted to a private lot—even land not suitable for development.

But if new housing in the suburbs need not follow the pattern of Levittown, it also need not conform entirely to the rules of the garden-city movement in Europe and America. Housing can be built in small developments in existing towns, or in new towns, or in larger developments around highway interchanges and commercial projects. Towns, moreover, can assure the preservation of large amounts of open space through such devices as "cluster zoning" and planned-unit development," which permit higher densities on portions of a tract if a certain amount of acreage is set aside for public recreational use. Nor would elimination of suburban exclusion prevent those who wish to own large amounts of land from doing so—a privilege guaranteed them by our economic system.

As the prospect of intensified development of the suburbs comes closer, private groups, sniffing profits, are investing in land for eventual massive building. One hopes that these developers will be guided by the principles of balancing industrial and commercial growth with new housing, and of a wide mixture of housing types and costs in open neighborhoods.

Nonprofit groups and public agencies should also be preparing for the future by negotiating for tracts of suburban land, on the theory that when the exclusionary laws are struck down, they had better be ready with plans for construction of low- and moderate-cost housing, or they will risk leaving the whole ball game to the private developers.

ARTICLE 39

Federal Policies and Equal Housing Opportunity

Richard M. Nixon

Of all the services, facilities, and other amenities a community provides, few matter more to the individual and his family than the kind of housing he lives in—and the kind of neighborhood of which that housing is a part. Through the ages, men have fought to defend their homes; they have struggled, and often dared the wilderness, in order to secure better homes.

It is not surprising, therefore, that public policies affecting the kind and location of homes available should be the subject of intense and widespread interest, and also of intense, far-ranging, and sometimes passionate debate.

One of the achievements of this administration of which I am most proud has been the dramatic progress we have made in increasing the supply of housing, including particularly low- and moderate-income housing, so as to expand the range of housing opportunities for Americans in search of a decent home. Housing starts are currently at the highest levels in 20 years. While our primary emphasis is on stimulating private construction, the number of federally assisted low- and moderate-income housing starts planned for fiscal year 1972 will be more than four times what it was as recently as fiscal 1968— an increase from some 150,000 to some 650,000. The remaining needs are still enormous. But this represents a giant step toward fulfilling the goal set forth in the Housing Act of 1949, of "a decent home and a suitable living environment for every American family."

The very fact that so much progress is being made, however, has sharpened the focus on what has come to be called "fair housing"—a term employed, but not defined, in the Civil Rights Act of 1968, and

Reprinted from "Federal Policies Relative To Equal Housing Opportunity." Statement by the President. *Weekly Compilation of Presidential Documents*, Vol. 7, No. 24 (June 14, 1971), pp. 892–905. Washington: U.S. Government Printing Office.

to which many persons and groups have ascribed their own often widely varied meanings.

In this statement, I shall set forth the policies, as they have been developed in this administration, that will guide our efforts to eliminate racial discrimination in housing, to enlarge housing opportunities for all Americans and to assist in stable and orderly community development. It is important to understand the laws that govern those policies, the limits within which they operate, the complexities they seek to address, and the goals they seek to achieve.

My purpose is not to announce new policies, but to define and explain the policies we have—setting forth what we will do and what we will not. The factors determining patterns of housing and community development are immensely complex and intricately balanced, many are uniquely local in nature, and the Federal Government operates in important but limited ways and under limited authorities. Within those limits, we intend to continue to move vigorously—not to restrict free choice, but to expand and protect it.

Underlying our housing policies—and embodied in our laws and our Constitution—are certain basic principles:

Denial of equal housing opportunity to a person because of race is wrong, and will not be tolerated.

Such denial will not be tolerated whether practiced directly and overtly, or under cover of subterfuges, or indirectly through such practices as price and credit discrimination.

To qualify for Federal assistance, the law requires a local housing or community development project to be part of a plan that expands the supply of low- and moderate-income housing in a racially nondiscriminatory way.

In terms of site selection for a housing development, the Federal role is one of agreeing or not agreeing to provide Federal subsidies for projects proposed by local authorities or other developers.

A municipality that does not want federally assisted housing should not have it imposed from Washington by bureaucratic fiat; this is not a proper Federal role.

Local communities should be encouraged in their own voluntary efforts to make more housing more widely available, and to reduce the extent of racial concentration.

Putting an end to racial discrimination, and building toward the goal of free and open communities, is a responsibility shared by Federal, State, and local governments, by business and private institutions, by civic leaders and by individual people everywhere.

A HISTORY OF HARDSHIP

The history of racial discrimination in housing in America runs deep; but, to the Nation's credit, so do efforts to correct it.

In earlier years, some local ordinances actually forbade minority group members to purchase property in blocks where they did not constitute a majority. Such ordinances were invalidated by the Supreme Court in 1917.

Covenants running with the land were widely used to restrict minority citizens in their access to housing. The efficacy of these covenants rested on their possible enforcement by courts and the awarding of damages for their breach. Judicial enforcement was invalidated by the Supreme Court in 1948.

Federal policy itself, quite unsurprisingly, in past eras reflected what then were widespread public attitudes. Policies which governed FHA mortgage insurance activities for more than a decade between the middle thirties and the late forties recognized and accepted restrictive covenants designed to maintain the racial homogeneity of neighborhoods.

Compounding the plight of minority Americans, locked as many of them were in deteriorating central cities, was the Federal urban renewal program. It was designed to help clear out blighted areas and rejuvenate urban neighborhoods. All too often, it cleared out but did not replace housing which, although substandard, was the only housing available to minorities. Thus it typically left minorities even more ill-housed and crowded than before.

Historically, then, the Federal Government was not blameless in contributing to housing shortages and to the impairment of equal housing opportunity for minority Americans. Much has been done to remedy past shortcomings of Federal policy, and active opposition to discrimination is now solidly established in Federal law. But despite the efforts and emphasis of recent years, widespread patterns of residential separation by race and of unequal housing opportunity persist.

RACIAL CONCENTRATION TODAY

In terms of racial concentration, the facts on housing occupancy revealed by the 1970 census are compelling. In our 66 largest metropolitan areas, accounting for more than half the U.S. population—of which 49 are in the North and West—the central city white population declined during the decade of the sixties by about 2 million (5%)—while the black population increased almost 3 million (35%). This meant overall black population in central cities increased from 18% in 1960 to 24% in 1970.

In the suburban areas of these cities, however, the story was different. White population increased by 12.5 million (30%) *and* black population increased by less than 1 million (44%). The result was that the total black proportion of suburban population increased only from 4.2% in 1960 to 4.5% in 1970.

In city after city the figures tell the same story. In New York City the white population declined by 617,000 while the black population rose by 579,000. In St. Louis whites declined by 169,000; blacks rose by 40,000. Thus the central cities grow ever more black, while the surrounding areas, for the most part, remain overwhelmingly white.

It is important to remember, of course, that simple divisions into "central city" and "suburban" can be misleading in this context. It makes a great deal of difference how large the city is, and what the patterns of distribution within the metropolitan area are in terms not only of housing, but of business, industry, recreational facilities, transportation, and all the many factors that enter into its internal dynamics as a functioning community.

One thing this points to is that no single set of rigid criteria can be laid down that will fit a wide variety of local situations. To speak of "opening up the suburbs," for example, may have widely differing implications in different metropolitan areas, just as the term "central city" means something quite different in New York or Chicago than it does in New Haven or Fresno.

To some extent, the persistence of racially separate housing patterns reflects the free choice of individuals and families in both the majority and minority communities. Economic factors have also played a part, since average income levels—even though the disparity is being narrowed—remain lower for minority Americans than for the Caucasian majority.

It also is inescapable, however, that continuing, often covert housing discrimination is thwarting or discouraging the efforts of many minority citizens to find better housing in better neighborhoods. This is wrong, constitutionally indefensible, and pragmatically unwise.

THE COST OF RACIAL SEPARATION

Separation of the races, particularly when it is involuntary, has damaging consequences. One is racial isolation—the social isolation of the races from each other—an estrangement that all too readily engenders unwarranted mistrust, hostility, and fear.

Another consequence of involuntary racial separation is the waste of human resources through the denial of human opportunity. No nation is rich enough and strong enough to afford the price which dehumanizing living environments extract in the form of wasted human potential and stunted human lives—and many of those living environments in which black and other minority Americans are trapped are dehumanizing.

Another price of racial segregation is being paid each day in dollars: in wages lost because minority Americans are unable to find housing near the suburban jobs for which they could qualify. Industry and jobs are leaving central cities for the surrounding areas. Unless minority workers can move along with the jobs, the jobs that go to the suburbs will be denied to the minorities—and more persons who want to work will be added to the cities' unemployment and welfare rolls.

Clearly, both outright racial discrimination and persisting patterns of racial concentration combine to create a serious set of problems that public policy must seek to meet. These problems are human, they are economic, they are social—and they pose a challenge of the first magnitude to the community of the metropolitan area that tries to meet them in a way most nearly fair to all those affected. It is encouraging that many communities are meeting this challenge, and meeting it successfully.

THE FEDERAL ROLE

The Law

The Federal Government's responsibilities for eliminating racial discrimination in housing derive partly from the Constitution, partly from the Government's own extensive involvement in housing and community development programs, and partly from a number of statutes and Executive orders.

The broad outlines of the law are contained in our Constitution, which in its 5th, 13th, and 14th amendments guarantees basic civil rights, including the right to seek shelter free from any racial discrimination fostered by Federal, State, or local governments.

Executive Order 11063, issued in 1962, expressly states that housing discrimination and segregation prevent the Nation from attaining the housing goals declared by the 1949 Housing Act. It further directs all Federal departments and agencies "to take all action necessary and appropriate to prevent discrimination" as to race, color, religion, or national origin in federally assisted housing and related projects.

Congress followed up this initiative 2 years later with the Civil Rights Act of 1964. A critical provision of that law, Title VI, provides that no person shall, "on the ground of race, color, or national origin, be excluded from participation in, be denied the benefits of, or be subjected to discrimination under any program or activity receiving Federal financial assistance." As a penalty for such discrimination, it provides for a cutoff of Federal funds to the program in which the discrimination occurs. The clear intent of the Congress in enacting this legislation was to insure that no program utilizing Federal financial aid should be tainted by racial or ethnic discrimination. A careful review of the legislative history indicates that the Congress intended that the cutoff of Federal funds resulting from a violation should apply only to the particular activity in which the unlawful racial discrimination took place, and not to all activities undertaken by the violator.

In the Civil Rights Act of 1968, the Congress declared that "It is the policy of the United States to provide, within constitutional limitations, for fair housing throughout the United States."

Title VIII of the 1968 act goes beyond the previous statutes (which in terms of housing, had dealt only with that which was federally assisted) to prohibit discrimination on account of race, color, religion, or national origin in most private real estate actions, whether sale or rental and regardless of whether Federal assistance is involved or not. In addition, this title also makes it the responsibility of "all executive departments and agencies" and the specific responsibility of the Secretary of Housing and Urban Development, to "administer their programs and activities relating to housing and urban development in a manner affirmatively to further the purpose of this title."

Antidiscrimination Enforcement

The provisions of the law aimed at barring racial discrimination in housing are administered primarily by the Departments of Justice and of Housing and Urban Development.

HUD's role under Title VI in the 1964 act is to guard against racial discrimination in any program or activity to which HUD gives financial assistance. Title VIII of the 1968 Civil Rights Act requires HUD to investigate complaints of housing discrimination and, where appropriate, to attempt to resolve such complaints through persuasion or conciliation. In calendar year 1970, HUD completed processing of 169 complaints; in 89 of these cases conciliation was successful. In the same year, HUD referred 19 of these cases where conciliation failed to the Department of Justice.

Under the terms of Title VIII of the 1968 Civil Rights Act, the Attorney General is empowered to bring suits in Federal court where he finds that racial discrimination in housing constitutes a "pattern or practice," or where housing discrimination cases raise issues of general public importance. Since January 1969, the Attorney General has brought or participated in 85 such suits against more than 250 defendants in 22 States and the District of Columbia. In addition, the Justice Department has negotiated out of court with several hundred other persons and companies and brought them into voluntary compliance.

These cases have involved not only outright racial discrimination in the sale or rental of homes, but also such practices as discriminatory real estate advertising and exclusion of minorities from multiple listing services. Several of the suits have been against municipal authorities. Several others have been against major companies controlling tens of thousands of dwelling units, and have resulted in orders that they take dramatic remedial efforts to attract minority families into buildings from which they have previously been barred or discouraged.

Not only have these suits directly opened to nonwhites a great deal of housing previously available only to whites; they also have had a significant wider impact in stimulating others to come into voluntary compliance with the antidiscrimination laws. This vigorous enforcement as required by law will continue.

Unlawful racial discrimination in housing extends beyond the barring of individuals from particular buildings or neighborhoods because of race. The courts have also held that, when its reasons for doing so are racial, a community may not rezone in order to exclude a federally assisted housing development. In such cases, where changes in land use regulations are made for what turns out to be a racially discriminatory purpose, the Attorney General, in appropriate circumstances, will also bring legal proceedings.

How Federal Programs Operate

In order to understand the way in which the broad "fair housing" mandates translate into specific actions, it is important to understand what some of the Federal housing programs are and how they operate.

HUD provides direct financial assistance in three broad areas:

Housing for low- and moderate-income families. This includes the Home Ownership and Rental Housing Assistance subsidy programs ("Section 235" and "Section 236" housing, respectively), the rent supplement program enacted in 1965, and assistance to low-rent public housing.

Grants for State, areawide, and local planning.

Aid for community development activities, such as urban renewal and water and sewer grants.

In addition, of course, HUD plays a major role in providing mortgage insurance and in facilitating the overall flow of mortgage funds.

In each of these areas, the Federal program role—as the governing statutes make clear—is essentially one of responding to local or private initiatives, rather than one of imposing its programs on State and local governments.

In none of HUD's grant programs does the Department act directly. The Department builds no housing, develops no land use plans, clears no slums, and constructs no sewers. Instead, HUD provides, within its statutory and regulatory framework, financial assistance to local developers and agencies, both public and private, who build and manage housing, and engage in planning and community development activities.

The extent to which HUD program activity is dependent on local initiative and execution is frequently overlooked, but is an important element in considering policy issues. Sites for HUD-assisted housing must be selected and acquired by local sponsors—public or private—and housing developed on those sites must conform to local zoning and local building codes. Planning performed with HUD assistance is done by State and local governmental bodies. Community development activities—urban renewal, water and sewer, or open space projects, for example—are initiated and executed by local government.

In short, HUD's role in the location of assisted housing is one not of site *selection*, but of ultimate site *approval*. It does not initiate local housing projects. With more applications than it can fund, it must select those for funding which it determines most fully satisfy the purposes of the enabling legislation—and in doing so it says "yes" or "no" to local requests for financial assistance for projects that have been locally planned and will be locally executed.

In responding to local and private initiatives, of course, the Department must follow the statutory mandates. For example:

As noted earlier, HUD may not make a grant under any of its programs if the recipient will discriminate or otherwise deny the benefits of the assisted activity or project to persons on account of race.

Where the "workable program" requirement—imposed on local communities by the Housing Act of 1949, as amended in 1954, in connection with urban renewal and related programs—is a condition of eligibility, HUD may not make a grant in the absence of a HUD-certified workable program for community improvement. The program must make reasonable provision for low- and moderate-income housing, which must of course be available on a nondiscriminatory basis.

Where comprehensive planning is supported by a Federal grant under the 1954 Housing Act, as amended in 1968, the plan must include a "housing element" to insure that "the housing needs of both the region and the local communities studied in the planning will be adequately covered in terms of existing and prospective in-migrant population growth." This provision has broad application, since such planning grants are often used to prepare the areawide plans which are a prerequisite for Federal financial assistance under the water and sewer, open space, and new communities programs.

Similarly, the statutory requirement of "fair housing" applies in the area of private housing construction, where the Federal role is substantial. The Federal Government provides billions of dollars in assistance and guarantees of mortgage credit for housing financing. The Federal Government sets standards widely used by industry, such as minimum property standards, credit standards, appraisal standards, and construction standards. The Federal Government makes market analyses which materially influence the private sector. The Federal Government approves mortgagees, builders, developers, and brokers with respect to their doing business with HUD. Local government and private initiative and Federal standards work together to produce new housing. And under the law, that new housing—like all the Nation's housing stock—must be open equally to all Americans regardless of race, religion, or national origin.

In approaching questions of "fair housing" for low- and moderate-income persons, it is important to remember that we are dealing with a rather imprecise term and with two separate matters.

One is the elimination of racial discrimination in housing. On this, the Constitution and the laws are clear and unequivocal: racial discrimination in housing will not be tolerated.

In public discussions of "fair housing" or "open housing," however, another issue has often become confused with that of racial discrimination. This is sometimes referred to as "economic integration." Frequently it arises in debates over whether subsidized low-rent public housing should be placed in the suburbs as a means of moving poor people out of the inner city and, if so, where, to what extent, and by what means.

One of the arguments frequently advanced is that poor people are often disadvantaged by living in low-income neighborhoods; that poverty thus perpetuates itself; and that the remedy therefore is to scatter the poor among the more affluent. Another argument often heard is that blacks and other minorities tend to be disproportionately poor, and that "economic segregation" is therefore equivalent to racial segregation.

It is important to remember, however, that the terms "poor" and "black" are not interchangeable. A higher percentage of blacks than of whites lives below the poverty line—but there are far more poor whites in America than there are poor blacks. Much of the Nation's most dismally inadequate housing is occupied by blacks; much of it is occupied by whites. Many of the worst slums are black; many are white. And by the same token, the skilled trades, the businesses, and professions increasingly are populated by affluent blacks whose children go to the best schools and colleges and who themselves have taken their deserved place in the leadership, not simply of inner-city neighborhoods, but of urban, suburban, and rural communities all across America.

To cite only one statistic, a recent special census study showed that in the North and West, black husband-wife families headed by persons under 25 had a median income equal to that of their white contemporaries. Although the income disparities among other ages and categories is still far too wide, this is one measure of how far we have come; also, because these young families represent the future, it is an indication of where we are heading. To equate "poor" with "black" does a disservice to the truth, and it blinks the fact—fundamental to anything so intensely personal as housing—that we are dealing with the needs not of an undifferentiated mass, but of millions of individual human beings, each separate and unique.

In many cases—when dealing with poor people who happen to be members of a racial minority—questions of where to locate housing for poor people and where to locate housing for members of the minority are related. But the issues involved are separate, and those who would treat effectively with race and poverty must take care to maintain the distinction. What is true of blacks in this regard is also true of Mexican-Americans, Indians, and members of other minorities.

When predominantly poor members of a racial minority are concentrated heavily in one particular area of a central city, the question of where to build housing designed to accommodate some but not all of them is often not easily answered. On the one hand, for example, concentrating the subsidized housing in the predominantly black area could have the effect of reinforcing the racial separation that already exists. On the other hand, failure to build at least a portion of it there could be unfair to the people who choose to live there, as well as reinforcing the housing blight that often prevails in such areas. Quite apart from racial considerations, residents of outlying areas may and often do object to the building in their communities of subsidized housing which they fear may have the effect of lowering property values and bringing in large numbers of persons who will contribute less in taxes than they consume in services. Beyond this, and whether rightly or wrongly, as they view the social conditions of urban slum life many residents of the outlying areas are fearful that moving large numbers of persons—of whatever race—from the slums to their communities would bring a contagion of crime, violence, drugs, and the other conditions from which so many of those who are trapped in the slums themselves want to escape.

In many other respects, the balances to be struck are often close and the considerations complex: For example, how are the interests of one part of a metropolitan area to be weighed against those of the area as a whole? What other housing opportunities are available? How do transportation patterns, job patterns, school locations, enter into the choice? What related efforts are being made to expand opportunity and end racial discrimination? And how and by whom are the determinations to be made?

By establishing "fair housing" as a policy but leaving the term undefined, Title VIII of the 1968 act added a complexity of its own: a lively debate about just what it means, and especially about the meaning of its requirement that Federal officials take "affirmative action" to promote it.

This and the other laws make abundantly clear that the Federal Government has an active, affirmative role to play in eliminating racial discrimination in either the sale or rental of housing. They also make it clear that those communities which seek Federal assistance for most housing and community development programs must work honestly and constructively to meet the housing needs of their low- and moderate-income families. The debate has arisen over the extent to which Federal agencies are either required or authorized to go beyond antidiscrimination efforts, and to use their program money leverage as a means of requiring local communities to subordinate their land use policies to the goal either of breaking up racial concentrations or of promoting "economic integration."

POLICIES OF THIS ADMINISTRATION

It will be the firm purpose of this administration to carry out all the requirements of the law fully and fairly.

Racial discrimination in housing is illegal, and will not be tolerated. In order to fulfill their responsibility for eliminating this discrimination, the Department of Housing and Urban Development and the Justice Department have been developing and elaborating a wide-ranging program aimed at creating equal housing opportunity.

By "equal housing opportunity," I mean the achievement of a condition in which individuals of similar income levels in the same housing market area have a like range of housing choices available to them regardless of their race, color, religion, or national origin.

At the outset, we set three basic requirements for our program to achieve equal housing opportunity: It must be aimed at correcting the effects of past discrimination; it must contain safeguards to ensure against future discrimination; and it must be results-oriented so its progress toward the overall goal of increasing housing opportunities can be evaluated.

The administration is embarked upon this course. It must and will press forward firmly.

The chief components of such a program include the firm enforcement of laws relating to equal housing opportunity; the development of appropriate equal housing opportunity criteria for participation in programs affecting housing; the development of information programs; and the development of policies relating to housing marketing practices.

It is obvious that not all individuals will exercise the full range of choices made available to them. Those are matters for individual decision.

What *is* essential is that all citizens be able to choose among reasonable locational alternatives within their economic means, and that racial nondiscrimination be scrupulously and rigorously enforced.

We will not seek to impose economic integration upon an existing local jurisdiction; at the same time, we will not countenance any use of economic measures as a subterfuge for racial discrimination.

When such an action is called into question, we will study its effect. If the effect of the action is to exclude Americans from equal housing opportunity on the basis of their race, religion, or ethnic background, we will vigorously oppose it by whatever means are most appropriate—regardless of the rationale which may have cloaked the discriminatory act.

Access to federally assisted housing, like access to all housing, must be nondiscriminatory as to race. But simply to apply this principle will not answer all the practical problems raised by our national commitment to expanded and equal housing opportunity.

Pressures for the construction of new housing and the rehabilitation of existing housing are growing all across the Nation—in central cities, in suburbs, in small towns, in rural America. Demand for housing at all income levels is increasing dramatically.

As a major part of our national effort to meet these housing needs—an effort which is both private and governmental—federally assisted housing is being built at a rate approaching ¾ of a million units a year. These units are needed. They are being built. And they must be built someplace. The question is where.

If all the federally assisted units are packed together in one type of community or one kind of location, we will only exacerbate the social and, in all probability, the racial isolation of our people from each other.

If we build federally assisted instant ghettos, we fail both our communities and the people we are trying to help.

If we impact or tip the balance of an established community with a flood of low-income families, we do a disservice to all concerned.

The answers to these practical considerations are not simple—but they are of great importance.

Based on a careful review of the legislative history of the 1964 and 1968 Civil Rights Acts, and also of the program context within which the law has developed, I interpret the "affirmative action" mandate of the 1968 act to mean that the administrator of a housing program should include, among the various criteria by which applications for assistance are judged, the extent to which a proposed project, or the overall development plan of which it is a part, will in fact open up new, nonsegregated housing opportunities that will contribute to decreasing the effects of past housing discrimination. This does not mean that no federally assisted low- and moderate-income housing may be built within areas of minority concentration. It does not mean that housing officials in Federal agencies should dictate local land use policies. It does mean that in choosing among the various applications for Federal aid, consideration should be given to their impact on patterns of racial concentration.

In furtherance of this policy, not only the Department of Housing and Urban Development but also the other departments and agencies administering housing programs—the Veterans Administration, the Farmers Home Administration, and the Department of Defense—will administer their programs in a way which will advance equal housing opportunity for people of all income levels on a metropolitan areawide basis.

This administration will not attempt to impose federally assisted housing upon any community.

We will encourage communities to discharge their responsibility for helping to provide decent housing opportunities to the Americans of low- and moderate-income who live or work within their boundaries.

We will encourage communities to seek and accept well-conceived, well-designed, well-managed housing developments—always within the community's capacity to assimilate the families who will live in them.

We will carry out our programs in a way that will be as helpful as possible to communities which are receptive to the expansion of housing opportunities for all of our people.

In these efforts we will be aided by a change that already is taking place in the way subsidized low- and moderate-income housing is planned, built, and managed: In terms of new construction, the old-style, massively concentrated high-rise public housing project is largely a thing of the past; the trend now is strongly toward low-rise dwellings, many of them one-, two-, three- or four-family, on scattered sites, so that they can blend in with the community without detracting from nearby properties. Under the newer Federal programs of financial assistance to low- and moderate-income housing of other sorts, the pattern has been one of variety, enabling the community to fit the development to its own needs.

By approaching local questions of land-use planning in a creative and sophisticated manner, local authorities should in most cases be able to work out site-selection problems in ways that provide adequate housing opportunities for those who need them without disrupting the community.

In other ways as well, we are and will be working to promote better and more open housing opportunities. For example:

By Executive Order 11512, issued in February 1970, I ordered that in the selection of sites for Federal facilities consideration should be given to the availability of adequate low- and moderate-income housing—and I have ordered that all agencies take specifically into account whether this housing is in fact available on a nondiscriminatory basis.

Guidelines have recently been issued by the Office of Management and Budget under the provisions of the Uniform Relocation Assistance Act of 1970, to assure that adequate housing is provided on a nondiscriminatory basis and within the financial means of persons displaced by federally financed projects.

The Department of Housing and Urban Development has been actively pressing the major Federal agencies regulating lending institutions to establish effective, affirmative measures against racial discrimination in home mortgage financing. The Federal Home Loan Bank Board, which regulates savings and loan institutions, has been the first to undertake the development of new rules and procedural safeguards. The Board is also working closely with industry leaders to improve financial services offered to members of minority groups.

HUD also engages in a number of other Title VIII activities intended to eliminate racial discrimination in housing. It publishes advisory guidelines to aid those subject to the jurisdiction of the law in understanding their responsibilities; it undertakes studies of housing practices and collects racial data on all of its housing programs in order to determine areas of noncompliance; it conducts continuing community education programs to inform individuals of their rights under law; it encourages national, State, and local private organizations in undertaking programs designed to expand housing options for minority group and low-income individuals; it works closely with State and local agencies having fair housing laws substantially equivalent to Title VIII and refers complaints to these agencies.

A FREE AND OPEN SOCIETY

On March 24, 1970, I issued a statement setting forth in detail the administration's policies on school desegregation. In a portion of that statement that applies equally to housing, I said the goal of this administration is "a free and open society"—and I added:

In saying this, I use the words "free" and "open" quite precisely.

Freedom has two essential elements: the *right* to choose, and the *ability* to choose. The right to move out of a mid-city slum, for example, means little without the means of doing so. The right to apply for a good job means without access to the skills that make it attainable. By the same token, those skills are of little use if arbitrary policies exclude the person who has them because of race or other distinction.

Similarly, an "open" society is one of open choices—and one in which the individual has the mobility to take advantage of those choices.

In speaking of "desegregation" or "integration," we often lose sight of what these mean within the context of a free, open, pluralistic society. We cannot be free, and at the same time be required to fit our lives into prescribed places on a racial grid—whether segregated or integrated, and whether by some mathematical formula or by automatic assignment. Neither can we be free, and at the same time be denied—because of race—the right to associate with our fellow-citizens on a basis of human equality.

An open society does not have to be homogeneous, or even fully integrated. There is room within it for many communities. Especially in a nation like America, it is natural that people with a common heritage retain special ties; it is natural and right that we have Italian or Irish or Negro or Norwegian neighborhoods; it is natural and right that members of those communities feel a sense of group identity and group pride. In terms of an open society, what matters is mobility: the right and the ability of each person to decide for himself where and how he wants to live, whether as part of the ethnic enclave or as part of the larger society—or, as many do, share the life of both.

We are richer for our cultural diversity; mobility is what allows us to enjoy it.

Economic, educational, social mobility—all these, too, are essential elements of the open society. When we speak of equal opportunity we mean just that: that each person should have an equal chance at the starting line, and an equal chance to go just as high and as far as his talents and energies will take him.

The Federal Government bears an important share of responsibility for achieving fair housing for all Americans. But fair housing is not the responsibility of the Federal Government alone, and not of government alone. Its achievement depends on all of us—on the

States and localities, on business and industry, on civic and professional leadership, and on each of us in his daily life.

For its part, the Federal Government will discharge fully its
own particular responsibilities and offer example and leadership for
others in the discharge of their responsibilities. We will be vigorous
in enforcing both the constitutional mandate and the statutory requirements that there not be housing discrimination on grounds of
race. In the more complex and difficult area of providing subsidized
housing in areas where it is needed, we will encourage communities
and local developers to take into account the broad needs of the various groups within the community and of the metropolitan area.

But we all must recognize that the kinds of land use questions
involved in housing site selection are essentially local in nature: They
represent the kind of basic choices about the future shape of a community, or of a metropolitan area, that should be chiefly for the people
of that community or that area to determine. The challenge of how to
provide fair, open and adequate housing is one that they must meet;
and they must live with their success or failure.

To local officials are entrusted the initial, and often the final,
determinations as to how much low- and moderate-income housing is
to be built, how well it is to be built, and where it is to be built. They
operate under the same antidiscrimination strictures that apply to
Federal officials. And in terms of site selection and residential zoning
—both sensitive and complex matters, and yet both central to the goal
of truly open housing in truly open communities—they operate in an
area little charted by the Supreme Court but increasingly being
navigated by the lower courts, as land use restrictions come under
mounting challenge on constitutional grounds.

Two recent court cases suggest the boundaries within which other
courts will be wrestling with these questions in the months and years
just ahead. In one of these cases (*James* v. *Valtierra*), the U.S.
Supreme Court decided that, absent any evidence of racially discriminatory intent, a State law requiring prior approval of low-rent housing projects by community referendum does not, on its face, violate
the Constitution. Noting California's long tradition of using referenda
on a wide range of issues of public policy and the factual finding in
the lower courts that legitimate economic considerations were involved
in the referendum in question, the court concluded that there was no
factual basis for a claim that the California law was "aimed at a
racial minority." On the other hand, in another case presenting sharply

contrasting circumstances (*Kennedy Park Homes Association* v. *City of Lackawanna, N.Y.*), a Circuit Court of Appeals recently held illegal certain zoning and other municipal restrictions used to block a subsidized low-income housing development in an all-white neighborhood. In that case the municipal practices were determined to be subterfuges and part of a pattern of racially motivated discrimination by municipal officials; the Supreme Court denied certiorari. In short, the one case did not present evidence of racially discriminatory intent; the other did.

If these cases define the outer limits, they also indicate the broad range within which cases will be pressed in the courts by those who would seek the mandate of judicial decree in setting aside local restrictions to achieve social purposes: for example, the right of a community to impose large-lot zoning, even in the absence of any racial discrimination, has lately been under court challenge.

If the infinitely varied individual questions that arise as our thousands of local governments hammer out their individual local land use policies are not appropriate for Federal determination—and they are not—neither would it be wise to allow a situation to develop in which they have to be hammered out in the courts. But they no doubt will end up in the courts if they are not satisfactorily dealt with outside the courts through timely and enlightened local action.

This administration will offer leadership in encouraging local and State governments and housing authorities to address this question creatively and imaginatively, and to address it with a keen understanding of the needs of those persons for whom the housing is being provided as well as the needs of the community at large.

Local and State authorities, for their part, should continue to respond constructively, pressing forward with innovative and positive approaches of their own. For it is they—and beyond them, it is millions of Americans individually—with whom the challenge primarily rests. We are dealing here in a realm in which Federal authority, while substantial in terms of enforcement, is very limited in terms of the many choices that must be made in each community.

There are some who assume that the Federal Government has the power to do anything it wants—or that they want. But we have maintained our freedom for nearly two centuries by insisting that the Federal Government's exercise of power not exceed its authority.

I believe in that principle. And because the authority of the Federal agencies is limited—quite properly, I believe—with respect to the essentially local and individual choices involved in local community planning, their power will be used in only limited ways.

This does not reduce the challenge to the States, the localities and the people; it heightens it. For the task of making our communities livable, not for some but for all—of achieving our goals of decent homes and of open communities in a free and open society—this task summons the best that is in each and every one of us, in a cause that touches our soul as a Nation. We cannot afford to fail. I believe that together we can succeed.

ARTICLE 40

Is the Large City Becoming Ungovernable?

Demetrios Caraley

When the question is raised about the large city becoming "ungovernable," what is really being asked is whether the gap has been sharply increasing in recent years between the performance of large city governments and the demands and expectations of their citizenry for alleviation of outstanding problems and for provision of traditional functions, including preservation of public order. Large city governments still perform some impressive feats. The sheer survival of large city governments without any major breakdowns since World War II, in the face of having to perform a constantly widening range of functions for more-demanding populations, while suffering slowly rising and in some cases declining tax bases, must be considered an achievement of the first order. Furthermore, it can be argued that with the extension of the merit system, technological advances, personnel training programs, data processing systems, and the like, urban governments are performing their housekeeping functions—e.g., fire, san-

Reprinted with permission from "Governing the City: Challenges and Options for New York," *Proceedings of the Academy of Political Science*, Vol. 29, (August 1969), pp. 206–223.

itation, water supply, street repair and lighting, and public health—with greater technical efficiency and honesty all the time.

The housekeeping functions in most large cities are, however, chronically underfinanced and understaffed and increasingly in recent years have been interrupted by strikes. Expenditures in most program areas have been rising, but so fast have employees' salaries, the cost of standard products, and the size of the population being serviced also been rising, that the extra funds seldom result in any improvement in the quality of performance. Thus what large city governments do in housekeeping matters is essentially conduct holding actions against any rapid worsening of services or deterioration of facilities. Rarely do they engage in a level of effort sufficiently intense to provide services or facilities of a quality normally expected of the federal government or of large private corporations. And as budgets become tighter, given the drain of financing poverty-related services and benefits, certain "nonessential" amenities like parks, zoos, museums, and libraries have in some cities had to be sharply curtailed. Strikes by municipal employees have already stopped the operation of public schools, garbage collection, transit facilities, welfare services, and hospitals in various cities, and not even police and fire departments have been free of strike threats, feigned mass illnesses, and slowdowns.

Much more serious than their underperformance of housekeeping functions is the little success large city governments have shown in ameliorating conditions of life of the poor that have come to be increasingly concentrated in urban slum ghetto areas. These poor are primarily black, but in certain cities they include sizable numbers of Puerto Ricans, Mexican-Americans, and Appalachian whites. They live in neighborhoods with large proportions of men without jobs or with jobs that do not pay enough to support a family and of families headed by women subsisting on welfare payments. Their schools are seemingly incapable of instilling fundamental skills of literacy in children. Much of their housing is overcrowded and dilapidated. Their neighborhoods also have extremely high rates of crimes.

True, census statistics suggest that the number of dilapidated housing units in all large cities combined has been declining, unemployment rates have been dropping as a result of the overheated economy, and the official count of persons subsisting on incomes below the poverty line has also been decreasing. But the proportions of dilapidated housing, unemployment, underemployment, and incomes below poverty level in certain large city neighborhoods are still two and three times the national average. According to the Kerner commission, in the worst neighborhoods, up to 91 per cent of the housing units are dilapidated, up to 15.6 per cent of the working force is unemployed, and as high as 47 per cent is underemployed. And although skilled, "successful working-class" and middle-class Negroes have recently been increasing their incomes rapidly and moving out of those slums, their places are constantly filled by the arrival of new unemployed migrants. These migrants, together with those "unsuccessful" slum-dwellers that are left behind, form a permanent contingent of two million hard-core urban poor. The Kerner commission found that during the current period of general prosperity the incomes of these hard-core poor "have not risen at all . . . unemployment rates have declined only slightly, the proportion of families with female heads has increased, and housing conditions have worsened even though rents have risen."

Furthermore, even for those black slum-dwellers whose conditions have been improving, the improvement in the standard of living of middle-class whites (and even blacks) has been so much faster, that the gap between their life in the slums and what they see depicted as the "normal American" style of life on the mass media has been widening. And unlike as recently as a decade ago, black slum-dwellers no longer believe that their color requires them to accept a permanently inferior standard of living or that governmental action is incapable of improving their situation. However much their conditions are getting better, they are still demanding more services and more benefits from city governments since their conditions have not yet reached equality with those of white Americans.

What many persons would probably consider to be the most critical evidence of ungovernability of large cities is their incapacity to stop increases in street crime and to contain mass violence. The chief victims of street crime are, of course, the people living in the lowest-income slum neighborhoods, where the rate of victimization is in some instances up to thirty-five times what it is in upper-income areas. But with the general spread of low-income neighborhoods in different parts of the city and with the mobility afforded by the automobile, middle-class areas have also experienced an increase in serious crime.

The outbreaks of riots by ghetto-dwellers that began in the summer of 1964 thus far have been directed primarily against police and stores in the ghetto areas. There is, however, increasing talk and apparently some preparation among the extremist black militants of starting citywide "urban guerilla warfare," which presumably would involve terroristic acts against white persons and property anywhere in a city. There has also been an increase in mass disruptions, vandalism, and arson of such places as welfare offices and schools and colleges. Until very recently, the participants in riots and disruptions have gone almost completely unpunished, as police have not made arrests or been largely unable to produce sufficient evidence in court to support successful prosecutions.

DRIFTING INTO THE "BLACK TINDERBOX" FUTURE

Given the continuation of existing trends, the most likely outcome, at least in many of the older large cities of the Northeast and Middle West, is to turn them within the next few decades into "black tinderboxes." First, the proportion of Negroes in the country's thirty largest cities has been increasing rapidly since World War II, almost doubling between 1950 and 1966. By 1985 Chicago, Philadelphia, St. Louis, Detroit, Cleveland, Baltimore, New Orleans, Newark, and Washington, D.C., are expected to have black majorities. Second, with a continuation of present discriminatory renting and selling practices in housing, the bulk of this population will be concentrated in the older, racially segregated, all-black neighborhoods, and in "changing" neighborhoods on their periphery. As these changing neighborhoods inexorably shift toward heavier Negro occupancy, "massive racial transition" will take place and the ghetto will spread. Third, without a sharp increase in the present level of effort to enrich schools, increase job skills and motivation, and provide greater job opportunities, the number of dropped-out, unemployed, and underemployed young Negro men will continue to be large and possibly larger than at present. Fourth, at the present level of building-code enforcement and renewal of central city housing, and with the present inability of slum dwellers to pay rents sufficient to enable landlords to keep their buildings in good repair, more and more blocks of older residential properties will continue to deteriorate and become dilapidated, and larger parts of central city populations will be forced to live under slum conditions. Fifth, as the number of tax dollars required to provide even the existing level of benefits and services to the poor and otherwise disadvantaged increases, and as the number of tax dollars available grows slowly or actually declines as still larger numbers of middle-income taxpayers move to suburbia and business volume and property value also go down, city governments will be caught in a constantly tighter fiscal squeeze. Even present levels of standard housekeeping services might have to be reduced.

The combustibility of a city with these conditions would obviously be very high. Nothing would be going on, as the Kerner commission put it, "to raise the hopes, absorb the energies, or constructively challenge the talents of the rapidly-growing number of young Negro men in central cities. . . . These young men have contributed disproportionately to crime and violence in the past, and there is danger, obviously, that they will continue to do so." An even more serious possibility in this kind of "black tinderbox" city is that a rising proportion of older blacks with better educations and higher incomes, strong majorities of whom according to opinion surveys still reject separatist thinking and violence, might also become embittered. Many of them might well come to look on continued poverty and oppressive slum-living of their lower-class racial brethren in the midst of plenty and on continued discrimination in housing or job opportunities for themselves as so outrageously unjust that they might decide to support not only riots and other violent protests, but also the tiny minority of revolutionaries who advocate outright rebellion and general urban guerrilla warfare.

Providing further fuel for combustion of the "black tinderbox," incidentally, will probably be those lower-middle and working-class whites not affluent or mobile enough to become suburbanites. These whites would in all likelihood feel increasingly alienated and deserted in what was becoming a predominantly Negro city, perceiving themselves as "penned-in" and "declassed" as Negroes moved closer to their neighborhoods and in increasing danger of losing their jobs to black competitors.

Despite the tightness of municipal budgets and the need for compensating contraction elsewhere, the resources allocated by city governments to police forces will almost certainly be steadily increased. The police will, therefore, probably be developing ever-greater capacity, with occasional assistance from the national guard, to respond quickly and with sufficient manpower to outbreaks of violence to be able to cut down sharply the frequency of the prolonged, multiday riots. And also, as city officialdom with strong black representation responded to precipitating incidents of violence in ghetto neighborhoods with what by then could be more heavily black police, the interracial character of the confrontations might be blurred and the possibility of escalation reduced. On the other hand, probably no amount of increase in police power will be sufficient to prevent sudden, "hit-and-run" burnings, lootings, and vandalism confined to small areas, nor is it likely to prevent periodic sniping at the police themselves.

Whether augmented police power, including an increase in the amount and quality of infiltration and undercover work, will be able to prevent serious outbreaks of terroristic violence directed against the white community generally remains an open question. If such violence were to begin—and it could be sustained at a highly disruptive level by even small numbers of determined nihilistic revolutionaries who were not concerned about their own eventual safety and apprehension—the nine-to-one white majority in the population would most likely retaliate massively and indiscriminately against all blacks, both through vigilantism and through the use of official governmental force.

Among the measures that might be resorted to by an angered majoritarian democracy or by the right-wing dictatorship that might conceivably emerge if democratically elected politicians fail to act repressively enough are the formalization of the urban *apartheid* alluded to by the Kerner commission and the drastic curtailment of civil liberties and procedural due process for all Americans, but particularly for Negroes.

If this kind of garrison-state "black tinderbox" future for large cities appears wildly fantastic and implausible, one should consider the following aspects of existing harsh realities: The rhetoric of revolution and guerrilla warfare and the display and some use of weaponry and fire-bombing is already increasing by extremist black militants. Opinion surveys[1] conducted over the past few years furthermore show that there is a hard core of Negroes who essentially hate all whites and are so alienated from the white community that they believe "close friendships between Negroes and whites are impossible" and that "there should be a separate black nation here." The percentage of Negroes who hold these views is small—only 5 to 12 per cent—but their absolute numbers are sizable, amounting to tens and possibly hundreds of thousands in each large city. Some 15 per cent of a sample of all Negroes, 20 per cent of the men, and up to

30 per cent of the youngest men believe that in order to gain their rights, black people should be "ready to use violence." Large minorities or majorities among Negroes believe that riots have been helpful to their cause, feel sympathetic with the rioters, and define the riots as essentially condonable protests against legitimate grievances. Finally, when asked after being specifically reminded that they were in a one-to-nine minority whether in any all-out confrontation with whites they would not lose, only 27 per cent of a national sample agreed, while 24 per cent of the overall sample and 15 per cent of the Northern ghetto contingent were not sure, *and 49 and 54 per cent respectively denied that they would lose in such a confrontation!*

There is already an increasing hardening of white attitudes toward blacks. Restrictive legislative action in Congress and various state legislatures and mounting electoral support for candidates who take strong "law and order" positions in the past two years all reflect this hardening. Recent opinion surveys of white attitudes also reveal, for example: Some two-thirds of a national sample believe Negroes "had gone too far in their demands," and 60 per cent feel an increase in themselves of anti-Negro sentiments as a result of the riots. Although there had been a long-term continuous downward trend in the acceptance by whites of unflattering stereotypes of Negroes, since the major riots of 1967 that trend has been reversed. Whereas as late as the summer of 1963, preponderant white majorities believed that demonstrations by Negroes were aimed at legitimate goals like "equal rights," "to be treated as human beings," and "equal education," only a minority of whites currently define riots as mainly spontaneous protests against unfair conditions, while varying-sized majorities characterize riots as being in part looting expeditions, planned and organized by "outside agitators" or "Communists" and calling in the short run for stronger police control. Some 5 per cent of all whites, 8 percent of the white males, and up to 21 per cent of the least-educated white males believe that if Negroes rioted in their city, they themselves should engage in counter-riot violence against Negroes.

Strong support exists among the American public for certain kinds of curtailment of civil liberties and safeguards of procedural due process. Political scientists have long documented that although Americans almost unanimously agree with various principles of free speech and legal procedure when stated in abstract terms, substantial minorities do not support various logical corollaries of those principles. Indeed, even majorities do not support specific applications to protect individuals or groups that become widely unpopular.[2] In early 1969 there was already serious consideration at the highest levels of American government of proposals for "preventive detention" of recidivists accused but not convicted of new crimes. The purpose of such detention would be to prevent the possibility of the accused committing further offenses while free on bail, as presumably permitted by the Constitution. Recent public opinion surveys on curtailment of Negro rights find that over a quarter of whites believe that even "orderly marches to protest against racial discrimination" are unjustified. More than two thirds think that nonviolent sit-in protests are also unjustified, and over a third are of the opinion that there is no "real difference" between nonviolent protest marches and demonstrations on the one hand and riots on the other. Majorities of two-to-one disagree with the Kerner commission findings that persons arrested during riots should have been given better legal counsel and fairer trials. A narrow majority believe that the "courts have been a major cause for the breakdown of law and order," the latter phrase being widely understood as code words referring in large part to Negro street crime and rioting.

GOVERNING THE CITY TOWARD A HEALTHY, MULTIRACIAL FUTURE

It is not inevitable that large cities become less and less governable and drift into "black tinderboxes." Admittedly city governments with only their own tax resources and present level of grants from the states and the federal government cannot develop the governing capacity to deal with the most serious problems within their jurisdictions. This is particularly true of the "tangle of pathology" associated with slum poverty. And, of course, some of the major causes of city problems, like suburbanization, black migration to cities, the unemployability of the unskilled, the high cost of new housing, and the loosening of inhibitions on the use of forcible tactics are national in scope or origin and are beyond any particular city's legal reach.

But certainly the American political system as a whole does have the capacity to brake the adverse trends affecting large cities and begin to actually "govern" them toward a healthy, multiracial future. Properly governed cities could have upgraded housekeeping services and sharply reduced levels of unemployment, underemployment, and poverty. Deteriorating neighborhoods could be rehabilitated and new housing constructed. More highly effective public schools could be developed to enable the next generation of slum ghetto children to break out of the "culture of poverty." The economy of these cities could still retain a fair share of top national firms and their downtown sections continue to be attractive as diversified shopping centers and as cultural and recreational hubs of their metropolitan areas. Such cities would also enjoy a greatly improved quality of law enforcement to control street crime in all areas of the city and to deal more effectively with riots and other mass violations of the law. Even though this "healthy" city would have a disproportionately high percentage of Negroes, and especially working-class Negroes, in its population relative to its surrounding suburbs, that percentage would be steady. Instead of increasing ghettoization there could be an expanding number of multiracial residential neighborhoods.

This future for large cities does not postulate any reversal of basic trends toward suburbanization of population and jobs or any reemergence of the central city as the overwhelmingly dominant force in the metropolis. It simply assumes that even within the limits set by those trends, the large city could be viable enough to be the preferred choice for work or residence or play for a substantial portion of the metropolitan population, whether white or black, low, middle, or upper income.

The large city could be revitalized if massive sums of money were fed into it for upgrading of housekeeping services, expanded job-creation and job-training including the guarantee of jobs by government as "employer of last resort," improved income supplementation, a concentrated attack on slum conditions, and sharply strengthened law enforcement efforts, and if strong efforts were made to stop increased ghettoization. Stopping ghettoization would not be easy. It would require some combination of reduced black in-migration to central cities, large-scale suburbanization of Negroes already there, a slowing down of mass white exodus to suburbia, and deliberate "managed integration" of central city neighborhoods.

OBSTACLES TO IMPROVED URBAN GOVERNABILITY

Given the unquestionable advantages of healthy, multiracial cities, why is not the American political system improving their governing capacity? Part of the answer is that there are important jurisdictional, organizational, technological, and fiscal obstacles that currently stand in the way of adopting and implementing the policies and programs required. The circumscribed legal powers often granted to city governments by their states, for example, prevent them from reaching some of the causes of the problems that they face, particularly those that are metropolitan in scope. The fragmentation of authority in most city governments often retards decisive, innovative decision making. The limited legal powers and staffs usually available to mayors, who normally are less parochial than the city bureaucracy, do not permit them to impart forceful direction to the city governments. The severe shortage of talented administrators limits the capacity of all governmental levels to design and operate complex urban programs at a high level of efficiency. The narrow channels for public participation in city-government decision making sometime interfere with its being responsive to the problems of the ghetto poor. The inadequate design, lack of coordination, and mismanagement of some existing urban-oriented federal programs prevent their making as great an impact on urban conditions as they should.

Also, complete knowledge is not available about psychological or sociological processes to permit the design of programs that get at the basic causes of such complex social phenomena as the "tangle of pathology" associated with slum living or the failure of ghetto children to learn. Moreover, under present tax rates and expenditure commitments, there is not sufficient money available to city governments to fund at the required level the various programs necessary to reverse trends toward a "black tinderbox."

It is reasonable, however, to assume that a country which twenty-five years ago could fight successfully a world war, supply logistically a worldwide alliance, and develop a nuclear weapon, and today can place a man on the moon, has sufficient organizational, legal, and administrative ability and can assemble sufficient knowledge to deal successfully with the most seriously oppressive symptoms of urban problems. And if there were a decision to do so, enough additional revenues could be extracted out of an overall economy of some $850 to $900 billion in gross national product to go a long way toward paying for the cost of healthy, multiracial large cities.

Admittedly, in many city governments, which rely primarily on the property tax, further sharp tax increases might prove counter-productive by stimulating an even faster flight of industry and middle-income taxpayers to the generally lower-tax suburbs. Though, to be sure, those city governments that are currently taxing their residents only one-third as much as others could probably make a greater local effort. The states making the highest tax efforts also must consider whether still higher rates will not lead to an erosion of their tax base to other jurisdictions. The federal government, however, need not fear the flight of tax-paying industries and individuals to lower-tax jurisdictions. Moreover, the federal revenue system, based heavily on income taxes, is highly growth-responsive so that in a prosperous economy a given tax rate takes in more money each year than the automatic rise in federal expenditures. This difference constitutes the so-called "fiscal dividend." There are, therefore, no fiscal reasons to prevent the federal government from providing most of the financing necessary to produce healthy large cities. Former U.S. Budget Director Charles L. Schultze estimates that if the Vietnam war were to end, there would be available within two years a "fiscal dividend" of about $10 billion and within four or five years one in the range of $35 to $40 billion, even if the 1968 ten per cent surcharge were discontinued.[3]

The most intractable obstacles to improving the governability of large cities are political ones. The political forces that oppose the courses of action necessary to solve city problems are stronger than those that support them. This political opposition is directed to three separate aspects of the strategy required: increased spending, stepped-up integration, and strengthened law enforcement.

Opposition to the increased spending necessary probably results first of all from the "optimistic denial" by most Americans of the seriousness of the urban situation and from the failure to recognize the consequences of present trends. Opposition also comes from public officials responsible for approving expenditures and raising revenues. Their opposition presumably reflects the widespread reluctance of the public to pay increased taxes, especially for financing programs that are perceived as being of greatest direct benefit only to the minority of Americans who are poor, black, and residents of large cities. It is important to recognize that while some 65 per cent of the American people live in metropolitan areas, only 30 per cent of Americans live in the central city portions and only 20 per cent in really large cities of 400,000 or more in population.

The opinion data suggests that there is probably little ideological opposition to spending money for improving the *physical* condition of slums. There is, however, such ideological opposition among some officials, particularly the great majority of Republican and Southern Democrat members of Congress who form the "conservative coalition," and much more among the public to improving the *social* conditions of the slum poor by having governmental programs redistribute income through increased welfare payments, negative income taxes, or rent supplements. Opposition to these programs is strongest among those parts of the white population closest in income, education, and status to groups who would receive the expanded benefits.

Political opposition to the residential integration of central city neighborhoods comes not only from those white racists who are against residential integration in principle but also from that much larger group of whites who incorrectly attribute to all Negroes the life style of lower class slum-dwellers. Their fear is that integration will lead to a deterioration in the quality of their children's education or the character of their own neighborhoods. Such opposition is likely to be strongest in those central city neighborhoods closest to the ghettos. Since suburbanization of Negroes sizable enough to halt the ghettoization of large cities would create a five- to ten-fold increase in the current growth rate of the Negro suburban population, suburban whites are opposed. Some are racists, but others simply fear that the problems of cities will be transferred to the suburbs.

Incidentally, some better-educated Negroes with higher incomes living in large cities also oppose these integration measures. Part of Negro opposition is based on their desire to turn large cities into black ghettos. Some of them are motivated by black racism and a commitment to separatism; others by an expectation of greater opportunities in such cities to capture top political offices and take over other major central-city institutions. Other Negro opposition is based on objection to the use of such means as "benign quotas" to maintain white dominance of white central-city neighborhoods. Such quotas are considered unacceptable and demeaning, even though their purpose would be to achieve real racial integration.

Finally, there is a considerable amount of sheer hostility among some whites toward all Negroes, which motivates them to be against anything that might benefit black people, even if no money had to be spent. Part of that hostility is no doubt based on the kind of long-term white racism cited by the Kerner commission, but opinion data suggest that probably more has been generated lately by the anti-white and violence-laden rhetoric and activities of the extremist black militants and by the rioting in black ghettos.

The political obstacles to strengthened law enforcement to reduce street crime and mass violence come from four diverse sources: the "antispenders," the police, the slum ghetto community, and some members of the liberal community. Slum conditions are not, of course, a sufficient cause for engaging in street crime and mass violence. Yet, slum living within the "culture of poverty" is highly conducive to criminal activity and does generate an underlying reservoir of grievances that provides fuel for crime and disorders. Thus the forces opposing spending for drastic amelioration of slums and poverty are perforce also obstructing law enforcement by preventing the removal of one basic cause of street crime and mass violence. Opposition to spending also blocks strenghtened law enforcement in a much more direct way. It prevents the expenditure of the large additional sums of money necessary for expansion of police forces, for additional prosecutors and judges, and for expansion and improvement of correctional institutions to give them capacity not only to incarcerate, but also to rehabilitate convicted criminals.

The political obstacles to strengthened law enforcement provided by the police themselves is based on the hostility many feel toward ghetto slum-dwellers and toward persons who defy, or sometimes even question, police authority. Varying proportions of police officers in different cities act out their hostility against black slum-dwellers by using insulting or abusive language during routine police contacts and chance encounters. Varying proportions of police also lose self-control when faced with rioting or nonviolent mass demonstrations, employing excessive gunfire and engaging in "police riots." This unauthorized verbal and physical brutality by police is, of course, no less illegal than any other crime. Furthermore, the resentments and hatred generated by this kind of brutality stimulates sniping and other violence against the police, and interferes with the kind of community cooperation that could help the police to reduce street crime.

The obstacle to strengthened law enforcement presented by the slum community is its deep hostility toward the police. Part of this hostility is, obviously, generated by police abuses and by the low level of protection afforded ghetto residents. But probably a larger part of that hostility is misdirected, with the police becoming the target for grievances felt against the shortcoming of city governmental performance in improving conditions, simply because police officers in the slums are the city's most visible and continuously available representatives. As a result, even when police are engaged in perfectly proper actions in black neighborhoods, such as stopping a speeding motorist or raiding an illegal business or intervening to stop an assault, bystanders will frequently treat the police officer as an enemy. This lack of support, indiscriminate hostility, and sometimes actual interference with the police when performing their legal duties predictably increase the sense of threat police feel and strengthens their belief that slum-dwellers are not really interested in better police protection. This in turn further stimulates their hostility toward the black community and makes them less likely to act in a restrained and discriminate manner.

The political obstacle to strengthened law enforcement that comes from the liberal community is based on the temperamental antipathy of many liberals to police as an intrinsically repressive force for whatever purpose used, but most especially when used against those perceived as unjustly deprived and downtrodden, like today's black slum-dwellers. This antipathy appears to be further buttressed by feelings of guilt over being part of the society responsible for allowing deplorable conditions like slum ghettos to exist. And these antipolice sentiments are often supported by an intellectual position that seems to hold that since by police action city governments can deal only with symptoms and not basic causes of urban problems, municipal governments should do neither until they can do both.

PROSPECTS FOR ENDING URBAN UNGOVERNABILITY

What possibility exists for overcoming the political opposition that currently exists to spending massively larger amounts of money on the problems of cities, to racially integrating central city neighborhoods as well as encouraging large numbers of central city Negroes to resettle in presently almost exclusively white suburbia, and to strengthening law enforcement sufficiently to control various forms of illegal violence without simultaneously curtailing nonviolent dissent, civil liberties, and procedural due process? Realistically speaking, the answer is "none" unless there develops a conscious and deliberate, long-term national commitment to alleviate the problems of cities much like the long-term commitment made for rebuilding the European economy after World War II through the Marshall Plan. And it is probably necessary that any expanded national commitment to aid cities be a part of a still larger one aimed at eliminating poverty and improving the quality of life of the less-affluent third of the population, whether urban or rural, black or white.

Actually, the supportive constituency for commitments to back the integrated package of policies and programs to bring about the healthy, multiracial future for large cities is potentially very broad. In terms of individuals and groups who stand to gain specific, tangible benefits, such a constituency would include:

Black slum-dwellers looking to improved incomes and other living conditions.

Other urban and rural poor, currently largely ignored, who would benefit from any general upgrading of incomes and quality of life for the nonaffluent.

Local and state elective and appointive officeholders, whose fiscal capacity to cope with demands and problems in their jurisdictions would be enhanced by federal absorption of the cost of welfare and poverty programs.

Large-city downtown retailers, bankers, utility and newspaper owners, restaurant, hotel, and theater operators, and other businessmen whose enterprises are largely "locked in" the central city's downtown section and whose economic success and survival depends on a healthy large city.

White upper-middle and upper-income devotees of apartment or townhouse big-city living, whose enjoyment would be increased by greater safety on the streets and by fewer slum sights.

Middle-income whites who prefer big-city living and who, with improved public safety and schools, might indulge these preferences.

White blue-collar and white-collar workers, who could see increased long-term security through "managed integration" against massive transition of their neighborhoods and who could also expect improved city services once poverty-related costs were absorbed by the federal government.

White suburbanites who want to patronize the recreational, cultural, and business facilities of the large city.

Persons who are highly disturbed by the increase in crime and riots and would be attracted by the strengthened law enforcement.

Incumbent national politicians of high visibility and competitive constituency, particularly the President, but also House members of the Administration party from close districts, who know that their reputations and reelection prospects will suffer if repeated outbreaks of violence occur during their own or their party's Administration.

On a higher level of generality, support for the package of policies and programs conducive to the healthy, multiracial city could come from all those whites who, regardless of actual place or residence, are ideologically or emotionally attached to large cities. They regard large cities as the nation's traditional centers of population, business, and culture, and oppose their becoming predominantly Negro possessions, particularly as this would entail the possible permanent loss of those specialized facilities necessary for a highly urbane style of life. For such facilities require a metropolitanwide clientele and probably cannot survive economically except at the geographic center of the area's population mass.

Finally, on the highest level of generality, a supportive constituency for a pro-city national commitment is potentially forthcoming from the great mass of middle-class Americans who have feelings of humanitarianism, justice, and fairness predisposing them to help the underprivileged and guarantee a minimally decent standard of living for everybody. These Americans do not feel comfortable with the prospects of an increasingly racially segregated society. They recognize that allowing large cities to drift into "black tinderboxes" and improving public order exclusively through strengthened law enforcement do not solve the problem of cities or race but merely postpone dealing with them until some time when their dimensions will be still larger. An optimistic opinion survey finding is that white majorities by five-to-one believe that "thinking about the next five to ten years . . . the best thing to do about the problem of riots" is *not* simply to "build up tighter police control in the Negro areas," but to "try harder to improve the condition of the Negroes" or "do both."

To say that support for a new pro-urban package will be forthcoming assumes that most white Americans, particularly younger, middle-class, and college-educated white Americans, are not unmitigated racists. Admittedly they are limited in the extent to which they are enthusiastic about converting their humanitarian feelings into actual sacrifices for the benefit of the black downtrodden. And they still harbor irrational prejudices against certain kinds of very close social contacts with Negroes. But there is no evidence to show that most white Americans are firmly committed to keeping Negroes in a position of permanent economic and social separation and inferiority. In this respect it was probably a mistake for the Kerner commission to refer to the racial prejudice interfering with Negro advancement by the term "white racism," with its strong implications that such prejudice is an inherent characteristic of all whites, all-encompassing in the relationships to which it attaches, and somehow fundamental and unchanging.

Whether or not the broad array of individuals, groups, and publics with tangible, ideological, and moral stakes in a healthy future for cities can be mobilized and their combined political resources brought to bear in support of a strategy necessary to bring it about is an open question. The answer will depend in great part on the kind of leadership that emerges, especially from national political officials such as the President, from large city mayors, from universities, from the mass media, and from business. Such leadership would have to instruct the American public in terms that will dispel its "optimistic denial" and capture its attention and sympathetic understanding about the harsh realities of the current urban situation and about the even harsher likely consequences of not changing present policies and allowing existing trends to continue. It would also have to explain that strategies, policies, and programs are available that when funded at a sufficiently high level can ameliorate current conditions and shift adverse trends. The most important targets of this kind of instruction will be that small stratum of politically active or attentive individuals who have disproportionately large influence over governmental decisions, especially solid working majorities in Congress for the authorization of necessary programs and the appropriation of sufficient funds.

The answer also depends on whether strong, responsible, and courageous black leadership will explain to the black community other harsh realities of the situation: that black time perspectives need to be lengthened as dramatic improvements in the most oppressive physical conditions are technically impossible to bring about immediately regardless of the sincerity and magnitude of the efforts made; that extremist antiwhite rhetoric and outbreaks of large-scale mass or guerrilla-type violence are almost certain to produce a backlash. For such black rhetoric and violence breed anxiety and hostility among whites that inevitably counteract support for ameliorative urban policies and provide backing for different political leadership that is oriented toward responding to urban problems solely by imposing order through repressive force.

How receptive either white or black publics would be if this leadership emerges depends on a number of additional factors. If national and local officials demonstrate clearly that they regard the problems of cities as urgent, if reasonable demands of responsible, nonviolent and nonseparatist black leaders are being met, and if ameliorative change is visibly taking place, the vast majority of the urban black community may well accede once again to pleas for more patience and keep relatively "cool." Similarly, if the national economy is experiencing rapid growth and the nation is not engaged in large-scale military operations, much or all of the huge monetary costs of the new policies could be borne "painlessly" out of the "fiscal dividends" generated by the federal tax system. Under those circumstances the dominant majority of the white public might well provide support for decisions by officials in the White House, in Congress, in various city halls, and in state houses to engage in an overall national commitment to achieve a better future for large cities.

If, on the other hand, the national economy should be less prosperous or the military budget remains high because of war or major new weapons-procurement programs or if any "fiscal dividend" were to be consumed by expansions of nonurban, nonpoverty related programs, the costs of achieving the healthy, multiracial future for cities would fall more painfully on much of its potential supportive constituency. Increased taxes might be required and, depending on how fast personal incomes were rising, even cuts in existing standards of living. Sustained support for any national commitment to improve the "governability" of large cities would then depend on how successful politicians and other leaders were in convincing the more affluent two-thirds of the American public to forego some personal income for a society whose cities would be healthy and multiracial and whose poor no longer had to live under conditions that might nauseate the average member of the middle class. And success in that task would depend ultimately on how receptive most Americans were to the idea that in such a society, a somewhat smaller income could actually lead to a more enjoyable life than a larger income in a society whose large cities had become "black tinderboxes," whose poor continued to live in degrading circumstances, where the two-thirds of the population that lived in or near those cities felt some degree of Hobbes' "continual feare, and danger of violent death," and where there existed for all Americans a risk of the ending of the present form of American democracy. It is not inconceivable that Americans might prove receptive.

NOTES

1. The opinion surveys primarily relied on for this paper have been reported by Angus Campbell and Howard Schuman, "Racial Attitudes in Fifteen Cities," *Supplemental Studies for the National Advisory Commission on Civil Disorders*, Praeger Edition, New York, 1968; by William Brink and Louis Harris, *Black and White*, New York, 1967; and by Louis Harris in the daily press. Specific citations will appear in my book *Urban Political Systems*, Englewood Cliffs, forthcoming.

2. See, for example, James W. Protho and Charles M. Griggs, "Fundamental Principles of Democracy: Bases of Agreement and Disagreement," *Journal of Politics*, XXII (1960), 276–294, and Herbert McClosky, "Consensus and Ideology in American Politics," *American Political Science Review*, LVIII (1964), 361–382.

3. "Budget Alternatives After Vietnam," in Kermit Gordon, ed., *Agenda for the Nation*, Washington, D.C., 1968.

SUGGESTIONS FOR FURTHER READING
(Combining Chapters 5 and 6)

I. Protests, Riots, and Community Order

Boskin, Joseph, ed. *Urban Racial Violence in the Twentieth Century.* Beverly Hills, Calif.: The Glencoe Press, 1969. (Selected essays with commentaries on the history of urban racial conflict.)

Connery, Robert H., ed. *Urban Riots.* New York: Random House, Inc., Vintage Books, 1969. (Original essays on violence and social change.)

Conot, Robert. *Rivers of Blood, Years of Darkness.* New York: Bantam Books, Inc., 1967. (A vivid, first-hand description of Watts, Los Angeles, riot of 1965.)

Fanon, Frantz. *The Wretched of the Earth.* New York: Grove Press, Inc., Evergreen Edition, 1966. (Strategy for guerrilla warfare and revolutionary upheaval.)

Gilbert, Ben W., and the Staff of *The Washington Post. Ten Blocks from the White House.* New York: Frederick A. Praeger, Publishers, 1968. (A journalistic account of Washington, D.C., riots of 1968.)

Governor's Select Commission on Civil Disorders. *Report for Action.* State of New Jersey, February 1968. (An analysis of 1967 New Jersey urban riots with an especially critical attack on the Newark city administration.)

Graham, Hugh D., and Ted R. Gurr., eds. *The History of Violence In America.* A Report to the National Commission on the Causes and Prevention of Violence. New York: Bantam Books, Inc., 1969. (An exhaustive and significantly revealing series of essays indicating the roots of violence in American society.)

Hayden, Tom. *Rebellion In Newark*. New York: Random House, Inc., Vintage Books, 1967. (A brief description of 1967 Newark riots.)

Hubbard, Howard. "Five Long Hot Summers and How They Grew." *The Public Interest* 12 (Summer 1968):3–24. (An analysis of black protest within a framework of bargaining and negotiation.)

Killian, Lewis M. *The Impossible Revolution? Black Power And The American Dream*. New York: Random House, Inc., 1968. (A pessimistic account of black prospects for change.)

Masotti, Louis H., and Don R. Bowen, eds. *Riots and Rebellion*. Beverly Hills, Calif.: Sage Publications, Inc., 1968. (A collection of original essays analyzing civil disorders.)

Oppenheimer, Martin. *The Urban Guerilla*. Chicago: Quadrangle Books, Inc., 1969. (Strategies for revolution and paramilitary insurgency in urban areas.)

Rainwater, Lee. "Open Letter on White Justice and the Riots." *Trans-Action* 4 (September 1967):22–32. (An analysis of the 1967 riots in which the author contends that many ghetto residents participated.)

Report of the National Advisory Commission on Civil Disorders. New York: Bantam Books, Inc., 1968. (A comprehensive analysis of 1967 city riots together with prescriptions for change. Highly recommended.)

Willis, Garry. *The Second Civil War*. New York: The New American Library, Inc., Signet Books, 1968. (Interviews with police officials preparing for civil disorders.)

Wilson, James Q. "The Urban Unease: Community vs. City," *The Public Interest* 12 (Summer 1968):25–39. (Neighborhood concern for public order.)

―――. "Why We Are Having A Wave of Violence." *The New York Times Magazine* (May 19, 1968):23–24, 116–120. (Contention that recent ghetto riots differ from past civil disturbances.)

II. The Police

Advisory Commission on Intergovernmental Relations. *Making the Safe Streets Act Work*. Washington: U.S. Government Printing Office, September 1970. (An analysis of 1968 federal legislation assisting local law enforcement, the first such comprehensive federal law providing grant-in-aid assistance.)

Becker, Theodore L., and Vernon G. Murray, eds. *Government Lawless-*

ness in America. New York: Oxford University Press, Inc., 1971. (An extensive collection of articles concerning police, crime, courts, and prisons, together with suggested remedies.)

Campbell, James S., Joseph R. Sahid, and David P. Stang, co-directors. *Law and Order Reconsidered.* Vol. 10, National Commission on the Causes and Prevention of Violence Staff Study Series. Washington: U.S. Government Printing Office, 1969. (A comprehensive report on problems of disorder, police response, and agencies of law enforcement.)

The Challenge of Crime in a Free Society. A Report by the President's Commission on Law Enforcement and Administration of Justice. New York: Avon Books, 1968. (A considerably detailed analysis of crime and police problems in American society.)

Chevigny, Paul. *Police Power.* New York: Random House, Inc., Vintage Books, 1969. (A study of police abuses and civil liberty violations in New York City.)

Doig, Jameson W., symposium ed. "The Police in a Democratic Society." *Public Administration Review* 28 (1968):393–430. (Four interesting articles on police problems and prospects.)

Lipset, Seymour. "Why Cops Hate Liberals—And Vice Versa." *The Atlantic Monthly* 233 (March 1969):76–83. (Reasons for polarization between police and liberal reformers.)

Masotti, Louis H., and Jerome R. Corsi. *Shoot-Out In Cleveland.* A Report to the National Commission on the Causes and Prevention of Violence. New York: Bantam Books, Inc., 1969. (An analysis of the events and causes related to the battle between black militants and the police in Cleveland on July 23, 1968.)

Newton, George D., and Franklin E. Zimring, directors. *Firearms and Violence in American Life.* Vol. 7, National Commission on the Causes and Prevention of Violence Staff Study Series. Washington: U.S. Government Printing Office, 1969. (A shocking study of the proliferation of violent weapons in American society.)

Niederhoffer, Arthur. *Behind The Shield.* Garden City, N. Y.: Doubleday & Co., Inc., Anchor Books, 1969. (An important evaluation of conflicts in police roles and perceptions.)

Saunders, Charles B., Jr., *Upgrading the American Police.* Washington: The Brookings Institution, 1970. (Recommendations for improving the quality of the police for better law enforcement.)

Skolnick, Jerome H., director. *The Politics of Protest.* A Report to the National Commission on the Causes and Prevention of Violence. New York: Ballantine Books, Inc., 1969. (A controversial study of protest strategies and tactics with an especially interesting chapter on the politicalization of the police.)

Summers, Marvin R., and Thomas E. Barth, eds. *Law and Order in a Democratic Society*. Columbus, Ohio: Charles E. Merrill Publishing Co., 1970. (Selected essays on criminal justice, urban violence, and political dissent.)

Walker, Daniel, director. *Rights In Conflict*. A Special Investigation Report to the National Commission on the Causes and Prevention of Violence. New York: Bantam Books, Inc., 1968. (A detailed study of the violent confrontation between demonstrators and police in Chicago during the Democratic National Convention of 1968.)

Wilson, James Q. *Varieties of Police Behavior*. New York: Atheneum, 1970. (A study of various police roles and styles.)

III. Poverty and Community Action

Alinsky, Saul D. *Reveille for Radicals*. New York: Random House, Inc., Vintage Books, 1969. (A new edition of a community organizer's strategies for local action against social disabilities.)

Bachrach, Peter, and Morton S. Baratz. *Power and Poverty*. New York: Oxford University Press, Inc., 1970. (An analytical study of community power and its application to the war on poverty in Baltimore.)

Beer, Samuel H., and Richard E. Barringer, eds. *The State and the Poor*. Cambridge, Mass.: Winthrop Publishers, Inc., 1970. (Twelve essays on the role of the states in alleviating poverty, with special emphasis on Massachusetts.)

Blaustein, Arthur I., and Roger R. Woock, eds. *Man Against Poverty: World War III*. New York: Random House, Inc., Vintage Books, 1968. (Problems of and prospects for American and international poverty conditions.)

Bloomberg, Warner, Jr., and Henry J. Schmandt, eds. *Urban Poverty*. Beverly Hills, Calif.: Sage Publications, Inc., 1968. (Twelve essays on poverty and the governmental response.)

Caplovitz, David. *The Poor Pay More*. New York: The Free Press, 1967. (Exploitative consumer practices against low-income ghetto residents.)

Clark, Kenneth, and Jeannette Hopkins. *A Relevant War Against Poverty*. New York: Harper & Row, Publishers, Inc., 1968. (An analysis of community action programs of the war on poverty.)

Donovan, John C. *The Politics of Poverty*. New York: Pegasus, 1967. (An evaluation of executive and legislative history leading to the passage of the 1964 Economic Opportunity Act.)

Ferman, Louis A., Joyce L. Kornbluh, and Alan Haber, eds. *Poverty in America.* Rev. ed. Ann Arbor: The University of Michigan Press, 1968. (An extensive collection of important essays and articles defining poverty and suggesting programs for change.)

Gladwin, Thomas. *Poverty U.S.A.* Boston: Little, Brown & Co., 1967. (Very perceptive arguments analyzing the political and social deprivations of America's poor. Highly recommended.)

Halloran, Daniel F. "Progress Against Poverty: The Governmental Approach." *Public Administration Review* 28 (1968): 205–213. (An examination of the federal government's role in alleviating poverty.)

Harrington, Michael. *The Other America: Poverty in the United States.* Baltimore: Penguin Books, Inc., 1964. (A classic study of poverty, deprivation, and hopelessness among low-income groups in America.)

Kershaw, Joseph A. *Government Against Poverty.* Chicago: Markham Publishing Co., 1970. (An analysis of 1964 EOA and OEO with the conclusion that antipoverty programs have been stymied by inadequate federal support.)

Kramer, Ralph M. *Participation of the Poor.* Englewood Cliffs, N. J.: Prentice-Hall, Inc., 1969. (Comparative case studies of CAP programs in four California communities.)

Levitan, Sar A. *The Great Society's Poor Law.* Baltimore: The Johns Hopkins Press, 1969. (A comprehensive examination of various programs of the war on poverty.)

Miller, S. M., and Martin Rein. "Participation, Poverty, and Administration." *Public Administration Review* 29 (1969):15–25. (A review of "maximum feasible participation" provisions of the 1964 EOA.)

Moynihan, Daniel P. *Maximum Feasible Misunderstanding.* New York: The Free Press, 1969. (A scathing attack on the CAP programs of the war on poverty.)

IV. The Welfare System and Proposed Reforms

Banfield, Edward C. "Welfare: A Crisis without Solutions." *The Public Interest* 16 (Summer 1969):89–101. (A description of how welfare dependency increases endlessly with proposals for reforms.)

Cloward, Richard A., and Frances Fox Piven. "The Weapon of Poverty: Birth of a Movement." *The Nation* 204 (May 8, 1967):582–588. (Burgeoning protests to inequities of public welfare programs.)

———. "The Weight of the Poor: A Strategy to End Poverty." *The Nation* 202 (May 2, 1966):510:517. (A strategy to overburden welfare programs so that a federal income distribution program can be achieved.)

————. "We've Got Rights! The No-Longer Silent Welfare Poor." *The New Republic* 157 (August 5, 1967):23–27. (Legal attacks on arbitrary denials of benefits to welfare recipients.)

Elman, Richard M. *The Poorhouse State.* New York: Dell Publishing Co., Delta Books, 1966. (Devastating personal interviews with welfare recipients in New York City.)

Glazer, Nathan. "Beyond Income Maintenance—A Note on Welfare in New York City." *The Public Interest* 16 (Summer 1969):102–120. (An examination of how even with massive welfare reforms, the nation's largest city would still have to support a considerably large poverty-stricken population.)

Gordon, David M. "Income and Welfare in New York City." *The Public Interest* 16 (Summer 1969):64–88. (A discussion of statistical analyses which indicate the persistence of poverty and welfare in the nation's largest city.)

Moynihan, Daniel P. "The Crises in Welfare." *The Public Interest* 10 (Winter 1968):3–29. (Suggestions that a program of family allowances should replace much of the existing welfare programs.)

Piven, Frances Fox, and Richard A. Cloward. "How the Federal Government Caused the Welfare Crisis." *Social Policy* 2 (May-June 1971):40–49. (A discussion of strategies of the National Welfare Rights Organization in response to the lack of governmental response to the welfare crisis.)

————. "The Relief of Welfare." *Trans-Action* 8 (May 1971):31–39, 52. (The AFDC program placed in historical perspective and criticized.)

Vadakin, James C. "A Critique of the Guaranteed Annual Income." *The Public Interest* 11 (Spring 1968):53–66. (An evaluation of five alternatives together with an argument for family allowances to replace the welfare system.)

V. Unemployment and Manpower Strategies

Bolino, August C. *Manpower and the City.* Cambridge, Mass.: Schenkman Publishing Co., 1969. (Major manpower programs in the urban setting together with future directions.)

Committee for Economic Development. *Training and Jobs for the Urban Poor.* New York: Committee for Economic Development, 1970. (Recommendations for a national manpower policy.)

Cross, Theodore L. *Black Capitalism: Strategy for Business in the Ghetto.* New York: Atheneum, 1969. (An analysis of black entrepeneurship and a thirteen-point attack on the wealth-repressive forces in the ghetto economy.)

Ferman, Louis A., Joyce L. Kornbluh, and J. A. Miller, eds. *Negroes and Jobs.* Ann Arbor: The University of Michigan Press, 1968. (A collection of articles on black unemployment problems.)

Foley, Eugene P. *The Achieving Ghetto.* Washington: The National Press, Inc., 1968. (The discussion of a former federal administrator of the Small Business Administration about economic development of ghettos.)

Hill, Herbert. "Racial Inequality in Employment: The Patterns of Discrimination." *The Annals* 357 (January 1965): 30–47. (The far-reaching consequences of black unemployment for American society.)

Jacobson, Julius, ed. *The Negro and the American Labor Movement.* Garden City, N. Y.: Doubleday & Co., Inc., Anchor Books, 1968. (A collection of articles on the history of blacks in unions.)

Levitan, Sar A., Garth L. Mangum, and Robert Taggert III. *Economic Opportunity in the Ghetto: The Partnership of Government and Business.* Baltimore: The Johns Hopkins Press, 1970. (An analysis of the NAB-JOBS program establishing job opportunities for minority groups in the corporate economy.)

Ruttenberg Stanley H., and Jocelyn Gutchess. *Manpower Challenge of the 1970's: Institutions and Social Change.* Baltimore: The Johns Hopkins Press, 1970. (An evaluation of federal manpower programs.)

Tabb, William K. *The Political Economy of the Black Ghetto.* New York: W. W. Norton & Co., Inc., 1970. (An argument that a colonial relationship exists between the ghetto and the larger society together with proposals for change.)

Wetzel, James R., and Susan S. Holland. "Poverty Areas Of Our Major Cities." *Monthly Labor Review* 89 (1966):1105–1110. (A statistical analysis of black unemployment and underemployment in big city ghettoes.)

VI. Public Education

Berube, Maurice R., and Marilyn Gittell, eds. *Confrontation At Ocean Hill-Brownsville.* New York: Frederick A. Praeger, Publishers, 1969. (A collection of essays dealing with the New York City School strikes of 1968 over the issues of decentralization and community control.)

Conant, James B. *Slums and Suburbs.* New York: The New American Library, Inc., Signet Books, 1964. (An analysis of unequal educational opportunity in the public schools.)

Crain, Robert L. *The Politics of School Desegregation.* Garden City, N. Y.: Doubleday & Co., Inc., Anchor Books, 1969. (A case analysis of northern and southern city school desegregation.)

Damerell, Reginald G. *Triumph In A White Suburb.* New York: William Morrow & Co., Inc., Apollo Editions, 1968. (An interesting and informative case history of school and housing integration by voluntary community efforts in Teaneck, New Jersey.)

Dentler, Robert A., Bernard Mackler, and Mary Ellen Warshauer, eds. *The Urban R's.* New York: Frederick A. Praeger, Publishers, 1967. (Eighteen essays which examine the effects of racial, economic, and class segregation in the schools together with analyses of what happens when school desegregation is achieved.)

Edwards, T. Bentley, and Frederick M. Wirt, eds. *School Desegregation in the North.* San Francisco: Chandler Publishing Co., 1967. (Case studies of the response to the challenge of *de facto* school segregation in four New York metropolitan area communities and six California communities.)

Kozol, Jonathan. *Death At An Early Age.* New York: Bantam Books, Inc., 1967. (Scathing attack on Boston public schools by a former teacher.)

Levin, Melvin R., and Alan Shank, eds. *Educational Investment In An Urban Society.* New York: Teachers College Press, Columbia University, 1970. (A collection of articles and essays dealing with cost-benefit analysis of education, manpower, and public policy.)

Mayer, Martin. *The Teachers Strike: New York, 1968.* New York: Harper & Row, Publishers, Inc., Perennial Books, 1969. (A brief and very critical account of school decentralization-community control issues in New York City.)

Meranto, Philip. *School Politics in the Metropolis.* Columbus, Ohio: Charles E. Merrill Publishing Co., 1970. (The relationship of public school politics to cities, suburbs, states, and the federal government.)

Rogers, David. *110 Livingston Street.* New York: Random House, Inc., Vintage Books, 1968. (Politics and bureaucracy in the New York City School system.)

Schrag, Peter. *Village School Downtown.* Boston: Beacon Press, 1967. (A critical attack on the Boston public school system together with a useful proposal for a metropolitan school district.)

U.S. Department of Health, Education, and Welfare. Office of Education. *Equality of Educational Opportunity,* Summary Report. Washington: U.S. Government Printing Office, 1966. (Summary findings of the landmark Coleman Report on the effects of unequal educational opportunity.)

VII. Housing

Abrams, Charles. *The City Is The Frontier.* New York: Harper & Row, Publishers, Inc., Colophon Books, 1967. (An important study of government roles in housing policies.)

Anderson, Martin. *The Federal Bulldozer*. New York: McGraw-Hill Book Company, 1967. (A highly critical, but somewhat debatable, attack on federal urban renewal programs.)

Babcock, Richard F. *The Zoning Game*. Madison: The University of Wisconsin Press, 1966. (A very useful study of different "players'" roles in local zoning policy making.)

Building The American City. Report of the National Commission on Urban Problems to the Congress and to the President. 91st Congress, 1st Session, House Document 91–34. Washington: U.S. Government Printing Office, 1968. (The comprehensive housing report by the Douglas Commission.)

Eley, Lynn W., and Thomas W. Casstevens, eds. *The Politics of Fair Housing Legislation*. San Francisco: Chandler Publishing Co., 1968. (State and local case studies concerning open housing laws.)

Freedman, Leonard. *Public Housing*. New York: Holt, Rinehart and Winston, Inc., 1969. (An analysis of legislative process and interest-group struggle over public housing together with an evaluation of public attitudes on race, poverty, and public ownership.)

Friedman, Lawrence M. *Government and Slum Housing: A Century of Frustration*. Chicago: Rand McNally & Co., 1968. (An analysis of relationships between law and slum housing in cities.)

Gans, Herbert J. "The Failure of Urban Renewal: A Critique and Some Proposals." *Commentary* 39 (April 1965):29–37. (The thesis that both suburban integration and improvement of slum conditions should be pursued in governmental policies.)

Goldwin, Robert A., ed. *A Nation of Cities*. Chicago: Rand McNally & Co., 1966. (A collection of essays in response to President Johnson's Model Cities proposal of 1966.)

Greer, Scott. *Urban Renewal and American Cities*. Indianapolis: The Bobbs-Merrill Co., Inc., 1965. (A discussion of how both the federal government and local agencies should evaluate the accomplishments of urban renewal policies.)

Lipsky, Michael. "Rent Strikes: Poor Man's Weapon." *Trans-Action* 6 (February 1969):10–15. (An evaluation of the strategies and tactics of Harlem rent strikes.)

Meyerson, Martin, and Edward C. Banfield. *Politics, Planning, and the Public Interest: The Case of Public Housing in Chicago*. New York: The Free Press of Glencoe, 1964. (An important decision-making study.)

Moore, William, Jr. *The Vertical Ghetto*. New York: Random House, Inc., 1969. (First-hand observations of everyday life in a public housing project.)

Sternlieb, George. *The Tenement Landlord.* New Brunswick, N. J.: Urban Studies Center, Rutgers—The State University, 1966. (A study of problems, maintenance, and eradication of slum housing.)

Vose, Clement E. *Caucasians Only.* Berkeley: University of California Press, 1969. (A case study of the restrictive covenant cases showing the important role of the NAACP before the United States Supreme Court.)

Weaver, Robert C. *Dilemmas of Urban America.* New York: Atheneum, 1965. (A discussion of housing and race problems.)

————. *The Urban Complex.* Garden City, N. Y.: Doubleday & Co., Inc., 1964. (An evaluation of urban renewal by the first federal cabinet Secretary of Housing and Urban Development.)

Wolman, Harold. *Politics of Federal Housing.* New York: Dodd, Mead & Co., Inc., 1971. (An analysis of federal housing policies with emphasis on interpretative interviews with 68 elites.)

VIII. Environmental and Ecological Problems

Anderson, Walt, ed. *Politics and Environment.* Pacific Palisades, Calif.: Goodyear Publishing Co., Inc., 1970. (A collection of articles on the ecological crisis.)

Caldwell, Lynton K., Symposium ed. "Environmental Policy: New Direction in Federal Action." *Public Administration Review* 28 (1968):301–347. (Seven essays on public policy problems connected with the environment.)

Carson, Rachel. *Silent Spring.* New York: Fawcett Publications, Inc., Crest Books, 1962. (Dangers of pesticides on the environment.)

Davies, J. Clarence, III. *The Politics of Pollution.* New York: Pegasus, 1970. (Federal legislation and the policy process relating to air and water pollution.)

Earth Day—The Beginning. New York: Bantam Books, Inc., 1970. (A diverse collection of speeches delivered across the nation during the first Earth Day, April 22, 1970.)

Editors of Fortune. *The Environment.* New York: Harper & Row, Publishers, Inc., Perennial Library, 1969. (Thirteen articles on various aspects of pollution problems.)

Goldman, Marshall I., ed. *Controlling Pollution.* Englewood Cliffs, N. J.: Prentice-Hall, Inc., Spectrum Books, 1967. (A collection of essays on American and European pollution difficulties.)

Man's Control of the Environment. Washington: Congressional Quarterly Inc., 1970. (A collection of articles and public documents indicating the development of public policy in abating pollution.)

Meek, Roy L., and John A. Straayer, eds. *The Politics of Neglect: The Environmental Crisis*. Boston: Houghton Mifflin Co., 1971. (A collection of articles on the environmental problems of the nation.)

Roos, Leslie L., Jr., ed. *The Politics of Ecosuicide*. New York: Holt, Rinehart and Winston, Inc., 1971. (A collection of nineteen articles on the politics of the environment.)

IX. Comprehensive Programs and Solutions

Advisory Commission on Intergovernmental Relations. "Federalism in the Sixties: A Ten-Year Review." In *Eleventh Annual Report*. Pp. 1–16. Washington: U.S. Government Printing Office, January 31, 1970. (A review of accomplishments and prospects of intergovernmental relations.)

Altshuler, Alan A. *Community Control*. New York: Pegasus, 1970. (An analysis of community control of public services in the nation's urban ghettoes.)

Banfield, Edward C. *The Unheavenly City*. Boston: Little, Brown & Co., 1970. (Controversial interpretations of the urban crisis.)

Bellush, Jewel, and Stephen M. David, eds. *Race and Politics in New York City*. New York: Praeger Publishers, Inc., 1971. (Five case studies of pluralism, race, and politics in the nation's largest city.)

Benson, Robert S., and Harold Wolman, eds. *Counterbudget*. New York: Praeger Publishers, Inc., 1971. (A blueprint for changing national priorities through the reallocation of funds in the federal budget over 1971–1976.)

Canty, Donald. *A Single Society*. New York: Praeger Publishers, Inc., 1969. (A comprehensive urban policy to change national priorities.)

Changing National Priorities. Hearings before the Subcommittee on Economy in Government of the Joint Economic Committee. 91st Congress, 2d Session, Parts I and II, June 1970. Washington: U.S. Government Printing Office. (The testimony of various witnesses on how the direction of national policies can be changed.)

Cleaveland, Frederic N., et. al. *Congress and Urban Problems*. Washington: The Brookings Institution, 1969. (A case analysis of major urban policies dealt with by Congress in the 1950's and 1960's.)

Donovan, John C. *The Policy Makers*. New York: Pegasus, 1970. (An interesting and informative study of political restraints on developing effective domestic policies.)

Downs, Anthony. *Urban Problems and Prospects*. Chicago: Markham Publishing Co., 1970. (Alternative suggestions for future urban public policies.)

Gardner, John W. *The Recovery of Confidence.* New York: Pocket Books, 1971. (Suggestions for changing the course of national policies and priorities.)

Moynihan, Daniel P., ed. *Toward A National Urban Policy.* New York: Basic Books, Inc., 1970. (Twenty-five original essays covering the wide range of past, present, and future urban policies.)

"Our Nation's Obligations To Its Cities." *Nation's Cities* 9 (March 1971): 8–17. (A summary of the national municipal policy by the 1971 National League of Cities.)

Schultze, Charles L., et. al. *Setting National Priorities: The 1972 Budget.* Washington: The Brookings Institution, 1971. (An examination of President Nixon's budget for 1972 with emphasis on controversial public policies.)

Sundquist, James L. *Making Federalism Work.* Washington: The Brookings Institution, 1969. (An evaluation of specific federal policies, including community action and model cities, within the framework of intergovernmental relations.)

————. *Politics and Policy.* Washington: The Brookings Institution, 1968. (The policy-making process from 1953 to 1966 in review and analysis.)

Urban America, Inc., and The Urban Coalition. *One Year Later.* New York: Frederick A. Praeger, Publishers, 1969. (Postmortems on the recommendations of the 1968 National Advisory Commission on Civil Disorders.)

Wilson, James Q., ed. *The Metropolitan Enigma.* Washington: U.S. Chamber of Commerce, 1967. (A collection of essays on urban problems and prospects.)

Index

Abernathy, Ralph Davis, 169
Abington School District v. *Schempp*, 114
Abrams, Charles, 681
Acculturation, 133, 139, 140, 141, 143
Addonızıo, Hugh J., 247, 249, 254
Adrian, Charles R., 121, 341-44
Advisory Commission on Intergovernmental Relations (ACIR), 122, 124, 352, 354, 373, 377ns, 405, 407-18, 431-32, 675, 684
Africa, 165, 169
   history, 173
   neocolonialism, 331
Aged, 45-46, 61, 543, 546, 604
Agnew, Spiro, 151, 154, 276-77, 337
Air pollution, 236, 315, 322, 431, 563, 566, 567, 569
Albuquerque, 137
Aleshire, Robert A., 434
Alford, Robert R., 341, 344
Alienation, 126, 162, 178, 259, 275, 489
   (*See also* Ghetto, Slum)
Alinsky, Saul D., 677
Aliota, Joseph, 301
Allen, Ivan, Jr., 345
Allen, Jesse, 254, 265
Allinsmith, Wesley and Beverly, 147
Alport, Gordon W., 147
Altshuler, Alan A., 684
American Civil Liberties Union, 634
American Economic Association, 30
American Indians, 35, 128, 524, 647 (*See also* Nonwhites)
American Museum of Natural History, 560
American Political Science Review, 131
American Revolution, 448
Amsterdam, 92
Anderson, Martin, 682
Anderson, Walt, 683
Anglo-Saxons, 150, 154, 278
Annexation, 379-80, 384, 387, 388
Antidiscrimination laws: enforcement, 643-44
Antidraft rioters, 446
Anti-exclusion laws, 632-33
   enforcement, 655
Anti-poverty programs, 167, 185, 191, 193, 236, 254, 472 (*See also* Job Corps)
Anti-urbanism, 5, 10
Antonovsky, Aaron, 148
Apollo II, 561

Appalachian whites, 657
Arc, M., 146
Arnold, Thurman, 264
Aronowitz, Stanley, 266
Asbell, Bernard, 345
Assimilation, 133, 140-44
Association of Bay Area Governments (ABAG), 370, 374, 377
Atlanta, Ga., 71, 73, 74, 207, 359-60, 366, 390, 446, 482
Atomic Energy Commission, 568

Babcock, Richard F., 682
Bachrach, Peter, 264, 267, 268, 677
Bailey, Harry A., Jr., 200, 346
Baisden, Richard, 73-77
Baker, Benjamin, 343
Baker, Russell, 210, 336-38
Baltimore, Md., 42, 52, 53, 71, 73-76, 427, 547
Baltzell, E. Digby, 147
Banfield, Edward C., 3, 4, 9, 11-33, 121, 122, 123, 139, 147, 239, 255, 263, 264, 266, 269, 272, 276, 340, 341, 343, 345, 365, 377, 390, 678, 682, 684
Banovetz, James M., 432
Baran, Paul, 263
Baratz, Morton S., 264, 267, 677
Barber, James D., 229, 269
Barbour, Floyd B., 346
Barringer, Richard E., 677
Barth, Thomas E., 677
Baton Rouge La., 357, 363, 364
Bay, Christian, 254-55, 266
Beardwood, Roger, 201
Becker, Theodore L., 675
Beckman, Norman, 402, 434
Beckwith, Burnham P., 573
Beer, Samuel H., 677
Bell, Alphonzo, 281
Bellush, Jewel, 684
Beltways, 72-75
Bensman, Joseph, 123
Benson, Robert S., 684
Berelson, Bernard R., 145
Berkeley, George E., 343
Bernards Township, N.J., 632
Bernstein, Lee, 247-48
Berube, Maurice R., 680
Birch, David L., 7, 91-101
Bish, Robert L., 432

Black:
  Americans, 154-55, 159-71, 585 (*See also* Negroes)
  crime, 163, 178-79, 659-63
  culture, 160, 172-73
  family income, 647
  ghettos, 667
  housing, 624-25 (*See also* Ghetto, Housing, Slum)
  insurgency, 326, 336
  leadership, 383-85, 387-91, 672-73 (*See also* Hatcher, Richard; Los Angeles Liberalism)
  militancy, 127-28, 130, 172-79, 198, 283, 292, 296, 310, 449, 659, 661, 667
    responses to, 176-79
  minority view, 127
  nonviolence, 161-62, 169-71, 174, 446
  Panthers, 128, 169, 175, 209
  police, 477, 481
  politics, 168, 172-74, 205, 211, 269n, 275, 379, 390, 667 (*See also* Hatcher, Richard; Los Angeles Liberalism)
  poor, 259
  power, 85-86, 125, 130, 160, 166-68, 472, 474
  racism, 667
  rule in urban South, 378-92
  "self-defense," 128, 174-76, 324
  separatism, 160-61, 162, 165-66, 447, 581, 660, 661, 667
  "tinderbox," 659-63, 665, 671, 673
Black, Gordon, 324
Blaustein, Arthur I., 677
Blind, 604
Bloomberg, Warner, Jr., 677
Blumenfeld, Hans, 31, 121
Board of Education v. *Watson*, 116
Bolino, August C., 679
Bollens, John C., 121, 200, 376, 432
Bond, Julian, 160-61, 169
Bone, Hugh A., 229, 344
Bordua, David, 483
Boskin, Joseph, 674
Boston, Mass., 33, 55, 135, 150, 302, 303, 308, 314, 356, 372, 551, 623
Bostonians, 15
Boulding, Kenneth, 572
Bowen, Don R., 675
Bradley, Thomas, 209, 211, 276-300, 334, 379
Branyan, Robert L., 122
Brathwaite, Yvonne, 160
Brink, William, 674

British Labor Party, 227
British Parliament, 448
Brockey, Harold, 75
Brodbeck, Arthur J., 145
Brookings Institution, 407
Brooks, Thomas R., 484
Brown, A. Theodore, 339
Brown v. *Board of Education*, 112, 531, 533, 534, 535, 539
Brown, Calude, 201
Brunswick, Ga., 390
Bryce, James, 231, 339
Buffalo, N.Y., 99
Burdick, Eugene, 145
Bureaucracy:
  city government, 234-38, 271, 329-33
  local governments, 422-23
Burger, Warren Earl, 531
Burke, J., 121
Burruss v. *Wilkerson*, 118
Burton, Richard P., 351-52, 354, 396-406

Caldwell, Lynton K., 572, 573, 574, 683
California, 472, 654
  Constitution, 103, 106, 110, 113
  population growth, 279
  state legislature, 398
  Supreme Court ruling, 8, 102-24, 633 (*See also* Serrano v. *Priest*)
Callow, Alexander B., Jr., 340
Campbell, Alan K., 353, 397, 399, 432
Campbell, Angus, 228, 674
Campbell, James S., 128, 172-79, 460, 676
Canty, Donald, 684
CAP (*see* Community Action Program)
Caplovitz, David, 677
Caraley, Demetrios, 577, 578, 656-74
Carmichael, Stokely, 160, 166, 169, 174, 323, 346
Carson City, Nev., 358
Carson, Rachel, 683
Carter, Luther J., 572
Casstevens, Thomas W., 682
Castro, Fidel, 323
Catholic church, 448
Catholics, 126, 131, 135-38, 150-51, 153, 156, 158, 293, 315, 320
Cavanagh, Jerome, 301, 303, 308
Chapman and Crockett, 485
Chapman, Samuel G., 485
Charleston, S.C., 359, 363, 390, 427
Charleston, W. Va., 427
Charlotte, N.C., 359, 363, 365, 390, 441
Charlotte-Mecklenburg school system, 364, 531, 538

Charlottesville, Va., 358, 369, 376n, 390
Chattanooga, Tenn., 360, 363, 390
Chevigny, Paul, 483, 485, 676
Chicago, Ill., 14, 16, 41, 42, 80, 100, 138, 173, 208, 221, 236, 316, 337, 422, 548 (*See also* Daley, Richard J.)
  blacks, 274-75, 269n
  Democratic Convention, 1968, 297, 303, 471, 484n
  machine politics, 231-32, 238-40
  riots, 446
Chicanos, 7, 128
Child, Irwin, 148
Childs, Richard S., 343, 344
Chinitz, Benjamin, 434
Chyz, Y.J., 146
Cincinnati, Ohio, 14, 16, 99
CIO, 157, 317
Citizen participation, 588-89
City: (*See also* Metropolis, Urban Party Politics)
  blacks, 42, 174, 274-75, 366, 640, 659
  central, defined, 37, 640
  composition, 40, 227, 640, 666
  crime, 301, 658-69 (*See also* Ghetto Riots, Police)
  expansion, 214-15
  Federal aid, 314, 590
  government and politics, 205-40, 656-74 (*See also* County government, Decentralization, Metropolitan government)
  corruption, 15, 206, 209, 219, 234, 279, 285
  efficiency, 232-37
  leadership, 672 (*See also* Mayor)
  life cycle, 98-101
  losses, 38-9, 190
  problems, 187, 205, 238, 313, 663-64
  residential integration, 664, 667, 670
  strikes, 657
  tax base, 271, 630, 656, 659-60, 665-66
City-manager system, 225
City-state, 598-99
Civil liberties, 662-63
Civil protest, 445-60, 472 (*See also* Police)
Civil Rights Acts, 488, 580, 632, 637, 642-43, 650
Civil War, 14, 194, 216, 443, 446, 579
Clague, Christopher, 324
Clark, Kenneth, 202, 267, 268, 677
Cleveland, Frederic N., 573, 684
Cleaver, Eldridge, 201
Cleveland, Ohio, 42, 55, 71, 76, 160, 210, 293, 324, 353, 379, 388, 389, 427
Cloward, Richard A., 347, 678, 679

Coleman, James S., 596
Coleman Report, 88, 441-42
Collins, John, 308
Columbia, Md., 636
Columbus, Ohio, 180, 183, 185
Committee for Economic Development (CED), 356, 376ns, 403-4, 432, 679
Commoner, Barry, 562
Communism, 154
Communist groups, 284-85, 287-88, 295, 318, 662
Communist party, 209, 253, 299, 317
Community Action Agencies (CAA's), 493-96, 504
Community Action Programs (CAP's), 129, 246, 439-40, 486-500 (*See also* Newark Community Union Project)
Community control, 309, 349, 390 (*See also* Poor, Poverty)
Commuting, 11-12, 14, 51-54, 629
  reverse, 22, 628, 630
Conant, James B., 680
Conant, Ralph W., 438, 445-60
Conflict, managing, 9, 257, 262, 313
Congress of Racial Equality (CORE), 496
Connecticut, 224, 623, 632
Connery, Robert H., 674
Conot, Robert, 674
Conservation funds, 570
Conservation interests, 570-71 (*See also* Environmental problems)
Consolidated metropolitan region (CMR), 405
Conspiracy, 292-3
Contini, Edgardo, 74
Converse, Philip E., 228
Coons, John E., 124
Corey, Lewis, 146
Cornwell, Elmer E., Jr., 228
Corsi, Jerome R., 676
Costikyan, Edward N., 239, 340
Coulter, Philip B., 432
Council of Economic Advisers, 23, 407, 564
Council on Environmental Quality, 563, 564
Council on Regional Issues, 370
Councils of governments (COG's), 374-75, 377, 403
County government, 369-71, 400-5, 422 (*See also* Metro-government, Metropolitan government)
  urban county, 401-3, 593-94
Crain, Robert L., 680

Crapsey, Edward, 31
Croker, Richard, 213, 214
Cross, Theodore L., 679
Crouch, William W., 400
Crouch, Winston W., 343
Cuba, 24
Cultural system, 133-34
Cutright, Phillips, 229, 341

Daddario, Emilio Qunicy, 563
Dade City, Fla., 362, 363-70, 401
Dahl, Robert A., 121, 131, 133, 136, 142,
    145, 148, 207, 222, 229, 243-44,
    255, 256, 261, 263, 265, 266, 267,
    268, 345
Daley, Richard J., 208, 211, 272-75, 303,
    495
Damerell, Reginald G., 680
Danielson, Michael N., 122, 379, 433
Davey, Tom, 572
David, Stephen M., 684
Davidoff, Linda and Paul, 576, 621-36
Davies, J. Clarence III, 683
Daytona Beach, Fla., 371
DDT, 557, 568, 569
Decentralization, 74, 199, 232-37, 309-
    310, 400-1, 404-6, 418, 488, 495-
    97, 499
Decision makers, 243, 255, 256, 262-63
Delaware River Basin Commission, 567
Democracy:
    majoritarian, 194
    pluralistic, 195, 200
Democratic Convention, 1968, 297, 303,
    471, 484n
Democratic party, 325-26
Demography, 313-14, 318 (See also
    Population)
Demonstration Cities and Metropolitan
    Development Act of 1966, 377n
Dentler, Robert A., 681
Department of Housing and Urban Devel-
    opment (see Housing and Urban
    Development, HUD)
DeSapio, Carmine, 226, 229n, 239
de Tocqueville, Alexis, 214
Detroit, Mich., 42, 55, 161, 222, 224,
    301-3, 308, 314, 393, 446, 456,
    579, 598
Deutscher, Irwin, 268
Disabled, aid to, 604
Disruption, 192-95, 198, 659
Dixon, Robert G., 343
Doccolo, Mario, 75
Dodd, Harold, 233
Doig, Jameson W., 676

Domhoff, G. William, 264
Donovan, John C., 677, 684
Dorsett, Lyle W., 122
Douglas v. California, 110, 117
Downes, Bryan T., 433
Downs, Anthony, 5, 6, 77-90, 129, 684
Dresden, 395
Duncombe, Herbert, 401
Dunn (Justice), 121
Dunstan, J. Leslie, 31
Duverger, Maurice, 231
Dye, Thomas R., 341, 433
Dymally, Mervyn M., 346

Eagle, Morris, 33
Earth Day, 571, 683
East, John P., 344
East St. Louis, Mo., 446
Eastman, George D., 484
ECCO project (East Central Citizens
    Organization), 180-86
Eckstein, Otto, 583
Ecological activism, 570
Economic integration, 646-47
Economic Opportunity Act, 490-92, 501
    Green Amendment, 495
Edelman, Murray, 256, 264, 267
Education, 4, 88, 111, 114, 121, 152, 440-
    42 (See also Serrano v. Priest;
    School Busing)
    equal opportunity, 518-30
    Federal aid, 430
    financing, 8-9, 625, 633
    research, 596
    Supreme Court decisions, 112-14
Edwards, T. Bentley, 681
Eisenhower, David and Julie, 338
Eisenhower, Dwight D., 167
Elazar, Daniel J., 123, 598
Eldersveld, Samuel J., 228
Election campaigns:
    government funding, 196
    nonpartisan, 279, 282
    role of money, 260-1
Electoral system:
    changes, 198
    at-large, 380, 384, 448
Elementary and Secondary Education Act,
    425
Eley, Lynn W., 682
Elites:
    power, 241-42
Elitists, 207, 208, 211
Elkins, Stanley M., 228
Ellis, John Tracy, 147
Elman, Richard M., 679

Elsing, William T., 33
Employment (*see* Jobs, Metropolis, Poor, Suburbs)
Endelman, Shalom, 484
Environmental problems, 442-44, 557-74, 597-98
  research needed, 569
Equal Employment Opportunity Act, 439, 444
Equal Employment Opportunity Commission, 54, 632-33
Equal housing opportunity, 637-56
Equal protection: (*See also* U.S. Constitution, U.S. Supreme Court)
  14th Amendment, 8, 102-3, 534
Equal rights, 168
Eskimos, 36
Ethnic Politics, 131-148 (*See also* Black, Nonwhites, White ethnics)
Etzioni, Amitai, 146, 147
Euclid v. *Ambler*, 633
Everglades National Park, 558
Evers, Charles, 160, 334
Exclusionary laws, 632-35

Fairfield, Conn., 632
Fanon, Frantz, 674
Farley, James A., 228
Farmers Home Administration, 651
Fayette, Miss., 160, 324
FBI, 151
Feagin, J.R., 268
Federal Communications Commission (FCC), 632
Federal Contract Compliance Office, 632
Federal Equal Employment Opportunity Commission, 632-33
Federal grants-in-aid, 352, 355, 373, 375-76, 424-25, 584, 590, 594-95
  conditional aid, 410, 413, 414, 416
Federal Home Loan Bank Board, 652
Federal Housing Administration (FHA), 16-17, 197, 639
Federalism, 415, 419-31, 568
Federalist, The, 419
Ferman, Louis A., 678, 680
Ferry, W.H., 561
Fesler, James W., 339
Field, John O., 340
Firth, R., 147
Financing public schools, 8-9 (*See also* Education, Serrano v. Priest, Suburbs)
Fisher, Joseph L., 375
Flaim, Paul O., 68
Flynn, Edward J., 228

Foley, Eugene P., 680
Foner, Philip S., 346
Food and Drug Administration, 557
Food budgets, 618
  USDA food plans, 617-19
Food stamps, 604, 617-19
Ford Foundation, 305, 307, 488-90
Ford Motor Company, 628-30
Forrester, Jay W., 587
Forthall, Sonya, 228
Fortune, 683
Foster, William Z., 317
Foundations, 305, 307, 308, 312, 328
Fowler, Edmund P., 340
Frankel, Charles, 235
Frankel, Max, 352, 419-31
Frankfurter, Felix, 119
Freedman, Leonard, 682
French, Robert M., 350, 353, 378-92
Freud, Sigmund, 152
Frieden, Bernard J., 31, 32
Friedman, Lawrence M., 682
Friedman, Morris, 137, 147
Friesma, H.P., 433
Frost, Richard T., 223, 229
Fuchs, Lawrence, 147, 200

Gallup Organization, 162
  poll, 407, 557
Gamson, William, 265
Gans, Herbert, 129, 135, 137, 146, 147, 186-202, 682
Gardner, John W., 685
Garvey, Marcus, 165
Gary, Ind., 42, 160, 210, 292, 379
  Liberation, 315-36
Ghetto: (*See also* Housing, Police, Slum)
  defined, 61, 79-80
  ballot power, 250-52, 260, 496
  black, 667
  dispersal, 6-7, 10, 86-90
  housing, 442
  improvement, 84-90, 129, 657
  police, 467, 468, 473-76, 481-82
  population, 80-82, 246
  problems, 82-90, 176, 246, 271, 439, 622
  riots, 125, 162, 171, 175, 177, 191-93, 254, 270, 301, 438, 443, 445-60, 658, 660-63, 667
  spread, 659
  unemployment rate, 629
G.I. Bill of Rights, 18, 424
Gibson, Kenneth, 324, 391
Gilbert, Ben W., 674
Gilbert, Charles E., 342

Gilbertson, H.S., 400
Ginger, Ray, 122
Ginsberg, Eli, 32
Gitlin, Todd, 245, 265, 268
Gittell, Marilyn, 270, 275, 345, 680
Glaab, Charles N., 30, 33, 339
Gladwin, Thomas, 678
Glazer, Nathan, 33, 54, 69, 70, 147, 148,
        201, 228, 589, 679
Glendening, Parris N., 385, 390
Goetcheus, Vernon M., 229
Goist, Park D., 123
Gold, Neil N., 576, 621-36
Goldberg, Paul, 265
Goldman, Marshall I., 683
Goldwater, Barry, 226
Goldwater, Barry, Jr., 284
Goldwin, Robert A., 682
Goodnow, Frank, 123
Gordon, David M., 679
Gordon, Kermit, 674
Gordon, Milton M., 146, 147
Gosnell, Harold F., 228, 230, 231, 239-40
Government Facilities Location Act, 631
Governments:
    elected, 589
    local, 422, 424-25, 587-90
    state, 593
Graham, Hugh D., 674
Gramsci, Antonio, 333
Grant, Daniel R., 376, 433
Greek-Americans, 138
Green, Arnold W., 146
Green, Constance McLaughlin, 31, 122
Green, Philip, 264, 269
Green v. *County School Board*, 532-33,
        539
Greenberg, Edward S., 346
Greenstein, Fred I., 145, 206, 212-230,
        275, 342
Greer, Edward, 210, 315-36, 346
Greer, Scott, 122, 136, 146, 201, 388, 682
Griffin v. *Illinois*, 110, 117
Griffin v. *School Board*, 116
Griggs, Charles M., 674
Grodzins, Morton, 201
Gross, Kenneth, 485
Guidici, John, 484, 485
Guinea, 327
Gurr, Ted R., 674
Gutchess, Jocelyn, 680
Guzman, Ralph, 147

Haber, Alan, 678
Hadden, Jeffrey K., 346
Hague, Frank, 213, 214

Haig and Associates, 284-85
Hall, Gus, 288
Hall v. *St. Helena Parish School Board*, 117
Halloran, Daniel F., 678
Halverson, Guy, 460
Hamilton, Alexander, 419
Hamilton, Charles, 174, 346
Handlin, Oscar, 30-31, 33, 145, 148, 201
Hansen, Marcus Lee, 147
Hanson, Royce, 377
Harper v. *Virginia Bd. of Elections*, 107,
        110
Harrington, Michael, 678
Harris, Louis, 674
Hart, Gary Warren, 573
Hartford, Conn., 427
Hatcher, Richard, 160, 161, 168, 209-11
        (*See also* Gary, Ind.)
    administration, 327-36
    mayoral campaign, 320-35
Hauser, Philip M., 67, 70, 339
Hawkins, Brett W., 341, 366, 377, 433
Hayden, Tom, 675
Hays, Samuel P., 340
Head Start, 494
Hechinger, Fred M., 343
Heller, Walter W., 352, 407, 413, 415,
        418, 434
Herson, Lawrence J.R., 122
Hester, L.A., 367, 377
Hickel, Walter, 557
Hicks, Louise Day, 303
Hiestand, Dale, 146
Higdon, Hal, 345
Hill, Herbert, 680
Hillenbrand, Bernard, 403
Hirsch, Werner Z., 123
Hobbes, Thomas, 673
Hodge, Patricia L., 67, 70
Hofstadter, Richard, 152, 339
Holden, Matthew, Jr., 572
Holland, Susan S., 680
Hollingshead, August B., 135, 146
Honolulu, Hawaii, 357, 615
Hopkins, Jeannette, 677
Hotchkiss, Preston, 284
Housing, 5, 11-14, 16-18, 20, 23, 25, 74,
        162, 163, 442, 444, 498-99 (*See
        also* Equal Housing Opportunity,
        Suburbs)
    abandoned, 540-56
    Acts, 374, 377, 442, 488, 637, 642,
        645-46
    code, 28, 548
    construction, 635-36, 650-51
    costs, 8, 63, 625, 626

dilapidated, 657-9 (*See also* Slum)
Federal policy, 577
Federal programs, 644-48, 650
financing, 544-45, 652
low-cost, 624-25, 632, 636-38, 644-46, 648, 652, 654
Newark protest, 247-48
open, 638, 640-44, 650-53
ownership, 553-55
rehabilitation, 542, 545, 551, 554-56, 650
rent strikes, 247-48, 250, 253, 262, 266n
segregation, 174, 576-77, 578, 592, 624-25, 639-41
substandard, 29, 31
remedies, 548-54
Housing and Urban Development Act, 374, 377
Housing and Urban Development Department (HUD), 442, 547, 549, 551-52, 554, 643-46, 649, 651, 652
Housing of Welfare Recipients, The, 542
Houston, Texas, 71, 73, 74, 99, 393, 427
Howe, Frederick C., 339
Howe, Harold, 124
Hubbard, Howard, 675
Human Rights Commission, 247
Humes, Samuel, 377
Humphrey, Hubert, 198, 303, 323
Hunter, David, 202
Hunter, Floyd, 207
Hyman, Herbert, 145
Hyman, Stanley Edgar, 140

Identificational durability, 139-41
Immigrants, 134-36, 148-49, 211, 216, 316-17, 447
votes, 219
Immigration, 16, 17, 19, 22, 24, 29, 136, 137, 153, 206, 317
laws, 146n
Income:
average family, 23
basic, 600, 602, 611-12
distribution, 11, 22, 30, 41-42
family support, 603, 614
"guaranteed adequate," 576, 609-21
Minimum Adequacy Budget, 615, 617-18
Negroes', 585
Poverty line, 613
redistribution, 498-99, 667
Indiana Acts of 1969, 376
Indianapolis, Ind., 358, 362, 390
Industrial Revolution, 3, 214, 627
Integrationists, 160-61, 162, 165
Irish, 126, 219

Italian-Americans, 17, 135, 138, 219
Italians, 126
IWW, 157

Jackson, Henry Martin, 563
Jackson v. Pasadena City School District, 112
Jacksonville-Duval City, Fla., 349, 350, 353, 358, 363-65, 367, 401
Jacksonville, Fla., 378-92
population 381-82
Jacobs, Paul, 268
Jacobson, Julius, 680
James v. Valtierra, 634, 654
Jefferson, Thomas, 181
Jesus Christ, 152
Jews, 17, 19, 90, 126, 135, 137-40, 150, 167
vote in Los Angeles, 282, 298-99
vote in New York City, 310
Job Corps, 440, 444, 501-18
Job patronage, 218, 220-22, 226-27, 272-73, 322
Jobs, 7, 11, 20, 51, 82-3, 163, 198
blue collar, 54, 198, 315, 629
government subsidized, 499 (*See also* Job Corps)
growth, 96-7
manufacturing, 368
segregation, 633
in suburbs, 628-29
unskilled, 21, 194
white collar, 54, 96, 136, 368
Johnson, LeRoy, 366
Johnson, Lyndon B., 297, 407, 438, 439, 568
Juvenile Delinquency and Youth Offenses Control Act, 489, 490

Kahn, Herman, 573
Kaiser Commission, 635
Kanin, Garson, 460
Kansas City, Mo, 402
Kariel, Henry, 264, 267
Karmin, Monroe W., 32
Katz, Daniel, 229
Katz, Ellis, 200
Kaufman, Herbert, 234
Kehaiyan, Haig, 284-85
Kendall, Willmoore, 213, 228
Keniston, Kenneth, 254, 266
Kennedy, John F., 125, 219, 293, 328
Kennedy Park Homes Assn. v. City of Lackawanna, N.Y., 655
Kennedy, Robert F., 125, 286, 288, 296, 297, 489
Kent, Frank R., 228

Kerner Commission (see Kerner Report or National Advisory Commission on Civil Disorders)
Kerner Report, 268, 382, 484n
Kershaw, Joseph A., 678
Kessel, John H., 344
Key, V.O., Jr., 132, 145, 240
Kiepper, Alan F., 365
Killian, Lewis M., 675
King, Coretta, 175
King, Martin Luther, 125, 159, 160, 162, 166, 168-71, 328, 457
Klapper, Joseph T., 229
Klein, Herbert T., 484n
Kneese, Allen V., 573
Kolodner, Ferne K., 439, 486-500
Korean war, 49
Kornbluh, Joyce L., 678, 680
Kotler, Milton, 128-29, 130, 180-86
Kozol, Jonathan, 681
Kramer, Ralph M., 678
Krause, Elliott A., 588
Kravitz, Sanford, 439, 486-500
Kristol, Irving, 202
Kroeber, A.L., 145
Krumholtz, Norman, 76
Ku Klux Klan, 174

Labor movement, 262, 316-18
Lackawanna, N.Y., 655
Lake Erie, 558
Land: (See also Suburbs)
  prices, 13, 21, 24, 26, 100, 627
  supply, 22-4, 622, 623-28, 635
  use, 15, 16, 28, 236, 355, 634, 650-51, 654-55
  zoning, 623-26, 632-34, 654-55
Landis, Judge, 119
Lane, Robert E., 229, 268
Langguth, Jack, 345
Larsen, Lawrence H., 122
Lasswell, Harold, 257, 267, 268
Law and order, 208, 209, 281, 283-84, 289, 290, 301, 302, 303-4, 310, 391, 443, 662-63
Law Enforcement Assistance Administration, 463
Lee, Eugene C., 341, 342
Lee, Richard C., 207, 222-23
Leichter, Franz, 632
Lemberg Center for the Study of Violence, 457, 460 (See also Ghetto riots, Police, Rioting, Violence)
Lenski, Gerhard, 138, 147, 148
Levin, Melvin R., 434, 681
Levinson, Sanford, 269
Levitan, Sar A., 678, 680

Levittowns, 626, 635, 636
Lewis, R., 146
Liberalism, 225-26, 290-91, 297, 299-300, 301
Liberals, 312, 313, 313-24
Lieber, Harvey, 443, 557-74, 573n
Lieberson, Stanley, 136, 146, 448
Lincoln, Abraham, 168
Lindbergh, Charles, 73
Lindsay, John V., 209-11, 301, 302-3, 312, 314, 345, 351-52, 354, 392-95, 633
Lindzey, Gardner, 145
Lineberry, Robert L., 340
Lipset, Seymour M., 145, 147, 676
Lipsky, Michael, 256, 267, 390, 682
Litt, Edgar, 201
Lockard, Duane, 342, 343
London, 395, 589
Los Angeles, 18, 41, 54, 55, 71, 73, 74, 160, 161, 301, 334, 337
  blacks, 293
  ethnic groups, 278
  legislature, 398
  liberalism, 276-300
  mayoral election, 1969, 209, 211, 276-300, 379
  migration, 278-79
  riot, 446
Los Angeles County, 102-3, 120, 369, 401 (See also Serrano v. Priest)
Los Angeles Times, 281
Louisville, Ky., 361-62
Low, Seth, 233, 339
Lowe, Jeanne R., 345
Lowi, Theodore J., 206, 230-40, 264, 340
Lutherans, 137, 156
Lyford, Joseph P., 123

McAvoy, Thomas T., 147
McCarthy, Eugene, 286, 288, 296, 297
McClosky, Herbert, 674
McComb, J., 121
McCone report, 54
McConnell, Grant, 263
McCoy, Charles, 259, 264, 265, 266, 268
McEntire, Davis, 31, 33
McInnis v. Shapiro, 118-120
McKelvey, Blake, 31
McNayr, Irving G., 364, 377
Mackler, Bernard, 681
Macon, Ga., 390
Madison Township, N.J., 634
Mahwah, N.J., 628-30
Maier, Henry W., 345
Mailer, Norman, 199, 396, 560
Majority rule, 186-202, 210

Malcolm X, 159, 166, 169, 201
Male franchise, 217
Mangum, Garth L., 680
Manjares, 113
Mann, Horace, 120
Manpower Training Act, 601
Mapp v. *Ohio*, 117
Marchi, John, 301
Marine, Gene, 346
Marshall Plan, 669
Martin, Roscoe C., 123, 381, 382, 434
Masotti, Louis H., 346, 675, 676
Mass media, 658
  influence, on voters, 225, 280, 290,
      295-96, 305, 307, 308, 312
  in riots, 450-53, 454, 458-59
Massachusetts, 112, 370-71, 580, 632
  Eastern Massachusetts Council of
      Governments, 370
Maulin, Richard L., 276-300
Mayer, Martin, 681
Mayor: (*See also* Richard J. Daley;
      Hatcher, Richard; Lindsay, John)
  audience vs. constituency, 304-12
  authority, 231, 234-37, 270, 313-14,
      665
  black, 312, 329, 334, 379, 384
  challenges, 270-72
  leadership, 269-76
  Los Angeles campaign, 276-300
  metromayors, 406
  "new breed," 300-14, 578, 579
  styles, 271
Medicaid, 613, 620
Mediterranean Sea, 559
Meek, Roy L., 684
Megalopolis, 38, 239, 376, 623
Meranto, Philip, 681
Meredith, James, 167
Merelman, Richard, 266
Metrogovernment, 378, 567
Metromayors, 406
Metropolis (SMSA), 37, 41, 58, 67, 95,
      374, 396
  developing, 3-10, 214-15, 406
  economic function, 91-101
  employment, 94-5, 97-9
  factors affecting, 11-12 (*See also* Ghetto,
      Slum, Suburbs)
  Negroes, 659 (see also Black)
  trends, 40-1, 63-4, 406, 585
Metropolitan areas
  racial concentration, 640
Metropolitan county, 405-6, 422
Metropolitan government, 348-53, 356,
      366, 370-71, 395, 589

charter, 351
county base, 363-64, 369-71, 400-1
ecumenicists, 373-75
planning agencies, 373-75
Metropolitan reform, 355-77
  consolidation, 356-69, 378, 380-92,
      404-5
  racial problems (*see* Black rule in urban
      South)
  surveys, 355-56, 376
  two-tier system, 369-71
Metropolitan state, 351-52, 353, 396-406
  statists, 371-73
Metropolitan Surveys: A Digest, 376
Metropolitan Washington Council of
      Governments, 374-75
Mexicans, 18
Mexican-Americans, 36, 138, 209, 524,
      647, 657
  in Los Angeles, 278, 281-83, 292,
      298-99
Meyerson, Martin, 682
Miami, Fla., 363, 364, 388
Michels, Robert, 229, 231
Middle West, 659
Migration, 137, 592-93, 658
  from Puerto Rico, 555
  from South, 17, 18, 22, 317, 488, 555,
      583, 586
Miliband, Ralph, 264
Miller, H.A., 145
Miller, J.A., 680
Miller, S.M. 678
Miller, Warren E., 228
Milliken, William G., 633
Milner, Neal, 346
Milwaukee, Wis., 401, 457
Minneapolis, Minn., 160, 224, 372
Minnesota, 372-73
Mississippi, 167
Model cities program, 305, 312, 328, 442,
      493, 548
Mogulof, Melvin, 403
Moore, Ferman, 161
Moore, Frank C., 355
Moore, Joan W., 147
Moore, William J., 682
Morlan, Robert L., 229, 343
Mormons, 138
Morris, Willie, 154
Mosk, J., 121
Mowry, George E., 339
Moynihan, Daniel P., 68, 147, 148, 151,
      418, 575, 578, 579-99, 678, 679,
      685
Muhammad Ali, 323

Muir, John, 570
Mumford, Lewis, 122, 123, 627
Munger, Frank, 132, 145
Murdy, Ralph G., 485
Murray, Vernon G., 675
Muskie, Edmund S., 563, 564, 573n

NAACP, 169, 481
Nam, C.B., 136, 146
Nashville, Tenn., 349, 353, 357, 358, 363,
    365, 366-67, 369, 378, 386-88
National Advisory Commission on Civil
    Disorders (Kerner Commission),
    177, 382, 438, 463, 658, 660, 661,
    663, 667, 671, 675 (See also
    Kerner Report)
National Association of Counties, 403
National Association of Manufacturers
    (NAM), 496
National cities, 351, 353, 392-95
National Commission on the Causes and
    Prevention of Violence, 172, 175,
    460, 675
National Commission on Urban Problems
    (Douglas Commission), 4, 34-70,
    356, 376n, 682
National Environmental Policy Act,
    563-65
National Goals Research Staff, 563
National Guard, 451, 457, 660
National health insurance, 613
National League of Cities, 685
National Planning Association, 96
National Welfare Rights Organization, 576,
    609-21
Nation's Cities, 122
Naughton, James M., 347
Negroes, 17-19, 20, 22, 23, 35, 41, 63, 90,
    138 (See also Black Americans)
    attitudes, 163-68, 171
    distribution in U.S., 37, 42, 51, 174, 593
    earnings, 585, 658
    education, 519-25, 528-30 (See also
        School Busing)
    ghettos, 79-81, 161, 162, 176, 178
    revolution, 159-60, 162
    unemployment, 49, 52, 54, 659 (See
        also Equal Employment
        Opportunity Act; Jobs; Poor)
Neier, Aryeh, 485
Neighborhood self-government, 180-86,
    309, 499-500 (See also Commu-
    nity control)
    Federal aid, 182, 185
Nelson, Gaylord, 563
Netzer, Dick, 7, 9, 124
Nevada, 138

New Canaan, Conn., 632, 633
New Deal, 206, 222, 231, 581
New England, 356
New Haven, Conn., 131, 135, 142, 207,
    222-24, 243
New Jersey, 223-24, 227, 390-91, 560,
    561, 623, 632, 634, 674 (See also
    Newark Community Union
    Project)
    Bureau of Motor Vehicles, 249
New Orleans, La., 42, 356, 561
New York City, 12, 14, 16, 19, 23-4, 41,
    53, 54, 55, 71, 100, 160, 198, 302,
    422, 626, 628 (See also Lindsay,
    John)
    budget, 393
    consolidation, 356, 358
    crime, 550
    election, 1961, 237-38
    housing, 26-30, 545, 547-48, 627
    Jews, 310
    Negroes, 17-18 (See also Black
        Americans, Ghetto, Slum)
    Nixon as mayor, 336-38
    police, 236, 310, 457, 470, 479
    population, 181, 640
    problems, 210
    reform, 231-40
    Regional Plan, 373
    riot, 446, 457
    schools, 595
    statehood, 199
    taxes, 427
New York State, 372, 376, 393, 623, 632
    Fleischman Commission, 633
New York Times, 5, 32, 33, 124, 151, 265,
    276, 320, 574
New Yorker, 152
Newark, N.J., 42, 161, 207, 265n, 334,
    379, 390-91, 628-30
    housing, 540, 551, 555
    riot, 446, 458
Newark Community Union Project
    (NCUP), 246-63
Newman, Dorothy K., 69
Newport Center, Calif., 73
Newspapers' influence, 240, 304 (See also
    Mass media)
Newsweek, 127, 147n
    Editors, 159-71
Newton, George D., 676
Niagara City, N.Y., 361
Niederhoffer, Arthur, 483, 484, 676
Nisbet, Robert A., 580
Nixon, Richard M., 153, 154, 167, 168,
    210, 304, 336-38, 419-31, 442,
    563, 565-66, 576-79, 620, 637-56

Administration, 164, 192, 352, 407, 440, 575, 610, 617
message from, 599-609
Nonpartisan ballot, 224-25
Nonwhites: (*See also* Black Americans, Negroes, *and by name of national origin*; Ghetto)
birthrate, 35
in cities, 40, 80-82
composition, 35-6
distribution in U.S., 36, 41
poor, 45-7, 59-62, 64
unemployed, 50-51, 54, 66
North Carolina, 364
North Carolina Acts of 1969, 376n
Northeast, 37, 58, 364, 583, 659
Novak, Michael, 126, 128, 130, 148-58

Oakland, Calif., 18, 42, 175
O'Connor, Edwin, 228
Office of Economic Opportunity, 197, 254, 608 (*See also* Community Action Programs; Job Corps)
Office of Juvenile Delinquency, 185
Olsen, Mancur, Jr., 267
Olson, David J., 346, 390
Omaha, Neb., 449-52
One man–one vote, 190, 195, 199-200, 300, 350, 379, 384
Open housing (*see* Housing)
Open Society, 653
Opinion Research of California, 288, 290
Oppenheimer, Martin, 675
Orientals, 35
Oriental-Americans, 523-24, 526-28
Orshansky, Mollie, 68, 69
Osofsky, Gilbert, 31
Ostrogorski, Moisei, 231, 340
Outer City, 70-76
Outvoted minorities, 190-202, 208

Paraprofessionals, 497-98
Parenti, Michael, 126, 129-30, 131-48, 207-8, 211, 241-76
Paris, 73, 92
Park, R.E., 145
Parsons, Talcott, 133, 139, 141, 145, 147
Pasadena, Texas, 74
Patillo, H.C., 73
Pechman, Joseph, 407
Pennsylvania, 149, 150
Supreme Court, 634
Pensacola, Fla., 361, 390
Pepsico, Inc., 628
Peters, J., 121
Philadelphia, Pa., 16, 41, 42, 52, 53, 55, 100, 161, 223-24, 337, 356, 393, 422, 547, 628
Philips, Channing, 334
Phoenix, Ariz., 55, 98, 596
Pinchot, Gifford, 570
Piper v. *Big Pine School District*, 112-13
Pittsburgh, Pa., 457
Piven, Frances Fox, 347, 678, 679
Playford, John, 264, 265, 266, 268
Plunkitt, George Washington, 217-18
Pluralism, 241-76
Pluralists, 207, 211, 255
Police, 128, 167, 174-75, 177-78, 270, 301, 438, 456 (*See also* Black Americans, Crime, Ghetto, Negroes, Violence)
Boston, 303
community relations, 443-44, 475-80, 482-83, 668-69
duties, 461-62, 478-80
Los Angeles, 281, 283-84, 289-91, 296, 297
New York City, 236, 310, 457, 470, 479
Newark, 253-54
Omaha, 449-52
problems, 439, 460-85, 668
riots, 446-48, 456-57
training, 457, 479
violence, 175, 192, 471-72, 660-62, 668
Polish-Americans, 135, 138, 148-49, 154
Political boss, 206, 208, 211-14, 219, 226 (*See also* Daley, Richard J.; Mayor, leadership; Political "machine")
Political campaigns (*see* Daley, Richard J.; Hatcher, Richard; Los Angeles Liberalism)
Political "machine," 206, 212, 213, 219, 226, 230-40
decline of, 220-22
new machines, 234-35
seniority system, 195-96
Political party organization:
changing rules, 262-63
Newark, 261-62
new patterns, 224-27
old style, 213-23, 227
Political T.V. debates, 285-86
Polsby, Nelson W., 229, 230, 243, 255, 258-59, 263, 264, 265, 267, 268, 339
Polycentric government, 402, 404
Polynesians, 35
Pomper, Gerald, 324
Poor, 44-70 (*See also* Black Americans, Ghetto, Housing, Jobs, Negroes, Nonwhites, Poverty areas, Slum, Welfare)

Poor,(continued)
black urban, 61, 586, 657
composition, 45-48, 657
direct help, 217-18
distribution, 57-63
fear, 258, 673
improving condition, 66, 439-40, 444,
    671
minority, 189, 208, 261
organizing, 197, 246-63
power (see Article 15, 241-69)
statistics, 44-5, 439
urban, 59-60, 80, 188-89, 585, 658
working, 56, 267n, 430, 600, 605, 608
Population:
age structure, 43-4, 65
density, 7, 58, 63
explosion, 34-6, 559, 583, 586
growth rates, 65, 586
impact of changes, 42-4
implosion, 36-8
increases, 4, 11, 22, 43, 63-4, 593
study of, 34-70
total U.S., 66, 81-2
urban, 583, 666
Populism, defined, 232-33
Poverty:
areas, 4, 54-5, 57-63, 592
causes, 56, 444
groups, 45
incidence, 45
programs (see Community Action Pro-
    grams, Job Corps, War on poverty,
    Welfare reform)
Poverty line income, 67n, 613, 620,
    657-58
Power elite, 151 (See also Elites, Elitists)
President's Commission on Law Enforce-
    ment and Administration of
    Justice, 463, 483, 676
President's Committee on Juvenile
    Delinquency, 489-90
President's Crime Commission, 462
Press, Charles, 121, 341, 343, 344
Price, Don K., 345
Procaccino, Mario, 301
Professionalism in city government,
    232-37, 307
Progressives, 206, 225
Proportional representation, 198
Protestant, 126, 131, 135, 138, 139, 140,
    141, 142, 150, 152, 153
rioters, 447
Protho, James W., 674
Providence, R.I., 219
Public Administration Review, 557, 572

Public opinion polls, 196, 259, 286, 288,
    290, 296, 301
Public policies, 575, 579-99
Public policy issues, 3, 9, 437-44
urban, 296, 306, 313
Public services:
child care, 606-7
competitive, 594-95
equal access, 591-92
Public welfare, 189, 191, 199, 338, 428-
    30, 488, 576 (See also National
    Welfare Rights Organization)
costs, 607-8
family assistance, 576, 578
"typical welfare family," 603
welfare reform, 599-609
Welfare Rights movement, 192
work incentive, 605-6
Public Works Administration (PWA), 17
Publius, 419, 420, 428, 431
Puerto Ricans, 7, 18, 19, 36, 128, 524,
    657
Puerto Rico, 555
Purchase, N.Y., 628

Race relations, U.S., 178, 451-52, 467,
    583, 661-62, 667
riots, 446
Racial prejudice, 293
Racial problems:
in government, 378-92
in housing, 637-656
in schools (see School Busing; Swann v.
    Charlotte-Mecklenburg Board of
    Education)
Racism, 253, 317, 322-23
corporate, 318-20
Racists, 154-55, 179, 209, 667, 671
Radical liberals, 276, 293
Rafferty, Max, 276-77
Rainwater, Lee, 202, 587, 675
Ramney, Austin, 213, 228
Ranney, David C., 434
Rashomon effect, 458, 460
Reagan, Ronald, 291, 304
Real estate practices, 7 (See also Housing;
    Land)
zoning, 576
Recentralization, 25-6
Reeves, Richard, 341
Referendum, 239-40
Reform politics, 220, 224-27, 231-39, 252,
    378-79, 388, 424
Regional Plan Association of New York,
    633
Regional Plan for New York and Its

Environs, 373
Regional planning, 403
Rehfuss, John A., 433
Reich, Charles A., 122
Reich, Larry, 73, 76
Reichley, A. James, 341, 353
Rein, Martin, 678
Reinhardt, Steven, 287
Reining, Henry, Jr., 433
Reiss, Albert J., 485
Reitman, Alan, 485
Religion, 131, 137, 156 (See also sects as
        Catholic, Lutheran)
Rent strikes, 266n (See also Housing,
        Newark Community Union
        Project)
Reps, John W., 316
Reston, Va., 636
Reuss, Henry S., 434
Revenue-sharing plan, 352, 356, 376, 407-
        18, 419-31, 590, 600
Revolutionary groups, 447, 660-61
Reynolds, Marcus T., 33
Reynolds v. Sims, 117
Ribicoff, Abraham, 631
Richards, Allan R., 339
Richardson, George, 251
Richmond, Va., 42, 362, 365, 390
Riesman, David, 263
Rights in Concord, 472
Riis, Jacob A., 29, 33
Riles, Wilson, 276-77
Riordon, William L., 228
Rioting: (See also Ghetto riots, Kerner
        Commission, Violence, Watts riots)
    anti-Negro, 447
    causes, 446-49, 456
    cure, 671
    defined, 445
    stages, 453-56
Roanoke, Va., 358-59, 390
Rockefeller, Nelson A., 372
Rodwin, Lloyd, 434
Rogers, David, 681
Roos, Leslie L., Jr., 684
Roosevelt Field, 73
Roosevelt, Franklin, 154, 206
Rose, Arnold, 263
Rosenthal, Erich, 146
Rosenthal, Jack, 4, 70-76
Rothenberg, Don, 287-88, 293
Rourke, Francis E., 123
Rovere, Richard, 579
Ruchelman, Leonard I., 346
Russell Sage Foundation, 373
Russians, 154, 191

Rustin, Bayard, 159, 347
Ruttenberg, Stanley H., 680

S 1075 (see National Environmental Policy
        Act)
Sacco-Vanzetti, 157
Sahid, Joseph R., 172, 460, 676
St. Louis, Mo., 14, 42, 53, 55, 353, 388,
        634, 640
Sales taxes, 8
Salisbury, Robert H., 342
Salsburg v. Maryland, 116, 117
Salt Lake City, Utah, 362
Salvatori, Henry, 284
San Antonio, Texas, 55
San Diego, Calif., 99, 401
San Francisco, Calif., 53, 54, 55, 138, 301,
        302, 370, 398, 558
San Francisco Unified School District v.
        Johnson, 112
Santa Barbara oil drilling, 562, 568-69
Saunders, Charles B., Jr., 676
Savannah, Ga., 360, 363, 390
Sayre, Wallace S., 230, 234, 339, 344
Scammon, 153
Schattschneider, E.E., 212, 214, 228, 267
Schmandt, Henry J., 121, 200, 376, 432,
        677
Schnore, Leo F., 31, 339
School busing, 441-42, 444, 531-40,
        634-35
    financing (see Serrano v. Priest)
    integration, 528-30
    racial balance, 534-36
    segregation, 161, 171, 440-42, 444,
        518-19, 652
Schrag, Peter, 681
Schultze, Charles L., 666, 685
Schuman, Howard, 674
Schumpeter, Joseph A., 231
Schwartz and Goldstein, 483, 484
Scoble, Harry M., 344
Seattle, Wash., 224, 427
Senate Subcommittee on Executive
        Reorganization, 128
Seniority system, 195-96 (See also Political
        "machine")
Serrano v. Priest, 8, 102-24
Serrin, William, 346
Shank, Alan, 269-76, 681
Shannon, James P., 147
Sheatsley, P.B., 268
Shils, Edward A., 228
Silberman, Charles E., 202
Silverman, Arnold, 448
Skolnick, Jerome H., 483, 676

Slavery, 177, 214, 445
Sloan, Lee, 350, 353, 378-92
Slovakia, 149
Slovaks, 150-51, 156, 158
Slum, 17-18, 64, 78, 128-29, 160, 189,
        271, 444, 546, 586, 601, 648,
        658-59, 665, 666-67 (*See also*
        Ghetto; Housing)
    landlords, 543-44
    residents, 54-5, 647
Smallwood, Frank, 433
Smelser, Neil J., 265
SNCC, 169, 173
Social Darwinism, 217, 580
Social Security, 431
Social Security Act, 488, 610, 620
    Administration, 607
    Aid to Dependent Children, 576
Socialism, 214
Social system, defined, 133-34
Social welfare agencies, 206
    bureaucracy, 207, 235-36
    programs, 5, 7, 222, 271, 428-31, 439
Sofen, Edward, 365, 377, 433
Sorauf, Frank J., 228
Southern Christian Leadership Conference
        (SCLC), 496
Southern states, 35, 37, 41, 57, 174, 350,
        353, 356 (*See also* Black rule in
        urban South; Migration from
        South)
    consolidation, 357-64, 376, 390
    growth, 100-1
Southwest, 350
Soviet Union, 78
Space costs (city vs. suburb), 91
Specialists (*see* Professionalism)
Spectorsky, A.C., 146
Spender, Stephen, 574
Spiegel, John P., 460
Springfield, Ill., 446
Springfield, Ohio, 446
Staats, Elmer B., 440, 501-18
Standard Metropolitan Statistical Areas
        (SMSA's), 98-100 (*See also*
        Metropolis)
    defined, 67
Stang, David P., 172, 439, 460-85, 676
Starr, Roger, 122
Staten Island, N.Y., 236
Steel strike, 1919, 317
Steelworkers Union, 318-19, 325
Steffens, Lincoln, 339
Steiner, Gilbert Y., 429
Sternlieb, George, 442, 540-56, 683
Stevenson, Adlai, 226, 572n
Stokes, Carl, 160, 168, 169, 210, 293, 324

Stokes, Donald E., 228
Stole, Leo, 145, 146
Stone, Chuck, 347
Stone, Harold A., 345
Stone, Kathryn H., 345
Stonequist, E.V., 145
Straayer, John A., 684
Straetz, Ralph A., 344
Strikes, 192, 266n, 317, 469, 657
Strong, Vivian, 449-52
Student militants, 281, 283, 285, 287,
        291-93, 295-96, 299
Students for a Democratic Society (SDS),
        209, 246-54, 291, 295
Subemployment, 56-7 (*See also* Jobs,
        Unemployment and Underem-
        ployment)
Suburban Action Institute, 632
Suburbanites, 349, 380, 388, 583, 635-36
Suburbanization, 187, 663-64, 667
Suburbs, 8, 67, 70-76, 136 (*See also*
        Housing; Outer City)
    flight to, 14-18, 137, 142, 188
        business and industry, 7, 51, 628,
                630-31, 641
    income, 41-42
    jobs, 97, 628-29
    opening, 621-36
    political power, 43, 227, 350
    poor, 63, 667
    population, 4, 38-9, 43, 583, 622, 640
    resources, 622
Sullivan, 485
Sullivan, J., 121
Summers, Marvin R., 677
Sundquist, James L., 566, 573, 685
Survey Research Center, 222
Sutton, Francis X., 264, 267
Swann et. al. v. *Charlotte-Mecklenburg
        Board of Education*, 441, 531-40
Swearer, Howard, 266
Sweezy, Paul, 264
Syed, Anwar, 123

Tabb, William K., 680
Taeuber, Conrad, 585
Taeuber, Karl, 596
Tager, Jack, 123
Taggert, Robert III, 680
Talbot, Allan R., 346
Tallahassee, Fla., 390
Tamm, Quinn, 484
Tammany, 217, 239
Tampa, Fla., 360-1, 386, 390
Taxes, 7, 8, 91, 187, 302, 337, 352, 364-
        65, 368, 410, 547, 633
    inequities, 426-29

personal income, 408-11, 425-26, 666
property, 7, 8, 10, 416, 426-27, 556,
    576, 625, 629-30, 665 (*See also*
    Serrano v. Priest)
sales, 410, 416, 426
state and local, 412-13, 416, 426-27, 666
Taxpayer resistance, 416
Taylorites, 561
Technological change, 16, 561, 563
Technology, 562-63, 592, 597
Terkel, Studs, 267, 268
Terris, Bruce J., 483, 485
Thermal pollution, 558
Thiessen, Victor, 346
Thomas, W.I., 145
Thomson, Elizabeth, 268
Tilly, Charles, 201
Tobriner, J., 121
Tokyo, 589
Toronto, Ont., 369, 404
Toure, Sekou, 327
Town meeting government, 128, 185 (*See
    also* Neighborhood self-govern-
    ment)
Towson, Md., 75
Transportation:
  costs, 91
  mass transit, 191, 197, 236
  radial pattern, 22
  studies, 355
  technology, 11, 14, 16, 21, 30
Troublemakers, The, 265
Truman, David, 263, 269
Tweed, William, 213, 214
Two-tier system (*see* Metropolitan reform)

Uhlman, Wes, 395
Uncle Tom, 296, 481
Unemployed and underemployed, 48-52,
    55-7, 439, 629, 657-58
  by color, 52
  ghetto, 629
  Negro, 488
  rates, 50, 55, 57, 440, 487-88
Uniform Relocation Assistance Act, 652
United Auto Workers, 288
United Freedom Ticket (UFT), 250-52,
    260
United Nations, 557
  Unesco, 560
U.S. Bureau of Labor Statistics, 50, 576,
    611, 612, 613, 615, 616-18, 620
U.S. Bureau of the Census, 41, 42, 43, 52,
    69-70, 81, 585
U.S. Chamber of Commerce, 496
U.S. Congress (91st), 563, 565, 599
  "conservative coalition," 667

U.S. Constitution, 262, 392, 394, 621,
    638, 642, 646, 654, 663,
    14th Amendment, 8, 102-24, 198,
    533, 634
U.S. Department of Agriculture, 507, 509,
    510, 568, 613, 616, 617-19
U.S. Department of Defense, 651
U.S. Department of Health, Education and
    Welfare (HEW), 568, 608, 681
U.S. Department of Justice, 325-26, 463,
    634, 643, 649
U.S. Department of Labor, 51, 56, 440
U.S. Department of the Interior, 507, 509,
    510, 557, 565, 566, 568
U.S. Employment Service (USES), 504,
    506, 629
U.S. foreign policy, 395, 418, 575
U.S. Office of Education, 441, 596
U.S. Steel Corporation, 315, 316, 320,
    326, 327
  black employees, 318-20
U.S. Supreme Court, 107, 109, 110,
    111-14, 119, 120, 161, 167, 190,
    350, 441, 464, 519, 531-40, 633,
    634, 639, 654-55
University of California, 291
  at Irvine, 73
Unskilled workers, 21, 187-88, 194
Urban Affairs Council, 565, 582, 608
Urban balance, 586-87
Urban Coalition, 496, 685
Urban environment, 598
Urban expansion, 214-15
Urban government, 215-16 (*See also* City
    government and politics; Metropol-
    itan government)
Urban Homestead Act, 554
Urban League, 169, 481
Urban party politics, 212-30
Urban problems and policies, 1960s,
    437-44
  research, 595-97
Urban redevelopment (*see* Urban renewal)
Urban renewal, 23, 24, 222, 246, 268n,
    274, 305, 307, 309, 374, 394, 442,
    587, 590, 627, 639, 644-45 (*See
    also* Housing)

Vadakin, James C., 679
Van Der Slik, Jack R., 347
Vernon, Raymond, 31, 32, 91-2, 101
Veterans Administration, 16, 651
Veterans relief, 429
Vidich, Arthur J., 123
Vietnam war, 125, 160, 163-64, 189, 191,
    270, 285, 446, 590-91, 666

Violence, 78-9, 88, 127, 192-93, 254, 301,
        328, 392, 445 (*See also* Black
        militancy; Disruption; Kerner
        Commission; Watts riots)
    black, 160-62, 168, 170-71, 175-79, 445,
        577, 585, 662
    police, 471-72, 658-61
    study of, 457, 460
*Violence in America: Historical and Com-
        parative Perspectives*, 472
Volusia City, Fla., 371
Vose, Clement E., 683
Votes, 244, 251, 261
    black, 252, 258-59, 302, 311
Voting Rights Act, 174

Wade, Richard C., 31, 123
Wagner, Robert, 238
Waldo, Dwight, 572
Walker, Daniel, 484, 677
Walker, Jack L., 265
Walker, Mabel L., 31
Wallace, George, 151, 198, 299, 301,
        441-42
Wall Street Journal, 32
Walzer, Michael, 269
Warner, Sam B., Jr., 31
Warner, W.L., 145, 146
War on Poverty, 129, 160, 305, 439, 440,
        491-93
    CAP, 498
Warshauer, Mary Ellen, 681
Washington, D.C., 42, 446, 480, 623
Washington Post, 574, 674
Water pollution, 236, 431, 557-58, 563,
        566, 567, 573n
    Federal Water Pollution Control
        Administration, 568
Wattenberg, 153
Watts riots, 54, 161, 175, 297, 446 (*See
        also* Ghetto riots; Police)
Weaver, Robert, 32, 683
Weber, Max, 147, 231
Weinberg, Kenneth G., 347
Weiner, Maury, 287
Wengert, Norman, 573
West, Ben, 388
Western states, 37, 100-1, 137-38
Wetzel, James R., 680
White, Andrew Dickson, 233
White ethnics, 126, 128, 130, 148-58
White, John Wesley, 385, 390
White, Kevin, 303, 308, 370
White, Morton and Lucia, 123
White racism, 671

Whyte, William Foote, 135, 146n
Whyte, William H., 146n
Wicker, Tom, 5, 147
Wiener, Anthony J., 573
Wiley, George A., 161, 576
Wilhelm, John, 264
Williams, Oliver P., 341, 342
Willie, Charles, 268
Willis, Garry, 675
Wilson, James Q., 31, 121, 139, 147, 201,
        209, 211, 228, 229, 239, 269, 270,
        272, 275, 276, 300-14, 340, 341,
        343, 347, 478-79, 483, 484, 485,
        590, 675, 677, 685
Wilson, O.W., 483
Wilson, Woodrow, 144, 233
Winchester, Va., 369
Wirt, Frederick M., 681
Wise, Arthur E., 124
Wolfinger, Raymond, 131, 132, 133, 136,
        142, 145, 148, 201, 229, 340
Wolman, Harold, 683, 684
Women:
    head of family, 585
    poor, 46-9
Women in Community Service, Inc., 504
Women's Liberation, 148
Woock, Roger R., 677
Wood, Edith Elmer, 17, 31
Wood, Robert C., 136, 146, 433
Woods, Robert A., 33
Workers (*see* Jobs; Unemployed and
        underemployed)
World Series, 314
World War I, 154, 317, 318, 486
World War II, 18, 21, 49, 317, 318, 583,
        594, 624, 656, 669
Wright, C.J., 121
Wright, Henry, 627

Yancey, William L., 202
Yavitz, Boris, 32
Yinger, J. Milton, 146
Ylvisaker, Paul, 406
Yorty, Samuel W., 209, 211, 276-300,
        301, 379
Youth, 49, 51, 125, 185, 192, 447, 455,
        489, 570 (*See also* Job Corps)

Zeller, Belle, 344
Zimmerman, Joseph F., 344, 349-50, 353,
        377, 434
Zimring, Franklin E., 676
Znanjecki, F., 145